Introduction to E-Commerce

Introduction to E-Commerce

Efraim Turban and **David King**

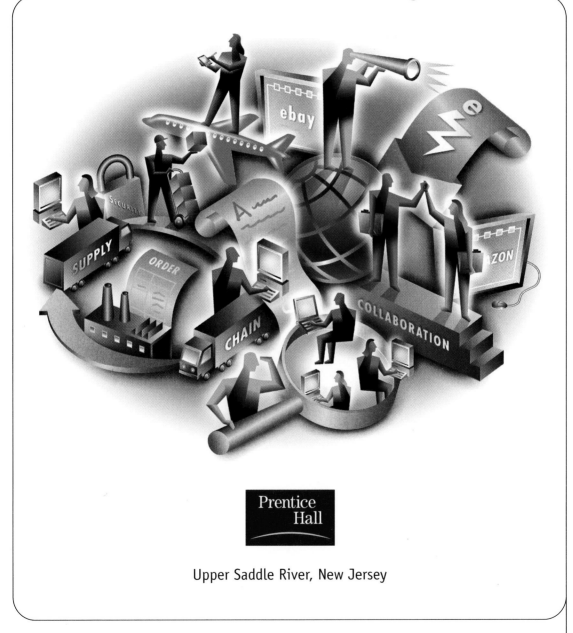

Prentice Hall

Upper Saddle River, New Jersey

Library of Congress Cataloging-in-Publication Data

Turban, Efraim.
    Introduction to e-commerce / Efraim Turban and David King
        p.   cm.
    Includes bibliographical references and index.
    ISBN 0-13-009406-4
      1. Electronic commerce.   I. King, David.   II. Title.

    HF5548.32 T87 2003
    658.8'4—dc21

                                    2002029310

Publisher and Vice President: Natalie E. Anderson
Executive Editor: Bob Horan
Project Manager, Editorial: Lori Cerreto
Editorial Assistant: Maat Van Uitert
Media Project Manager: Joan Waxman
Senior Marketing Manager: Sharon Turkovich
Marketing Assistant: Scott Patterson
Production Manager: Gail Steier de Acevedo
Project Manager, Production: April Montana
Associate Director, Manufacturing: Vincent Scelta
Manufacturing Buyer: April Montana
Design Manager: Maria Lange
Art Director: Pat Smythe
Interior Design: Quorum Creative Services
Cover Design: Joan O'Connor
Interior/Cover Art: John Bleck
Manager, Print Production: Christy Mahon
Composition: BookMasters, Inc.
Full-Service Project Management: BookMasters, Inc.
Cover Printer: Phoenix Color
Printer/Binder: Quebecor World

10 9 8 7 6 5 4 3 2 1

ISBN: 0-13-009406-4

Pearson Education LTD
Pearson Education of Australia Pty. Limited, Sydney
Pearson Education (Singapore) Pte. Ltd.
Pearson Education North Asia Ltd
Pearson Education, Canada, Ltd
Pearson Educación de Mexico, S.A. de C.V.
Pearson Education—Japan
Pearson Education Malaysia, Pte, Ltd
Pearson Education Upper Saddle River, New Jersey

Dedicated to all those who are interested in
learning about electronic commerce

Contents in Brief

Online Chapter

Online Technical Appendixes

Online Tutorials

www.prenhall.com/turban

Contents

Part II Internet Retailing   93

Part III Business-to-Business E-Commerce   201

Part IV Other EC Models and Applications   289

Part V Supporting EC Applications   381

Part VI Strategy and Implementation   455

Online Chapter

Online Tutorials

As we enter the third millennium, we are experiencing one of the most important changes to our daily lives—the move to an Internet-based society. The U.S. Department of Commerce reported that in January 2002 more than 55 percent of all Americans (141 million) surfed the Internet. More interesting is the fact that over 90 percent of people 5 to 17 years old surf the Internet on a regular basis. It is clear that this percentage will continue to increase. Similar trends exist in most other countries. As a result, much has changed at home, school, work, and in the government—and even in our leisure activities. Some changes are already here and are spreading around the globe. Others are just beginning. One of the most significant changes is in how we conduct business, especially in how we manage marketplaces and trading.

Electronic commerce (EC), also known as e-business, describes the manner in which transactions take place over networks, mostly the Internet. It is the process of electronically buying and selling goods, services, and information. Certain EC applications, such as buying and selling stocks on the Internet, are growing very rapidly. In Korea, for example, 70 percent of all stock trading is already conducted on the Internet. Electronic commerce will impact a significant portion of the world, affecting businesses, professions, and, of course, people. Electronic commerce is not just about buying and selling, it is also about electronically communicating, collaborating, and discovering information. It is about e-learning, e-government, and much more.

The impact of EC is not just in the creation of Web-based corporations. It is the building of a new industrial order. Such a revolution brings a myriad of opportunities as well as risks. Bill Gates is aware of this, as the company he founded, Microsoft, is continually developing Internet and EC products and services. Yet, Gates has stated that Microsoft is always 2 years away from failure—that somewhere out there is an unknown competitor who could render your business model obsolete. Bill Gates knows that competition today is not among products or services, but among business models. What is true for Microsoft is true for just about every other company. The hottest and most dangerous new business models out there are on the Web.

The purpose of this book is to describe the essentials of EC—how it is being conducted and managed as well as assessing its major opportunities, limitations, issues, and risks. As electronic commerce is an interdisciplinary topic, it should be of interest to managers and professional people in any functional area of the business world. People in government, education, health services, and other areas will benefit from learning about EC.

Today, EC is going through a period of consolidation in which enthusiasm for new technologies and ideas is now being accompanied by careful attention to proper strategy and implementation. Most of all, people recognize that e-business has two parts; it is not just about technology, it is also about business.

This book is one of the first textbooks dedicated solely to EC. It is written by experienced authors who share academic as well as real-world practices. It is a comprehensive text, yet it is small enough so that it can be used for one semester or quarter. It also can be used to supplement a text on Internet fundamentals, MIS, or marketing.

FEATURES OF THIS BOOK

Several features are unique to this book.

MANAGERIAL ORIENTATION

Electronic commerce (e-commerce) can be approached from two major aspects: technological and managerial. This text uses the second approach. Most of the presentations are about EC applications and implementation. However, we do recognize the importance of the technology; therefore, we present the essentials of security in Chapters 9 and 10 and the essentials of infrastructure and system development in Chapter 12, which is located on the book's Web site (prenhall.com/turban). We also provide some detailed technology material in the appendices and tutorials on the book's Web site.

USER-FRIENDLY BEGINNERS' TEXT

This book is written for beginners in e-commerce. It is clear, simple, and well organized, and it provides all the basic definitions as well as logical support. Relevant review questions are provided at the end of each section so the reader can pause to review and digest the new material.

INTERDISCIPLINARY APPROACH

E-commerce is interdisciplinary, and we illustrate this throughout the book. Major related disciplines include accounting, finance, information systems, marketing, management, and human resources management. In addition, some nonbusiness disciplines are related, especially public administration, computer science, engineering, psychology, political science, and law. Finally, economics plays a major role in the understanding of EC.

REAL-WORLD ORIENTATION

Extensive, vivid examples from large corporations, small businesses, and government and not-for-profit agencies from all over the world make concepts come alive by showing students the capabilities of EC, its cost and justification, and the innovative ways real corporations are using EC in their operations.

SOLID THEORETICAL BACKGROUND

Throughout the book we present the theoretical foundations necessary for understanding EC, ranging from consumer behavior to economic theory of competition.

Furthermore, we provide Web site addresses, many exercises, extensive references, and lists of additional readings to supplement the theoretical presentations.

MOST CURRENT

The book presents the most current topics of EC, as evidenced by the many 2000, 2001, and 2002 citations. Topics such as e-learning, e-government, e-strategy, Web-based supply chain systems, collaborative commerce, mobile commerce, and EC economics are presented both from the theoretical point of view and from the application side.

INTEGRATED SYSTEMS

In contrast to other books that highlight isolated Internet-based systems, we emphasize those systems that support the enterprise and supply chain management. Intra- and interorganizational systems are particularly highlighted, including the latest innovations in global EC and in Web-based electronic data interchange (EDI).

GLOBAL PERSPECTIVE

The importance of global competition, partnerships, and trade is rapidly increasing. E-commerce facilitates export and import, the management of multinational companies, and electronic trading around the globe. International examples are provided throughout the book.

EC FAILURES AND LESSONS LEARNED

In addition to EC success stories, we also present EC failures, and, where possible, analyze the causes of those failures.

COMPREHENSIVENESS AND EASE OF READING

All major EC topics are covered by the text. Furthermore, the book is easy to understand and is full of interesting real-world examples and "war stories" that keep the reader's interest at a high level.

THEMES FOR EC APPLICATION CASES

In order to highlight the relevance of the EC Application Cases to the major categories of EC, we elected four major themes to be associated with the cases. In instances where a case might be associated with more than one category, we selected the most relevant one. The categories, and the icons used to identify them throughout the book, are as follows.

1. **Individuals and society.** These are cases that emphasize the relationship of EC to individuals or to society in general. Such cases discuss customer service, e-learning, selling to individuals, and online transactions between individuals. Examples of societal issues discussed include protection of privacy and provision of social services online. Finally, all government services to individuals belong to this category.

2. **Interorganization and collaboration.** All interactions between two or more organizations fall into this category. These interactions include selling and buying, exchanging information, collaborations of various types, services provided to organizations, and more. Organizations considered in this category can be private or public, profit or not for profit.

3. **Intraorganization.** All EC activities conducted *within* an organization belong to this category. These activities include transactions among employees, transactions between the organization and its employees, and all internal communication and collaboration within organizations.

4. **Implementation and strategy.** All issues related to EC strategy and implementation of EC applications belong to this category. Topics include justifying EC applications, planning for EC, deciding on development strategies, and deciding whether to go global.

ORGANIZATION OF THE BOOK

The book is divided into 11 chapters grouped into six parts. One additional chapter, four technology appendices, and three tutorials are available as online supplements.

PART I—INTRODUCTION TO EC

In Part I we provide an overview of the entire book as well as the fundamentals of EC and some of its terminology (Chapter 1) and a discussion of electronic markets and their mechanisms (Chapter 2). An online appendix to Chapter 2 provides additional discussion of auctions.

PART II—INTERNET RETAILING

In Part II we describe EC B2C applications in two chapters. Chapter 3 addresses e-tailing and electronic service industries. An online appendix to Chapter 3 describes how to build electronic storefronts; two related tutorials are also available online. Chapter 4 deals with consumer behavior online, market research, and online advertising.

PART III—BUSINESS-TO-BUSINESS E-COMMERCE

In Part III we examine the one-to-many B2B models (Chapter 5), including auctions, and the many-to-many models (Chapter 6), including exchanges. Collaborative commerce is also covered in Chapter 5. An online appendix to Chapter 5 provides discussion of the transition from traditional EDI to Internet-based EDI, and an online appendix to Chapter 6 provides additional material on extranets.

PART IV—OTHER EC MODELS AND APPLICATIONS

Part IV begins with a description of several interesting applications such as e-government, intrabusiness applications, consumer-to-consumer EC, and e-learning (Chapter 7). Chapter 8 explores the developing applications in the world of wireless EC (m-commerce and l-commerce).

PART V—SUPPORTING EC APPLICATIONS

Chapter 9, the first chapter of Part V, begins with a discussion of the need to protect privacy and intellectual property. It also describes various types of computer fraud and crime and discusses how to minimize these risks through appropriate security programs. Chapter 10 describes the major EC support services: electronic payments and order fulfillment. An online appendix to Chapter 10 explores issues surrounding content generation, delivery, and management.

PART VI—STRATEGY AND IMPLEMENTATION

Chapter 11 discusses strategic issues in implementing and deploying EC. The chapter also presents electronic communities, global EC, and EC for small businesses. This chapter closes the book with an overview of future EC directions. An interactive online tutorial deals with creation of a business plan for Internet companies and a business case for EC applications.

LEARNING AIDS

The text offers a number of learning aids to the student:

CHAPTER OUTLINES

Detailed outlines ("Content") at the beginning of each chapter provide a quick overview of the major topics covered.

LEARNING OBJECTIVES

Learning objectives at the beginning of each chapter help students focus their efforts and alert them to the important concepts to be discussed.

OPENING VIGNETTES

Each chapter opens with a real-world example that illustrates the importance of EC to modern corporations. These cases were carefully chosen to call attention to the major topics covered in the chapters. Following each vignette, a short section titled "What We Can Learn . . ." links the important issues in the vignette to the subject matter of the chapter.

EC APPLICATION CASES

In-chapter cases highlight real-world problems encountered by organizations as they develop and implement EC. Questions follow each case to help direct student attention to the implications of the case material.

INSIGHTS AND ADDITIONS

Topics sometimes require additional elaboration or demonstration. Insights and Additions boxes provide an eye-catching repository for such content.

EXHIBITS

Numerous attractive exhibits (both illustrations and tables) extend and supplement the text discussion.

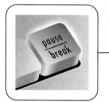

REVIEW QUESTIONS

Each section ends with a series of review questions about the specific section. Signaled by the "Pause/Break" icon shown here, these questions are intended to help students summarize the concepts introduced and to digest the essentials of each section before moving on to another topic.

MARGINAL GLOSSARY AND KEY TERMS

Each bolded Key Term is defined in the margin when it first appears. In addition, an alphabetical list of Key Terms appears at the end of each chapter with a page reference to the location in the chapter where the term is discussed.

MANAGERIAL ISSUES

The final section of every chapter explores some of the special concerns managers face as they adapt to doing business in cyberspace. These issues are framed as questions to maximize readers' active engagement with them.

CHAPTER SUMMARY

The chapter summary is linked one-to-one to the learning objectives introduced at the beginning of each chapter.

END-OF-CHAPTER EXERCISES

Different types of questions measure students' comprehension and their ability to apply knowledge. Discussion Questions are intended to promote class discussion and develop critical thinking skills. Internet Exercises are challenging assignments that require students to surf the Internet and apply what they have learned. Over 200 hands-on exercises send students to interesting Web sites to conduct research, investigate an application, download demos, or learn about state-of-the-art technology. The Team Assignment and Role Playing exercises are challenging group projects designed to foster teamwork.

REAL-WORLD CASES

Each chapter ends with a real-world case, which is presented in somewhat more depth than the in-chapter EC Application Cases. Questions follow each case.

SUPPLEMENTARY MATERIALS

The following support materials are also available.

INSTRUCTOR'S RESOURCE CD-ROM

This convenient *Instructor's CD-ROM* includes all of the supplements: Instructor's Manual, Test Item File, Windows PH Test Manager, PowerPoint Lecture Notes, and Image Library (text art). The Instructor's Manual, written by Professor Jon C. Outland of National American University, includes answers to all review and discussion questions, exercises, and case questions. The Test Item File (Test Bank), written by Professor James Steele of Chattanooga State Technical Community College, includes multiple-choice, true-false, and essay questions for each chapter. The Test Bank is provided in Microsoft Word, as well as in the form of the Windows PH Test Manager. The PowerPoint Lecture Notes, by Judy Lang, are oriented toward text learning objectives. They are also available at the book's Web site at prenhall.com/turban.

WEB SITE

The book is supported by a Companion Website that includes:

a. An online chapter (Chapter 12 on EC applications and infrastructure).

b. Four technology appendices.

c. Three interactive tutorials, two on storefront development (store.yahoo and bigstep.com), and one on preparation of an EC business plan.

d. A password-protected faculty area where instructors can download the Instructor's Manual.

e. PowerPoint Lecture Notes.

f. Interactive Study Guide, by Professor Jon C. Outland of National American University, includes multiple-choice, true-false, and essay questions for each chapter. Each question includes a hint and coaching tip for students' reference. Students receive automatic feedback upon submitting each quiz.

g. All of the Internet Exercises from the end of each chapter in the text are provided on the Web site for convenient student use.

h. Chapter Updates are posted periodically to help both students and instructors stay up to date with what's happening in e-commerce and e-business today and how it relates to chapter material.

i. EC case studies, some with teaching notes.

j. Links to a large number of case studies, including customer success stories and academically oriented cases.

k. Links to many EC vendors' sites.

l. Supplementary material to some chapters.

WEB STRATEGY PRO

Prentice Hall is pleased to offer this powerful educational version of Web Strategy Pro software. This Windows-based, easy-to-use program allows you to bring the entire process of planning an Internet strategy alive in your classroom in seven easy steps. Web Strategy Pro is not available as a stand-alone item but can be packaged with the Turban text at an additional charge. Contact your local Prentice Hall representative for more details.

ONLINE COURSES

WebCT (prenhall.com/webct). Gold Level Customer Support, available exclusively to adopters of Prentice Hall courses, is provided free of charge upon adoption and provides you with priority assistance, training discounts, and dedicated technical support.

BlackBoard (prenhall.com/blackboard). Prentice Hall's abundant online content combined with BlackBoard's popular tools and interface result in robust Web-based courses that are easy to implement, manage, and use—taking your courses to new heights in student interaction and learning.

CourseCompass (prenhall.com/coursecompass). CourseCompass is a dynamic, interactive online course management tool powered exclusively for Pearson Education by BlackBoard. This exciting product allows you to teach market-leading Pearson Education content in an easy-to-use customizable format.

ACKNOWLEDGMENTS

Many individuals helped us create this text. Faculty feedback was solicited via reviews and through a focus group. We are grateful to the following faculty for their contributions.

CONTENT CONTRIBUTORS

The following individuals contributed material:

- ▶ Matthew Lee, City University of Hong Kong, an Internet lawyer and IS professor, contributed to Chapter 9.

- ▶ Merrill Warkentin of Mississippi State University contributed to Chapter 3. Merrill is a co-author of our *Electronic Commerce 2002*.

- ▶ Jae K. Lee of Korea Advance Institute of Science and Technology contributed Chapters 5 and 6. Lee is also a co-author of *Electronic Commerce 2002*.

- ▶ Mohamed Khalifa, City University of Hong Kong, contributed to online Chapter 12.

- ▶ Dennis Viehland of Massey University in New Zealand read the entire manuscript and provided valuable comments and additional material in many places.

REVIEWERS

We wish to thank the faculty who participated in reviews of this text and our other EC titles.

David Ambrosini, Cabrillo College

Deborah Ballou, University of Notre Dame

Martin Barriff, Illinois Institute of Technology

Stefan Brandle, Taylor University

Joseph Brooks, University of Hawaii

John Bugado, National University

Ernest Capozzolli, Troy State University

Jack Cook, State University of New York at Geneseo

Larry Corman, Fort Lewis College

Mary Culnan, Georgetown University

Ted Ferretti, Northeastern University

Ken Griggs, California Polytechnic University

Varun Grover, University of South Carolina

James Henson, Barry University

Paul Hu, University of Utah

Jeffrey Johnson, Utah State University

Morgan Jones, University of North Carolina

Douglas Kline, Sam Houston State University

Byungtae Lee, University of Illinois at Chicago

Lakshmi Lyer, University of North Carolina

Michael McLeod, East Carolina University

Susan McNamara, Northeastern University

Mohon Menon, University of South Alabama

Ajay Mishra, SUNY–Binghamton

Bud Mishra, New York University

William Nance, San Jose State University

Katherine Olson, Northern Virginia Community College

Craig Peterson, Utah State University

Greg Rose, California State University, Chico

Linda Salchenberger, Loyola University of Chicago

George Schell, University of North Carolina at Wilmington

Sri Sharma, Oakland University

Sumit Sircar, University of Texas at Arlington

Kan Sugandh, DeVry Institute of Technology

Linda Volonino, Canisius College

Gregory Wood, Canisius College

James Zemanek, East Carolina University

Many students at City University of Hong Kong participated in this project in several ways. Some helped us to find materials while others provided feedback. They are too many to name individually, but thanks goes to all of you.

Several individuals helped us with the administrative work. Special mention goes to Judy Lang of Eastern Illinois University who helped in editing, typing, URL verification, and more. We also thank Grace Choi of City University of Hong Kong for her help in typing and editing. Several student assistants helped with library searches, typing, and diagramming. Most of the work was done by Mavis Chan. We thank all these people for their dedication and superb performance shown throughout the project.

The Information System Department of City University of Hong Kong was extremely supportive in providing all the necessary assistance. Many faculty member provided advice and support material. Special thanks go to Chris Wagner, the department head, and to Doug Vogel, Matthew Lee, and Louis Ma.

We also recognize the various organizations and corporations that provided us with permission to reproduce material.

Thanks also to the Prentice Hall team that helped us from the inception of the project to its completion under the leadership of Executive Editor Bob Horan and Publisher and Vice President Natalie Anderson. The dedicated staff includes Project Manager-Editorial Lori Cerreto, Production Manager Gail Steier de Acevedo, Project Manager-Production April Montana, Art Director Pat Smythe, Editorial Assistant Maat Van Uitert, Marketing Manager Sharon Turkovich, Marketing Assistant Scott Patterson, and Media Project Manager Joan Waxman.

Last, but not least, we thank Ann Torbert, the book's development editor, who spent long hours in contributing innovative ideas and providing the necessary editing.

OVERVIEW OF ELECTRONIC COMMERCE

Content

Learning objectives

Upon completion of this chapter, you will be able to:

▶ Define electronic commerce (EC) and describe its various categories.

▶ Describe and discuss the content and framework of EC.

▶ Describe the major types of EC transactions.

▶ Describe some EC business models.

▶ Discuss the benefits of EC to organizations, consumers, and society.

▶ Describe the limitations of EC.

▶ Describe the role of the digital revolution in EC and the economic impact of EC.

▶ Discuss the contribution of EC in helping organizations respond to environmental pressures.

▶ Discuss some major managerial issues regarding EC.

QANTAS AIRWAYS—A NEW WAY TO COMPETE

The Problem

In 1999 and 2000, rising fuel costs placed pressure on the airline industry. Increased fuel prices arrived quickly and without warning. For Qantas Airways (*qantas.com.au*), Australia's largest airline, the increase in fuel prices was just one of several problems. The airline faced two new domestic competitors, Impulse and Virgin Blue, as well as higher fees at Sydney Airport. In 2001 traffic dwindled, especially after the September 11 disaster. In addition, the airline needed to upgrade its fleet to stay competitive, replacing aging aircraft and purchasing new 500-seat planes. Finally, the Australian economy slowed down in 2000 and 2001, and the Australian dollar was sinking against the U.S. dollar. Can Qantas, the world's second-oldest airline, survive against such business pressures?

The Solution

In addition to traditional responses, such as buying fuel contracts for future dates, Qantas took major steps to implement *electronic commerce* (e-commerce, EC), which involves buying, selling, and exchanging goods, services, information, and payments electronically. Qantas undertook a number of major initiatives:

- Joined Airnew Co., a procurement *business-to-business (B2B) electronic-marketplace* (e-marketplace), that links dozens of major airlines with suppliers of fuel, fuel services, flight maintenance services, catering, and other services and suppliers. The e-marketplace uses electronic catalogs and conducts a variety of auctions.

- Joined *Corprocure.com.au* together with 13 other large corporations in Australia to electronically purchase general goods and services, such as office supplies, light bulbs, and maintenance services.

- Formed a Pan-Pacific electronic marketplace that provides a full spectrum of travel services (airline tickets, hotels, cars, etc.). This e-marketplace provides products and services to business partners, such as travel agencies, who can use the same marketplace to sell directly to individual consumers. This type of transaction is known as a business-to-business-to-consumer (B2B2C) transaction.

Qantas also implemented the following EC activities:

- Sends e-mails to all 2.4 million of its frequent-flyer members, inviting them to book a flight online. As an incentive to book online, customers are rewarded with mileage bonuses and an opportunity to win $10,000 AU.

- Provides information on arrival and departure times, as well as flight delays, to travelers via mobile phones and other wireless devices.

- Increases brand visibility by providing online training to travel agents.

- Assists in the training of its 30,000 employees in 32 countries via Qantas College Online. This program is part of Qantas's *business-to-employees (B2E)* initiative (*qfcollege.edu.au*).

- Operates a credit union with 50,000 members worldwide (another B2E project). Members make over 100,000 transactions a month at *qantascu.com.au*. Services are comparable with those of commercial online banks.

The Results

Leading an old-economy company into e-commerce is not easy. It requires changing existing organization structures and processes and fitting new-economy strategies with old-economy ways of thinking. Qantas knows that this is the path it must take. Results are not expected overnight. It will take years and hundreds of millions of dollars to implement these and dozens more EC initiatives. Yet, Qantas expects to see an estimated $85 million AU in cost reductions per year by 2003. It also expects to increase annual revenues by $700 million from nontravel sales. One piece of bright news for Qantas is that it has successfully outlasted competitor Impulse, which went out of business in 2001.

What We Can Learn . . .

As the story about Qantas demonstrates, traditional brick-and-mortar companies are facing increasing competitive and other environmental pressures. A possible response to these pressures is to introduce a variety of e-commerce initiatives that can reduce costs, increase customer service, and open markets to more customers. The implementation of such e-commerce initiatives and the issues involved will be explored in this chapter and throughout this textbook.

Chapter 1 will define e-commerce and discuss the content of the field and the various EC business models.

It also will illustrate the benefits and limitations of e-commerce. Finally, the chapter will demonstrate the economics of EC that make it so attractive and the role EC plays in today's economy.

1.1   ELECTRONIC COMMERCE DEFINITIONS AND CONCEPTS

ELECTRONIC COMMERCE

Electronic commerce (EC, e-commerce) describes the process of buying, selling, or exchanging products, services, and information via computer networks, including the Internet. Kalakota and Whinston (1997) define EC from four perspectives:

▶ **From a communications perspective**, EC is the delivery of goods, services, information, or payments over computer networks or by any other electronic means.

▶ **From a business process perspective**, EC is the application of technology toward the automation of business transactions and workflow.

▶ **From a service perspective**, EC is a tool that addresses the desire of firms, consumers, and management to cut service costs while improving the quality of customer service and increasing the speed of service delivery.

▶ **From an online perspective**, EC provides the capability of buying and selling products and information over the Internet and other online services.

We add two more perspectives to this list:

▶ **From a collaborations perspective**, EC is the facilitator for inter- and intra-organizational collaboration.

▶ **From a community perspective**, EC provides a gathering place for community members, to learn, transact, and collaborate.

electronic commerce (EC)
The process of buying, selling, or exchanging products, services, and information via computer networks.

E-BUSINESS

Some people define the term commerce as describing transactions conducted between business partners. When this definition of commerce is used, some people find the term electronic commerce to be fairly narrow. Thus, many use the term **e-business**. E-business refers to a broader definition of EC, not just the buying and selling of goods and services, but also servicing customers, collaborating with business partners, and conducting electronic transactions within an organization. In this book we use the broadest meaning of electronic commerce, which is basically equivalent to e-business. The two terms will be used interchangeably throughout the text.

e-business
A broader definition of EC that includes not just the buying and selling of goods and services, but also servicing customers, collaborating with business partners, and conducting electronic transactions within an organization.

PURE VS. PARTIAL EC

brick-and-mortar organizations
Old-economy organizations (corporations) that perform all of their business off-line, selling physical products by means of physical agents.

pure online virtual organizations
New-economy organizations that sell products or services only online.

click-and-mortar organizations
Organizations that conduct e-commerce activities, but do their primary business in the physical world.

Electronic commerce can take several forms depending on the degree of digitization (the transformation from physical to digital) of (1) the product (service) sold, (2) the process, and (3) the delivery agent (or intermediary). Choi et al. (1997) created a framework, shown in Exhibit 1.1, that explains the possible configurations of these three dimensions. A product can be physical or digital, the process can be physical or digital, and the delivery agent can be physical or digital. These alternatives create eight cubes, each of which has three dimensions. In traditional commerce, all three dimensions are physical (lower-left cube), and in pure EC, all dimensions are digital (upper-right cube). All other cubes include a mix of digital and physical dimensions.

If there is at least one digital dimension, we consider the situation EC, but only *partial EC*. For example, buying a book from Amazon.com is partial EC, because the physical book is delivered by FedEx. However, buying an e-book from Amazon.com or a software product from buy.com is *pure EC*, because the product delivery, payment, and agent are all digital.

Pure physical organizations (corporations) are referred to as **brick-and-mortar** or old-economy organizations, whereas pure EC organizations are considered **pure online virtual organizations**. **Click-and-mortar organizations** are those that conduct some e-commerce activities, yet their primary business is done in the physical world. Gradually, many brick-and-mortar companies are changing to click-and-mortar ones (e.g., Qantas Airways).

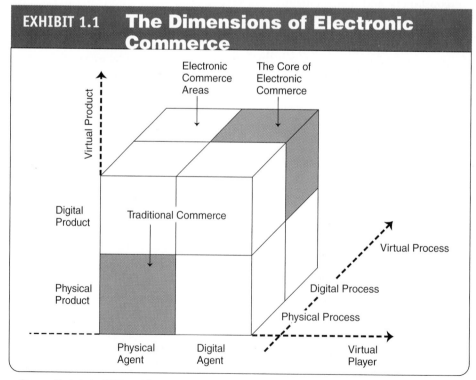

EXHIBIT 1.1   The Dimensions of Electronic Commerce

Source: Choi et al., 1997, p. 18.

INTERNET VS. NON-INTERNET EC

Most EC is done over the Internet. EC can also be conducted on private networks, such as *value-added networks* (VANs, networks that add communication services to existing common carriers), on *local area networks* (LANs), or even on a single computerized machine. For example, buying food from a vending machine and paying with a smart card or a cell phone can be viewed as an EC activity.

ELECTRONIC MARKETS VS. INTERORGANIZATIONAL SYSTEMS

E-commerce can be conducted in an **electronic market** where buyers and sellers meet to exchange goods, services, money, or information. Or, it can be done in **interorganizational information systems (IOSs)**, where routine transaction processing and information flow take place between two or more organizations. E-commerce is enabling a large number of organizations, both private and public, in manufacturing, agriculture, and services, not only to excel, but also in many cases to survive.

electronic market
An online marketplace where buyers and sellers meet to exchange goods, services, money, or information.

interorganizational information systems (IOSs)
Communications systems that allow routine transaction processing and information flow between two or more organizations.

▶ Define EC and e-business.
▶ Distinguish between pure and partial EC.
▶ Define click-and-mortar organizations.

1.2   THE EC FRAMEWORK AND FIELD

The EC field is a diversified one, involving many activities, organizational units, and technologies (e.g., see Shaw et al. 2000). Therefore, a framework to describe its content is useful.

AN EC FRAMEWORK

There are dozens of EC applications, some of which were illustrated in the opening vignette about Qantas; others will be shown throughout the book (also see Huff et al. 2001 and Farhoomand and Lovelock 2001). To execute these applications, companies need the right information, infrastructure, and support services. Exhibit 1.2 shows how EC applications are supported by infrastructure and by five support areas (shown as supporting pillars): people, public policy, technical standards, business partners, and support services.

▶ **People.** Sellers, buyers, intermediaries, employees, and any other participants.
▶ **Public policy.** Legal and other policy issues, such as privacy protection, that are determined by the government. (Legal and security issues are the topic of Chapter 9.)

EXHIBIT 1.2   A Framework for Electronic Commerce

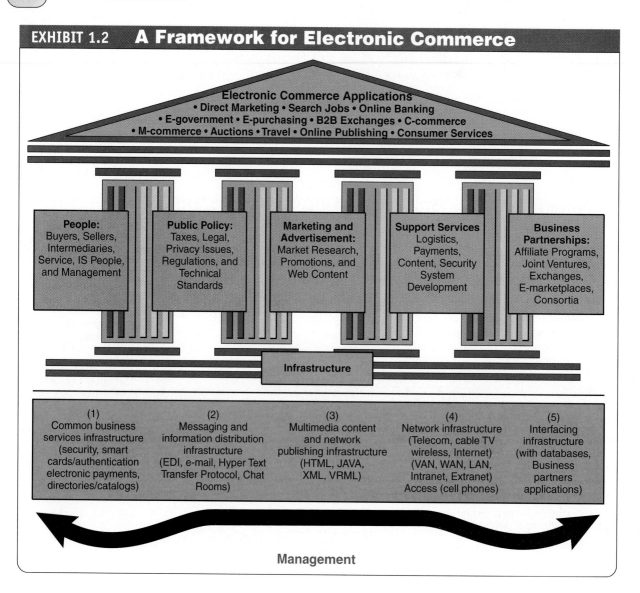

Electronic Commerce Applications
• Direct Marketing • Search Jobs • Online Banking
• E-government • E-purchasing • B2B Exchanges • C-commerce
• M-commerce • Auctions • Travel • Online Publishing • Consumer Services

People:
Buyers, Sellers, Intermediaries, Service, IS People, and Management

Public Policy:
Taxes, Legal, Privacy Issues, Regulations, and Technical Standards

Marketing and Advertisement:
Market Research, Promotions, and Web Content

Support Services
Logistics, Payments, Content, Security System Development

Business Partnerships:
Affiliate Programs, Joint Ventures, Exchanges, E-marketplaces, Consortia

Infrastructure

(1)
Common business services infrastructure (security, smart cards/authentication electronic payments, directories/catalogs)

(2)
Messaging and information distribution infrastructure (EDI, e-mail, Hyper Text Transfer Protocol, Chat Rooms)

(3)
Multimedia content and network publishing infrastructure (HTML, JAVA, XML, VRML)

(4)
Network infrastructure (Telecom, cable TV wireless, Internet) (VAN, WAN, LAN, Intranet, Extranet) Access (cell phones)

(5)
Interfacing infrastructure (with databases, Business partners applications)

Management

▶ **Technical standards and protocols.** Security and payment protocols, such as SSL (secure socket layer). Companies need standards and protocols so that they can communicate with one another or move money online in a secured manner. (Standards are discussed in Chapters 8 and 9.)

▶ **Business partners.** Joint ventures, exchanges, and business partnerships of various sorts. E-commerce occurs frequently throughout the *supply chain* (the interactions between a company and its suppliers, customers, and other partners) and between or among business partners. (Business partnerships are discussed in Chapters 5 and 6.)

▶ **Support services.** Market research (Chapter 4), advertising (Chapter 4), payments (Chapter 10), logistics (Chapter 10), and security (Chapter 9). Many support services are needed in EC. All of these infrastructure components require good management practices. This means that companies need to plan, organize, motivate, devise strategy, and reengineer processes as needed.

Exhibit 1.2 can be viewed as a framework for understanding the relationships among the EC components and for conducting research in the EC field. In this text we will provide details on most of these topics. The infrastructures of EC technologies are described in Appendices A–D at the book's Web site and in Chapter 12 online.

CLASSIFICATION OF EC BY THE NATURE OF THE TRANSACTION

A common classification of EC is by the nature of the transaction or the relationship among participants. The following types of EC are commonly distinguished.

▶ **Business-to-business (B2B).** All of the participants in **business-to-business (B2B)** e-commerce are businesses or other organizations. Today most EC is B2B (Cunningham 2001).

▶ **Business-to-consumer (B2C). Business-to-consumer (B2C)** EC includes retail transactions from businesses to individual shoppers. The typical shopper at Amazon.com is a *consumer,* or *customer.* This EC type is also called **e-tailing.**

▶ **Business-to-business-to-consumer (B2B2C).** In business-to-business-to-consumer (B2B2C) EC, a business provides some product or service to a client business. The client business maintains its own customers, to whom the product or service is provided. An example is Qantas' Pan-Pacific market cited earlier. The term B2B frequently is used to describe B2B2C as well.

▶ **Consumer-to-business (C2B).** This category includes individuals who use the Internet to sell products or services to organizations, as well as individuals who seek sellers to bid on products or services they need. Priceline.com is a well-known C2B organizer.

▶ **Consumer-to-consumer (C2C).** In the **consumer-to-consumer (C2C)** category, consumers sell directly to other consumers. Examples include individuals selling residential property, cars, and so on in online classified ads. The advertisement of personal services over the Internet and the selling of knowledge and expertise online are other examples of C2C (e.g., guru.com). In addition, several auction sites allow individuals to place items up for auction. A special type of C2C is where people exchange music, videos, software, and other digitizable goods electronically using a *peer-to-peer* (P2P) technology. A well-known organizer of P2P is Napster (napster.com). (As a result of legal challenges, Napster no longer offers free exchanges; in 2002 it tried offering only digital goods that people pay for.)

▶ **Mobile commerce.** E-commerce transactions and activities conducted in a wireless environment are referred to as **mobile commerce,** or **m-commerce.** Such transactions targeted to individuals in specific locations, at specific times, are referred to as **location-based commerce,** or **l-commerce.**

▶ **Intrabusiness (organizational) EC.** The **intrabusiness EC** category includes all internal organizational activities that involve the exchange of goods, services, or information among various units and individuals in that organization. Activities can range from selling corporate products to employees to online training and collaborative design efforts. Intrabusiness EC is usually performed on intranets or corporate portals (in general, gateways to the Web).

business-to-business (B2B)
E-commerce model in which all of the participants are businesses or other organizations.

business-to-consumer (B2C)
E-commerce model in which businesses sell to individual shoppers.

e-tailing
Online retailing, usually B2C.

consumer-to-consumer (C2C)
E-commerce model in which consumers sell directly to other consumers.

mobile commerce (m-commerce)
E-commerce transactions and activities conducted in a wireless environment.

location commerce (l-commerce)
M-commerce transactions targeted to individuals in specific locations, at specific times.

intrabusiness EC
E-commerce category that includes all internal organizational activities that involve the exchange of goods, services, or information among various units and individuals in an organization.

business-to-employees (B2E)
E-commerce model in which an organization delivers services, information, or products to its individual employees.

collaborative commerce (c-commerce)
E-commerce model in which individuals or groups communicate or collaborate online.

e-government
E-commerce model in which a government entity buys or provides goods, services, or information to businesses or individual citizens.

exchange
A public electronic market with many buyers and sellers.

exchange-to-exchange (E2E)
E-commerce model in which electronic exchanges formally connect to one another for the purpose of exchanging information.

▶ **Business-to-employees (B2E).** The **business-to-employees (B2E)** category is a subset of the intrabusiness category in which the organization delivers services, information, or products to individual employees, as Qantas Airways is doing with its College Online.

▶ **Collaborative commerce.** When individuals or groups communicate or collaborate online they may be engaged in **collaborative commerce (c-commerce)**. For example, business partners in different locations may design a product together, using screen sharing, or they may jointly forecast market demand.

▶ **Nonbusiness EC.** An increasing number of nonbusiness institutions such as academic institutions, not-for-profit organizations, religious organizations, social organizations, and government agencies are using EC to reduce their expenses or to improve their general operations and customer service. (Note that in the previous categories one can usually replace the word *business* with *organization*.)

▶ **E-government: Government-to-citizens (G2C) and to others.** In **e-government** EC, a government entity buys or provides goods, services, or information to businesses or individual citizens.

▶ **Exchange-to-exchange (E2E).** An **exchange** describes a public electronic market with many buyers and sellers. As these proliferate, it is logical for exchanges to connect to one another. **Exchange-to-exchange (E2E)** EC is a formal system that connects exchanges.

We will provide many examples of the various types of EC transactions throughout this book.

THE INTERDISCIPLINARY NATURE OF EC

Because EC is a new field, it is just now developing its theoretical and scientific foundations. From just a brief overview of the different EC models and infrastructure, you can probably see that EC is based on several different disciplines. The major EC disciplines are marketing, computer science, consumer behavior, finance, economics, management information systems, accounting, management, business law, robotics, public administration, and engineering.

A BRIEF HISTORY OF EC

electronic data interchange (EDI)
Technology to electronically transfer documents such as purchase orders between firms doing business.

EC applications were first developed in the early 1970s with innovations such as *electronic funds transfers (EFT)*, in which funds could be transferred electronically. However, the extent of the applications was limited to large corporations, financial institutions, and a few other daring businesses. Then came **electronic data interchange (EDI)**, a technology to electronically transfer documents such as purchase orders, invoices, and electronic payments between firms doing business. (See Chapter 5 for more on EDI.) This new application enlarged the pool of participating companies from financial institutions to manufacturers, retailers, services, and many other types of businesses. More new EC applications followed, ranging from stock trading to travel reservation systems. Such systems were called IOS (interorganizational systems) applications, and their strategic value has been widely recognized.

As the Internet became more commercialized and users flocked to participate in the World Wide Web in the early 1990s, the term *electronic commerce* was coined. EC applications rapidly expanded. One reason for this rapid expansion was the development of new networks, protocols, software, and specifications. The other reason was an increase in competition and other business pressures.

Since 1995, Internet users have witnessed the development of many innovative applications ranging from interactive advertisements to virtual reality experiences. Almost every medium- and large-sized organization in the world now has a Web site, and most large U.S. corporations have comprehensive portals through which employees, business partners, and the public can access corporate information. Many of these sites contain tens of thousand of pages and links. In 1999, the emphasis of EC shifted from B2C to B2B. Also, consolidation of organizations engaging in EC is now taking place following a number of industry failures in the late 1990s, 2000, and 2001.

EC Successes

During the last few years we have seen extremely successful pure online EC companies such as eBay, VeriSign, AOL, and Checkpoint. We also have witnessed major successes in click-and-mortar companies such as General Electric, IBM, Intel, and Schwab. Many small companies, for example, Alloy.com (a young-adults-oriented portal) and Campusfood.com, have also been successful (see EC Application Case 1.1).

EC Failures

However, starting in 1999, a large number of EC companies, especially e-tailing ones, began to fail (see startupfailures.com, disobey.com/ghostsites, and Useem 2000). (We will discuss reasons for these failures in detail in Chapters 3 and 11.) Does this mean that EC is just a buzzword and its days are numbered? Absolutely not! The EC field is basically experiencing consolidation as companies test different business models and organizational structures. Most EC companies, including giants such as Amazon.com, are not yet making a profit, but they are expanding operations and generating increasing sales. It is believed that by 2003, many of the major EC companies will begin to generate profits. (Amazon.com posted its first quarterly profit in the fourth quarter of 2001, largely on the strength of holiday sales, though it still lost money for the year.)

THE FUTURE OF EC

In 1996, Forrester Research Institute (forrester.com) predicted that B2C would be a $6.6 billion business in 2000, up from $518 million in 1996. B2C sales in the United States in 2000 actually were about 1 percent of total retail sales, and they are increasing at about 40 percent a year. In 2000, B2C sales totaled about $18 billion, greatly exceeding the 1996 estimate. Today's predictions on the future size of EC vary. For 2004, total online shopping and B2B transactions in the United States are estimated to be in the range of $3 to $7 trillion. Some EC applications,

EC APPLICATION CASE 1.1

Individuals and Communities

THE SUCCESS STORY OF CAMPUSFOOD.COM

Campusfood.com's recipe for success was a simple one: Provide interactive menus to college students, using the power of the Internet to enhance traditional telephone ordering of meals. Launched at the University of Pennsylvania (Penn), the company took thousands of orders for local restaurants, bringing pizzas, hoagies, and wings to the Penn community.

Founder Michael Saunders began developing the site in 1997 while he was a junior at Penn. With the help of some classmates, the site was launched in 1998. After graduation, Saunders began building the company's customer base. This involved registering other universities, attracting students, and generating a list of restaurants from which students could order food for delivery. Currently, some of these activities are outsourced to a marketing firm, enabling the addition of dozens of schools nationwide.

Financed through private investors, friends, and family members, the site was built on an investment of less than $1 million. (For comparison, another company with services also reaching the college-student market invested $100 million.) Campusfood.com's revenue is generated through transaction fees; the site takes a 5 percent commission on each order.

When you visit *campusfood.com*, you can:

▶ Navigate through a list of local restaurants, their hours of operation, addresses, phone numbers, and other information.

▶ Browse an interactive menu. The company takes a restaurant's standard print menu and researches each one in order to convert it to an electronic menu that lists every topping, every special, and every drink offered, along with the latest prices.

▶ Bypass "busy" telephone signals to place an order online, and in doing so, avoid miscommunications.

▶ Get access to special foods, promotions, and restaurant giveaways. The company is working to set up meal deals that are available exclusively online for Campusfood.com customers.

▶ Arrange electronic payment of your order.

Sources: Compiled from M. Prince, "Easy Doesn't Do It," *Wall Street Journal,* July 17, 2000, and *campusfood.com*, 2002.

Questions

▶ Classify this application by EC type and business model.

▶ Explain the benefits of Campusfood.com for students and for restaurants.

▶ Trace the flow of digitized information in this venture.

▶ How does the outsourcing of marketing activities contribute to the business?

such as online auctions and online stock trading, were initially growing at a rate of 10 to 15 percent per month. The number of Internet users worldwide is predicted to reach 750 million by 2008. Experts predict that as many as 50 percent of all Internet users will shop online. (See Chapter 11 for further discussion about the future of EC.) (Note: The predictions in this chapter were compiled from AMR Research, emarketer.com, and Forrester.com.)

▶ List the major components of the EC framework.

▶ List the major transactional types of EC.

▶ Describe the major landmarks in EC history.

1.3   E-COMMERCE BUSINESS PLANS, CASES, AND MODELS

One of the major characteristics of EC is that it enables the creation of new business models. A **business model** is a method of doing business by which a company can generate revenue to sustain itself. The model spells out where the company is positioned in the value chain. Some models are very simple. For example, Nokia makes cellular phones, sells them, and generates a profit. In contrast, a TV station provides free broadcasting. Its survival depends on a complex model involving advertisers and content providers. Public Internet portals, such as Yahoo!, also use a complex business model. One company may have several business models. Business models are a component of a business plan or a business case.

business model
A method of doing business by which a company can generate revenue to sustain itself.

BUSINESS PLANS AND BUSINESS CASES

A **business plan** is a written document that identifies the company's business goals and outlines a plan on how to achieve them. Business plans are used for various purposes. Entrepreneurs use business plans to get funding from investors, such as *venture capitalists*. Or, a business plan can be used for the purposes of restructuring or reengineering an organization. The term is a very broad one, and its content and meaning vary with the type, purpose, and size of the plan and the amount of money involved. The content of a typical business plan is shown in the Insights and Additions box at the top of the next page. Several software packages are available for the creation of business plans (e.g., see bplans.com and planware.org).

business plan
A written document that identifies the business goals and outlines the plan how to achieve them.

A **business case** is a written document that is used by managers to garner funding for specific applications or projects. Its major emphasis is the justification for a specific investment. A business case is usually conducted in existing organizations that want to embark on new projects, for example, an e-procurement project. The business case provides the bridge between the initial plan and its execution. Its purpose is not only to gain approval and funding, but also to provide the foundation for tactical decision making and technology risk management. The business case helps to clarify how the organization will best use its resources to accomplish the e-strategy. [A complete coverage of business cases for e-commerce is provided by Kalakota and Robinson (2001) and in online Tutorial 3 on the book's Web site.] Software for the business case of e-commerce is commercially available (e.g., from paloalto.com and bplans.com).

business case
A written document that is used by managers to garner funding for specific applications or projects; its major emphasis is the justification for a specific investment.

Note that a business plan concentrates on the *viability* of a company, whereas a business case concentrates on justification, risk management, and fit with the organization's mission. One business plan or business case may contain several business models. (For more discussion of business plans and business cases, see Chapter 11.)

THE STRUCTURE OF BUSINESS MODELS

The structure of business models varies because there are many ways that companies can generate revenues. All business models, however, must specify their revenue model. A **revenue model** outlines how the company or the EC project will earn

revenue model
Description of how the company or an EC project will earn revenue.

Insights and Additions   The Content of a Business Plan

The following is a suggested structure for a dot-com business plan based on Eglash (2001).

▶ Mission statement and company description.

▶ The management team: Who they are, their experience, etc.

▶ The market and the customers: Who the potential customers are (demographics, location, etc.), the size of the market, and how the company and proposed product will serve the market. What the perceived *value proposition* is.

▶ The industry and competition: What companies and products the proposed business is going to compete with. The competitive advantage of the proposal.

▶ The specifics of the products and/or services to be offered, and how they will be developed.

▶ Marketing and sales plan: How marketing and sales will be done. Advertising and promotion plans. How customer service will be provided. Is there a need for market research? If so, how will it be done?

▶ Operations: How the business will be run. What operations will be done in-house and what will be outsourced?

▶ Financial projections and plans: The *revenue generation model,* cash flow, cost of financing, and so on.

▶ Risk analysis: How risky is the venture? What are the contingencies?

▶ Technology analysis: What technology is necessary and how is it going to be obtained?

revenue. For example, in our opening vignette, the revenue model for Qantas's Pan-Pacific project showed revenue from online sales. Other typical revenue models are:

- **Transaction fees.** A company receives commission paid on the volume of transactions made. For example, what you pay when you buy or sell a house would be a transaction fee; the more you pay, the higher the transaction fee.

- **Subscription fees.** Customers pay a fixed amount, usually monthly, to get some type of service. An example would be a customer's access fee to America Online (AOL). Thus, AOL's primary revenue model is subscription based.

- **Advertisement fees.** Companies charge others to place a banner on their sites (see Chapter 4).

- **Affiliate fees.** Companies receive commissions for referring customers to other Web sites.

- **Sales.** Companies generate revenue from selling on their Web sites or from providing a service. An example is when Walmart.com sells a product line.

- **Other models.** Some companies allow you to play games for a fee or watch a sports competition in real time (e.g., msn.espn.go.com).

Exhibit 1.3 (on page 14) summarizes the five most common revenue models. A company uses its business model to describe *how* it will earn income, and its business model to describe the *process* it will use to earn those revenues. For example, the revenue model of 7-Eleven stores in Japan is the sales model. Its business model would show that customers can order different products online (using a PC, cell phone, or at 7-Eleven stores, where they can pay). It also would show that customers can pick up the merchandise at 7-Eleven stores (only in Japan) or have it shipped to their homes for an extra charge.

Value Proposition

A **value proposition** refers to the benefits a company can derive from using EC. In B2C e-commerce, for example, a value proposition defines how a company product or service fulfills a customer need. The value proposition is an important part of the marketing plan of any product or service.

> **value proposition**
> Description of the benefits a company can derive from using EC.

TYPICAL BUSINESS MODELS IN EC

There are many types of EC business models. Examples and details can be found throughout this text (and also in Timmers 1999; Applegate 2000; and Afuah and Tucci 2000). The following list describes some of the most common or visible models.

1. **Online, direct marketing.** The most obvious model is that of selling online, from manufacturers to customers (eliminating intermediaries) or from retailers to consumers (making distribution more efficient). Such a model is especially efficient for digitizable products and services. It is practiced in B2C and B2B types of EC.

2. **Electronic tendering systems.** Large organizational buyers, private or public, usually make their purchases through a tendering (bidding) system, also known as a **reverse auction** (Chapter 2). Such a tendering can be done online, saving time and money. Pioneered by General Electric Corp. (gxs.com), e-tendering systems are gaining popularity (for more on e-tendering, see

> **reverse auction**
> A tendering system in which sellers are invited to bid on the fulfillment of an order to produce a product or provide a service; the lowest bid wins.

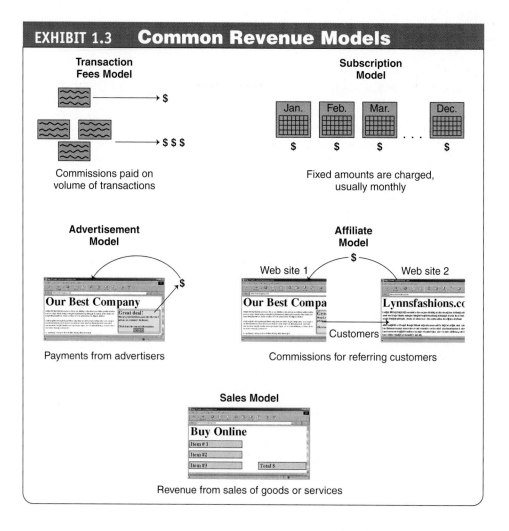

EXHIBIT 1.3 Common Revenue Models

Transaction Fees Model

Commissions paid on volume of transactions

Subscription Model

Jan. Feb. Mar. . . . Dec.

Fixed amounts are charged, usually monthly

Advertisement Model

Our Best Company

Payments from advertisers

Affiliate Model

Web site 1 Web site 2

Our Best Compa Lynnsfashions.cc

Customers

Commissions for referring customers

Sales Model

Buy Online

Item # 1
Item #2
Item #3   Total $

Revenue from sales of goods or services

Chapter 5). Several government agencies mandate that all agency procurement must be done through e-tendering.

3. **Name your own price.** Pioneered by Priceline.com, this model allows buyers to set the price they are willing to pay for a specific product or service. Priceline.com will try to match the customer's request with a supplier willing to sell the product or service at that price. Customers, usually individuals, may have to increase their bids before they get the product or service.

4. **Find the best price.** According to this model, a customer specifies a need and then an intermediate company, such as Hotwire.com, matches the customer's need against a database, locates the lowest price, and submits it to the consumer. The potential buyer then has 60 minutes to accept or reject the offer. A variation of this model is available for insurance. For example, a consumer can submit a request for insurance to Insweb.com and receive several quotes. Many companies employ similar models to find the lowest price. For example, consumers can go to E-LOAN (eloan.com) to find the best interest rate for auto or home loans.

5. **Affiliate marketing. Affiliate marketing** is an arrangement whereby a marketing partner (a business, an organization, or even an individual) refers consumers to the selling company's Web site. The referral is done by placing a banner ad or the logo of the selling company on the affiliated company's Web site. The affiliated partner receives a 3 to 15 percent commission on the purchase price whenever a customer it refers to the selling company's Web site and makes a purchase there. In other words, by using affiliate marketing, a selling company creates a virtual commissioned sales force. Pioneered by CDNow (see Hoffman and Novak 2000), the concept is now employed by thousands of retailers or manufacturers (see affiliateworld.com). For example, Amazon.com has close to 500,000 affiliates, and even tiny Cattoys.com offers individuals and organizations the opportunity to put its logo and link on their Web sites to generate commissions.

6. **Viral marketing.** According to the viral marketing model, one can increase brand awareness or even sales by inducing people to send messages to other people or to recruit friends to join certain programs. It is basically Web-based word-of-mouth marketing. (See Chapter 4 for more details.)

7. **Group purchasing.** Discounts are usually available for quantity purchasing. EC has spawned the concept of electronic aggregation, wherein a third party finds individuals or SMEs (small-to-medium enterprises), aggregates their orders, and then negotiates (or conducts a tender) for the best deal. Thus, using the concept of **group purchasing**, a small business or even an individual can get a discount. Some leading aggregators are Accompany.com and Shop2gether.com (see Rugullis 2000).

8. **Online auctions.** Almost everyone has heard of eBay.com, the world's largest online auction site. Several hundred other companies, including Amazon.com and Yahoo.com, also conduct online auctions. In these auctions, online shoppers make consecutive bids for various goods and services, and the highest bidders get the auctioned items.

9. **Product and service customization. Customization** of products or services means creating a product or service according to the buyer's specifications. Customization is not a new model; in fact, it is as old as commerce itself! What is new is the ability to quickly customize products online for consumers at prices not much higher than their noncustomized counterparts. Dell Computer is a good example of a company that customizes products for its customers. Many other companies are following Dell's lead: The automobile industry is customizing its products, and expects to save billions of dollars in inventory reduction alone every year by producing cars made-to-order (see Wiegram and Koth 2000). Mattel's My Design lets fashion-doll fans custom-build a friend for Barbie at Mattel's Web site; the doll's image is displayed on the screen before the customer orders. Nike allows customers to customize shoes, which can be delivered in a week. De Beers allows consumers to design their own engagement ring.

10. **Electronic marketplaces and exchanges.** Electronic marketplaces existed in isolated applications for decades (e.g., stock and commodities exchanges). But as of 1999, thousands of e-marketplaces have introduced new efficiencies to the process. If they are well organized and managed, e-marketplaces can provide significant benefits to both buyers and sellers. Of special interest are

---

affiliate marketing
An arrangement whereby a marketing partner (a business, an organization, or even an individual) refers consumers to the selling company's Web site.

viral marketing
Word-of-mouth marketing in which customers promote a product or service to friends or other people.

group purchasing
Quantity purchasing that enables purchasers to obtain a discount price on the products purchased.

customization
Creation of a product or service according to the buyer's specifications.

vertical marketplace
A marketplace that concentrates on one industry; also called *vertical portals* or *vortals*.

vertical marketplaces (also called vertical portals, or vortals), which concentrate on one industry (e.g., e-steel.com for the steel industry and Chemconnect.com for the chemical industry).

11. **Supply chain improvers.** One of the major contributions of EC is in the creation of new models that change or improve supply chain management. Most interesting is the conversion of a *linear* supply chain, which can be slow, expensive, and error prone, into a *hub*. An example of such an improvement is provided in EC Application Case 1.2.

Any of the preceding business models can be independent or they can be combined among themselves or with traditional business models. One company may use several different business models.

> ▶ Define business plan, business case, and business model.
> ▶ Describe the content of a business plan and its relationship to the business model.
> ▶ Identify business models related to selling.
> ▶ Identify business models related to buying.
> ▶ Describe how a linear supply chain is changed to a hub.

1.4   BENEFITS AND LIMITATIONS OF EC

THE BENEFITS OF EC

Few innovations in human history encompass as many potential benefits as EC does. The global nature of the technology, the opportunity to reach hundreds of millions of people, the interactive nature of EC, the variety of possibilities for its use, and the resourcefulness and rapid growth of its supporting infrastructures, especially the Web, result in many potential benefits to organizations, individuals, and society. These benefits are just starting to materialize, but they will increase significantly as EC expands. It is not surprising that some maintain that the EC revolution is as profound as the change that accompanied the Industrial Revolution (Clinton and Gore 1997).

Benefits to Organizations

The benefits of e-commerce to organizations fall into several main categories, as described in the following list.

> ▶ **EC expands the marketplace.** With minimal capital outlay, a company can easily and quickly locate more customers, the best suppliers, and the most suitable business partners nationally or worldwide. For example, Boeing Corporation reported a savings of 20 percent after it posted on the Internet a request for a proposal to manufacture a subsystem. A small vendor in Hungary answered the request and won the electronic bid. Not only was the subsystem cheaper, but it was delivered about twice as quickly as Boeing had anticipated. EC also enables companies not only to find new customers, but also to interact more closely with them. This promotes better customer relationship management (CRM) and increases customer loyalty.

EC APPLICATION CASE 1.2

Interorganization and Collaboration

ORBIS CORP. CHANGES A LINEAR PHYSICAL SUPPLY CHAIN TO AN ELECTRONIC HUB

ORBIS Corp. is a small Australian company that provides Internet and EC services. One of its services, ProductBank (*productbank.com.au*), revolutionized the flow of information and products in the B2B advertising field. To put together a retail catalog or brochure, someone must first gather pictures of the many products to be advertised. These pictures are obtained from each manufacturer, such as Sony or Nokia. The traditional process is linear, as shown in the figure below.

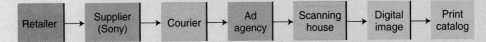

The traditional process works like this: When retailers need a photo of a product, they contact the manufacturers, who send the photos via a courier to an ad agency. The ad agency decides which photos to use and how to present them. The agency then sends out the photos to be scanned and converted into digital images, which are transferred to the printer. The cycle time for each photo is 4 to 6 weeks, and the total transaction cost of preparing one picture for the catalog is about $150 AU.

ProductBank simplifies this lengthy process. It has changed the linear flow of products and information into a digitized hub as shown in the following figure.

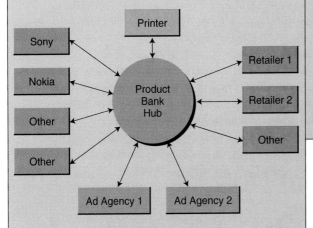

With the new process, manufacturers send digitized photos to ORBIS, and ORBIS enters and organizes the photos in a database. When retailers need pictures, they can view the digitized images in the database, decide which they want to include in their catalog, and communicate that information electronically to their ad agency. When the ad agency completes its design, the picture can be downloaded by the printer. The transaction cost per picture (usually paid by the manufacturer) is 30 to 40 percent lower than with the linear model, and the cycle time is 50 to 70 percent shorter than in the traditional catalog production method.

The ORBIS case provide some tips for succeeding in the digital economy:

▶ Digitize as much as you can; eliminate paper and other physical transactions.

▶ Digitize at the beginning of the transaction process.

▶ Change the supply chain from a linear model to a hub-based model.

▶ Aggregate many business partners into one place, such as an information hub or an electronic marketplace.

Sources: Compiled from *vibesglobal.com* 2000, 2001, 2002.

Questions

▶ Identify the benefits of the hub-based model to the supply-chain participants.

▶ Where does the cost reduction in the ProductBank process come from?

▶ Where does the cycle-time reduction come from?

▶ Explain the benefits of electronic collaboration between the catalog owner and the ad agency.

▶ **EC offers significant cost savings.** With EC, companies no longer need to bear the costs of creating, processing, distributing, storing, and retrieving paper-based information. For example, by introducing an electronic procurement system, companies can cut purchasing administrative costs by as much as 85 percent. EC also lowers telecommunications costs—the Internet is much cheaper to access than VANs. Further, EC enables efficient e-procurement that can reduce administrative costs by 80 percent or more, reduce purchasing prices by 5 to 15 percent, and reduce purchasing cycle time by more than 50 percent. By reducing the length of the operating cycle (the transition from cash to inventories to receivables and back to cash), companies are able to spend less on financing costs. The Insights and Additions box, on facing page, lists some specific examples of savings from EC.

▶ **EC improves business organization and processes.** EC allows for many innovative business models that provide strategic advantages and/or increase profits. Pull-type production processing, such as that used by Dell, allows for inexpensive customization of products and services, and it provides a competitive advantage for companies that implement this strategy. In addition, supply chain inefficiencies, such as excessive inventories and delivery delays, can be minimized with EC. For example, by building cars to order instead of for dealers' showrooms, the automotive industry expects to save tens of billions of dollars annually, just from inventory reduction. Group purchasing (Chapter 5) combined with electronic bidding is another example of an innovative business model. In short, e-commerce provides organizations with an unparalleled level of strategic control, offering a tremendous competitive edge (Evans and Wurster 2000; Slywotzky and Morrison 2001).

▶ **EC promotes interactivity.** EC allow companies to interact with their customers and business partners and to receive quick and accurate feedback.

Other benefits of EC include improved corporate image, simplified business processes, compressed time-to-market (time from the inception of an idea to its implementation), significantly increased productivity, reduced paper and paperwork, increased access to information, and increased flexibility. EC also allows for a high degree of specialization that is not economically feasible in the physical world. For example, a store that sells only dog toys can operate in cyberspace (dogtoys.com); in the physical world, such a store would not have enough customers to be profitable.

Benefits to Consumers

The benefits of EC to consumers center mostly around *convenience, speed,* and *cost.* EC allows consumers to shop or perform other transactions year round, 24 hours a day, from almost any location. It provides consumers with more choices of more products, from many vendors. Consumers can locate relevant and detailed product and service information and conduct comparisons in seconds, rather than in days or weeks. By enabling consumers to shop in many places and conduct quick comparisons, EC facilitates competition, which results in substantially lower prices for consumers. In some cases, especially with digitized products, EC also allows for quick delivery. Another benefit to customers is the ability to buy *customized products* and *personalized services* at a very reasonable cost.

EC offers consumers new forms of interaction, both commercial and social. On-line auctions, for example, allow individuals to sell things quickly and buyers to locate

Insights and Additions   Cutting Organizations' Costs with EC

▶ It costs a bank $1.08 to perform a simple teller transaction at a branch. On the Web, the same transaction costs between $0.02 and $0.10.

▶ The cost of issuing and processing an airline ticket on the Web is $1. With a physical system the same transaction costs $8.

▶ It costs $70 to arrange an average medical appointment, including lab work, over the phone (counting the time of the employee involved), but only $10 on the Internet.

▶ Each transaction to process one order of appliances and other high-cost items costs a brick-and-mortar retailer $12 to $20; selling over the Internet reduces the cost to $2.

▶ It costs between $3 and $15 for a vendor to handle a customer-service call. Letting the customers do it by themselves (e.g., track orders, use FAQs to answer routine inquiries) reduces the cost to $1 per inquiry.

▶ Procuring a large sales order in a company can cost between $100 and $140 in administrative costs per order. In e-procurement, the cost ranges between $7 and $10.

▶ The administrative cost to send a bill (invoice) is $1.60. This amount can be cut in half if bills are sent electronically.

▶ It costs the U.S. government $0.43 to issue a paper check versus $0.02 to issue the same payment electronically.

collectors' items and find bargains. EC also allows customers to design their own products and services, from a car to a shirt. Finally, EC enables customers to interact with other customers in **virtual communities**, groups of individuals linked on the Internet, where they can exchange ideas as well as compare experiences (see Chapter 11).

virtual communities
Groups of individuals linked on the Internet.

Benefits to Society

EC benefits to society are *improvements in the standard of living and delivery of public services.* For example, people in less-developed countries and in rural areas are now able to enjoy products and services that were otherwise unavailable. This includes opportunities to learn skilled professions or earn college degrees. Also, EC enables more individuals to work at home and do less traveling for work or shopping, resulting in less traffic on the roads and reduced air pollution. Public services, such as health care, education, and distribution of government social services, can be delivered via EC at a reduced cost and/or with improved quality. For example, EC provides rural doctors access to information and technologies with which they can better treat their patients.

THE LIMITATIONS OF EC

EC has both technological and nontechnological limitations. The major limitations are summarized in Exhibit 1.4.

Despite these limitations, EC is expanding rapidly. For example, the number of people in the United States who buy and sell stocks electronically increased from 300,000 at the beginning of 1996 to over 25 million by the spring of 2002. In Korea, about 67 percent of all stock market transactions took place over the Internet in the spring of 2002 (versus 2 percent in 1998). According to the major financial institution J. P. Morgan, the number of online brokerage customers in Europe will reach 17.1 million in 2003 (versus 1.4 million in 1999). As experience accumulates and technology improves, the cost-benefit ratio of EC will increase, resulting in greater rates of EC adoption.

The benefits presented here may not be convincing enough reasons for a business to implement EC. Much more compelling are the economic impact of EC and the digital revolution, along with the effects of EC on business competition, discussed in the next two sections.

EXHIBIT 1.4 Limitations of Electronic Commerce

Technological Limitations

1. There is a lack of universally accepted standards for quality, security, and reliability.
2. The telecommunications bandwidth is insufficient.
3. Software development tools are still evolving.
4. There are difficulties in integrating the Internet and EC software with some existing (especially legacy) applications and databases.
5. Special Web servers in addition to the network servers are needed (added cost).
6. Internet accessibility is still expensive and/or inconvenient.

Nontechnological Limitations

1. Security and privacy concerns deter customers from buying.
2. Trust in EC and in unknown sellers hinders buying.
3. National and international government regulations sometimes get in the way.
4. It is difficult to measure the benefits of EC, such as the effectiveness of online advertising. There is a lack of mature methodology.
5. Some customers like to feel and touch products. Customers are resistant to the change from a real to an online store.
6. People do not yet sufficiently trust paperless, faceless transactions.
7. There is an insufficient number (critical mass) of sellers and buyers needed for profitable EC operations.

> Describe some EC benefits to individuals, organizations, and society.

> List the major technological and nontechnological limitations of EC.

> Which limitations do you think will be more easily overcome—the technological or the nontechnological, and why?

1.5 THE DIGITAL REVOLUTION AND THE ECONOMIC IMPACT OF EC

THE DIGITAL REVOLUTION

The **digital economy** refers to an economy that is based on digital technologies, including digital communication networks (the Internet, intranets, extranets, and private VANs), computers, software, and other related information technologies. The digital economy is also sometimes called the *Internet economy,* the *new economy,* or the *Web economy.* In this new economy, digital networking and communication infrastructures provide a global platform over which people and organizations interact, communicate, collaborate, and search for information. This platform includes the following characteristics (Choi and Whinston 2000):

> A vast array of digitizable products—databases, news and information, books, magazines, TV and radio programming, movies, electronic games, musical CDs, and software—that are delivered over a digital infrastructure any time, anywhere in the world.

> Consumers and firms conducting financial transactions digitally through digital currencies or financial tokens, carried via networked computers and mobile devices.

> Microprocessors and networking capabilities embedded in physical goods such as home appliances and automobiles.

The term *digital economy* also refers to the convergence of computing and communication technologies on the Internet and other networks and the resulting flow of information and technology that is stimulating e-commerce and vast organizational changes. This convergence enables all types of information (data, audio, video, etc.) to be stored, processed, and transmitted over networks to many destinations worldwide. The digital economy is creating an economic revolution, which, according to the *Emerging Digital Economy II* (ecommerce.gov), is evidenced by unprecedented economic performance and the longest period of uninterrupted economic expansion in history (about 10 years) combined with low inflation. The Insights and Additions box presents, on page 22, some relevant statistics related to this digital revolution in the United States.

Web-based EC systems are accelerating the digital revolution by providing competitive advantage to organizations. In a study conducted by Lederer et al. (1998), "enhancing competitiveness or creating strategic advantage" was ranked as the number-one benefit of Web-based systems. Let's see what economic impact EC is having on competitiveness.

digital economy
An economy that is based on digital technologies, including digital communication networks, computers, software, and other related information technologies; also called the *Internet economy,* the *new economy,* or the *Web economy.*

Insights and Additions   Statistics Related to the Digital Revolution in the United States

▶ Information technology industries have been growing at more than double the rate of the overall economy. In 2000, they reached close to *9 percent of GDP,* up from 4.9 percent in 1985.

▶ IT industries by themselves have driven *over one-quarter of total real economic growth* (not including any indirect effects) each year between 1996 and 2001.

▶ Without information technology, overall inflation would have been *3.1 percent in 1997,* more than a full percentage point higher than the *2.0 percent* it actually was. Similar differences exist in other years.

▶ Companies throughout the economy are betting on IT to boost productivity. In the 1960s, business spending on IT equipment represented only *3 percent* of total business equipment investment. By 2001, IT's share rose to *45 percent* of business spending per year.

▶ In 2001, over 8.5 million people worked in IT-related jobs across the economy. There were nearly 2.5 million Internet jobs in the United States in early 2000, up *36 percent* in just a 12-month period. The average salary for IT workers was about $49,000 per year, compared to an average of $29,000 for the private sector as a whole.

▶ Worldwide cost savings from the use of Internet applications, according to Giga Information Group (*gigaweb.com*), will reach $1.25 trillion in 2002, of which about $600 billion are in U.S. organizations.

Source: *ecommerce.gov.*

THE ECONOMICS OF DIGITAL SYSTEMS

The economics of EC are based on principles that sometimes differ from those underlying traditional markets. These EC principles are drawn from information and network economics. Consider the following examples.

Products' Cost Curves

The average-cost (AVC) curve of many physical products and services is U-shaped (see Exhibit 1.5a). This indicates that, at first, as quantity increases, the average cost declines. As quantity increases still more, the cost goes back up due

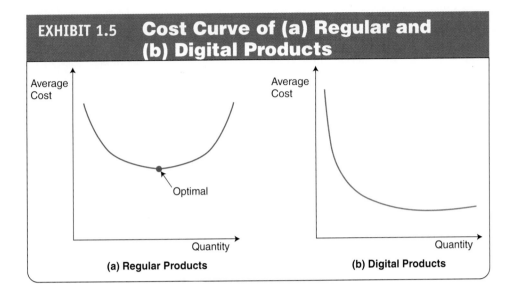

EXHIBIT 1.5   Cost Curve of (a) Regular and (b) Digital Products

to increasing variable costs (especially administrative and marketing costs) in the short run, when production capacity is fixed.

In contrast, the variable cost per unit of digital products is very low (in most cases) and almost fixed, regardless of the quantity. Therefore, as illustrated in Exhibit 1.5b, total cost per unit will decline as quantity increases, as the fixed costs are spread (prorated) over more units. This relationship results in increasing returns with increased sales.

Other Cost Curves

EC has other economic advantages over traditional commerce. In Exhibit 1.6 we show three cost components—the production function, transaction costs, and agency/administration costs—and the effect of EC on each.

Production function. The production function is shown in Exhibit 1.6a. It indicates that for the same quantity of production, Q, companies can either use a certain amount of labor or they can invest in more automation (they can substitute IT capital for labor). For example, for a quantity $Q = 1,000$, the lower the amount of labor needed, the higher the required IT investment. When EC enters the picture, it shifts the function inward (from Q_1 to Q_2), lowering the amount of labor and/or capital needed to produce the same $Q = 1,000$.

Transaction costs. The economics of the firm's transaction costs (costs associated with conducting a sale) are shown in Exhibit 1.6b. Traditionally, in order to reduce this cost, firms had to grow in size (as depicted in curve T_1). In the digital economy, the transaction cost is shifted inward, to position T_2. This means that EC makes it possible to have low transaction costs with smaller firm size or to enjoy much lower transaction costs when firm size increases.

Agency costs. Exhibit 1.6c shows the economics of the firm's administrative (agency) costs. In the "old economy," administrative costs (A_1) grew with the size (and complexity) of the firm, preventing companies from growing to a very large size. In the digital economy, the administrative costs curve is shifted outward, to

EXHIBIT 1.6   The Economic Effects of EC

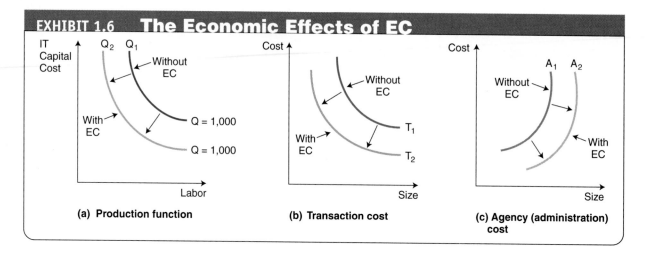

(a) Production function

(b) Transaction cost

(c) Agency (administration) cost

A_2. This means that as a result of EC, companies can significantly expand their business without too much increase in administrative costs.

Reach vs. Richness

Another economic impact of EC is the trade-off between the number of customers a company can reach (called "reach") and the amount of interactions and information services they can provide to customers (called "richness"). According to Evans and Wurster (2000), for the same amount of cost (resources), there is a trade-off between reach and richness. The more customers a company wants to reach, the fewer services they can provide to them. This economic relationship is depicted in Exhibit 1.7a. Using EC, it is possible to shift the curve outward.

Exhibit 1.7b shows an implementation of the reach versus richness concept at Charles Schwab brokerage house. Initially, Schwab attempted to increase its reach. To do so the company went downward along the curve, reducing its richness. However, with its Web site (eschwab.com), Schwab was able to drastically increase its reach and at the same time provide richness in terms of customer service and

EXHIBIT 1.7   Reach vs. Richness

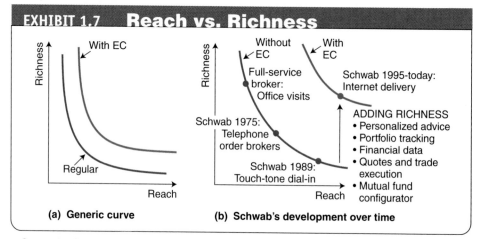

(a) Generic curve

(b) Schwab's development over time

financial information to customers. For example, Schwab's *Mutual Fund Screener* allows customers to design their own investment portfolios by selecting from an array of mutual funds. This service may be combined with other tools such as the *Asset Allocator* and the *Performance Monitor*. Providing such services (richness) allows Schwab to increase the number of its customers (larger reach), as well as to charge higher fees than competitors that provide little or no value-added service (for additional details, see Slywotzky and Morrison 2001).

▶ Define the digital economy.

▶ List the three characteristics of the digital revolution cited by Choi and Whinston.

▶ Describe how traditional economic relationships have changed in the digital era.

▶ Describe the contribution of EC to the reach/richness relationship.

1.6   THE CONTRIBUTION OF E-COMMERCE TO ORGANIZATIONS

To understand the contribution of EC to organizations, it is worthwhile to examine today's business environment, the pressures it creates on organizations, the organizational responses to those pressures, and the potential role of EC in responding to them.

THE NEW WORLD OF BUSINESS

Economic, societal, and technological factors have created a highly competitive business environment in which customers are becoming more powerful. These factors can change quickly, sometimes in an unpredictable manner. For example, James Strong, the CEO of Qantas, once said (*Business Review Weekly of Australia,* August 25, 2000), "The lesson we have learned is how quickly things can change. You have to be prepared to move fast when the situation demands." Companies need to react quickly to both the problems and the opportunities resulting from this new business environment. Because the pace of change and the level of uncertainty are expected to accelerate, organizations are operating under increasing pressures to produce more products faster and with fewer resources.

In order to succeed, and frequently to survive, in the face of this dramatic change, companies must take not only traditional actions such as lowering costs and closing unprofitable facilities, but also innovative actions such as customizing or creating new products or providing superb customer service (Boyett and Boyett 1995). We refer to these activities as *critical response activities*.

Critical response activities can take place in some or all organizational processes, from the daily processing of payroll and order entry to strategic activities such as the acquisition of a company. Responses can also occur in the supply chain, as demonstrated by Qantas. A response can be a reaction to a specific pressure already in existence or it can be an initiative that will defend an organization against future pressures. It can also be an activity that exploits an opportunity created by changing conditions. Many response activities can be greatly facilitated by EC. In some cases, EC is the *only* solution to these business pressures (Tapscott et al. 1998; Callon 1996; Turban et al. 2002a).

Organizations respond to business pressures with activities supported by IT in general and EC in particular. The relationship among business pressures, organizational responses, and EC is shown in Exhibit 1.8. Now, let's examine the three components of this model in more detail.

BUSINESS PRESSURES

The term *business environment* refers to the social, economic, legal, technological, and political actions that affect business activities. In this text, business pressures are divided into the following categories: market (economic), societal, and technological. The main types of business pressures in each category are listed in Exhibit 1.9.

ORGANIZATIONAL RESPONSES

Because some traditional response activities may not work in today's turbulent and competitive business environment, many of the old solutions need to be modified, supplemented, or discarded. Alternatively, new responses can be devised. Here we present some examples from among the many EC-supported response activities.

Strategic Systems

Strategic systems provide organizations with strategic advantages, enabling them to increase their market share, better negotiate with their suppliers, or prevent com-

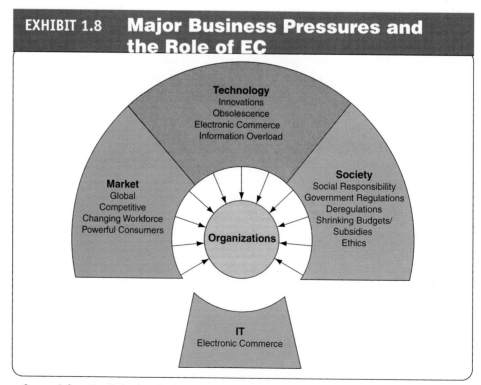

EXHIBIT 1.8   Major Business Pressures and the Role of EC

Source: Information Technology for Management, 3rd ed., E. Turban, E. R. McLean, and J. C. Wetherbe. Copyright © 2001 John Wiley & Sons, Inc. This material is used by permission of John Wiley & Sons, Inc.

EXHIBIT 1.9 Major Business Pressures

Market and Economic Pressures	Societal and Environmental Pressures	Technological Pressures
▸ Strong competition ▸ Global economy ▸ Regional trade agreements (e.g., NAFTA) ▸ Extremely low labor costs in some countries ▸ Frequent and significant changes in markets ▸ Increased power of consumers	▸ Changing nature of workforce ▸ Government deregulation leads to more competition ▸ Shrinking government subsidies ▸ Increased importance of ethical and legal issues ▸ Increased social responsibility of organizations ▸ Rapid political changes	▸ Rapid technological obsolescence ▸ Increasing innovations and new technologies ▸ Increases in information overload ▸ Rapid decline in technology cost vs. performance ratio

petitors from entering into their territory (Callon 1996). There are a variety of EC-supported strategic systems. One example is FedEx's tracking system, which allows FedEx to identify the status of every individual package, anywhere in the system. Most of FedEx's competitors have already copied its system. In response, FedEx is now introducing new Web-based initiatives (see EC Application Case 1.3 on page 28).

Continuous Improvement Efforts and Business Process Reengineering

Many companies continuously conduct programs to improve their productivity, quality, and customer service. Examples of such programs include customer relationship management (CRM) and total quality management (TQM). Here are two examples of how EC can help: Dell Computer takes its orders electronically and immediately moves them via enterprise resources planning (ERP) software into the just-in-time assembly operation. Intel tracks the consumption of its products by 11 of its largest customers using an almost real-time extranet-based monitoring system to plan production schedules and deliveries.

However, continuous improvement programs may not be the best solution for some business problems. Strong business pressures may require a radical change. Such an effort is referred to as *business process reengineering* (BPR). E-commerce is frequently interrelated with BPR.

Business Alliances

Many companies realize that alliances with other companies, even competitors, can be beneficial. For example, General Motors, Ford, and others in the automotive industry created a huge B2B e-marketplace called Covisint (see Chapter 6). There are several types of business alliances, such as resource-sharing partnerships, permanent supplier-company relationships, and joint research efforts.

One of the most interesting types of business alliances is the electronically supported temporary joint venture in which companies form a special organization for a specific, time-limited mission. This is an example of a *virtual corporation*, which could be a common business organizational structure in the future. In a virtual corporation, an organization outsources most of its activities to business partners. A more permanent type of virtual corporation that links manufacturers,

EC APPLICATION CASE 1.3
Interorganization and Collaboration
FEDEX SOLUTIONS

FedEx provides a host of Web-based logistics solutions to enterprise (business) customers. The major services provided to these customers are as follows.

- **FedEx distribution centers.** This service uses a worldwide network of warehouses to provide ready-to-use warehousing services to businesses. This allows for instant expansion of distribution capabilities, and is especially helpful to small businesses. The network is managed electronically, and all communication with the shippers and receivers is done online.

- **FedEx express distribution depots.** This service is primarily limited to U.S. businesses and provides a one-stop source of express distribution capabilities. Goods in these depots are available for delivery 24 hours a day. This service is targeted at time-critical businesses. Again, all communication is done online.

- **FedEx returns management.** FedEx NetReturn is designed to streamline the process of return of unwanted products to retailers or manufacturers. FedEx business customers can use the Internet-based system to schedule pickup of packages from consumers and to obtain time-definite delivery as well as online status tracking and customized reporting.

- **Other value-added services.** FedEx offers several Web-based value-added services. For example, products can be shipped from a FedEx-operated warehouse instead of the business customer's warehouse. In addition, FedEx can provide a "merge-in-transit" service to customers, such as Micron Computers, that operate on rapid turnaround and delivery. Under the merge-in-transit program, FedEx stores peripherals such as monitors and printers for Micron at its Memphis, Tennessee, air hub. FedEx then matches those products with the computers en route to a customer. If a customer in Boston, Massachusetts, for example, orders a popular PC model online, Micron sends the electronic order to FedEx, which will transport the computer from Micron's warehouse to FedEx's Boston station. FedEx electronically matches the computer with a standard Micron monitor and printer shipped from a FedEx-managed warehouse in Memphis. The FedEx driver then delivers the computer, monitor, and printer together to the customer's home.

Sources: Compiled from Rao et al., 1999 and from FedEx press releases, 2001.

Questions

- What are the benefits to a company of outsourcing logistics (shipping, etc.) to FedEx?
- Visit *fedex.com* and identify more EC-related business services.

---

suppliers, and finance corporations is known as *keiretsu* (a Japanese term meaning a permanent business alliance). These various types of alliances are heavily supported by EC technologies ranging from electronic transmission of maps and drawings to use of real-time collaborative technologies.

Electronic Markets

Electronic markets, private or public, can optimize trading efficiency, enabling their members to compete globally. Most electronic markets require the collaboration of different companies, sometimes even competitors. As will be shown in Chapter 6, there are thousands of e-markets.

Reductions in Cycle Time and Time to Market

Cycle time reduction—shortening the time it takes for a business to complete a productive activity from its beginning to end—is extremely important for increasing productivity and competitiveness (Wetherbe 1996). Similarly, reducing the time from the inception of an idea to its implementation (*time-to-market*) is important because those who are first on the market with a product or who can provide customers with a service faster than their competitors enjoy a distinct competitive advantage. Extranet-based applications can expedite the various steps in the process of product or service development, testing, and implementation. An example of cycle time reduction in bringing new drugs to the market is described in EC Application Case 1.4 (page 30).

cycle time reduction
Shortening the time it takes for a business to complete a productive activity from its beginning to end.

Empowerment of Employees and Collaborative Work

Giving employees the authority to act and make decisions on their own is a strategy used by many organizations as part of productivity improvement programs or customer relationship management (CRM). Management delegates authority to individuals or teams (see Lipnack and Stamps 1997) who can then execute the work faster and with fewer delays. EC allows the decentralization of decision making and authority via collaborative commerce, but simultaneously supports centralized control. Empowered sales people and customer service employees can make customers happy and do it quickly, helping to increase customer loyalty.

Supply Chain Improvements

EC, as will be shown throughout the book and especially in Chapter 11, can help reduce supply chain delays, reduce inventories, and eliminate other inefficiencies. The Orbis case presented earlier (EC Application Case 1.2) illustrated supply chain improvements from EC.

Mass Customization

As today's customers demand customized products and services, the business problem is how to provide customization and do it efficiently. This can be done, in part, by changing manufacturing processes from mass production to mass customization (Pine and Gilmore 1997). In mass production, a company produces a large quantity of identical items. In **mass customization**, items are produced in a large quantity but are customized to fit the desires of each customer. EC is an ideal facilitator of mass customization, for example, by enabling electronic ordering to reach the production facility in minutes.

mass customization
Production of large quantities of customized items.

▶ List the major business pressures faced by organizations today.
▶ List the major organizational responses to business pressures.
▶ Describe how EC supports organizational responses to business pressures.

EC APPLICATION CASE 1.4

Interorganization and Collaboration

THE INTERNET AND THE INTRANET SHORTEN TIME-TO-MARKET FOR NEW DRUGS

The Federal Drug Administration (FDA) must be extremely careful in approving new drugs. However, there is public pressure on the FDA to approve new drugs quickly, especially those for cancer and HIV. The problem is that to ensure quality, the FDA requires companies to conduct extensive research and clinical testing. The development programs for such research and testing cover 300,000 to 500,000 pages of documentation for each new drug. The subsequent results and analyses are reported on 100,000 to 200,000 additional pages. These pages then are reviewed by the FDA prior to approval of a new drug. Manual processing of this information significantly slows the work of the FDA, so that the total approval process takes 6 to 10 years.

A software program called Computer-Aided Drug Application Systems (Research Data Corporation, New Jersey) offers a computerized solution. The software uses a network-distributed document-processing system that enables the pharmaceutical company to scan all related documents into a database. The documents are indexed, and full-text search and retrieval software is attached to the system. Using keywords, corporate employees can search the database via their company's intranet. The database is also accessible, via the Internet, to FDA employees, who no longer have to spend hours looking for a specific piece of data. Information can be processed or printed at the user's desktop computer. Today, the U.S. government is able to offer an electronic submission and online review process for approval of new drugs (*fas.gov/cder*).

This system not only helps the FDA, but also the companies' researchers who now have every piece of required information at their fingertips. Remote corporate and business partners can also access the system. The overall result: The time-to-market of a new drug is reduced by up to a year. (Each week saved can be translated into the saving of many lives and can also yield up to $1 million profit.) The system also reduces the time it takes to patent a new drug.

An interesting use of this technology is the case of ISIS Pharmaceuticals, Inc. (*isip.com*), which developed an extranet-based system similar to the one described here. The company uses CD-ROMs to submit reports to the FDA and opens its intranet to FDA personnel. This step alone could save 6 to 12 months from the average 15-month review time. Simply by submitting an FDA report electronically, the company can save 1 month of review time. To cut even more time, SmithKline Beecham Corporation is using electronic publishing and hypertext links to enable FDA reviewers to quickly navigate its submissions.

Source: Compiled from *IMC Journal*, May/June 1993, *INCTechnology*, No. 3, 1997, and *openmarket.com*.

Questions

▶ How does the computerized drug application system facilitate collaboration?

▶ How is cycle time reduced in the drug development process?

1.7 PUTTING IT ALL TOGETHER

EC could become a significant global economic element within 10 to 20 years (forrester.com, February 2001). The task facing each organization is how to put together the components that will enable the organization to gain competitive advantage by using EC. The first step is to put in the right connective networks.

The vast majority of EC is done on computers connected to the Internet or to its counterpart within organizations, an intranet. An **intranet** is an internal corporate or government network that uses Internet tools, such as Web browsers, and Internet protocols. Another EC computer environment is an **extranet**, a network that uses the Internet to link multiple intranets. (For more detail on intranets and extranets, see Fingar et al. 2000 and Chapter 6.)

The major concern of many companies today is how to transform themselves in order to take part in the digital economy, where e-business is the norm. If the transformation is successfully completed, many companies will reach the status of our hypothetical company, Toys, Inc., shown in Exhibit 1.10 (page 32), which uses the Internet, intranets, and extranets in an integrated manner to conduct various EC activities.

Toys, Inc. conducts all of its internal communications, collaboration, dissemination of information, and database access over an intranet. The company uses an extranet (upper left of Exhibit 1.10) to cooperate with its large business partners, such as suppliers, distributors, noncorporate retail stores, and liquidators. In addition, the company is connected via an extranet to a toy exchange (upper right of Exhibit 1.10), which includes other manufacturers, professional associations, and large suppliers.

Additionally, the company is networked to other e-marketspaces and large corporations. For example, some major corporations allow Toys, Inc. to connect to their intranets via their own extranets. Toys, Inc. is also connected with its banks and other financial institutions (loan providers, stock issuers) over a highly secured EDI (electronic data interchange) that runs on a VAN. The company is also using the VAN-based EDI with some of its largest suppliers and other business partners. An Internet-based EDI is used with smaller business partners that are not on the corporate EDI. The company communicates with others via the Internet.

The company's business partners and employees interact with each other and with the company via a corporate portal. A **corporate portal** is a major gateway through which employees, business partners, and the public can access corporate information and communicate and collaborate as needed. (In contrast, **public portals** such as Yahoo! enable the general public to access Internet resources.) Many companies are moving towards a network configuration similar to that of Toys, Inc. Today, it is almost impossible to do business without being connected to business partners through the Internet, extranets, or EDIs.

It may take 5 to 10 years for companies to become fully digitized like the hypothetical Toys, Inc. Major companies such as Schwab, IBM, Intel, and General Electric are moving rapidly toward such a status (Slywotzky and Morrison 2001). The major characteristics of such a company are shown in Exhibit 1.11 (page 33), where they are compared to those of a brick-and-mortar business.

> **intranet**
> An internal corporate or government network that uses Internet tools, such as Web browsers, and Internet protocols.

> **extranet**
> A network that uses the Internet to link multiple intranets.

> **corporate portal**
> A major gateway through which employees, business partners, and the public can enter a corporate Web site.

> **public portal**
> A gateway, such as Yahoo!, through which the general public can access the Internet.

▶ Define intranets and extranets.

▶ What is a corporate portal?

▶ Why would one company conduct multiple EC initiatives?

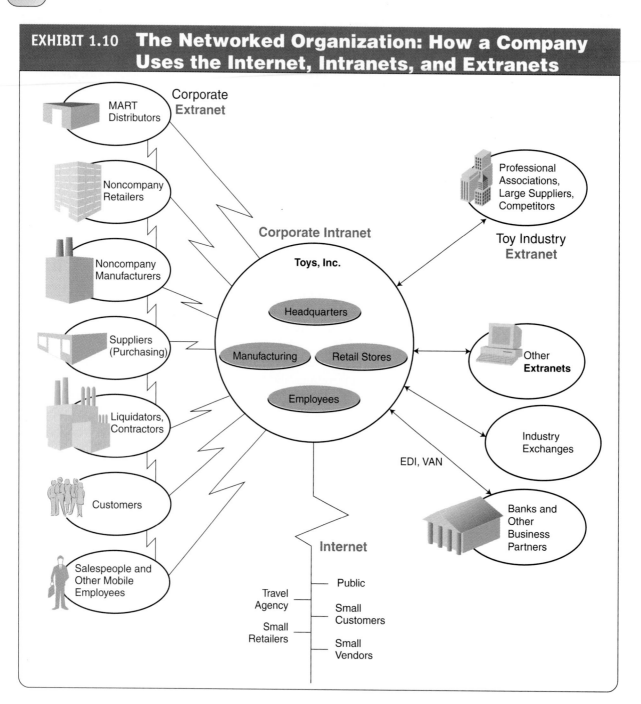

EXHIBIT 1.10 **The Networked Organization: How a Company Uses the Internet, Intranets, and Extranets**

1.8 TEXT OVERVIEW

This book is composed of 11 chapters divided into six parts, as shown in Exhibit 1.12 (page 34). In addition, more content is available online at the book's Web site. There you will find a seventh part, with an additional chapter (Chapter 12 on EC infrastructure and application development processes and methods), as well as four technology appendices and three tutorials.

EXHIBIT 1.11 The Digital vs. Brick-and-Mortar Company

Brick-and-Mortar Organizations	Digital Organizations
Selling in physical stores	Selling online
Selling tangible goods	Selling digital goods
Internal inventory/production planning	Online collaborative inventory forecasting
Paper catalogs	Smart electronic catalogs
Physical marketplace	Marketspace (electronic)
Use of VANs and traditional EDI	Use of the Internet and extranets
Physical and limited auctions	Online auctions, everywhere, any time
Broker-based services, transactions	Electronic infomediaries, value-added services
Paper-based billing	Electronic billing
Paper-based tendering	Electronic reverse auctions, tendering
Push production, starting with demand forecast	Pull production, starting with an order
Mass production	Mass customization, build-to-order
Physical-based commission marketing	Affiliated, virtual marketing
Word-of-mouth, slow and limited advertisement	Explosive viral marketing
Linear supply chains	Hub-based supply chains
Large amount of capital is needed for mass production	Little capital is needed for build-to-order
Large fixed cost is required for plant operation	Small fixed cost is required for plant operation
Customers' value proposition is frequently a mismatch (cost > value)	Perfect match of customers' value proposition (cost = value)

PART I: INTRODUCTION TO EC

Part I includes an overview of EC, its content, benefits, and limitations, which have been presented in Chapter 1. Chapter 2 presents the major EC market mechanisms, including electronic catalogs and auctions.

PART II: INTERNET RETAILING

Part II consists of two chapters. Chapter 3 describes e-tailing (B2C), including some of its most innovative applications. We also describe delivery of services, such as online banking. Chapter 4 is dedicated to the explanation of consumer behavior in cyberspace, market research, customer service, and Internet advertising.

PART III: BUSINESS-TO-BUSINESS E-COMMERCE

Part III is composed of two chapters. In Chapter 5 we introduce B2B EC and describe primarily company-centric models (one buyer–many sellers, one seller–many buyers). Electronic exchanges (many buyers–many sellers) are described in Chapter 6.

PART IV: OTHER EC MODELS AND APPLICATIONS

In Part IV we present several different topics. In Chapter 7 we introduce intra-business EC, e-government, C2C, corporate portals, and e-learning. In Chapter 8 we discuss mobile commerce (m-commerce) and its many applications.

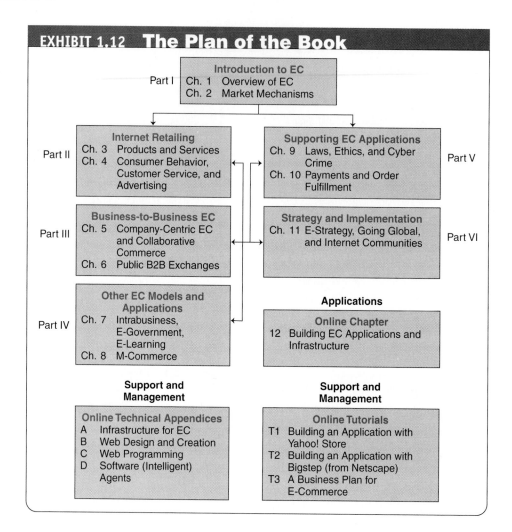

EXHIBIT 1.12   The Plan of the Book

Part I
- **Introduction to EC**
  - Ch. 1   Overview of EC
  - Ch. 2   Market Mechanisms

Part II
- **Internet Retailing**
  - Ch. 3   Products and Services
  - Ch. 4   Consumer Behavior, Customer Service, and Advertising

Part III
- **Business-to-Business EC**
  - Ch. 5   Company-Centric EC and Collaborative Commerce
  - Ch. 6   Public B2B Exchanges

Part IV
- **Other EC Models and Applications**
  - Ch. 7   Intrabusiness, E-Government, E-Learning
  - Ch. 8   M-Commerce

Part V
- **Supporting EC Applications**
  - Ch. 9   Laws, Ethics, and Cyber Crime
  - Ch. 10   Payments and Order Fulfillment

Part VI
- **Strategy and Implementation**
  - Ch. 11   E-Strategy, Going Global, and Internet Communities

Applications
- **Online Chapter**
  - 12   Building EC Applications and Infrastructure

Support and Management
- **Online Technical Appendices**
  - A   Infrastructure for EC
  - B   Web Design and Creation
  - C   Web Programming
  - D   Software (Intelligent) Agents

Support and Management
- **Online Tutorials**
  - T1   Building an Application with Yahoo! Store
  - T2   Building an Application with Bigstep (from Netscape)
  - T3   A Business Plan for E-Commerce

PART V: SUPPORTING EC APPLICATIONS

Part V examines issues involving the support of EC applications. Chapter 9 delves into privacy and other legal issues, as well as EC security. Of the many diverse EC support activities, we concentrate on three: payments, order fulfillment, and content creation and maintenance, which are presented in Chapter 10.

PART VI: STRATEGY AND IMPLEMENTATION

In this final part of the text, Chapter 11 deals with e-strategy and planning. The chapter also covers the issues of global EC, small businesses in EC, and virtual communities. We conclude the text with a discussion on the future of EC.

ONLINE PART VII: MORE EC APPLICATIONS

An additional chapter is online at the book's Web site (prenhall.com/turban). Chapter 12 addresses infrastructure and application development processes and methods.

APPENDICES AND TUTORIALS

Four appendices and three online tutorials are available on the book's Web site (prenhall.com/turban):

- ◗ Appendix A: Infrastructure for EC
- ◗ Appendix B: Web Page Design and Creation
- ◗ Appendix C: Web Programming
- ◗ Appendix D: Software (Intelligent) Agents
- ◗ Tutorial T1: Building an Application with Yahoo! Store
- ◗ Tutorial T2: Building an Application with Bigstep (from Netscape)
- ◗ Tutorial T3: A Business Plan for E-Commerce

MANAGERIAL ISSUES

Many managerial issues are related to EC. These issues are discussed throughout the book and summarized in a separate section (like this one) near the end of each chapter. Some managerial issues related to this introductory chapter are as follows:

1. **Is it real?** For those not involved in EC, the first question that comes to mind is, "Is it real?" We believe that the answer is an emphatic "yes." Just ask anyone who has banked from home, purchased stocks online, or bought a book from *Amazon.com.* An interesting tip for organizations and managers was given by Randy Mott, Wal-Mart's Chief Information Officer (CIO), "Start EC as soon as possible; it is too dangerous to wait." Jack Welch, former Chief Executive Officer (CEO) of General Electric, has commented, "The Internet and e-commerce are as important as breathing. Where does the Internet rank in priority? It's number one, two, three, and four" (*Business Week*, June 18, 1999).

2. **How should we evaluate the magnitude of the business pressures?** The best approach is to solicit the expertise of research institutions, such as GartnerGroup or Forrester Research, which specialize in EC. Otherwise, by the time you determine what is going on, it may be too late. The big certified public accounting companies may be of help too. (PriceWaterhouseCoopers, Accenture, and others provide considerable EC information on their Web sites.) It is especially important for management to know what is going on in its own industry.

3. **Why is the B2B area so attractive?** The simple answer is that some B2B models are easier to implement. In contrast, B2C has several major problems ranging from channel conflict with existing distributors to lack of a critical mass of buyers. Also, the volume of B2B transactions is larger. Rather than waiting for B2C problems to be worked out, many companies can start B2B buying or selling electronically in a matter of days by joining existing marketplaces. The problem is determining which marketplaces to join.

4. **There are so many EC failures—how can one avoid them?** As of early 2000, we have witnessed the failure of many EC projects within companies, as well as the failure of many dot-com "Internet companies." Industry consolidation often occurs after a "gold rush." About 100 years ago, hundreds of companies tried to manufacture cars, following Ford's success in the United States; only three survived. The important thing is to learn from the failures of others (see Useem 2000 and Chapter 11).

5. **What should be my company's strategy toward EC?** There are three basic strategies: lead, wait, or experiment. This issue is revisited in Chapter 11, together with related issues such

as the cost-benefit trade-offs of EC, integration of EC into the business, outsourcing, and how to handle resistance to change. Another strategic issue is the prioritization of the many initiatives and applications available to a company (see Rosen 1999).

6. **How do we transform our organization into a digital one?** Once a company determines its strategy and decides to move to EC, it must plan an implementation strategy. This process is shown in Chapter 11 (and is discussed at length by Slywotzky and Morrison 2001).

SUMMARY

In this chapter you learned about the following EC issues as they relate to the learning objectives.

1. **Definition of EC and description of its various categories.** EC involves conducting transactions electronically. Its major categories are pure vs. partial EC, Internet- vs. non-Internet–based EC, and electronic markets vs. interorganizational systems and intraorganizational transactions.

2. **The content and framework of EC.** The applications of EC, and there are many of them, are based on infrastructures and supported by people, public policy and technical standards, marketing and advertising, logistics, and business partners—all brought together by management.

3. **The major types of EC transactions.** The major types of EC transactions are B2B, B2C, B2B2C, C2C, m-commerce, intrabusiness e-commerce, B2E, c-commerce, G2C, and E2E.

4. **The major business models.** The major EC business models include online direct marketing, electronic tendering systems, name your own price, find the best price, affiliate marketing, viral marketing, group purchasing, online auctions, mass customization (make-to-order), electronic marketplaces, and supply chain improvers.

5. **Benefits of EC to organizations, consumers, and society.** EC provides numerous benefits to organizations, consumers, and society. Because these benefits are substantial, it looks as though EC is here to stay, and it cannot be ignored.

6. **Limitations of EC.** The many limitations of EC can be categorized as technological and nontechnological. As time passes, the barriers posed by technological limitations diminish, as capacity, security, and accessibility continue to improve through technological innovations. Nontechnological limitations will also diminish with time, but some of them, especially the behavioral ones, may persist for many years in some organizations.

7. **The digital revolution and the economic impact of EC.** E-commerce is a major product of the digital revolution, which enables companies to simultaneously increase growth and profit, "reach" and "richness," and more.

8. **The role of EC in combating pressures in the business environment.** Market (economic), technological, and societal pressures force organizations to respond. Traditional responses may be insufficient because of the magnitude of the pressures and the pace of change. Therefore, organizations frequently must innovate and reengineer their operations. In many cases, EC is the major facilitator of such organizational responses.

KEY TERMS

Affiliate marketing,	p. 14	Business plan,	p. 11	Business-to-consumer (B2C),	p. 7
Brick-and-mortar,	p. 4	Business-to-business (B2B),	p. 7	Business-to-employee (B2E),	p. 8
Business case,	p. 11				
Business models,	p. 11				

DISCUSSION QUESTIONS

1. Compare and contrast viral marketing with affiliate marketing.

2. Carefully examine the nontechnological limitations of EC. Which are company-dependent and which are generic?

3. Compare and contrast brick-and-mortar and click-and-mortar organizations.

4. Why is it said that EC is a catalyst of fundamental changes in organizations?

5. Explain how EC facilitates supply chain management.

6. Explain how EC can reduce cycle time, improve employees' empowerment, and facilitate customer support.

7. How does EC facilitate customization of products and services?

8. Why is buying with a smart card from a vending machine considered EC?

9. Compare EC with catalog-based mail-order shopping.

10. Why is distance learning considered EC?

INTERNET EXERCISES

1. Go to bigboxx.com and identify the services the company provides to its customers. What type of EC is this? What business model does Bigboxx use?

2. Locate recent information on Amazon.com in the following areas:

   a. Enter Amazon's site and find the top-selling books on EC.

   b. Find a review of one of these books.

   c. Review the customer services you can get from Amazon and describe the benefits you receive from shopping there.

   d. Review the products directory.

3. Enter priceline.com and identify the various business models it uses.

4. Go to ups.com and find information about recent EC projects that are related to logistics and supply chain management.

5. Go to musicmaker.com and create a CD. Then go to nike.com and design a pair of shoes.

Next visit iprint.com and create a business card. Finally, enter jaguar.com and configure the car of your dreams. What are the advantages of each activity? The disadvantages?

6. Enter chemconnect.com. What kind of EC does this site offer? What benefits can it provide to buyers? To sellers?

7. Try to sell or buy an item on an online auction. You can try eBay.com, auction.yahoo.com, or an auction site of your choice. You can participate in an auction from almost any country. Prepare a short report describing your experiences.

8. Try to save on your next purchase by using group purchasing. Visit shop2gether.com, letsbuyit.com, and zwirl.com. Which site do you prefer? Why?

TEAM ASSIGNMENTS AND ROLE PLAYING

1. Assign each team two failed or failing Internet companies (e.g., musicmaker.com, accompany. com, comdex.com). Use startupfailures.com to identify companies that are in distress. Fortune. com is a good source of details for particular business failures. Have each team prepare a report on why the companies the team examined failed or are failing.

2. Each team will research two EC success stories. Members of the group should examine companies that operate solely online and some that extensively utilize a click-and-mortar strategy. Each team is responsible for identifying the critical success factors for its companies and presenting a report to the class. (See prenhall.com/turban for case studies and relevant URLs.)

REAL-WORLD CASE

E-COMMERCE CURES HOSPITALS

Changes in U.S. government regulations and strong competition in the health care industry in the late 1990s and early 2000 caused headaches for many health care institutions. Even Kaiser Permanente, the largest U.S. health maintenance organization (HMO), could not escape the problem, losing $288 million in 1998 alone. Kaiser Permanente serves about 10 million members with 361 hospitals and clinics, 10,000 doctors, and tens of thousands of support employees.

The company realized that the old way of doing business, working with old-fashioned paper records and communicating with telephones, faxes, and letters, would aggravate its financial problems. So in a bold move, Kaiser Permanente decided to move toward EC by investing $2 billion in various Web-based systems. Here are some of the projects that were undertaken:

▶ An Internet-based communications system was implemented. The system includes customized Web pages for each organization with which Kaiser has a contract. Staff from those organizations can locate particular rates or coverage online, and do not have to call Kaiser's employees for the information.

▶ Kaiser's portal allows patients to schedule and check their appointments via the Internet and to e-mail routine queries to Kaiser employees.

▶ Kaiser's corporate intranet allows doctors and other employees to electronically order supplies, equipment, and services.

▶ The corporate intranet has an application that checks the drugs that a doctor suggests for each patient. The computer suggests cheaper or less dangerous alternatives, and the doctor can then decide if the substitution is acceptable.

- As an HMO, Kaiser has to compete with other HMOs for customers, both organizational (with all their employees) and individuals. The intranet allows for real-time quotes, enabling Kaiser's sales force of over 4,000 brokers to provide customers with customized rates within minutes.

- Digital records of patients' tests are kept on Kaiser's intranet and can be accessed by authorized personnel in seconds. This means that staff no longer need to repeat 10 to 15 percent of patient tests due to lost or misread paper records.

- An e-procurement system expedites shipments, reduces inventories, and cuts costs.

- All medical records are digitized. A doctor can instantly tap into a patient's records from a keyboard and a flat-panel computer screen attached to the wall. The doctor can also add notes to the electronic file.

Dozens of other EC applications are in the works. All of the EC applications will be part of a huge network that will be completed in 2003.

EC implementation has not been easy. The HMO started phasing in EC in the northwestern states in 1999. During the phase-in, some employees resisted, mistakes were made, and vendors had to be managed. But the results are clear. The Internet is the most effective medicine for large health care organizations. In the first 2 years, processing costs in the Internet system were about 60 percent lower than costs in comparable non-Internet systems. Most importantly, the use of EC has also improved the quality of delivery, and that is what really matters.

Sources: Compiled from *Business Week E.BIZ,* February 7, 2000, and from Kaiser Permanente press releases, 2000, 2001.

Questions

1. Review the EC applications listed and classify them as B2C, B2B, etc.

2. What factors drove Kaiser Permanente to implement EC?

3. Identify the EC applications related to supply chain management.

4. It is said that placing a large computer screen in an examination room increases the doctor's productivity and improves doctor–patient interaction. Why might that be so?

E-COMMERCE MARKET MECHANISMS

Learning objectives

Upon completion of this chapter, you will be able to:

▶ Define e-marketplaces and list their components.

▶ List the major types of electronic markets and describe their features.

▶ Define supply chains and value chains and understand their roles.

▶ Describe the role of intermediaries in EC.

▶ Discuss competition, quality, and liquidity issues in e-marketplaces.

▶ Describe electronic catalogs, shopping carts, and search engines.

▶ Describe the various types of auctions and list their characteristics.

▶ Discuss the benefits, limitations, and impacts of auctions.

▶ Describe bartering and negotiating online.

▶ Describe the impact of e-marketplaces on organizations.

▶ Define m-commerce and explain its role as a market mechanism.

Content

How Raffles Hotel Is Conducting E-Commerce

Managerial Issues

Real-World Case:

FreeMarkets.com Revolutionizes Procurement

HOW RAFFLES HOTEL IS CONDUCTING E-COMMERCE

The Problem

Raffles Hotel, one of Singapore's colonial-era landmarks, is the flagship of Raffles Holding Ltd., which owns and manages luxury and business hotels worldwide. Raffles Hotel operates in a very competitive environment. To maintain its world-renowned reputation, the hotel spent lavishly on every facet of its operation. For example, it once stocked 12 different kinds of butter, at a high cost. The success of the company and each of its hotels depends on the company's ability to lure customers to its hotels and facilities and on its ability to contain costs.

The Solution

To maintain its image and contain costs, Raffles must address two types of issues—business-to-consumer and business-to-business. On the business-to-consumer side, Raffles maintains a diversified public *portal* (*raffles.com*) that introduces customers to the company and its services. The portal includes information on the hotels, a reservation system, links to travelers' resources, a customer relationship management (CRM) program, and an online store for Raffles products.

On the business-to-business side, Raffles has interorganizational systems that enable efficient contacts with its suppliers. To do business with Raffles, each of 5,000 potential vendors must log on to Raffles' private marketplace. As for purchasing, Raffles conducts e-procurement using *reverse auctions* among qualified suppliers, in which sellers bid for the sales contract, and the lowest bidder wins. With the reverse auction, the number of suppliers is reduced and the quantity purchased from each increases, which leads to lower purchasing prices. For example, butter is now purchased from only two suppliers. Procurement negotiations now take place online. Buyer–seller relationships have been strengthened by the private, online marketplace.

The e-marketplace also has a sell-side, allowing other hotels to buy Raffles-branded products, such as tiny shampoo bottles and bathrobes, from electronic catalogs. Even competitors buy Raffles-branded products because they are relatively inexpensive. Also, the luxury products make the hotel that purchases them look upscale.

The Results

The public portal helps in customer acquisition. Using promotions and direct sales, the hotel is able to maintain high occupancy rates in difficult economic times. The private marketplace is strategically advantageous to Raffles in forcing suppliers to disclose their prices, thus increasing competition among suppliers. The company is saving about $1 million a year on procurement of eight high-volume supplies (toiler paper, detergents, etc.) alone. The success of the company is evidenced by its aggressive expansion in the Asian markets.

What We Can Learn . . .

For an old-economy hotel to transform itself into a click-and-mortar business, it had to create two separate electronic markets: a B2C private market for selling its services to consumers and a B2B market to buy from its suppliers and to sell products to other hotels. In addition, it had to use several e-commerce mechanisms: a corporate portal, electronic catalogs, and e-procurement using reverse auctions. Electronic markets and some of their supporting mechanisms are described in this chapter. We also will examine the economics of e-commerce and its impacts on organizations.

2.1   ELECTRONIC MARKETPLACES

According to Bakos (1998), markets play a central role in the economy, facilitating the exchange of information, goods, services, and payments. In the process, they create economic value for buyers, sellers, market intermediaries, and for society at large.

Markets (electronic or otherwise) have three main functions: (1) matching buyers and sellers; (2) facilitating the exchange of information, goods, services, and payments associated with market transactions; and (3) providing an institutional infrastructure, such as a legal and regulatory framework, that enables the efficient functioning of the market (Exhibit 2.1).

In recent years, markets have seen a dramatic increase in the use of IT and EC (Turban et al. 2002). EC has increased market efficiencies by expediting or improving the functions listed in Exhibit 2.1. Furthermore, EC has been able to significantly decrease the cost of executing these functions.

The emergence of electronic marketplaces, also called **marketspaces**, especially Internet-based marketspaces, changed several of the processes used in trading and in supply chains. These changes, driven by IT, resulted in even greater economic efficiencies. EC leverages IT with increased effectiveness and lower transaction and distribution costs, leading to more efficient, "friction-free" markets. An example of such efficiency can be seen in the NTE case (EC Application Case 2.1). Another example is provided in the Real-World Case at the end of this chapter.

marketspace
A marketplace in which sellers and buyers exchange goods and services for money (or for other goods and services), but do so electronically.

MARKETSPACE COMPONENTS

Similar to a marketplace, in a marketspace sellers and buyers exchange goods and services for money (or for other goods and services if bartering is used), but they do it electronically. A marketspace includes electronic transactions that bring

EXHIBIT 2.1   Functions of a Market

Matching of Buyers and Sellers	Facilitation of Transactions	Institutional Infrastructure

▸ Determination of product offerings
    Product features offered by sellers
    Aggregation of different products
▸ Search (of buyers for sellers and of sellers for buyers)
    Price and product information
    Organizing bids and bartering
    Matching seller offerings with
      buyer preferences
▸ Price discovery
    Process and outcome in
      determination of prices
    Enabling price comparisons
	▸ Logistics
	    Delivery of information, goods,
	      or services to buyers
	▸ Settlement
	    Transfer of payments to sellers
	▸ Trust
	    Credit system, reputations, rating
	      agencies like Consumers Reports
	      and BBB. Special escrow and
	      trust online agencies
		▸ Legal
		    Commercial code, contract law,
		      dispute resolution, intellectual
		      property protection
		    Export and import law
		▸ Regulatory
		    Rules and regulations,
		      monitoring, enforcement

Source: Bakos, Y., "The Emerging Role of Electronic Marketplaces on the Internet." *Communications of the ACM*, August © 1998 ACM, Inc., p. 35. Used with Permission.

Interorganization and Collaboration
NTE EVENS THE LOAD

The hauling industry is not very efficient. Though trucks are likely to be full on outbound journeys, they are often empty on the way back. (About 50 percent of the trucks on America's roads at any one time are not full.) National Transportation Exchange (NTE) is attempting to solve this problem.

NTE (*nte.com*) uses the Internet to connect shippers who have loads they want to move cheaply with fleet managers who have space to fill. NTE helps create what is called a *spot market* (a very short-term market) by setting daily prices based on information from several hundred fleet managers about the destinations of their vehicles and the amount of space they have available. It also gets information from shippers about their needs and flexibility in dates. NTE then works out the best deals for the shippers and the haulers. When a deal is agreed upon, NTE issues the contract and handles payments. The entire process takes only a few minutes. NTE collects a commission based on the value of each deal, the fleet manager gets extra revenue that they would otherwise have missed out on, and the shipper gets a bargain price, at the cost of some loss of flexibility.

When NTE was first set up in 1995, it used a proprietary network that was expensive and limited the number of buyers and sellers who could connect through it. By using the Internet, NTE has been able to extend its reach down to the level of individual truck drivers and provide a much wider range of services. Today, drivers can use wireless Internet access devices to connect to the NTE Web site on the road.

In 2001, NTE expanded its services to improve inventory management, scheduling, and vendor compliance along the entire supply chain. NTE's software is integrated with its customers' operations and systems. NTE's business is currently limited to ground transportation within the United States. In Hong Kong, *arena.com.hk* (called Line) provides similar port services.

Source: Compiled from *The Economist*, June 26, 1999; Davidson, April 2001, and *arena.com.hk*, April 2001.

Questions

▶ What type of B2B is done at NTE? Classify this B2B model.

▶ What are the benefits of NTE's services to truckers? To shippers?

---

about a new distribution of goods and services. The major components and players of a marketspace are customers, sellers, goods (physical or digital), infrastructure, a front end, a back end, intermediaries and other business partners, and support services. A brief description of each follows.

▶ **Customers.** The tens of millions of people worldwide that surf the Web are potential buyers of the goods and services offered or advertised on the Internet. These consumers are looking for bargains, customized items, collectors' items, entertainment, and more. They are in the driver's seat. They can search for detailed information, compare, bid, and sometimes negotiate. Organizations are the major consumers, accounting for over 85 percent of EC activities.

▶ **Sellers.** Hundreds of thousands of storefronts are on the Web, advertising and offering millions of items. Every day it is possible to find new offerings of products and services. Sellers can sell direct from their Web site or from e-marketplaces.

digital products
Goods that can be transformed to digital format and delivered over the Internet.

front end
The portion of an e-seller's business processes through which customers interact, including the seller's portal, electronic catalogs, a shopping cart, a search engine, and a payment gateway.

back end
The activities that support online order-taking and fulfillment, inventory management, purchasing from suppliers, payment processing, packaging, and delivery.

intermediary
A third party that operates between sellers and buyers.

▶ **Products.** One of the major differences between the marketplace and the marketspace is the possible digitization of products and services in a marketspace. Although both types of markets can sell physical products, the marketspace also can sell **digital products**, which are goods that can be transformed to digital format and delivered over the Internet. In addition to digitization of software and music, it is possible to digitize dozens of other products and services, as shown in Exhibit 2–2. As described in Chapter 1, digital products have different cost curves than those of regular products. In digitization, most of the costs are fixed and the variable cost is very small. Thus, profit will increase very rapidly as volume increases once the fixed costs are paid for. This is one of the major potentials of electronic markets.

▶ **Infrastructure.** An electronic market infrastructure includes hardware, software, and networks.

▶ **Front end.** Customers interact with a marketspace via a **front end**. The business processes in the front end include the seller's portal, electronic catalogs, a shopping cart, a search engine, and a payment gateway.

▶ **Back end.** All the activities that are related to order aggregation and fulfillment, inventory management, purchasing from suppliers, payment processing, packaging, and delivery, are done in what is termed the **back end** of the business.

▶ **Intermediaries.** In marketing, an **intermediary** typically is a third party that operates between sellers and buyers. Intermediaries of all kinds offer their services on the Web. The role of these electronic intermediaries, as will be seen throughout the text and especially in Chapters 3, 6, and 10, is different from that of regular intermediaries (such as wholesalers). Online intermediaries cre-

---

EXHIBIT 2.2   Examples of Digital Products

Information and Entertainment Products	**Symbols, Tokens, and Concepts**	**Processes and Services**
▶ Paper-based documents: books, newspapers, magazines, journals, store coupons, marketing brochures, newsletters, research papers, and training materials	▶ Tickets and reservations: airlines, hotels, concerts, sports events, transportation	▶ Government services: forms, benefits, welfare payments, licenses
▶ Product information: product specifications, catalogs, user manuals, sales training manuals	▶ Financial instruments: checks, electronic currencies, credit cards, securities, letters of credit	▶ Electronic messaging: letters, faxes, telephone calls
▶ Graphics: photographs, postcards, calendars, maps, posters, x-rays		▶ Business-value-creation processes: ordering, bookkeeping, inventorying, contracting
▶ Audio: music recordings, speeches, lectures, industrial voice		▶ Auctions, bidding, bartering
▶ Video: movies, television programs, video clips		▶ Remote education, telemedicine and other interactive services
▶ Software: programs, games, development tools		▶ Cybercafes, interactive entertainment, virtual communities

Source: Adapted from Choi et al., 1997, p. 64.

ate and manage the online markets (such as in the NTE case). They help match buyers and sellers, provide some infrastructure services, and help customers and/or sellers to institute and complete transactions. Most of these online intermediaries are computerized systems.

▶ **Other business partners.** In addition to intermediaries, there are several types of partners, such as shippers, that collaborate on the Internet, mostly along the supply chain.

▶ **Support services.** Many different support services are available, ranging from certification and trust services, which ensure security, to knowledge providers. These services are created to address implementation issues.

These components are available in different types of e-markets.

▶ What is the difference between a marketplace and a marketspace?

▶ List the components of a marketspace.

▶ Define a digital product and provide five examples.

2.2 TYPES OF ELECTRONIC MARKETS: FROM STOREFRONTS TO PORTALS

There are several types of e-marketplaces. In B2C the major e-marketplaces are *storefronts* and *Internet malls*. In B2B we observe private *sell-side* (one seller–many buyers), and *buy-side* (one buyer–many sellers), e-marketplaces and public *exchanges*. Let's elaborate on these as well as on the gateways to the e-marketplaces—the portals.

ELECTRONIC STOREFRONTS

An electronic or Web **storefront** refers to a single company's Web site where products and services are sold. It is an electronic store. The storefront may belong to a manufacturer (e.g., geappliances.com), to a retailer (e.g., walmart.com), to individuals selling from their home, or to another type of business.

A storefront includes several mechanisms that are necessary for conducting the sale. The most common features are:

▶ Electronic catalogs

▶ A search engine that helps the consumer to find products in the catalog

▶ An electronic cart for holding items until check-out

▶ E-auction facilities

▶ A payment gateway where payment arrangements can be made

▶ A shipment court where shipping arrangements are made

▶ Customer services, including product information and a register for warranties

We will describe the first three mechanisms in Section 2.6; e-auction facilities are described in Section 2.7; and mechanisms for payments and shipments are

storefront
A single company's Web site where products and services are sold.

described in Chapter 10. Customer services, which can be fairly elaborate, are covered in Chapter 4.

ELECTRONIC MALLS

e-mall

An online shopping center where many stores are located.

In addition to shopping in individual storefronts, consumers can shop in electronic malls (e-malls). Similar to malls in the physical world, an **e-mall** is an online shopping location where many stores are located. For example, hawaii.com is an e-mall that aggregates Hawaiian products and stores. It contains a directory of product categories and the stores in each category. When a consumer indicates the category they are interested in, they are transferred to the appropriate independent *storefront* to conduct their shopping. This kind of a mall does not provide any shared services. Other malls do provide shared services (e.g., choicemall.com). Some malls are actually large click-and-mortar retailers, and some (e.g., buy.com) are virtual retailers.

TYPES OF STORES AND MALLS

There are several types of stores and malls:

- **General stores/malls.** These are large marketspaces that sell all types of products. Examples are choicemall.com, shop4.com, spree.com, and the major public portals (yahoo.com, aol.com, and lycos.com). All major department and discount stores fall into this category.

- **Specialized stores/malls.** These sell only one or a few types of products, such as books, flowers, wine, cars, or pet toys. Amazon.com started as a specialized e-bookstore, but today is a generalized store. At buy.com you can only purchase computers and consumer electronic products. Beautyjungle.com specializes in beauty tips, trends, and products.

- **Regional vs. global stores.** Some stores, such as e-groceries or sellers of heavy furniture, serve customers that live in a close-by area. For example, parknshop.com serves the Hong Kong community; it will not deliver groceries to New York. However, some local stores will sell to customers in other countries if the customer will pay the shipping, insurance, and other costs.

- **Pure online organizations vs. click-and-mortar stores.** Stores can be pure online ("virtual") organizations, such as Amazon.com, buy.com, or cattoys.com. They do not have physical stores. Others are physical ("brick-and-mortar") stores that also sell online (e.g., Walmart.com, 1800flowers.com, or woolworths.com.au). This second category is called click-and-mortar. Both categories will be discussed in Chapter 3.

MARKETPLACES

In general conversation, the distinction between a mall and a marketplace is not always clear. In the physical world, we view a mall as a collection of stores (a shopping center) where the stores are isolated from each other and prices are generally fixed. In contrast, markets/marketplaces, some of which are open air, imply a place where people are looking for bargains and are expected to negotiate prices.

On the Web, the term *marketplace* has a different and distinct meaning. If individual customers want to negotiate prices, they may be able to do so in some storefronts or malls. However, the term **e-marketplace** usually implies B2B, not B2C. We distinguish three types of such e-marketplaces: private, public, and consortia.

Private E-Marketplaces

Private e-marketplaces are those owned by a single company. As can be seen in the Raffles Hotel story, two types of such markets exist: sell-side and buy-side. In a **sell-side e-marketplace**, a company such as Cisco Systems will sell either standard or customized products to qualified companies. This is similar to a storefront in B2C. In a **buy-side e-marketplace**, a company conducts purchasing from invited suppliers. For example, Raffles Hotel buys butter from two approved vendors. We will return to the topic of private e-marketplaces in Chapter 5.

Public E-Marketplaces

Public e-marketplaces are B2B markets that include many sellers and many buyers. These markets are usually owned and/or managed by an independent third party. These markets are also known as *exchanges* (e.g., a stock exchange), and they are regulated by the government or the exchange's owners. We will look at public e-marketplaces in more detail in Chapter 6.

Consortia

A small group of major buyers may create an e-marketplace to deal with suppliers, usually in their same industry. A group of sellers may also create an e-marketplace to deal with industry buyers. Such e-marketplaces are called **consortia** (singular, a *consortium*). They can be completely private, where only invited suppliers can participate, or they can be open to more suppliers, resembling a public e-marketplace. Regardless of whether they are owned by buyers or sellers, these markets can be *vertical*, meaning they are confined to one industry, or *horizontal*, meaning that different industries trade there. We will revisit consortia in Chapter 6.

INFORMATION PORTALS

With the growing use of intranets and the Internet, many organizations encounter information overload at a number of different levels. Information is scattered across numerous documents, e-mail messages, and databases at different locations and systems. Finding relevant and accurate information is often time consuming and requires access to multiple systems.

As a consequence, organizations lose a lot of productive employee time. One solution to this problem is to use portals. A portal is simply a gateway. It attempts to address information overload through an intranet-based environment to search and access relevant information from disparate IT systems and the Internet, using advanced search and indexing techniques. An **information portal** is a personalized, single point of access through a Web browser to critical business information located inside an organization. In Chapter 1 we discussed public portals and corporate portals. Both of these are types of information portals.

Portals appear under many descriptions and shapes. One way to distinguish among them is to look at their content, which can vary from narrow to broad,

e-marketplace
An online market, usually B2B, in which buyers and sellers negotiate; the three types of e-marketplaces are private, public, and consortia.

private e-marketplaces
Online markets owned by a single company; can be either sell-side or buy-side marketplaces.

sell-side e-marketplace
A private e-market in which a company sells either standard or customized products to qualified companies.

buy-side e-marketplace
A private e-market in which a company makes purchases from invited suppliers.

public e-marketplaces
B2B markets, usually owned and/or managed by an independent third party, that include many sellers and many buyers; also known as *exchanges*.

consortia
E-marketplaces that deal with suppliers and buyers in a single industry.

information portal
A personalized, single point of access through a Web browser to business information inside an organization.

and their community or audience, which can also vary. We distinguish five types of portals:

1. **Publishing portals** are intended for large communities with diverse interests. These portals involve relatively little customization of content except online search and some interactive capabilities, which would be typical for the Web. Examples are techweb.com and zdnet.com.

2. **Commercial portals** offer narrow content for diverse communities and are the most popular portals for online communities. Although they offer customization of the user interface, they are still intended for broad audiences and offer fairly simple content (a stock ticker and news on a few preselected items). Examples are My Yahoo!, lycos.com, and msn.com.

3. **Personal portals** target specific filtered information for individuals. As with commercial portals, they offer relatively narrow content but are typically much more personalized, effectively having an audience of one.

4. **Corporate portals** coordinate rich content within a relatively narrow community. They are also known as enterprise portals or enterprise information portals. Corporate portals are described in more detail in Chapter 6.

5. **Mobile portals** are portals that are accessible from mobile devices. Although most of the other portals mentioned here are PC-based, increasing numbers of portals are accessible via mobile devices. One example of such a **mobile portal** is iMode, which we will discuss in Section 2.9.

mobile portal
A portal accessible via a mobile device.

▶ Describe electronic storefronts and e-malls.

▶ List the various types of stores and malls.

▶ Differentiate between private and public marketspaces.

▶ What are information portals?

2.3   SUPPLY CHAINS AND VALUE CHAINS

Electronic markets differ from regular markets in that the customers do not physically travel to the market. Although they are physically disconnected from their customers in the purchasing process, electronic markets are connected to the physical world through market mechanisms for production and logistics. To better understand these and other market mechanisms and how they operate, we look first at the essential concepts of the supply and value chains.

SUPPLY CHAINS

supply chain
The flow of materials, information, money, and services from raw material suppliers through factories and warehouses to the end customers.

A **supply chain** is the flow of materials, information, money, and services from raw material suppliers through factories and warehouses to the end customers. A supply chain also includes the *organizations* and *processes* that create and deliver these products, information, and services to the end customers. The term supply chain comes from a picture of how the partnering organizations are linked together.

As shown in Exhibit 2.3, a simple linear supply chain links a company that manufactures or assembles a product (middle of the chain) with its suppliers (on the left) and distributors and customers (on the right). The upper part of the figure shows a generic supply chain. The bottom part shows a specific example of the toy-making process. The solid lines in the figure show the flow of materials among the various partners. Not shown is the flow of returned goods (e.g., defective products) and money, which are flowing in the *reverse direction*. The broken lines, which are shown only in the upper part of Exhibit 2.3, indicate the bidirectional flow of information.

As you can see, a supply chain involves activities that take place during the entire *product life cycle,* from "dirt to dust." However, a supply chain is more than that, as it also includes movement of information and money and procedures that support the movement of a product or a service. Finally, the organizations and individuals involved are considered a part of the supply chain as well.

Supply Chain Components

A supply chain can be broken into three parts: upstream, internal, and downstream.

Upstream supply chain. The upstream part of the supply chain includes the activities of suppliers (which can be manufacturers and/or assemblers) and their

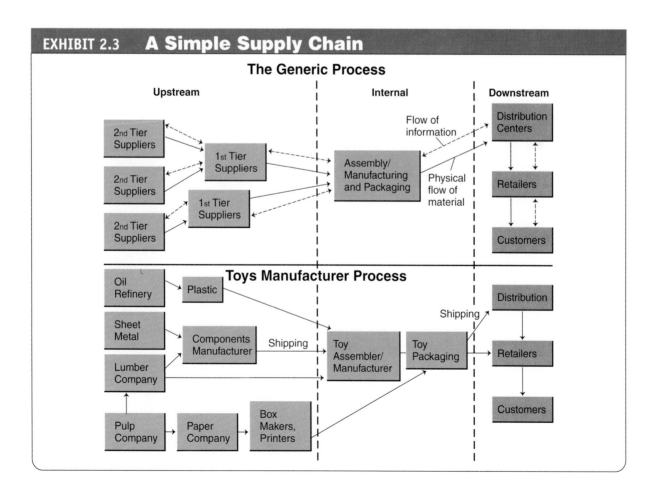

EXHIBIT 2.3   A Simple Supply Chain

suppliers. The supplier relationship can be extended to the left in several tiers, all the way to the origin of the material (e.g., mining ores, growing crops).

Internal supply chain. The internal part of the supply chain includes all the in-house processes used in transforming the inputs received from the suppliers into the organization's outputs. It extends from the time the inputs enter an organization to the time that the products go to distribution outside of the organization.

Downstream supply chain. The downstream part of the supply chain includes all the activities involved in delivering the product to the final customers. Looked at very broadly, the supply chain actually ends when the product reaches its after-use disposal—presumably back to Mother Earth somewhere.

TYPES OF SUPPLY CHAINS

The supply chain that was shown in Exhibit 2.3 is typical for a manufacturing company. However, supply chains can be much more complex. The following are four very common types of supply chains.

Integrated Make-to-Stock

The *integrated make-to-stock* supply chain model focuses on tracking customer demand so that the production process can efficiently restock the inventory of finished goods. To accomplish this goal, the company must integrate customer demand for products and services in real time, which can be in one or several marketing channels, and the sources of supply of the products and services. For example, Starbucks Coffee (starbucks.com) uses several distribution channels, selling not only hot coffee to consumers, but also coffee to businesses, such as airlines, supermarkets, department stores, and ice-cream makers. Sales are also done through direct mail, as well as the Internet. Starbucks is successfully integrating all sources of demand and matching it with supply by using Oracle's automated information system for manufacturing (called GEMMS). The system does distribution planning, manufacturing scheduling, and inventory control. The coordination of supply with multiple distribution channels requires timely and accurate information flow about demand, inventories, storage capacity, transportation scheduling, and more.

Continuous Replenishment

The idea of the *continuous replenishment* model is to constantly replenish the inventory as it declines, by working closely with suppliers and/or intermediaries. However, if the replenishment process involves many shipments, shipping costs may be too high, causing the supply chain to collapse. For example, daily deliveries in small amounts or unplanned shipments cost more for both an organization and its supplier than would biweekly shipments in larger amounts. To avoid this cost problem, real-time information on changes in demand is required in order to plan ahead and maintain the desired replenishment schedules and levels. Such information can be provided by EDI, extranets, and other EC systems. A continuous replenishment distribution channel which is suitable for a stable environment is shown in Exhibit 2.4a for McKesson Co., a leading distributor of pharmaceuticals to retail pharmacies.

EXHIBIT 2.4   Supply Chains: Integrated and Build-to-Order

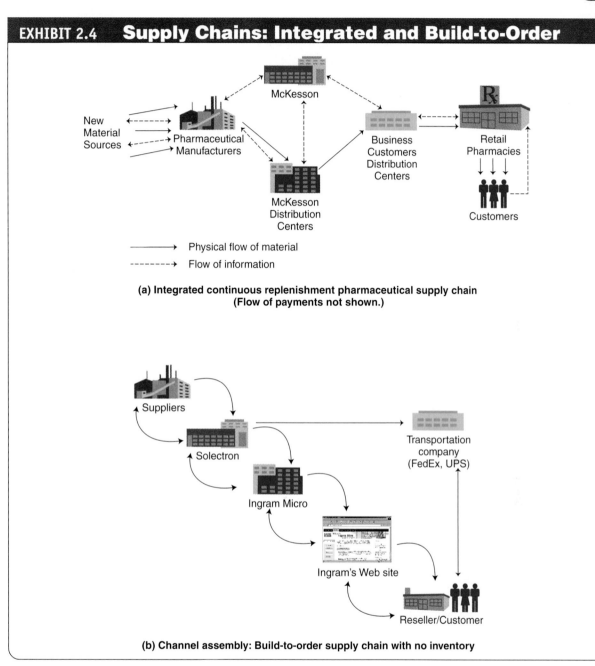

(a) Integrated continuous replenishment pharmaceutical supply chain
(Flow of payments not shown.)

(b) Channel assembly: Build-to-order supply chain with no inventory

Source: (b) Kalakota and Robinson, 2000, p. 301.

Build-to-Order

Dell Computer is best known for its application of the **build-to-order** supply chain model. The concept behind this model is to begin assembly of the customer's order almost immediately upon receipt of the order. This requires careful management of the component inventories and supply chain in order to have the needed materials on hand (or be able to obtain quickly, at the right cost) at each point in the production process. A solution to this potential inventory problem is to utilize

build-to-order
Supply chain model in which a manufacturer begins assembly of the customized order almost immediately upon receipt of the order.

many common components across several production lines and in several locations. With such planning, it is easy to make customized products.

Channel Assembly

A slight modification to the build-to-order supply chain model is *channel assembly*. In this model, the product is assembled as it moves through the distribution channel. This is accomplished through strategic alliances with *third-party logistics* (3PL) firms, such as Federal Express or UPS. These services sometimes involve physical assembly of a product at a 3PL facility, or collection of finished components for delivery to the customer. With this model, the customer's order would come together only once all items were placed on a vehicle for final delivery. Dell Computer is an excellent example. Dell makes and ships the computer via United Parcel Service (UPS) in a "From Dell" box. Dell sends the monitor order to Sony (or others) for shipping via UPS in a "From Dell" box. Dell also sends the software order to a software clearinghouse, which ships the software via UPS in a "From Dell" box. When all three items are in the UPS depot nearest the customer's house (within 1 to 2 days after the order was placed), UPS delivers all three boxes together to a customer who thinks that all of this came from Dell. By this model, Dell moves information down the supply chain, rather than moving physical product up the supply chain.

A channel assembly may have low or zero inventories. In the preceding example, Dell saves on warehousing costs and inventory management overhead. Channel assembly is popular in the computer technology industry. An example of this model is shown in Exhibit 2.4b, with a large distributor, Ingram Micro, at the center of the supply chain. (For further discussion of Ingram Micro, see Section 2.4.)

THE VALUE CHAIN

value chain
The series of activities a company performs to achieve its goal(s) at various stages of the production process; each activity adds value to the company's product or service, contributes to profit, and enhances competitive position.

The **value chain** is the series of activities that an organization performs to achieve its goal(s) at various stages of the production process, from resource acquisition to product delivery. The added value of these activities contributes to profit and enhances the asset value as well as the competitive position of the company in the market. Activities can be primary, such as manufacturing, or secondary (support), such as accounting. These activities are interconnected and sequenced and can be shown graphically for each product/or process. The value chain is used mainly to analyze the activities by looking at their cost in comparison to the value delivered. The value chain can be drawn for supply chain participants, and therefore the value provided to business partners and customers also can be analyzed.

Michael Porter, the creator of the value-chain concept, examined the impact of the Internet on the value chain (Porter 2001). He showed that the Internet can be incorporated into every type of activity in the value chain. The magnitude and nature of the integration depends on the specific industry and company. Porter views this impact as a step of an evolutionary process in which information technologies increasingly penetrate the value chain. Currently, the Internet enables the integration of the value chain and entire **value systems**, which are a set of value chains in an entire industry, including the value chains of tiers of suppliers, distribution channels, and customers.

value system
A set of value chains in an entire industry, including the value chains of tiers of suppliers, distribution channels, and customers.

The value chain and the supply chain concepts are interrelated. The value chain shows the activities performed by an organization and the values added (the contribution) by each. The supply chain shows flows of materials, money, and information that support the execution of these activities. E-commerce, as will be shown throughout the book, increases the value added by introducing new business models, automating business processes, and so on. It also smoothes the supply chain by reducing problems in the flows of material, money, and information. Finally, EC facilitates the restructuring of business activities and supply chains. Intermediaries are found in many supply chains.

⬥ Define supply chains and list their components.

⬥ Describe the four major types of supply chains.

⬥ Describe value chains.

2.4 INTERMEDIATION AND SYNDICATION IN E-COMMERCE

Intermediaries (brokers) play an important role in commerce by providing value-added activities and services to buyers and sellers. There are many types of intermediaries. The most well-known intermediaries in the physical world are wholesalers and retailers. In cyberspace there are, in addition, intermediaries that control information flow. These electronic intermediaries are known as **infomediaries**. Frequently, they aggregate information and sell it to others. As we continue our study of e-commerce market mechanisms, we need to examine the roles of intermediaries.

infomediaries
Electronic intermediaries that control information flow in cyberspace, often aggregating information and selling it to others.

THE ROLES AND VALUE OF INTERMEDIARIES IN E-MARKETS

Producers and consumers may interact directly in an e-marketplace: Producers provide information to customers, who then select from among the available products. In general, producers set prices, but sometimes prices are negotiated. However, direct interactions are sometimes undesirable or unfeasible. In that case, intermediation is needed. Intermediaries, whether human or electronic, can address the following five important limitations of direct interaction.

1. **Search costs.** It may be expensive for providers and consumers to find each other. In electronic bazaars, thousands of products are exchanged among millions of people. Producers may have trouble accurately gauging consumer demand for new products; many desirable items may never be produced simply because no one recognizes the demand for them. Some intermediaries maintain databases of customer preferences, and they can predict demand and reduce search costs by selectively routing information from providers to consumers and by matching customers with products and/or services.

2. **Lack of privacy.** Either the buyer or seller may wish to remain anonymous or at least protect some information relevant to a trade. Intermediaries can relay messages and make pricing and allocation decisions without revealing the identity of one or both parties.

3. **Incomplete information.** The buyer may need more information than the seller is able or willing to provide, such as information about product quality, competing products, or customer satisfaction. An intermediary can gather product information from sources other than the product provider, including independent evaluators and other customers. Many third-party Web sites provide such information (e.g., bizrate.com, mysimon.com, and consumerguide.com).

4. **Contract risk.** A consumer may refuse to pay after receiving a product or a producer may provide inferior products or give inadequate postpurchase service. Intermediaries have a number of tools to reduce such risks. First, the broker can disseminate information about the behavior of providers and consumers. The threat of publicizing bad behavior or removing a seal of approval may encourage both producers and consumers to meet the broker's standard for fair dealing. Or, the broker may accept responsibility for the behavior of parties in transactions it arranges and act as a policeman on its own. Third, the broker can provide insurance against bad behavior. The credit card industry uses all three approaches to reduce providers' and consumers' exposure to risk.

   In the online auction area, there are companies that act as "escrow agencies," accepting and holding payment from the buyer while the seller completes delivery of the product or service to the escrow agency. Then, if the product is satisfactory, the agency releases payment to the seller and the product to the buyer.

5. **Pricing inefficiencies.** By jockeying to secure a desirable price for a product, providers and consumers may miss opportunities for mutually desirable trades. This is particularly likely in negotiations over unique or custom products, such as houses, and in markets for information products and other public goods where freeloading is a problem. Intermediaries can use pricing mechanisms that induce just the appropriate trades, for example, dealing with an imbalance of buy and sell orders in stock markets.

E-DISTRIBUTORS ON B2B

e-distributor
An e-commerce intermediary that connects manufacturers (suppliers) with buyers by aggregating the catalogs of many suppliers in one place—the intermediary's Web site.

A special type of intermediary in e-commerce is the B2B **e-distributor**. These intermediaries connect manufacturers (suppliers) with buyers, such as retailers (or resellers in the computer industry). E-distributors basically aggregate the catalogs of many suppliers, sometimes thousands of them, in one place—the intermediary's Web site. In the past such intermediaries worked with paper catalogs. For buyers, e-distributors offer a one-stop location from which to place an order. The items purchased are mostly *maintenance*, *repair*, and *operation* items (MROs), that is, items that are usually not under regular contract with suppliers. One of the most well-known distributors that moved aggressively online is W. W. Grainger (grainger.com), the largest U.S. distributor of MROs. Grainger actually buys products from manufacturers and, like a retailer in B2C, sells them, but to businesses.

Another B2B e-distributor is Ingram Micro (ingrammicro.com), the largest global wholesale provider of technology products and supply chain management services. Of its many EC initiatives, one of the more interesting is IM-Logistics, which connects leading technology and consumer electronic manufacturers to more than 7,500 retailers in the United States. Ingram Micro is operating in a complex supply chain, which was shown in Exhibit 2.4(b), page 51. Note that there is an additional intermediary in the chain, Solectron. The job of Solectron is to match customized orders collected by Ingram and arrange for one or more suppliers to fulfill them.

Many e-distributors also provide support services, such as payments, deliveries, or escrow services. E-distributors aggregate buyers' and or sellers' orders, they provide valuable services such as security, payments, escrows, and they may arrange delivery.

DISINTERMEDIATION AND REINTERMEDIATION

Intermediaries provide two types of services: (1) they provide relevant information about demand, supply, prices, and requirements, and in doing so, help match sellers and buyers; (2) they offer value-added services such as consulting or assistance in finding a business partner. The first type of service can be fully automated, and thus is likely to be assumed by e-marketplaces, infomediaries, and portals that provide free or low-commission services. The second type requires expertise, such as knowledge of the industry, the products and technological trends, and it can only be partially automated. Intermediaries who provide only (or mainly) the first type of service may be eliminated, a phenomena called **disintermediation**. For example, discount stockbrokers that only execute trades will disappear. On the other hand, brokers who provide the second type of service or who manage electronic intermediation are not only surviving, but may actually be prospering. This phenomenon is called **reintermediation**.

The Web offers new opportunities for reintermediation. First, brokers are especially valuable when the number of market participants is enormous, as with the stock market, or when complex information products are exchanged. Second, many brokering services require information processing. Electronic versions of these services can offer more sophisticated features at a lower cost than is possible with human labor. Finally, for delicate negotiations, a computer mediator may be more predictable, and hence trustworthier, than a human. For example, suppose a mediator's role is to inform a buyer and a seller whether a deal can be made, without revealing either side's initial price to the other, as such a revelation would influence subsequent price negotiations. A software-based mediator will reveal only the information it is supposed to; a human mediator's fairness is less easily ensured. Intermediation and reintermediation are discussed further in Chapters 3, 6, and 11.

disintermediation
Elimination of intermediaries between sellers and buyers.

reintermediation
Establishment of new intermediary roles for traditional intermediaries that were disintermediated.

SYNDICATION AS AN EC MECHANISM

According to Werbach (2000), **syndication** involves the sale of the same good to many customers, who then integrate it with other offerings and resell it or give it away free. Syndication is extremely popular in the world of entertainment, but was rare elsewhere until the arrival of the Internet. The digitization of products and services and the ease with which information flows, makes syndication a popular business model. Let's look at a few examples.

Virtual stockbrokers, such as E*Trade, offer considerable information on their portals (e.g., financial news, stock quotes, research, etc.). Yahoo! and other portals offer other types of information. These brokers and portals buy the information from information creators or originators, such as Reuters, who sell the same

syndication
The sale of the same good (e.g., digital content) to many customers, who then integrate it with other offerings and resell it or give it away free.

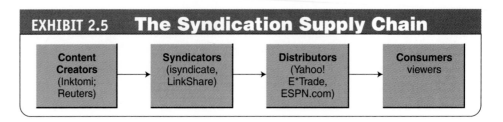

EXHIBIT 2.5   The Syndication Supply Chain

Content Creators (Inktomi; Reuters) → Syndicators (isyndicate, LinkShare) → Distributors (Yahoo! E*Trade, ESPN.com) → Consumers viewers

information to many portals or other users. Customers may buy directly from the information creators, but in many cases creators use a supply chain of syndicators and distributors to move news and information to the end consumers, as shown in Exhibit 2.5. Content creators, such as Inktomi (see Carr 2000) and Reuters, make their money by selling the same information to many syndicators and/or distributors. The information distributors, such as E*Trade, then distribute free information to the public (customers).

Syndication is especially popular with software and other digitizable items. For example, companies syndicate EC services such as payments and shopping-cart ordering systems for e-tailers. Logistics, security, and systems integration tools are frequently syndicated.

Syndication can be done in several ways. Therefore, there are a number of different revenue-sharing models along the supply chain in Exhibit 2.5. For example, the *affiliate* program discussed in Chapter 1, which is used by CDNow, Amazon.com, and many other e-tailers, is a variation of syndication (Helmstetter and Metivier 2000). For discussion of the organizational impacts of syndication, see Werbach (2000) and Carr (2000).

▶ List the roles of intermediaries in e-markets.
▶ Describe e-distributors.
▶ What are disintermediation and reintermediation?
▶ Explain how syndication works in e-commerce.

2.5   ISSUES IN E-MARKETS: COMPETITION, LIQUIDITY, QUALITY, AND SUCCESS FACTORS

COMPETITION IN THE INTERNET ECOSYSTEM

The *Internet ecosystem* is the business model of the online economy. The prevailing model of competition in the Internet economy is more like a web of interrelationships than the hierarchical, command-and-control model of the industrial economy. The Internet economy has low barriers to entry. Just like an ecosystem in nature, activity in the Internet economy is self-organizing: The process of *natural selection* takes place around company profits and value to customers. As the Internet ecosystem evolves, both technologically and in population, it will be even easier and likelier for countries, companies, and individuals to participate in the

Internet economy. Already, there is $1 trillion in technical infrastructure in place, ready and available for anyone to use at any time—free of charge. New ideas and ways of doing things can come from anywhere at any time in the Internet economy, some of the old rules no longer apply.

Competitive Factors

EC competition is very intense for the following reasons.

Lower buyers' search costs. E-markets reduce the cost of searching for product information, frequently to zero. This can significantly impact competition, enabling customers to find cheaper (or better) products and forcing sellers, in turn, to reduce prices and/or improve customer service. Companies that do just that can exploit the Internet to gain a considerably larger market share.

Speedy comparisons. Not only can customers find inexpensive products online, but they can find them quickly. For example, a customer does not have to go to several bookstores to quickly find the best price for a particular book. Using shopping search engines such as allbookstores.com or bestwebbuys.com/books, customers can find what they want and compare prices. Companies that trade online and provide information to search engines will gain a competitive advantage.

Differentiation and personalization. **Differentiation** involves providing a product or service that is not usually available elsewhere. For example, Amazon.com differentiates itself from other book retailers by providing customers with information that is not available in a physical bookstore, such as communication with authors, almost real-time book reviews, and book recommendations. In addition, EC provides for personalization or customization of products and services. **Personalization** refers to the ability to tailor a product, service, or Web content to specific user preferences. For example, Amazon.com will notify you by e-mail when new books on your favorite subject or by your favorite author are published.

Consumers like differentiation and personalization and are frequently willing to pay more for them. Differentiation reduces the substitutability between products. Also, price cutting in differentiated markets does not impact market share very much: Many customers are willing to pay a bit more for the personalized products or services.

Lower prices. Buy.com and other companies can offer low prices due to their low costs of operation (no physical facilities, minimum inventories, and so on). If volume is large enough, prices can be reduced by 40 percent or more.

Customer service. Amazon.com provides superior customer service. As we will see in Chapters 3 and 4, such a service is an extremely important competitive factor.

Certain other competitive factors have become less important as a result of EC. For example, the size of a company may no longer be a significant competitive advantage (as will be shown later). Similarly, location (geographical distance from the consumer) now plays an insignificant role, and language is becoming less important, as translation programs remove some language barriers. Finally, product condition is unimportant for digital products, which are not subject to normal wear and tear. (See discussion in Choi and Whinston 2000.)

All in all, EC supports efficient markets and could result in almost perfect competition. In such markets, a *commodity* (undifferentiated product) is produced when the consumer's willingness to pay equals the marginal cost of producing the

differentiation
Providing a product or service that is unique.

personalization
The ability to tailor a product, service, or Web content to specific user preferences.

commodity, and neither sellers nor buyers can influence supply or demand conditions individually. The characteristics necessary for *perfect competition* are the following:

1. Many buyers and sellers must be able to enter the market at no entry cost (no barriers to entry).

2. Large buyers or sellers are not able to individually influence the market.

3. The products must be homogeneous (no product differentiation). (For customized products, there is no perfect competition.)

4. Buyers and sellers must have comprehensive information about the products and about the market participants' demands, supplies, and conditions.

EC could provide, or come close to providing, these conditions. It is interesting to note that the ease of finding information benefits both buyers (finding information about products, vendors, prices, etc.) and sellers (finding information about customer demands, competitors, etc.).

It can be said that competition between companies is being replaced by competition between networks. The company with better networks, advertisement capabilities, and relationships with other Web companies (such as Amazon.com) has a strategic advantage. It can also be said that competition is between *business models*. The company with a better business model will win.

Porter's Competitive Analysis in an Industry

Porter's (2001) *competitive forces model* applied to an industry, views five major forces of competition that determine the industry's structural attractiveness. These forces, in combination, determine how the economic value created in an industry is divided among the players in the industry. Such an industry analysis helps companies develop their competitive strategy.

As the five forces are affected by both the Internet and e-commerce, it is interesting to examine how the Internet influences the industry structure portrayed by Porter's model. Porter divided the impacts of the Internet into either positive or negative for the industry. As shown in Exhibit 2.6, most of the impacts are negative (marked by a minus sign). (Of course, there are variations and exceptions to the impacts shown in the illustration, depending on the industry, its location, and its size.) A negative impact means that competition will intensify in most industries as the Internet is introduced. The competition is not only between online and off-line companies, but also among the online newcomers. This competition, which is especially strong in commodity-type products (toys, books, CDs), was a major contributor to the collapse of many dot-com companies in 2000 to 2001. To survive and prosper in such an environment, a company needs to use innovative strategies.

LIQUIDITY: THE NEED FOR A CRITICAL MASS OF BUYERS AND SELLERS

A critical mass of buyers is needed for an EC company or initiative to survive. As indicated earlier, the fixed cost of deploying EC can be high, sometimes very high. Without a large number of buyers, sellers will not make money. In 2001, the num-

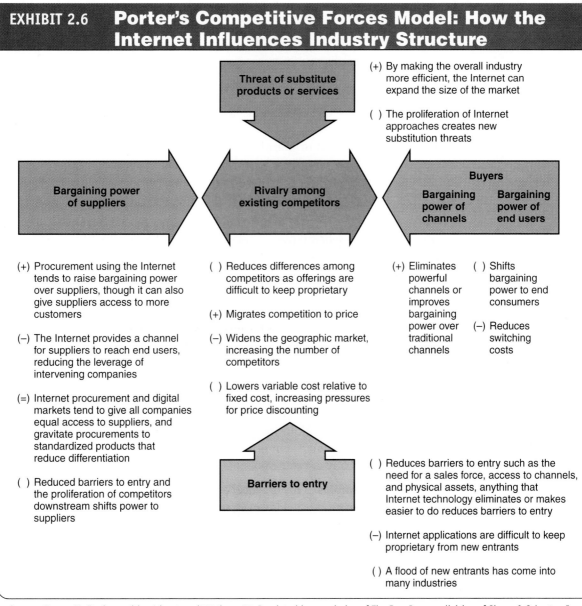

EXHIBIT 2.6 **Porter's Competitive Forces Model: How the Internet Influences Industry Structure**

Threat of substitute products or services

(+) By making the overall industry more efficient, the Internet can expand the size of the market

( ) The proliferation of Internet approaches creates new substitution threats

Bargaining power of suppliers

Rivalry among existing competitors

Buyers
Bargaining power of channels | **Bargaining power of end users**

(+) Procurement using the Internet tends to raise bargaining power over suppliers, though it can also give suppliers access to more customers

(−) The Internet provides a channel for suppliers to reach end users, reducing the leverage of intervening companies

(=) Internet procurement and digital markets tend to give all companies equal access to suppliers, and gravitate procurements to standardized products that reduce differentiation

( ) Reduced barriers to entry and the proliferation of competitors downstream shifts power to suppliers

( ) Reduces differences among competitors as offerings are difficult to keep proprietary

(+) Migrates competition to price

(−) Widens the geographic market, increasing the number of competitors

( ) Lowers variable cost relative to fixed cost, increasing pressures for price discounting

(+) Eliminates powerful channels or improves bargaining power over traditional channels

( ) Shifts bargaining power to end consumers

(−) Reduces switching costs

Barriers to entry

( ) Reduces barriers to entry such as the need for a sales force, access to channels, and physical assets, anything that Internet technology eliminates or makes easier to do reduces barriers to entry

(−) Internet applications are difficult to keep proprietary from new entrants

( ) A flood of new entrants has come into many industries

ber of Internet users worldwide was estimated by Forrester Research to be between 350 million and 450 million, and many of them do not shop online. This number is small compared with an estimated 2 billion television viewers worldwide. This situation will change, especially when TV/PC integration becomes widespread and wireless devices become a popular way to access the Internet (see Section 2.9).

At the global level, governments are assisting industry to achieve a critical mass of buyers. Canada, for example, has a goal to be recognized as an EC-friendly country in order to attract international investments and business. Hong Kong is developing a multibillion-dollar "cyberport" that will facilitate EC development and may position the country as a center for global EC in Southeast Asia. Korea supports nine major B2B exchanges that relate to the country's major industries (e.g., semiconductors). Finally, in 2001, the U.S. government introduced buyUSA.com to facilitate global trade.

Having a critical mass of buyers and sellers is referred to as *liquidity*. One of the major success factors for a start-up B2B vendor is **early liquidity**—achieving a critical mass of buyers and sellers as fast as possible, before the company's cash disappears (see Ramsdell 2000 and Chapter 6). Finally, in addition to the issue of profitability, critical mass of both buyers and sellers is needed for markets to be truly efficient, so that strong and fair competition can develop.

early liquidity
Achieving a critical mass of buyers and sellers as fast as possible, before a start-up company's cash disappears.

QUALITY UNCERTAINTY AND QUALITY ASSURANCE

Although price is a major factor for any buyer, quality is extremely important in many situations, especially when buyers cannot see and feel a product before they purchase it. When a consumer buys a brand-name PC from Dell, IBM, or Compaq, they are fairly sure about the quality of the product or service purchased. When a consumer buys from a not-so-well-known vendor, however, quality can become a major issue. The issue of quality is related to the issues of trust (discussed in Chapter 4) and consumer protection (in Chapter 9). Quality assurance can be provided through a trusted third-party intermediary. For example, TRUSTe and the BBBOnLine provide a testimonial seal for participating vendors. BBBOnLine is known for its quality-assurance system and its physical testing of products.

quality uncertainty
The uncertainty of online buyers about the quality of products that they have never seen, especially from an unknown vendor.

The problem of quality is frequently referred to as **quality uncertainty**. Customers have a cognitive difficulty accepting products that they have never seen, especially from an unknown vendor. The BBBOnLine and TRUSTe seals can convince some customers, but not all. Those who remain skeptical are not sure what they will get. Here are some possible solutions to quality uncertainty.

▶ **Provide free samples.** This is a clear signal that the vendor is confident about the quality of its products. However, samples cost money. It is a sunk cost that will need to be recovered from future sales. The cost for digital samples, however, is minimal. Shareware-type software is based on this concept.

▶ **Return if not satisfied.** This policy is common in several countries and is used by most large retailers and manufacturers. This policy, which provides a guarantee or a full refund for dissatisfied customers, is helpful in facilitating trust in EC. Such a policy, however, might not be feasible for digital products for the following reasons.

First, many digital products, such as information, knowledge, or educational materials, are fully consumed when they are viewed by consumers. After they are consumed, returning the products has little meaning. Unlike physical products, returning a digital product does not prevent the consumer from using the product in the future. Also, the vendor cannot resell the returned product.

Second, returning a product or refunding a purchase price may be impractical due to transaction costs. For example, a **microproduct**, a small digital product costing a few cents, must be transported twice over the network, so the cost of the refund may exceed the price. Therefore, for microproducts sup-

microproduct
A small digital product costing a few cents.

ported by micropayments (small payments, see Chapter 10), some companies do not offer a quality guarantee or a refund. (For further discussion of quality uncertainty, see Choi et al. 1997 and Choi and Whinston 2000.)

▶ **Insurance, escrow, and other services.** Many services, such as insurance and escrow, are available to ensure quality and prevent fraud. Of special interest are those offered by auction houses, such as eBay.com, as discussed in Chapter 9 and Appendix 2A online.

E-MARKET SUCCESS FACTORS

Based on an analysis of the EC examples we have discussed, it is apparent that EC will impact some industries more than others. The question is, "What are some of the factors that determine this level of impact?" Strader and Shaw (1997) have identified factors that fall within one of four categories: product, industry, seller, and consumer characteristics.

Product Characteristics

Digitizable products are particularly suited for e-markets because they can be electronically distributed to customers, resulting in very low distribution costs. Digitization also allows the order-fulfillment cycle time to be minimized.

A product's price may also be an important determinant to its success. The higher the product price, the greater the level of risk involved in the market transaction between buyers and sellers who are geographically separated and may have never dealt with each other before. Therefore, some of the most common items currently sold through e-markets are low-priced items such as CDs and books.

Finally, computers, electronic products, consumer products, and even cars can be sold electronically because the consumer knows exactly what they are buying. The more product information available, the better. The use of multimedia, for example, can dramatically facilitate product description.

Industry Characteristics

Electronic markets are most useful when they are able to directly match buyers and sellers. However, some industries require transaction brokers, so they may be affected less by e-markets than are industries where no brokers are required. Stockbrokers, insurance agents, and travel agents may provide services that are still needed, but in some cases software may be able to reduce the need for these brokers. This is particularly true as intelligent systems become more available to assist consumers.

Seller Characteristics

Electronic markets reduce search costs, allowing consumers to find sellers offering lower prices. In the long run, this may reduce profit margins for sellers that compete in e-markets, although it may also increase the number of transactions that take place. If sellers are unwilling to participate in this environment, then the impact of e-markets may be reduced. However, in highly competitive industries with low barriers to entry, sellers may not have a choice but to join in.

Consumer Characteristics

Consumers can be classified either as impulse, patient, or analytical (as we will discuss further in Chapter 4). Electronic markets may have little impact on industries where a sizable percentage of purchases are made by impulse buyers. Because e-markets require a certain degree of effort on the part of the consumer, e-markets are more conducive to consumers who do some comparisons and analyses before buying (the patient and analytical buyers). Analytical buyers can use the Internet to evaluate a wide range of information before deciding where to buy. On the other hand, m-commerce is banking on impulse buyers.

- ❭ Why is competition so intense online?
- ❭ Describe Porter's competitive forces model on the Internet.
- ❭ What is early liquidity? Why is it important?
- ❭ How can quality be assured in EC?
- ❭ Describe the success factors for e-markets.

2.6   ELECTRONIC CATALOGS AND OTHER MARKET MECHANISMS

To enable selling online, one usually needs *EC merchant server software* (see Chapter 12, online). The basic functionality offered by such software includes electronic catalogs, search engines, and shopping carts.

ELECTRONIC CATALOGS

electronic catalogs
The presentation of product information in an electronic form; the backbone of most e-selling sites.

Catalogs have been printed on paper for generations. Recently, electronic catalogs on CD-ROM and the Internet have gained popularity. **Electronic catalogs** consist of a product database, directory and search capabilities, and a presentation function. They are the backbone of most e-commerce sites. For merchants, the objective of electronic catalogs is to advertise and promote products and services. For the customer, the purpose of such catalogs is to provide a source of information on products and services. Electronic catalogs can be searched quickly with the help of search engines.

The majority of early online catalogs were replications of text and pictures from printed catalogs. However, online catalogs have evolved to become more dynamic, customized, and integrated with selling and buying procedures. As the online catalog is integrated with shopping carts, order taking, and payment, the tools for building online catalogs are being integrated with merchant sites (e.g., see store.yahoo.com).

Electronic catalogs can be classified according to three dimensions:

1. **The dynamics of the information presentation.** Catalogs can be static or dynamic. In *static catalogs*, information is presented in text and static pictures. In *dynamic catalogs*, information is presented in motion pictures or animation, possibly with supplemental sound.

2. **The degree of customization.** Catalogs can be standard or customized. In *standard catalogs*, merchants offer the same catalog to any customer. In *customized catalogs*, content, pricing, and display are tailored to the characteristics of specific customers.

3. **Integration with business processes.** Catalogs can be classified according to the degree of integration with the following business processes or features: order taking and fulfillment; electronic payment systems; intranet workflow software and systems; inventory and accounting systems; suppliers' or customers' extranets; and paper catalogs. For example, when you place an order with Amazon.com, your order will be transferred automatically to a computerized inventory check.

Although used occasionally in B2C commerce, customized catalogs are especially useful in B2B e-commerce. For example, e-catalogs can show only the items that the employees are able to purchase and can exclude items the buying company's managers do not want their employees to see or to buy. E-catalogs can be customized to show the same item to different customers at different prices, reflecting discounts or purchase contract agreements. They can even show the buyer's item, model, or stock-keeping unit (SKU) numbers, rather than the seller's numbers. Extranets, especially, can deliver customized catalogs to different business customers.

For a comprehensive discussion of online catalogs see jcmax.com/advantages.html and purchasing.about.com.

Comparison of Online Catalogs with Paper Catalogs

The advantages and disadvantages of online catalogs are contrasted with those of paper catalogs in Exhibit 2.7 (page 64). Although online catalogs have significant advantages, such as ease of updating, ability to integrate with the purchasing process, coverage of a wide spectrum of products, and a strong search capability, they do have disadvantages and limitations. To begin with, customers need computers and the Internet to access online catalogs. However, as computers and Internet access are spreading rapidly, we can expect a large portion of paper catalogs to be replaced by, or at least be supplemented by, electronic catalogs. On the other hand, considering the fact that printed newspapers and magazines have not diminished due to the online ones, we can guess that paper catalogs will not disappear. There seems to be room for both media, at least in the near future. However, in B2B, paper catalogs may disappear more quickly.

Representative tools for building online catalogs are Boise Cascade's Marketing Service (Boise), IBM's Net.commerce (IBM), and Oracle's Internet Commerce Server (ICS).

Customized Catalogs

A *customized catalog* is a catalog assembled specifically for a company, usually a customer of the catalog owner. It can also be tailored to loyal individual shoppers or a segment of shoppers (e.g., frequent buyers). There are two approaches to customized catalogs.

EXHIBIT 2.7	**Comparison of Online Catalogs with Paper Catalogs**	
Type	**Advantages**	**Disadvantages**
Paper Catalogs	▷ Easy to create without high technology ▷ Reader is able to look at the catalog without computer system ▷ More portable than electronic catalog	▷ Difficult to update changed product information promptly ▷ Only a limited number of products can be displayed ▷ Limited information through photographs and textual description is available ▷ No possibility for advanced multimedia such as animation and voice
Online Catalogs	▷ Easy to update product information ▷ Able to integrate with the purchasing process ▷ Good search and comparison capabilities ▷ Able to provide timely, up-to-date product information ▷ Provision for globally broad range of product information ▷ Possibility of adding on voice and animated pictures ▷ Long-term cost savings ▷ Easy to customize ▷ More comparative shopping ▷ Ease of connecting order processing, inventory processing, and payment processing to the system	▷ Difficult to develop catalogs, large fixed cost ▷ There is a need for customer skill to deal with computers and browsers

The first approach is to let the customers identify the interesting parts out of the total catalog, as is done by software products such as One-to-One from broadvision.com. Customers then do not have to deal with topics that are irrelevant to them. Such software allows the creation of catalogs with branded value-added capabilities that make it easy for customers to find the products they want to purchase, locate the information they need, and quickly compose their order.

The second approach is to let the system automatically identify the characteristics of customers based on their transaction records. However, to generalize the relationship between the customer and items of interest, data-mining technology (Chapter 4) may be needed. This second approach can be effectively combined with the first one.

As an example of the second approach, consider this scenario, which uses Oracle's ICS:

Scenario: Joe Public logs on to the Acme Shopping site, where he has the option to register as an account customer and record his preferences in terms of address details, preferred method of payment, and interest areas. Acme Shopping offers a wide range of products, including electronics, clothing, books, and sporting goods. Joe is interested only in clothing and electronics. He is not a sportsman nor a great book lover. Joe also has some very distinct hobby areas—one is photography.

After Joe has recorded his preferences, each time he returns to Acme's electronic store, the first page will show him only the clothing and electronics departments. Furthermore, when Joe goes into the electronics department, he sees only products related to photography—cameras and accessories. Some of the products are out of Joe's price range, so Joe further can refine his preferences to indicate that he is interested only in electronics that relate to photography and cost $300 or less. Such personalization gives consumers a value-added experience and adds to their reasons for revisiting the site, thus building brand loyalty to that Internet store. Against the backdrop of intense competition for Web time, personalization provides a valuable way to get consumers matched to the products and information in which they are most interested as quickly and painlessly as possible. An example of how corporations customize their catalogs for corporate clients is provided in EC Application Case 2.2 (page 66).

SEARCH ENGINES AND INTELLIGENT AGENTS

A **search engine** is a computer program that can access a database of Internet resources, search for specific information or keywords, and report the results. For example, customers tend to ask for information (e.g., requests for product information or pricing) in the same general manner. This type of request is repetitive, and answering such requests is costly when done by a human. Search engines deliver answers economically and efficiently by matching questions with FAQ templates, which include standard questions and "canned" answers to them.

Google, AltaVista, and Lycos are popular search engines. Portals such as AOL, Netscape, and MSN have their own search engines. Special search engines, organized to answer certain questions or search in specified areas, include AskJeeves and Looksmart. There are over 3,000 different search engines.

Unlike a search engine, a **software (intelligent) agent** can do more than just "search and match." It has capabilities that can be used to perform routine tasks that require intelligence. For example, it can monitor movements on a Web site to check whether a customer seems lost or ventures into areas that may not fit their profile. If it detects such confusion, the agent can notify the customer and provide assistance. Software agents can be used in e-commerce to support tasks such as shopping, interpreting information, monitoring activities, and working as an assistant. Users can even chat or collaborate with agents.

In e-commerce, users use both search engines and intelligent agents. If customers are inside a storefront or an e-mall, they can use the search engine to find a product or a service. They will also use Web search engines, such as google.com, to find general information about a product or service. Finally, they will use software agents, such those that do comparisons (e.g., mysimon.com) and conduct other tasks. The essentials of software agents are provided in online Appendix D. Applications of software agents are described in several chapters, especially in Chapters 3, 4, and 5.

search engine
A computer program that can access a database of Internet resources, search for specific information or keywords, and report the results.

software (intelligent) agent
Software that can perform routine tasks that require intelligence.

Implementation and Strategy

ELECTRONIC CATALOGS
AT BOISE CASCADE

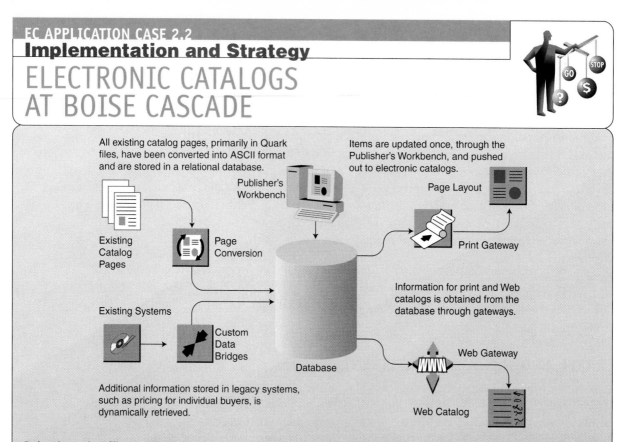

All existing catalog pages, primarily in Quark files, have been converted into ASCII format and are stored in a relational database.

Publisher's Workbench

Items are updated once, through the Publisher's Workbench, and pushed out to electronic catalogs.

Page Layout

Existing Catalog Pages

Page Conversion

Print Gateway

Existing Systems

Custom Data Bridges

Database

Information for print and Web catalogs is obtained from the database through gateways.

Web Gateway

Additional information stored in legacy systems, such as pricing for individual buyers, is dynamically retrieved.

Web Catalog

Boise Cascade Office Products is a $3-billion office products wholesaler. Its customer base includes over 100,000 large corporate customers and 1 million small ones. The company's 900-page paper catalog used to be mailed to customers once each year. Throughout the year, Boise also sent minicatalogs tailored to customers' individual needs based on past buying habits and purchase patterns. The company sells over 200,000 different items.

In 1996, the company placed its catalogs online. Customers view the catalog at *boiseoffice.com* and can order straight from the site or submit orders by e-mail. The orders are shipped the next day. Customers are then billed. In 1997, the company generated 20 percent of its sales through the Web site. In early 1999, the figure was over 30 percent. The company acknowledges that its Internet business is the fastest growing segment of its business. It expects the Internet business to generate 80 percent of its total sales by 2004.

Boise prepares thousands of individualized catalogs for its customers. In 2002, the company was sending paper catalogs only when specifically requested. As indicated earlier, the vast majority of customers use the online catalogs. It used to take about 6 weeks to produce a single paper customer catalog, primarily because of the time involved in pulling together all the data. Now the process of producing a Web catalog takes only 1 week. One major advantage of customized catalogs is pricing. If everyone has the same catalog, you cannot show the customized price for each buyer, which is based on the type of the contract signed and the volume of goods being purchased.

Boise estimates that electronic orders cost approximately 55 percent less to process than paper-based orders. The figure above shows the process of working with the electronic catalogs. Some catalogs on Web sites provide text and pictures without linking them to order taking. For instance, Coca-Cola's Web site (*cocacola.com*) is not set up to take Coke's orders online; it just reminds people about the taste of Coca-Cola. However, you can buy Coca-Cola collectors items and more at the online store.

Source: Compiled from *boiseoffice.com, about/netscape.com*, 2001, and *ecommerce.shtml*, 2001. Above figure used with permission of AOL/Netscape.

Questions

▶ What are the advantages of the electronic catalog to Boise Cascade? To its customers?

▶ How are the customized catalogs created?

SHOPPING CARTS

An **electronic shopping cart** is an order-processing technology that allows customers to accumulate items they wish to buy while they continue to shop. In this respect, it is similar to a physical-world cart. The software program of an electronic shopping cart allows customers to select items, review what has been selected, make changes, and then finalize the list. A click on "buy" will trigger the actual purchase.

Shopping carts for B2C are fairly simple (visit amazon.com to see an example), but for B2B, a shopping cart may be more complex. A B2B shopping cart could enable a business customer to shop at several sites while keeping the cart on the buyer's Web site to integrate it with the buyer's e-procurement system. A special B2B cart was proposed for this purpose by Lim and Lee (2002) where, in addition to the cart offered at the seller's site, there is a buyers' cart ("b-cart") that resides on the buyers' sites and is sponsored by the participating sellers.

Shopping-cart software is sold or provided for free as an independent component (e.g., monstercommerce.com, e-shopping-cart-software.com). It also is embedded in merchants' servers such as store.yahoo.com.

electronic shopping cart
An order-processing technology that allows customers to accumulate items they wish to buy while they continue to shop.

▶ List the benefits of electronic catalogs.

▶ Explain how customized catalogs are created and used.

▶ List the dimensions by which electronic catalogs can be classified.

▶ Compare search engines with software agents.

▶ Describe an electronic shopping cart.

2.7   AUCTIONS

One of the most interesting market mechanisms in e-commerce is electronic auctions. They are used in B2C, B2B, C2C, G2B, G2C, and more.

DEFINITION AND CHARACTERISTICS

An **auction** is a market mechanism by which a seller places an offer to sell a product and buyers make bids sequentially and competitively until a final price is reached. A wide variety of online markets qualify as auctions using this definition. Auctions, an established method of commerce for generations, deal with products and services for which conventional marketing channels are ineffective or inefficient. For example, auctions can expedite the disposal of items that need liquidation or a quick sale. They offer trading opportunities for both buyers and sellers that are not available in the conventional channels, and they ensure prudent execution of contracts.

auction
A market mechanism by which a seller places an offer to sell a product and buyers make bids sequentially and competitively until a final price is reached.

There are several types of auctions, each with its own motives and procedures. Klein (1997) classified them into four major categories. Auctions can be done *online* or *off-line*. They can be conducted in *public* auction sites, such as at eBay. They can also done by invitation to *private* auctions.

In this section we present the essential information about auctions that is necessary for understanding Chapters 3–11. An even fuller treatment of auctions is available in online Appendix 2A.

Limitations of Traditional Auctions

Traditional auctions, regardless of their type, have the following limitations: They generally last only a few minutes, or even seconds, for each item sold. This rapid process may give potential buyers little time to make a decision, so they may decide not to bid. Therefore, sellers may not get the highest possible price, and bidders may not get what they really want or they may pay too much for the item. Also, in many cases, the bidders do not have much time to examine the goods. As bidders must usually be physically present at auctions, many potential bidders are excluded.

Similarly, it may be difficult for sellers to move goods to the auction site. Commissions are fairly high, as a place must be rented, the auction needs to be advertised, and an auctioneer and other employees need to be paid. Electronic auctioning removes these deficiencies.

Electronic Auctions

The Internet provides an infrastructure for executing auctions electronically at lower cost, with a wide array of support services, and with many more sellers and buyers. Individual consumers and corporations both can participate in this rapidly growing and very convenient form of e-commerce. The Internet auction industry is projected to reach $100 billion in sales by 2004.

electronic auctions (e-auctions)
Auctions conducted online.

Electronic auctions (e-auctions) have been in existence for several years on local area networks and were started on the Internet in 1995. They are similar to off-line auctions except that they are done on a computer. Host sites on the Internet serve as brokers, offering services for sellers to post their goods for sale and allowing buyers to bid on those items. Many sites have certain etiquette rules that must be adhered to in order to conduct fair business. (For examples, see ebay.com and infospace.com.) The usaweb.com site provides an Internet auction list and a search engine. bidfind.com is an auction aggregator that enters hundreds of auction sites and lets consumers know which items are being auctioned at which sites.

Major online auctions offer consumer products, electronic parts, artwork, vacation packages, airline tickets, and collectibles, as well as excess supplies and inventories being auctioned off by B2B marketers. Another type of B2B online auction is increasingly used to trade special types of commodities, such as electricity transmission capacities and gas and energy options. Furthermore, conventional business practices that traditionally have relied on contracts and fixed prices are increasingly being converted into auctions with bidding for online procurements (e.g., Raffles Hotel).

Of course, many consumer goods are not suitable for auctions, and for these items, conventional selling—such as posted-price retailing—is more than adequate. Yet the flexibility offered by online auction trading offers innovative market processes for many other goods. For example, instead of searching for products and vendors by visiting sellers' Web sites, a buyer may solicit offers from all potential sellers. Such a buying mechanism is so innovative that it has the potential to be used in almost all types of consumer goods (as will be shown later when we discuss reverse auctions and "name-your-own-price" auctions).

DYNAMIC PRICING AND TYPES OF AUCTIONS

A major characteristic of auctions is that they are based on dynamic pricing. **Dynamic pricing** refers to prices that change based on supply-and-demand relationships at any given time. That is, the prices are not fixed, but are allowed to change as supply and demand in a market change. In contrast, catalog prices are fixed, as are prices in department stores, supermarkets, and many electronic storefronts.

Dynamic pricing appears in several forms. Perhaps the oldest ones are negotiation and bargaining, which have been practiced for many generations in open-air markets. It is customary to classify dynamic pricing into four major categories, depending on how many buyers and sellers are involved. These four categories are shown in Exhibit 2.8 and discussed in the following sections.

dynamic pricing
Prices that change based on supply and demand relationships at any given time.

One Buyer, One Seller

In this configuration, one can use negotiation, bargaining, or bartering. The resulting price will be determined by each party's bargaining power, supply and demand in the item's market, and (possibly) business environment factors.

One Seller, Many Potential Buyers

In this configuration, the seller uses **forward auctions**, auctions in which a seller entertains bids from buyers. (Because forward auctions are the most common and traditional form, they are often simply called auctions.) There are four major types of forward auctions: English, Yankee, Dutch, and free-fall.

forward auction
An auction in which a seller entertains bids from buyers.

English auction. In an **English auction**, one item is sold at a time and buyers bid on it in sequence and the price increases with time. A minimum bid that specifies the smallest amount that can be entered is usually part of an English auction. (The seller can also set a reserve price, the lowest acceptable price that the seller is willing to accept for the item.) The auction will continue until no more bids are rendered or until the auction time is over. The winner is the one with the highest bid. English auctions can take days on the Internet, but they can also be conducted in real time ("live") and take only minutes. English auctions are used in

English auction
An auction in which buyers bid on an item in sequence and the price increases with time.

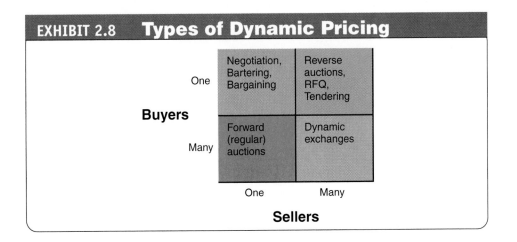

EXHIBIT 2.8   Types of Dynamic Pricing

	One Seller	Many Sellers
Buyers One	Negotiation, Bartering, Bargaining	Reverse auctions, RFQ, Tendering
Buyers Many	Forward (regular) auctions	Dynamic exchanges

C2C, B2C, B2B, and G2B markets. The English auction process is shown in Exhibit 2.9.

Yankee auction. In a **Yankee auction**, a seller offers multiple identical items, usually with a minimum bid. Bidders can bid for any number of the items offered. The winner is the one with the highest bid.

Dutch auction. Like Yankee auctions, **Dutch auctions** are designed for multiple identical items. The difference is that prices in Dutch auctions start at a very high level and are reduced as the auction time passes. The bidders specify the quantity they want to buy at a posted price. An example is the international flower market in the Netherlands. Before the Internet, the process was done manually, using a big clock whose hands showed the price. Now the clock is computerized (see Chapter 6, p. 264). Once a bidder is willing to pay the price indicated by the auctioneer, the quantity available is adjusted until the entire quantity is sold. Dutch auctions happen very fast. There are several variations of this method.

- The following describes how a Dutch auction is conducted at eBay: Sellers list a starting price for one item and the number of items for sale. If no bids are made, the starting price is reduced.

- Bidders specify both a bid price and the quantity they want to buy. All winning bidders pay the same price per item, which is the *lowest* bid when the time expires (This might be less than a bidder's last bid!)

- If there are more buyers than items, the earliest successful bids get the goods. Higher bidders are more likely to get the quantities they have requested.

- Winning bidders can refuse partial quantities. For example, if a bidder places a bid for 10 items and only 8 are available after the auction, the bidder does not have to buy any of them.

Yankee auction

Auction of multiple identical items in which bidders can bid for any number of the items offered, and the highest bid wins.

Dutch auction

Auction of multiple identical items, with prices starting at a very high level and declining as the auction time passes.

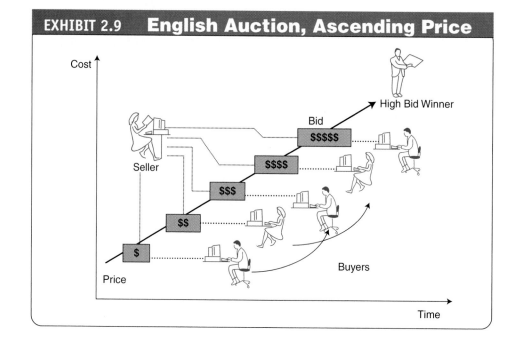

EXHIBIT 2.9   English Auction, Ascending Price

Cost

High Bid Winner

Bid

$$$$$

$$$$

$$$

$$

$

Seller

Price

Buyers

Time

Free-fall (declining-price) auction. A **free-fall (declining-price) auction** is a variation of the Dutch auction in which only one item is auctioned at a time. The price starts at a very high level, and then is reduced at fixed time intervals. The lowest bid when the time expires is the winning bid. This type of auction is used with popular items where many bidders are expected. In such a case, the free-fall auction moves very fast.

One Buyer, Many Potential Sellers

There are two types of auctions in which there is one buyer and many potential sellers: reverse and "name-your-own-price." These are two of the most popular auction models on the Internet.

Reverse auctions. When there is one buyer and many potential sellers, one uses a **reverse auction** (also called a **bidding** or **tendering system**). In a reverse auction, the buyer places an item for bid (or *tender*) on a *request for quote* (RFQ) system. Potential suppliers bid on the job, reducing the price sequentially (see Exhibit 2.10). In electronic bidding in a reverse auction, several rounds of bidding take place until the bidders do not reduce the price. The winner is the one with the lowest bid (assuming that only price is considered). Reverse auctions are primarily a B2B or G2B mechanism. (For further discussion and examples, see Chapter 5.)

The name-your-own-price model. Priceline.com pioneered the **"name-your-own-price" model**. In this model, a would-be buyer specifies the price (and other terms) they are willing to pay to any willing and able seller. Priceline.com presents consumer requests to sellers who can fill as much of the guaranteed demand as they wish at prices and terms requested by buyers or Priceline.com searches its own database that contains vendors' lowest prices and tries to match supply against requests. Priceline.com asks customers to guarantee acceptance of the offer if it is

free-fall (declining-price) auction
A variation of the Dutch auction in which only one item is auctioned at a time; the price starts at a very high level and declines at fixed time intervals; the winning bid is the lowest one when the time expires.

reverse auction (bidding or tendering system)
Auction in which the buyer places an item for bid (*tender*) on a request for quote (RFQ) system, potential suppliers bid on the job, with price reducing sequentially, and the lowest bid wins; primarily a B2B or G2B mechanism.

"name-your-own-price" model
Auction model in which a would-be buyer specifies the price (and other terms) they are willing to pay to any willing and able seller. It is a C2B model, pioneered by Priceline.com.

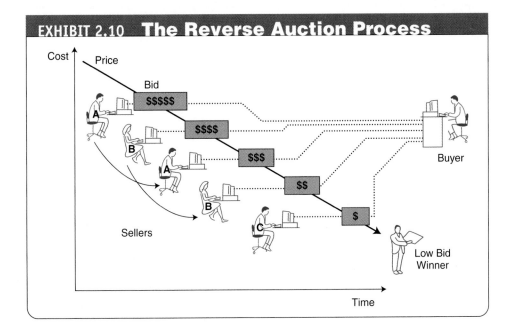

EXHIBIT 2.10 The Reverse Auction Process

consumer-to-business (C2B) model
EC model in which consumers place a bid for a product or service and suppliers compete to get the job.

at or below the requested price by giving a credit card number. This is basically a **consumer-to-business (C2B) model**, although some businesses use it too.

Priceline.com is currently selling multiple products and services, mainly across the following product categories: a travel service that offers leisure airline tickets, hotel rooms, and rental cars; a personal finance service that offers home refinancing and home equity loans; an automotive service that offers new cars; credit cards; and long-distance calling plans. In 2000, the company teamed up with Hutchison Whampoa of Hong Kong, to offer a range of services in Asia.

Many Sellers, Many Buyers

When there are many sellers and many buyers, buyers and their bidding prices and sellers and their asking prices are matched, considering the quantities on both sides. Stocks and commodities markets are typical examples of this configuration. Buyers and sellers can be individuals or businesses. Such an auction is called a **double auction**.

double auction
Auction in which buyers and their bidding prices and sellers and their asking prices are matched, considering the quantities on both sides.

BENEFITS, LIMITATIONS, AND IMPACTS OF E-AUCTIONS

Electronic auctions are becoming important selling and buying channels for many companies and individuals. E-auctions enable buyers to access goods and services anywhere auctions are conducted. Moreover, almost perfect market information is available about prices, products, current supply and demand, and so on. These characteristics provide benefits to all.

Benefits of E-Auctions

A listing of the benefits of e-auctions to sellers, buyers, and e-auctioneers is provided in the following Insights and Additions box.

Insights and Additions   Benefits of Electronic Auctions

BENEFITS TO SELLERS	BENEFITS TO BUYERS	BENEFITS TO E-AUCTIONEERS
▸ Increased revenues from broadening customer base and shortening cycle time	▸ Opportunities to find unique items and collectibles.	▸ Higher repeat purchases. Jupiter Media Metrix (jmm.com) found that auction sites such as eBay tend to garner higher repeat-purchase rates than the top e-commerce B2C sites, such as Amazon.com.
▸ Optimal price setting, determined by the market (more buyers).	▸ Chance to bargain instead of buying at a fixed price.	
▸ Sellers can gain more customer dollars by offering items directly (disintermediation). Also saves on the commission to intermediaries. (Physical auctions' fees are very expensive compared to e-auctions.)	▸ Entertainment. Participation in e-auctions can be entertaining and exciting.	▸ High "stickiness" to the Web site (the tendency of customers to stay at sites longer and come back more often). Auction sites are frequently "stickier" than fixed-priced sites. Stickier sites generate more ad revenue for the e-auctioneer.
	▸ Anonymity. With the help of a third party, buyers can remain anonymous.	
▸ Can liquidate large quantities quickly.	▸ Convenience. Buyers can trade from anywhere, even with a cell phone; they do not have to travel to an auction place.	▸ Expansion of the auction business.
▸ Improved customer relationship and loyalty (in the case of specialized B2B auction sites and electronic exchanges).		

Limitations of E-Auctions

E-auctions have several limitations. The most significant limitations are the following:

▶ **Possibility of fraud.** Auction items are in many cases unique, used, or antique. Because the buyer cannot see the items, the buyer may get defective products. Also, buyers can commit fraud by receiving goods or services without paying for them; thus, the fraud rate is very high. For a discussion of fraud by both buyers and sellers and of fraud prevention, see online Appendix 2A.

▶ **Limited participation.** Some auctions are by invitation only, whereas others are open to dealers only.

▶ **Lack of security.** Some of the C2C auctions conducted on the Internet are not secure because they are done in an unencrypted environment and credit card numbers could be stolen during the payment process. Recent payment methods such as paypal.com (Chapter 10) can solve the payment problem. However, some B2B auctions are conducted on highly secure private lines.

▶ **Limited software.** Unfortunately, there are only a few "complete" or "off-the-shelf" market-enabling solutions that can completely support the functionality required for optimizing auctions.

Impacts of Auctions

Because the trade objects and contexts for auctions are very diverse, the rationale behind auctions and the motives of the different participants for setting up auctions are quite different. Representative impacts of e-auctions include the following:

▶ **Auctions as a coordination mechanism.** Auctions are increasingly used as an efficient coordination mechanism for establishing an equilibrium in price. An example is auctions for the allocation of telecommunications bandwidth.

▶ **Auctions as a social mechanism to determine a price.** For objects not being traded in traditional markets, such as unique or rare items, or for items that may be offered randomly or at long intervals, an auction creates a marketplace that attracts potential buyers, and often experts. By offering many of these special items at a single time, and by attracting considerable attention, auctions provide the requisite exposure of purchase and sale orders, and hence liquidity of the market in which an optimal price can be determined. Typical examples are auctions of fine arts or rare items, as well as auctions of communication frequencies, Web banners, and advertising space. For example, winebid.com is a global auction site for wine collectors.

▶ **Auctions as a highly visible distribution mechanism.** Another type of auction is similar to the previous one, but deals with special offers. In this case, a supplier typically auctions off a limited amount of items, using the auction primarily as a mechanism to gain attention and to attract those customers who are bargain hunters or have a preference for the gambling dimension of the

EC APPLICATION CASE 2.3
Individuals and Communities
REVERSE MORTGAGE AUCTIONS IN SINGAPORE

Homebuyers like to get the lowest possible mortgage rates. In the United States, *Priceline.com* will try to find you a mortgage if you "name your own price." However, a better deal may be available to homebuyers in Singapore, where reverse auctions are combined with "group purchasing," saving about $20,000 over the life of a mortgage for each homeowner, plus $1,200 in waived legal fees. *Dollardex.com* offers the service in Singapore, Hong Kong, and other countries.

Here is how Dollardex arranged its first project: The site invited potential buyers in three residential properties in Singapore to join the service. Applications, including financial credentials, were made on a secure Web site. Then, seven lending banks were invited to bid on the loans. In a secure electronic room, borrowers and lenders negotiated. After 2 days of negotiations of interest rates and special conditions, the borrowers voted on one bank. In the first project, 18 borrowers agreed to give the job to United Overseas Bank (UOB), paying about 0.5 percent less than the regular rate. The borrowers negotiated the waiver of the legal fee as well. From this first project, UOB generated $10 million of busi-

ness. Today, Dollardex allows customers to participate in an individual reverse auction if they do not want to join a group.

The banks involved in the auctions can see the offers made by competitors. Flexibility is high; in addition to interest rates, banks are willing to negotiate down payment size and the option of switching from a fixed to variable rate loan. On average, there are 2.6 bank bids per customer.

As of spring 2000, in addition to mortgages, Dollardex.com offers car loans, insurance policies, and travel services. It also allows comparisons of mutual funds that have agreed to give lower front-end fees.

Sources: Compiled from Moneyq.com.hk, 2002 and *Dollardex.com*, 2002.

Questions

▶ How is the group purchasing organized at *dollardex.com*? What services are offered?

▶ Why does a reverse auction take place?

▶ Can this model exist without an intermediary?

auction process. The airline-seat auctions by Cathy Pacific, American Airlines, and Lufthansa fall into this category.

▶ **Auctions as a component in e-commerce.** Auctions can stand alone or they can be combined with other e-commerce activities. An example is the combination of group purchasing with reverse auctions, as described in EC Application Case 2.3.

▶ Define auctions and describe how they work.

▶ Describe the benefits of electronic auctions over traditional (nonelectronic) auctions.

▶ List the general types of auctions.

▶ Distinguish between forward and reverse auctions.

▶ Describe the "name-your-own-price" model.

▶ List the major benefits of auctions to buyers, sellers, and auctioneers.

▶ What are the major limitations of auctions?

▶ List the major impacts of auctions trading on markets.

2.8 BARTERING AND NEGOTIATING ONLINE

ONLINE BARTERING

Bartering, an exchange of goods and services, is the oldest method of trade. Today, it is usually done primarily between organizations. The problem with bartering is that it is difficult to find trading partners. Businesses and individuals may use e-classified ads to advertise what they need and what they offer.

bartering
An exchange of goods and services.

E-bartering (electronic bartering) can improve the matching process by attracting more customers to the barter. In addition, matching can be done faster and ass a result, better matches can be found. Items that are frequently bartered online include office, storage, and factory space; idle facilities; as well as labor, products, and banner ads. Representative bartering Web sites include allbusiness.com, intagio.com, ubarter.com, and whosbartering.com. (Note that e-bartering may have tax implications that need to be considered.)

e-bartering
Bartering conducted online, usually by a bartering exchange.

E-bartering is usually done in a **bartering exchange**, a marketplace in which an intermediary arranges the transactions. These can be very effective. The process works like this:

bartering exchange
A marketplace in which an intermediary arranges barter transactions.

1. You tell the bartering exchange what you want to offer.
2. The exchange assesses the value of your products or services and offers you certain "points" or "bartering dollars."
3. You use the "points" to buy the things you need from a participating member in the exchange.

The problem with manual matching by a third-party bartering exchange is that the commission is very high (30 percent or more). (The commission is much lower in an e-bartering exchange; in the range of 5 to 10 percent.) Also, it may take a long time to arrange a transaction in a manual barter.

Bartering sites must be financially secure. Otherwise users may not have a chance to use the points they accumulate. (For further details, see "virtual bartering 101" at fortune.com/smallbusiness and Lorek 2000).

ONLINE NEGOTIATING

Dynamic prices can also be determined by *negotiation*, especially for expensive or specialized products. Much like in auctions, negotiated prices result from interactions and bargaining among sellers and buyers. However, in contrast with auctions, negotiation also deals with nonpricing terms, such as payment method and credit. Negotiation is a well-known process in the off-line world, for example in real estate, automobile purchases, and contract work. In addition, in cases where there is no standard service or product to speak of, some digital products and services can be personalized and "bundled" at a standard price. Preferences for these bundled services differ among consumers, and thus they are frequently negotiated.

According to Choi and Whinston (2000), negotiating in the electronic environment is easier than in the physical environment. Also, due to customization and bundling of products and services, it is necessary to negotiate both prices and terms. E-markets allow such negotiations to be conducted for virtually all products and services. Three factors may facilitate **online negotiation**:

1. Products and services that are bundled and customized.
2. Computer technology that facilitates the negotiation process.
3. Software (intelligent) agents that perform searches and comparisons, thereby providing quality customer service and a base from which prices can be negotiated.

online negotiation
Electronic negotiation, usually supported by software (intelligent) agents that perform searches and comparisons; improves bundling and customization of products and services.

▶ Define bartering and describe the advantages of e-bartering.
▶ Explain the role of online negotiation in EC.

2.9 MOBILE COMMERCE

The widespread adoption of wireless and mobile networks, devices, and middleware (software that links application modules from different computer languages and platforms) is creating exciting new opportunities. These new technologies are making **mobile computing** possible—meaning fully portable, real-time access to information, applications, and tools that, until recently, were accessible only from a desktop computer. **Mobile commerce (m-commerce)** refers to the conduct of e-commerce via wireless devices. It is also sometimes called **m-business** when reference is made to its broadest definition (Kalakota and Robinson 2001), in which the e-business environment is wireless.

There is a reason for the strong interest in the topic of mobile commerce. According to the International Data Corporation and Gartner Group, the number of mobile devices is projected to top 1.3 billion by 2004 (predictions made in March 2002). These devices can be connected to the Internet, allowing users to conduct transactions from anywhere. Gartner Group estimates that at least 40 percent of all B2C transactions, totaling over $200 billion by 2004, will be initiated from smart wireless devices. Others predict much higher figures because mobile devices (handsets, PDAs, etc.) will soon overtake PCs as the predominant Internet access device, creating a global market of over 500 million subscribers.

mobile computing
Permits real-time access to information, applications, and tools that, until recently, were accessible only from a desktop computer.

mobile commerce (m-commerce)
E-commerce conducted via wireless devices.

m-business
The broadest definition of m-commerce, in which e-business is conducted in a wireless environment.

THE PROMISE OF M-COMMERCE

Since 1999, m-commerce has become one of the hottest topics in IT in general and in EC in particular. Mobility significantly changes the manner in which people and customers interact, communicate, and collaborate, and mobile applications are expected to change the way we live, play, and do business. Much of the

Internet culture, which is currently PC-based, may change to one based on mobile devices. As a result, m-commerce creates new business models for EC, notably location-based applications (which we cover in Chapter 8).

Although there are currently many hurdles to the widespread adoption of m-commerce, it is clear that many of these will be reduced or eliminated in the future. Many companies are already shifting their strategy to the mobile world. Many large corporations with huge marketing presence—Microsoft, Intel, Sony, AT&T, AOL-Time-Warner, to name a few—are transforming their businesses to include m-commerce-based products and services. Nokia emerged as a world-class company not just because it sells more cell phones than anyone else, but also because it has become the major player in the mobile economy. Similarly, major telecommunications companies, from Verizon to Vodafone, are shifting their strategies to wireless products and services. In Europe alone, over 200 companies offer mobile portal services. In the United States, over 2 million subscribers used General Motors' OnStar in-vehicle mobile services in 2002 (see onstar.com). DoCoMo, the world's largest mobile portal, with more than 30 million customers in Japan, is investing billions of dollars to expand its services to other countries, via its i-Mode services.

I-MODE: A SUCCESSFUL MOBILE PORTAL

To illustrate the potential spread of m-commerce, let's examine DoCoMo's i-Mode, the pioneering wireless service that took Japan by storm in 1999 and 2000. With a few clicks on a handset, i-Mode users can conduct a large variety of m-commerce activities ranging from online stock trading and banking to purchasing travel tickets and booking Karaoke rooms. Users can also use i-Mode to send and receive color images. Launched in February 1999, i-Mode went international in 2000 and had over 15 millions users by the end of that year (nttdocomo.com). Here are some interesting applications of i-Mode:

▶ **Shopping guides.** Addresses and telephone numbers of the favorite shops in the major shopping malls in Tokyo and other cities are provided with a supporting search engine. Consumers can locate information about best-selling books and then buy them. Users can purchase music online to enjoy anywhere.

▶ **Maps and transportation.** Digital maps show detailed guides of local routes and stops of the major public transportation systems in all major cities. Users can access train and bus timetables, guides to shopping areas, and automatic notification of train delays.

▶ **Ticketing.** Airline tickets and movie tickets can be purchased online.

▶ **News and reports.** Fast access to global news, local updated traffic conditions, the air pollution index, and weather reports are provided continuously.

▶ **Personalized movie service.** Updates on the latest movies with related information, such as casting and show times, are provided. Also, subscribers can search for their own favorite movies by entering the name of the movie or the name of the movie theater.

▶ **Entertainment.** Up-to-date personalized entertainment, such as playing favorite games, can be searched easily. Online "chatting" is also provided, and users can send or receive photos. Also, users can subscribe to receive Tamagotchi's characters each day for only $1 a month. These virtual pets (the translation of their Japanese name means "cute little eggs") exhibit intelligent behavior; for example, a Tamagotchi cat will purr if you pet it, but "bite" if it is hungry.

▶ **Dining and reservations.** The exact location of a selected participating restaurant is shown on a digital map. Subscribers can also find a restaurant that provides a meal in a particular price range. Reservations can be made online. Discount coupons are also available online.

▶ **Additional services.** Additional services such as banking, stock trading, telephone directory searches, dictionary services, and a horoscope are available.

These applications are for individual users and are provided via a mobile portal. An even greater number of applications is available in the B2B area and in the intrabusiness area. For a complete coverage of m-business applications, see Chapter 8 and Kalakota and Robinson (2001).

▶ Define computing mobility and mobile commerce.

▶ How does mobile commerce differ from EC?

▶ What major services are provided by i-Mode?

2.10 IMPACTS OF E-MARKETS ON BUSINESS PROCESSES AND ORGANIZATIONS

Because the field of EC is relatively new, little statistical data or empirical research on it are available. Therefore, the discussion in this section is based primarily on experts' opinions, logic, and some actual data. The discussion here is also based in part on the work of Bloch et al. (1996), who approached the impact of e-markets from a value-added point of view. Their model, which is shown in Exhibit 2.11 (page 79), divides the impact of e-markets into three major categories: improving direct marketing, transforming organizations, and redefining organizations. We will look at each of these impacts, in turn.

IMPROVING DIRECT MARKETING

Traditional direct marketing was done by mail order (catalogs) and telephone (telemarketing). According to the U.S. Department of Commerce, in 2001, direct mail generated sales of over $110 billion in the United States, of which only $5 billion was via e-markets. This figure is small, but growing.

Bloch et al. (1996) suggested the following impacts of e-markets on B2C direct marketing:

EXHIBIT 2.11 The Analysis-of-Impacts Framework

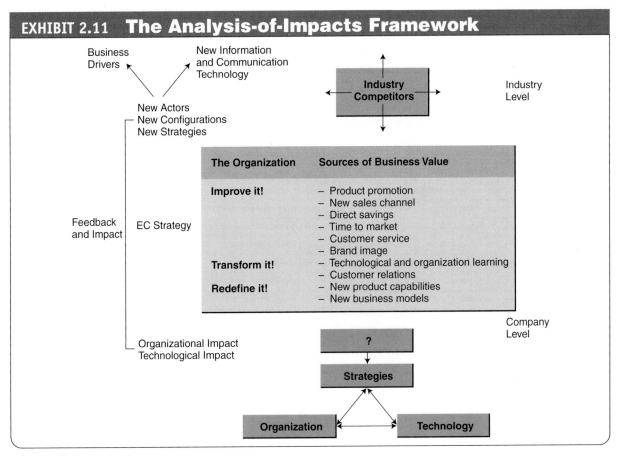

Source: Bloch et al., 1996.

Product promotion. The existence of e-markets has increased the promotion of products and services through direct marketing. Contact with customers has become more information-rich and interactive.

New sales channel. Because of the direct reach to customers and the bidirectional nature of communications in EC, a new distribution channel for existing products has been created.

Direct savings. The cost of delivering information to customers over the Internet results in substantial savings to senders. Major savings are also realized in delivering digitized products (such as music and software) versus delivery of physical products.

Reduced cycle time. The delivery time of digitized products and services can be reduced to seconds. Also, the administrative work related to physical delivery, especially across international borders, can be reduced significantly, cutting the cycle time by more than 90 percent. One example of this is TradeNet in Singapore, which reduced the administrative time of port-related transactions from days to minutes. Cycle time can be reduced through improvements along the supply chain.

Customer service. Customer service can be greatly enhanced by enabling customers to find detailed information online. For example, FedEx and other shippers allow customers to trace the status of their packages. Also, software (intelligent) can answer standard e-mail questions in seconds. Finally, human experts' services can be expedited using help-desk software.

Brand or corporate image. On the Web, newcomers can establish corporate images very quickly. What Amazon.com did in just 3 years took traditional companies generations to achieve. A good corporate image facilitates trust, which is necessary for direct sales. Traditional companies such as Intel, Disney, Wal-Mart, Dell, and Cisco use their Web activities to affirm their corporate identity and brand image.

In addition to the preceding impacts suggested by Bloch et al. (1996), other impacts of e-markets on direct marketing include the following:

Customization. EC enables customization of products and services. In contrast, buying in a store or ordering from a television advertisement usually limits customers to a supply of standard products. Dell Computer is the classic example of customization success. Today, customers can configure not only computers, but also cars, jewelry, gifts, and hundreds of other products and services. If properly done, a company can achieve mass customization that provides a competitive advantage, as well as increases the overall demand for certain products and services. Customization will change marketing and sales activities both in B2C and in B2B.

Advertising. With direct marketing and customization comes one-to-one or direct advertising, which can be much more effective than mass advertising. This creates a fundamental change in the manner in which advertising is conducted, not only for online transactions, but also for products and services that are ordered and shipped in traditional ways. As we will see in Chapter 4, the entire concept of advertising is going through a fundamental change due to EC.

Ordering systems. Taking orders from customers can be drastically improved if it is done online, reducing both processing time and mistakes. Electronic orders can be quickly routed to the appropriate order-processing site. This process reduces expenses and also saves time, freeing salespeople to sell products. Also, when ordering online, customers can configure their own orders and compute the costs, saving time for all parties involved.

Market operations. Direct e-marketing is changing traditional markets. Some physical markets may disappear, as does the need to make deliveries of goods to intermediaries in the marketplace. In an electronic marketspace, goods are delivered directly to buyers upon completion of the purchase, making markets much more efficient and saving the cost of the shipment into and from the brick-and-mortar store.

For digitally based products—software, music, and information—the changes brought by e-markets will be dramatic. Already, small but powerful software packages are delivered over the Internet. The ability to deliver digitized products electronically affects (eliminates) packaging and greatly reduces the need for specialized distribution models.

New sales models such as shareware, freeware, and pay-as-you-use are emerging. Although these models currently exist only within particular sectors, such as the software and publishing industries, they will eventually pervade other sectors.

All of these impacts of e-markets on direct marketing provide companies with a competitive advantage over the traditional direct-sales methods. Furthermore, because the competitive advantage is so large, e-markets are likely to replace many nondirect marketing channels. Some people predict the "fall of the shopping mall," and many retail stores and brokers of services (stocks, real estate, and insurance) are labeled by some as soon-to-be-endangered species.

TRANSFORMING ORGANIZATIONS

The second impact of e-markets suggested by Bloch et al. (1996) is the transformation of organizations. Here, we look at two key organizational transformations: organizational learning and the nature of work.

Technology and Organizational Learning

Rapid progress in EC will force a Darwinian struggle: To survive, companies will have to learn and adapt quickly to the new technologies. This struggle will offer them an opportunity to experiment with new products, services, and business models, which may lead to strategic and structural changes. These changes may transform the way in which business is done. Bloch et al. (1996) believe that as EC progresses, it will have a large and durable impact on the strategies of most organizations.

Thus, new technologies will require new organizational structures and approaches. For instance, the structure of the organizational unit dealing with e-marketspaces might have to be different from the conventional sales and marketing departments. Specifically, a company's e-commerce unit might report directly to the chief information officer (CIO) rather than to the sales and marketing vice president. To be more flexible and responsive to the market, new processes must be put in place. For a while, new measurements of success may be needed. For example, the measures (called "metrics") used to gauge success of an EC project in its early stages might need to be different from the traditional revenues–expenses framework. However, in the long run, as many dot-coms have found out, no business can escape the traditional revenue–expenses framework.

In summary, corporate change must be planned and managed. Before getting it right, organizations may have to struggle with different experiments and learn from their mistakes.

The Changing Nature of Work

The nature of some work and employment will be transformed in the Digital Age; it is already happening before our eyes. For example, driven by increased competition in the global marketplace, firms are reducing the number of employees down to a core of essential staff and outsourcing whatever work they can to countries where wages are significantly less. The upheaval brought on by these changes is creating new opportunities and new risks, and is forcing us into new ways of thinking about jobs, careers, and salaries.

Digital-Age workers will have to be very flexible. Few will have truly secure jobs in the traditional sense, and many will have to be willing and able to constantly learn, adapt, make decisions, and stand by them. Many will work from home.

The Digital-Age company will have to prize its core of essential workers as its most valuable asset. It will have to constantly nurture and empower them and provide them with every means possible to expand their knowledge and skill base.

REDEFINING ORGANIZATIONS

Some of the ways in which e-markets will redefine organizations are presented in the following sections.

New and Improved Product Capabilities

E-markets allow for new products to be created and/or for existing products to be customized in innovative ways. Such changes may redefine organizations' missions and the manner in which they operate. Customer profiles (see Chapter 4), as well as data on customer preferences, can be used as a source of information for improving products or designing new ones.

Mass customization, as described earlier, enables manufacturers to create specific products for each customer, based on the customer's exact needs. For example, Motorola gathers customer needs for a pager or a cellular phone, transmits the customer's specifications electronically to the manufacturing plant where the device is manufactured, and then sends the finished product to the customer within a day. Dell Computer and General Motors use the same approach in building their products. Using the Web, customers can design or configure products for themselves. For example, customers can use the Web to design T-shirts, furniture, cars, jewelry, Nike shoes, and even a Swatch watch. Using mass-customization methods, the cost of customized products is at or slightly above the comparable retail price of standard products.

New Business Models

E-markets affect not only individual companies and their products, but also entire industries. The wide availability of information and its direct distribution to consumers will lead to the use of new business models (e.g., the name-your-own-price model of Priceline.com). Another example of a new business model is that of DM & S Trucking Company, which added an online bidding system. The system not only improved the company's operations, but eventually expanded to be a matching e-marketplace for small trucking companies, as described in EC Application Case 2.4 (page 84).

Improving the Supply Chain

One of the major benefits of e-markets is the potential improvement in supply chains. A major change is the creation of a hub-based chain, shown in Exhibit 2.12.

Impacts on Manufacturing

EC is changing manufacturing systems from mass production lines to demand-driven, just-in-time manufacturing. These new production systems are integrated with finance, marketing, and other functional systems, as well as with business partners and customers. Using Web-based enterprise resource planning (ERP) systems (supported by software such as SAP R/3), companies can direct customer orders to designers and/or to the production floor within seconds. Production cycle time is cut by 50 percent or more in many cases, especially if production is done in a different country from where the designers and engineers are located.

An interesting organizational concept is that of **virtual manufacturing**, which is the ability to run multiple manufacturing plants as though they were at one location. A single company controls the entire manufacturing process, from the supply

virtual manufacturing
Running global manufacturing plants as though they were one location, by a single company electronically controlling the entire manufacturing process.

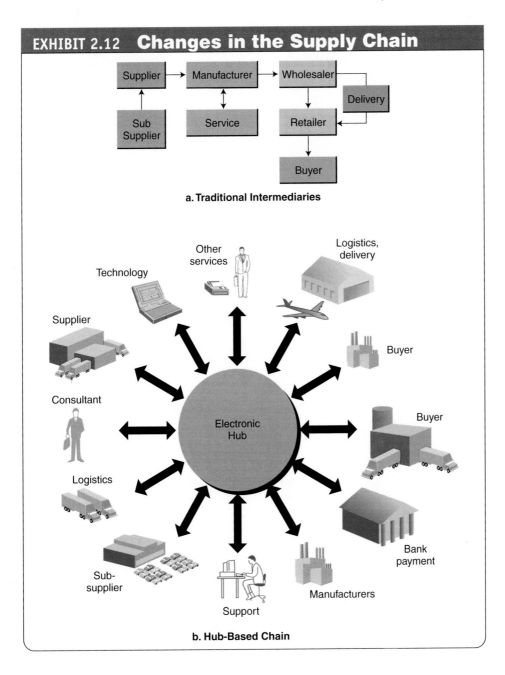

EXHIBIT 2.12 Changes in the Supply Chain

a. Traditional Intermediaries

b. Hub-Based Chain

of components to shipment, while making it completely transparent to customers and employees. For example, Cisco System works with 34 plants globally, 32 of which are owned by other companies. Each of Cisco's products will look exactly alike, regardless of where it was manufactured. Up-to-the-minute information sharing is critical for the success of this mass-production approach (Pine 1999).

Companies such as IBM, General Motors, General Electric, and Boeing assemble products from components that are manufactured in many different locations, even different countries. Sub-assemblers gather materials and parts from their vendors, and they may use one or more tiers of manufacturers. Communication,

EC APPLICATION CASE 2.4
Implementation and Strategy
A NEW MODEL FOR SMALL MOVERS

DM & S is a small trucking company with $1.8 million in annual sales. In early 2000, the U.S. economy started to slow down, and fuel prices increased. DM & S started to lose money, as did many other small movers.

A major problem in the trucking industry is that trucks need to move cargos at certain times, but they may not have a full load. Furthermore, on return trips, trucks are usually not completely full. Unused cargo space is lost revenue. Bert Lampers, owner and CEO of DM & S, had an idea: Create a service in which small moving companies bid on jobs of moving goods for individuals. Customers with flexible moving dates can benefit the most. This is basically a reverse-auction process.

Lampers spent $15,000 to create an auction site, *dickerabid.com*, for the new service. Once customers place notice of their job on the site, small truckers start to bid. For a trucker with a destination and travel date that matches the customers' requirement, hauling almost anything is better than going with empty space. Customers can get huge discounts, and winning truckers can earn money to help cover their fuel expenses.

Starting with four truckers and increasing to 20, the auction site increased DM & S's revenues by $14,000 during the first few months of operation. Additional revenue is generated by advertisers that cater to people who are relocating, such as furniture and window-blind companies. The Web site won third place in *Inc.*'s Web innovations in 2000.

DM & S is a third-party auction maker, as well as a buyer of small truckers' services. Larger truckers (moving companies) also have their own Web site, *imove.com*, which provides a considerable amount of services and information.

Source: *Inc.* Magazine Innovation Award, 2000.

Questions

▶ Why is *dickerabid.com* useful for a small moving company?

▶ What kind of service is *dickerabid.com* providing?

▶ Compare this model with the *Priceline.com* model.

▶ Compare the service provided to an individual who wants to move using *dickerabid.com* with what is offered at *imove.com* (check "Moving").

---

collaboration, and coordination are critical in such multitier systems. Using electronic bidding, assemblers get subassemblies 15 to 20 percent cheaper than before and 80 percent faster (e.g., see the GE case in Chapter 5). Furthermore, such systems are flexible and adaptable, allowing for fast changes with minimum cost. Also, costly inventories that are part of mass-production systems can be minimized.

Build-to-Order. The biggest change in manufacturing will be the move to build-to-order systems. Manufacturing or assembly will start only after an order is received. This will change not only the production planning and control, but also the entire supply chain.

Impacts on Finance and Accounting

E-markets require special finance and accounting systems. Most notable of these are electronic payment systems. Traditional payment systems are ineffective or inefficient for electronic trade. The use of new payment systems such as electronic cash is complicated because legal issues and agreements on international standards are involved. Nevertheless, electronic cash is certain to come soon, and it will change how payments are made. It could also change consumers' financial lives and shake the foundations of financial systems.

Executing an electronic order triggers an action in what is called the back office. *Back-office* transactions include buyers' credit checks, product availability checks, order confirmation, changes in accounts payable, receivables, billing, and much more. These activities must be efficient, synchronized, and fast so the electronic trade will not be slowed down. An example of this is online stock trading. In most cases, orders are executed in less than 1 second, and the trader can find an online confirmation of the trade immediately.

One of the most innovative concepts in accounting and finance is the "virtual close," which would allow companies to close their accounting records within a day. This Cisco Systems project is described in the following Insights and Additions box.

Insights and Additions   Cisco's Virtual Close

Cisco Systems, the company that supplies vast networks that connect computers to the Internet, is using technology to develop a product, Virtual Close, with which a company can close its accounting records (its "books") more quickly. This will be done by connecting the accounting and financial records of an entire company, even one with operations in dozens of countries, via an intranet. Cisco's infrastructure will permit information sharing almost instantly.

Cisco is implementing such a system for itself. Closing the quarterly accounts used to take up to 10 days. Within 4 years, the chief financial officer worked the close down to 2 days (and significantly cut its cost). Cisco's goal is to be able to close the books with 1 hour's notice, on any day in the quarter, by 2002 or 2003.

The advantages for Cisco and any other company that uses Virtual Close are:

▶ Companies can become proactive, spotting problems at any time, instead of just once a quarter. Problems that would otherwise have remained unseen for months can be quickly addressed and their damage minimized.

▶ New opportunities can be detected early, allowing companies to exploit them quickly.

▶ Virtual Close will enable quick "drill down" analysis, which locates the causes of either poor or excellent performance.

▶ It will bring huge productivity gains related to corporate financial reporting.

Implementing Virtual Close is a lengthy process that may end in failure due to the project's complexity. However, not implementing it might result in a competitive disadvantage.

Source: Compiled from "Business and the Internet," *The Economist*, June 26, 1999, and *cisco.com* press releases, 2000 and 2001.

Impact on Human Resources Management and Training

EC is changing how people are recruited, evaluated, promoted, and developed (Chapter 3). EC also is changing the way training and education are offered to employees. Online distance learning is exploding, providing opportunities that never existed in the past. Companies are cutting training costs by 50 percent or more, and virtual courses and programs are mushrooming.

New e-learning systems offer two-way video, on-the-fly interaction, and application sharing. Such systems provide for interactive remote instruction systems, which link sites over a high-speed intranet (as shown in Chapter 7). At the same time, corporations are finding that e-learning may be their ticket to survival as changing environments, new technologies, and continuously changing procedures make it necessary for employees to be trained and retrained constantly.

▶ List the major parts of Bloch et al.'s model.
▶ Describe how EC improves direct marketing.
▶ Describe how EC transforms organizations.
▶ Describe how EC redefines organizations.

MANAGERIAL ISSUES

Some managerial issues related to this chapter are as follows.

1. **How do we compete in the digital economy?** Although the basic theories of competition are unchanged, the rules are different. Of special interest are digital products and services, whose variable costs are very low. Competition involves both old-economy and new-economy companies. The speed of changes in competitive forces can be rapid, and the impact of new business models can be devastating. As Bill Gates once said, "Competition is not among companies, but among business models."

2. **What about intermediaries?** Many EC applications will change the role of intermediation. This may create a conflict between a company and its distributors. It may also create opportunities. In many cases, the distributors will need to change their roles. This is a sensitive issue that needs to be planned for during the transformation plan.

3. **What organizational changes will be needed?** Companies should expect organizational changes in all functional areas once e-commerce reaches momentum. At minimum, purchasing will be done differently in many organizations, but introducing models such as name-your-own-price and affiliate programs may also have a major impact on business operations.

4. **Should we auction?** A major strategic issue is whether or not to do auctions. Auctions do have risks, and forward auctions may create conflicts with other distribution channels. If a company decides to do an auction, it needs to select an auction mechanism and determine pricing. These strategies determine the success of the auction and the ability to attract and retain visitors on the site. Auctions also require support services. Decisions about how to provide these services and to what extent to use business partners are critical to the success of repeated high-volume auctions.

5. **What should be auctioned?** Both individuals and companies would like to auction everything. However, is it ethical or even legal to do so? Ask eBay, which is trying, for example, to clean up pornographic auctions by banning some items and directing some items into a "mature audi-

ences" area. Another issue is pirated software, which is offered on about 2,000 auction sites worldwide. In fact, eBay was sued in 2000 by video-game manufacturers Nintendo, Sega, and Electronic Arts for auctioning pirated video games. (For further discussion, see Beato 2000.)

6. **Should we have our own auction site or use a third-party site?** This is a strategic issue, and there are pluses and minuses to each alternative. However, if a company decides to auction from their own site, they will need to advertise and attract visitors, which may be expensive. Also, the company will need to install fraud-prevention mechanisms and provide other services. Either way, the company may need to consider connectivity to its back-office and logistics system.

7. **Should we barter?** Bartering can be an interesting strategy, especially for companies that need cash and have some surplus inventory. However, the valuation of what is bought or sold may be hard to determine, and the tax implications in some countries are not clear.

8. **What m-commerce opportunities are available?** A company should develop an m-commerce strategy if it will be impacted by it. The opportunities presented by m-commerce are enormous, but so are the risks. However, doing nothing may be even riskier. (For further discussion, see Kalakota and Robinson 2001 and Sadeh 2002).

SUMMARY

In this chapter you learned about the following EC issues as they relate to the learning objectives.

1. **E-marketplaces and their components.** A marketspace or e-marketplace is a virtual market that does not suffer from limitations of space, time, or borders. As such, it can be very effective. Its major components include sellers, buyers, products (some digital), electronic intermediaries, electronic catalogs, search engines, and more.

2. **The major types of e-markets.** In the B2C area there are storefronts and e-malls. In the B2B area there are private and public e-marketplaces, which can be vertical (by industry) or horizontal. Different types of portals provide access to e-marketplaces.

3. **Supply chains and value chains.** A supply chain is the flow of materials, information, money, and services among business partners. The value chain is the series of activities done by an organization to create its products or services. These activities create economic value for which customers are willing to pay. Both concepts are critical to understanding the benefits and limitations of e-commerce.

4. **The role of intermediation.** The role of intermediaries will change as e-markets develop; some will be eliminated, others will prosper. New value-added services that range from content creation to syndication are mushrooming.

5. **Competition, quality, and liquidity in e-markets.** Three major e-market issues are strong online competition, the need for quality assurance, and the need for a large number of participating sellers and buyers.

6. **Electronic catalogs, search engines, and shopping carts.** The major mechanisms in e-markets are electronic catalogs, search engines and software (intelligent) agents, and electronic shopping carts. These mechanisms facilitate EC by providing a user-friendly shopping environment.

7. **Types of auctions and their characteristics.** In forward auctions, bids from buyers are placed sequentially, either in increasing (English) mode or in decreasing (Dutch) mode. In reverse auctions, buyers place an RFQ and suppliers submit offers in one or several rounds. In "name-your-own-price" auctions, buyers specify how much they are willing to pay for a product or service and an intermediary tries to find a supplier to fulfill the request.

8. **The benefits and limitations of auctions.** The major benefits for sellers are the ability to reach many buyers, to sell quickly, and to save on commissions to intermediaries. Buyers have a chance to obtain collectibles while shopping from their homes, and they can find bargains. The major limitation is the possibility of fraud.

9. **Bartering and negotiating.** Electronic bartering can greatly facilitate the swapping of goods and services among organizations, thanks to improved search and matching capabilities. Search engines can facilitate online negotiation.

10. **The role of m-commerce.** Mobile commerce is emerging as a phenomenon that can provide Internet access to millions of people. It also creates new location-related applications.

11. **The impact of e-markets on organizations.** All functional areas of an organization are affected by e-markets. Broadly, e-markets improve direct marketing and transform and redefine organizations. Direct marketing (manufacturers to customers) and one-to-one marketing and advertisement are becoming the norm, and mass customization and personalization are taking off. Production is moving to a pull model, changing supply-chain relationships and reducing cycle time. Virtual manufacturing is on the rise. Financial systems are becoming more efficient as they become networked with other business functions, and the human resources activities of recruiting, evaluation, and training are being managed more efficiently due to employees' interactions with machines.

KEY TERMS

Auction,	p. 67	Electronic auctions		Online negotiation,	p. 76
Back end,	p. 44	(e-auctions),	p. 68	Personalization,	p. 57
Bartering,	p. 75	Electronic catalogs,	p. 62	Private e-marketplaces,	p. 47
Bartering exchange,	p. 76	Electronic shopping		Public e-marketplaces,	p. 47
Bidding system,	p. 71	carts,	p. 67	Quality uncertainty,	p. 60
Build-to-order,	p. 51	English auction,	p. 69	Reintermediation,	p. 55
Buy-side e-marketplace,	p. 47	Forward auction,	p. 69	Reverse auction,	p. 71
Consortia,	p. 47	Free-fall auction,	p. 71	Search engine,	p. 65
Consumer-to-business		Front end,	p. 44	Sell-side e-marketplace,	p. 47
(C2B) model,	p. 72	Infomediaries,	p. 53	Software (intelligent)	
Differentiation,	p. 57	Information portal,	p. 47	agent,	p. 65
Digital products,	p. 44	Intermediary,	p. 44	Storefront,	p. 45
Disintermediation,	p. 55	M-business,	p. 77	Supply chain,	p. 48
Double auction,	p. 72	Marketspace,	p. 42	Syndication,	p. 55
Dutch auction,	p. 70	Microproduct,	p. 60	Tendering system,	p. 71
Dynamic pricing,	p. 69	Mobile commerce		Value chain,	p. 52
E-bartering,	p. 75	(m-commerce),	p. 77	Value system,	p. 52
E-distributor,	p. 54	Mobile computing,	p. 77	Virtual manufacturing,	p. 83
E-mall,	p. 46	Mobile portal,	p. 48	Yankee auction,	p. 70
E-marketplace,	p. 47	"Name-your-own-price"			
Early liquidity,	p. 60	model,	p. 71		

DISCUSSION QUESTIONS

1. Compare marketplaces with marketspaces. What are the advantages and limitations of each?

2. What are the major benefits of syndication to the various participants?

3. Compare and contrast competition in traditional markets with that in digital markets.

4. Discuss the differences between a supply chain and a value chain. How are they related?

5. Explain how NTE provides real-time procurement services (EC Application Case 2.1).

6. Which type of e-marketplace is NTE (EC Application Case 2.1)? Why?

7. The "name-your-own-price" model is considered a reverse auction. However, this model does not include RFQs or consecutive bidding. Why is it called a reverse auction?

8. Discuss the advantages of dynamic pricing over fixed pricing. What are the potential disadvantages of dynamic pricing?

9. Discuss the need for search and software agents in EC and in auctions.

10. Why are sell-side and buy-side markets in the same company usually separated, whereas in an exchange they are combined?

11. Discuss the advantages of m-commerce over e-commerce.

INTERNET EXERCISES

1. Enter arena.com.hk and examine the products and services provided. Which are similar to those offered by NTE? Examine the Global Cargo exchange and other initiatives. Classify the services according to the models presented in Chapter 1.

2. Go to cisco.com, google.com, and cio.com and locate information about the status of the "virtual close." Write a report based on your findings.

3. Visit ebay.com and examine all the quality-assurance measures available, either for a fee or for free. Prepare a list of the mechanisms.

4. Visit ticketmaster.com, ticketonline.com, and other sites that sell event tickets online. Assess the competition in online ticket selling. What services do the different sites provide?

5. Examine how bartering is conducted online at tradeaway.com, abarter.com, and intagio.com.

6. Enter ebay.com/anywhere and investigate the use of "anywhere wireless." Review the wireless devices and find out how they work.

7. Enter imandi.com and review the process by which buyers can send RFQs to merchants of their choice. Also, evaluate the services provided in their choice. Also, evaluate the services provided in the areas of marketing, staffing, and travel. Write a report based on your findings.

8. Examine the process used by office.com regarding auctions. Review its reverse auction arrangement with bigbuyer.com. Write a report based on your findings.

9. Enter bidder-network.co.nz/software/ and view all the different types of auction software and auction hosting available. Find what the site has for a company-centric auction and learn about exchanges.

10. Enter ingrammicro.com and go to its IM-Logistics product. Identify all the services provided by IM-Logistics to both suppliers and buyers.

11. Enter respond.com and send a request for a product or a service. Once you receive replies, select the best deal. You have no obligation to buy. Write a short report on your experience.

12. Enter onstar.com and review its services. Comment on the usability of each.

TEAM ASSIGNMENTS AND ROLE PLAYING

1. Several competing exchanges operate in the steel industry (e.g., newview.com and isteelasia.com). Assign one group to each exchange. Look at its market structure, at the services it offers, and so on. The group then will make a presentation to convince buyers and sellers to join its exchange.

2. Assign each team an auction method (English, Dutch, etc.). Each team should convince a company that wants to liquidate items that its method is the best. Items to be liquidated include:
   a. Five IBM top-of-the-line mainframe systems valued at about $500,000 each.
   b. 750 PCs valued at about $1,000 each.
   c. A real estate property valued at about $10 million.

   Present different arguments for each type of item.

3. Assign teams to major auction sites from your country and from two other countries. Each team should present the major functionalities of the sites and the fraud protection measures they use.

REAL-WORLD CASE

FREEMARKETS.COM REVOLUTIONIZES PROCUREMENT

FreeMarkets.com began in 1995 with an idea: By conducting auctions online, procurement professionals could raise the quality of the direct materials and services they buy while substantially lowering the prices they pay for them.

FreeMarkets.com is a leader in creating B2B online auctions for buyers of industrial parts, raw materials, commodities, and services around the globe. The company has created auctions for goods and services in more than 70 industrial-product categories. In 1999, FreeMarkets.com auctioned more than $2.7 billion worth of purchase orders and saved buyers an estimated 2 to 25 percent.

FreeMarkets.com has helped customers find sources for billions of dollars worth of goods and services in hundreds of product and service categories through its B2B Global Marketplace. FreeMarkets.com also has helped companies improve their asset-recovery results by getting timely market prices for surplus assets through the FreeMarkets.com Asset Exchange.

FreeMarkets.com Asset Exchange addresses even the most complex transactions over a flexible trading platform. It bridges the gaps in information, geography, and industry that make traditional surplus-asset markets so inefficient. With a combination of online and onsite sales venues, FreeMarkets.com Asset

Exchange offers the following solutions to help companies meet their asset recovery goals:

▶ **FreeMarkets.com online markets.** An effective method for asset disposal that delivers timely, market-based pricing.

▶ **FreeMarkets.com online marketplace.** A self-service venue where sellers post available assets. This service is useful when getting the right price is more important than a quick sale.

▶ **FreeMarkets onsite auctions.** Live auction events that are ideal for clearing a facility, time-critical sales, or selling a mix of high- and low-value assets.

When the commercial situation demands, the company also combines onsite auctions and online markets into a single asset-disposal solution. FreeMarkets Onsite Auctions provide the following:

▶ **Asset-disposal analysis.** Market makers work with sellers to determine the best strategy to meet asset-recovery goals.

▶ **Detailed sales offering.** The company collects and consolidates asset information into a printed or online sales offering for buyers.

▶ **Targeted market outreach.** FreeMarkets conducts targeted marketing to a global database of 500,000 buyers and suppliers.

▶ **Event coordination.** The company prepares the site, provides qualified personnel, and enforces auction rules.

▶ **Sales implementation.** FreeMarkets summarizes auction results and assists in closing sales.

Emerson Corp., a global diversified manufacturing firm, faced the difficult challenge of consolidating millions of dollars of printed circuit board (PCB) purchases across 14 global divisions. The company wanted to consolidate its supply base and standardize data to understand future buying patterns. It turned to FreeMarkets for assistance. Using an RFQ, Emerson received 755 bids and achieved the following:

▶ Obtained buy-in from 14 divisions to participate in a corporate-wide event.

▶ Standardized data on more than 1,000 PCB designs across 19 divisions.

▶ Introduced several qualified suppliers from Asian countries.

▶ Consolidated its supplier's base from 58 to nine.

The company saved more than $10 million in 1 year.

Questions

1. Enter *freemarkets.com* and explore its current activities and services.

2. Look at five customer success stories. What common elements can you find?

3. If you work for a company, register and examine the process as a buyer and as a seller.

4. Compare the use of FreeMarkets.com to the option of building your own auction site.

5. How does surplus asset recovery become more efficient with FreeMarkets?

CHAPTER 3

RETAILING IN E-COMMERCE: PRODUCTS AND SERVICES

Content

Amazon.com: The King of E-Tailing

Managerial Issues

Real-World Case:

Wal-Mart Goes Online

Learning objectives

Upon completion of this chapter, you will be able to:

▶ Define and describe the primary business models of electronic retailing ("e-tailing").

▶ Discuss various e-tail markets, such as those for books, music, and cars.

▶ Identify the principles of "click-and-mortar" strategies for traditional retailers.

▶ Describe how online travel and tourism operate.

▶ Discuss the online employment market, including its drivers and benefits.

▶ Describe online real estate, insurance, and stock trading.

▶ Discuss cyberbanking and online personal finance.

▶ Describe on-demand delivery by e-grocers.

▶ Describe the delivery of digital products and online entertainment.

▶ Discuss various e-tail consumer aids, including comparison-shopping aids.

▶ Identify the critical success factors for direct marketing and e-tailing.

▶ Describe reintermediation, channel conflicts, and personalization in e-tailing.

AMAZON.COM: THE KING OF E-TAILING

The Problem

Entrepreneur Jeff Bezos saw the potential for retail sales over the Internet and selected books as the most logical product for e-tailing. In July 1995, he started Amazon.com, an e-tailing pioneer, offering books via an electronic catalog from its Web site. Over the years, the company has recognized that it must continually enhance its electronic store by expanding product selection and improving the customer experience.

The Solution

In addition to its initial electronic bookstore, Amazon.com now offers specialty stores, such as its professional and technical store. It has also expanded its book editorial content through partnerships with experts in certain fields and has increased product selection with the addition of millions of used and out-of-print titles. Key features of the Amazon.com superstore are easy browsing and searching, useful product information, reviews, recommendations and personalization, broad selection, low prices, One-Click order technology, secure payment systems, and efficient order fulfillment.

The Amazon.com Web site also has a number of features that make the online shopping experience more enjoyable. Its "Gift Ideas" section features seasonally appropriate gift ideas and services. Its "Community" section provides product information and recommendations shared by customers. Through its e-cards section, customers can send free animated electronic greeting cards to friends and family.

Amazon.com also offers various marketplace services. Amazon Auctions hosts and operates auctions on behalf of individuals and small businesses throughout the world. The zShops service hosts electronic storefronts for a monthly fee, offering small businesses the opportunity to have customized storefronts supported by the richness of Amazon.com's order-fulfillment processing.

Amazon.com is recognized as an online leader in creating sales through customer intimacy and CRM, which are cultivated by informative marketing front-ends and one-to-one advertisements. In addition, sales are supported by highly automated, efficient back-end systems. When a customer makes a return visit to Amazon.com, a cookie file (see Chapter 4) identifies the user and says, for example, "Welcome back, Sarah Shopper," and then proceeds to recommend new books from the same genre of previous customer purchases. The company tracks customer purchase histories and sends purchase recommendations via e-mail to cultivate repeat buyers. It also provides detailed product descriptions and ratings to help consumers make informed purchase decisions. These efforts usually result in satisfactory shopping experiences and encourage customers to return to the site.

Customers can personalize their account and manage orders online with the patented "One-Click" order feature. This personalized service allows customers to view their order status, cancel or combine orders that have not entered the shipping process, edit the shipping options and addresses on unshipped orders, modify the payment method for unshipped orders, and more.

Starting in 2000, Amazon.com has undertaken alliances with "trusted partners" that provide knowledgeable entry into new markets. For example, Amazon's alliance with *carsdirect.com* allows it to sell cars online. Clicking "Health and Beauty" on the Amazon.com Web site takes the visitor to a site Amazon.com operates jointly with *Drugstore.com*, clicking on "Wireless Phones" will suggest a service plan from an Amazon.com partner in that market. (Later in this chapter, we discuss the successful alliance between Amazon.com and Toys R Us.) Amazon.com also is becoming a Web fulfillment outsourcer for national chains such as Target and Circuit City.

The Results

Annual sales for Amazon.com have trended upward, from $15.7 million in 1996 to $600 million in 1998 to about $4 billion by 2002. This pioneer e-tailer now offers over 17 million book, music, and DVD/video titles to some 20 million customers.

Amazon.com also offers several features for international customers, including over 1 million Japanese-language titles.

In January 2002, Amazon.com declared its first profit for the 2001 first quarter. Yet the company's financial success is by no means assured.

What We Can Learn . . .

The case of Amazon.com demonstrates some of the features and managerial issues related to electronic retailers, also known as e-tailers. Amazon.com is the most recognized e-tailer worldwide. The case study demonstrates the evolution of e-tailing, some of the problems encountered by e-tailers, and the solutions employed by Amazon.com. In this chapter we will look at the delivery of both products and services online to individual customers. We also will discuss e-tailing failures and successes.

3.1   ELECTRONIC RETAILING (E-TAILING) AND THE B2C MARKET

A retailer is a sales *intermediary*, a seller that operates between manufacturers and customers. In the physical world, retailing is done in stores that customers must visit in order to make a purchase. Companies that produce a large number of products, such as Procter & Gamble, use retailers for efficient distribution. However, even if you sell only a relatively few products (e.g., Kodak), you still may need retailers to reach a large number of customers.

Catalog sales free a retailer from the need for a physical store from which to distribute products. Customers can browse catalogs on their own time, rather than shopping in a physical store. With the ubiquity of the Internet, the next logical step was for retailing to move online. Online retail sales are called **electronic retailing**, or **e-tailing**, and those who conduct retail business online are called **e-tailers**. E-tailing can be also be conducted through auctions, discussed in Chapter 2. E-tailing makes it possible for a manufacturer to sell directly to the customer, cutting out the intermediary. In this chapter we will deal with the various types of e-tailing and related issues.

The concept of retailing and e-tailing implies sales to individual customers. However, the distinction between B2C and B2B e-commerce is not always clear cut. Amazon.com sells books mostly to individuals, but it also sells to corporations. Amazon.com's chief rival, Barnes & Noble, has a special division that caters only to business customers. Walmart.com sells to both individuals and businesses (via Sam's Club). Dell sells its computers to both consumers and businesses, and insurance sites sell to both to individuals and corporations.

SIZE AND GROWTH OF THE B2C MARKET

The statistics for the volume of B2C EC sales, including forecasts for future sales, come from many sources (e.g., emarketer.com, jmm.com), and there is substantial deviation in the reported data due to how the numbers are derived. Some of the variation stems from the use of different definitions of EC. When tallying the financial data, some analysts include the investment costs in Internet infrastructure, whereas others merely include just the amount of the actual transactions conducted via the Internet. Another issue is how the items for sale are categorized. Some sources combine certain products and services, others do not.

electronic retailing (e-tailing)
Retailing conducted online, over the Internet.

e-tailers
Those who conduct retail business over the Internet.

Here are some statistics: According to emarketer.com (July 2001), during 2001, about 75 million individual Internet users participated in some form of online shopping. Worldwide B2C revenues, according to another eMarketer report (May 2001), ranged from $53 billion to $238 billion (depending on the source), and are forecast in the range of $428 billion to $2.134 trillion in 2004.

The following sites provide statistics on e-tailing:

▌ Jupiter Media Metrix (Jmm.com)

▌ Cyberdialogue.com

▌ emarketer.com

▌ Business2.com

▌ Cyberatlas.com

▌ Gomez.com

▌ Statmarket.com

▌ Forrester.com

▌ AMRResearch.com

What Sells Well on the Internet

Thousands of items are available on the Web from tens of thousands of vendors. The most recognizable one are the following:

▌ **Computers and electronics.** Dell and Gateway are the major vendors, with more than $12 billion in sales in 2001. Hardware is most popular, but more and more people buy software online as well.

▌ **Sporting goods.** According to PC Data Online, second to PCs, sporting goods are sold on the Internet more than any other product. However, it is difficult to verify this information as there are only a few e-tailers that sell sporting goods exclusively online (e.g., fogdog.com).

▌ **Office supplies.** Office supply sales by Officedepot.com and Staples.com alone reached over $2.5 billion in 2001 (Jupiter Media Metrix). Both B2C and B2B sales of office supplies are increasing rapidly, all over the world.

▌ **Books and music.** As can be learned from their Web sites, Amazon.com and Barnesandnoble.com are the major sellers of books (over $5 billion in 2001). However, hundreds of other e-tailers sell books on the Internet, especially specialized books (e.g., technical books, children's books).

▌ **Toys.** After two rocky Christmas seasons in which toy e-tailers had problems delivering ordered toys, toy sales are now moving successfully to the click-and-mortar mode. With the Toys R Us/Amazon alliance leading the pack, and Kbkids.com following, consumers can buy their favorite toys online at discount stores, department stores, or direct from some manufacturers (e.g., mattel.com, lego.com).

▌ **Health and beauty.** A large variety of health and beauty products, from vitamins to cosmetics to jewelry, are sold online by most large retailers and by specialty stores.

▶ **Entertainment.** This is another area where dozens of products, ranging from tickets to events (e.g., ticketmaster.com) to paid fantasy games (e.g., espn.com), are embraced by millions of shoppers worldwide.

▶ **Apparel.** With the possibility of buying customized shirts, pants, and even shoes, the online sale of apparel is also growing.

▶ **Services.** Sales in service industries, especially travel, stock trading, electronic banking, real estate, and insurance, are increasing, in some cases, more than doubling every year.

▶ **Cars.** The sale of cars over the Internet is just beginning (people still like to "kick the tires"), but they could be a top seller on the Internet by 2007.

▶ **Others.** Many other products, ranging from flowers to food to pet supplies, are offered on the Internet. As more and more retailers sell online, virtually every item that is available in a physical store may be sold online as well. Many of these items are specialized or niche products. The Internet offers an open and global market to shops that are trying to sell specialized products they would not be able to market in any other way (e.g., antique Coca-Cola bottles at antiquebottles.com, tea tree oil at teatree.co.uk).

CHARACTERISTICS OF SUCCESSFUL E-TAILING

Retail and e-tail success comes from offering quality merchandise at good prices, coupled with excellent service. In that sense, the online and traditional channels are not very different. However, e-tailers can offer expanded consumer services not offered by traditional retailers. These services will be discussed later in this and the following chapter. But with all else being equal in the online environment, goods with the following characteristics are expected to facilitate higher sales volumes:

▶ High brand recognition (e.g., Lands' End, Sony)

▶ A guarantee provided by highly reliable or well-known vendors (e.g., Dell, L.L. Bean)

▶ Digitized format (e.g., software, music, or videos)

▶ Relatively inexpensive items (e.g., office supplies, vitamins)

▶ Frequently purchased items (e.g., groceries, prescription drugs)

▶ Commodities with standard specifications (e.g., books, CDs, air tickets), making physical inspection unimportant

▶ Well-known packaged items that cannot be opened even in a traditional store (e.g., foods, vitamins)

In the next section we will look at the business models that have proved successful in e-tailing.

▶ Describe the nature of B2C e-commerce.

▶ What sells well in B2C?

▶ What are the characteristics of high-volume products and services?

3.2   E-TAILING BUSINESS MODELS

E-tailing business models can be classified in several ways. For example, some in the industry classify e-tailers by the scope of items handled (general-purpose versus specialty e-tailing) or by scope of the sales region covered (global versus regional). The two main models, which we will discuss here, are classification by revenue model and classification by distribution channel.

CLASSIFICATION BY REVENUE MODEL

As discussed in Chapter 1, e-commerce business models are often categorized by the way that revenues are generated. Typical B2C e-tailing models include product sales, subscription, transaction-fee, advertising-supported, and sponsorship models.

- **Product sales models.** Charge customers directly for products or services they buy.
- **Subscription models.** Charge a fixed monthly or annual subscription fee for the service provided to the customer.
- **Transaction-fee models.** Charge a service fee based on the volume and value of transactions offered.
- **Advertising-supported models.** Instead of charging users, the company charges advertisers. Alternatively, the ad revenues can be an additional source of income in subscription and/or transaction-fee models.
- **Sponsorship models.** Some companies may sponsor an e-business for non-financial reasons (e.g., for marketing purposes). This model is usually a supplementary source of income.

CLASSIFICATION BY DISTRIBUTION CHANNEL

Another common way of classifying e-tailing business models is to look at the distribution channel. Here we distinguish three categories:

- **Direct marketing.** Manufacturers, such as Dell, Nike, Lego, or Sony, market directly from company sites to individual customers.
- **Pure-play e-tailers.** These e-tailers have no physical stores, only an online sales presence. Amazon.com is an example of a pure-play e-tailer.
- **Click-and-mortar retailers.** These are traditional retailers with a supplementary Web site (e.g., Walmart.com or Homedepot.com).

Direct Marketing by Manufacturers or Mail-Order Companies

direct marketing
Broadly, marketing that takes place without intermediaries between manufacturers and buyers; in the context of this book, marketing done online between the seller and the buyer.

In a broad sense, **direct marketing** describes marketing that takes place without intermediaries between manufacturers and buyers. Direct marketers take orders directly from consumers, bypassing traditional wholesale distribution. The term is used to refer to mail-order catalog sales, supported, if necessary, by telephone interaction with the customer. The Web offers another mechanism for interaction between the manufacturer and the customer. Firms with established, mature mail-order businesses have a distinct advantage in online sales, given their existing payment processing, inventory management, and order fulfillment operations, as shown in EC Application Case 3.1.

Using the Internet, manufacturers can sell directly to customers and provide customer support online. In this sense, the traditional intermediaries are eliminated, or disintermediated. **Disintermediation** refers to the removal of organizations or business process layers responsible for certain intermediary steps in a given supply chain. In the traditional distribution channel, there are intermediating layers between the manufacturer and consumer, such as wholesalers, distributors, and retailers, as shown in Exhibit 3.1. In some countries, such as Japan, one may find inefficient distribution networks with as many as 10 layers of intermediaries. These extra layers can add as much as a 500 percent markup to the manufacturers' prices.

disintermediation
The removal of organizations or business process layers responsible for certain intermediary steps in a given supply chain.

EC APPLICATION CASE 3.1
Individuals and Communities
LANDS' END: HOW A MAIL-ORDER COMPANY MOVED ONLINE

Some of the most successful B2C e-tailers are mail-order companies that were once based solely on paper catalogs. One reason for their success was the logistics system such companies already had in place. Here we look at Lands' End, a successful direct-marketing company that served over 6.2 million customers in 2000. The company is well known for its quality products, casual-styled clothing, and customer service. Internet sales in 2000 were 10 percent of the company's $1.3 billion total, doubling the 5 percent Internet sales of 1999. Projected Internet sales are 20 percent in 2003.

Lands' End's Web site (*landsend.com*) offers all the company's catalog products. (To show how far the company has come with e-tailing, in 1995, it offered only 100 products online; in 2002, it offered over 300.) Besides the product offerings, the Web site allows women customers to build and store a 3D model of their body (called the Personal Model). The model then recommends outfits that flatter certain body profiles and suggests sizes based upon the customer's measurements. Male customers can use a feature called "Oxford Express" to sort through hundreds of fabrics, styles, collar and cuff options, and sizes within seconds. Personal shopping accounts are also available on the Web site.

In addition, customers can track their order status online and request catalogs using the Internet.

The company has an affiliates network that pays 5 percent commission for every sale that comes from a referral. It also maintains a B2B "store" at *landsend.com/corpsales*. Land's End Live allows online customers to shop with the assistance of a "real" personal shopper. Land's End extends its presence globally by having localized sites in Japan, Germany, and the United Kingdom.

Lands' End operates 16 physical outlets in the United States and 3 in the United Kingdom. Orders made online are shipped from these distribution outlets. Because of their order fulfillment capabilities, U.S. customers usually receive their orders 2 days after they are placed.

As 88 percent of the company's customers are college graduates, most having computers, the company expects its online business to continue to grow rapidly during the next few years.

Source: Compiled from *landsend.com*.

Questions

▶ Discuss the advantage of Lands' End over stores such as the Gap.

▶ Identify the company's critical success factors.

▶ Enter *landsend.com* and configure your ideal outfit. Report on your experience.

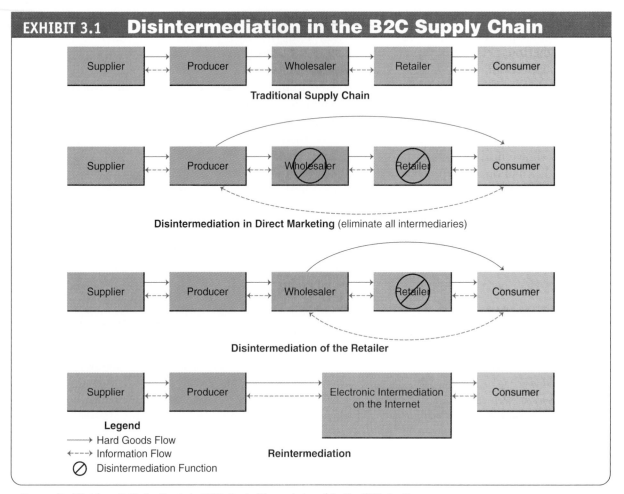

EXHIBIT 3.1   Disintermediation in the B2C Supply Chain

Source: Modified from M. Warkentin et al., 2000. Used with permission of Dr. Merrill Warkentin.

When manufacturers connect directly with consumers and shorten the distribution chain, inefficiencies can be eliminated, product delivery time can be decreased, and manufacturers can build closer relationships with consumers. When the Internet can serve as a replacement for the intermediary in managing information flow from consumers back to the manufacturers, demand can be gauged more accurately and orders can be placed quickly. When the Internet also can provide the opportunity for manufacturers to directly contact consumers to provide product information or information about orders, the need for the traditional intermediaries is reduced or eliminated.

Dell Computer has established itself as one of the world's most successful e-tailers by profitably selling its computers directly to millions of consumers over the Internet. Besides the cost advantages, the parties in direct marketing have a greater opportunity to influence each other. Sellers can understand their markets better because of the direct connection to consumers, and consumers gain greater information about the products through their direct connection to the manufacturers.

Make-to-order online Direct sales by manufacturers are gaining popularity due to the ability to customize products or services, a concept championed by Dell.

Customization is usually an *additional* marketing channel (e.g., see nike.com, lego.com). Direct marketing can more effectively support the consumer's build-to-order requests. EC Application Case 3.2 describes the process by which customers can build cars to order online.

Pure Play E-Tailers

Virtual (pure-play) e-tailers are firms that sell directly to consumers over the Internet without maintaining a physical sales channel. Amazon.com is a prime example of this type of e-tailer. Virtual e-tailers have the advantage of low

virtual (pure-play) e-tailers
Firms that sell directly to consumers over the Internet without maintaining a physical sales channel.

EC APPLICATION CASE 3.2
Individuals and Communities
BUYING CARS ONLINE: BUILD TO ORDER

The world's automobile manufacturers are complex enterprises with thousands of suppliers and millions of customers. Their traditional channel for distributing cars has been the automobile dealer, who orders cars and then sells them from the lot. When a customer wants a particular feature or color, the dealer may have to wait until the "pipeline" of vehicles has that particular car in a delivery.

In the traditional system, the manufacturers conduct market research in order to estimate which features and options will sell well, and then make the cars they wish to sell. In some cases, certain cars are ultimately sold from stock at a loss when the market exhibits insufficient demand for a particular vehicle. The carmakers have long operated under this "build-to-stock" environment where they build cars that are carried as inventory during the outbound logistics process (ships, trucks, trains, and dealers' lots). General Motors estimates that it holds as much as $40 billion worth of parts and unsold vehicles in its distribution channels. Other automakers hold similar amounts.

Ford and GM, along with many other carmakers around the world, have announced plans to implement a "build-to-order" program much like the Dell approach to building computers. These auto giants intend to transform themselves from build-to-stock companies to build-to-order companies, thereby cutting inventory requirements in half (Simison 2000), while at the same time giving customers exactly what they want.

As an example of this trend toward build-to-order mass customization in the new car market, Jaguar car buyers can build a dream car online. On Jaguar's Web site, consumers are able to custom configure their car's features and components, see it online, price it, and have it delivered to a nearby dealer. Using a virtual car on the Web site, customers can view in real time more than 1,250 possible exterior combinations, rotate the image 360 degrees, and see the price updated automatically with each selection of trim or accessories. After storing the car in a virtual garage, the customer can decide on the purchase and select a dealer at which to pick up the completed car. (Thus conflicts with the established dealer network channel are avoided.) The Web site helps primarily with the research process—it is not a fully transactional site. The configuration, however, is transmitted to the production floor, thereby reducing delivery time and contributing to increased customer satisfaction.

Questions

▶ Relate this case to the concept of mass customization.

▶ How is channel conflict avoided?

▶ What are the benefits of customization to the company? To the customer?

overhead costs and streamlined processes. Virtual e-tailers may be general purpose or specialized.

General purpose e-tailers sell a broad range of products to a large number of consumers. They leverage their expertise in order fulfillment or personalization to reach great numbers of customers so they can maximize revenues. Amazon.com, which started as a book and music e-tailer, now sells many other types of products, either directly or through their alliances with other firms.

Specialty or *niche e-tailers* sell to a specific market segment. They leverage their expertise in one specific product area to assemble the items that are in greatest demand and use the most effective practices to appeal to their potential customers. Some examples of market segments for which there are specialty e-tailers include flowers, consumer electronic products, computer hardware and software, automobiles, books, CDs, and clothing. Specialty e-tailers can operate in a very narrow market. See the CatToys.com example in EC Application Case 3.3 for an example. Such a specialized business could not survive in the physical world; it would not have enough customers.

brick-and-mortar retailers
Retailers who do business in the non-Internet, physical world in traditional brick-and-mortar stores.

click-and-mortar retailers
Brick-and-mortar retailers with a transactional Web site from which to conduct business.

Click-and-Mortar Retailers

Brick-and-mortar retailers are retailers that conduct business in the physical world, in traditional brick-and-mortar stores. The third type of online retailer is a **click-and-mortar retailer**, a brick-and-mortar retailer with an added-on transactional Web site. Traditional retailing frequently involves a single distribution

---

EC APPLICATION CASE 3.3
Individuals and Communities
CATTOYS.COM, A SPECIALTY E-TAILER

CatToys.com is a specialized e-tail site that sells cat toys to cat owners. The Web site is designed to appeal to cat enthusiasts, with cat images everywhere and informal fonts to put buyers at ease. It has no banner ads, is easy to navigate, is updated weekly, and displays products in clear categories. The company's retail prices are comparable to those of pet stores and are kept low through aggressive cost control. The site offers weekly specials and wholesale prices for qualified businesses. Buyers can receive discounts by donating cat toys to animal shelters. Marketing is mostly accomplished through search engines and an affiliate program. The site has no membership or personalization features.

CatToys.com hosts its site on Yahoo!, which allows it to use sophisticated technology (cookies for the shopping-cart process and payment security), while having access to a large audience. This enables

CatToys.com to concentrate on its core competency, selecting the right cat toys and marketing them effectively. CatToys.com is an example of a low-volume specialized store that attracts people with specific shopping needs.

Source: Compiled from *CatToys.com*.

Questions

▶ Enter *cattoys.com* and examine the company's revenue model.

▶ Examine the relationship between *cattoys.com* and *dogtoys.com*. Can you guess the reason for this relationship?

▶ What are the advantages of *cattoys.com* over *toysrus.com*? What are the disadvantages?

channel, the physical store. In some cases, traditional sellers may also operate a mail-order business. In today's new economy, click-and-mortar retailers sell via stores, through voice phone calls to human operators, with touch-tone phones, over the Internet through interactive Web sites, and by mobile devices. A firm that operates both physical stores and an online e-tail site is said to be a *multichannel store*.

Although there may be practical advantages to being a virtual seller, such as lower overhead costs, there are many drawbacks, which we will discuss later. Therefore, many experts suggest that the ultimate winners in many market segments will be the companies that are able to leverage the best of both worlds using the click-and-mortar approach.

OTHER BUSINESS MODELS

Several other business models are used in B2C. They are discussed in various places throughout the book. Some of these are used in B2B, G2B, etc. A summary of these models is provided in Exhibit 3.2.

In the following sections we will describe some of the successful B2C e-tailers.

EXHIBIT 3.2 Other B2C Business Models

Model Name	Description	Reference in Book
Electronic mall	Like a regular mall, but online. Some provide only links to storefronts, in others you can shop. Examples: *mallchoicemall.com, fashionmall.com* at *beautyjungle.com*.	Chapter 2
Transaction brokers	Electronically mediate between buyers and sellers. Popular in services, travel, job market, stocks, insurance.	Chapters 2, 3, 6
Information portals	Besides information, most provide links to merchants, for which they are paid a commission (affiliate marketing). Some provide hosting and software (e.g., *store.yahoo.com*), some also sell.	Chapters 1, 2
Communities portal	Combining community services with selling or doing affiliate marketing (e.g., *hometownconnections.com*)	Chapters 11
Content creator or disseminators	Provide content to the masses (news, stock data). Also participate in the syndication chain. Examples: *espn.com, reuters.com, cnn.com*.	Chapters 2, 10 (online material)
Viral marketing	Using e-mail or SMS to advertise. Also can sell direct or via affiliates. Example: *blueskyfrog.com*	Chapter 8 (online material)
Market makers	Create and manage many-to-many markets (e.g., *chemconnect.com*); also auction sites (e.g., *ebay.com, dellauction.com*). Aggregating buyers and/or sellers (*ingrammicro.com*).	Chapters 2, 6, and 7
Make-to-order	Manufacturers that customize their products and services via online orders (*dell.com, nike.com, jaguar.com*)	Chapters 1, 2, 3, 5
Service providers	Offer online payments, order fulfillment (delivery), and security. Examples: *paypal.com, netship.com*.	Chapters 3, 10

▶ List the B2C revenue models.

▶ List the B2C distribution channel models.

▶ Describe the direct marketing model.

▶ Describe virtual e-tailing.

▶ Describe the click-and-mortar approach.

▶ List other B2C models.

3.3   TRAVEL AND TOURISM SERVICES ONLINE

The Internet is an ideal place to plan, explore, and arrange almost any trip. Convenience and potential savings are available through special sales and the elimination of travel agents by buying directly from service providers.

Some major travel-related Web sites are expedia.com, orbitz.com, travelocity.com, asiatravel.com, trip.com, travelweb.com, eurovacations.com, priceline.com, and lonelyplanet.com. Online travel services also are provided by all major airlines, vacation services, large conventional travel agencies, car rental agencies, hotels, and tour companies. Publishers of travel guides such as Fodors and Lonely Planet provide considerable amounts of travel-related information on their Web sites (fodors.com and lonelyplanet.com).

SERVICES PROVIDED

Virtual travel agencies offer almost all the services provided by conventional travel agencies, from providing general information to reserving and purchasing tickets, accommodations, and entertainment. In addition, they often provide services that most conventional travel agencies do not offer, such as travel tips provided by people who have experienced certain situations (e.g., a visa problem), electronic travel magazines, fare comparisons, currency conversion calculators, fare tracking (free e-mail alerts on low fares to favorite destinations), worldwide business and place locators, an outlet for travel accessories and books, experts' opinions, major international and travel news, detailed driving maps and directions for the United States and several other countries (see biztravel.com), chat rooms and bulletin boards, and frequent-flier deals. In addition, some offer several other innovative services, such as online travel auctions.

SPECIAL SERVICES

Many online travel services offer travel bargains. For special bargain fares consumers need to go to special sites, such as those offering stand-by tickets. Lastminute.com offers very low airfares and discount accommodations prices to fill otherwise-empty seats and hotel rooms. Last-minute trips can also be booked on americanexpress.com, sometimes at a steep discount. Special vacation destinations can be found at priceline.com, rent-a-holiday.com, stayfinder.com, and greatrentals.com.

Also of interest are sites that offer medical advice and services for travelers. This type of information is available from the World Health Organization (who.int), governments (e.g., cdc.gov/travel), and private organizations (e.g., tripprep.com, medicalert.com, webmd.com).

Wireless Services

Several airlines (e.g., Cathay Pacific, Delta, Qantas Airways) allow customers with WAP cell phones to check their flight status, update frequent flyer miles, and book flights with their cell phones.

Direct Marketing

Airlines sell electronic tickets over the Internet. Using direct marketing techniques, airlines are able to build customer profiles and target specific customers with tailored offers. Many airlines offer "specials" or "cyber offers" on their Web sites (e.g., cathaypacific.com).

Alliances and Consortia

Airlines and other companies are creating alliances to increase sales or reduce purchasing costs (see the Qantas case in Chapter 1). Several alliances exist in Europe, the United States, and Asia. For example, some consortia aggregate participants' Internet-only fares.

BENEFITS AND LIMITATIONS OF ONLINE TRAVEL SERVICES

The benefits of online travel services to travelers are enormous. The amount of free information is tremendous, and it is accessible at anytime from any place. Substantial discounts can be found, especially for those who have time and patience. Providers of travel services also benefit: Airlines, hotels, cruise lines, and so on are selling otherwise-empty spaces.

Online travel services do have some limitations. First, many people do not use the Internet. Second, the amount of time and the difficulty of using virtual travel agencies may be significant, especially for inexperienced Internet surfers. Finally, complex trips require specialized knowledge and arrangements, which may be better done by a knowledgeable, human travel agent. Therefore, the need for travel agents as intermediaries remains, at least for the immediate future. However, as we will show later, intelligent agents may lessen some of these limitations, further reducing the reliance on travel agents.

IMPACT OF EC ON THE TRAVEL INDUSTRY

Bloch and Segev (1997) classify the impacts of EC on the travel industry into 10 categories, ranging from product promotion to new products and new business models. They predict that travel agencies as we know them today will disappear. Only the value-added activities of travel agencies will not be automated, and these will be performed by a new type of organization. These new organizations will serve certain targeted markets and customers (see Van der Heijden 1996). Travel superstores, which will provide many products, services, and entertainment, may enter the industry, as will innovative individuals operating as travel agents from their homes.

CORPORATE TRAVEL

Corporations can use all of the travel services mentioned earlier. However, many large corporations receive additional services from large travel agencies. To reduce corporate travel costs, companies can make arrangements that enable employees to plan and book their own trips. Using online optimization tools provided by travel companies (such as those offered at rosenbluth.com), companies can try to reduce travel costs even further. Travel authorization software that checks availability of funds and compliance with corporate guidelines is usually provided by travel companies such as Rosenbluth International.

The corporate travel market is huge and has been growing rapidly in recent years. One online service that is trying to tap this market is Oracle's e-Travel, which provides software to automate and manage online booking. American Express has teamed with Microsoft and MCI to provide an interactive corporate travel reservation system called AXI, which displays airline seat charts, maps showing hotels, information about nearby health clubs, and weather information. In trying to reduce costs to the corporate client, AXI creates profiles for travelers and their preferences and, thus, tries to satisfy both travelers and corporate travel managers.

INTELLIGENT AGENTS IN TRAVEL SERVICES

There is no doubt that EC will play an even greater role in the travel industry in the future. One area that is very promising is the use of software (intelligent) agents. The agents emulate the work and behavior of human agents in executing organizational processes, such as travel authorization (Bose 1996). Each agent is capable of acting autonomously, cooperatively, and collectively to achieve the stated goal. The system increases organizational productivity by carrying out several tedious watchdog activities, thereby freeing humans to work on more challenging and creative tasks.

Intelligent agents could be involved in buyer–seller negotiations, as shown in the following scenario: You want to take a vacation in Hawaii. First you called a regular travel agent who gave you the impression he was too busy to help you; finally, though, he gave you a plan and a price that you do not like. A friend suggested you use an intelligent agent. Here is how the process works:

1. You visit an online travel site and enter your desired destination, dates, available budget, special requirements, and desired entertainment.
2. Your computer dispatches an intelligent agent that "shops around," entering the Internet and communicating electronically with the databases of airlines, hotels, and other vendors.
3. Your agent attempts to match your requirements against what is available, negotiating with the vendors' agents. These agents may activate other agents to make special arrangements, cooperate with each other, activate multimedia presentations, or make special inquiries.

4. Your agent returns to you within minutes with suitable alternatives. You have a few questions and you want modifications. No problem. Within a few minutes, it's a done deal. No waiting for busy telephone operators and no human errors. Once you approve the deal, the intelligent agent will make the reservations, arrange for payments, and even report to you about any unforeseen delays in your departure.

How do you communicate with your software agent? By voice, of course. This scenario is not as far off as it may seem. Such a scenario may be possible by 2005.

> ▶ What travel services are available online that are not available off-line?
>
> ▶ List the benefits of online travel services to travelers and to service providers.
>
> ▶ What role do intelligent agents have in travel services?

3.4 EMPLOYMENT PLACEMENT AND THE JOB MARKET

The online job market connects individuals who are looking for a job with employers who are looking for employees with specific skills. The job market is very volatile, and supply and demand are frequently unbalanced. Traditionally, job matching has been done in several ways, ranging from ads in classified sections of newspapers to the use of corporate recruiters, commercial employment agencies, and headhunting companies. The job market has now moved online. Advantages of the online job market over the traditional one are listed in Exhibit 3.3.

EXHIBIT 3.3 Traditional vs. Online Job Markets

	Traditional Job Market	Online Job Market
Cost	Expensive, especially in prime space	Can be very inexpensive
Life cycle	Short	Long
Place	Usually local and limited if global	Global
Context updating	Can be complex, expensive	Fast, simple, inexpensive
Space for details	Limited	Large
Ease of search by applicant	Difficult, especially for out-of-town applicants	Quick and easy
Ability of employers to find applicants	May be very difficult, especially for out-of-town applicants	Easy
Matching of supply and demand	Difficult	Easy
Reliability	Material can be lost in mail	High
Communication speed between employees and employers	Can be slow	Fast
Ability of employees to compare jobs	Limited	Easy, fast

THE INTERNET JOB MARKET

The Internet offers a perfect environment for job seekers and companies searching for hard-to-find employees. The online job market is especially effective for technology-oriented companies and jobs because these companies and workers use the Internet regularly. However, there are thousands of other types of companies that advertise available positions, accept resumes, and take applications over the Internet. The following parties use the Internet job market:

1. **Job seekers.** Job seekers can reply to employment ads. Or, they can take the initiative and place their resumes on their own home pages or on others' Web sites, send messages to members of newsgroups asking for referrals, and use recruiting firms such as headhunter.net, asiajobsearch.org, hotjobs.com, and monster.com. For entry-level jobs and internships for newly minted graduates, job seekers can use jobdirect.com.

2. **Employers seeking employees.** Many organizations advertise openings on their Web sites. Others advertise job openings on popular public portals, online newspapers, bulletin boards, and with recruiting firms. Employers can conduct interviews and administer tests on the Web.

3. **Job agencies.** Hundreds of job agencies are active on the Web. They use their own Web pages to post available job descriptions and advertise their services in e-mails and at other Web sites. Recruiters use newsgroups, online forums, bulletin boards, Internet commercial resume services, and portals such as Yahoo! and AOL.

4. **Government agencies and institutions.** Many government agencies advertise openings for government positions on their Web sites and on other sites. In addition, some government agencies use the Internet to help job seekers find jobs elsewhere, as done in Hong Kong and the Philippines (see EC Application Case 3.4).

BENEFITS AND LIMITATIONS OF THE ELECTRONIC JOB MARKET

As indicated earlier, the electronic job market offers a variety of benefits for both job seekers and employers. These advantages are shown in Exhibit 3.4.

Probably the biggest limitation of the online job market is the fact that many people do not use the Internet. This limitation is even more serious with nontechnology-oriented jobs. To overcome this problem, companies may use both traditional advertising approaches and the Internet. However, the trend is clear: Over time, more and more of the job market will be on the Internet. One solution to the problem of limited access is the use of kiosks (as described in EC Application Case 3.4).

Security and privacy may be another limitation. For one thing, resumes and other online communications are usually not encrypted, so one's job-seeking activities may not be secure. For another, there is the possibility that someone at your current place of employment (possibly even your boss) may find out that you are job hunting. The electronic job market may also create high turnover costs for

EC APPLICATION CASE 3.4
Individuals and Communities

MATCHING WORKERS WITH JOBS IN THE PHILIPPINES

The Philippines is a country with many skilled employees but with few open jobs. In January 1999, the government created a special Web site that matches people with jobs. The site is part of a computerized project of the Department of Labor, and it is a free service.

For those who do not have computers or Internet access, the government located computer terminals (kiosks) in hundreds of locations throughout the country. The kiosk system is also connected with Philippine embassies, especially in countries where there are many overseas Filipino workers, so that they can find a job and return home. Government employees help those applicants who do not know how to use the system.

This system gives job seekers a chance to find a job that would best suit their qualifications. At the heart of the system is its matchmaking capabilities.

For the matchmaking process, a database stores all the job vacancies submitted by different employers. Another database stores the job applications fed into the system. The system matches qualified applicants with companies. It also automatically does a ranking based on the matches. This job-matching feature differentiates this site from other online job sites. Everything is done electronically, so job seekers can see the match results in seconds.

Source: Anonymous, *Computerworld Hong Kong*, January 14, 1999.

Questions

▶ What is the role of Internet kiosks?
▶ How are jobs matched with applicants?

EXHIBIT 3.4 Advantages of the Electronic Job Market for Job Seekers and Employers

Advantages for Job Seekers

▶ Can find information on a large number of jobs worldwide
▶ Can communicate quickly with potential employers
▶ Can market themselves directly to potential employers (e.g. *discoverme.com*)
▶ Can write and post resumes for large-volume distribution (e.g., *careerbuilder* at *headhunter.net*, *jobweb.com*, *brassring.com*).
▶ Can search for jobs quickly from any location
▶ Can obtain several support services at no cost (e.g., career planning is provided by *hotjobs.com* and *monster.com*)
▶ Job seekers can assess their market value (e.g., *wageweb.com* and *rileyguide.com*; look for salary surveys).
▶ Can learn how to use their voice effectively in an interview (*greatvoice.com*)
▶ Can access newsgroups that are dedicated to finding jobs (and keeping them)

Advantages for Employers

▶ Can advertise to a large numbers of job seekers
▶ Can save on advertisement costs
▶ Can reduce application processing costs by using electronic application forms
▶ Can provide greater equal opportunity for job seekers
▶ Increased chance of finding highly skilled employees

employers, by accelerating employees' movement to better jobs. Finally, finding candidates online is more complicated than most people think, mostly due to the large number of resumes available online. Some sites offer prescreening of candidates (e.g., jobtrak.com), which may alleviate this problem.

INTELLIGENT AGENTS IN THE ELECTRONIC JOB MARKET

The large number of available jobs and resumes online makes it difficult both for employers and employees to search the Internet for useful information. Intelligent agents can solve this problem by matching openings and jobs (see Exhibit 3.5).

Intelligent Agents for Job Seekers

A free service that uses intelligent agents to search the Internet's top job sites and databases for job postings based on users' profiles is offered at careershop.com. Users can create as many as five different profiles based on more than 100 different job categories, geographic regions, and key words. Users receive a daily e-mail containing job opportunities from over a dozen top job sites around the Internet (e.g., careermosaic at headhunter.net), that match their career interests. This saves the users a tremendous amount of time.

Intelligent Agents for Employers

A special intelligent-agent powered search engine helps employers find resumes that match specific job descriptions. Here is how the search engine Resumix describes its product on its Web site (resumix.com):

> From the time a position becomes available or a resume is received, Resumix gives you the control while dispersing the work. Hiring mana-

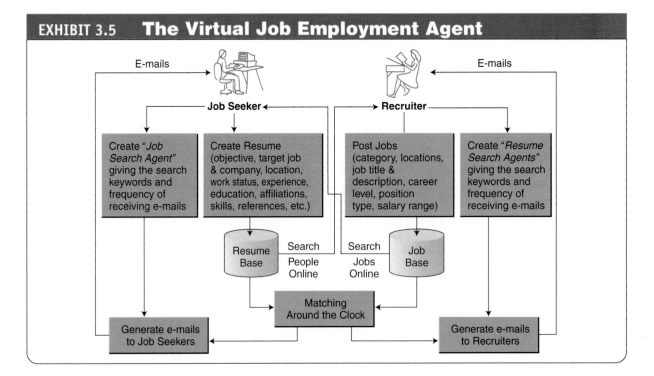

EXHIBIT 3.5   The Virtual Job Employment Agent

gers can open jobs; operators can scan resumes; and you can search for a candidate or identify employees for training programs, redeployment opportunities, or new initiatives.

The core of this powerful system is Resumix's Knowledge Base. As an expert system, it goes beyond simply matching words. The Knowledge Base interprets a candidate's resume, determining skills based on context and matching those skills to the position criteria. For example, you might be looking for a product manager. Being a member of the AMA (American Marketing Association) might be one of the desirable properties for the job. However, with a basic keyword search, you might get candidates who have listed AMA, but are really members of the American Medical Association or American Meatpackers Association. Those are not relevant to your search. Resumix Knowledge Base would select only the candidates with relevant skills.

▶ What are the driving forces of the electronic job market?

▶ What are the major advantages of the electronic job market to the candidate? To employers?

▶ Describe the role of intelligent agents in the electronic job market.

3.5   REAL ESTATE, INSURANCE, AND STOCK TRADING ONLINE

REAL ESTATE ONLINE

Real estate transactions are an ideal area for EC for a number of reasons. First, potential home buyers can view many properties online, saving time for the buyer and for the broker. Second, potential home buyers can sort and organize properties according to specific criteria and preview the exterior and interior design of the properties, shortening the search process. Finally, potential home buyers can find detailed information about the properties and frequently get more detailed real estate listings than brokers will provide.

In some locations, real estate databases are only available to realtors over private networks in their offices, but in many cities, this information is available to potential buyers from their personal Internet connections. For example, realtor.com allows buyers to search a database of over 1 million homes located all over the United States. The database is composed of local multiple listings of all available properties and of properties just sold, in hundreds of locations. Realtor Cushman and Wakefield of New York (cushwake.com) also uses the Internet to sell commercial property.

Builders, too, now use virtual reality technology on their Web sites to demonstrate three-dimensional floor plans to home buyers. "Virtual models" enable buyers to "walk through" three-dimensional mock-ups of homes.

Real Estate Applications

The real estate industry is just starting to discover EC. Some real estate applications and services, with their representative Web addresses, are shown in the following list. More applications and services are sure to proliferate in the coming years.

- Assist2sell.com offers advice to consumers on buying or selling a home.
- International Real Estate Directory and News (ired.com) is a comprehensive real estate Web site.
- A national listing of properties for sale can be found at homesinamerica.com.
- Commercial real estate listings can be found at commercialproperty.com.
- Listings of residential real estate in multiple databases can be viewed at homescout.com and realestate.yahoo.com.
- The National Association of Realtors, realtor.com, has links to house listings in all major cities.
- Maps are available on mapquest.com and realestate.yahoo.com.
- Information on current mortgage rates is available at bankrate.com, eloan.com, and quickenloans.quicken.com.
- Mortgage comparisons and calculations and other financing information are available from eloan.com and quickenloans.quicken.com.
- Mortgage brokers can pass loan applications over the Internet and receive bids from lenders who want to issue mortgages (e.g., eloan.com).
- Online lenders such as arcsystems.com can approve loans online.
- To automate the closing of real estate transactions, which are notorious for the paperwork involved, see closeyourdeal.com.
- Home seller sites such as owners.com provide a place for persons who want to sell their homes privately, without using a real estate agent. Decided not to buy? Rental properties are listed on homestore.net. Several services are available, including a virtual walk-through of some listings.

In general, online real estate is supporting rather than replacing existing agents. Due to the complexity of the process, real estate agents are still charging high commissions. However, several Web sites have started to offer services at lower commissions (e.g., see Assist2sell.com).

Real Estate Mortgages

Large numbers of companies compete in the residential mortgage market. Several online companies are active in this area (e.g., lendingtree.com, eloan.com). Many sites offer loan calculators. Mortgage brokers can pass loan applications over the Internet and receive bids from lenders who want to issue mortgages. Priceline.com offers its "name your own price" model for residential loans. In another case, a Singaporean company aggregates loan seekers and then places the package for bid on the Internet. Some institutions approve loans online in 10 minutes and settle in 5 days (e.g., homeside.com.au).

INSURANCE ONLINE

An increasing number of companies use the Internet to offer standard insurance policies such as auto, home, life, or health at a substantial discount. Furthermore, third-party aggregators offer free comparisons of available policies. Several large insurance and risk-management companies offer comprehensive insurance contracts online. Although many people do not trust the faceless insurance agent, others are eager to take advantage of the reduced premiums. For example, a visit to insurerate.com will show a variety of different policies. Order.com allows customers and businesses to compare car insurance offerings and then make a purchase online. Some other popular insurance sites include quotesmith.com, insweb.com, insurance.com, ebix.com, and quicken.com. Many insurance companies use a dual strategy (MacSweeney 2000), keeping human agents but also selling online.

ONLINE STOCK TRADING

Although U.S. stock traders were among the first to embrace the Internet, traders in Korea really love it. By 2002, more than 67 percent of all stock trades in Korea were transacted online (versus about 30 percent in the United States). Why trade online? Because it makes a lot of "dollars and sense" (Schonfeld 1998).

The commission for an online trade is between $5 and $29, compared to an average fee of $100 from a full-service broker or $35 from a discount broker. With online trading, there are no busy telephone lines, and the chance for error is small as there is no oral communication in a frequently noisy environment. Orders can be placed from anywhere, anytime, day or night, and there is no biased broker to push a sale. Furthermore, investors can find a considerable amount of free information about specific companies or mutual funds.

Several discount brokerage houses initiated extensive online stock trading, notably Charles Schwab, in 1995. Full-service brokerage companies such as Merrill Lynch followed in 1998–1999. By 1999, there were more than 120 brokerage firms offering online trading. In the United States alone, the volume of trading has increased significantly in the last 3 years.

How does online trading work? Let's say an investor has an account with Schwab. The investor accesses Schwab's Web site (schwab.com), enters their account number and password, and clicks on stock trading. Using a menu, the investor enters the details of the order (buy, sell, margin or cash, price limit, or market order). The computer tells the investor the current "ask" and "bid" prices, much as a broker would do over the telephone, and the investor can approve or reject the transaction. The flow chart of this process is shown in Exhibit 3.6 (page 114) for execution on the floor of the New York Stock Exchange. However, companies such as Schwab are now also licensed as exchanges. This allows them to match the selling and buying orders of their own customers for many securities in about 1 to 2 seconds.

Some well-known companies that offer online trading are E*TRADE, Ameritrade, TD Waterhouse, Datek Online, Suretrade, Discover, and Lombard. E*TRADE offers many finance-related services and also challenges investors to participate in a simulated investment game. (For further details on brokers and services provided online, see Gilbert et al. 2000.)

EXHIBIT 3.6 Online Electronic Stock Trading

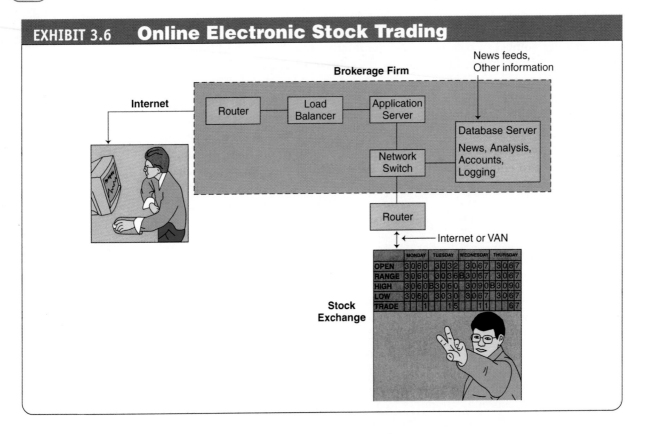

Of the many brokers online, of special interest are datek.com, which provides extremely fast executions, and webstreet.com, which charges no commissions on trades of 1,000 shares or more on NASDAQ. However, the most innovative service is that of E*TRADE. Note that in 1999, E*TRADE started its own portfolio of mutual funds. E*TRADE is expanding rapidly into several countries, enabling global stock trading.

Investment Information

There is an almost unlimited amount of investment-related information available online, mostly free (usually in exchange for a registration). Here are some examples:

▸ Current financial news is available at CNN Financial (money.cnn.com). This portal also has large amounts of company information, all free. Similar information is available at Hoover's (hoovers.com) and Bloomberg (bloomberg.com).

▸ Municipal bond prices are available at bloomberg.com.

▸ A good source of overall market information, with many links to other financial sites, is cyberinvest.com.

▸ Free "Guru" advice is available from upside.com and thestreet.com.

▸ Stock screening and evaluation tools are available at multexinvestor.com and money.cnn.com.

▶ Articles from the *Journal of the American Association of Individual Investors* can be read at aaii.com.

▶ The latest on funding and pricing of initial public offerings (IPOs) is available at hoovers.com/ipo and at ipodata.com.

▶ Chart lovers will enjoy bigcharts.com. Charts are also available on many other sites.

▶ Mutual fund evaluation tools and other interesting investment information are available from Morningstar (morningstar.com).

▶ Earnings estimates and much more are available at firstcall.com.

▶ Almost anything that anyone would need to know about finance and stocks can be found at finance.yahoo.com.

Most of these services are free. Many other services relating to global investing, portfolio tracking, and investor education are also available. An example of finding free information on a mutual fund is shown in the Insights and Additions box below.

Related Markets

In addition to stocks, online trading is expanding to include mutual funds, commodities, financial derivatives, and more. Futures exchanges around the world are moving to electronic trading. For example, the Chicago Board of Trade, the world's largest futures exchange, is offering full-range electronic trading.

▶ List the major online real estate applications.

▶ What are the advantages of online stock tracking?

▶ What investment information is available online?

Insights and Additions   **Can the Web Simplify the Picking of a Mutual Fund?**

A number of free Web sites allow you to scan mutual-fund offerings to find a suitable investment sector, country to invest in, and risk profile. For example, *Morningstar.com* not only rates mutual funds, but also provides a search engine to help you narrow your search. Use the "Fund selector" option and go to "Morningstar category." For example, if you want to invest in Southeast Asia, you can find funds operating not only from the United States, but also from Hong Kong, Singapore, or Malaysia. Once you have picked your market, you can segment it by the size of the fund, by return on investment during the last 5 or 10 years, and other criteria. You can consider the fund's risk level and even the fund-manager's tenure. The site has news and chat rooms for each fund. It also lets you look at the top-10 holdings of most funds.

Other evaluation sites similar to Morningstar, such as *Lipperweb.com*, also rank funds by volatility. You can get fund details and charts showing past performance against a relevant index for each fund.

3.6 BANKING AND PERSONAL FINANCE ONLINE

electronic banking (e-banking)
Various banking activities conducted from home or the road using an Internet connection; also known as *cyberbanking, virtual banking, online banking,* and *home banking.*

Electronic banking (e-banking), also known as cyberbanking, virtual banking, online banking, and home banking, includes various banking activities conducted from home, business, or on the road instead of at a physical bank location. Consumers can use e-banking to pay bills online or to secure a loan electronically. Today, many traditional banks around the world offer diversified e-banking services (e.g., see main.hangseng.com).

Electronic banking saves time and money for users. For banks, it offers an inexpensive alternative to branch banking and a chance to enlist remote customers. Many physical banks are beginning to offer home banking services, and some use EC as a major competitive strategy. One such bank is Wells Fargo (wellsfargo.com). Overall, 15 million online bank accounts were active in 2002 in the United States; 25 million are projected by 2004.

HOME BANKING CAPABILITIES

The major capabilities of home banking include the following:

- **Get current account balances at anytime.** Consumers can easily check the status of their checking, savings, credit card, and money market accounts.
- **Obtain charge and credit card statements.** Users can even set up their account to pay off cards automatically every month.
- **Pay bills.** Electronic payments from accounts are normally credited the same day or the next. The cost of paying bills electronically may be less than the postage involved in sending out a large number of payments each month.
- **Download account transactions.** Account transactions can easily be imported into money management software such as Quicken.
- **Transfer money between accounts.** No more waiting in lines, filling out deposit slips, and running to the ATM.
- **Balance accounts.** If you are the kind of person who forgets to record ATM withdrawals, online banking may help you get organized. Just download the transactions and import them into your register.
- **Send e-mail to the bank.** Got a problem with an account? Users can send a quick note to their online bank representative.
- **Expand the meaning of "banker's hours."** Consumers can manage their money and bills on their own schedules.
- **Handle finances when traveling.** Consumers can access accounts when they are on the road and even arrange for bill payments to be made in their absence.
- **Use additional services.** Customers of some banks receive free phone banking with their online banking service, all for a $5 to $7 monthly fee. Union Bank of California throws in free checking, ATM withdrawals, and bill paying (for 1 year). Several banks, such as Bank of America, waive regular checking charges if consumers sign up for online banking.

Electronic banking offers several of the EC benefits listed in Chapter 1, both to the bank and to its customers, such as expanding the bank's customer base and saving on the cost of paper transactions (Gosling 2000). In addition to regular banks adding online services, virtual banks have emerged that only conduct online transactions. The Security First Network Bank (SFNB) was the first such bank to offer secure banking transactions on the Web (sfnb.com). Its home page looked like the lobby of a bank. The bank offered savings and checking accounts, certificates of deposit, money market accounts, joint accounts, check imaging, and other services. To attract customers, SFNB offered very-high-interest yields for CDs and money market accounts and allowed access to information from various locations. In March 1998, SFNB sold its online banking operations to Royal Bank of Canada, which needed the online services to serve its customers while they are vacationing in the United States. SFNB created a software company that is marketing the online banking software to other banks. Other representative virtual banks in the United States are netbank.com and First Internet Bank (firstib.com). Virtual banks exist in many other countries (e.g., bankdirect.co.nz). In some countries, virtual banks are involved in stock trading (e.g., see Bank One at oneinvest.com) and stockbrokers are doing banking (e.g., see etrade.com).

A word of caution about virtual banking: Before sending money to any cyberbank, especially those that promise high interest rates for your deposits, make sure that the bank is a legitimate one. Several cases of fraud have already occurred.

INTERNATIONAL AND MULTIPLE-CURRENCY BANKING

International banking and the ability to handle trades in multiple currencies are critical for international trading. Although some international retail purchasing can be done by providing a credit card number, other transactions may require international banking support. Examples of such cross-border support include:

- Hong Kong Bank developed a special system called HEXAGON to provide electronic banking in Asia. Using this system, the bank has leveraged its reputation and infrastructure in the developing economies of Asia to become a major international bank rapidly, without developing an extensive new branch network (Peffers and Tunnainen 1998). For details of this system, see the HEXAGON case on the Web site (prenhall.com/turban).

- Tradecard and MasterCard have developed a multiple-currency system for global transactions (see tradecard.com).

- Bank of America and most other major banks offer international capital raising, cash management, trades and services, foreign exchange, risk management investments, merchant services, and special services for international traders.

- Fxall.com is a multidealer foreign exchange service that enables faster and cheaper foreign exchange transactions. Special services are being established for stock market traders who need to pay for foreign stocks (e.g., Charles Schwab).

IMPLEMENTATION ISSUES IN ONLINE FINANCIAL TRANSACTIONS

As you might expect, the implementation of online banking and online stock trading are interrelated. In many instances, one financial institution offers both services. The following are some implementation issues for online financial transactions.

Securing Financial Transactions

Financial transactions such as home banking and online trading must be very secure. In Chapter 10, we discuss the details of secure EC payment systems. In EC Application Case 3.5, we give an example of how Bank of America provides security and privacy to its customers.

Using Banks' Intranets

Many banks provide their large business customers with personalized service by allowing them access to the bank's intranet. For example, Bank of America allows its customers access to accounts, historical transactions, and other data, including intranet-based decision-support applications, which may be of interest to large-business customers. Bank of America also allows its small-business customers to apply for loans through its Web site.

Using Imaging Systems

Several financial institutions (e.g., Bank of America) allow customers to view images of all of their incoming checks, invoices, and other related online correspondence. Image access can be simplified with the help of a search engine.

Pricing Online Versus Off-Line Services

Computer-based banking services are offered free by some banks, whereas others charge $5 to $10 a month. Also, some banks charge fees for individual transactions (e.g., fee per check, per transfer, and so on). Financial institutions must carefully think through the pricing of online and off-line services. Pricing issues must take into account the costs of providing the different types of services, the organization's desire to attract new customers, and the prices offered by competitors.

Risks

Online banks, as well as click-and-mortar banks, may carry some risks and problems, especially in international banking. Some believe that virtual banks carry liquidity risk (the risk of not having sufficient funds to pay obligations as they come due) and could be more susceptible to panic withdrawals. Regulators are grappling with the safeguards that need to be imposed on e-banking.

PERSONAL FINANCE ONLINE

Individuals often combine electronic banking with portfolio management and personal finance. Also, brokerage firms such as Schwab offer personal finance services such as retirement planning. However, specialized personal finance vendors

EC APPLICATION CASE 3.5

Individuals and Communities

ONLINE SECURITY AT BANK OF AMERICA

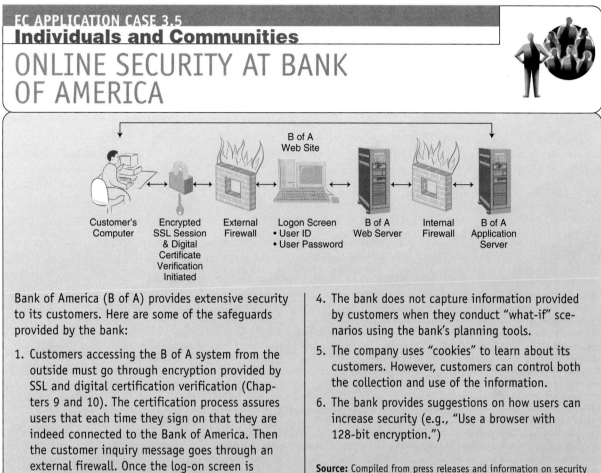

Bank of America (B of A) provides extensive security to its customers. Here are some of the safeguards provided by the bank:

1. Customers accessing the B of A system from the outside must go through encryption provided by SSL and digital certification verification (Chapters 9 and 10). The certification process assures users that each time they sign on that they are indeed connected to the Bank of America. Then the customer inquiry message goes through an external firewall. Once the log-on screen is reached, a user ID and a password are required. This information flows through a direct Web server, then goes through an internal firewall to the application server. (See the above illustration.)

2. The bank maintains accurate information. Corrections are made quickly.

3. Information is shared among the company's family of partners only for legitimate business purposes. Sharing information with outside companies is done with extreme care.

4. The bank does not capture information provided by customers when they conduct "what-if" scenarios using the bank's planning tools.

5. The company uses "cookies" to learn about its customers. However, customers can control both the collection and use of the information.

6. The bank provides suggestions on how users can increase security (e.g., "Use a browser with 128-bit encryption.")

Source: Compiled from press releases and information on security from Bank of America's Web site (*bankofamerica.com*).

Questions

▶ Why is security so important for the bank?

▶ Why is there a need for two firewalls?

▶ Who is protected by the bank's security system—the customer, the bank, or both? Elaborate.

---

offer more diversified services (Tyson 2000). For example, both Quicken (from Intuit) and Microsoft's Money offer the following capabilities:

▶ Bill paying and electronic check writing.

▶ Tracking of bank accounts, expenditures, and credit cards.

▶ Portfolio management, including reports and capital gains (losses) computations.

▶ Investment tracking and monitoring of securities.

▶ Stock quotes and past and current prices of stocks.

▶ Personal budget organization.

▶ Record keeping of cash flow and profit and loss computations.

▶ Tax computations and preparations (Also see riahome.com and taxlogic.com).

▶ Retirement goals, planning, and budgeting.

Although Quicken is the most popular personal finance software, there are more sophisticated packages such as Prosper (from Ernst & Young) and CAPTOOL (captools.com). All of these products are available as independent software programs for the Internet or are coupled with other services, such as those offered by America Online (AOL).

Online Billing and Bill-Paying

In August 1998, 90 percent of people surveyed in the Bay Area of California indicated a desire to pay their bills on the Internet. People prefer to pay monthly bills, such as telephone, utilities, credit cards, cable television, and so on, online. The recipients of such payments are even more eager than the payers to receive money online, as online payments have lower processing costs.

The following are the major existing payment systems:

▶ **Automatic transfer of mortgage payments.** This method has existed since the late 1980s. The payee authorizes their bank to pay the mortgage directly from their bank account, including escrow for tax payments.

▶ **Automatic transfer of funds to pay monthly utility bills.** Since fall 1998, the city of Long Beach has allowed its customers to pay their gas and water bills automatically from their bank accounts. Many other utilities worldwide provide such an option.

▶ **Paying bills from online banking accounts.** Payments from online bank accounts can be made into any bank account. Many people pay their monthly rent and other bills directly into the payees' bank accounts.

▶ **Merchant-to-customer direct billing.** Under this model, a merchant such as American Express posts bills on its Web site where customers can then view and pay them. Several utilities in Los Angeles allow customers to pay bills on the utilities' Web sites, charging customers 20 cents per transaction, which is less than the price of a stamp. However, this means that customers have to go to many Web sites to pay all their bills.

▶ **Using an intermediary.** In this model, a third party such as MSFDS (Microsoft and First Data Corporation) consolidates all of a customer's bills at one site and in a standard format. Collecting a commission on each transaction, the intermediary makes it convenient both to the payee and payer to complete transactions. This latest model is of interest to many vendors, including E*TRADE and Intuit.

▶ **Person-to-person direct payment.** An example of this is Paypal (paypal.com). This service enables you to send funds to another individual over the Internet, by opening an account with Paypal and charging on a credit card or bank account the amount you want to send. Paypal alerts by e-mail the person to whom you want to send the funds, and he or she accesses the account and transfers the funds to a credit card or bank account. Paypal is being followed by a number of competitors (see Chapter 10).

Online billing and bill-paying can be classified into B2C, B2B, or C2C. In this section, we have focused largely on B2C services, which help consumers to save time and payees to save on processing costs. However, large opportunities also exist in B2B services, which can save businesses about 50 percent of billing costs. In Hong Kong, for example, CitiCorp links suppliers, buyers, and banks on one platform, enabling automatic payments.

- ▶ List the capabilities of online banking. Which of these capabilities would be most beneficial to you?
- ▶ Discuss some implementation issues of financial services.
- ▶ List the major personal finance services available online.
- ▶ Explain online bill paying.

3.7   ON-DEMAND DELIVERY SERVICES

Most e-tailers use common carriers to deliver product to customers. They may use the postal system within their country or they may use private shippers such as Airborne Express, Tiger, FedEx, or UPS. Delivery can be made within days or overnight if the customer is willing to pay for the expedited shipment.

Some e-tailers and direct marketing manufacturers own a fleet of delivery vehicles and incorporate the delivery function into their business plan in order to provide greater value to the consumer. These firms will either provide regular deliveries on a daily or other regular schedule or will deliver items within very short periods of time, usually 1 hour. They may also provide additional services to increase the value proposition for the buyer. The online grocer, or **e-grocer**, is a typical example of businesses in this category. Home delivery of food from restaurants is another example. In addition, there is a class of firms (groceries, office supplies, repair parts, and pharmaceutical products) that promise virtually instantaneous or at least same-day delivery of third-party goods to consumers.

Whether the delivery is made by company-owned vehicles or outsourced to a carrier, an express delivery model is referred to as an **on-demand delivery service**. In such a model, shown in Exhibit 3.7, the delivery must be done fairly quickly after an order is received. (For more on this topic, see Chapter 10.) A variation of this model is *same-day delivery*. According to this model, delivery is done faster than "overnight" but slower than the 30 to 60 minutes expected in on-demand delivery. E-grocers often deliver using the same-day delivery model.

e-grocer
A grocer that will take orders online and provide regular deliveries on a daily or other regular schedule or will deliver items within a very short period of time.

on-demand delivery service
Express delivery made fairly quickly after an online order is received.

THE CASE OF E-GROCERS

The U.S. grocery market is valued at over $300 billion annually. Online grocery sales exceeded $5 billion in 2000, and Andersen Consulting projects that the market will top out at $85 billion by 2007, capturing about 15 percent of

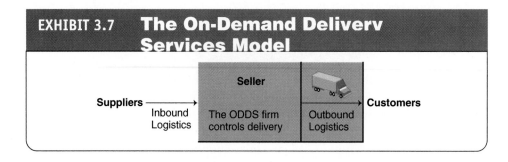

EXHIBIT 3.7   The On-Demand Delivery Services Model

U.S. households. Most e-grocers are click-and-mortar retailers that operate in the countries where they have physical stores, such as Woolworths in Australia (woolworths.com.au).

All e-grocers offer consumers the ability to order items online and have them delivered to their houses. Some e-grocers offer free regular "unattended" weekly delivery (e.g., to your garage), based on a monthly subscription model. Others offer on-demand deliveries (if you are at home), with a surcharge added to the grocery bill and sometimes an additional delivery charge. One e-tail grocer sells only nonperishable items shipped via common carrier. Many offer additional services, such as dry cleaning pickup and delivery. Other add-on features include "don't run out" automatic reordering of routine foods or home-office supplies, as well as fresh flower delivery, movie rentals, meal planning, recipe tips, multimedia features, and nutritional information.

Who Are the E-Grocery Shoppers?

An extensive survey conducted by the Consumer Direct Cooperative pointed to six major groups of potential online grocery shoppers, some of whom are more likely to use online grocers than others. The survey identified the following groups:

- Shopping avoiders; people who dislike going to the grocery store.
- Necessity users who are limited in their ability to shop (e.g., disabled and elderly people, shoppers without cars).
- "New technologists" who are young and comfortable with technology.
- Time-starved, extremely busy consumers who will pay to free up time in their schedules.
- Consumers who gain a sense of self-worth from online shopping.
- Older individuals who enjoy shopping in any type of store.

Online grocery customers are generally repeat customers who order week after week in a tight ongoing relationship with the grocer. The user interaction with the Web site is much more substantial than with other B2C Web sites, and user feedback is also more prevalent. Shopping for groceries online is a very sophisticated purchase compared to most EC shopping transactions. At Amazon.com you may buy one to four items. In an e-grocery purchase, the average order has 54 different items in different food categories (Kruger 2000).

Around the world, many e-tailers are targeting the busy consumer with the promise of home delivery of groceries. Parknshop is the largest supermarket chain in Hong Kong. Parknshop.com offers a "personal shopping list" that helps customers easily order repetitive items on each visit. (The Web site also uses advertising as an additional source of revenue to make the business model a bit more solid.) The Tesco chain in the United Kingdom (tesco.com) is another successful e-grocer. So far, online sales are usually not as profitable as sales in physical grocery stores, due to the delivery costs and low volume of online sales. However, this additional channel allows grocers to increase their sales volume and serve customers who are unable to visit their physical stores. In addition, they can increase their publicity by maintaining an Internet presence.

However, despite the promise that on-demand delivery seems to hold, virtual e-grocers have not been successful in this competitive market. For example, StreamLine.com and ShopLink.com folded in 2000. HomeGrocer.com, WebVan.com (a grocer and delivery company), and Kozmo.com (a well-publicized express delivery company) folded in 2001. Other virtual e-grocers, such as Peapod.com and NetGrocer.com, were struggling as of spring 2002.

▶ Explain on-demand delivery service.

▶ Describe e-grocers and how they operate.

▶ Who are the typical e-grocery shoppers? (Would you shop online for groceries?)

3.8 ONLINE DELIVERY OF DIGITAL PRODUCTS, ENTERTAINMENT, AND MEDIA

Certain goods, such as software, music, or news stories, may be distributed in a physical form (such as CD-ROM, DVD, and newsprint) or they may be digitized and delivered in digital format over the Internet. For example, a consumer may purchase a shrink-wrapped CD-ROM containing software (along with the owner's manual and a warranty card) or they may pay for the software at a Web site and immediately download it onto their computer [usually through File Transfer Protocol (FTP), a fast way to download large files].

As described in Chapter 2, products that can be transformed to digital format and delivered over the Internet are called *digital products*. Exhibit 3.8 (page 124) shows some digital products that may be distributed either physically or digitally. There are advantages and disadvantages to each delivery method for both sellers and buyers. Customers, for example, may prefer the formats available through physical distribution. They perceive value in holding a physical CD-ROM or music CD as opposed to a downloaded file. In addition, the related packaging of a physical product may be significant. Current technology makes a standard music CD more versatile for use in cars and portable devices than a downloaded MP3 file. In some cases, customers enjoy the "liner notes" that accompany a music CD. Paper-based software user manuals and other materials also have value, and may be preferred over online help features. On the other hand, customers may have to wait days for physical products to be delivered.

EXHIBIT 3.8	Distribution of Digital vs. Physical Products	
Type of Product	**Physical Distribution**	**Digital Distribution**
Software	Boxed, shrink-wrapped	FTP, direct download, e-mail
Newspapers, magazines	Home delivery, postal mail	Display on Web, "e-zines"
Greeting cards	Retail stores	E-mail, URL link to recipient
Images (e.g., clipart, graphics)	CD-ROM, magazines	Web site display, downloadable
Movies	DVD, VHS, NTSB, PAL	MPEG3, streaming video: RealNetwork, AVI, QuickTime, etc.
Music	CD, cassette tape	MP3, WAV, RealAudio downloads

For sellers, the costs associated with manufacture, storage, and distribution of physical products (DVDs, CD-ROMs, paper magazines, etc.) can be enormous. Inventory management also becomes a critical cost issue. The need for retail intermediaries requires the establishment of relationships with channel partners and revenue-sharing plans. Direct sales of digital content through digital download, however, allow a producer of digital content to bypass the traditional retail channel, thereby reducing overall costs and capturing greater profits. However, retailers are often crucial in creating demand for a product through in-store displays, advertising, and human sales efforts, all of which are lost when the producer "disintermediates" the traditional channel.

THE NAPSTER EXPERIENCE

With improvements in Internet technologies, the possibility exists for widespread distribution of digital content from businesses to consumers and from consumers to consumers. The rise in importance of Napster, a person-to-person file-sharing tool, coincided with the near universality of computer availability on college campuses and the widespread adoption of MP3 as a music file compression standard. MP3 files are much smaller than earlier file alternatives and allow individuals to download a standard song in far less time. The Napster network does not require the use of a standard Web browser, such as Netscape or Internet Explorer. Nor does the user's client machine actually download the MP3 files from Napster's servers. Rather, Napster only shares "libraries," or lists of songs, and then enables a *peer-to-peer* file-sharing environment in which the individual users literally download the music from each others' machines (called *peers*).

The growth of the "Napster community" (with over 60 million registered users by the end of 2002 and as many as 1.3 million using the service at the same time) was nothing short of phenomenal. It is said to have grown faster than any other community in history. Because of the potential challenge to their revenue sources, the Recording Industry Association of America and five major record labels engaged in a legal battle with Napster, suing it for copyright infringement. Napster argued that its file-sharing never actually published music that could be "pirated" or copied illegally in violation of internationally recognized copyright and licensing laws. However, the court ruled that as a manager of file exchanges, Napster must observe copyright laws (see Chapter 9). Thus free file-sharing is no longer allowed; Napster now must charge customers for use of its file-sharing service.

Napster surprised everyone when it entered into an agreement with Bertelsmann AG, the large global music label based in Germany and a major shareholder in Napster. As part of the deal, Bertelsmann's BMG music unit, which participated in the lawsuit against Napster, agreed to withdraw from the complaint. The latest version of Napster's file-swapping software features a "buy button" that links to CDNow, a Bertelsmann-owned Web site that sells traditional, physical music CDs. The future of this consumer environment is clearly in doubt, though it is clear that technological developments will probably continue to outpace the ability of the market and legal structures to react and adapt. Meanwhile, other peer-to-peer tools have emerged, including Freenet, Gnutella, and P2P.

NEW DEVELOPMENTS IN THE DELIVERY OF DIGITAL PRODUCTS

An interesting development in music distribution is the availability of custom-publishing music CD sites (e.g., see angelfire.com and grabware.com). These sites enable consumers to collect their favorite songs from various artists and master a "personal favorites" compilation CD, which is then shipped to the consumer. The CD mastering sites pay royalties to the various artists through established channels.

Another trend is the disintermediation of traditional print media. Several journals and magazines ceased publishing "dead paper" versions and have become strictly online distributors of digital content, generating revenues through advertising or by online subscriptions. (Some of these transformations were subsequently reversed, due to lack of financial success of the online version.) Other prominent publications, including the *Wall Street Journal*, now offer either a paper-only subscription, an online-only subscription (at a lower subscription price), or a dual-mode subscription for consumers who want to access their business news through both methods.

Similarly, Egghead Software closed all of its brick-and-mortar stores and became a pure-play software store called Egghead.com. In doing so, the company dramatically cut operating costs and streamlined its inventory requirements, but lost certain advantages offered by a physical presence. Egghead.com went out of business in 2001, and its assets were picked up by Amazon.com. Time will tell if digital delivery replaces or enhances traditional delivery methods for various types of digital content.

▶ Describe digital goods and their delivery.

▶ Explain the Napster business model.

▶ What are the benefits and the limitations of digital delivery?

3.9   ONLINE PURCHASE DECISION AIDS

Many sites and tools are available to help online consumers with purchasing decisions. Consumers must decide which product or service to purchase, which site to use for the purchase (a manufacturer site, a general purpose e-tailer, a niche intermediary, or some other site), and what other services to employ. Some sites offer price comparisons as their primary tool, others evaluate services, trust, quality, and other factors. There are shopping portals, shopping robots ("shopbots"), business ratings sites, trust verification sites, and other shopping aids.

SHOPPING PORTALS

shopping portals
Gateways to storefronts
and malls; may be
comprehensive or
niche-oriented.

Shopping portals are gateways to storefronts and e-malls. Like any other portal, they may be comprehensive or niche-oriented. Comprehensive or general-purpose portals have links to many different sellers that evaluate a broad range of products. Comprehensive portals include Gomez Advisors (gomez.com) and activebuyersguide.com. Several general portals also offer shopping opportunities and comparison aids. Examples are altavista.dealtime.com, shopping.yahoo.com, eshop.msn.com, and webcenter.shop.aol.com. These are all clear links from the main page of the portal, and they generate revenues by directing consumers to their affiliates' sites. Some of these portals even offer comparison tools to help identify the best price for a particular item. Several of these evaluation companies have purchased shopbots or other, smaller shopping aids and incorporated them into their portals.

Shopping portals may also offer specialized niche aids, with information and links for purchasers of automobiles, toys, computers, travel, or some other narrow area. Examples include bsilly.com for kid's products and zdnetshopper.cnet.com or shopper.cnet.com for computer equipment. The advantage of niche shopping portals is their ability to specialize in a certain line of products and carefully track consumer tastes within a specific and relevant market segment. Some of these portals seek only to collect the referral fee from their affiliation with sites they recommend. Others have no formal relationship with the sellers; instead, they sell banner ad space to advertisers who wish to reach the communities who regularly visit these specialized sites. In other cases, shopping portals act as intermediaries by selling directly to consumers, though this may harm their reputation for independence and objectivity.

SHOPBOTS AND AGENTS

Savvy Internet shoppers may bookmark their favorite shopping sites, but what if they want to find other stores with good service and policies that sell similar items at lower prices? **Shopping robots** (also called **shopping agents** or **shopbots**) are tools that scout the Web for consumers who specify search criteria. Different shopbots use different search methods. For example, mysimon.com searches the Web to find the best prices for thousands of popular items. This is not a simple task. The shopbot may have to evaluate different SKU (stock-keeping unit) numbers for the same item, as each e-tailer may have a different SKU rather than a standardized data-representation code.

**shopping robots (also
shopping agents or
shopbots)**
Tools that scout the
Web on behalf of con-
sumers who specify
search criteria.

Some agents specialize in certain product categories or niches. For example, autobytel.com, autovantage.com, and carpoint.com help consumers shop for cars. Zdnet.com/computershopper searches for information on computers, software, and peripherals. A shopping agent at office.com helps consumers find the best price for office supplies. A shopping agent for books is isbn.nu. In addition, agents such as pricegrabber.com are able to identify customers' preferences. Dealtime.com allows consumers to compare over 1,000 different merchant sites, and keeps seeking lower prices on their behalf. There are even negotiation agents and agents that assist auction bidders (e.g., auctionbid.com) by automating the bid process using the bidder's instructions.

BUSINESS RATINGS SITES

Many Web sites rate various e-tailers and online products based on multiple criteria. Bizrate.com and gomez.com (Gomez Advisors) are two such sites. At gomez.com, the consumer can actually specify the relative importance of different criteria when comparing online banks, toy sellers, or e-grocers. Bizrate.com has a network of shoppers that report on various sellers and uses the compiled results in its evaluations.

TRUST VERIFICATION SITES

A number of companies purport to evaluate and verify the trustworthiness of various e-tailers. The TRUSTe seal appears at the bottom of each TRUSTe-approved e-tailer's Web site. E-tailers pay TRUSTe for use of the seal (which they call a "trustmark"). TRUSTe's 1,300-plus members hope that consumers will use the seal as an assurance and as a proxy for actual research into their privacy policy and personal information protection. With so many sellers online, many consumers are not sure whom they should trust. Even TRUSTe is not foolproof. It has been criticized for its lax verification processes, and a number of high-profile privacy violations and other problems with TRUSTe members have led to publication of a study that investigated a TRUSTe "Hall of Shame" (Rafter 2000). The most comprehensive trust verification sites are Verisign, BBBOnline, and WebTrust (cpawebtrust.org). Verisign tends to be the most widely used.

Other sources of trust verification include BBBOnLine and Secure Assure, which charge yearly license fees based on a company's annual revenue. In addition, Ernst and Young, the global public accounting firm, has created it own service for auditing e-tailers in order to offer some guarantee of the integrity of their business practices.

OTHER SHOPPER TOOLS

Other digital intermediaries assist buyers or sellers, or both, with the research and purchase processes. For example, escrow services (e.g., tradenable.com, escrow.com) assist buyers and sellers in the transfer of funds. As buyers and sellers do not see or know each other, there is frequently a need for a trusted third party to facilitate the proper exchange of money and goods. Escrow sites may also provide payment-processing support, as well as letters of credit (see Chapter 10).

Other decision aids include communities of consumers who offer advice and opinions on products and e-tailers. One such site is epinions.com, which has searchable recommendations on thousands of products. Pricescan.com is a price comparison engine, and pricegrabber.com is a comparison shopping tool that covers over 1 million products. DealTime.com specializes in electronics, and iwon.com specializes in apparel, health and beauty, and other categories. Other software agents and comparison sites are presented in Exhibit 3.9 (page 128).

EXHIBIT 3.9   Representative Comparison of Software Agents

Agent Classification	Product (URL)	Description
Learning agents	Empirical (empirical.com)	Surveys user's reading interests and uses machine learning to find Web pages using neural-network-based collaborative filtering technology.
Comparison shopping agents	Jango (jango.com)	Constructs a lot of shopping guides such as Yahoo!, Visa, Compaq, Hot Blot, and so on. Adapted to Excite's shopping guide.
	MySimon (mysimon.com)	Using VLA (virtual learning agent) technology, shops for the best price from merchants in hundreds of product categories, with a real-time interface.
	CompareNet (compare.net)	Interactive buyer's guide that educates shoppers and allows them to make direct comparisons between brands and products.
AI/Logic-supported approaches	Cnetshopper (shopper.cnet.com)	Makes price comparisons.
Computer-related shopping guide	Netbuyer (netbuyer.co.uk/)	Supplies sales and marketing solutions to technology companies, by delivering information about computer and communications industry trends, products developments, and buyer activity.
Car-related shopping guide	Auto-by-Tel (autobytel.com)	A low-cost, no-haggle car-buying system used by leading search engines and online programs such as Excite, NetCenter, Lycos, and AT&T WorldNet Services.
	Autovantage (cendant.com)	Provides the Web's premier savings site for great deals on autos. (Also offers travel, shopping, dining, and other services.)
	CarPoint (carpoint.msn.com)	A one-stop shopping place for searching and purchasing automobiles.
Microsoft-related agent technology	Agentmart (microsoft.com/ products/msagent)	Provides Microsoft's agent infospace and agent directory. First Web site with animated conversational characters such as Genie, Merlin, and so on.

EXHIBIT 3.9 (CONTINUED)

Agent Classification	Product (URL)	Description
Aggregator portal	Pricing Central (*pricingcentral.com*)	Aggregates information from other shopping agents and search engines. Comparison shopping is done in real time (latest pricing information).
Real-time agents	Gold Digger (*mygolddigger.com*)	Finds the lowest price automatically when you visit a store.
	EdgeGain (*edgegain.com*)	Compares prices.

▶ Define shopping portals and provide two examples.

▶ What are shopbots?

▶ Explain the role of business rating and site verification tools in the purchase-decision process.

▶ Why are escrow services useful for online purchases?

3.10 SUCCESSFUL CLICK-AND-MORTAR STRATEGIES

Although thousands of companies have evolved their online strategies into mature Web sites with extensive interactive features that add value to the consumer purchase process, many sites remain simple "brochureware" sites with limited interactivity. Many traditional companies are in a transitional stage. According to International Data Corp., by 2003, 32 percent of companies that have Web sites will fully support interactive online transactions.

Mature transactional systems include features for payment processing, order fulfillment, logistics, inventory management, and a host of other tasks. In most cases, a company must replicate each of its physical business processes and design many more that can only be performed online. Today's environment includes sophisticated access to order information, shipping information, product information, and more through Web pages, touch-tone phones, Web-enabled cellular phones, and PDAs over wireless networks. Faced with all of these variables, the challenges to implementing EC can be daunting.

The real gains for traditional retailers will come from leveraging the benefits of their physical presence and the benefits of their online presence. Web sites frequently offer better prices and selection, whereas physical stores offer a trustworthy staff and opportunities for customers to examine items before purchasing. (Physical examination is critical for clothing and ergonomic devices, for example, but not for commodities, music, or software.) Large, efficient established retailers, such as Wal-Mart (walmart.com), Marks & Spencer (marksandspencer.com), and Takashimaya (takashimaya.co.jp) are able to create the optimum value proposition for their customers by providing a complete offering of services.

A traditional brick-and-mortar store with a mature Web site uses a click-and-mortar strategy to do the following.

Speak with one voice. A firm can link all of its back-end systems to create an integrated customer experience. Regardless of how a customer interfaces with a company, the information received and service provided should be consistent.

Empower the customer. The seller needs to create a powerful 24/7 channel for service and information. Through various technologies, sellers can ensure that customers are empowered with information and give customers the opportunity to use online technologies to perform various functions interactively, at any time. Such functions include the ability to find store locations, product information, and inventory availability online. Circuitcity.com, for example, allows customers to receive rich product comparisons between various models of consumer electronics products.

Leverage the channels. The innovative retailer will offer the advantages of each marketing channel to customers from all channels. Whether the purchase is made online or at the store, the customer should benefit from the presence of both. For example, customers who purchase from the Web site should be allowed to return items to the physical store (Eddie Bauer's policy). In addition, combining both channels can enhance the inventory of available items. (Established mail-order direct marketers such as Eddie Bauer have a distinct advantage due to the ready availability of order processing systems, payment processing systems, and supply management expertise.) Many physical stores, such as BestBuy, now have terminals in the store to order items from the Web site if they are not available in the store. In addition, many companies allow customers to have those items shipped to their home or to the store to evaluate the item before purchasing. Needless to say, prices should be consistent to avoid "channel conflict" (discussed in Section 3.12).

TRANSFORMATION TO CLICK-AND-MORTAR OPERATIONS: CIRCUIT CITY

Circuit City is the second-largest U.S. retailer of consumer electronics (behind BestBuy), operating about 650 stores located across the United States. Prior to the summer of 1999, Circuit City's Web site was largely a brochureware site, capable only of selling gift certificates. When Circuit City launched the new circuitcity.com in 1999, it already had some of the needed EC systems in place—the credit card authorization and inventory-management systems at its brick-and-mortar stores. However, linking the company's brick-and-mortar systems with the EC system was neither cheap nor easy. "It's safe to say that millions of dollars need to be spent to have a *Fortune* 500 kind of presence on the Web in a transactional way," indicated George Barr, Circuit City's director of Web development. "It's just not something you could do for $100,000" (Calem 2000).

A few features of the circuitcity.com site deserve special attention. First, the site educates customers about the various features and capabilities of different products, cutting through the jargon to help the customer understand why these features may be desirable and what the trade-offs are. In this personal and non-threatening way, customers can gain valuable knowledge to assist them in the purchase decision. (Some consumers find shopping in the traditional brick-and-mortar Circuit City store to be intimidating because they do not understand the terms and product features discussed by store personnel.) Second, at the Web site, customers can perform powerful searches on a product database to help find the appropriate models to consider. Third, the site offers an extensive amount of information about electronics and other products, organized in a very flexible way. This assists buyers as they gather information before a purchase is made, whether or not they eventually buy from circuitcity.com. Visitors can select several models and compare them by viewing a dynamically created table of purchase criteria, displayed side-by-side, with drill-down details if necessary.

Circuit City has engineered the online purchase to be smooth, secure, and seamless. Poor process design will scare off many customers. It has been reported that in other stores only 17 percent of all purchase processes are completed (versus over 50 percent for Circuit City). Customers who abandon the purchase typically do so because of confusion and complexity, surprises (such as shipping costs), concerns about security and privacy of personal information, system errors, slow transmission speeds, and other factors.

Finally, circuitcity.com's order fulfillment method is flexible. The customer is given three choices: (1) receive the purchase via common carrier with no sales tax, but with a small shipping charge for 3-day delivery, or (2) pay a larger shipping charge for overnight delivery, or (3) pick up the item at the nearby brick-and-mortar store and pay sales tax but no shipping, and thus have the item almost immediately. If the customer chooses the self-pickup, the customer prints a confirmation page and takes it to the front desk of the store, along with a picture ID. The customer can pick up a new purchase, such as a DVD player, in under 2 minutes.

ALLIANCE OF VIRTUAL AND TRADITIONAL RETAILERS: AMAZON.COM AND TOYS R US

In online toy retailing, eToys was the pioneer. However, as electronic orders, particularly during the peak holiday season, increased, eToys could not meet its delivery requirements due to its limited logistics capability. Price wars and high customer acquisition costs also caused problems for this e-tailer. Eventually, eToys closed, and its assets were sold to KB Toys and its Web channel, kbtoys.com.

Meanwhile, giant toy retailer Toys R Us, a competitor of KB Toys, had been unsuccessful in creating an independent e-tailing business. One solution seemed promising: an alliance between Toys R Us and Amazon.com. Amazon.com is known as a premier site for creating customer loyalty and for driving sales through its execution of CRM with efficient back-office order fulfillment systems. Toys R Us, backed by 40 years of toy-industry experience, is known for its broad product offering and a deep understanding of the market, customer tastes, and suppliers. It has strong B2B supplier relationships and a well-developed inventory system.

Before the alliance with Toys R Us, Amazon.com had failed in the toy business because it lacked the strong B2B supplier relationships with toy manufacturers. It could not get the best toys and did not know how to manage inventory against product demand (Karpinski 2000). Toys R Us also had problems. It could not figure out how to effectively manage a direct-to-consumer distribution center or how to balance its retail-store business with its online business (Karpinski 2000).

During the 1999 Christmas season, before their alliance, both companies failed to profitably deliver toys on time. Amazon.com miscalculated inventory requirements, and was left with millions of toys it had to write off. ToysRUs.com badly bungled the operations side by creating a Web site that was unable to handle large amounts of traffic and order shipping. ToysRUs.com could not execute its Web business effectively due to a lack of experience with both the front-end design and the back-end order fulfillment processes. As a result, 1 in 20 children failed to get presents in time for Christmas from ToysRUs.com.

After bad press, lost business, and rebates to customers, these two companies decided to combine their efforts for 10 years, commencing with the 2000 Christmas season. They have pooled their expertise to form a single online toy store. Their alliance allows the partners to leverage each other's core strengths (Schwartz 2000). Under the 10-year agreement, ToysRUs.com identifies, purchases, and manages inventory, using the parent company's clout to get the best lineup of toys. Since Amazon.com has a distribution network with plenty of excess capacity and a solid infrastructure, it is responsible for order fulfillment and customer service. Amazon.com applies its expertise in front-end site design, offering a powerful customer-support environment. Revenues will be split between the two companies, the risks also are equally shared.

This is an innovative model. The two companies must coordinate disparate systems—operational, technological, and financial—as they merge their corporate cultures. If they succeed and execute this strategy successfully, this kind of partnership could be a prime model for the future of e-tailing. In the alliance's first Christmas season, things went "so-so"; in the second season, business was even better.

▶ What motivates a brick-and-mortar company to offer Web services?

▶ What customer services are provided by Circuit City on its Web site?

▶ Describe the logic of the alliance between Amazon.com and ToysRUs.com.

3.11 PROBLEMS WITH E-TAILING AND LESSONS LEARNED

As the experiences of eToys and others indicate, e-tailing is no panacea. It offers some serious challenges and tremendous risks for those who fail to provide value to the consumer, who fail to establish a profitable business model, or who fail to execute the model they establish. The road to e-tail success is littered with dead companies that could not deliver on their promises. The shakeout from mid-2000 to mid-2001 caused many companies to fail; others learned and adapted. Some enduring principles have been distilled from the failures, and these "lessons learned" are discussed next (see Chapter 11 for further discussion).

DON'T IGNORE PROFITABILITY

One fundamental lesson is that each marginal sale should lead to marginal profits. It has been said that in business, "If it doesn't make cents, it doesn't make sense." The trouble with most virtual e-tailers is that they lose money on every sale as they try to grow to a profitable size and scale. Amazon.com may generate about $5 per book order, but it still loses about $7 per sale on nonbook sales. Some e-tailers will have to adjust prices or refocus their market targets to concentrate on profitable sales.

Many pure-play e-tailers were initially funded by venture capital firms that provided enough financing to get the e-tailers started and growing. However, in many cases, the funding ran out before the e-tailer achieved sufficient size and maturity to break even and become self-sufficient. In some cases, the underlying cost and revenue models were not sound—the firms would never be profitable without major changes in their funding sources, proper revenue model, and controlled costs. Long-run success requires financial viability.

MANAGE NEW RISK EXPOSURE

The Internet creates new connectivity with customers and offers the opportunity to expand markets. However, it also has the potential to expose a retailer to more sources of risk. Local companies have to contend with local customers and local regulations, whereas national firms have more constituents with which to interact. Global firms have to contend with numerous cultural perspectives. Will they offend potential customers because of a lack of awareness of other cultures? Global Internet firms also have to manage their exposure to risk from the mosaic of international legal structures, laws, and regulations. Can they be sued in other countries for their business practices?

Groups of disgruntled employees or customers can band together to contact the news media, file a class action lawsuit, or launch their own Web site to publicize their concerns. One example of this was the walmartsucks.com site, which was created by a customer who felt he was mistreated at one Wal-Mart store. He created a repository of all the negative news stories he could find about Wal-Mart and anecdotal accounts from fired employees and unhappy customers. Similar information about other corporations and government agencies is available at sucks500.com. When disgruntled individuals used to tell 50 to 100 friends and coworkers about their frustration, it may have resulted in a few lost sales; with the Internet, these people can now reach thousands or even millions of potential customers.

WATCH THE COST OF BRANDING

Branding has always been considered a key to retail success. Consumers are thought to be more willing to search out products with strong brand recognition, as well as pay a bit more for them. However, in e-tailing, the drive to establish brand recognition quickly often leads to excessive spending. In one case, an upstart e-tailer spent over 50 percent of its venture capital funding on one 30-second television advertisement during the Super Bowl game! In other cases, e-tailers offered extravagant promotions and loss-leader offers to drive traffic to their sites, and then lost money on every sale. The huge volume of site traffic merely served to increase their losses. The lesson from success stories is that most customers, especially long-term loyal customers, come to a Web site from affiliate links, search engines, or personal recommendations—not from Super Bowl ads.

DON'T START WITH INSUFFICIENT FUNDS

It may seem obvious that a venture will not succeed if it lacks funds at the start, but many people are so excited about their business idea that they decide to try anyway. An example of this is the failure of Garden.com. Garden.com was a Web site that provided rich, dynamic content (how to plant bulbs, tips on gardening, an "ask the expert" feature, etc.) and a powerful landscape design tool, which allowed a visitor to lay out an entire garden and then purchase all the necessary materials with one click. Garden.com also hosted various "community" features with discussions about various types of gardening-related topics. Gardeners are often passionate about their hobby and like to learn more about new plants and gardening techniques. The business idea sounded good. However, the site failed due to the company's inability to raise sufficient venture capital necessary to cover losses until enough business volume was reached.

A COMPANY MUST PERFORM

Today's savvy Internet shoppers expect Web sites to offer superior technical performance—fast page loads, quick database searches, streamlined graphics, and so forth. Web sites that delay or frustrate consumers will not experience a high sales volume because of a high percentage of abandoned purchases.

KEEP IT INTERESTING

Web sites without dynamic content will bore returning visitors. Static design is a "turn-off." Today, most e-tailers offer valuable tips and information for consumers, who often come back just for that content and may purchase something in the process. L. L. Bean, for example, offers a rich database of information about parks and recreational facilities as well as its buying guides. Visitors who visit the site to find a campground or a weekend event may also purchase a tent or a raincoat.

Although there have been many e-tailing failures (mostly pure-play e-tailers, but some click-and-mortar companies, too), there are many success stories. Some are described in Chapter 11. The successful case of a floral business is presented in EC Application Case 3.6. In general, while pure-play online retailing is risky and its future is not clear, online retailing is growing very rapidly as a complementary distribution channel to physical stores and mail-order catalogs. In other words, the click-and-mortar model appears to be winning.

▶ Why are virtual e-tailers usually not profitable?

▶ Relate branding to profitability.

▶ Why are technical performance and dynamic site content important?

EC APPLICATION CASE 3.6
Individuals and Communities

A BLOOMING SUCCESS

Jody Yan had been running a steady floral business in downtown Hong Kong since 1987. In 1997, an online auction site asked Jody to sponsor gifts for auctions and she agreed. Intrigued by the potential of the Internet, in 1998, she set up an online store named *ambassador.com.hk*. When the orders started to flow in, Jody decided to expand the business by adding functions such as online payments.

Ambassador sells customized designer flower baskets, flower bouquets, cakes, and fruit and gourmet gift baskets, all attractively packaged, at an average price of US $100 each. Colorful pictures of all products are displayed on the online storefront. The firm runs a warehouse on the south side of Hong Kong. In addition to sourcing from local wholesalers, fresh flowers are air-shipped from Holland and New Zealand.

Jody realized that it would be very difficult to develop and maintain in-house software to address the requirements of an online store. So she hired an IT consulting firm to develop the online store from scratch and also retained them for maintenance, hosting, employee training, and operational support. "There is absolutely no need to build an in-house IT function when you can outsource it to reliable experts," says Jody. To stay ahead of competitors, Jody emphasized good product design. Another strength was her loyal staff, most of them having been with her for over 6 years.

In the first year of operations, the online store accounted for about 10 percent of firm's revenue. Online sales have since doubled every year and accounted for 30 percent of the firm's total revenue of around HK $5 million (US $640,000) in 2000. In 2001, the company closed its physical retail shop. The remaining sales channel comprises mail-order catalogs and the online store. Local telephone purchase orders are also accepted. Customers receive a detailed picture of the actual product at the time of delivery via e-mail. Both an in-house team and an outsourced company support local deliveries, helping Ambassador to cope with seasonal fluctuations. Courier companies carry out all international deliveries. This multichannel business model for floral gift products works very well.

The following success factors helped Ambassador's online business blossom.

▌ Jody's extensive experience in the floral gift products business

▌ Jody's analysis that floral gift products are suitable for Internet sales

▌ Back-end operations for the online floral gift shop were already in place, hence additional costs were marginal

▌ Identification of the online store as part of a multichannel retailing strategy

▌ An initial pilot implementation that resulted in orders

▌ Plans and budgets prepared for experimentation

▌ The decision to outsource the implementation from scratch; hosting, maintenance, and training done by one vendor.

▌ Integration of online store functions with other business models and IT systems

Source: This case was provided by Matthew K. O. Lee, City University of Hong Kong, 2001.

Questions

▌ Why was the physical store closed?

▌ What are the major success factors of *Ambassador.com*?

3.12 ISSUES IN E-TAILING

DISINTERMEDIATION AND REINTERMEDIATION

Intermediaries traditionally provided trading infrastructure (such as a sales network), and they manage the complexity of matching buyers' and sellers' needs. The introduction of EC resulted in the automation of many tasks provided by intermediaries. Does this mean that travel agents, real estate brokers, job agency employees, insurance agents, and other such jobs will disappear?

As you may recall from Exhibit 3.1, the manufacturer bypassed the wholesalers and retailers, selling directly to consumers. As defined earlier, this phenomenon is called disintermediation, meaning the elimination of the intermediaries, such as the retailers. However, consumers have a wide selection of online vendors. Thus, new online assistance is needed, and it may be provided by the traditional intermediaries. In such cases, the traditional intermediaries fill new roles, providing added value and assistance. This process is referred to as **reintermediation**. Thus, for the intermediary, the Internet offers new ways to reach new customers, new ways to bring value to customers, and perhaps new ways to generate revenues.

An example of reintermediation is that of Rosenbluth International. This travel company completely changed its business model by providing value-added services to its business customers. At a time when many travel agencies were losing their role as intermediaries, Rosenbluth was able to survive, and even prosper, by using EC-based business models.

Bloch et al. (1996) think that the intermediary's role will shift to one that emphasizes value-added services such as:

▶ Assisting customers in comparison shopping from multiple sources.

▶ Providing total solutions by combining services from several vendors.

▶ Providing certifications and trusted third-party control and evaluation systems.

In the world of online new and used car sales, there are many electronic intermediaries that assist buyers and/or sellers. These are new **reintermediaries**, namely intermediaries that have restructured their role in the purchase process, selling cars to consumers without the involvement of traditional car dealers. Some of these sites include Kelly Blue Book (kbb.com), which offers pricing information for consumers, edmunds.com, which gives consumers information about the dealer's true costs, carfax.com, which will research a specific used car and tell you if it has ever been in an accident or had an odometer rollback, and imotors.com, which gives members discounts on insurance, gas, and repairs. Additionally, there are "lead services" that direct buyers to member dealers and, in some cases, also offer direct sales of new cars. The leading site in this category is autobytel.com; others include carsdirect.com (Amazon.com's partner) and cars.com.

Some reintermediaries are newcomers, rivaling the traditional retail stores, whereas others are operations established by the traditional retailers. Some reintermediaries cooperate with manufacturers or retailers to provide a needed service to the seller or distributor in the online environment. Other reintermediaries are virtual e-tailers that fill a unique niche. Intermediaries such as online retailers (walmart.com), shopping portals, directories, and comparison-shopping agents

reintermediation
The process whereby intermediaries (either new ones or those that had been disintermediated) take on new intermediary roles.

reintermediaries
Intermediaries that have restructured their roles.

can also act as reintermediaries. The evolution and operation of these companies is critical to the success of e-commerce.

Cybermediation

In addition to reintermediation, there is a completely new role in EC called **cyber-mediation**, or **electronic intermediation**. These terms describe special Web sites that use intelligent agents to facilitate intermediation. Cybermediators can perform many roles in EC. To illustrate the diversity of such roles, Giaglis et al. (1999) examined the market functions listed in Exhibit 3.10 and found that cyber-mediation can affect most market functions. For example, intelligent agents can find when and where an item that a consumer wants will be auctioned. The matching services described in this chapter are done by cybermediator agents. Cybermediator agents also conduct price comparisons of insurance policies, long-distance calls, and other services. Cybermediation services are spreading rapidly around the globe (Vandermerwe 1999; Berghel 2000; and Kauffman et al. 2000).

cybermediation (electronic intermediation)
The use of software (intelligent) agents to facilitate intermediation.

Hypermediation

In some cases, many EC transactions require extensive human and electronic intermediation. In many cases, EC requires content providers, affiliate sites, search engines, portals, ISPs, software makers, and more. A large e-tailer, such as Amazon.com, for example, includes all of the these services, and also uses auction services, payments services, logistics support, and more. According to Carr (2000), this phenomenon, called **hypermediation**, runs opposite to disintermediation, providing intermediaries with a chance to profit from EC.

hypermediation
Extensive use of both human and electronic intermediation to provide assistance in all phases of an e-commerce venture.

EXHIBIT 3.10 Opportunities and Threats to Intermediaries in Electronic Markets

Market Function	Electronic Market Influence	Likely Effects on Intermediation
Determination of product offerings	Personalization of products	Disintermediation (especially in digital products)
	Aggregation	Cybermediation (aggregators)
	Disaggregation	Disintermediation (pay-per-use)
Searching	Lower search costs	Disintermediation
	More complex search requirements	Cybermediation
	Lower barriers to entry	Cybermediation/Reintermediation
Price discovery	Redistribution of mechanisms	Cybermediation/Reintermediation
	New markets	Cybermediation
Logistics	Lower logistical costs	Disintermediation
	Economics of scale	Reintermediation
Settlement	New cost structures	Reintermediation
	New payment mechanisms	Cybermediation/Reintermediation
Trust	Increased protection requirements	Cybermediation/Reintermediation
Legal and regulatory	Institutional support for electronic markets	Reintermediation

Source: Giaglis et al., 1999, p. 401. Used with permission of Dr. George Giaglis.

CHANNEL CONFLICT

Many traditional retailers establish a new marketing channel when they start selling online. Similarly, some manufacturers have instituted direct marketing initiatives in parallel with their established channels of distribution, such as retailers or dealers. In such cases, channel conflict may occur. **Channel conflict** refers to any situation in which the online marketing channel upsets the traditional channels due to real or perceived damage from competition.

Another type of a marketing conflict may occur within a click-and-mortar company, that between the online and off-line departments. For example, the online department may want to offer lower prices and have more online advertisements than the off-line department offers. The off-line department wants the opposite. Because the two departments are competing in different markets, they need different strategies. The conflict occurs when corporate resources are limited and an action by one department may be at the expense of another. There also may be staff conflict, as staff members want to join the new, future-oriented, online department, and those in the off-line department feel left behind.

channel conflict
Situation in which an online marketing channel upsets the traditional channels due to real or perceived damage from competition.

PERSONALIZATION

One significant characteristic of many online marketing business models is the ability of the seller to create an element of *personalization* for each individual consumer. For example, an e-tailer can utilize cookie files and other technologies to track the specific browsing and buying behavior of each consumer and create a marketing plan tailored to that consumer's pattern by showing items of interest, offering incentives that appeal to that consumer's sense of value, or providing certain services that will attract that consumer back to the Web site. The Internet also allows for easy self-configuration ("design it your way"). This creates a large demand for personalized products and services. Manufacturers can meet it by using a *mass customization* strategy. As indicated earlier, many companies offer customized products from their Web sites.

Although pure-play e-tailing is risky, and its future is unclear, e-tailing is growing rapidly as a complementary distribution channel to stores and catalogs. In other words, the click-and-mortar model is winning.

▶ Define disintermediation.
▶ Explain reintermediation.
▶ Describe the two types of channel conflict.
▶ Explain personalization and mass customization.

MANAGERIAL ISSUES

Some managerial issues related to this chapter are as follows.

1. **Should we grab a first-mover advantage or wait and learn?** It has often been suggested that the first firm to enter a new marketspace and sell products online in that category will be able to dominate that niche by establishing its brand and becoming the recognized seller. This is known as the "first-mover advantage," and it seems to apply in certain categories. For example, Amazon.com was the first major online bookseller, and despite competition, it remains the most recognized Web site for online consumer purchases of books. However, in many cases, the "first-to-market" firms make many mistakes, and if they are not agile enough to adapt to the market or other conditions, they may fail, leaving room for the "second-to-market" firms to rush in and attract the online customers who leave the first mover.

    In many cases, the second-mover firm or firms can learn from the initial company's mistakes and avoid the expense and losses associated with those mistakes. If the first mover makes a strategic mistake that upsets buyers, such as failure to ship items in a timely way or violation of their customers' privacy, the buyers will look for another, similar e-tailer.

2. **What should our strategic position be?** The most important decision for retailers and e-tailers is the overall *strategic position* they establish within their market. What niche will they fill? What business functions will they execute internally and which functions will be outsourced? What partners will they use? How will they integrate brick-and-mortar facilities (retail stores, warehouses, etc.) with their online presence? What are their revenue sources in the short and long term, and what are their fixed and marginal costs? An e-business is still a business and must establish solid business practices in the long run in order to ensure profitability and viability.

3. **Are we financially viable?** The collapse of the dot-com bubble as of April 2000 provided a wake-up call to many e-tailers. A return to business fundamentals was pursued by some, whereas others sought to redefine their business plan in terms of click-and-mortar strategies or alliances with traditional retailers (as Amazon.com did with Toys R Us). Because most easy sources of funding have dried up and revenue models are being scrutinized, many e-tailers are also pursuing new partners, and consolidation will continue until there is greater stability within the e-tail segment. Ultimately, there will likely be a smaller number of larger sellers, resulting in fewer comprehensive sites and many smaller, specialized niche sites.

4. **Should we recruit out of town?** Out-of-town recruitment can be an important source of skilled workers. Using video teleconferencing, recruiters can interview potential employees from a distance. Aptitude tests also can be taken from a distance. Furthermore, for many jobs, companies can use telecommuters. This could be a major strategy in the twenty-first century. However, online recruiting may result in too many irrelevant resumes and wasted time.

5. **Are there international legal issues regarding online recruiting?** Various international legal issues must be considered with online recruiting. For example, online recruitment of people from other countries may be complicated. The validity of contracts signed in different countries must be checked by legal experts.

6. **Do we have ethics and privacy guidelines?** Ethical issues are extremely important in an agentless system. In traditional systems, human agents play an important role in assuring the ethical behavior of buyers and sellers. Will ethics and the rules of etiquette be sufficient to guide behavior on the Internet? Only time will tell. For example, as job-applicant information travels over the Internet, security and privacy become even more important. It is management's job to make sure that information from

applicants is secure. Also, e-tailers need to establish guidelines for protecting the privacy of customers who visit their Web sites.

7. **How will intermediaries act in cyberspace?** It will take a few years before the new roles of Internet intermediaries will be stabilized, as well as their fees. Also, the emergence of support services, such as escrow services in global EC, will have an impact on intermediaries and their role.

8. **Should we set up alliances?** Alliances for online initiatives are spreading rapidly. For example, in Hong Kong, four banks created a joint online e-bank (to save on capital costs and share the risk). Online trading brokers are teaming up with banks. Banks are teaming up with telecommunications companies, software companies, and even airlines. Finally, eBay and Wells Fargo Bank have an alliance for C2C payment transactions and auctions.

SUMMARY

In this chapter, you learned about the following EC issues as they relate to the learning objectives.

1. **E-tailing business models.** The major e-tailing business models can be classified as a manufacturer selling direct to consumers, pure-play e-tailing, and a click-and-mortar strategy that has both online and traditional channels.

2. **The major e-tail markets.** Computers and electronics are the major items sold online. Books, CDs, toys, and other standard commodities also sell well. Sales of airline ticket and travel services, as well as stocks and services such as insurance, also are growing.

3. **Click-and-mortar strategy.** An increasing number of traditional retailers and manufacturers are adding an online channel. This may create channel conflict with their regular distributors. Strategies used to resolve channel conflict range from avoiding the conflict by not selling online to attempts to reconcile the differences.

4. **How online travel/tourism services operate.** Most services available through a physical travel agency are also available online. In addition, customers get much more information, much more quickly through online resources. Customers can even receive bids from travel providers. Finally, travelers can compare prices, participate in auctions and chat rooms, and view videos and maps.

5. **The online job market, its drivers, and benefits.** The online job market is growing rapidly, with millions of jobs matched with job seekers each year. The major drivers of online job markets are the ability to reach a large number of job seekers at low cost, to provide detailed information online, to take applications, and even to conduct tests. Also, using intelligent agents, resumes can be checked and matches made quickly. Millions of job offers on the Internet help job seekers, who also post their resumes on the Web.

6. **The electronic real estate market.** The online real estate market is basically supporting rather than replacing existing agents. However, both buyers and sellers can save time and effort in the electronic market. Buyers can purchase distant properties much more easily and in some places have access to less expensive services. Eventually, commissions on regular transactions are expected to decline as a result of the electronic market for real estate, and more sales "by owner" will materialize.

7. **Online stocks and bonds.** One of the fastest growing online businesses is the online trading of securities. It is inexpensive, convenient, and supported by a tremendous amount of financial and advisory information. Trading is very fast and efficient, almost fully automated, and moving toward 24/7 global trading. The traditional brokers are slowly disappearing. IPOs also are moving online.

8. **Cyberbanking and personal finance.** Branch banking is on the decline due to less expensive, more convenient online banking. The world is moving toward online banking; today, most routine banking services can be done from home. Banks can reach customers in remote places, and customers can bank with faraway institutions. This makes the financial markets more efficient.

9. **On-demand delivery service.** On-demand delivery service is needed when items are perishable or when delivering medicine, express documents, or urgently needed supplies. One example of on-demand delivery is groceries that are shipped within 24 hours, or even 4.

10. **Delivery of digital products.** Anything that can be digitized can be successfully delivered online. Delivery of digital products such as music, movies, and other entertainment online is has been a success. Some print media, such as electronic versions of magazines (e.g., hotwired.com) or electronic books (see Chapter 7), are also having success delivering their products digitally.

11. **Aiding consumer purchase decisions.** The available purchase-decision aids are shopping portals, shopbots and agents, business rating sites, trust verification sites, and so on.

12. **Critical success factors.** Critical success factors for direct online sales to consumers and e-tailing are managing risk properly, creating a profitable site, and watching the cost of branding.

13. **Disintermediation and reintermediation.** Direct electronic marketing by manufacturers results in disintermediation by removing wholesalers and retailers. However, online reintermediaries provide additional value, such as helping consumers make selections among multiple manufacturers. Traditional retailers may pressure manufacturers not to sell online at cheaper prices, causing channel conflict.

KEY TERMS

Brick-and-mortar retailers,	p. 102	Electronic banking (e-banking),	p. 116	Reintermediaries,	p. 136
Channel conflict,	p. 138	Electronic intermediation,	p. 137	Reintermediation,	p. 136
Click-and-mortar retailers,	p. 102	Electronic retailing (e-tailing),	p. 95	Shopping robots (shopbots, shopping agents),	p. 126
Cybermediation,	p. 137	Hypermediation,	p. 137	Shopping portals,	p. 126
Direct marketing,	p. 98	On-demand delivery service,	p. 121	Virtual (pure-play) e-tailers,	p. 101
Disintermediation,	p. 99				
E-grocer,	p. 121				
E-tailers/E-tailing,	p. 95				

DISCUSSION QUESTIONS

1. What are the success factors of Amazon.com? Should Amazon.com limit its sales to books, music, and movies, or is a broader selection of items a good direct marketing strategy? With the broader selection, do you think the company will dilute its brand or extend the value proposition to its customers?

2. Compare the major e-tail business models.

3. Will direct marketing of automobiles be a successful strategy? How should the dealers' inventory and the automakers' inventory and manufacturing scheduling be coordinated to meet a specific order with a quick due date?

4. Discuss the advantages of established click-and-mortar companies such as Wal-Mart Online over pure-play e-tailers such as Amazon.com.

5. Discuss the advantages of a partnership such as that of Amazon and Toy R Us. Are there any disadvantages?

6. Discuss the advantages of shopping aids to the consumer. Should a vendor provide a comparison tool on its site? Why or why not?

7. Discuss the advantages of a specialized e-tailer, such as dogtoys.com. Can such a store survive in the physical world? Why or why not?

8. Discuss the benefits of build-to-order to buyers and sellers. Are there any disadvantages?

9. Why are online travel services such a popular Internet application? Why do so many Web sites provide free travel information?

10. Compare the advantages and disadvantages of online stock trading with off-line trading.

11. Why do Internet job placement services provide free advice on how to write a resume?

12. Intelligent agents read resumes and forward them to potential employers. What are the benefits of this use of intelligent agents? Do they violate the privacy of job seekers?

13. Online employment services make it easy to change jobs; therefore, turnover rates may increase. This could result in total higher costs because of increased costs for recruiting and training new employees and the need to pay higher salaries and wages to attract or keep employees. What can companies do to ease this problem?

14. How can companies offer very low commissions for online stock purchases (as low as $5 per trade, with some even offering no commission for certain trades)? Why would they choose to offer such low commissions? Over the long run, do you expect commissions to increase or continue to decrease?

15. Explain what is meant by the statement, "Intermediaries will become knowledge providers rather than transaction providers."

INTERNET EXERCISES

1. Visit peapod.com and epinions.com. Compare the products and services offered by the two companies and evaluate their chances for success. Why do you think "unattended delivery" e-grocers such as shoplink.com failed?

2. There are many consumer portals that offer advice and ratings of products or e-tailers. Identify and examine two separate general-consumer portals that look at other sites and compare prices or other purchase criteria. Try to find and compare prices for a hat, a microwave oven, and an MP3 player. Summarize your experience. Comment on the strong and weak points of such shopping tools.

3. Design a trip to Kerala, India (use stayfinder.com). Find accommodations, restaurants, health clubs, festival information, and art. Arrange a tour for two people for 7 days. How much will it cost?

4. Almost all car manufacturers allow consumers to configure their car online. Visit a major automaker's Web site and configure a car of your choice (e.g., jaguar.com). Also visit one electronic intermediary (e.g., autobytel.com). After you decide what car you want, examine the payment options and monthly payments. Print your results. How does this process compare to visiting an auto dealer? Do you think you found a better price online? Would you consider buying a car this way?

5. Visit amazon.com and identify at least three specific elements of its personalization and customization features. Browse specific books on one particular subject, leave the site, and then go back and revisit the site. What do you see?

Are these features likely to encourage you to purchase more books in the future from Amazon.com? List the features and discuss how they may lead to increased sales. Now visit Amazon zShop (go to amazon.com, and click on zShops) to identify and compare three sellers of food and beverages. Can you find items not normally available in your local grocery store?

6. Use a statistics source (e.g., jmm.com, emarketer.com, or cyberatlas.com) and look for recent statistics about the growth of Internet-based consumer-oriented EC in your country and in three other countries. Where is the greatest growth occurring? Which countries have the largest total e-tail sales? Which countries have the highest per-capita participation (the "penetration rate")? What are the forecasts for continued growth in the coming years?

7. Visit nike.com and prepare a customized order for a pair of shoes. Describe the process. Do you think this will result in a better-fitting shoe? Do you think this personalization feature will lead to greater sales volume for Nike?

8. Make your resume accessible to millions of people. Ask Careerbuilder at headhunter.net for help in rewriting your resume. Consult jobweb.org in planning your career. Get prepared for a job interview (hotjobs.com). Also, use wageweb.com to determine what salary you can get in the city of your choice in the United States.

9. Visit homeowners.com, decisionaide.com, or a similar site and compute the mortgage payment on a 30-year loan at 7.5 percent fixed interest. Also check current interest rates. Estimate your closing costs on a $200,000 loan. Compare the monthly payments of the fixed rate with that of an adjustable rate for the first year. Finally, compute your total payments if you take the loan for 15 years at the going rate. Compare it to a 30-year mortgage. Comment on the difference.

10. Access virtualtrader.co.uk and register for the Internet stock game. You will be bankrolled with £100,000 in a trading account every month. You can also play investment games at investorsleague.com, E*TRADE (etrade.com, stocks, options), and fantasystockmarket.com.

11. Enter etrade.com and boom.com and find out how you can trade stocks in countries other than the one you live in. Prepare a report.

12. Enter wellsfargo.com and examine its global and B2B services. For each service that is being offered, comment on the advantages of online versus off-line options.

13. Examine the consolidated billing process. Start with e-billingonline.com, alysis.com, and intuit.com. Identify other contenders in the field. What standard capabilities do they all offer? What capabilities are unique to certain sites?

14. Try to compare the price of a Sony digital camera at dealtime.com, mysimon.com, bottomdollar.com, and pricescan.com. Which site locates the best deal?

TEAM ASSIGNMENTS AND ROLE PLAYING

1. Each team is to investigate the services of online car selling in the following list. When teams have finished, they should bring their research together and discuss their findings.

   a. Buying new cars through an intermediary (autobytel.com, carsdirect.com, or amazon.com)

   b. Buying used cars (autotrader.com)

   c. Buying used cars from dealers (manheim.com)

   d. Support for used car dealers (autotrader.com/dealer)

   e. Automobile ratings sites (carsdirect.com, autoinvoices.com, and fueleconomy.gov)

   f. Car-buying portals (thecarportal.com and cars.com)

g. Sites where antique cars can be purchased (yesterdays-cars.com, classiccars.com).

2. Each team will represent a broker-based area (e.g., real estate, insurance, stocks, job finding). Each team will find a new development that has occurred in the assigned area over the last 3 months. Look for the site vendor's announcement and search for more information on the development with google.com or another search engine. Examine the business news at bloomberg.com. After completing your research, as a team, prepare a report on disintermediation in your assigned area.

3. Airline consortiums are competing with Travelocity, Expedia, and other online travel agents. Research several of these consortiums (each team will examine one) and analyze the competitive advantage of the airlines over the online agents. Prepare a report based on your findings. Make a presentation that will predict a winner from among the following: airline sites, travel agencies, or online sites such as Expedia.

REAL-WORLD CASE

WAL-MART GOES ONLINE

Wal-Mart is the largest retailer in the world with over 2,700 stores in the United States and about 750 stores in other countries. Its standard company cheer ends with, "Who's number one? The customer." Wal-Mart has established itself as a master of the retail process by streamlining its supply chain process and undercutting competitors with low prices. But one problem with its strategy for growing online sales is the demographics of its primary customer base. Wal-Mart's target demographic is households with $25,000 in annual income, whereas the median income of online consumers is perhaps $60,000.

Despite these demographics, online sales (primarily in music, travel, and electronics) already account for about 10 percent of Wal-Mart's U.S. sales. One way that its long-time chief rival, Kmart, Inc., tried to attract its demographic audience to its Web site (bluelight.com) was to offer free Internet access. This appealed to its cost-conscious, lower-income constituency, and also provided the opportunity for those customers to access the site to conduct purchases! However, this move decreased company profits in the short run and was one of the factors that led Kmart to file for bankruptcy in 2002.

Wal-Mart also has concerns about cannibalizing its in-store sales. Its recent alliance with AOL was designed to provide cobranded $9.94/month Internet access to dwellers in both very rural and very urban areas, where there are no nearby Wal-Mart stores. The intent is to lure in a new market segment and thus cancel the effect of cannibalization. Ultimately, a hybrid e-tailer that can offer a combination of huge selection with the click-and-mortar advantages of nearby stores may prove to be the 800-pound gorilla of online consumer sales.

In 2002, *walmart.com* matured, offering order status and tracking, a help desk, a clear return policy and return mechanisms, a store locator, and information on special sales and liquidations. Also, community services such as photo sharing are provided.

Questions

1. Compare *walmart.com* with *amazon.com*. Which features do the sites have in common?

2. Will Wal-Mart.com become the dominant e-tailer in the world, replacing Amazon.com? What factors would contribute to its success in the online marketplace? What factors would detract from its ability to dominate online sales the way it has been able to dominate physical retail sales in many markets?

3. Perform a strategic analysis of Walmart.com. Who are its competitors, customers, and

suppliers? What is its relative strength or power in each of these relationships? What is its distinctive competence? What environmental factors influence its success? How much of its strength is borrowed from its knowledge of physical stores?

4. Visit *walmart.com*, *target.com*, and *sears.com*. Identify the common features of their online marketing and at least one unique feature evident at each site. Do these sites have to distinguish themselves primarily in terms of price, product selection, or Web site features?

CONSUMER BEHAVIOR, CUSTOMER SERVICE, AND ADVERTISING

Learning objectives

Upon completion of this chapter, you will be able to:

▶ Describe the factors that influence consumer behavior online.

▶ Understand the decision-making process of consumer purchasing online.

▶ Describe how companies are building one-to-one relationships with customers.

▶ Discuss the issues of e-loyalty and e-trust in EC.

▶ Explain how personalization is accomplished online.

▶ Describe consumer market research in EC.

▶ Explain the implementation of customer service online and describe its tools.

▶ Describe the objectives of Web advertising and its characteristics.

▶ Describe the major advertising methods used on the Web.

▶ Describe various online promotions.

▶ Describe the issues involved in measuring the success of Web advertisements as it relates to different pricing methods.

▶ Understand the role of intelligent agents in consumer issues and advertising applications.

Content

Ritchey Design Learns About Customers

4.1 Learning about Consumer Behavior Online

4.2 The Consumer Decision-Making Process

4.3 One-to-One Marketing and Personalization in EC

4.4 Market Research for EC

4.5 Delivering Customer Service in Cyberspace

4.6 Web Advertising

4.7 Advertising Methods

4.8 Advertising Strategies and Promotions

4.9 Special Advertising Topics

4.10 Software Agents in Customer-Related and Advertising Applications

Managerial Issues

Real-World Case:

Chevron's World of Car Characters

RITCHEY DESIGN LEARNS ABOUT CUSTOMERS

The Problem

Ritchey Design, Inc. of Redwood City, California, is a relatively small ($15 million sales per year) designer and manufacturer of mountain-bike components. The company sells its products to distributors and/or retailers, who then sell them to individual consumers. The company opened a Web site in 1995 (*ritcheylogic.com*), but like so many companies' Web sites, Ritchey's was more a status symbol than a business tool. Most of the site's visitors came to get information on Team Ritchey (now Ritchey Yahoo! Team), the company's world-class mountain-bike team, or to find out where Ritchey products were sold, but that was where the site's usefulness ended. It did not give customers all the information they wanted or enable the company to gain insight into its customers' wants and needs.

The Solution

In late 1995, Philip Ellinwood, Ritchey's chief operating officer and IS director, decided to rework the Web site so that the company could hear from its customers directly. First, Ellinwood set up customer surveys on the site. To induce visitors to participate, the company offers visitors who answer the surveys a chance to win free Ritchey products. Visitors are asked to enter their names and addresses and then to answer questions about the company's products. A special software program, Web Trader, automatically organizes and saves the answers in a database. The information is later used to help make marketing and advertising decisions.

Ellinwood can easily change the questions to learn customers' opinions about any of about 15 new products Ritchey develops each year. In the past, the company knew little about how consumers might react to a new product until it was in the stores. Ellinwood says, "The process could save us as much as $100,000 a year on product development."

To educate retailers and consumers about the technological advantages of Ritchey's high-end components over competitors' parts, Ellinwood also created an electronic catalog, accessible through the Web site. Visitors can browse through the product catalog, which includes detailed descriptions and graphics of Ritchey's products.

The Results

As of this writing, Ritchey does not yet sell directly to individuals online, because the company wants to maintain its existing distribution system. However, dealers can place orders on the site, and they can learn about new products quickly, so they no longer push only those products about which they know the most. The site is basically used for market research and advertising.

Source: Compiled from *ritchylogic*, 2000, 2001.

What We Can Learn . . .

This case illustrates the benefits a company can derive from changing its Web site from a passive one to one with interactivity. Ritchey can now hear from its customers directly, even though it uses intermediaries for its sales. The new interactive Web site allows the company to learn more about its customers, while educating customers at the same time. The company also uses the site for advertising and customer service. These topics are the subjects of this chapter.

4.1 LEARNING ABOUT CONSUMER BEHAVIOR ONLINE

Companies today operate in an increasingly competitive environment. Therefore, they treat customers like royalty, as they try to lure them to buy their goods and services. Finding and retaining customers is a major critical success factor for most businesses, off-line and online. One of the keys to building effective customer relationships is an understanding of consumer behavior online.

A MODEL OF EC CONSUMER BEHAVIOR ONLINE

For decades, market researchers have tried to understand consumer behavior, and they have summarized their findings in various models of consumer behavior. Exhibit 4.1 shows the basics of these consumer behavior models, adjusted to fit the EC environment. According to this model, the purchasing decision process is triggered by a customer's reaction to stimuli (on the left). The process is then influenced by the buyer's characteristics, by the purchasing environment, by the relevant technology, by the EC logistics, and by other seller-controlled factors. Exhibit 4.1 identifies some of the variables in each category. In this chapter, we deal mainly with the following issues: personal characteristics, the decision process, seller–customer relationship building, customer service, and advertising. Discussion of other issues can be found in Internet marketing books, such as Strauss and Frost (2001).

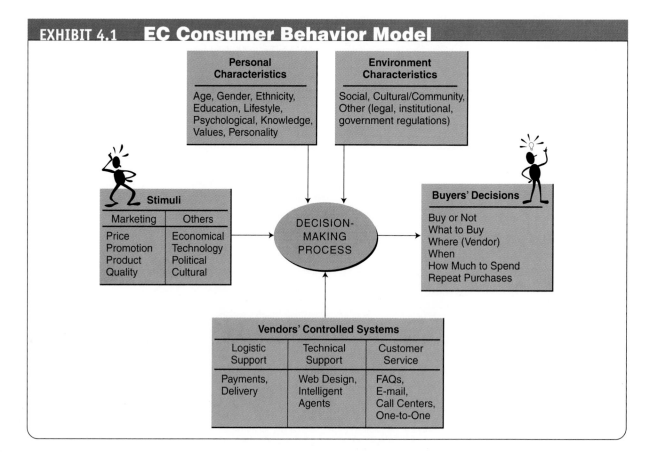

EXHIBIT 4.1 EC Consumer Behavior Model

First, though, who are the EC consumers? Online consumers can be divided into two types: *individual consumers,* who get much of the media attention, and *organizational buyers,* who do most of the actual shopping in cyberspace. Organizational buyers include governments, private corporations, resellers, and public organizations. Purchases by organizational buyers are generally used to create other products (services) by adding value to the products. Also, organizational buyers may purchase products for resale without any further modifications. We will return to organizational purchasing in Chapter 5. In this chapter, we deal with individual consumers.

The Variables in the Purchasing Environment

Let's look at the components of the individual consumer model of Exhibit 4.1. As shown in the box in the top-right portion of the figure, environmental variables can be grouped into the following categories:

▶ **Social variables.** These variables play an important role in EC purchasing. People are influenced by family members, friends, coworkers, and "what's in fashion this year." Of special importance in EC are Internet communities (covered in Chapter 11) and discussion groups, which communicate via chat rooms, electronic bulletin boards, and newsgroups. These topics are discussed in various places in the text.

▶ **Cultural/community variables.** It makes a big difference if a consumer lives near Silicon Valley in California or in the mountains in Nepal. (For further discussion of the impact of these variables, see Hasan and Ditsa 1999.)

▶ **Other environmental variables.** These include the available information, government regulations, legal constraints, and situational factors.

Personal Characteristics and Personal Differences

Personal characteristics include age, gender, and other demographic variables. Several Web sites provide information on customer buying habits online (e.g., emarketer.com, jmm.com). The major demographics that such sites track are gender, age, marital status, educational level, ethnicity, occupation, and household income. These are correlated with Internet and EC data. Exhibit 4.2 summarizes the sources and types of Internet and EC statistics.

EXHIBIT 4.2	**Sources and Types of Internet and EC Statistics**
Data sources	*ecominfocenter.com,* AMR Research, *cyberdialogue.com, forrester.com, gartnergroup.com, headcount.com, idc.com, jup.com, jmm.com, nua.ie/surveys, statmarket.com, yankeegroup.com*
Available data	Age, buying patterns (items, price), country of residence, educational level, ethnicity, gender, household income, Internet access options, Internet usage patterns, occupation, length and frequency of use, marital status

EXHIBIT 4.3   Amount of Money Spent on the Web

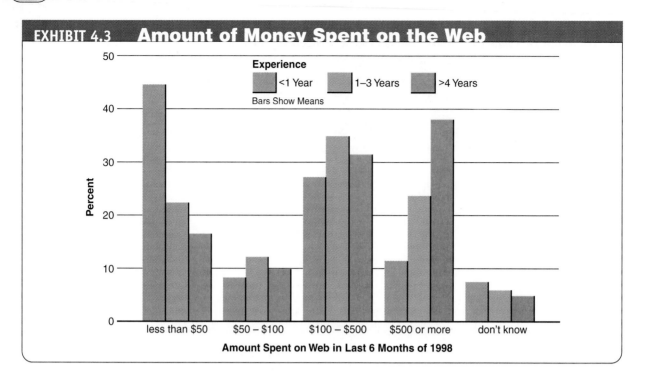

Amount Spent on Web in Last 6 Months of 1998

It is interesting to note that the more experience people have with Internet shopping, the more likely they are to spend money online, as shown in Exhibit 4.3. From Internet statistics we can learn not only what people buy, but also why they *do not* buy. The two most-cited reasons for not making purchases on the Web are security (30 percent) and the difficulty in judging the quality of the product (20 percent). Some users, about 9.3 percent, do not make purchases because they have heard that buying on the Web is not reliable or trustworthy. An additional 4.5 percent of users do not purchase online because they consider the process complicated. Only 1.9 percent of online consumers have actually had an unfavorable experience (the least-cited reason for not making more purchases on the Web).

Psychological variables are another personal characteristic studied by marketers. Such variables include personality and lifestyle characteristics. These variables are briefly mentioned in several places throughout the text. The reader who is interested in the details of psychological variables should see Solomon (2002).

▶ Describe the major components of the consumer online purchasing behavior model.

▶ List the major environmental variables of the purchasing environment.

▶ List some major personal characteristics that influence consumer behavior.

4.2 THE CONSUMER DECISION-MAKING PROCESS

Let's return to the central part of Exhibit 4.1, where consumers are shown making purchasing decisions. First, let's clarify the roles people play in the decision-making process. The major roles are as follows (Kotler and Armstrong 2002):

▶ **Initiator.** The person who first suggests or thinks of the idea of buying a particular product or service.

▶ **Influencer.** A person whose advice or view carries some weight in making a final purchasing decision.

▶ **Decider.** The person who ultimately makes a buying decision or any part of it—whether to buy, what to buy, how to buy, or where to buy.

▶ **Buyer.** The person who makes an actual purchase.

▶ **User.** The person who consumes or uses a product or service.

If one individual plays all of these roles, the marketer seeks to understand and target that individual. However, it is difficult to properly target advertising and marketing when more than one individual plays these different roles. How marketers deal with such an issue is beyond the scope of this book.

Several models have been developed in an effort to describe the details of the decision-making process that leads up to and culminates in a purchase. These models provide a framework for learning about the process in order to predict, improve, or influence consumer decisions. Here we introduce two popular models.

A GENERIC PURCHASING-DECISION MODEL

A general purchasing-decision model consists of five major phases. In each phase we can distinguish several activities and, in some of them, one or more decisions. The five phases are: (1) need identification, (2) information search, (3) evaluation of alternatives, (4) purchase and delivery, and (5) after-purchase evaluation. Although these phases offer a general guide to the consumer decision-making process, do not assume that consumers' decision making will necessarily proceed in this order. In fact, the consumer may proceed to a point and then revert back to a previous phase.

The first phase, *need identification,* occurs when a consumer is faced with an imbalance between the actual and the desired states of a need. A marketer's goal is to get the consumer to recognize such imbalance and then convince them that the product or service the seller offers will fill in this gap.

After identifying the need, the consumer *searches for information* (phase 2) on the various alternatives available to satisfy the need. Here, we differentiate between a decision of what product to buy, **product brokering**, and from whom to buy it, **merchant brokering**. These two decisions can be separate or combined. In the consumer's search for information, catalogs, advertising, promotions, and reference groups influence the decision making. During this phase, online product search and comparison engines, such as compare.com and mysimon.com, can be very helpful.

The consumer's information search will eventually generate a smaller set of preferred alternatives. From this set, the would-be buyer will further *evaluate the*

product brokering
Deciding what product to buy; may be done with the help of software agents.

merchant brokering
Deciding from whom to buy a specific product; may be done with the help of software agents.

alternatives (phase 3) and, if possible, will negotiate terms. In this phase, a consumer will use the information collected to develop a set of criteria. These criteria will help the consumer evaluate and compare alternatives. In phase 4, the consumer will make the *purchasing decision,* arrange payment and delivery, buy warranties, and so on.

Finally, there is a *postpurchase phase* (fifth phase) of customer service and evaluation of the usefulness of the product (e.g., "This is really great!" or "What was I thinking?").

A CUSTOMER DECISION MODEL IN WEB PURCHASING

The purchasing-decision model was used by O'Keefe and McEachern (1998) to build a framework for a Web-purchasing model, called the Consumer Decision Support System (CDSS). According to their framework, shown in Exhibit 4.4, each of the phases of the purchasing model can be supported by both CDSS facilities and generic Internet and Web facilities. The CDSS facilities support the specific decisions in the process. Generic EC technologies provide the necessary mechanisms, and they enhance communication and collaboration. Specific implementation of this framework is demonstrated throughout the text.

Others have developed similar models. The point here is that the planner of B2C marketing needs to consider a Web purchasing model in order to better influence the customer's decision making (e.g., by effective promotion).

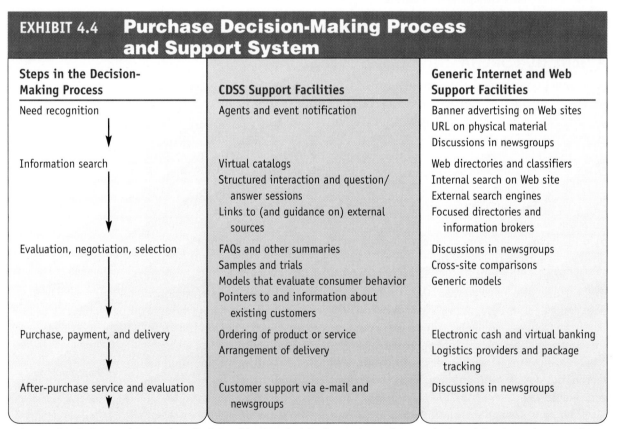

EXHIBIT 4.4	**Purchase Decision-Making Process and Support System**	
Steps in the Decision-Making Process	**CDSS Support Facilities**	**Generic Internet and Web Support Facilities**
Need recognition	Agents and event notification	Banner advertising on Web sites URL on physical material Discussions in newsgroups

Information search	Virtual catalogs
	Structured interaction and question/
	  answer sessions
	Links to (and guidance on) external
	  sources
		Web directories and classifiers
		Internal search on Web site
		External search engines
		Focused directories and
		  information brokers

Evaluation, negotiation, selection	FAQs and other summaries Samples and trials Models that evaluate consumer behavior Pointers to and information about existing customers	Discussions in newsgroups Cross-site comparisons Generic models
Purchase, payment, and delivery	Ordering of product or service Arrangement of delivery	Electronic cash and virtual banking Logistics providers and package tracking
After-purchase service and evaluation	Customer support via e-mail and newsgroups	Discussions in newsgroups

Source: O'Keefe, R. M., and T. McEachern, "Web-Based Customer Decision Support System." *Communications of the ACM* March © 1998 ACM, Inc. Used with permission.

▶ List the roles people play in purchasing.
▶ List the five stages in the generic purchasing-decision model.
▶ Describe the Web-based purchasing-decision model.

4.3 ONE-TO-ONE MARKETING AND PERSONALIZATION IN EC

One of the greatest benefits of EC is its ability to match products and services with individual consumers. Such a match is a part of **one-to-one marketing**, which treats each customer in a unique way to fit the customer's needs and other characteristics. The ability of EC to match individuals with products/services includes *personalization* or *customization* of products/services. Let's first look at the one-to-one relationship in EC.

one-to-one marketing
Marketing that treats each customer in a unique way.

HOW ONE-TO-ONE RELATIONSHIPS ARE PRACTICED

Although some companies have had one-to-one marketing programs for years, it may be much more beneficial to institute a corporate-wide policy of building one-to-one relationships around the Web. There are several ways to do this. For example, the Gartner Group, an IT consulting company, proposed what it calls "the new marketing cycle of relationship building." This proposal, illustrated in Exhibit 4.5, views relationships as a two-way street: First, customer information is collected and placed in a database. Then, a customer's profile is developed and the so-called *"Four P's"* of marketing (product, place, price, and promotion) are generated on a

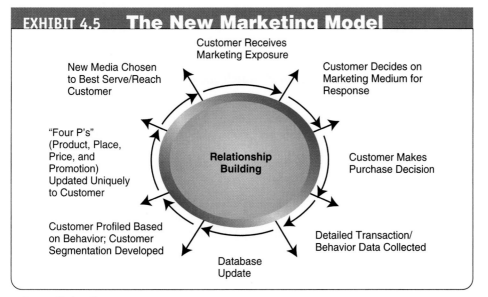

EXHIBIT 4.5 The New Marketing Model

Source: Gartner Group.

one-to-one basis. Based on this individualized profile, appropriate advertisements are prepared that will hopefully lead to a purchase by the customer. The detailed transaction is then added to the database, and the cycle is repeated. All this can, and should, be done in the Web environment.

One of the benefits of doing business over the Internet is that it enables companies to better communicate with customers and better understand customers' needs and buying habits. These improvements, in turn, enable companies to improve and frequently customize their future marketing efforts. For example, amazon.com can e-mail customers announcements of books published in their areas of interest, as soon as they are published.

Here we will address the key issues related to one-to-one marketing: personalization, collaborative filtering, customer loyalty, and trust. (For details on these and other issues related to implementing EC-based one-to-one marketing, see Peppers et al. 1999; Sindell 2000; and Todor and Todor 2001.)

PERSONALIZATION

personalization
The matching of services, products, and advertising content to individual consumers.

As discussed in Chapter 2, **personalization** refers to the matching of services, products, and advertising content to individuals. The matching process is based on what a company knows about the individual user. This knowledge is usually referred to as a **user profile**. The user profile defines customer preferences, behaviors, and demographics.

user profile
The requirements, preferences, behaviors, and demographic traits of a particular customer.

There are several ways to build user profiles. The major strategies used to compile user profiles include:

▶ **Solicit information directly from the user.** This is usually done by asking the user to fill in a questionnaire.

▶ **Use cookies or other methods to observe what people are doing online.** A cookie is a data file that is stored on the user's hard drive, frequently without disclosure or the user's consent. Sent by a Web server over the Internet, the information stored will surface when the user's browser again accesses the specific Web server, and the cookie will collect information about the user's activities at the site (see cookiecentral.com and online Chapter 9).

cookie
A data file that is placed on a user's hard drive by a Web server, frequently without disclosure or the user's consent, that collects information about the user's activities at a site.

▶ **Perform marketing research.** Research the market using tools such as Web mining.

▶ **Build from previous purchase patterns.** For example, Amazon.com builds customer profiles to recommend books and CDs based on what customers purchased before, rather than asking customers, using cookies, or doing market research.

Once a profile is constructed, a company matches the profile with a database of products, services, or contents. The actual matching process is usually done by software agents, as will be described later. Manual matching is too time-consuming and expensive.

Personalization can be applied through several different methods. One well-known method is *collaborative filtering*.

COLLABORATIVE FILTERING

Once a company knows a consumer's preferences (e.g., what music they like), it would be useful if the company could predict, without asking, what other products or services this consumer might enjoy. One way to do this is through **collaborative filtering**, which uses customer data to infer customer interest in other products or services. This prediction is based on special formulas derived from behavioral studies (see sins.berkeley.edu/resources.collab/ for details). The prediction can be extended to other customers with similar profiles. One of the pioneering filtering systems was Firefly (now part of Microsoft Network). Many personalization systems are based on collaborative filtering (e.g., backflip.com, c5corp.com, and blink.com). The following are some variations of collaborative filtering:

> **Rule-based filtering.** A company asks the consumers a series of yes/no or multiple-choice questions. The questions may range from personal information to the specific information the customer is looking for on a specific Web site. Certain behavioral patterns are predicted using the collected information. From this information, the collaborative filtering system derives behavioral and demographic rules such as, "If customer age is greater than 35, and customer income is above $100,000, show Jeep Cherokee ad. Otherwise, show Mazda Protégé."

> **Content-based filtering.** With this technique, vendors ask users to specify certain favorite products. Based on these user preferences, the vendor's system will recommend additional products to the user. This technique is fairly complex because mapping among different product categories must be completed in advance.

> **Activity-based filtering.** Filtering rules can also be built from watching the user's activities on the Web.

For more about personalization and filtering see personalization.com and cio.com.

Legal and Ethical Issues in Collaborative Filtering

Information is frequently collected from users without their knowledge or permission. This raises several ethical and legal questions, including invasion-of-privacy issues. Several vendors offer *permission-based* personalization tools. With these, companies request the customer's permission to receive questionnaires and ads (e.g., see knowledgestorm.com). For more on privacy issues, see Chapter 9.

CUSTOMER LOYALTY

One of the major objectives of one-to-one marketing is to increase customer loyalty. *Customer loyalty* is the degree to which a customer will stay with a specific vendor or brand. Customer loyalty is expected to produce more sales and increased profits over time. Also, it costs a company between five to eight times more to acquire a new customer than to keep an existing one. Customer loyalty strengthens a company's market position because loyal customers are kept away from the competition. Furthermore, increased loyalty can bring cost savings to a company in

collaborative filtering
A personalization method that uses customer data to predict, based on formulas derived from behavioral studies, what other products or services a customer may enjoy; predictions can be extended to other customers with similar profiles.

many ways: lower marketing costs, lower transaction costs, lower customer turnover expenses, lower failure costs such as warranty claims, and so on.

The introduction of EC decreases loyalty in general because customers' ability to shop, compare, and switch to different vendors becomes easier, faster, and less expensive given the aid of search engines and other technologies. On the other hand, companies have found that loyal customers end up buying more when they have a Web site to shop from. For example, grainger.com, a large industrial-supply company, found that loyal B2B customers increased their purchases substantially when they began using Grainger's Web site. Also, loyal customers may refer other customers to a site. Therefore, the company's goal is to increase customer loyalty. The Web offers ample opportunities to increase loyalty.

E-Loyalty

e-loyalty
Customer loyalty to an e-tailer.

E-loyalty refers to customers' loyalty to an e-tailer. Customer acquisition and retention is a critical success factor in e-tailing. The expense of acquiring a new customer can be over $100; even at Amazon.com, which has a huge reach, it is more than $15. In contrast, the cost of maintaining an existing customer at Amazon.com is $2 to $4.

Companies can foster e-loyalty by learning about their customers' needs, interacting with customers, and providing superb customer service, as Richey Design did. A major source of information about e-loyalty is e-loyaltyresource.com. One of its major services is an online journal, the *Journal of Customer Loyalty*, which offers numerous articles describing the relationships among e-loyalty, customer service, personalization, CRM, and Web-based tools. A comprehensive review of the use of the Web and the Internet to foster e-loyalty is provided by Reichheld (2001) and Reichheld and Schefter (2000).

TRUST IN EC

trust
The psychological status of involved parties who are willing to pursue further interaction to achieve a planned goal.

Trust is the psychological status of involved parties who are willing to pursue further interactions to achieve a planned goal. If you trust someone, you have confidence that as transaction partners they will keep their promises. However, both parties in a transaction assume some risk. In the marketspace, sellers and buyers do not meet face to face. The buyer can see a picture of the product but not the product itself. Promises of quality and delivery can be easily made—but will they be kept? To deal with these issues, EC vendors need to establish high levels of trust with current and potential customers. Trust is particularly important in global EC transactions due to the difficulty in taking legal action in cases of a dispute or fraud and the potential for conflicts caused by differences in culture and business environments.

How to Increase Trust in EC

How does one establish the necessary level of trust for EC? The desired level of trust is determined by the following factors (Shapiro et al. 1992): the degree of initial success that each party experienced with EC and with each other, well-defined roles and procedures for all parties involved, and realistic expectations as to outcomes from EC. Conversely, trust can be decreased by any user uncertainty regarding the technology, by lack of initial face-to-face interactions, and by lack of enthusiasm among the parties.

Brand recognition is very important in EC trust. For example, when a consumer buys online from Dell or Wal-Mart, the consumer probably will have a great deal of trust. Obviously, the consumer needs to be assured that Dell is the actual seller. Therefore, EC security mechanisms can also help solidify trust. In addition, it is necessary for EC vendors to disclose and update their latest business status and practices to potential customers and build transaction integrity into the system. They must also guarantee information and protection privacy through various communication channels.

Working against EC trust are stories of a considerable amount of fraud on the Internet, especially when unknown parties are involved. In Chapter 9, we describe measures that are being taken to reduce fraud and increase trust. In addition to trust between the buyers and sellers, it is necessary to have trust in the EC infrastructure and in the EC environment. (For comprehensive treatment of EC trust, see Camp 2000 and Keen et al. 2000.)

▶ Describe one-to-one marketing.

▶ Explain how personalization (matching people with goods/services) is done.

▶ Define loyalty and describe e-loyalty.

▶ Describe the issue of trust in EC and how to increase it.

4.4   MARKET RESEARCH FOR EC

The goal of market research is to find information and knowledge that describes the relationships among consumers, products, marketing methods, and marketers. Its aim is to discover marketing opportunities and issues, to establish marketing plans, to better understand the purchasing process, and to evaluate marketing performance. Market research includes gathering information about topics such as the economy, industry, firms, products, pricing, distribution, competition, promotion, and consumer purchasing behavior. Here we focus on the latter.

Various tools are used by businesses, educational institutions, and even governments to conduct consumer market research. For example, business representatives with questionnaires in shopping malls collect information from people about clothing, consumer products, or Internet usage. Surveyors may appear just about anywhere there is high traffic, such as supermarkets, theaters, and airport terminals, and replicating a survey in various cities can yield fairly generalized results. Another conventional way of conducting market research is by telephone surveys, where an interviewer calls current or prospective customers or a randomly selected sample of customers and asks questions regarding a specific product or service. Questionnaires may also be sent to specific individuals in a company or household.

In addition, *focus groups* can be useful. In these, groups of selected individuals are asked to discuss products or services in order for marketers to identify differences in attributes, benefits, and values of various potential markets. Analyzing these differences among groups of consumers is important when companies seek new target markets.

Because EC also has to identify an appropriate customer group for specific products and services, it is important first to understand how groups of consumers are classified. This classification is called segmentation.

MARKET SEGMENTATION

For years companies used direct mail to contact customers. However, they frequently did it regardless of whether the products or services were appropriate for the individuals on the company's mailing list. The cost of the direct mailings was about $1 per customer, and only 1 to 3 percent responded. This meant that the cost per responding customer was between $33 and $100. Obviously, this type of direct marketing was frequently not cost-effective. Instead, markets can be segmented in order to formulate effective marketing strategies that appeal to specific consumer groups.

market segmentation
The process of dividing a consumer market into logical groups for conducting marketing research, advertising, and sales.

Market segmentation is the process of dividing a consumer market into logical groups for conducting marketing research, advertising, and sales. A consumer market can be segmented in several ways, for example, by geography, demographics, psychographics, and benefits sought, as shown in Exhibit 4.6. A company can separate even millions of customers into smaller segments and tailor its campaigns to each of those segments. For example, advertisers may try to find people interested in travel and then send them travel information.

Segmentation is done with the aid of tools such as data modeling and data warehousing (e.g., see Levinson 2000). Using data mining (Berry and Linoff 2000) and Web mining, businesses can look at consumer buying patterns to slice segments even finer. This is not an easy process, and it requires considerable resources and computer support. Most of the segmentation success stories involve large companies. For example, Royal Bank of Canada segments its 10 million customers at least once a month to determine credit risk, profitability, and so on. This segmentation has been very successful: The response to Royal Bank of Canada advertising campaigns has increased from 3 to 30 percent. Segmentation can be very effective in the Web environment.

EXHIBIT 4.6	Consumer Market Segmentation in the United States (a partial list)
Segmentation	**Bases/Descriptors**
Geographic	Region; size of city, county, or Standard Metropolitan Statistical Area (SMSA); population density; climate
Demographic	Age; occupation; gender; education; family size; religion; race; income; nationality
Psychosocial	Social class; lifestyle; personality
Cognitive, affective, behavioral	Attitudes; benefits sought; loyalty status, readiness stage; usage rate; perceived risk; user status; innovativeness; usage situation; involvement

CONDUCTING MARKET RESEARCH ONLINE

EC market research can be conducted by conventional methods, such as those described earlier, or it can be done with the assistance of the Internet. Although telephone or shopping mall surveys will continue, interest in Internet research methods is on the rise. Market research that utilizes the Internet is frequently faster and more efficient, and allows the researcher to access a more geographically diverse audience than those found in off-line surveys. Also, on the Web, market researchers can conduct a very large study much more cheaply than with other methods. The larger the sample size, the larger the accuracy and the predictive capabilities of the results. Telephone surveys can cost as much as $50 per respondent. This may be too expensive for a small company that needs several hundred respondents. An online survey will cost a fraction of a similarly sized telephone survey.

What Are We Looking for in EC Market Research?

By looking at a personal profile that includes observed behaviors on the Web, it is possible for marketers to predict online buying behavior. Major factors that are used for prediction are (in descending order of importance): product information requested; number of related e-mails; number of orders made; what products/services are ordered; and gender. Typical questions that online market research attempts to answer are: What are the purchase patterns for individuals and groups (segmentation)? What factors encourage online purchasing? How can we identify those who are real buyers from those who are just browsing? How does an individual navigate—does the consumer check information first or do they go directly to ordering? What is the optimal Web page design? Knowing the answers to questions such as these helps a vendor to advertise properly, to price items, to design the Web site, and to provide appropriate customer service. Online market research can provide such data about individuals, about groups, and even about the entire Internet.

Internet-based market research is often done in an interactive manner, allowing personal contact with customers, and it provides marketing organizations with greater ability to understand the customer, the market, and the competition. For example, it can identify early shifts in product and customer trends, enabling marketers to identify products and marketing opportunities and to develop those products that customers really want to buy. It also tells management when a product or a service is no longer popular. To learn more on market research on the Web, see the tutorials at webmonkey.com. The following discussion describes some online market research methods.

Online Market Research Methods

Online research methods range from one-to-one communication with specific customers, usually by e-mail, to moderated focus groups conducted in chat rooms, to surveys placed on Web sites, to tracking of customers' movements on the Web. A typical Internet-based market research process is shown in Exhibit 4.7 (page 160).

Using questionnaires, companies collect information from customers before they are allowed to play games, win prizes (see opening case study), or download

---

EXHIBIT 4.7   Online Market Research Process and Results

Steps in Collecting Market Research Data
1. Define the research issue and the target market.
2. Identify newsgroups and Internet communities to study.
3. Identify specific topics for discussion.
4. Subscribe to the pertinent groups; register in communities.
5. Search discussion group topic and content lists to find the target market.
6. Search e-mail discussion group lists.
7. Subscribe to filtering services that monitor groups.
8. Read FAQs and other instructions.
9. Visit chat rooms.

Content of the Research Instrument
1. Post strategic queries to groups.
2. Post surveys on your Web site.
3. Offer rewards for participation.
4. Post strategic queries on your Web site.
5. Post relevant content to groups with a pointer to your Web site survey.
6. Post a detailed survey in special e-mail questionnaires.
7. Create a chat room and try to build a community of consumers.

Target Audience of the Study
1. Compare your audience with the target population.
2. Determine your editorial focus.
3. Determine your content.
4. Determine what Web services to create for each type of audience.

Source: Based on Vassos, 1996, pp. 66–68.

---

free software. However, according to recent surveys conducted by the Georgia Institute of Technology, more than 40 percent of the information people place on such questionnaires is incorrect (1998; 1999). Therefore, appropriate design of Web questionnaires and incentives for true completion are critical for the validity of the results. Professional pollsters and marketing research companies frequently conduct online voting polls (e.g., see cnn.com, acnielsen.com).

Online market researchers have to address numerous issues. For example, customers may refuse to answer certain questions. Also, the analysis of questionnaires can be lengthy and costly. Furthermore, researchers risk losing respondents to online questionnaires because the respondents may not have the latest computers or a fast Internet connection.

Web-based surveys. Web-based surveys are becoming popular among companies and researchers. For example, Mazda North America used a Web-based survey to help design its Miata line. Free software to create survey forms and analyze results is available at zoomerang.com. For more information and additional software tools, see supersurvey.com, websurveyor.com, clearlearning.com, and tucows.com/webforms. For an introduction on how to conduct Web-based surveys, see Lazar and Preece (1999), and for some hands-on experiences, see Compton (1999).

Online focus groups. Several research firms create panels of qualified Web regulars to participate in online focus groups. For example, NPD's panel (npd.com) consists of 15,000 consumers recruited online and verified by telephone; Greenfield Online picks users from its own database, then calls them periodically to verify that they are who they say they are. Another online research firm, Research Connections, recruits in advance by telephone, and takes the time to help new users connect to the Internet, if necessary. Use of these preselected focus group participants helps overcome some of the problems (e.g., sample size and partial responses) that sometimes limit the effectiveness of Web-based surveys.

Tracking customer movements. To avoid some of the problems of online surveys, especially the provision of false information, some marketers choose to learn about customers by observing their behavior rather than by asking them questions. Many marketers keep track of consumers' Web movements using either transaction logs or cookie files. For example, Internet Profile Corporation will collect data from a company's client/server logs and provide the company with periodic reports that include demographic data such as where customers come from or how many customers have gone straight from the home page to placing an order. IPC also translates Internet domain names into real company names and includes general and financial corporate information in their reports.

Transaction logs. A **transaction log** records user activities at a company's Web site. It is not simple to analyze transaction logs (e.g., see webtrends.com). The transaction-log method is especially useful if the visitors' names are known (e.g., when they have registered with the site). Also, one can combine actual shopping data from the shopping-cart database. Note that as customers move on the Net, they establish their **clickstream behavior**, a pattern we can see in their transaction logs.

Cookies and Web bugs. Cookies and Web bugs can supplement transaction-log methods. As discussed earlier, *cookies* allow a Web site to store data on the user's PC, which can be used to find what the customer did in the past when they return to the site. Cookies are frequently combined with **Web bugs**, tiny graphics files embedded on e-mail messages and on Web sites. Web bugs transmit information about the user and their movements to a monitoring site.

With both cookies and Web bugs, there is controversy about whether their use invades customer privacy (see privacyfoundation.org). Tracking customers' activities *without their knowledge or permission* may be unethical or even illegal.

Limitations of Online Research Methods

We have already noted some of the limitations of online research methods: accuracy of responses, loss of respondents because of equipment problems, and the ethics and legality of Web tracking. In addition, focus group responses can lose something in the translation from an in-person group to an online group. You may get people online to talk to each other and play off each other's comments, but eye contact and body language are two interactions of traditional focus group research that are lost in the online world. On the other hand, just as it hinders the two-way assessment of visual cues, Web research can actually permit some participants the anonymity necessary to elicit an unguarded response.

transaction log
A record of user activities at a company's Web site.

clickstream behavior
Customer movements on the Internet.

Web bugs
Tiny graphics files embedded on e-mail messages and in Web sites that transmit information about the user and their movements to a Web server.

DATA MINING

data mining
The process of searching a large database to discover previously unknown patterns; automates the process of finding predictive information.

Data mining derives its name from the similarities between searching for valuable business information in a large database and mining a mountain for a vein of valuable ore. Both processes require either sifting through an immense amount of material or intelligently probing it to find exactly where the value resides. Given databases of sufficient size and quality, data mining technology can generate new business opportunities by providing these capabilities:

▶ **Automated prediction of trends and behaviors.** Data mining automates the process of finding predictive information in large databases. Questions that traditionally required extensive hands-on analysis can now be answered directly and quickly from the data. A typical example of a predictive problem is targeted marketing. Data mining can use data on the response to past promotional mailings to identify the targets most likely to respond favorably to future mailings. For an example of using data mining to predict trends and customer behavior, see EC Application Case 4.1.

▶ **Automated discovery of previously unknown patterns.** Data mining tools identify previously hidden patterns. An example of pattern discovery is the analysis of retail sales data to identify seemingly unrelated products that are often purchased together, such as baby diapers and beer. Other pattern-discovery targets include detecting fraudulent credit card transactions and identifying anomalous data that may represent data entry keying errors.

EC APPLICATION CASE 4.1

Implementation and Strategy

BRITISH TELECOM USES DATA MINING

British Telecom is a large telecommunications company in the United Kingdom. Its 1.5 million business users make about 90 million calls a day. The company provides 4,500 products and services. The company was looking for the best way to reach out and touch individual customers. The solution was a customer data warehouse and neural computing technology for conducting data mining.

The company uses the system to analyze customers' buying habits in order to better understand customer needs and target marketing opportunities. For example, the company identified purchasing profiles for individual products, packages of products, and customers. One goal of the system is to identify customers who could be at risk of capture by the competition. Data mining is also useful in identifying trends in products that have a high sales value, such as a call-waiting feature. Finding such trends improves the relationship between marketing and sales and helps guide the sales force on where to put their resources. Prior to data mining, the sales and marketing personnel were analyzing data that were 6 months to 1 year old. Now they have almost real-time marketing information.

Source: Compiled from *bt.com* and *emarketer.com*.

Questions

▶ What is being mined?

▶ What are the advantages of data mining in this case?

Data miners can use the following tools and techniques:

- **Neural computing.** Neural computing is a machine-learning approach by which historical data can be examined for patterns.
- **Intelligent agents.** One of the most promising approaches to retrieving information from the Internet or from intranet-based databases is through the use of intelligent agents.
- **Association analysis.** This approach uses a specialized set of algorithms that sorts through large sets of data and expresses statistical rules among items.

It is estimated that at least half of all *Fortune* 1,000 companies worldwide use data mining technologies (Tiedrich, 2001). Data mining can be very helpful, as shown by the examples in Exhibit 4.8. Data mining is useful in analyzing data in both databases and data warehouses. It can also be used to conduct Web mining, as described next.

Web Mining

Web mining is the application of data mining techniques to discover meaningful patterns, profiles, and trends from Web sites. The term Web mining is being used in two different ways. The first, *Web content mining* is the process of discovering information from millions of Web documents. The second, *Web usage mining*, is the process of analyzing Web access logs (or other information connected to user browsing and access patterns) on one or more Web localities.

    Web mining can be used for various purposes: to filter information from e-mail, magazines, and newspapers; to conduct surveillance of competitors' Web sites; for assisted browsing for funding information; and to fight crime on the Internet.

Web mining
The application of data mining techniques to discover meaningful patterns, profiles, and trends from both the content and usage of Web sites.

EXHIBIT 4.8	Sample Data Mining Applications
Industry	**Applications**
Retailing and sales distribution	Predicting sales; determining inventory levels and schedules
Banking	Forecasting bad loans and fraudulent credit card use; predicting credit card spending by new customers; predicting customer response to offers
Airlines	Capturing data on where customers are flying and the ultimate destination of passengers who change carriers mid-trip so airlines can identify popular locations that they do not service and check the feasibility of adding routes to capture lost business
Broadcasting	Predicting the best programming to air during prime time and how to maximize returns by interjecting advertisements
Marketing	Classifying customer demographics that can be used to predict which customers will respond to a mailing or buy a particular product

Web mining is critical for EC due to the large number of visitors to EC sites (about 2.4 billion during the Christmas 2001 season alone). For additional discussions of Web mining, see Parsa (1999) and sas.com.

LIMITATIONS OF ONLINE MARKET RESEARCH

Concerns have been expressed over the potential lack of representativeness in samples composed of online users. Online shoppers tend to be wealthy, employed, and well educated. Although this may be a desirable audience for some products and services, the research results may not be extendable to other markets. Although the Web-user demographic is rapidly diversifying, it is still skewed toward certain population groups, such as those with Internet access. Another important issue concerns the lack of clear understanding of the online communication process and how online respondents think and interact in cyberspace.

It is important that a company verifies the target audience or demographic it wants, so it can perform the right kind of sampling. Web-based surveys typically have a lower response rate than e-mail surveys, and there is no respondent control for public surveys. If your target respondents are allowed to be anonymous, it may encourage them to be more truthful in their opinions. However, with anonymity, you lose valuable information about the demographics and characteristics of the respondents. Finally, there are still concerns about the security of the information transmitted, which may also have an impact on the truthfulness of the respondents.

Some researchers are wildly optimistic about the prospects for market research on the Internet; others are more cautious. One expert predicts that in the next few years, 50 percent of all market research will be done on the Internet. "Ten years from now, national telephone surveys will be the subject of research methodology folklore," he proclaims. "That's a little too soon," cautions another expert. "But in 20 years, yes."

- Describe the objectives of market research.
- Define and describe segmentation.
- Describe how market research is done online.
- Describe data mining and how it is done.
- Define Web mining.
- Describe the limitations of online market research.

4.5 DELIVERING CUSTOMER SERVICE IN CYBERSPACE

When customers engage in EC purchasing, they may sometimes require assistance. For example, customers may need assistance in finding out what item they should buy to satisfy a particular need. Customers often have questions about a product's characteristics before they make a purchase, as well as questions on proper maintenance and repair after the sale. Sellers must be able to assist in any and all of the customers' questions. Such assistance is a major objective of customer service.

Customer service is a series of activities designed to enhance customer satisfaction (the feeling that a product or service has met the customer's expectations). EC customer service improves on traditional customer service by means of easier communications and speedier resolution of customer problems, frequently by automatic responses to questions or customer self-service. Today, in order to satisfy the increased customer expectations, EC marketers must respond by providing the best, most powerful, and innovative systems and software.

E-SERVICE

When customer service is supplied over the Internet, it is referred to as **e-service**. E-service often provides online help for online transactions (e.g., searchhp.com). In addition, even if a product is purchased off-line, customer service may be offered online. For example, if a consumer purchases a product off-line and needs expert advice on how to use it, they may find detailed instructions online (e.g., livemanuals.com).

According to Voss (2000), there are three levels of e-service:

1. **Foundation of service.** This includes the minimum necessary services such as site responsiveness (e.g., how quickly and accurately the service is provided), site effectiveness, and order fulfillment.
2. **Customer-centered services.** These services include order tracing, configuration and customization, and security/trust. These are the services that matter the most to customers.
3. **Value-added services.** These are extra services such as dynamic brokering, online auctions, and online training and education.

Customer service should be provided throughout the entire product life cycle. The value chain for Internet service is composed of four parts (Plant 2000):

▶ **Customer acquisition (pre-purchase support):** A service strategy that reflects and reinforces the company's brand and provides information to potential customers to encourage them to buy.

▶ **Customer support during purchase:** The service strategy provides a shopping environment that the consumer sees as efficient, informative, and productive.

▶ **Customer fulfillment (purchase dispatch):** This involves timely delivery, including keeping the customer informed about the fulfillment process, especially if there are any delays.

▶ **Customer continuance support (post-purchase):** Information and support help maintain the customer relationship between purchases.

CUSTOMER RELATIONSHIP MANAGEMENT (CRM)

A new way of looking at customer service is an approach called **customer relationship management (CRM)**. CRM recognizes that customers are the core of a business and that a company's success depends on effectively managing its relationship

---

customer service
A series of activities designed to enhance customer satisfaction (the feeling that a product or service has met the customer's expectations).

e-service
Customer services supplied over the Internet.

customer relationship management (CRM)
A customer service approach that focuses on building long-term and sustainable customer relationships that add value both for the customer and the company.

with them (see Brown 2000). CRM focuses on building long-term and sustainable customer relationships that add value both for the customer and the company (Kalakota and Robinson 2001). (See also crm-forum.com and crmassist.com.)

Seybold and Marshak (1998) highlight some important steps in building an EC strategy that is centered on the customer. These steps include: a focus on the end customer; systems and business processes that are designed for ease of use and from the end-customer's point of view; and efforts to foster customer loyalty, the key to profitability in EC. To successfully make these steps, businesses must take the following actions:

- Deliver personalized services (e.g., dowjones.com).
- Target the right customers (e.g., aa.com, nsc.com).
- Help the customers do their jobs (e.g., boeing.com).
- Let customers help themselves (e.g., iprint.com).
- Streamline business processes that impact the customers (e.g., ups.com, amazon.com).
- "Own" the customer's total experience by providing every possible customer contact (e.g., amazon.com, hertz.com).
- Provide a 360-degree view of the customer relationship (e.g., wellsfargo.com, verizon.com).

Many of these steps are valid for both B2C and for B2B EC.

CUSTOMER SERVICE FACILITIES AND TOOLS

Customer service on the Web can take many forms, ranging from providing search and comparison capabilities to allowing customers to track the status of their order. These services are summarized in Exhibit 4.9. Notice that several of these services are performed by the customers themselves (self-service). This saves money and expedites the service. The last three items in the table are described in more detail in the following sections.

Personalized Web Pages

Many companies provide customers with tools to create their own individual Web pages. These Web pages can then be used to record customer purchases and preferences. Companies can efficiently deliver customized information such as product information and warranty information when the customer logs on to the personalized page. Not only can a customer pull information from the vendor's site, but the vendor can also push information to the consumer.

Vendors can use customer information collected from customized Web sites to facilitate customer service and enhance sales. Information that previously may have been provided to the customer 1 to 3 months after a transaction was completed is now provided in real or almost-real time, and it can be traced and analyzed for an immediate response or action. Companies now use customer information to help market additional products by matching valuable information about product performance and consumer behavior. American Airlines is an example of

EXHIBIT 4.9   Customer Service Facilities and Tools

Facility or Tool	Description
Search and comparison tools	Search for items, compare prices (see Chapter 3)
Free services, samples, and entertainment	Customers love free stuff (e.g., *netbank.com* provides free bill payment)
Tracking accounts or order status	Self-service for finding current information; popular in e-banking, online stock trading, shipping (e.g., FedEx, UPS, USPS), and checking the status of an order (e.g., *amazon.com*)
Frequently asked questions (FAQs)	Self-service for answering common questions
Chat rooms and discussion boards	A place to discuss problems and opinions with others; creates a community of users; company experts monitor discussion and help customers resolve problems
Product (service) customization and configuration	Customers can use customization tools to customize thousands of products and services (e.g., *dell.com*, *nike.com*); also popular in B2B.
Detailed product information, tutorials, demos, and more	Customers can access expert information (*1-800-flowers.com*), tutorials, technical advice, and more (e.g., *livemanuals.com* provides information on how to assemble products; and people can learn about tires at *goodyear.com*)
Support services, maps, news	Information of general interest to the site visitors; supports the interest of the community visitor
Troubleshooting tools	Self-service problem resolution; intelligent diagnosis and recommendation tools (e.g., *prismnet.com*, *woodfinishsupply.com*).
Arrange for live communication	Customers may arrange to talk or chat in real time with a company representative.
Animated agents	Animated agents on a Web site provide guided tours and make the customer feel as if they have personalized service.
Personalized Web pages	Can be used to display a customer's frequent flyer mileage, bank balance, or purchase history; vendors also use the accumulated information from these pages for advertisement and cross-selling.
Automatic response to e-mail inquiries	Customers get a quick response to queries. Answers are first provided by software agents. If answer is not satisfactory, a human answer can be provided.
Call centers	Call centers aggregate all inquiries, distribute them so they can be answered, and manage all communication.

one company that uses personalized Web sites to help increase the bottom line, as shown in EC Application Case 4.2.

Automated Response to E-Mail

The most popular online customer service tool is e-mail. Inexpensive and fast, e-mail is used to disseminate information and to conduct correspondence on many topics, including responses to customer inquiries.

The ease of sending e-mail messages has resulted in a flood of customer e-mail. Some companies receive tens of thousands of e-mails a week, or even a day. Answering these e-mails manually would be expensive and time-consuming. Customers want quick answers, usually within 24 hours (a policy of many organizations). Several vendors offer automated e-mail reply systems, which provide answers to commonly asked questions (see egain.com, firepond.com, and quark.com).

The eGain system, for example, looks for certain phrases or key words such as "complaint" or "information on a product," and then taps into a knowledge base to generate a canned, matching response. For messages that require human atten-

---

EC APPLICATION CASE 4.2
Individuals and Communities
AMERICAN AIRLINES OFFERS PERSONALIZED WEB SITES

In late 1998, American Airlines (AA) unveiled a number of features on its Web site (*aa.com*) that some thought made the site the most advanced for personalized, one-to-one interactions and transactions on the Web. The most innovative feature of this site is its ability to generate personalized Web pages for each of about 1 million registered, travel-planning customers. How can AA handle such a large amount of information and provide real-time customized Web pages for each customer? The answer—intelligent agents.

The AA site was developed by Broadvision (*broadvision.com*), a major developer of one-to-one marketing applications, using a complex software called One-to-One Application. One of the core components needed to generate personalized Web pages is intelligent agents, which dynamically match customer profiles (built on information supplied by the customer, observed by the system, or derived from existing customer databases) to the database of contents. The output of the matching process triggers the creation of a real-time customized Web page, which for AA can contain information on the consumer's home airport and preferred destinations.

By using intelligent-agent technology, American Airlines built a considerable edge over its competitors. Personalizing Web pages is becoming more important because of its potential in increasing customer loyalty and cementing relationships with customers. The Web site also fostered the community of American Airlines frequent flyers.

Source: Compiled from *aa.com* and *broadvision.com*.

Questions

▌ What are the benefits of the personalized pages to American Airlines?

▌ What role do intelligent agents play in the personalization process?

tion, the query is assigned an ID number and passed along to a customer agent for a reply.

Many companies do not provide actual answers in their automatic responses, but only acknowledgement that a query has been received. Customer queries are classified in a decision-support repository until a human agent logs in and responds. This is usually part of a call center.

Call Centers

A **call center** is a comprehensive customer service entity in which EC vendors take care of customer-service issues communicated through various contact channels. Providing well-trained customer service representatives who have access to data such as customer history, purchases, and previous contacts is one way to improve customer service.

call center
A comprehensive service entity in which EC vendors address customer-service issues communicated through various contact channels.

New products are extending the functionality of the conventional call center to e-mail and Web interactivity, integrating them into one product. An example of a well-managed integrated call center is that of Bell Advanced Communication in Canada, whose subscribers can submit customer service queries over the Web. From the Bell Advanced Web site, a customer can fill out an e-mail form with drop-down menus that help pinpoint the customer's problem. The e-mail then is picked up by the call center, which either answers the question immediately or tries to have a human response within 1 hour. Another example is eFrontOffice (epicor.com/efrontoffice), which combines Web channels such as automated e-mail reply, Web knowledge bases, and portal-like self-service, with call center agents or field service personnel. Such centers are sometimes called **telewebs**. For another example of a Web-based call center, see the Application Case about Canadian Tire's integrated call center in the Chapter 4 material at the book's Web site. A comprehensive description of Web-based call centers, including tutorial, articles, and information on leading vendors is available at call-centers.org.

telewebs
Call centers that combine Web channels with portal-like self-service.

Today's various customer service facilities and tools—personalized Web pages, automated responses to e-mails, and multimedia-based, Web-enabled call centers—can arrange quick contact with humans, mobile device connections, and more. However, as you might imagine, such customer service programs are expensive to develop. How do companies justify investing in them?

JUSTIFYING CUSTOMER SERVICE AND CRM PROGRAMS

Two major problems arise when companies try to justify expenditures for customer service and CRM programs. The first problem is the fact that most of the benefits are intangible, and the second is that substantial benefits can be reaped only from loyal customers. This, of course, is true for both off-line and online organizations. In a 1990 study published in *Harvard Business Review* titled, "Zero Defections: Quality Comes to Services," (see details at Reichheld and Schefer 2000), researchers demonstrated that the high costs of acquiring customers renders many customer relationship programs unprofitable during their early years. Only in later years, when the cost of retaining loyal customers falls and the volume of their purchases rises, do CRMs generate big returns (Reichheld and Schefer 2000).

Therefore, companies are very careful about determining how much customer service to provide (see Petersen 1999).

Metrics

One way to determine how much service to provide is to compare a company against a set of standards known as **metrics**. Metrics can be either quantitative or qualitative measures. Here are some Web-related metrics a company can use to determine the appropriate level of customer support:

metrics
Measures of performance; may be quantitative or qualitative.

- ❯ **Response time.** Many companies have a target response time of 24 to 48 hours. If a company uses intelligent agents, a response can be made in real time or the system can provide an acknowledgement that the customer's message has been received.

- ❯ **Site availability.** Customers should be able to reach the company Web site at any time (24 hours a day). This means that downtime should be as close to zero as possible.

- ❯ **Download time.** Users usually will not tolerate downloads that last more than 10 to 20 seconds.

- ❯ **Timeliness.** Information on the company site must be up-to-date. The company sets an interval (say every month) at which information must be revised.

- ❯ **Security and privacy.** Web sites must provide sufficient privacy statements and an explanation of security measures.

- ❯ **On-time order fulfillment.** Order fulfillment must be fast and when promised to the customer. The company can measure the time it takes to fulfill orders, and it can count the number of times it fails to meet its fulfillment promises.

- ❯ **Return policy.** In the United States and several other countries, return policies are a standard service. Having a return policy increases customer trust and loyalty. The ease by which customers can make returns is important to customer satisfaction.

- ❯ **Navigability.** A Web site must be easy to navigate. Companies might measure the number of customers who get part way into an order and then "bail out."

Once they have planned solid products or services, backed by superb customer service, organizations also put much time, money, and effort into advertising. Like many other businesses, e-commerce sites need to advertise their products and services. This topic is discussed in the remaining sections of the chapter.

- ❯ Define customer service and describe its importance.
- ❯ Define e-service.
- ❯ Define CRM and describe how it is practiced in EC.
- ❯ List the customer service functions provided online.
- ❯ Describe help desks and call centers in EC.
- ❯ Describe metrics related to customer service.

4.6   WEB ADVERTISING

OVERVIEW OF WEB ADVERTISING

Advertising is an attempt to disseminate information in order to affect a buyer–seller transaction. In *traditional* marketing, advertising was impersonal, one-way mass communication, paid for by sponsors. Telemarketing and direct mail were attempts to personalize advertisement in order to make it more effective. These *direct marketing* approaches worked fairly well but were expensive and slow and seldom truly one-to-one interactive. For example, as mentioned earlier, a direct mail campaign costs about $1 per person, with a response rate of only 1 to 3 percent. This makes the cost per responding person in the range of $33 to $100. Such an expense can be justified only for high-ticket items (e.g., cars).

One of the problems with direct mail advertising was that the advertisers knew very little about the recipients. Segmentation helped a bit, but did not solve the problem. The Internet introduces the concept of **interactive marketing**, which has enabled advertisers to interact directly with customers. In interactive marketing, a consumer can click on an ad in order to obtain more information or send an e-mail to ask a question. Besides the two-way communication and e-mail capabilities provided by the Internet, vendors also can target specific groups and individuals on which they want to spend their advertising dollars. Finally, the Internet enables truly one-to-one advertising. A comparison of mass advertising with interactive advertising is shown in Exhibit 4.10.

Companies use Internet advertising as *one* of their advertising channels. At the same time, they may use also TV, newspapers, or other channels. In this chapter, we deal with Internet advertising in general. (For additional resources on Internet advertisement, see adage.com and hotwired.com/webmonkey).

INTERNET ADVERTISING TERMINOLOGY

The following glossary of terms will be of use as you read about Web advertising.

- **Ad views.** **Ad views** are the number of times users call up a page that has a banner on it during a specific time period (e.g., "ad views per day"). They are also known as *impressions* or *page views*.
- **Button.** A *button* is a small banner that is linked to a Web site. It may contain downloadable software.
- **Page.** A *page* is an HTML (Hypertext Markup Language) document that may contain text, images, and other online elements, such as Java applets and multimedia files. It may be statically or dynamically generated.
- **Click.** A **click** (or **ad click** or **click-through**) is counted each time a visitor clicks on an advertising banner to access the advertiser 's Web site.
- **CPM.** The **CPM** is the **cost per thousand impressions**. This is the fee the advertiser pays for each 1,000 times a page with a banner ad is viewed.

---

interactive marketing
Marketing that allows a consumer to interact with an online seller (e.g., requesting information by e-mail).

ad views
The number of times users call up a page that has a banner on it during a specific time period; known as *impressions* or *page views*.

click
A count made each time a visitor clicks on an advertising banner to access the advertiser's Web site.

CPM (cost per thousand impressions)
The fee an advertiser pays for each 1,000 times a page with a banner ad is viewed.

EXHIBIT 4.10	From Mass Advertising to Interactive Advertising		
	Mass Advertising	**Direct Mail Advertising**	**Interactive Advertising**
Best outcome	Volume sales	Customer data	Customer relationships
Consumer behavior	Passive	Passive	Active
Leading products	Food, personal care products, beer, autos	Credit cards, travel, autos	Upscale apparel, travel, financial services, autos
Market	High volume	Targeted goods	Targeted individual
Nerve center	Madison Avenue	Postal distribution centers	Cyberspace
Preferred media vehicle	Television, magazines	Mailing lists	Online services
Preferred technology	Storyboards	Databases	Servers, on-screen navigators, the Web
Worst outcome	Channel surfing	Recycling bins	Log off

Source: Based on *InformationWeek*, October 3, 1994, p. 26. Used with permission.

hit
A request for data from a Web page or file.

visit
A series of requests during one navigation of a Web site; a pause of request for a certain length of time ends a visit.

▶ **Hit.** A **hit** refers to any request for data from a Web page or file. Hits are often used to determine the popularity/traffic of a site in the context of getting so many "hits" during a given period.

▶ **Visit.** A user may make a sequence of requests during one **visit** to a site. Once the visitor stops making requests from a site for a given period of time, called a *time-out* (usually 15 or 30 minutes), the next hit by this visitor is considered a new visit.

WHY INTERNET ADVERTISING?

The major traditional advertising media are television (about 36 percent), newspapers (about 35 percent), magazines (about 14 percent), and radio (about 10 percent). Although Internet advertisement is a small percentage of the $120-billion-a-year industry (less than 5 percent in 2001), it is growing rapidly. For example, in 1995, Internet advertising expenditures were about $43 million. This amount grew to over $1 billion in 1998 (iab.net) and to close to $5 billion in 2002. The estimate for 2005 is $15 billion.

There are several reasons why companies advertise on the Internet. To begin with, television viewers are migrating to the Internet. Numerous studies have found that over three-quarters of PC users are giving up some television time to spend more time on their computers. A November 2001 study done at UCLA confirms this trade-off (ccp.ucla.edu, November 2001). Finally, many Internet users are well educated and have high incomes. Therefore, many Internet surfers are a desired target for advertisers.

Meeker (1997) examined the length of time it took for each ad media to reach 50 million U.S. users. Meeker found that it took radio 38 years, television 13 years, and cable television 10 years to reach 50 million viewers. Remarkably, it took only about 5 years for the Internet to reach 50 million users! Exhibit 4.11 extends the study to the year 2000, at which time more than 300 million people had used the Internet. According to these statistics, the Internet is by far the fastest growing communication medium. Of course, advertisers are interested in a medium with such potential reach, both locally and globally.

EXHIBIT 4.11   Adoption Curves for Various Media

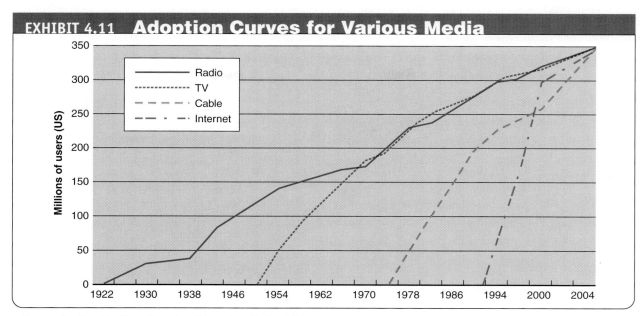

Source: Developed by the authors, based in part on Meeker, 1997.

Other reasons why Web advertising is growing rapidly include:

▶ **Cost.** Online ads are sometimes cheaper than those in other media. In addition, ads can be updated at any time with minimal cost.

▶ **Richness of format**. Web ads can effectively use the convergence of text, audio, graphics, and animation. In addition, games, entertainment, and promotions can easily be combined in online advertisements.

▶ **Personalization.** Web ads can be interactive and targeted to specific interest groups and/or individuals.

As of 1998, these factors began to convince large, consumer-products companies to shift an increasing share of their advertising dollars away from traditional media to Web advertisements. Toyota is a prime example of the power of Internet advertising. Saatchi and Saatchi, a major ad agency, developed Toyota's Web site (toyota.com) and also placed Toyota 's traffic-luring banner ads on other popular Web sites such as espn.com. Within a year, the Web site overtook Toyota's 1-800 telephone number as its best source of sale leads.

Of course, each advertising medium, including the Internet, has its advantages and limitations. Exhibit 4.12 (page 174) compares the advantages and limitations of Internet advertising against the traditional advertising media.

ADVERTISING NETWORKS

One of the major advantages of Internet advertising is the ability to customize ads to fit individual viewers. Specialized firms have sprung up to offer this service to companies that wish to locate customers through targeted advertising. Called **advertising networks** (or *ad server networks*) these firms offer special services such as brokering banner ads for sale, bringing together online advertisers and providers

advertising networks
Specialized firms that offer customized Web advertising, such as brokering ads and helping target ads to selected groups of consumers.

EXHIBIT 4.12 Advantages and Limitations of Internet Advertising Compared to Traditional Media

Medium	Advantages	Limitations
TV	▶ Intrusive impact—high attention getter ▶ Ability to demonstrate product and feature "slice of life" situations ▶ Very "merchandisable" with media buyers	▶ Fragmented ratings, rising costs, "clutter" ▶ Heavy "downscale" audience skew ▶ Time is sold in multiprogram packages. Networks often require major up-front commitments. Both limit the advertiser's flexibility.
Radio	▶ Highly selective by station format ▶ Allows advertisers to choose the time of day or the day of the week to exploit timing factors ▶ Copy can rely on the listener's mood or imagination.	▶ Audience surveys are limited in scope, do not provide socioeconomic demographics ▶ Difficult to buy with so many stations to consider ▶ Testing of copy is difficult because there are few statistical guidelines
Magazines	▶ Offer unique opportunities to segment markets, both demographically and psychographically ▶ Ads can be studied and reviewed at leisure ▶ High impact can be attained with good graphics and literate, informative copy	▶ Reader controls ad exposure, can ignore campaign ▶ Difficult to exploit "timing" aspects
Newspapers	▶ High single-day reach opportunity ▶ Reader often shops for specific information when ready to buy ▶ Portable format	▶ Lack of demographic selectivity, despite increased zoning, many markets have only one paper. ▶ High cost for large-size ads ▶ Lack of creative opportunities for "emotional" selling campaigns ▶ Low-quality reproduction, lack of color
Internet	▶ Internet advertisements are available 24 hours a day, 365 days a year, and costs are the same regardless of audience location ▶ Accessed primarily because of interest in the content, so market segmentation opportunity is large ▶ Opportunity to create one-to-one direct marketing relationship with consumer ▶ Multimedia will increasingly create more attractive and compelling ads ▶ Distribution costs are low (just technology costs), so reaching millions of consumers costs the same as reaching one ▶ Advertising and content can be updated, supplemented, or changed at any time, and are therefore always up-to-date. ▶ Response (click-through rate) and results (page views) are immediately measurable. ▶ Logical navigation—you click when and where you want, and you can spend as much time as you want at the site	▶ No clear standard or language of measurement ▶ Immature measurement tools and metrics ▶ Although the variety of ad content format and style that the Internet allows can be considered a positive in some respects, it also makes apples-to-apples comparisons difficult for media buyers ▶ Difficult to measure size of market, therefore it is difficult to estimate rating, share, or reach and frequency ▶ Audience is still small

Source: Based on Meeker, 1997, pp. 1–10.

of online ad space, and helping target ads to consumers who are presumed to be interested in categories of advertisements based on technology-based consumer profiling. DoubleClick is the premier company in this area. DoubleClick prepares millions of ads for its clients every week, following the process shown in EC Application Case 4.3.

EC APPLICATION CASE 4.3
Intraorganization

TARGETED ADVERTISEMENTS: THE DOUBLECLICK APPROACH

One-to-one targeted advertisements can take many forms. Assume that 3M Corp. wants to advertise its multimedia projectors that cost $10,000. It knows that potential buyers are people who work in advertising agencies or in IS departments of large corporations or companies that use UNIX as their operating system. 3M approaches DoubleClick, Inc. and asks the firm to identify such potential customers. How does DoubleClick find them? The answer is clever and simple.

As of 1997, DoubleClick (*doubleclick.com/us*) monitors people browsing the Web sites of several hundred cooperating companies such as Quicken (*quicken.com*) and Travelocity (*travelocity.com*). By inspecting the Internet addresses of the visitors to these companies' Web sites and matching them against a database with about 100,000 Internet domain names that include a line-of-business code (code that tells the classification of each industry), DoubleClick can find those people working for advertising agencies. By checking the users' browsers, it can also find out which visitors are using UNIX. Although DoubleClick cannot find out your name, it can build a dossier on you that is attached to an ID number that was assigned to you during your first visit to any of the cooperating sites. As you continue to visit the sites, an intelligent (software) agent builds a relatively complete dossier on you, your spending, and your computing habits. This process is done with a cookie, so the Web site can "remember" your past behavior on the Internet.

DoubleClick then prepares an ad about 3M projectors. The ad is targeted to people whose profiles match the criteria listed earlier. If you are a UNIX user or work for an advertising agency, on your next browsing trip to *any* of the participating Web sites, you will be greeted with an ad that 3M hopes will be of interest to you—an ad for the multimedia projector.

How is this financed? DoubleClick charges 3M for the ad. The fee is then split with the participating Web sites that carry the 3M ads, based on how many times the ad is matched with visitors.

In 1998, DoubleClick expanded the service, called Dynamic Advertising Reporting and Targeting (DART), from pinpoint target and ad design to advertising control, ad frequency determination, and providing verifiable measures of success. DoubleClick brings the right advertisement, to the right person, at the right time. DART works with 22 criteria that it tries to find on each consumer (e.g., location, time of day, etc.).

In June 1999, DoubleClick announced the purchase of Abacus Direct, whose database contains the buying habits of 88 million U.S. households. DoubleClick wanted to tie its online consumer data with that of Abacus to collect personal information online. This way, names and addresses would be in DoubleClick's database. Privacy-protection groups opposed the merger, asking the FTC to open an investigation. Under pressure, DoubleClick agreed to limit the connection.

Sources: Compiled from Rothenberg, 1999 and *doubleclick.com*, 2001.

Questions

▶ How does DoubleClick build dossiers on people?

▶ How are ads matched with individual viewers?

▶ What role do the "participating sites" play in the DART system?

One-to-one targeted advertising and marketing can be expensive, but it can be very rewarding. According to Taylor (1997), successful targeted ads were proven very effective for Lexus cars (at a cost of $169 per car sold). Targeting ads to groups (based on segmentation) rather than to individuals can also be very cost-effective.

▶ Define Web advertising and the major terms associated with it.
▶ Describe the reasons for the growth in Web advertising.
▶ List the major characteristics of Web advertising.
▶ Explain the role of ad networks in Web advertising.

4.7   ADVERTISING METHODS

BANNERS

banner
On a Web page, a graphic advertising display linked to the advertiser's Web page.

A **banner** is a graphic display on a Web page that is used for advertising. The size of the banner is usually 5 to 6.250 inches in length, 0.5 to 1 inch in width, and is measured in pixels. A banner ad is linked to an advertiser's Web page. When a user "clicks" on the banner, they will be transferred to the advertiser 's site. Advertisers use tricks or go to great lengths to design a banner that catches consumers' attention. Banners often include video clips and sound. Banner advertising is the most commonly used form of advertising on the Internet.

There are two types of banners: keyword banners and random banners. **Keyword banners** appear when a predetermined word is queried from a search engine. They are effective for companies that want to narrow their target audience. **Random banners** appear randomly, and not as a result of some action by the viewer. Companies that want to introduce new products (e.g., a new movie or CD) use random banners.

keyword banners
Banner ads that appear when a predetermined word is queried from a search engine.

random banners
Banner ads that appear at random, not as the result of the viewer's action.

If an advertiser knows something about a visitor, such as the visitor's user profile, it is possible to match a specific banner to that customer. Obviously, such targeted, personalized banners are the most effective.

Benefits and Limitations of Banner Ads

The major benefit of banner ads is that by clicking on them users are transferred to an advertiser's site. Another advantage of using banners is the ability to customize them to the target audience or market segment. Also, customers are forced to see banner ads before they can get free information or entertainment they like to see (a strategy called "forced advertising"). Finally, banners may include attention-grabbing multimedia.

click ratio
The ratio between the number of clicks on a banner ad and the number of times it is seen by viewers; measures the success of a banner in attracting visitors to click on the ad.

The major disadvantage of banners is their cost. If a company demands a successful marketing campaign, it will need to allocate a large percentage of the advertising budget to place banners on a high-volume Web site. Another drawback is that a limited amount of information can be placed on the banner. Hence, advertisers need to think of a creative but short message to attract viewers. Additionally, it seems that viewers have become somewhat immune to banners, and simply do not notice them as they once did. The **click ratio**, which measures the success of a banner in attracting visitors to click on it, has been declining over time. For example, if a page received

1,000 views and there are 30 "clicks" on a banner, the click ratio is 3 percent. The University of Michigan found the average click ratio today is less than 1 percent.

Therefore, it is important to decide where to place banners. For example, a study of Web ads, conducted by the University of Michigan, showed that ads placed in the lower-right-hand corner of the screen, next to the scrollbar, generate 228 percent higher click-through than ads at the top of the page (Doyle et al., 1997). The study also found that ads placed one-third of the way down the page and centered increased click-through 77 percent over ads at the top of the page, where ads are usually positioned.

Banner Swapping

Banner swapping means that company A agrees to display a banner of company B in exchange for company B displaying company A's banner. This is probably the least expensive form of banner advertising, but it is also difficult to arrange. A company must locate a site that could generate a sufficient amount of quality traffic. Then, the company must contact the owner/Webmaster of the site and inquire if they would be interested in a reciprocal banner swap. Because individual swaps are difficult to arrange, many companies use banner exchanges.

banner swapping
An agreement between two companies to each display the other's banner ad on its Web site.

Banner Exchanges

Banner exchanges are markets where companies can trade or exchange placement of banner ads on each other's Web sites. A multicompany banner match may be easier to arrange than a two-company swap. For example, company A can display B's banner to good advantage, but B cannot display A's banner optimally. However, B can display C's banner, and C can display A's banner. Such bartering may involve many companies. Banner exchange organizers arrange the trading, which works much like an off-line bartering exchange. Firms that are willing to display others' banners join the exchange. Each time a participant displays a banner for one of the exchange's other members, it receives a credit. After a participant has "earned" enough credits, its own banner is displayed on another member's site. Most exchanges offer members the opportunity to purchase additional display credits.

banner exchanges
Markets in which companies can trade or exchange placement of banner ads on each other's Web sites.

Bcentral.com, via its Link Exchange, acts as a banner-ad clearinghouse for thousands of small Web sites. The site is organized into more than 1,600 categories. Bcentral.com also monitors the content of the ads of all its members.

Banner exchanges are not without their disadvantages. Some banner exchanges will not allow certain types of banners. In addition, there are tax implications for companies that barter banners.

Overall, banner advertising can be very valuable, and although its share of the market is declining, it is still the largest Internet advertising medium.

POP-UNDER ADS

A **pop-under ad** is an ad that appears underneath the current browser window. When users close the active window, they see the ad. This method is controversial: Many users strongly object to these ads, which they consider intrusive. There are pop-under exchanges (see popunder.com) that function much like banner exchanges.

pop-under ad
An ad that appears underneath the current browser window, so when the user closes the active window, they see the ad.

INTERSTITIALS

An **interstitial** is an initial Web page, or a portion of one, that is used to capture the user's attention for a short time, either as a promotion or a lead-in to the site's home page or to advertise a product or a service. These ads appear while content is loading. (The word *interstitial* comes from *interstice*, which means a small space between things.) Interstitials are pages or boxes that appear after you click on a link. They pop onto the PC screen much like a TV commercial.

The major advantages of an interstitial over any other online advertising method is that advertisers can create innovative multimedia effects and provide sufficient information for delivery in one visit. Also, viewers tend to look at them while they wait for the requested content to appear. (However, viewers can remove interstitials in several ways, by simply closing them or installing software to block them.)

E-MAIL

A popular way to advertise on the Internet is to e-mail company information to people or companies listed in mailing lists. E-mail messages may be combined with brief audio or video clips promoting a product and with on-screen links that users can click on to make a purchase (see aceconcept.com). E-mail is an interactive medium, and it can combine advertising and customer service. The advantages of the e-mail approach are its low cost and the ability to reach a wide variety of targeted audiences. Most companies have a database of customers to which they can then send e-mail messages. However, using e-mail to send ads (sometimes floods of ads) without the receivers' permission is considered **spamming** (see Chapter 9).

Undoubtedly, the quantity of e-mail that consumers receive is exploding. In light of this, marketers employing e-mail must take a long-term view and work toward motivating consumers to continue to read the messages they receive. This is especially important as nearly one-third of consumers read e-mail only from senders with whom they have a relationship. As the volume of e-mail increases, consumers' tendency to screen messages will rise as well. Many e-mail services permit users to block messages from specific sources (e.g., see hotmail.com).

A list of e-mail addresses can be a very powerful tool with which a company can target a group of people it knows something about. For information on how to create a mailing list, consult groups.yahoo.com (the service is free) or topica.com. E-mail can also be sent to PDA devices (e.g., Palm i705) and to mobile phones. Mobile phones offer advertisers a real chance to advertise interactively and on a one-to-one basis with consumers. In the future, ads will be targeted to individuals based not only on their user profiles, but also on their physical location at any point in time. See Chapter 8 for a description of this concept (l-commerce).

STANDARDIZED ADS

On February 26, 2001, the Internet Advertising Bureau, an industry trade group, adopted five standard ad sizes for the Internet. These standardized ads are larger and more noticeable than banner ads. They look like the ads in a newspaper or magazine, so advertisers like them. In preliminary tests, users read these ads four times more frequently than banners (Tedeschi 2001). The ads appear on Web sites in columns or boxes. One of the most popular of the standardized ads is a full-column-deep ad called a *skyscraper ad*. Publishers, such as the *New York Times* online (nytimes.com) and corp.ign.com, publish these standardized ads, sometimes as many as four on one Web page. Some of these ads are interactive; users can click on a link inside the ad for more information about a product or service.

CLASSIFIED ADS

Another newspaper-like ad is the *classified* ad. There are special sites for such ads (e.g., classifieds2000.com), and they also appear in online newspapers, exchanges, portals, and so on. In many cases, posting regular-size classified ads is free, but placing them in a larger size or with some noticeable features is done for a fee.

URLS

Most search engines allow companies to submit their Internet addresses (URLs; Universal Resource Locators) for free. After submitting a URL to a search engine, the search engine spider can crawl through the submitted site, indexing its content and links. Then, the site will be included in future searches. Because there are several thousand search engines, advertisers who use this method should register URLs with as many search engines as possible.

The major advantage of using URLs as an advertising tool is that it is free. Anyone can submit a URL to a search engine and be listed. Also, by using URLs, it is more likely that searchers of the correct key words will come to the Web site, rather than finding it by accident. However, the URL method has several drawbacks. The major one has to do with location: The chance that a specific site will be placed at the top of a search engine's list (say, in the first 10 sites) is very slim. Furthermore, even if your URL makes it to the top, others can quickly displace your URL from the top slot. Second, different search engines index their listings differently, so it is difficult to make the top of several lists. One may have the correct keywords, but if the search engine indexed its listing using the "title" or "content description" in the meta tag, then the effort could be fruitless.

Improving a Company's Search-Engine Ranking

By simply adding, removing, or changing a few sentences, a Web designer may alter the way a search engine's spider ranks its findings (see Nobles and O'Neil 2000), and so improve a company's ranking on the search engine's list. Several companies have services that optimize Web content so that a site has a better chance of being discovered by a search engine (e.g., keywordcount.com). More tips for improving a site's listing in various search engines can be found at searchenginewatch.com.

Paid Search-Engine Inclusion

Several search engines charge fees for including URLs near the top of the search results. For example, overture.com charges firms for placement. The more the company pays, the closer it will be to the top. Overture works with AltaVista, Lycos, and other search engines. Many major search engines allow for paid inclusion. A debatable issue is the ethics of this strategy. Basically, promotion is given to those that pay more. Although this is a fact of advertising in general (you pay more for a TV ad in the Super Bowl than for one during the late-night news), it is a fact that may not be known to customers who use the search engines.

ADVERTISING IN CHAT ROOMS

A chat room can be used to build a community, to promote a political or environmental cause, to support people with medical problems, or to let hobbyists share their interest. It can be used for advertising as well.

Vendors frequently sponsor chat rooms. The sponsoring vendor places a chat link on its site, and the chat vendor does the rest, including placing the advertising that pays for the session. The advertising in a chat room merges with the activity in the room, and the user is conscious of what is being presented.

The main difference between an advertisement that appears on a static Web page and one that comes through a chat room is that the latter allows advertisers to cycle through messages and target the chatters again and again. Also, advertising can become more thematic. An advertiser can start with one message and build upon it to a climax, just as an author does with a good story. For example, imagine you are a toy maker and you have a chat room dedicated to electronic toys. You can use the chat room to pose a query such as, "Can anyone tell me about the new Electoy R3D3?" Also, you can go to your competitors' chat rooms and observe the conversation there.

Chat rooms also are used as one-to-one connections between a company and their customers. For example, Mattel (mattel.com) sells about one-third of its Barbie dolls to collectors. These collectors use the chat room to make comments or ask questions that are then answered by Mattel's staff.

OTHER FORMS OF ADVERTISING

advertorial
An advertisement "disguised" to look like an editorial or general information.

Online advertising can be done in several other ways, ranging from ads in newsgroups to ads in computer kiosks. Advertising on Internet radio is just beginning, and soon advertising on Internet television will commence. Some use an **advertorial**, which is material that looks like editorial content or general information but is really an advertisement. Others advertise to members of Internet communities (Chapter 11). Community sites, such as geocities.com, offer direct advertising opportunities, and usually offer discounts to members on the advertised products. There are also ads that link users to other sites that might be of interest to community members, and targeted ads that can also go to the members' portals. Finally, the domain name itself can be used for brand recognition. This is why some companies are willing to pay millions of dollars to keep certain domain names in their own control (see alldomains.com) or buy popular names.

▌ Define banner ads and describe their benefits and limitations.

▌ Describe banner swapping and banner exchanges.

▌ Explain how e-mail and chat rooms are used for advertising.

▌ Describe advertising via URLs and advertorials.

4.8   ADVERTISING STRATEGIES AND PROMOTIONS

Several advertising strategies can be used over the Internet. In this section, we will present the major strategies used.

ASSOCIATED AD DISPLAY

Sometimes it is possible to associate the content of a Web page with a related ad. Suppose you are interested in finding material on e-loyalty. If you use Yahoo! to search for e-loyalty, you will receive a list of sources and a banner ad that will say, "Search Books!, Barnes and Noble, E-Loyalty." The same banner ad will appear when you click on the top sites that deal with e-loyalty. This strategy, of displaying a banner ad related to a term entered in a search engine, is called **associated ad display** or **text links**. For example, when using MapQuest (mapquest.com), which supports hotel reservations, the user may select an indexed category such as "lodging" within a city, and an associated ad for a Radisson hotel may be displayed.

> **associated ad display (text links)**
> An advertising strategy that displays a banner ad related to a term entered in a search engine.

Another example of associated ad display can be found at amazon.com. When a customer reads about a book, a list of books is displayed under the heading "'Customers who bought this book also bought. . . .'" To support this kind of service, Amazon.com's system uses data mining capabilities. Keyword banners are also a kind of associated ad. The associated ads appear only as a reaction to user actions.

Companies usually implement the associated ad display strategy through their *affiliates programs* (e.g., see Helmstetter and Metivier 2000), as is done by Yahoo!

ADS AS A COMMODITY

With the *ads-as-a-commodity* approach, the time spent viewing an ad is sold as a product. This approach is used by CyberGold (now mypoints.com) and others. At mypoints.com, interested consumers read ads in exchange for payments made by the advertisers. Consumers fill out data on personal interests, and then receive targeted banners based on their personal profiles. Each banner is labeled with the amount of payment that will be paid if the consumer reads the ad. If interested, the consumer clicks the banner to read it and, passing some tests as to its content, is paid for the effort. Readers can sort and choose what they read, and the advertisers can vary the payment level reflecting the frequency and desirability of readers. Payments can be cash (e.g., $0.50 per banner) or discounts on products.

VIRAL MARKETING

Viral marketing refers to word-of-mouth marketing in which customers promote a product or service by telling others about it. The idea is to have people forward messages to friends, asking them, for example, to "check out this idea." This approach has been used for generations, but now its speed and reach are multiplied manyfold by the Internet. This ad model can be used to build brand awareness at a minimal cost (Helm 2000), as the people who pass on the messages are paid very little or nothing for their efforts.

> **viral marketing (advocacy marketing)**
> Word-of-mouth marketing by which customers promote a product or service by telling others about it.

Viral marketing has long been a favorite strategy of online advertisers pushing youth-oriented products. For example, advertisers might distribute, embedded within a sponsor's e-mail, a small game program that is easy to forward. By releasing a few thousand copies of the game to some consumers, vendors hope to reach hundreds of thousands of other consumers. Viral marketing also was used by the founder of Hotmail, a free e-mail service, which grew from zero to 12 million subscribers in just 18 months and to over 50 million in about 4 years. Each e-mail sent via Hotmail carried an invitation for free Hotmail service. Known also as **advocacy marketing**, this innovative approach, if properly used, can be effective, efficient, and relatively inexpensive.

One of the downsides of this strategy is that several e-mail hoaxes have been spread this way. Another danger of viral advertising is that a destructive virus can be added to an innocent advertisement-related game or message.

advocacy marketing
Word-of-mouth marketing by which customers promote a product or service by telling others about it; also called viral marketing.

CUSTOMIZING ADS

There is too much information on the Internet for customers to view. Filtering irrelevant information by providing consumers with customized ads can reduce this information overload. BroadVision (broadvision.com) provides a customized ad service platform, called One-to-One. The heart of One-to-One is a customer database, which includes registration data and information gleaned from site visits. The companies use the database to send customized ads to consumers. Using this feature, a marketing manager can customize display ads based on users' profiles.

Another model of personalization can be found in **Webcasting**, a free Internet news service that broadcasts personalized news and information. A user signs into the Webcasting system and selects the information they would like to receive, such as sports, news, headlines, stock quotes, or desired promotions. When you request free information, you get that information and personalized advertisements based on your interests, or general ads based on your profile.

Webcasting
A free Internet news service that broadcasts personalized news and information in categories selected by the user.

ONLINE EVENTS, PROMOTIONS, AND ATTRACTIONS

In the winter of 1994, the term EC was hardly known and people were just starting to discover the Internet. Yet, one company demonstrated that there was a new way of doing business on the Internet. DealerNet, which was selling new and used cars in physical lots, started a virtual showroom. It let people "visit" dozens of dealerships and compare prices and features. At that time, this was a revolutionary way of selling cars. To get people's attention, DealerNet gave away a car over the Internet.

This promotion, unique at the time, received a lot of off-line media attention and was a total success. Today, such promotions are regular events on thousands of Web sites. Contests, quizzes, coupons, and giveaways, designed to attract visitors, are as much a part of online marketing as they are of off-line commerce (see Giannoni 2000 and Wong 2000). Some innovative ideas used to encourage people to read online advertising are provided in the nearby Insights and Additions box.

Bargain hunters can find lots of bargains on the Internet. Special sales, auctions, and coupons are frequently combined with ads. Of special interest are sites such as coolsavings.com, hotcoupons.com, supercoups.com, clickrewards.com, mypoints.com, and windough.com. A popular lottery site is world-widelotto.com. Free samples are of interest to many consumers, and "try-before-you buy" gives

Insights and Additions   How to Attract Web Surfers

There are dozens of innovative ways that advertisers lure consumers into viewing online ads. The following is only a sample:

▶ Yoyodyne, Inc. (*yoyo.com*) conducts give-away games, discount contests, and sweepstakes. Entrants agree to read product information from advertisers ranging from Major League Baseball to Sprint Communications. For example, Yoyodyne organized a contest in 1997 in which tax preparer H&R Block paid $20,000 toward the winner's federal income taxes.

▶ Retailers can provide online shoppers with special offers while they are purchasing or "checking out." If a shoppers' profile or shopping history is known, the ads can be targeted. See *@pos.com* (*atpos.com*).

▶ Netstakes runs sweepstakes that require no skill. Users register only once and win prizes at random (*webstakes.com*). The sponsors pay Netstakes to send them traffic. Netstakes also runs online ads, both on the Web and through e-mail lists that people subscribe to.

▶ *Cydoor.com* places ads, news, and other items on software applications. Consumers who download the software receive a reward each time they use the software (and presumably read the ads).

▶ *Promosinmotion.com* and others painted Volkswagen Bugs with advertisers' logos, tag lines, or ad messages. The painted cars were displayed on Web sites and even driven on the streets, attracting considerable attention.

▶ Sometimes a catchy name draws Web surfers. For example, an old-economy seller of hard-to-find light bulbs changed its name to *topbulb.com* and created an online catalog, named the Bulbguy, through which to sell light bulbs online at a discount. The Web site is advertised both online and off-line, and business is booming!

▶ To promote its sport utility, the 4Runner, Toyota wanted to reach as many Internet users as possible. The company displayed Toyota banners on the search engine AltaVista (*altavista.com*): Whenever someone used AltaVista to search for anything automotive related, they would see the Toyota banner. Also, Kelly Blue Book's new-car pricing catalog (*kbb.com*) has links to Toyota's car. In the first 2 months of the campaign, over 10,000 potential car buyers clicked on the banner ads looking for more detailed information about the Toyota 4Runner.

▶ To promote its recruiting visits on U.S. college campuses, IBM created over 75,000 college-specific banners such as: "There is life after Boston College: click to see why." The students clicked on the banners at a very high rate (5 to 30 percent). As a result, IBM restructured its traditional media plans using the "Club Cyberblue" scheme.

▶ Each year, almost 500,000 brides-to-be use *theknot.com* to plan their wedding. A "Knot Box" with insert folders is sent to users by regular mail. Each insert is linked to a corresponding page at theknot.com. Advertisers underwrite the mail campaign. The Web site provides brides with information and help in planning the wedding and selecting vendors. Orders can be placed by phone or online (not all products can be ordered online). *Weddings411.com* is a similar service, operating primarily online.

consumers confidence in what they are buying. Freesamples.com began to offer free samples in June 2000.

Running promotions on the Internet is similar to running off-line promotions. According to Chase (1998) and Clow and Baack (2002), some of the major considerations when implementing an online ad campaign include the following:

▶ The target audience needs to be clearly understood and should be online surfers.

▶ The traffic to the site should be estimated, and a powerful enough server must be prepared to handle the expected volume of traffic.

▶ Assuming the promotion is successful, what will the result be? This assessment is needed to evaluate the budget and promotion strategy.

▶ Consider cobranding; many promotions succeed because they bring together two or more powerful partners. For more information about promotions and ad strategies, see Clow and Baack (2002).

▶ Describe the associate ad (text links) strategy.
▶ How does the "ads as a commodity" strategy work?
▶ Describe viral marketing.
▶ How are ads customized?
▶ List some typical Internet promotions.

4.9   SPECIAL ADVERTISING TOPICS

PRICING OF ADVERTISING

Justifying the cost of Internet advertisement is more difficult than doing so for conventional advertisements for two reasons: (1) the difficulty in measuring the effectiveness of online advertising and (2) disagreements on pricing methods. Several methods are available for measuring advertising effectiveness, conducting cost-benefit analyses, and pricing ads. Four representative methods are discussed in the following sections.

PRICING BASED ON AD VIEWS

Traditional ad pricing is based on exposure or circulation. So far, this model has been the standard advertising rate-pricing tool for Web sites as well, usually using *ad views* to measure circulation. Because advertisers pay an agreed-upon multiple of the number of "guaranteed" ad views, it is very important that ad views are measured accurately in the context of the advertising business model. Generally, CPMs seem to average on the order of $40, resulting in a cost of $0.04 per impression viewed (per ad view).

Some companies, such as *USA Today*, charge their clients according to the number of *hits* (about $0.03 per hit in 2001). However, hits are not an accurate measure of visitation as there may be several hits in one ad view.

PRICING BASED ON CLICK-THROUGH

Ad pricing based on click-through is an attempt to develop a more accountable way of charging for Web advertising. In this model, the payment for a banner ad is based on the number of times visitors actually click on it. Payment based upon click-through guarantees not only that the visitor was *exposed to* the banner ad, but also that the visitor was sufficiently interested to click on the banner and view the target ad (Hoffman and Novak 2000).

However, a relatively small proportion of those exposed to a banner ad (about 1 to 3 percent of viewers) actually click on the banner. Therefore, space providers usually object to this method, claiming that simply viewing a banner ad may lead to a purchase later or to an off-line purchase, much as newspaper or TV ads do. Advertisers, on the other hand, do not like to pay for ad views; they prefer the click-through method, which they feel is more accurate. Only large advertisers such as Procter & Gamble can pressure space sellers to accept click-through payment methods, or even better, interactivity.

PAYMENT BASED ON INTERACTIVITY

Although payment based on click-through guarantees exposure to target ads, it does not guarantee that the visitor liked the ad or even spent a substantial time viewing it. The interactivity model suggests basing the ad pricing on how the visitor interacts with the target ad. Such an interactivity measure could be based on the duration of time spent viewing the ad, the number of pages of the target ad accessed, the number of additional clicks generated, or the number of repeat visits to the target ad. Obviously, this method is more complex to administer than the previous methods.

PAYMENT BASED ON ACTUAL PURCHASE

Many advertisers prefer to pay for ads only if an actual purchase has been made. But because space providers generally do not prefer this payment basis, such arrangements usually take place through *affiliate programs*. Merchants ask partners, known as *affiliates*, to place the merchant's logo on the affiliate's Web site. The merchants promise to pay the affiliate a commission of 5 to 15 percent whenever a customer clicks on the merchants' logo on the affiliate's Web site and eventually moves to the merchant site and makes a purchase (e.g., see cdnow.com and cattoys.com). For example, if a customer saw amazon.com's banner at AOL's Web site, clicked on it, moved to Amazon.com, and completed the purchase, AOL would receive a referral fee of say 5 percent of the purchase price of the book. This method can work only at sites where actual purchases can be made. At the Web site of Ritchey Design or Coca-Cola (cocacola.com), you only get information and brand awareness, so this method would be inappropriate for these types of merchants.

WHICH IS THE MOST APPROPRIATE PRICING METHOD?

In addition, still other methods can be used to pay for ads. For example, some space providers charge a fixed monthly fee to host a banner, regardless of the traffic. Others use a hybrid approach, a combination of some of the previous methods. The question is, which is the most appropriate method?

Web publishers push for CPM. They argue that the problem with activity-based measures, such as click-through or interactivity, is that the Web publishers cannot be held responsible for activity related to an advertisement. (If the customer sees an ad, but it is a poor ad that does not inspire further activity, it is not the fault of the Web publisher.) They also argue that traditional media, such as newspapers or television, charge for ads whether or not they lead to sales. So why should the interactive condition be applied on the Net?

Advertisers and their agencies, on the other hand, argue that since the Web medium allows for accountability, models can and should be developed that measure actual consumer activities. The answer to the question of the most appropriate method, therefore, has not been settled. It depends on whose seat you are sitting in.

PERMISSION ADVERTISING

One of the major issues of one-to-one advertising is the flooding of users with unwanted (junk) e-mail, banner ads, pop-up screens, and so on. One of the authors of this book experienced a flood of X-rated ads. Each time such an ad arrived, he blocked receipt of further ads from this source. That helped for a day or two, but then the same ads arrived from another e-mail address. His e-mail service provider, hotmail.com, was very helpful in providing several options to minimize this problem. Hotmail can place software agents to delete such junk mail. This problem is spamming, where users are flooded by unsolicited e-mails. In either case, the user is upset, and this may keep useful advertising from reaching users.

permission advertising (permission marketing)
Advertising (marketing) strategy in which customers agree to accept advertising and marketing materials.

To overcome the problem, advertisers use **permission advertising (permission marketing)**, where users register with advertisers and agree to accept advertising. For example, the authors of this book agreed to receive large numbers of e-commerce newsletters that include ads. This way we can keep abreast of what is happening in the field. We also agree to accept e-mail from research companies, newspapers, travel agencies, and more. These vendors push, for free, very valuable information to us. The accompanying ads pay for such service.

MEASURING, AUDITING, AND ANALYZING WEB TRAFFIC

Before a company decides to advertise on someone's Web site, it is important that the company knows that the number of hits, clicks-through, or other data it was told about are legitimate. A *site audit* validates the number of ad views and hits claimed by the site, assuring advertisers that they are getting their money's worth. An impartial, external analysis is crucial to advertisers to verify the accuracy of any counts claimed by sites.

The Audit Bureau of Circulation (ABC) (see abc.org.uk) is a not-for-profit association created by advertisers, advertising agencies, and publishers who came together to establish advertising standards and rules. The ABC verifies circulation reports by auditing circulation figures of newspapers, TV, radio, and now the Internet. It provides credible and objective information to the buyers and sellers of advertising. Several other independent third-party Internet auditing companies also are in operation, such as BPA International (bpai.com) and Audit at (ipro.com).

Related to auditing is the rating of sites. This is done by companies such as Accure, Accipiter, Ipro, Netcount, Interse, Hotstats, and CNet. Rating is done by looking at multiple criteria such as content, attractiveness, ease of navigation, and privacy protection. Sites with higher ratings can command higher prices for advertising placed on their sites. In addition to outside independent monitoring, several vendors sell software that allows Webmasters to self-monitor traffic on their own Web sites. Examples are webconnect.com, webtrends.com, siteguage.com, and netratings.com. Additionally, Webmasters can measure who is coming to a site and from where (e.g., see leadspinner.com). Using such software, companies can assess if placing ads really increases traffic to their sites.

LOCALIZATION

Localization is the process of converting media products developed in one country to a form culturally and linguistically acceptable in countries outside the original target market. It is usually done by a set of *internationalization* guidelines. Web-page translation (Chapter 11) is only one aspect of internationalization. There are several more. For example, a jewelry manufacturer that displayed its products on a white background was astonished to find that this might not appeal to some customers in countries where a blue background is preferred.

If a company aims at the global market (and there are millions of potential customers out there), it must make an effort to localize its Web pages. This may not be a simple task because of the following factors:

> Many countries use English, but the English used may differ in terminology, culture, and even spelling (e.g., United States vs. United Kingdom vs. Australia).

> Some languages use accented characters. If text includes an accented character, the accent will disappear when converted into English.

> Hard-coded text and fonts cannot be changed, so they remain in their original format in the translated material.

> Graphics and icons look different to viewers in different countries. For example, a U.S. mailbox resembles a European trashcan.

> When translating into Asian languages, significant cultural issues must be addressed, for example, how to address the elderly in a culturally correct manner.

> Dates that are written mm/dd/yy (e.g., June 8, 2002) in the United States are written dd/mm/yy (e.g., 8 June 2002) in many other countries.

> Consistent translation over several documents can be very difficult to achieve. (For free translation in six languages, see freetranslation.com.)

Using Internet Radio for Localization

Internet radio is a Web site that provides music, talk, and other entertainment, both live and stored, from a variety of radio stations. It is especially useful in presenting programming from local communities. For example, kiisfmi.com is a Los Angeles site that features music from up-and-coming L.A. bands, live concerts, interviews with movie stars, and so forth. About 40 percent of the site's traffic comes from listeners in California, and the rest from listeners around the world. The big advantage of Internet radio is that there are few limits on the type or number of programs it can offer, as compared to traditional radio stations. The company that powers kiisfmi.com also operates sites focused on country music, Latin music, and so forth. Advertisers can reach fairly narrow audience segments by advertising on Internet radio.

localization
The process of converting media products developed in one country to a form culturally and linguistically acceptable in countries outside the original target market.

Internet radio
A Web site that provides music, talk, and other entertainment, both live and stored, from a variety of radio stations.

▶ List the various methods of pricing Internet ads.

▶ Describe the reasons for using payment methods other than CPM payments.

▶ Describe permission advertising.

▶ Discuss how Web traffic is measured and audited.

▶ What is localization?

4.10 SOFTWARE AGENTS IN CUSTOMER-RELATED AND ADVERTISING APPLICATIONS

As the volume of customers, products, vendors, and information increases, it becomes uneconomical, or even impossible, for customers to consider all relevant information and to manually match their interests with available products and services. The practical solution to handling such information overload is to use software (intelligent) agents. In Chapter 3, we demonstrated how intelligent agents help online shoppers find and compare products, resulting in significant time savings.

In this section, we will concentrate on how software agents can assist customers in the online purchasing decision-making process. Depending on their level of intelligence, agents can do many other things (see Appendix D on the book's Web site).

A FRAMEWORK FOR CLASSIFYING EC AGENTS

Exhibit 4.4 (page 152) detailed the customer's purchase decision-making process. A logical way to classify EC agents is by relating them to this decision-making process (in a slightly expanded form), as shown in Exhibit 4.13. (In the decision-making model in Exhibit 4.4, the second step was information search. Because of the vast quantity of information that software (intelligent) agents can supply, we have split this step into two types of agents: those that first answer the question, "what to buy?" and those that answer the next question, "from whom?") Let's see how agents support each of the phases of the decision-making process.

Agents That Support Need Identification (Recognition)

Agents can help buyers recognize their need for products or services by providing product information and stimuli. For example, expedia.com notifies customers about low airfares to a customer's desired destination whenever they become available. Auctionrover.com watches auctions and notifies the consumer where and when an item they want is being auctioned.

Several commercial agents can facilitate need recognition directly or indirectly. Here are several examples:

▶ Salesmountain.com helps people who are looking for certain items when they are put "on sale." If customers specify what they want, salesmountain.com will send notification when the item is discounted.

▶ Findgift.com asks customers questions about the person they are buying a gift for and helps them hunt down the perfect gift.

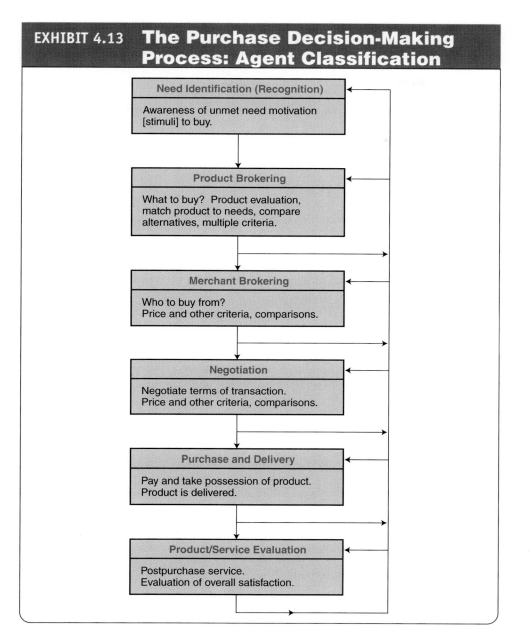

EXHIBIT 4.13   The Purchase Decision-Making Process: Agent Classification

Need Identification (Recognition)
Awareness of unmet need motivation [stimuli] to buy.

Product Brokering
What to buy? Product evaluation, match product to needs, compare alternatives, multiple criteria.

Merchant Brokering
Who to buy from?
Price and other criteria, comparisons.

Negotiation
Negotiate terms of transaction.
Price and other criteria, comparisons.

Purchase and Delivery
Pay and take possession of product.
Product is delivered.

Product/Service Evaluation
Postpurchase service.
Evaluation of overall satisfaction.

▶ Querybot.com/shopping not only looks for deals, but also finds related information such as newsgroup discussions about the type of product for which the consumer is searching.

Agents That Support Product Brokering

Once a need is established, customers search for a product (or service) that will satisfy the need. Several agents are available to assist customers with this task. The comparison agents cited in Chapter 3 belong to this category. Exhibit 4.14 shows the product-comparison screen from a search engine. Other examples of

EXHIBIT 4.14 An Illustrative Screen for Product Comparison

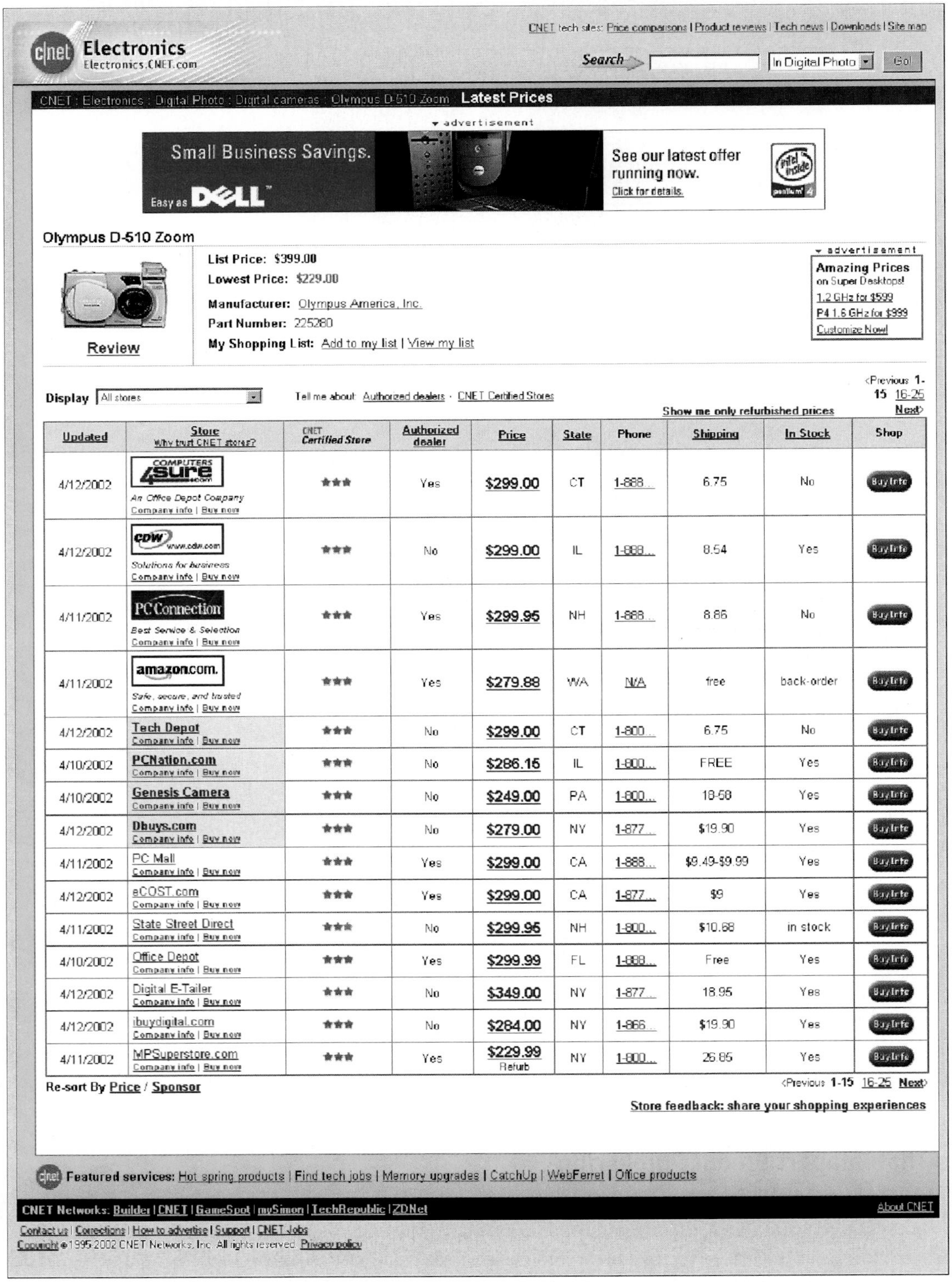

CNET tech sites: Price comparisons | Product reviews | Tech news | Downloads | Site map

Electronics
Electronics.CNET.com

Search [ ] In Digital Photo Go!

CNET : Electronics : Digital Photo : Digital cameras : Olympus D-510 Zoom **Latest Prices**

Olympus D-510 Zoom

Review

List Price: $399.00
Lowest Price: $229.00
Manufacturer: Olympus America, Inc.
Part Number: 225280
My Shopping List: Add to my list | View my list

Display All stores   Tell me about: Authorized dealers · CNET Certified Stores

Show me only refurbished prices   <Previous **1-15** 16-25 Next>

Updated	Store (Why trust CNET stores?)	CNET Certified Store	Authorized dealer	Price	State	Phone	Shipping	In Stock	Shop
4/12/2002	Computers 4sure.com — An Office Depot Company — Company info | Buy now	★★★	Yes	$299.00	CT	1-888...	6.75	No	Buy Info
4/12/2002	CDW www.cdw.com — Solutions for business — Company info | Buy now	★★★	No	$299.00	IL	1-888...	8.54	Yes	Buy Info
4/11/2002	PC Connection — Best Service & Selection — Company info | Buy now	★★★	Yes	$299.95	NH	1-888...	8.86	No	Buy Info
4/11/2002	amazon.com. — Safe, secure, and trusted — Company info | Buy now	★★★	Yes	$279.88	WA	N/A	free	back-order	Buy Info
4/12/2002	Tech Depot — Company info | Buy now	★★★	No	$299.00	CT	1-800...	6.75	No	Buy Info
4/10/2002	PCNation.com — Company info | Buy now	★★★	No	$286.15	IL	1-800...	FREE	Yes	Buy Info
4/10/2002	Genesis Camera — Company info | Buy now	★★★	No	$249.00	PA	1-800...	18-58	Yes	Buy Info
4/12/2002	Dbuys.com — Company info | Buy now	★★★	No	$279.00	NY	1-877...	$19.90	Yes	Buy Info
4/11/2002	PC Mall — Company info | Buy now	★★★	Yes	$299.00	CA	1-888...	$9.49-$9.99	Yes	Buy Info
4/12/2002	eCOST.com — Company info | Buy now	★★★	Yes	$299.00	CA	1-877...	$9	Yes	Buy Info
4/11/2002	State Street Direct — Company info | Buy now	★★★	No	$299.95	NH	1-800...	$10.68	in stock	Buy Info
4/10/2002	Office Depot — Company info | Buy now	★★★	Yes	$299.99	FL	1-888...	Free	Yes	Buy Info
4/12/2002	Digital E-Tailer — Company info | Buy now	★★★	No	$349.00	NY	1-877...	18.95	Yes	Buy Info
4/12/2002	ibuydigital.com — Company info | Buy now	★★★	No	$284.00	NY	1-866...	$19.90	Yes	Buy Info
4/11/2002	MPSuperstore.com — Company info | Buy now	★★★	Yes	$229.99 Refurb	NY	1-800...	26.85	Yes	Buy Info

Re-sort By Price / Sponsor   <Previous **1-15** 16-25 Next>

Store feedback: share your shopping experiences

Featured services: Hot spring products | Find tech jobs | Memory upgrades | CatchUp | WebFerret | Office products

CNET Networks: Builder | CNET | GameSpot | mySimon | TechRepublic | ZDNet   About CNET

Contact us | Corrections | How to advertise | Support | CNET Jobs

Source: cnet.com. Used with permission of CNET.com.

product brokering would be the software agents used by Fastparts (fastparts.com) and classifieds2000.com. An example of how these agents are used in advertising is provided in EC Application Case 4.4.

Some agents can match people that have similar interest profiles. Even more ambitious agents try to predict which brands of computers, cars, and other goods will appeal to customers, based on market segmentation preferences in a variety of different product categories such as wine, music, or breakfast cereal. (See the earlier discussion on *collaborative filtering*.)

Agents That Support Merchant Brokering and Comparison

Once a customer has a specific product in mind, they need to find a place to buy it. BargainFinder (from Andersen Consulting) was the pioneering agent in this category. The agent, used in online CD shopping, queried the price of a specific CD from a number of online vendors and returned a list of prices. However, this system encountered problems because vendors who did not want to compete on price managed to block out the agent's requests. (Today's version is at cdrom-guide.com/pricegrabber.html.) The blocking problem has been solved by Inktomi Shopping Agent, My Simon (mysimon.com), and Junglee (of amazon.com). These agents originate the requests from the user's site instead of from the agents'. This way vendors have no way of determining whether the request is from a real customer or from the agent.

In finding an online merchant, fraud is a major concern, as buyers cannot see the products or the sellers. Several vendors offer agent-based fraud detection systems. One such system is HNC Risk Suite from hnc.com. It is based on pattern recognition driven by neural computing.

EC APPLICATION CASE 4.4

Individuals and Communities

FUJITSU USES AGENTS FOR TARGETED ADVERTISING IN JAPAN

Fujitsu (*fujitsu.com*) is a Japanese-based global provider of Internet-focused information technology solutions. Since the end of 1996, Fujitsu has been using an agent-based technology called Interactive Marketing Interface (iMi). The system allows advertisers to interact directly with specific segments of the consumer market through the use of software agents while ensuring that consumers remain anonymous to advertisers. Consumers submit a personal profile to iMi, indicating such characteristics as product categories of interests, hobbies, travel habits, and the maximum number of e-mail messages per week that they are willing to receive. In turn, customers receive product announcements, advertisements, and marketing surveys by e-mail from advertisers, based on their personal profile information. By answering the marketing surveys or acknowledging receipt of advertisements, consumers earn iMi points, redeemable for gift certificates and phone cards.

Source: Compiled from *fujitsu.com*, 1999.

Questions

▶ Why would customers agree to have a personal profile built on them?

▶ What is the role of the software agent in this case?

Comparison agents. Part of the merchant brokering process is determining price and other purchase criteria. Large numbers of agents enable consumers to perform all kinds of comparisons, as was shown in Chapter 3. Here are some additional examples:

- Allbookstores.com and bestbookbuys.com are two of several agents that help consumers find the lowest prices of books available online.
- Bottomdollar.com, compare.net, pricewonders.com, shopper.com, robo-shopper.com, and bargainvillage.com are examples of agents (out of several dozen) that suggest brands and compare prices once consumers specify what they want to buy.
- Pricescan.com guides consumers to the best prices on thousands of computer hardware and software products.
- Buyerzone.com is a B2B portal at which businesses can find the best prices on many products and services.

Agents That Support Buyer–Seller Negotiation

The traditional concept of "market" implies negotiation, mostly about price. Whereas many retail stores engage in fixed-price selling, many small retail stores and most markets use negotiation extensively. In several cultures (e.g., Chinese), negotiation is very common. In many B2B transactions, negotiation is common too. The benefit of dynamically negotiating a price is that the pricing decision is shifted from the seller to the marketplace. In a fixed-price situation, if the seller fixes a price that is too high, sales will suffer. If the price is set too low, profits will be lower.

Negotiations, however, are time-consuming and often disliked by individual customers who cannot negotiate properly because they lack information about the marketplace and prices (or haven't learned to negotiate). Many vendors do not like to negotiate either. Therefore, electronic support of negotiation can be extremely useful.

Agents can negotiate in pairs or one agent can negotiate for a buyer with several sellers' agents. In the latter case, the contact is done with each seller's agent individually, and the buyer's agent can conduct comparisons (Yan et al. 2000). Also, customers can negotiate with sellers' agents.

Agents That Support Purchase and Delivery

Agents are used extensively during the actual purchase, often arranging payment and delivery. For example, if a customer makes a mistake when completing an electronic order form, an agent will point it out immediately. When a customer buys stocks, for example, the pricing agent will tell the customer when a stock they want to buy on margin is not marginable or when the customer does not have sufficient funds. Delivery options at amazon.com, for example, are posted by agents and the total cost of the transaction is calculated in real time.

Agents That Support After-Sale Service and Evaluation

Agents can also be used to facilitate after-sale service. For example, the automatic answering agents described earlier are usually effective in answering customer queries. A non-Internet agent can monitor automobile usage and notify you when it is time to take your car in for periodic maintenance. Agents that facilitate feedback from customers are also useful.

CHARACTER-BASED INTERACTIVE AGENTS

Several agents enhance customer service by interacting with customers via animated characters. Animated characters are software agents with personalities. They are versatile and employ friendly front ends to communicate with users. They are not necessarily intelligent. These animated agents are also called avatars. **Avatars** are animated computer representations of human-like movements and behaviors in a computer-generated 3D world. Advanced avatars can "speak" and exhibit behaviors such as gestures and facial expressions. They can be fully automated to act like robots. The purpose of avatars is to introduce believable emotions so that the agents can gain credibility with users.

Avatars are considered a part of **social computing**, an approach aimed at making the human–computer interface more natural. Studies conducted by extempo.com showed that interactive characters can improve customer satisfaction and retention by offering personalized, one-to-one service (extempo.com/company_info/press/webtechniques.shtml 1999). They can also help companies get to know their customers (see the Real-World Case at the end of this chapter).

avatars
Animated computer characters that exhibit human-like movements and behaviors.

social computing
An approach aimed at making the human–computer interface more natural.

Chatterbots

A special category of animation characters are those that can chat, known as **chatterbots**. Chatterbots can do many things to enhance customer service, such as greeting a consumer when they enter a site or giving the consumer a guided tour of the site. For example, consider the following chatterbot agents:

chatterbots
Animation characters that can talk (chat).

- Mr. Clean (mrclean.com) guides consumers to cleaning-related Procter & Gamble products.
- "Katie" is an interactive agent that provides personalized and interactive information about Dove's skincare products (dove.com).
- The Personal Job Search Agent at monster.com helps users find a job.
- "Ed, Harmony, and Nina" are virtual guides who help visitors who wish to learn more about products and tools available at extempo.com (a vendor specializing in avatars).

For additional information on interactive characters, see Hayes-Roth et al. (1999), microsoft.com/msagent/, extempo.com, and nativeminds.com.

AGENTS THAT SUPPORT AUCTIONS

Several agents support auction-related activities. Agents often act as auction aggregators, which tell consumers where and when certain items will be auctioned. Examples are bidxs.com, rubylane.com, auctionwatch.com, and bidfind.com. Some aggregators provide real-time access to auctions.

Almost all auctions require users to personally execute the bidding. However, AuctionBot allows users to create intelligent agents that will take care of the bidding process for them. With AuctionBot, users create auction agents by specifying a number of parameters that vary depending on the type of the auction selected. After that, it is up to the agent to manage the auction until a final price is met or the auction deadline is reached. At yahoo.com, a bidding agent places bids on the user's behalf at the lowest possible increments. The user enters the highest amount they will pay, and the agent will try to win the bid at a lower price.

OTHER EC AGENTS

Other agents support consumer behavior, customer service, and advertising activities. For example, resumix.com (now part of TMP Worldwide) is an application that wanders the Web looking for Web pages containing resume information. If it identifies a page as being a resume, it tries to extract pertinent information from the page, such as the person's e-mail address, phone number, skill description, and location. The resulting database is used to connect job seekers with recruiters. For current lists of various EC agents see botspot.com, agentland.com, and agents.umbc.edu (look at Agents 101 Tutorial). For a comprehensive guide to EC agents, see Fingar 1998.

▶ List the major types of software (intelligent) agents used in customer-related and advertising applications.

▶ What role do software agents play in need identification?

▶ How do software agents support product brokering and merchant brokering?

▶ What are avatars and chatterbots? Why are they used on Web sites?

▶ What type of support do software agents provide to online auctions?

MANAGERIAL ISSUES

Some managerial issues related to this chapter are as follows.

1. **Do we understand our customers?** Understanding the customers, specifically what the customer needs and how to respond to those needs, is the most critical part of consumer-centered marketing. To excel, companies need to satisfy and retain customers, and management must monitor the entire process of marketing, sales, maintenance, and follow-up service.

2. **What do customers want from technology?** Complex lifestyles, a more diverse and fragmented population, and the power of technology all contribute to changing consumer needs and expectations in the digital age. Moreover,

today, consumers want more control over their time. In certain societies, EC has become more and more popular because it saves time, not because it saves money. Technology also provides consumers the ability to get customized products quickly. Vendors should understand these relationships and take advantage of them in their marketing efforts.

3. **How is our response time?** Acceptable standards for response in customer service must be set. For example, customers want acknowledgment of their query within 24 to 48 hours. Many companies seek to provide this response time and do so at a minimum cost.

4. **How do we improve and measure customer service?** The Internet provides an excellent platform for delivery of superb customer service via a variety of tools. The problem is that the returns are mostly intangible and may only be realized in the distant future.

5. **Should we use intelligent agents?** Any company engaged in EC must examine the possibility of using intelligent agents to enhance customer service, and possibly to support market research. Commercial agents are available on the market at a reasonable cost. For heavy usage, companies may develop customized agents.

6. **Is our market research leading to customer acquisition?** B2C requires extensive market research. This research is not easy to do, nor is it inexpensive. Deciding whether to outsource to a market research firm or maintain an in-house market research staff is a major management issue. Customer acquisition is a major success factor in B2C. Without a large number of customers, an EC business will not survive.

7. **Are customers satisfied with our Web site?** This is a key question, and it can be answered in several ways. Many vendors are available to assist you; some provide free software. For discussion on how to improve customer satisfaction, see *webhelp.com* and *e-satisfy.com*.

8. **Should we advertise anywhere but our own site?** Web advertising is a complex undertaking, and outsourcing should be seriously considered. Companies should examine the *adage.com* site, which contains an index of Web sites, their advertising rates, and reported traffic counts, before selecting a site on which to advertise. Companies should also consult third-party audits.

9. **What is our commitment to Web advertising, and how will we coordinate Web and traditional advertising?** Once a company is totally committed to advertising on the Web, it must remember that a successful program is multifaceted. It requires input and vision from marketing, cooperation from the legal department, and strong technical leadership from the corporate information systems (IS) department. A successful Web advertising program also requires coordination with non-Internet advertising and top management support.

10. **Should we integrate our Internet and non-Internet marketing campaigns?** Many companies are integrating their TV and Internet marketing campaigns. For example, a company's TV or newspaper ads direct the viewers/readers to the Web site, where short videos and sound ads, known as *rich media*, are used. With click-through ratios of banner ads down to less than 0.5 percent at many sites, innovations such as the integration of off-line and online marketing are certainly needed.

11. **What ethical issues should we consider?** Several ethical issues relate to online advertising. One issue that receives a great deal of attention is spamming, which is now subject to legislation. Another issue is the selling of mailing lists and customer information. Some people believe that not only does a company need the consent of the customers before selling a list, but that the company should share the profits derived from the sale with them. Using cookies without an individual's consent is another ethical issue.

12. **Have we integrated advertising with ordering and other business processes?** This is an important requirement. When a user goes to *Amazon.com*, they are directed to the shopping cart, then to the catalog, then to ordering and paying. Next, inventory availability is checked, and delivery is arranged. Such integration of business processes should be seamless.

13. **How important is branding?** Market research attempts to find out how important a brand name is on the Internet. Obviously, a strong brand helps to increase trust. However, many online shoppers are more concerned with low prices than with purchasing a particular brand. Each company must decide its optimal balance of advertising its brand versus promotion based on low price. Also, it is important for newcomers in a market to know how much to invest in a brand name.

SUMMARY

In this chapter, you learned about the following EC issues as they relate to the learning objectives.

1. **Essentials of consumer behavior.** Consumer behavior in EC is similar to that of any consumer behavior. It is described in a stimuli-based decision model that is influenced by personal characteristics and the shopping environment. The model also includes a significant vendor-controlled component that deals with logistics, technology, and customer service. All of these characteristics and systems interact to influence the decision-making process.

2. **The online consumer decision-making process.** The goal of marketing and advertising efforts is to understand the consumers' online decision-making process and formulate an appropriate strategy to influence their behavior. For each step in the process, sellers can develop appropriate strategies. Also, it is possible to use intelligent agents to automate some of the activities in each step.

3. **Building one-to-one relationships with customers.** EC offers companies the opportunity to build one-to-one relationships with customers that are not possible in other marketing systems. Product customization, personalized service, and getting the customer involved interactively (e.g., in feedback, order tracking, and so on) are all practical in cyberspace. In addition, advertisements can be matched with customer profiles so that ads can be presented on a one-to-one basis.

4. **Increasing loyalty and trust.** Customers can switch loyalty online easily and quickly. Therefore, enhancing e-loyalty is a must. Similarly, trust is a critical success factor that must be nourished.

5. **Online personalization.** Companies can allow customers to self-configure the products or services they want. Personalization can also be done by matching products with customers' profiles.

6. **EC customer market research.** Several fast and economical methods of online market research are available. The two major approaches to data collection are soliciting voluntary information from the customers and using cookies to track customers' movements on the Internet. Understanding market segmentation by grouping consumers into categories is also an effective EC market research method. However, online market research has several limitations, including data accuracy.

7. **Implementing customer service.** Retaining customers by satisfying their needs is the core of customer service. Customer service on the Web is provided by e-mail, on the corporate Web site, in customized Web pages, at integrated call centers, and by intelligent agents. Online customer service is media rich, effective, and less expensive than off-line services.

8. **Objectives and characteristics of Web advertising.** Web advertising attempts to attract surfers to an advertiser's site. Once at the advertiser's site, consumers can receive lots of information, interact with the seller, and in many cases, immediately place an order. With Web advertising, ads can be customized to fit groups of people with similar interests or even individuals. In addition, Web advertising can be interactive, is easily updated, can reach millions at a reasonable cost, and offers dynamic presentation by rich multimedia.

9. **Major online advertising methods.** Banners are the most popular online advertising method. Other frequently used methods are e-mail (including e-mail to mobile devices), registration of URLs with search engines, standardized ads, and interstitials.

10. **Various advertising strategies.** The major advertising strategies are ads associated with search results (text links), pay incentives for customers to view ads, and ads customized on a one-to-one basis.

11. **Types of promotions on the Web.** Web promotions are similar to off-line promotions. They

include giveaways, contests, quizzes, entertainment, coupons, and so on. Customization and interactivity distinguishes Internet promotions from conventional ones.

12. **Measuring the advertising success and pricing ads.** The traditional concept of paying for ads by exposure (by CPM) is also used on the Internet, but this is being challenged. Although space sellers prefer the CPM approach, advertisers prefer to pay for actions such as click-throughs. Paying commissions for electronic referrals is becoming a popular method.

13. **Intelligent agents.** Intelligent agents can gather and interpret data about consumer purchasing behavior. Advanced agents can even learn about customer behavior and needs by observing their Web movements. Agents can facilitate or support all aspects of the customer purchasing process. For example, agents can generate automatic e-mail replies and support customer service and market research.

KEY TERMS

Avatars,	p. 193	CPM (cost per thousand impressions),	p. 171	Permission advertising (permission marketing),	p. 186
Ad views,	p. 171	Customer service,	p. 165	Personalization,	p. 154
Advertising networks,	p. 173	Customer relationship management (CRM),	p. 165	Pop-under ads,	p. 177
Advertorial,	p. 180	Data mining,	p. 162	Product brokering,	p. 151
Advocacy marketing,	p. 182	E-loyalty,	p. 156	Random banner,	p. 176
Associated ad display,	p. 181	E-service,	p. 165	Social computing,	p. 193
Banner,	p. 176	Hit,	p. 172	Spamming,	p. 178
Banner exchanges,	p. 177	Interactive marketing,	p. 171	Telewebs,	p. 169
Banner swapping,	p. 177	Internet radio,	p. 187	Text links,	p. 181
Call center,	p. 169	Interstitial,	p. 178	Transaction log,	p. 161
Chatterbots,	p. 193	Keyword banners,	p. 176	Trust,	p. 156
Click ratio,	p. 176	Localization,	p. 187	User profile,	p. 154
Click (click-through or ad click),	p. 171	Market segmentation,	p. 158	Visit,	p. 172
Clickstream behavior,	p. 161	Merchant brokering,	p. 151	Viral marketing,	p. 181
Collaborative filtering,	p. 155	Metrics,	p. 170	Web bugs,	p. 161
				Web mining,	p. 163
Cookie,	p. 154	One-to-one marketing,	p. 153	Webcasting,	p. 182

DISCUSSION QUESTIONS

1. What would you tell an executive officer of a bank about the critical success factors for increasing customer loyalty by using the Internet?

2. Why is data mining becoming an important element in EC? How is it used to learn about consumer behavior? How can it be used to facilitate customer service?

3. Discuss the contribution of a call center to CRM.

4. Compare banner swapping with a banner exchange.

5. Explain why third-party audits of Web site traffic are needed.

6. Discuss why banners are so popular in Internet advertising.

7. Compare and contrast Internet and television advertising.

8. Discuss the advantages and limitations of listing a company's URL with various search engines.

9. How might a chat room be used for advertising?

10. Compare the use of the click-through pricing method with more interactive approaches to ad pricing.

11. Is it ethical for a vendor to enter a chat room operated by a competitor and pose queries under an assumed name?

INTERNET EXERCISES

1. Go to priceline.com. Review the strategies used to attract and retain customers. What additional efforts could this site exercise to retain its customers?

2. Survey two department store Web sites, such as JCPenney (jcpenney.com), Marks & Spencer (marksandspencer.com), or Sears (sears.com). Write a report that highlights the different ways they provide customer service online.

3. Surf the Home Depot Web site (homedepot.com) and check whether (and how) the company provides service to customers with different skill levels.

4. Examine a market research Web site (e.g., acnielsen.com). Discuss what might motivate a consumer to provide answers to market research questions.

5. Enter mysimon.com and share your experiences about how the information you provide might be used by the company for marketing in a specific industry (e.g., the clothing market).

6. Enter nativeminds.com and extempo.com. Find information about the "virtual representative," and check demos and customers' stories. Pre-

pare a report that compares the two sites.

7. Go to reflect.com. Examine how this company provides a personalized service. Examine ecommerceand marketing.com and personalization.com, and identify new developments in product and service personalization.

8. Enter the Web site of ipro.com. Find what Internet traffic management, Web results, and auditing services are provided. What are the benefits of each service? Find at least one competitor in each category (e.g., netratings.com; observe their "demo"). Compare the services provided and the prices.

9. Investigate the tools available to self-monitor Web sites. What are the major capabilities of these tools? Start with webarrange.com, webtrends.com, and doubleclick.com.

10. Enter hotwired.com and espn.com. Identify all of the advertising methods used on each site. Can you find those that are targeted advertisements? What revenue sources can you find on this site? (Try to find at least seven.)

TEAM ASSIGNMENTS AND ROLE PLAYING

1. Each team should select an overnight delivery service company (FedEx, DHL, UPS, U.S. Postal Service, and so on). The team will then identify all of the online customer service features offered by their company. The team then

will try to convince the class that its company provides the best customer service.

2. Go to webmonkey.com and find the market research tutorial. Each team member should

explore two different tools. As a group, compare the tools and prepare a written report.

3. As a team, examine the various advertising options offered by m-commerce companies. Start with I-MODE at nttdocomo.com. Move on to nokia.com, motorola.com, and ericsson.com. Also check adage.com and any other sources you might find. Prepare a report based on your findings.

4. Each team will choose one advertising method and conduct an in-depth investigation of the major players in that part of the ad industry. For example, direct e-mail is relatively inexpensive. Visit the-dma.org to learn about direct mail. Then visit bulletmail.com, e-target.com, permissiondirect.com, and venturedirect.com. Each team will prepare and present an argument as to why its method is superior.

REAL-WORLD CASE

CHEVRON'S WORLD OF CAR CHARACTERS

To have its brand more easily recognized, especially among children, Chevron Corp. (now ChevronTexaco), a major oil and gas company, ran a promotional campaign that featured an animated toy car and was centered around the Web site *chevroncars.com*. Chevron built one of the freshest, most innovative corporate sites on the Web. Within 3 months, traffic at the site increased from about 1,500 hits per day to over 150,000 hits per day. The site won the 1997 Best of the Internet (BOTI) Award and generated about 100 suggestions per day from viewers, mostly children, ranging from ideas for new Claymation characters to new product designs.

Among the highlights at chevroncars.com are a question-and-answer section of frequently asked questions (FAQs), the ability to customize toy cars and put them in "My Garage," free stuff (e.g., a car-themed screen saver), and a knowledge base about cars. A squirrel points out commercial messages and tasks for which children may need adult permission. At the Kidshop, users can grab a shopping cart and buy a plastic version of one of Chevron's animated vehicles or other Chevron items. Finally, a "playground" with games such as crossword puzzles, connect the dots, and a concentration-like activity is available. The game that allows users to check how they did against players nationwide seems to be the hands-down favorite. If the user provides an incorrect response to any question in any game at the site, the site provides an empathetic "bummer" response.

The site has a definite commercial and branding message: Chevron is a responsible, necessary, and even fun type of business, and the company is ecologically aware, doing things such as protecting baby owls nesting in pumps. The company is thinking of ways to use the site to promote Chevron's math and science awards and to help teachers locate videos and other educational materials. In addition, the site lets users find out how a company like Chevron operates.

So what is the most popular part of the Chevron site? Shopping for the toy cars, of course. The largest buying group tends to be the parents of children between ages three and nine. Next comes the 18-to-21-year-old demographic, followed by "kids" 35 years and older.

For a national gasoline company that operated in just 26 markets (before its merger with Texaco), the real success of Chevron's site was in the brand recognition it afforded for both existing and future customers. The fun message also reflects the changing nature of the gasoline business—pumps giving way to service complexes including commercial markets, car washes, fast-food chains, and even hotels. The company believes that the site's success has had as much to do with listening to what people want as any static master plan it could have dreamed up at corporate headquarters.

Sources: Compiled from *chevroncars.com/awardpage/BOTI.html*; C. Hudgins-Bonafield, "BOTI Awards: Most Innovative Site— chevroncars.com," *Internet Week*; and *polyweb.com/danno/ toycars_awards/chevroncars_com_awards.html*, December 16, 1999.

Questions

1. Explain the logic of using Claymation cars to advertise the Chevron brand. How would you compare the Web advertising with TV ads?

2. Why would Chevron want to target the 5-to-12-year-old demographic? They certainly do not buy gasoline, and, by the time they drive cars, the market for gasoline sales may be completely different.

3. From what you have learned in this chapter, what factors do you think contributed to the site's success?

COMPANY-CENTRIC B2B AND COLLABORATIVE COMMERCE

Content

Learning objectives

Upon completion of this chapter, you will be able to:

▶ Describe the B2B field.

▶ Describe the major types of B2B models.

▶ Discuss the characteristics of the sell-side marketplace.

▶ Describe the sell-side intermediary models.

▶ Describe the characteristics of the buy-side marketplace and e-procurement.

▶ Explain how forward and backward auctions work in B2B.

▶ Describe B2B aggregation and group purchasing models.

▶ Describe collaborative e-commerce and interorganizational systems.

▶ Describe infrastructure and standards requirements for B2B.

GENERAL MOTORS' B2B INITIATIVES

The Problem

General Motors (GM) is the world's largest vehicle manufacturer. The company sells cars in 190 countries and has manufacturing plants in about 50. Because the automotive industry is very competitive, GM is always looking for ways to improve its effectiveness. Its most publicized new initiative is a futuristic build-to-custom project with which GM expects to custom build the majority of it cars by 2005. Using the new system, the company hopes to save billions of dollars by reducing its inventory of finished cars. In the meantime, GM must effectively manage its resources to free up funds that can be put to use in this and other new automotive projects.

One ongoing financial challenge has been what to do with manufacturing machines that are no longer sufficiently productive. These capital assets depreciate (lose value) over time, and eventually must be replaced. GM traditionally has sold these assets, through intermediaries, at auction. The problem was that the auctions took weeks, even months. Furthermore, the prices obtained in the auctions seemed to be too low, and a 20 percent commission had to be deducted for the intermediary.

A second resource problem relates to procurement of commodity products, which can be either direct materials going into the cars or indirect materials such as light bulbs or office supplies. GM buys about 200,000 different products from 20,000 suppliers, spending close to $100 billion annually. GM was using a manual bidding process to negotiate with potential suppliers. Specifications of the needed materials were sent by mail to potential suppliers, the suppliers would submit a bid, and GM would select a winner if a supplier offered a low enough price. If all the bids were too high, second and third rounds of bidding were conducted. In some cases the process took weeks, even months, before GM was confident that the best deal, from a price and quality standpoint, had been achieved. The preparation costs involved in this process kept some bidders from submitting bids, so a less than optimal number of suppliers participated.

The Solution

The solution to both problems was online B2B auctions. To address the capital assets problem, GM implemented its own electronic market, now part of covisint.com, to conduct *forward auctions*. The first items put up for bid in early 2000 were eight 75-ton stamping presses. GM invited 140 certified bidders to view the pictures and service records of the presses online. On January 27, after only 1 week of preparation, the auction went live online.

For the resource procurement problem, GM automated the bidding, creating online *reverse auctions* on its e-procurement site. Qualified suppliers use the Internet to bid on each item GM needs to purchase. Bids are "open," meaning that all bidders can see the bids of their competitors. GM is able to accept bids from many suppliers concurrently, and can award jobs quickly to the most suitable bidder based on predetermined criteria, such as price, delivery date, and payment terms.

The Results

Both types of auctions have produced significant savings. Within just 89 minutes after the first forward auction opened, the eight presses were sold for $1.8 million. With the old off-line method, a similar item would have sold for less than half of its online price, and the process would have taken 4 to 6 weeks. In 2001, GM conducted over 150 other electronic auctions. Other sellers were encouraged to put their items up for sale at the site as well, paying a commission on the final sales price to GM.

In the first online reverse auction, GM purchased a large volume of rubber sealing packages for vehicle production. The price GM paid was significantly lower than the price GM had been paying for the same items that had been negotiated by manual tendering. Now, many similar bids are conducted on the site every week. The administrative costs per order have been reduced by 40 percent or more.

What We Can Learn . . .

The GM case demonstrates how a large company engaged in two EC activities: (1) electronically auctioning used equipment to customers and (2) conducting purchasing via electronic bidding. Both activities were conducted from GM's *private e-marketplace,* and the transactions were business-to-business (B2B). In B2B transactions, the company can be a seller, offering goods or services to many corporate buyers, or it can be a buyer, seeking goods/services from many corporate sellers (suppliers). When conducting such trades, a company can employ auctions, as GM did, or it can use other market mechanisms. These mechanisms and methods are the subject of this chapter.

5.1   CONCEPTS, CHARACTERISTICS, AND MODELS OF B2B EC

BASIC B2B CONCEPTS

Business-to-business e-commerce (B2B EC), also known as *eB2B* (*electronic B2B*) or just *B2B*, refers to transactions between businesses conducted electronically over the Internet, extranets, intranets, or private networks. Such transactions may be conducted between a business and its supply chain members, as well as between a business and any other business. In this context, a business refers to any organization, private or public, for profit or nonprofit. The major characteristic of B2B is that companies attempt to automate the trading process in order to improve it. (Note that B2B commerce can also be done without the Internet, but in this book we use the term B2B to mean specifically B2B e-commerce. To avoid confusion, any non-EC B2B will be designated as such.)

business-to-business e-commerce (B2B EC) Transactions between businesses conducted electronically over the Internet, extranets, intranets, or private networks; also known as *eB2B* (*electronic B2B*) or just *B2B*.

MARKET SIZE AND CONTENT OF B2B

First let's look at the B2B market. Market forecasters estimate that by 2005 the global B2B market may reach $10 trillion, continuing to be the major component of the EC market (Retter and Calyniuk 1998; Forrester Research 2001). The percentage of Internet-based B2B EC as a proportion of total non-Internet B2B commerce increased from 0.2 percent in 1997 to 2.1 percent in 2000, and is expected to grow to 10 percent by 2005 (see gs.com, special report, February 15, 2001). Chemicals, computer electronics, utilities, agriculture, shipping and warehousing, motor vehicles, petrochemicals, paper and office products, and food are the leading items in B2B.

Different B2B market forecasters use different definitions and methodologies. Because of this, there are often frequent changes in predictions and differences in predictions and other statistical data. Therefore, we will not provide any data here. Data sources are provided in Exhibit 4.2 (page 149).

B2B CHARACTERISTICS

Similar to the classic story of the blind men trying to describe an elephant, B2B can be described in a variety of ways, depending on what characteristic one is focusing on. Here we examine various qualities by which B2B transactions can be characterized.

Parties to the Transaction

B2B commerce can be conducted *directly* between a buyer and a seller or it can be conducted via an **online intermediary**. The intermediary is an online third party that brokers the transaction between the buyer and seller; it can be a virtual intermediary or a click-and-mortar intermediary. The electronic intermediaries for consumers mentioned in Chapter 3 can also be referenced for B2B by replacing the individual consumers with business customers.

Types of Transactions

There are two basic *types* of B2B transactions: spot buying and strategic sourcing. **Spot buying** refers to the purchasing of goods and services as they are needed, usually at prevailing market prices, which are determined dynamically by supply and demand. The buyers and the sellers may not know each other. Stock exchanges and commodity exchanges (oil, sugar, corn, etc.) are examples of spot buying. In contrast, **strategic sourcing** involves purchases made in long-term contracts that are usually based on private negotiation between sellers and buyers.

Spot buying may be conducted most economically on the third-party exchanges. Strategic purchases can be supported more effectively and efficiently through direct buyer–seller negotiations.

Types of Materials

Further, two types of materials and supplies are traded in B2B: direct and indirect. **Direct materials** are materials used in making the product, such as steel in a car or paper in a book. The characteristics of direct materials are that their use is scheduled, they are usually not shelf items, and they are usually purchased in large quantities and after negotiation and contracting.

Indirect materials, such as office supplies or light bulbs, support production. They are usually used in *maintenance*, *repairs*, and *operations* activities, and are known collectively as **MROs**, or nonproduction materials.

Direction of Trade

B2B marketplaces can be classified as either vertical or horizontal. **Vertical marketplaces** are those that deal with one industry or industry segment. Examples include electronics, cars, steel, or chemicals. **Horizontal marketplaces** are those that concentrate on a service or a product that is used in all types of industries. Examples are office supplies, PCs, or travel services.

These various characteristics of B2B transactions are presented in summary form in the nearby Insights and Additions box. (The final two categories are discussed in the next section.) Basic types of B2B models are discussed and illustrated in the next section.

---

online intermediary
An online third party that brokers a transaction between a buyer and a seller; can be virtual or click-and-mortar.

spot buying
The purchase of goods and services as they are needed, usually at prevailing market prices.

strategic sourcing
Purchases involving long-term contracts that are usually based on private negotiations between sellers and buyers.

direct materials
Materials used in the production of a product (e.g., steel in a car or paper in a book).

indirect materials
Materials used to support production (e.g., office supplies or light bulbs).

MROs (maintenance, repairs, and operations)
Indirect materials used in activities that support production.

vertical marketplaces
Markets that deal with one industry or industry segment (e.g., steel, chemicals).

horizontal marketplaces
Markets that concentrate on a service or a product that is used in all types of industries (e.g., office supplies, PCs).

Insights and Additions — Summary of B2B Characteristics

PARTIES TO TRANSACTIONS	TYPES OF TRANSACTIONS
Direct, seller to buyer or buyer to seller	Spot buying
Via intermediaries	Strategic sourcing

TYPES OF MATERIALS SOLD	DIRECTION OF TRADE
Direct	Vertical
Indirect (MROs)	Horizontal

NUMBER AND FORM OF PARTICIPATION	DEGREE OF OPENNESS
One-to-many: sell-side	Private
Many-to-one: buy-side	Private
Many-to-many: exchanges	Public
Many, connected: collaborative	Public

THE BASIC B2B TRANSACTION TYPES

The basic types of B2B transactions are:

- **Sell-side.** One seller to many buyers.
- **Buy-side.** One buyer from many sellers.
- **Exchanges.** Many sellers to many buyers.
- **Collaborative commerce.** Communication and sharing of information, design, and planning among business partners.

EXHIBIT 5.1   Types of B2B E-Commerce

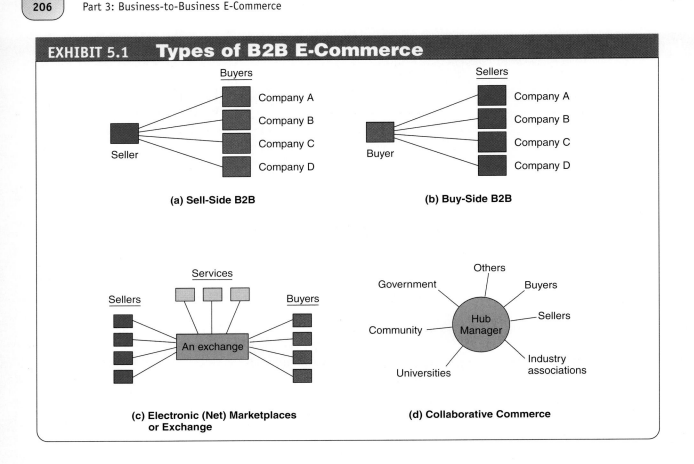

Exhibit 5.1 gives a graphic presentation of these B2B types, which we discuss in more detail in the following sections.

One-to-Many and Many-to-One: Company-Centric Transactions

company-centric EC
E-commerce that focuses on a single company's buying needs (many-to-one, or buy-side) or selling needs (one-to-many, or sell-side).

In one-to-many and many-to-one markets, one company does either all of the selling (*sell-side market*) or all of the buying (*buy-side market*). Because they are focused on a single company's buying or selling needs, they are referred to as **company-centric EC**. Company-centric marketplaces are the topic of this chapter.

In the company-centric marketplaces, the individual sell-side or buy-side company has complete control over who participates in the selling or buying transaction and the supporting information systems. Thus, these transactions are essentially private, and sell-side and buy-side markets are considered **private e-marketplaces**.

private e-marketplaces
Markets in which the individual sell-side or buy-side company has complete control over participation in the selling or buying transaction.

Most company-centric markets are conducted without the help of intermediaries. However, when it comes to auctions or to aggregating small buyers, an intermediary may be used. (Even when an intermediary is used, the market is still considered private, because the single buyer or seller that hires the intermediary maintains control of who is invited to participate in the market.) Several selling and buying methods are used in company-centric marketplaces, as we will demonstrate throughout the chapter.

Many-to-Many: Exchanges

In many-to-many e-marketplaces, many buyers and many sellers meet electronically for the purpose of trading with each other. There are different types of e-marketplaces, which are also known as **exchanges, trading communities**, or **trading exchanges**. We will use the term *exchanges* in this book. Exchanges are usually owned and run by a third party or by a consortium. They are described in more detail in Chapter 6. Exchanges are open to all interested parties (sellers and buyers), and so are considered **public e-marketplaces**.

Other B2B Models and Services

Businesses deal with other businesses for purposes other than just selling or buying. One example is that of *collaborative commerce*, which is communication, design, planning, and information sharing among business partners. To qualify as collaborative commerce, the activities that are shared must represent far more than just financial transactions. For example, they may include activities related to design, manufacture, and management. Collaborative commerce is described later in the chapter (Section 5.8).

Other B2B models include services and relationships such as value-chain integrators, value-chain service providers, and information brokers.

SUPPLY CHAIN RELATIONSHIPS IN B2B

In the various B2B transaction types, business activities are usually conducted along the supply chain of a company (see Chapter 2). The supply chain process consists of a number of interrelated subprocesses and roles. These extend from the acquisition of materials from suppliers to the processing of a product or service, to packaging it and moving it to distributors and retailers, and end with its eventual purchase by the end-consumer. B2B can make supply chains more efficient and effective or change the supply chain completely, eliminating one or more intermediaries.

Historically, many of the segments and processes in the supply chain, especially the upstream and downstream activities, have been managed through paper transactions (e.g., purchase orders, invoices, and so forth). B2B applications are done online so they can serve as supply chain enablers that offer distinct competitive advantages. Supply chain management also encompasses the coordination of order generation, order taking, and order fulfillment/distribution. (See Chapters 2 and 10 for more discussion of supply chain management.)

VIRTUAL SERVICE INDUSTRIES IN B2B

In addition to trading products between businesses along the supply chain, services can also be provided in B2B. Just as service industries such as banking, insurance, real estate, job matching, and stock trading can be conducted electronically for individuals, as described in Chapter 3, so too can they be supplied electronically to businesses. The major B2B services are:

1. **Travel services.** Many large corporations arrange special travel discounts through B2B travel agents. To further reduce costs, companies can make special arrangements that enable employees to plan and book their own trips online.

exchanges
Many-to-many e-marketplaces, usually owned and run by a third party or a consortium, in which many buyers and many sellers meet electronically to trade with each other; also called *trading communities* or *trading exchanges*.

public e-marketplaces
Third-party exchanges that are open to all interested parties (sellers and buyers).

For instance, Rosenbluth International (rosenbluth.com) provides an agentless service to corporate clients.

2. **Real estate.** Commercial real estate transactions can be very large and complex. Therefore, the Web may not be able to completely replace existing human agents. Instead, the Web can help businesses find the right properties, compare properties, and assist in negotiations. Some government-run foreclosed real estate auctions are open only to real estate dealers (companies) and are conducted online.

3. **Electronic payments.** Internet banking is an economical way of making business payments, transferring funds, or performing other financial transactions. For example, electronic funds transfer (EFT) is popular with businesses. Transaction fees over the Internet are less costly than any other alternative method.

4. **Online stock trading.** Corporations are important stock investors. Because fees for online trading are very low (as low as $5 per transaction) and flat, regardless of the trading amount, online trading services are very attractive to institutional investors.

5. **Online financing.** Business loans can be solicited online from lenders. Bank of America, for example, offers its commercial customers a matching service on IntraLoan, which uses an extranet to match business loan applicants with potential lending corporations. Several sites, such as garage.com, provide information about venture capital.

6. **Other online services.** Consulting services, law firms, health organizations, and others sell knowledge online. Many other online services, such as the purchase of electronic stamps (similar to metered postage, but generated on a computer), are available online (estamp.com).

THE BENEFITS OF B2B

The benefits of B2B EC depend on which model is used. In general, though, the major benefits of B2B are that it:

- Eliminates paper and reduces administrative costs.
- Expedites cycle time.
- Lowers search costs and time for buyers.
- Increases productivity of employees dealing with buying and/or selling.
- Reduces errors and/or improves quality of services.
- Reduces inventory levels and costs.
- Increases production flexibility, permitting just-in-time delivery.
- Facilitates mass customization.
- Increases opportunities for collaboration.

The introduction of B2B may eliminate the distributor and/or the retailer, which may be a benefit to the seller and the buyer (though not a benefit to the distributor or retailer). In previous chapters we referred to such a phenomenon as *disintermediation*.

In the remainder of the chapter, we will look in more depth at the B2B models and topics introduced in this opening section.

> ⬤ Define B2B.
>
> ⬤ Discuss the following: spot buying versus strategic sourcing, direct materials versus indirect materials, and vertical markets versus horizontal markets.
>
> ⬤ What are buy-side and sell-side transactions? How are they different?
>
> ⬤ What are company-centric marketplaces? Are they public or private?
>
> ⬤ Define B2B exchanges.
>
> ⬤ Relate the supply chain to B2B transactions.
>
> ⬤ List the B2B service industries.

5.2 SELL-SIDE MARKETPLACES: ONE-TO-MANY

SELL-SIDE MODELS AND ACTIVITIES

In Chapter 3, we introduced the direct-selling model in which a manufacturer or a retailer sells electronically directly to consumers. The **sell-side e-marketplace** is the analogous market for business buyers. That is, the sell-side e-marketplace delivers a Web-based, private-trading sales channel, frequently over an extranet, to business customers. The seller can be a manufacturer selling to a wholesaler, to a retailer, or to a large business. Intel, Cisco, and Dell are examples of such sellers. Or, the seller can be a distributor selling to wholesalers, to retailers, or to businesses. In either case, sell-side involves one seller and many potential buyers. In this model, both individual consumers and business buyers may use the same sell-side marketplace, as shown in Exhibit 5.2 (page 210).

sell-side e-marketplace
A Web-based marketplace in which one company sells to many business buyers, frequently over an extranet.

The architecture of this B2B model is similar to that of B2C EC. The major differences are in the process. For example, in B2B, large customers may get customized catalogs and prices. Usually, companies will separate B2C orders from B2B orders. One reason for the separation is the different order fulfillment process (see Chapter 10).

There are three major methods for direct sale in the one-to-many model: selling from electronic catalogs; selling via forward auctions (as GM does with its old equipment); and one-to-one selling, usually under a negotiated, long-term contract. Such one-to-one negotiating is familiar; we describe the other two methods in this chapter, the first method in this section and the second in Section 5.3.

Real or Virtual Sellers

Sellers in the sell-side marketplace can be click-and-mortar manufacturers or intermediaries, usually distributors or wholesalers. The intermediaries may even be virtual, as in the case of bigboxx.com.hk described in EC Application Case 5.1 (page 211).

Customer Service

Online sellers can provide sophisticated customer services. For example, General Electric receives 20 million calls a year regarding appliances. Although most of these calls come from individuals, many come from businesses. By using the Internet

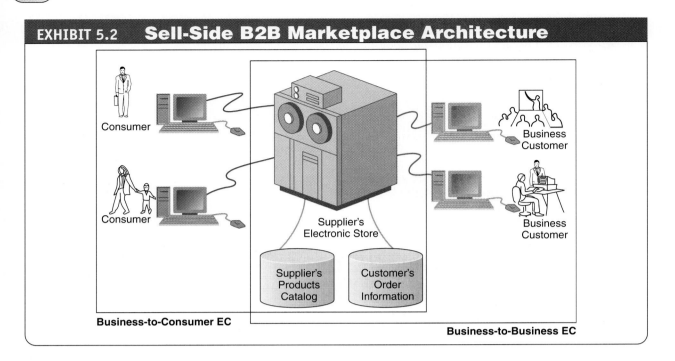

EXHIBIT 5.2   Sell-Side B2B Marketplace Architecture

Consumer

Consumer

Business-to-Consumer EC

Supplier's
Electronic Store

Supplier's
Products
Catalog

Customer's
Order
Information

Business
Customer

Business
Customer

Business-to-Business EC

and automatic-response software agents, GE has reduced the cost of calls from $5 per call by phone to $0.20 per call through an automatic response.

Another example of B2B customer service is that of Milacron, Inc., which produces consumable industrial products for metalworking. The company launched an award-winning EC site aimed at its more than 100,000 *small and medium enterprise (SME)* customers. The site provides an easy-to-use and secure way of selecting, purchasing, and applying Milacron's 55,000 products. From this site, the SMEs also can access a level of technical service beyond that provided previously to even Milacron's largest customers (see milacron.com).

DIRECT SALES FROM CATALOGS

Companies can use the Internet to sell directly from their online catalogs. A company may offer one catalog for all customers or a customized catalog for each customer.

In Chapter 2, we presented the advantages of e-catalogs over paper catalogs and showed how Boise Cascade Corp. uses e-catalogs for B2B sales. Without enhancements, this model may not be convenient for large and repetitive business buyers, because the buyer's order information is stored in the supplier's server and is not easily integrated with the buyer's corporate information system. In order to facilitate the B2B direct sale, the seller can provide the buyer with a buyer-customized shopping cart, which can store order information that can be integrated with the buyer's information system. This is particularly important when buyers have to visit several sites in one or several shopping malls.

Interorganization and Collaboration

BUYING FROM VIRTUAL SELLER BIGBOXX.COM

Bigboxx.com (*bigboxx.com*) is a Hong Kong–based B2B office supply retailer. It has no physical stores and sells products through its online catalog, so it is an online intermediary. The company has three types of customers: large corporate clients, medium corporate clients, and small offices (SOHO). The company offers more than 10,000 items from 300 suppliers. Bigboxx.com's goal is to sell its products in various countries in Southeast Asia. The company began operations in spring 2000. By fall 2001, it had over 6,500 registered customers.

The company's portal is attractive and easy to use. The company also has a tutorial that instructs users on how to use the Web site. Once a user registers, the user can start shopping using the online shopping cart. Users can look for items by browsing through the online catalog or by searching the site with a search engine.

Users can pay by cash or by check (upon delivery), via automatic bank drafts, by credit card, or by purchasing card. Soon users will be able to pay through Internet-based direct debit, by electronic bill presentation, or by Internet banking.

Using its own trucks and warehouses, deliveries are made within 24 hours or even on the same day. Delivery is scheduled online. The ordering system is integrated with an SAP-based back-office system.

Bigboxx.com provides numerous value-added services for customers:

- The ability to check item availability in real time.
- The ability to track the status of each item in an order.
- Promotions and suggested items based on customers' user profiles.
- Customized prices, for every product, for every customer.
- For customers with multibranching (e.g., using multiple branches of the same bank), a group account by branch.
- A control and a central-approval feature.
- Automatic activation at desired time intervals of standing orders for repeat purchasing.
- A large number of Excel reports and data, including comparative management reports.

Questions

- Enter *bigboxx.com* and *staples.com* and compare their offerings and purchase processes. (Take the tutorial at *bigboxx.com*.)
- One day, customers may be used to buying office supplies online. They may then try to buy directly from the manufacturers. Will *Bigboxx.com* then be disintermediated?

Many sellers provide separate pages and catalogs to their major buyers. For example, staples.com, an office supply vendor, offers its business customers personalized catalogs and pricing at StaplesLink.com, which uses several vendors' e-procurement systems (e.g., Ariba, Oracle).

Configuration and Customization

As with B2C e-commerce, B2B direct sales from catalogs offer an opportunity for efficient customization. As we will see in the case of Cisco (described in detail later in the chapter), manufacturers can provide online tools for self-configuration.

Business customers can customize products, get a price quote, and submit the order for production, all online.

Benefits and Limitations of Direct Sales

Successful examples of the B2B direct sales model include Dell, Intel, IBM, and Cisco. Sellers that use this model may be successful as long as they have a superb reputation in the market and a large enough group of loyal customers.

The major benefits of direct sales are:

1. Lower order-processing costs (including commissions) and less paperwork.
2. A faster ordering cycle.
3. Fewer errors in ordering and product configuration.
4. Lower search costs for buyers (who can more easily compare prices among sellers).
5. Lower search costs for sellers (who can advertise online).
6. Lower logistics costs (due to less inventory, fewer shipments, and less handling).
7. The ability to offer different catalogs and prices to different customers (personalization, customization) and to customize products and services efficiently.

In terms of limitations, one of the major issues facing smaller direct sellers is how to find buyers. Many small companies know how to advertise in traditional channels but are still learning how to contact would-be buyers online. Also, B2B sellers may experience channel conflicts with their existing distribution systems. Another limitation is that if traditional electronic data interchange (EDI; the computer-to-computer direct transfer of business documents) is used, the cost to the customers can be high, and they will be reluctant to go online. (The solution to this problem is the transfer of documents over the Internet or extranets.) Finally, the number of business partners online must be large enough to justify the system infrastructure and operation and maintenance expenses.

> ▌ List the types of sell-side B2B transactions.
> ▌ Distinguish between use and non-use of intermediaries in B2B sell-side transactions.
> ▌ Describe direct sales from catalogs.
> ▌ Discuss the benefits and limitations of direct sales.
> ▌ Describe customer service in B2B systems.

5.3   SELLING VIA AUCTIONS

USING AUCTIONS ON THE SELL SIDE

As you read in the opening case study, GM uses auctions to sell capital assets. In a *forward auction*, items are displayed on an auction site (private or public) for quick disposal. Forward auctions offer a number of benefits to B2B sellers:

▸ **Revenue generation.** Forward auctions as a new sales channel support and expand online and overall sales. For example, Weirton Steel Corp. doubled its customer base when it started auctions (Fickel 1999). Forward auctions also offer businesses a new venue for quickly and easily disposing of excess, obsolete, and returned products.

▸ **Cost savings.** In addition to generating new revenue, conducting auctions electronically reduces the costs of selling auction items. These savings also help increase the seller's profits.

▸ **Increased page views.** Forward auctions give Web sites "stickiness." **Stickiness** is a characteristic describing customer loyalty to a site demonstrated by the number and length of visits to a site. Stickiness at an auction site, for example, means that auction users spend more time on a site, generate more page views than other users, and buy more.

> **stickiness**
> The characteristic of customer loyalty to a Web site, demonstrated by the number and length of visits to a site.

▸ **Member acquisition and retention.** All bidding transactions result in additional registered members, who are future business contacts. Further, auction software enables sellers to search and report on virtually every relevant auction activity for future analysis and use.

There are two different ways to conduct forward auctions. A company may conduct its forward auctions from its own Web site or it can sell from an intermediary auction site, such as eBay or freemarkets.com. Let's examine these options.

SELLING FROM THE COMPANY'S OWN SITE

For large and well-known companies that conduct auctions frequently, such as GM, it makes sense to build an auction mechanism on the company's own site. Why should a company pay a commission to an intermediary if the intermediary cannot provide the company with much added value? Of course, if a company decides to auction from its own site, the company will have to pay for infrastructure and operate and maintain the auction site. But, if the company already has an electronic marketplace for selling from e-catalogs, the additional cost for conducting auctions may not be too high.

USING INTERMEDIARIES

Large numbers of intermediaries offer B2B auction sites (e.g., see freemarkets.com). An intermediary may conduct private auctions for a seller, either from the intermediary's or the seller's site. Or, a company may choose to conduct auctions in a public marketplace, using a third-party hosting company (e.g., eBay, which has a special "business exchange" for small companies). The market in which such intermediaries operate online is called an **intermediary-oriented e-marketplace**.

> **intermediary-oriented e-marketplace**
> An e-marketplace in which intermediaries operate.

Using a third-party hosting company for conducting auctions has many benefits. The first is that no additional resources (e.g., hardware, bandwidth, engineering resources, or IT personnel) are required. Nor are there any hiring costs or opportunity costs associated with the redeployment of corporate resources. B2B auctions also offer fast time to market: They enable a company to have a robust, customized auction up and running immediately. Without the intermediary, it may take a company weeks to prepare an auction site in-house.

A second benefit of using an intermediary relates to who owns and controls the auction information. When a private auction is conducted, the intermediary sets up the auction to show the branding (company name) of the merchant, rather than the intermediary's name. (For example, if an intermediary prepares a private auction for Blue Devils Company, customers see the Blue Devils name and logo.) Yet the intermediary does the work of controlling data on Web traffic, page views, and member registration; setting all the auction parameters (transaction fee structure, user interface, and reports); and integrating the information flow and logistics.

Another benefit of using intermediaries to run auction sites relates to billing and collection efforts, which are handled by the intermediary rather than the company. For example, intermediaries calculate merchant-specific shipping weights and charge customers for shipping of auctioned items. All credit card data are encrypted for secure transmission and storage, and all billing information can be easily downloaded by the merchant company for integration with existing systems. These services are not free, of course. They are provided as part of the merchant's commission to the intermediary, a cost often deemed worth paying in exchange for the ease of the service.

▶ List the benefits of using B2B auctions for selling.
▶ List the benefits of using auction intermediaries.

5.4   SELL-SIDE CASES

In this section, we look in some detail at three examples of successful sell-side marketplaces: a direct-sales model, Cisco Systems, and at two B2B intermediaries, Marshall Industries and Boeing.

CISCO CONNECTION ONLINE (CCO)

Cisco Systems (cisco.com) is the world's leading producer of routers, switches, and network interconnect services. Cisco's portal has evolved over several years, beginning with technical support for customers and developing into one of the world's largest direct-sales EC sites. Today, Cisco offers about a dozen Internet-based applications to both end-user businesses and reseller partners.

Customer Service

Cisco began providing electronic support in 1991 using value-added networks (VANs). Software downloads, defect tracking, and technical advice were the first applications offered. In spring 1994, Cisco placed its system on the Web and named its site Cisco Connection Online (CCO). By 2001, Cisco's customers and reseller partners were logging onto Cisco's Web site about 1.3 million times a month to receive technical assistance, place and check orders, or download software. The online service has been so well received that nearly 85 percent of all customer service inquiries and 95 percent of software updates are delivered online. It is delivered globally in 14 languages. The CCO is considered a model for B2B success, and several books have been written about it (e.g., Bunnel and Brate 2000; Stauffer 2000).

Online Ordering

Cisco builds virtually all its products made-to-order, so it has very few off-the-shelf products. Before the CCO, ordering a product was a lengthy, complicated, and error-prone process, because it was done by fax or by "snail mail." Cisco began deploying Web-based commerce tools in July 1995, and within a year, its Internet Product Center allowed users to purchase any Cisco product over the Web. Today, a business customer's engineer can sit down at a PC, configure a product, and find out immediately if there are any errors in the configuration (some feedback is given by intelligent agents). The customer can then route the order to its procurement department, which submits the order electronically to Cisco.

By providing online pricing and configuration tools to customers, almost all orders (about 98 percent) are now placed through CCO, saving time for both Cisco and its customers. In the first 5 months of online ordering operation in 1996, Cisco booked over $100 million in online sales. This figure grew to $4 billion in 1998 and to over $8 billion in 2002.

Order Status

Each month Cisco used to receive over 150,000 order-status inquiries such as, "When will my order be ready? How should the order be classified for customs? Is the product eligible for NAFTA agreement? What export control issues apply?" Cisco provides customers with tracking and FAQ tools so that customers can find the answers to their questions by themselves. In addition, the company's primary domestic and international freight forwarders update Cisco's database electronically about the status of each shipment. CCO can record the shipping date, the method of shipment, and the current location of each product. All new information is made available to customers immediately. As soon as an order ships, Cisco sends the customer a notification by e-mail.

Benefits to Cisco

Cisco reaps many benefits from the CCO system. The most important benefits are:

- **Reduced operating costs for order taking.** By automating its order process online in 1998, Cisco has saved $363 million per year, or approximately 17.5 percent of its total operating costs. This is due primarily to increased productivity of the employees who take and fulfill orders.

- **Enhanced technical support and customer service.** With more than 85 percent of its technical support and customer service calls handled online, Cisco's technical support productivity has increased by 250 percent per year.

- **Reduced technical support staff cost.** Online technical support reduced technical support staff costs by roughly $125 million in 1998 alone.

- **Reduced software distribution costs.** Customers download new software releases directly from Cisco's site, saving the company $180 million in distribution, packaging, and duplicating costs each year. Having product and pricing information on the Web and Web-based CD-ROMs saves Cisco an additional

$50 million annually in printing and distributing catalogs and marketing materials to customers.

▸ **Faster service.** Lead times were reduced from 4 to 10 days to 2 to 3 days.

Benefits to Customers

The CCO system also benefits customers. Cisco customers can configure orders more quickly, immediately determine costs, and collaborate much more rapidly and effectively with Cisco's staff. Also, technical support is faster.

MARSHALL INDUSTRIES

Marshall Industries, now part of Avnet Electronics Marketing (avnet.com), is a large distributor of electronic components. Prior to its merger with Avnet in 1999, Marshall posted $1.7 billion in sales in fiscal year 1999, and served over 30,000 business customers, many of which are small in size. Marshall distributed over 130,000 different products worldwide. Avnet was a competitor. Now, together, they have sales of close to $10 billion a year.

The electronics industry is very competitive. Distributors compete against each other and against direct marketing by the manufacturers, and they may face disintermediation. Thus, providing value-added services is key to a distributor's survival. Marshall adds value through IT support. The company is known for its innovative use of information technologies and the Web (e.g., see Wilson 1998). The company won a first prize in the 1997 SIM International awards competition (simnet.org) for the best paper describing how the company uses IT and EC. In 1999, the company was the first ever to use the XML-based interoperable solution for B2B integration. (XML stands for eXtensible Markup Language, a standard for defining data elements on a Web page and B2B documents.)

Marshall has pioneered the use of the Internet and IT applications, with a view to reengineering its business and creating new competitive strengths. Its major Web-based initiatives, which are interconnected, are listed in Exhibit 5.3.

In addition to the physical distribution of components, distributors such as Marshall have increasingly taken on value-added tasks such as technical support, logistics, processing payments and accounts receivable, offering credit, logistics, and more. The semiconductor industry, for example, is cyclical, causing major delivery and inventory problems that distributors seek to solve. In addition, large customers are global, requiring global sourcing. Time-to-market competition and customization at the customer end require a fast and flexible response from distributors. Just-in-time and supplier-managed inventories are increasingly required from distributors. These demands require tight integration of information and provision of value-added services along the value chain. Marshall met these demands in its e-commerce initiative by providing value-added services that enabled the company to survive as an intermediary.

Marshall's Survival Strategy

Marshall's use of e-commerce was combined with other innovations and with *business process reengineering* (BPR), the introduction of a fundamental change in the way a company does business. For example, Marshall:

EXHIBIT 5.3	**Marshall Industries' EC Initiatives**
Initiative	**Description**
MarshallNet	An intranet supporting sales people in the field via wireless devices and portable PCs. Real-time access to corporate database, DSS applications, workflow, and collaboration.
Marshall on the Internet (portal)	A B2B portal for customers offering information, ordering, and tracking (using UPS software) capabilities. Discussion, chat, connection to call centers. Special pages for value-added resellers. Troubleshooting capabilities.
Strategic European Internet	A strategic partner in Europe, offering MarshallNet in 17 languages, plus additional local information.
Electronic Design Center	Includes an online configuration tool. Provides technical specs. A simulation capability for making virtual components. Marshall can produce sample products designed by customers.
PartnerNet	Customized Web pages for major customers and suppliers. Accessibility to Marshall's intranet. Electronic payments. Historical data and records. Planning tools online.
NetSeminar	Training online; bringing together suppliers and customers for live interactions.
Education and News Portal	Education, news and entertainment services, including consulting, sales training, and interactive public product announcements.

▶ Provided continuous improvement programs and innovations, jointly with its business partners.

▶ Used a team-based organization with a flat hierarchy, decentralizing decision making.

▶ Changed the salesperson's compensation from commission-based to profit sharing.

▶ Promoted the use of customer relationship management (CRM).

▶ Provided new Web-based services to continuously create value between suppliers and customers.

▶ Changed the internal organizational structure and procedures to fully support e-commerce initiatives.

Marshall was very successful and profitable. Its EC initiatives are now practiced at Avnet-Marshall as well. (For additional information, see Timmers 1999 and El-Sawy et al. 1999.)

BOEING'S PART MARKETPLACE

Boeing Company (boeing.com) is the world's largest maker of airplanes for commercial and military customers. It also plays the role of intermediary in supplying replacement and maintenance parts to airlines. Unlike other online B2B intermediaries such as ProcureNet, revenue as an intermediary may be a minor concern to Boeing, which makes most of its revenue from selling airplanes. The major goal of PART (Part Analysis and Requirement Tracking) is supporting customers' maintenance needs as a customer service.

The objective of PART is to link airlines that need maintenance parts with suppliers who are producing the parts for Boeing aircraft (boeing.com/assocproducts/ bpart/partpage). Boeing's online strategy is to provide a single point of online access through which airlines (the buyers of Boeing's aircraft) and the maintenance and parts providers (Boeing's suppliers) can access data about the parts they need. These data might come from the airframe builder, the component supplier, the engine manufacturer, or the airline itself. Thus, Boeing is acting as an intermediary between the airlines and the parts suppliers. With data from 300 key suppliers of Boeing's airplane parts, Boeing's goal is to provide its customers with one-stop shopping for online maintenance information and ordering capability.

The Spare Parts Business Using Traditional EDI

Ordering spare parts had been a multistep process for many of Boeing's customers. For example, an airline's mechanic informed the purchasing department of his company that a specific part was needed; purchasing approved the purchase order and sent it to Boeing by phone or fax. At that point, the mechanic did not need to know who produced the part, because the aircraft was purchased from Boeing as one body. However, Boeing had to find out who produced the part and then ask the producer to deliver the part to the customer (unless Boeing happened to keep an inventory of that part).

The largest airlines began to streamline the ordering process nearly 20 years ago. Because of the volume and regularity of their orders, they established EDI connections with Boeing over VANs. Not all airlines were quick to follow suit, however. It took until 1992 to induce 10 percent of the largest customers, representing 60 percent of the volume, to order through EDI. The numbers did not change much until 1996, due to the cost and complexity of VAN-based EDI.

Debut of PART on the Internet

Boeing viewed the Internet as an opportunity to encourage more of its customers to order parts electronically. With the initial investment limited to a standard PC and basic Internet access, even its smallest customers can now participate. Because of its interactive capabilities, many customer service functions that were handled over the telephone are now handled over the Internet.

In November 1996, Boeing debuted its PART page on the Internet, giving its customers around the world the ability to check part availability and pricing, order parts, and track order status, all online. Less than a year later, about 50 percent of Boeing's customers used PART for parts orders and customer-service inquiries. In its first year of operation, the Boeing PART page handled over half a million inquiries and transactions from customers around the world. Boeing's spare parts business processed about 20 percent more shipments per month in 1997 than it did in 1996 with the same number of data entry people. In addition, as many as 600 phone calls a day to customer-service staff were eliminated because customers had access to information about pricing, availability, and order status online. Over time, Boeing anticipates that PART online will result in fewer parts being returned due to administrative errors. Furthermore, the service may encourage airlines to buy Boeing aircraft the next time they make an aircraft purchase.

As a result of PART's success, Boeing has started a complementary EC initiative, called BOLD, which provides technical support.

Portable Access to Technical Drawings/Support

Airline maintenance is spread over a wide geographical area, taking place anywhere in the world an aircraft flies. At an airport, maintenance activities may take place at the gate or at the maintenance operations center. Mechanics traditionally have had to make repeated, time-consuming trips to the operations center to consult paper or microfilm reference materials. A single manual may contain as many as 30,000 pages.

For this reason, in April 1996, Boeing On Line Data (BOLD) went into operation. This online data resource not only incorporates engineering drawings, but also manuals, catalogs, and other technical information. By 2001, BOLD had about 10,000 users from 100 different airlines. In addition, Portable Maintenance Aid (PMA) was developed to enable wireless access to BOLD from anywhere. Because of BOLD and PMA, mechanics and technicians are able to access all the information they need to make decisions about necessary repairs at the time and place they need the information.

Early users of BOLD and PMA report that spending less time searching for information has freed up engineers and maintenance technicians to focus on more productive activities. One U.S. airline saved $1 million a year when it gave 400 users access to Boeing's BOLD program. Seeing the results of the initial implementation, the airline expanded the service to 2,000 users. A European airline saved $1.5 million from BOLD in the first year alone, due to a nearly 4 percent boost in production and engineering staff productivity. In addition, with maintenance information available online at the gate, delays at the gate resulting from missing information can be reduced. The European airline mentioned earlier estimates that PMA will reduce flight delays by 5 to 10 percent.

A final benefit is that quicker maintenance checks are expected to lead to increased airline revenues. Every 3,000 hours, an airline does a "schedule-C" maintenance check that can keep an aircraft grounded for up to a week, and not having maintenance information readily available can lengthen the process. The longer the maintenance check, the more revenue an airline loses. (Idle aircraft cost tens of thousands of dollars a day.) Through BOLD and PMA, the European airline estimates it will save 1 to 2 days of idle time per year for each aircraft, resulting in a $43 million in increased revenue. Boeing's expectation is that all of these benefits will make airlines want to buy Boeing aircraft.

▶ Describe the online services that CCO offers.

▶ What are the benefits of CCO to Cisco? To Cisco's customers?

▶ Draw Marshall's supply chain.

▶ Being an intermediary, how does Marshall protect its existence?

▶ Draw Boeing's PART supply chain.

▶ What activities in Boeing's supply chain are improved by its online initiatives?

5.5   BUY-SIDE MARKETPLACES: ONE-FROM-MANY

A unique feature of B2B EC is the buy-side market and its use for procurement. *Procurement* is the purchase of goods and services for organizations. It is usually done by *purchasing agents* (also known as *corporate buyers*). EC procurement is usually done in buy-side marketplaces.

PROCUREMENT METHODS

Companies use different methods to procure goods and services depending on what they buy, the quantities needed, how much money is involved, and more. The major procurement methods are:

- Buy from manufacturers, wholesalers, or retailers at their storefronts, from catalogs, and by negotiation.
- Buy from the catalog of an intermediary that aggregates sellers' catalogs.
- Buy from an internal-buyer's catalog in which company-approved vendors' catalogs, including preagreed prices, are aggregated.
- Conduct a bidding or tendering system (a reverse auction) in a systems where suppliers compete against each other. This method is used for large-ticket items or large quantities.
- Buy at private or public auction sites in which the organization participates as one buyer.
- Join a group-purchasing system. The group will negotiate or enter into a bidding process.

Some of these activities are done in private marketplaces, others in public exchanges.

INEFFICIENCIES IN PROCUREMENT MANAGEMENT

procurement management
The coordination of all the activities relating to purchasing goods and services needed to accomplish the mission of an organization.

Procurement management refers to the coordination of all the activities pertaining to purchasing goods and services necessary to accomplish the mission of an enterprise. Approximately 80 percent of an organization's purchased items, mostly MROs, constitute 20 to 25 percent of the total purchase value. Furthermore, a large portion of corporate buyers' time is spent on non-value-added activities such as data entry, correcting errors in paperwork, expediting delivery, or solving quality problems.

For the high-value items, purchasing personnel need to spend a lot of time and effort on upstream procurement activities such as qualifying suppliers, negotiating prices and terms, building rapport with strategic suppliers, and carrying out supplier evaluation and certification. If buyers are busy with the details of the smaller items, usually the MROs, they do not have enough time to properly deal with the purchase of the high-value items. Organizations try to address this imbalance by implementing new purchasing models.

There are many other potential inefficiencies in procurement. These range from delays to paying too much for rush orders. Another procurement inefficiency is **maverick buying**. It involves making unplanned purchases of items needed quickly and buying from nonapproved vendors at higher prices. The traditional procurement process, shown in Exhibit 5.4, is inefficient. To correct the situation, companies reengineer their procurement systems, and in particular, introduce e-procurement.

maverick buying
Unplanned purchases of items needed quickly, often from nonapproved vendors or at higher prices.

THE GOALS OF E-PROCUREMENT

The reengineering of procurement has been attempted for decades, usually by using new information technologies. The real opportunity for reengineering lies in the use of **e-procurement**, the electronic acquisition of goods and services for organizations. The general e-procurement process (with the exception of tendering) is shown in Exhibit 5.5 (page 222).

e-procurement
The electronic acquisition of goods and services for organizations.

By automating and streamlining the laborious routines of the purchasing function, purchasing professionals can focus on more strategic purchases, achieving the following goals:

▶ Increasing purchasing agent productivity.

▶ Lowering purchase prices through product standardization and consolidation of purchases.

▶ Improving information flow and management (e.g., supplier's information and pricing information).

▶ Minimizing the purchases made from noncontract vendors (eliminating maverick buying).

▶ Improving the payment process.

▶ Streamlining the purchasing process, making it simple and fast. Sometimes this involves authorizing requisitioners to perform purchases from their desktops, bypassing the procurement department.

▶ Reducing the administrative processing cost per order by as much as 90 percent. (In many cases, GM achieved a reduction from $100 to $10.)

▶ Finding new suppliers and vendors, which can provide goods and services faster and/or cheaper.

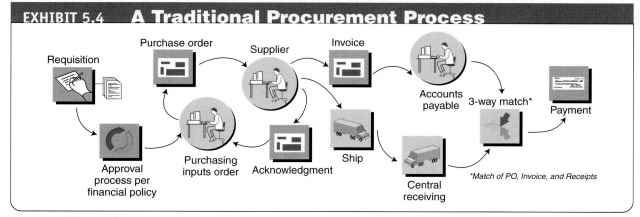

EXHIBIT 5.4 A Traditional Procurement Process

Source: *Ariba.com*, February 2001.

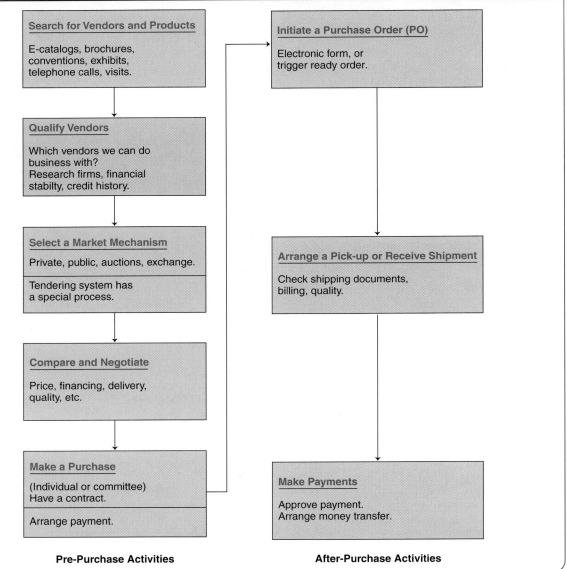

EXHIBIT 5.5   The E-Procurement Process: A Buyer's View

Search for Vendors and Products

E-catalogs, brochures,
conventions, exhibits,
telephone calls, visits.

Qualify Vendors

Which vendors we can do
business with?
Research firms, financial
stabilty, credit history.

Select a Market Mechanism

Private, public, auctions, exchange.

Tendering system has
a special process.

Compare and Negotiate

Price, financing, delivery,
quality, etc.

Make a Purchase

(Individual or committee)
Have a contract.

Arrange payment.

Initiate a Purchase Order (PO)

Electronic form, or
trigger ready order.

Arrange a Pick-up or Receive Shipment

Check shipping documents,
billing, quality.

Make Payments

Approve payment.
Arrange money transfer.

Pre-Purchase Activities   **After-Purchase Activities**

> ▌ Integrating the procurement process with budgetary control in an efficient
> and effective way.

> ▌ Minimizing human errors in the buying or shipping process.

E-procurement is relatively easy to implement. There are usually no channel conflicts, and the resistance to change is minimal. Also, a wide selection of software packages and other infrastructure are available at a reasonable cost.

MROs are often the initial target for e-procurement. However, improvement can be made in purchasing of direct materials as well. All existing manual processes of requisition creation, requests for quotation, invitation to tender, purchase order issuance, receiving goods, and making payment can be streamlined and automated. However, to most effectively implement such automated support, the people involved in procurement must collaborate with the suppliers' Web sites.

IMPLEMENTING E-PROCUREMENT

Putting the buying department on the Internet may be the easy part of e-procurement. The more difficult part is dealing with the following issues:

▶ Fitting e-procurement into the company EC strategy.

▶ Reviewing and changing the procurement process itself. E-procurement may have an effect on how many purchasing agents exist, where they are located, and how purchases are being approved. Also important is the degree of purchasing centralization.

▶ Providing interfaces between e-procurement with integrated enterprise-wide information systems such as enterprise resources planning (ERP) or supply chain management (SCM). If the company does not have such systems, it may be beneficial to do some BPR prior to the installation of e-procurement.

▶ Coordinating the buyer's information system with that of the sellers. Sellers have many potential buyers. For this reason, some major suppliers, such as SKF (a Swedish automotive parts maker, skf.com), developed an integration-oriented procurement system for its buyers. For example, the SKF information system is designed to make it easier for the procurement systems of others (notably the distributors in other countries) that buy the company's bearings and seals to interface with the SKF system. The SKF system allows distributors to gain real-time technical information on the products, as well as details on product availability, delivery times, and commercial terms and conditions.

Despite these challenges, many companies that have implemented e-procurement have been extremely satisfied with the payoffs.

▶ Describe the inefficiencies of traditional procurement.

▶ Describe the goals of e-procurement.

▶ Differentiate direct materials from MROs; why are MROs good candidates for e-procurement?

▶ Describe the implementation of e-procurement.

5.6 BUY-SIDE E-MARKETPLACES: REVERSE AUCTIONS

When a buyer goes to a sell-side marketplace, such as Cisco's, the buyer's acquisition department sometimes has to manually enter the order information into its own corporate information system. Furthermore, searching e-stores and e-malls to find and compare suppliers and products can be very slow and costly. As a

buy-side e-marketplace
A Web-based market-place in which a buyer opens an electronic market on its own server and invites potential suppliers to bid on the items the buyer needs; also called the *reverse auction, tendering,* or *bidding model.*

request for quote (RFQ)
The "invitation" to a buy-side marketplace (reverse auction).

solution, large buyers can open their own marketplace, which we call the **buy-side e-marketplace**, as depicted in Exhibit 5.6. Under this model, a buyer opens an electronic market on its own server and invites potential suppliers to bid on the items the buyer needs. The "invitation" to such reverse auctions is a form or document called a **request for quote (RFQ)**. The RFQ process is called the *reverse auction, tendering,* or *bidding model.*

The reverse auction is the most common model for large purchases. Governments and large corporations frequently mandate this approach, which may provide considerable savings. To understand why this is so, study the nearby Insights and Additions box on the next page, which compares the pre-Internet tendering process with the Web-based reverse auction process. The electronic process is faster and administratively much less expensive. It can also result in locating the cheapest possible products or projects.

CONDUCTING REVERSE AUCTIONS

Thousands of companies use the reverse auction model. Reverse auctions may be administered from a company's Web site, as with GM in the opening case. The bidding process conducted by companies such as GE lasts a day or more. In some cases the bidders bid only once. In other cases the bidders can view the lowest bid and rebid several times.

As the number of reverse auction sites increases, suppliers will not be able to manually monitor all such tendering sites. This problem has been addressed with the introduction of online directories that list open RFQs. Another way to solve this problem is through the use of software search-and-match agents. Other software agents can reduce the human burden in the bidding process.

EXHIBIT 5.6 Buy-Side B2B Marketplace Architecture

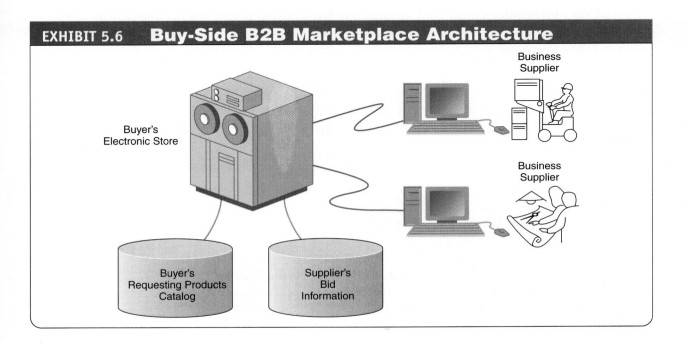

Insights and Additions   Comparison of Pre-Internet and Web-Based Reverse Auction Processes

THE PRE-INTERNET TENDERING SYSTEM PROCESS	THE WEB-BASED REVERSE AUCTION PROCESS
The buyer prepares a paper-based description of the product (project) that needs to be produced. The description includes specifications, blueprints, quality standards, delivery date, and required payment method.	The buyer gathers product information automatically from online sources.
The buyer announces the RFQ via newspaper ads, direct mail, fax, or telephone.	The buyer posts the RFQ on its secured corporate portal or sends e-mail to selected vendors.
Bidders (suppliers) that express interest receive detailed information (sometimes for a fee), usually by postal mail or a courier.	The buyer identifies potential suppliers from among those who responded to the online request for bids (RFQ) and invites suppliers to bid on the project. Bidders download the project information from the Web.
Bidders prepare proposals. They may call the company for additional information. Sometimes changes are made that must be disseminated to all interested bidders.	Bidders conduct real-time, or open time, reverse auctions. Requests for more information can be made online. Changes in specifications can be disseminated electronically.
Bidders submit proposals, usually several copies of the same documents, by a preestablished deadline.	Bidders submit proposals in electronic format.
Proposals are evaluated, usually by several departments at the buyer's organization. Communication and clarification may take place via letters or phone/fax.	The buyer evaluates the suppliers' bids. Communications, clarifications, and negotiations to achieve the "best deal" take place electronically.
Buyer awards a contract to the bidder(s) that best meets its requirements. Notification is usually done via postal mail.	Buyer awards a contract to the bidder(s) that best meets its requirements. Notification is done online.

Alternatively, a third-party intermediary may run the electronic bidding, as they do for forward auctions. General Electric's GXS TPN (described in detail in the next section) opened its bidding site to other buyers so that they can post their requests for quotations. This site, therefore, can be regarded as an intermediary-oriented marketplace. Auction sites such as A-Z Used Computers (a-zuc.com) and freemarkets.com also belong to this category. An example of bidding managed by an intermediary is shown in EC Application Case 5.2 (page 226).

THE PROCUREMENT REVOLUTION AT GENERAL ELECTRIC

General Electric's material costs increased 16 percent between 1982 and 1992 (gegxs.com, 1999). During those same years, GE's product prices remained flat and for some products even declined. In response to the cost increases, GE began an all-out effort to improve its purchasing system. The company analyzed its procurement process and discovered that its purchasing was inefficient, involved too many transactions, and did not leverage GE's large volumes to get the best price. In addition, more than one-quarter of its 1.25 million invoices per year had to be reworked because the purchase orders, receipts, and invoices did not match.

EC APPLICATION CASE 5.2
Interorganization and Collaboration
BIDDING THROUGH A THIRD-PARTY AUCTIONEER: FREEMARKETS

Imagine this scenario: United Technologies Corp. needs suppliers to make $24 million worth of circuit boards. Twenty-five hundred suppliers, whose names were found in electronic registries and directories, were identified as possible contractors. The list of possible suppliers was submitted to FreeMarkets (*freemarkets.com*), a third-party auctioneer. Experts at FreeMarkets reduced the list to 1,000, based on considerations ranging from plant location to the size of the supplier. After further analysis of plant capacity and customer feedback, the list was reduced to 100. A detailed evaluation of the potential candidates resulted in 50 qualified suppliers, who were then invited to bid. Those 50 suppliers received a password to review the circuit board specifications online.

A 3-hour auction of online competitive bidding was conducted. FreeMarkets divided the job into 12 lots, each of which was put up for bid. At 8:00 A.M., the first lot, valued at $2.25 million, was placed online. The first bid was $2.25 million, which was seen by all bidders. Minutes later, another bidder placed a $2.0 million bid. Using the reverse auction approach, the bidders further reduced their bids.

Minutes before the bid closed, at 8:45 A.M., the 42nd bid, which was for $1.1 million, was received. No other bids were received. When the bidding ended, the bids for all 12 lots totaled $18 million (about a 35 percent savings to United Technologies).

To finalize the process, FreeMarkets conducted a comprehensive analysis of several of the lowest bidders of each lot, attempting to look at other criteria in addition to cost. Based on the bid amount as well as other factors, FreeMarkets then recommended the winners and collected its commission fees.

Source: Compiled from A. Jahnke, "How Bazaar," *CIO Magazine*, August 1, 1998, and *freemarkets.com*, 1999.

Questions

▶ What type of auction is this?

▶ What role does FreeMarkets play in the procurement process?

▶ Why would a large company such as United Technologies need an intermediary?

TPN at GE's Lighting Division

General Electric took a number of steps to improve its procurement, the most recent of which involves the Internet. One of the first initiatives was an electronic tendering system for GE's Lighting Division.

Factories at GE Lighting used to send hundreds of RFQs to the corporate sourcing department each day, many for low-value machine parts. For each requisition, the accompanying blueprints had to be requested from storage, retrieved from the vault, transported to the processing site, photocopied, folded, attached to paper requisition forms with quote sheets, stuffed into envelopes, and mailed out to bidders. This process took at least 7 days and was so complex and time-consuming that the sourcing department normally sent out bid packages for each part only to two or three suppliers.

In 1996, GE Lighting piloted the company's first online procurement system, the Trading Process Network (TPN) Post. With the online system, the sourcing department receives the requisitions electronically from its internal customers and sends off a bid package to suppliers around the world via the Internet. The system automatically pulls the correct drawings and attaches them to the electronic requisition forms. Within 2 hours from the time the sourcing department starts the process, suppliers are notified of incoming RFQs by e-mail, fax, or EDI. They are given 7 days to prepare a bid and send it back electronically to GE Lighting. Then the bid is transferred internally, over the corporate intranet, to the appropriate evaluators, and a contract can be awarded that same day.

Benefits of TPN

As a result of implementing TPN, GE has realized a number of benefits:

- Labor involved in the procurement process declined by 30 percent. At the same time, material costs declined 5 to 50 percent due to the procurement department's ability to reach a wider base of competing suppliers online.
- GE has been able to cut by 50 percent the number of staff involved in the procurement process, and has redeployed those workers into other jobs. The sourcing department has at least 6 to 8 free days a month to concentrate on strategic activities rather than on paperwork, photocopying, and envelope stuffing.
- It used to take 18 to 23 days to identify suppliers, prepare a request for bid, negotiate a price, and award the contract to a supplier. It now takes 9 to 11 days.
- With the transaction handled electronically from beginning to end, invoices are automatically reconciled with purchase orders, reflecting any modifications that happen along the way.
- GE procurement departments around the world now share information about their best suppliers. In February 1997 alone, GE Lighting found seven new suppliers through the Internet, including one that charged 20 percent less than the second-lowest bid.

TPN has changed to GXS Express Marketplaces, which is operated by GE Global Exchange Services (gxs.com), a public marketplace on which other companies can place RFQs. So, not only is GE realizing savings on its own purchases through GXS, but it also has a new revenue source in the commissions it is receiving from companies that are participating in the public marketplace.

Benefits to GE's buyers. The benefits of GXS to GE's purchasing departments are:

- Identifying and building partnerships with new suppliers worldwide.
- Strengthening relationships and streamlining sourcing processes with current business partners.
- Rapidly distributing information and specifications to business partners.
- Transmitting electronic drawings to multiple suppliers simultaneously.
- Cutting sourcing cycle times and reducing costs for sourced goods.
- Quickly receiving and comparing bids from a large number of suppliers so as to negotiate better prices.

By 2001, most of GE's divisions were using GXS for some of their procurement needs. The company bought over $1 billion worth of goods and supplies over the Internet during 1997. By 2000, 12 of GE's divisions were purchasing their non-production and MRO materials over the Internet, for an annual total of $5 billion.

General Electric estimates that streamlining these purchases alone can save the company $500 to $700 million annually.

Benefits to suppliers. Suppliers in the GE GXS system can gain instant access to global buyers (including GE) with billions of dollars in purchasing power. In addition, they may dramatically improve the productivity of their own bidding and sales activities. Other benefits are increased sales volume, expanded market reach and ability to find new buyers, lower administration costs for sales and marketing activities, shorter requisition cycle time, improved sales staff productivity, and a streamlined bidding process.

General Electric reports that the benefits of GXS extend beyond its own walls. A computer reseller, Hartford Computer Group, reports that since joining GXS, it has increased its exposure to different GE business units so that its business with GE has grown by over 250 percent. In addition, GXS has introduced Hartford Computer Group to other potential customers.

Deployment Strategies

The GE case also demonstrates two deployment strategies for EC initiatives. The first is to start EC in one division (GE started in its Lighting Division) and slowly go to all divisions. The second is to also use the site as a public bidding marketplace to generate commission income. In 1998, GE opened tpn.com to public bidding and started with 2,500 registered suppliers. The site is powered by TPN Register, a service that facilitates trading communities. TPN Register was acquired in 2001 by GE Global Exchange Services (gxs.com).

> ▶ Describe a manual tendering system.
> ▶ How do online reverse auctions work?
> ▶ List the benefits of Web-based reverse auctions.
> ▶ Describe the business drivers of GE's TPN (GXS).
> ▶ What are the benefits of GXS to GE? To suppliers?
> ▶ Why was TPN converted to a public exchange?

5.7   AGGREGATING CATALOGS, GROUP PURCHASING, AND BARTERING

Three additional e-purchasing methods are used by companies: aggregating catalogs, group purchasing, and bartering.

AGGREGATING SUPPLIERS' CATALOGS: AN INTERNAL MARKETPLACE

Large organizations have many corporate buyers or purchasing agents, usually located in different places. These agents buy from a large number of suppliers. The problem is that even if all purchases are made from approved suppliers, it is difficult to plan and control procurement. In many cases, in order to save time, buyers engage in maverick buying: they purchase from the most convenient supplier and pay a premium.

In addition, an organization needs to control the purchasing budget. This situation is especially serious in government agencies and multinational entities where many buyers and large numbers of purchases are involved. For example, Bristol-Myers Squibb Corporation (bms.com) has over 30,000 corporate buyers all over the world.

One effective solution to the procurement problem in large organizations is to aggregate in one place, at the corporate headquarters, the catalogs of all approved suppliers. Prices can be negotiated in advance or determined by a tendering so that the buyers do not have to negotiate each time they place an order. By aggregating the suppliers' catalogs on the organization's server, it is possible to centralize and control all procurement.

Benefits of Internal Marketplaces

Using a search engine, corporate buyers can find what they want, check availability and delivery times, and complete an electronic requisition form. Another advantage of such aggregation is that the company can reduce the number of suppliers. For example, Caltex, a multinational oil company, reduced the number of its suppliers from over 3,000 to 800. The reason for this reduction is that the central catalog enables buyers at multiple corporate locations to buy from remote but fewer sellers. Buying from fewer sellers typically increases the quantities bought and lowers the per unit price. Another example of a successful aggregation of suppliers' catalogs is that of MasterCard International (see EC Application Case 5.3 on page 230).

Finally, such internal marketplaces allow for easy financial controls. As buyers make purchases, their account balances are displayed. Once the budget is depleted, the system will not allow the purchase order to go through. Therefore, this model is popular in public institutions and government entities.

GROUP PURCHASING

An increased number of companies are moving to group purchasing. With **group purchasing**, the orders from several buyers are aggregated into volume purchases, so that better prices can be negotiated. Two models are in use: *internal aggregation* and *external* (third-party) *aggregation*.

group purchasing
The aggregation of orders from several buyers into volume purchases, so that better prices can be negotiated.

Internal Aggregation

Large companies, such as GE, buy billions of dollars of MROs every year. Company-wide orders for such items are aggregated, using the Web, and are replenished automatically. Besides economies of scale (lower prices for large purchases) on many items, GE saves on the administrative cost of the transactions, reducing transaction costs from $50 to $100 per transaction to $5 to $10 (Rudnitsky, 2000). With 4 million transactions annually at GE, this is a substantial savings.

External Aggregation

Many SMEs would like to enjoy quantity discounts but have difficulty finding others to join them to increase the procurement volume. Such matching can be accomplished by an external third party such as buyerzone.com and allbussiness.com. The

EC APPLICATION CASE 5.3
Interorganization and Collaboration
BUYING FROM MASTERCARD'S INTERNAL CATALOG

Pleased with the progress of a 6-month pilot program, MasterCard International expanded the use of its online buying program throughout the company. The program allows corporate buyers to select goods and services from MasterCard's own electronic catalog, which aggregates more than 10,000 items from the catalogs of approved suppliers. The goal of this project is to consolidate buying activities from multiple corporate sites, improve processing costs, and reduce the supplier base.

The procurement department defines the scope of products or projects to buy and invites vendors to bid or negotiate prices. Then, the agreed-upon prices (contract prices) are stored in the internal electronic catalog. The final buyer at MasterCard (not the procurement department) can compare the available alternatives in the electronic catalogs, and an organizational purchasing decision can be tightly coupled with an internal workflow management system. The internal electronic catalog can be updated manually or by software agents.

The procurement system software, initially pilot-tested by more than 250 buyers, was rolled out to 2,300 users in 1998. Over 9 months in 1998, purchasing agents placed thousands of transactions with the company's preferred suppliers. Payments are made with MasterCard's corporate procurement card. By 2002, the system was being used by more than 2,500 buyers. In conjunction with the expanded deployment, MasterCard is continuously adding suppliers and catalog content to the system.

Source: Based on work by students at the Korea Advanced Institute of Science and Technology, 1999.

Questions

▶ What are the advantages of the internal marketplace to the company's purchasing agents?

▶ Some say that this model may eliminate corporate purchasing departments. Do you think it will? Explain why or why not.

▶ What purchasing model is this?

idea is to provide SMEs with better prices, selection, and services by aggregating demand online and then either negotiating with suppliers or conducting reverse auctions. One can appreciate the importance of this market by taking into consideration some data about small businesses: In the United States, according to the U.S. Department of Commerce, 90 percent of all businesses have fewer than 100 employees, yet they account for over 35 percent of all MRO business volume. Therefore, the potential for external aggregators is huge. The external aggregation group purchasing process is shown in Exhibit 5.7.

Several big companies, including large CPA firms, EDS, and Ariba, are providing similar services, mainly to their regular customers. Yahoo! and AOL offer such services too. Many start-ups, such as shop2gether.com, are competing with mobshop.com. A key to the success of these companies is a critical mass of buyers. An interesting strategy is for a company to outsource aggregation to a third party. For example, biztobiz21.com provides group buying for community site partners such as about.com.

Group purchasing, which started with commodity items such as MROs and consumer electronic devices, has now moved to services ranging from travel to payroll processing and Web hosting. Some aggregators use Priceline's "name-your-

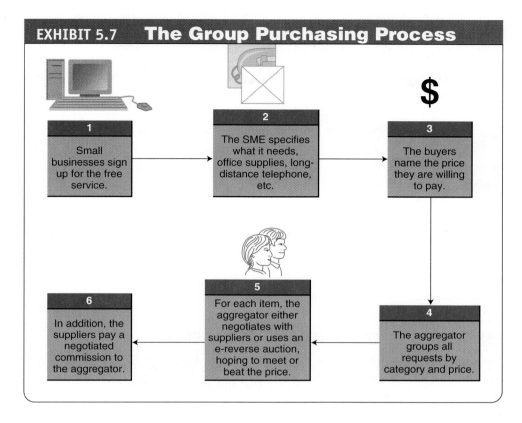

EXHIBIT 5.7   The Group Purchasing Process

1 Small businesses sign up for the free service.

2 The SME specifies what it needs, office supplies, long-distance telephone, etc.

3 The buyers name the price they are willing to pay.

4 The aggregator groups all requests by category and price.

5 For each item, the aggregator either negotiates with suppliers or uses an e-reverse auction, hoping to meet or beat the price.

6 In addition, the suppliers pay a negotiated commission to the aggregator.

own-price" approach. Others try to find the lowest possible price. Similar approaches are used in B2C, and several vendors serve both markets.

ELECTRONIC BARTERING

Bartering is the exchange of goods and/or services without the use of money. The basic idea is for a company to exchange its surplus for something that it needs. Companies can advertise their surpluses in a classified area and may find a partner to make an exchange, but usually a company will have little success in finding an exact match. Therefore, companies ask an intermediary to help. The intermediary can use a manual search-and-match approach or create an electronic bartering exchange. With a **bartering exchange**, a company submits its surplus to the exchange and receives points of credit, which can be used to buy items that the company needs. Popular bartering items are office space, idle facilities and labor, products, and even banner ads (see Chapter 4). In Chapter 2, we explained how this process works electronically and provided the names of some electronic bartering exchanges.

Until 2001, most B2B implementation was in the sell-side of large vendors (Cisco, Intel, IBM) and in the procurement of MROs. However, MROs make up from 20 to 50 percent of the purchasing budget of companies. The majority of corporate expenditures are related to the purchase of *direct materials*. Therefore, it is probable that much greater benefits will come from introducing e-purchasing of

bartering exchange
An intermediary that links parties in a barter; a company submits its surplus to the exchange and receives points of credit, which can be used to buy the items that the company needs from other exchange participants.

direct goods, so that companies can get them to the market faster, reduce the unit cost, reduce inventories, and avoid shortages of materials. Thus, a greater challenge for the future is the e-procurement of direct materials. Sourcing direct materials typically involves more complex transactions requiring *collaboration* and greater information exchange. This leads us to collaborative commerce.

▶ Describe an internal marketplace and list its benefits.

▶ Explain the logic of group purchasing and how it is organized.

▶ How does B2B bartering work?

5.8   COLLABORATIVE COMMERCE

In the previous sections we introduced you to B2B activities related to selling and buying. However, e-commerce can be used for other purposes. A major area of application is collaborative commerce.

ESSENTIALS OF COLLABORATIVE COMMERCE

collaborative commerce (c-commerce)
E-commerce consisting of activities between business partners in jointly planning, designing, developing, managing, and researching products and services.

Collaborative commerce (c-commerce) refers to the use of digital technologies that enable companies to collaboratively plan, design, develop, manage, and research products, services, and innovative EC applications. These activities differ from selling and buying. An example would be a company that it is collaborating electronically with a vendor that designs a product or a part for the company. C-commerce implies communication, information sharing, and collaborative planning done electronically through tools such as groupware and specially designed EC collaboration tools.

C-commerce activities are usually conducted between and among supply chain partners. In Chapter 1 we provided an example of Orbis, a small Australian company that uses a hub to get all its business partners together. A similar model is used by Webcor Builders, as shown in EC Application Case 5.4.

There are many varieties of c-commerce, ranging from joint design efforts to forecasting. Collaboration can be done both between and within organizations. For example, a collaborative platform can help in communication and collaboration between headquarters and subsidiaries or between franchisers and franchisees. The platform provides e-mail, message boards and chat rooms, and online corporate data access around the globe, no matter what the time zone. The following sections demonstrate some types and examples of c-commerce.

RETAILER–SUPPLIER COLLABORATION: TARGET CORPORATION

Target Corporation (targetcorp.com) is a large retail conglomerate (owner of Target, Marshall's, Marshall Field's, Mervyn's, Dayton's, Hudson's, among others). It needs to conduct EC activities with about 20,000 trading partners. In 1998, operating under the name Dayton Hudson Corporation, the company established an extranet-based system for those partners that were not connected to its VAN-based EDI.

Implementation and Strategy
WEBCOR CONSTRUCTION GOES ONLINE WITH ITS PARTNERS

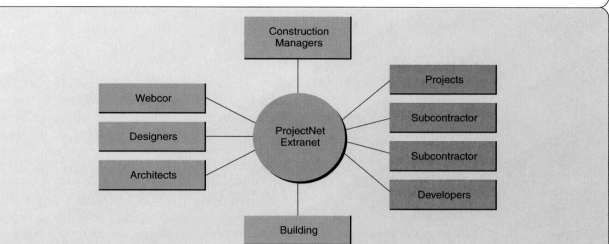

Webcor Builders (*webcor.com*) builds apartment buildings, hotels, and office parks and earns revenues of about $500 million a year. For years the company suffered from poor communication with its partners (architects, designers, building owners, subcontractors) and struggled with too much paperwork. Reams of documents were sent back and forth through snail mail. In a very competitive industry, inefficiencies can be costly. So, Webcor decided to introduce c-commerce into its operations. Webcor's goal was to turn its computer-aided design (CAD) drawings, memos, and other information into shared digital information.

To enable online collaboration, Webcor is using an application service provider (ASP) that hosts Webcor's projects using ProjectNet software on a secured extranet. The major problem was getting everyone to accept ProjectNet. The software is complex, and some user training is necessary. However, Webcor found itself in a strong enough position to be able to say that in the near future, it would not partner with anyone who would not use ProjectNet.

With everyone on the ProjectNet system, Webcor's business partners can post, send, or edit complex CAD drawings, digital photos, memos, status reports, and project histories. Everyone involved in a project is more accountable, because there is a digital trail, and partners now get instant access to new building drawings. ProjectNet provides a central meeting place where users can both download and transmit information to all parties, all with a PC.

One of the major benefits of ProjectNet is that people now spend more time managing their work and less time on administrative paperwork. Several clerical workers were laid off, and the cost of their salaries saved is covering the software rental fees.

Sources: Compiled from *Webcor.com*, 2000 and DiCarlo, 1999.

Questions

▶ Draw the supply chain of Webcor before ProjectNet.

▶ What B2B model is this (e.g., sell-side, buy-side, etc.)?

▶ What are the benefits of this c-commerce project to Webcor?

▶ What are the benefits of this project to Webcor's clients?

The extranet enabled Dayton Hudson not only to reach many more partners, but also to use many applications not available on the traditional EDI. The system (based on GE's InterBusiness Partner Extranet platform, geis.com) enabled the company to streamline its communications and collaboration with suppliers. It also allowed Dayton Hudson's business customers to create personalized Web pages that were accessible via either the Internet or GE's private VAN (see the textbook's Web site, prenhall.com/turban for a figure that shows the suppliers' extranet).

CONTINUOUS REPLENISHMENT: WARNER-LAMBERT

Large manufacturers of consumer goods such as Warner-Lambert (WL) and Procter & Gamble (P&G) have superb supply chains resulting from their use of a program called Collaborative Planning, Forecasting, and Replenishment (CPFR). This was a retail-industry project in which WL served as a pilot site. As part of the pilot project, WL shared strategic plans, performance data, and market insight with Wal-Mart. The company realized that it could benefit from Wal-Mart's market knowledge, just as Wal-Mart could benefit from WL's product knowledge. In CPFR, trading partners collaborate on making *demand forecasts*. Using CPFR, WL increased its products' shelf-fill rate (the extent to which a store's shelves are fully stocked) from 87 percent to 98 percent, earning the company about $8 million a year in additional sales. P&G also deploys CPFR to integrate consumer demand data from several sources. The goal of CPFR is to streamline the product flow from manufacturing plants all the way to customers' homes.

Warner-Lambert is involved in another collaborative retail industry project, the Supply-Chain Operations Reference (SCOR), an initiative of the Supply-Chain Council in the United States. SCOR divides supply chain operations into parts, giving manufacturers, suppliers, distributors, and retailers a framework with which to evaluate the effectiveness of their processes along the same supply chains.

REDUCTION OF DESIGN CYCLE TIME: ADAPTEC, INC.

Adaptec, Inc. is a large microchip manufacturer that supplies critical components to electronics-equipment makers. The company outsources manufacturing tasks, concentrating on product research and development. Outsourcing production, however, puts the company at a disadvantage against competitors that have their own manufacturing facilities and can optimize their delivery schedules. It took Adaptec up to 15 weeks to deliver products to customers; competitors were able to deliver similar chips in only 8 weeks.

The longer delivery time was mainly caused by the need to coordinate design activities between Adaptec headquarters in California and its three principal fabrication factories in Hong Kong, Japan, and Taiwan. To solve this problem, the company introduced an extranet and enterprise-level supply chain integration software, which incorporates automated workflow and EC tools.

One initial benefit of the new system was a reduction in the time required to generate, transmit, and confirm purchase orders. Adaptec now uses e-mail to communicate with manufacturers across several time zones to automatically start the flow of raw materials, which in turn reduces invoicing and shipping times. In addition to business transaction documents, Adaptec can send chip design diagrams over the extranet, enabling the manufacturers to prepare for product changes and new designs. This faster communication method required Adaptec to adjust its decision-making processes that were based on the old assumption that at least 2 weeks were needed to put an order into production. The overall result was a reduction in its order-to-product-delivery time from 15 weeks to between 10 and 12 weeks.

REDUCTION OF PRODUCT DEVELOPMENT TIME: CATERPILLAR, INC.

Caterpillar, Inc. is a multinational heavy-machinery manufacturer. In the traditional mode of operation, cycle time along the supply chain was long because the process involved paper document transfers among managers, salespeople, and technical staff. In 1998, Caterpillar connected its engineering and manufacturing divisions with its active suppliers, distributors, overseas factories, and customers through a global extranet. By means of the extranet, a request for a customized tractor component, for example, can be transmitted from a customer to a Caterpillar dealer and on to designers and suppliers, all in a very short time. Customers also can use the extranet to retrieve and modify detailed order information while the vehicle is still on the assembly line. Remote collaboration capabilities between the customer and product developers decreases cycle time delays caused by rework time. Suppliers produce and deliver the final product directly to the customer. The extranet also is used for expediting maintenance and repairs.

OTHER C-COMMERCE EXAMPLES

Leading businesses are moving quickly to realize the benefits of c-commerce. For example, the real estate franchiser RE/MAX uses a c-commerce platform to improve communications and collaboration among its nationwide network of independently owned real estate franchises, sales associates, and suppliers. Similarly, Marriott International, the world's largest hospitality company, started with an online brochure and then developed EC systems that link corporations, franchisees, partners, and suppliers, as well as customers, around the world. (See Intel 1999a and 1999b for details.) In addition, as described in EC Application Case 5.5 (page 236), Nygard of Canada has developed a collaborative system along the entire supply chain.

BARRIERS TO C-COMMERCE

Despite the many potential benefits, c-commerce is moving ahead fairly slowly. Reasons cited in various studies include technical reasons involving integration, standards, and networks; security and privacy concerns over who has access control to information stored in a partner's database; internal resistance to new models and approaches; and lack of internal skills to conduct collaborative commerce (Schram 2001).

Specialized software tools for c-commerce can be expected to break down some of the barriers to c-commerce. (C-commerce tools are provided by seecommerce.com, allegis.com, lotus.com, and ca.com.) In addition, as they hear about the major benefits of c-commerce, such as smoothing the supply chain, reducing inventories

Interorganization and Collaboration

INTERORGANIZATIONAL COLLABORATION AT NYGARD OF CANADA

The apparel industry is one of the most competitive industries, and global manufacturers are willing to operate with razor-thin margins. One of the major issues in the apparel industry is the transfer of manufacturing operations to countries where labor is inexpensive. Nygard International of Winnipeg, Canada (*nygard.com*), a large apparel manufacturer, decided against overseas operations because they would increase (perhaps double) product cycle time as well as inventory levels. So in order to remain in Canada and stay competitive, the company must use EC to control its labor and manufacturing costs. In fact, Nygard has become a leader in adopting IT and e-commerce in the apparel industry.

Nygard developed an ERP and supply chain management that controls all internal operations, purchasing, product development, accounting, production planning, and sales. This enabled the company to develop tight integration with its trading partners. For example, the moment that a customer buys a pair of pants at a partner's retail store, the information moves from the POS terminal to automatically generate a reorder at Nygard. In production planning, the SCM not only matches customers' orders with the right fabrics, but it searches the market pool for the most efficient combinations of other material for use with those fabrics. Similarly, when sales trigger orders, Nygard's manufacturing automatically triggers records on all raw materials, such as fabrics, zippers, and buttons. The

moment that raw material is used, an automatic reorder of the material is generated. This allows just-in-time production and quick order delivery; deliveries are sometimes made the same day that orders are received.

In the apparel industry, it is most important to use EC tools on the procurement side. To ensure just-in-time delivery, Nygard must have the ability to have visibility, not only into their suppliers' systems, but also into their suppliers' suppliers. This way Nygard can make commitments to their customers that they can fulfill (penalties are paid for late deliveries).

A Web-based control system enables the company to conduct detailed profitability studies, so every proposal and decision is evaluated by its impact on the bottom line. Decision support systems (DSS) models are used for this purpose.

Sources: Stephenson, W., "Nygard Goes Electronic," *Winnipeg Sun*, June 3, 1999.

Questions

▶ Which e-commerce activities are conducted on the internal supply chain?

▶ Which activities of e-commerce are done with partners' collaboration?

▶ Discuss the considerations of moving production to a country with inexpensive labor.

and operating costs, and increasing customer satisfaction and the competitive edge, companies will rush to jump on the c-commerce bandwagon.

▶ Define collaborative commerce.

▶ List the major types of collaborative commerce.

▶ Describe some examples of collaborative commerce.

▶ List the major barriers to c-commerce.

5.9 INFRASTRUCTURE, INTEGRATION, AND B2B AGENTS

INFRASTRUCTURE FOR B2B

Large numbers of vendors, including Ariba, Oracle, Microsoft, and IBM, offer all the necessary B2B tools. The major infrastructures needed for B2B marketplaces are:

- Server(s) for hosting the databases and the applications.
- Software for executing the sell-side activities, including catalogs.
- Software for conducting auctions and reverse auctions.
- Software for e-procurement (buy side).
- Software for CRM, possibly related to a call center.
- Security for hardware and software.
- Software for building a storefront.
- Software for building exchanges.
- Telecommunications networks and protocols (including EDI, extranets, and XML).

Most companies use vendors to build their B2B applications, as shown in the Real-World Case at the end of this chapter. The vendor sells or leases all of the necessary software to create the e-marketplace. One of the major B2B product vendors is Ariba; see the book's Web site, prenhall.com/turban for a description of Ariba's B2B offerings.

EDI and Extranets

In order for business partners to communicate online, companies must implement some type of secure interorganizational network, such as an extranet, and a common protocol, such as EDI. **Electronic data interchange (EDI)** is the electronic movement of specially formatted standard business documents, such as bills, orders, and confirmations sent between business partners. Traditional EDI systems, which have been around for about 30 years, were implemented in **value-added networks (VANs)**, which are private, third-party-managed common carriers that also provide communications services and security. However, VANs are relatively expensive, and so small companies found EDI over VANs to be unaffordable. However, **Internet-based EDI** is accessible to most companies in the world. It can be used to replace or supplement traditional EDI. In addition, Internet-based EDI provides several capabilities that are not available in traditional EDI.

Briefly, **extranets** ("extended intranets") are secured networks, usually Internet-based, that allow business partners to access portions of each other's intranets. Extranets and their core technology, virtual private networks (VPNs), are explained more fully in Chapters 6 and 9.

electronic data interchange (EDI)
The electronic movement of specially formatted standard business documents, such as bills, orders, and confirmations sent between business partners.

value-added networks (VANs)
Private, third-party-managed networks that add communications services and security to existing common carriers; used to implement traditional EDI systems.

Internet-based EDI
EDI that runs on the Internet and so is widely accessible to most companies, including SMEs.

extranets
Secured networks by VPN, usually Internet-based, that allow business partners to access portions of each other's intranets; "extended intranets."

INTEGRATION

Integration with Existing Internal Infrastructure and Applications

EC applications of any kind need to be connected to the existing internal information systems. For example, an ordering system in sell-side B2B is usually connected to a payment verification system and to an inventory management application. Systems that must be integrated with EC applications include marketing and other databases; legacy systems and their applications; ERP software; catalog (product) information; the payment system; CRM software; logistics and inventory systems; workflow systems; sales statistics; and supply chain management (SCM) and decision support system (DSS) applications. All major EC software vendors, such as Ariba, IBM, Microsoft, Oracle, Commerce One, and SAP, provide for such integration.

Integration with Business Partners

EC can be integrated more easily with internal systems than with external ones. For instance, in the sell-side e-marketplace, it is not easy for the many buying companies to connect to each seller. Similarly, a buy-side e-marketplace needs to be connected to hundreds or even thousands of suppliers. One solution is a buyer-owned shopping cart (Lim and Lee 2002). The interface with back-end information systems allows the customer to put items from different sellers in a single cart. This makes shopping much more convenient as you pay once even though you shopped in five different locations.

Systems integrators and middleware vendors (e.g., tibco.com) provide many solutions for both internal and external integration. Details on systems integrations are provided in online Chapter 13 (prenhall.com/turban) and in Linthicum (2001).

THE ROLE OF XML IN B2B INTEGRATION

For B2B companies of all kinds to interact with each other easily and effectively, they must be able to connect their servers, applications, and databases. For this to happen, standard protocols and data-representation schemes are needed. EDI is one such standard, but it has several limitations and is not structured for the Internet.

The Web is based on the standard communication protocols of *TCP/IP* (Transmission Control Protocol/Internet Protocol) and *http* (Hypertext Transfer Protocol). Further, Web pages are written in the universally recognized standard notation of *HTML* (Hypertext Markup Language). However, this standard environment is useful only for displaying static visual Web pages. To further extend the functionality of EC sites, one can use JavaScript and other Java and ActiveX programs. These tools allow for human interaction, but they still do not address the need to interconnect back-end database systems and applications. For that purpose, the industry is pursuing several alternatives for standardized data representation.

One of the most promising standards is **XML (eXtensible Markup Language)** and its variants. XML is used to improve compatibility between the

XML (eXtensible Markup Language)
Standard (and its variants) used to improve compatibility between the disparate systems of business partners by defining the meaning of data in business documents.

disparate systems of business partners by defining the meaning of data in business documents. (For details, see online Appendix B and xml.com). An example of an XML variant is voice XML, which is used to increase interactivity and accessibility with speech recognition systems. For an example of how XML works, see EC Application Case 5.6.

As XML and other related standards (see Appendix B) require national and international agreements and cooperation, there are several organizations devoted to these topics. See the book's Web site (prenhall.com/turban) for a list of some important standards organizations with links to their Web sites.

THE ROLE OF SOFTWARE AGENTS IN B2B EC

Software (intelligent) agents play multiple roles in B2B.

Agent's role in the sell-side marketplace. In Chapter 3, we discussed how software agents are used to aid customers in the comparison-shopping process. The major role of software agents in that case was collecting data from multiple

---

EC APPLICATION CASE 5.6
Interorganization and Collaboration
XML UNIFIES AIR CARGO TRACKING SYSTEM

TradeVan Information Services of Taiwan provides information services about the cargo flights of different airlines. As such, it can be classified as a B2B intermediary. Because different airlines have different information systems, the query results from each airline differ in format. XML can facilitate data exchange between heterogeneous databases. A special application was developed by Li and Shue (2001) to unify different document presentations for cargo status information in Taiwan. In addition, the information can be presented on wireless application protocol (WAP)-based cell phones (see Chapter 8).

Shippers and receivers can use the system to track the status of deliveries. Prior to the installation of the system, an air cargo shipment spent 80 percent of its transport time waiting and only 8 percent in the air. The new system is expected to reduce delays significantly, to the benefit of all members of the supply chain.

The system offers a uniform cargo status inquiry and returns with a standardized yet personalized presentation for different airlines. This standardization enables customs brokers to reduce the cycle time by preparing declarations of imports faster. Buyers and

other supply chain partners can schedule production lines with precision and in advance. Finally, the quality of door-to-door delivery companies such as FedEx and UPS can be improved due to quick communication between shippers and delivery companies. At present, the answers to queries are generated in carriers' databases, including those of China Air and Eva Air. XML helps to centralize information, so answers to queries can be derived much faster. A fast delivery of unified information helps to improve the supply chain by reducing both delivery lead times and inventory levels.

Sources: Compiled from S.Li and L. Shue, "Towards XML-Enabling E-Commerce Infomediary: A Case Study in Cargo Tracking," *Proceedings fo the 34th Annual Hawaii International Conference on System Sciences*, HICSS-34, January 2001, Maui, HI, *computer.org/ Proceedings/hicss/0981/volume%207/098147007abs.htm.*

Questions

▶ What problem does XML solve?

▶ What are the benefits of this system to shippers and receivers?

commercial sites. Similarly, in B2B, agents will collect information from sellers' sites for the benefit of the buyers.

Agent's role in the buy-side marketplace. Suppose that a large number of customers need to request quotes from multiple potential suppliers in buy-side marketplaces. Doing so manually will be slow, physically impossible, or uneconomical. Therefore, software agents are needed to assist both buyers and sellers.

> ▌ List the major infrastructures required for B2B EC.
> ▌ Describe the difficulties of integration with business partners.
> ▌ Describe the roles of EDI and extranets in interorganizational networks.
> ▌ Describe the purpose of XML.

MANAGERIAL ISSUES

Some managerial issues related to this chapter are as follows.

1. **Can we justify the cost?** Because there are several B2B models, each of which can be implemented in different ways, it becomes critical to conduct a cost-benefit analysis of the proposed applications (projects). Such an analysis should include organizational impacts, such as possible channel conflicts and how to deal with resistance to change within the organization.

2. **Which vendor(s) should we select?** Vendors normally develop B2B applications. Two basic approaches to vendor selection exist: (1) select a primary vendor such as IBM, Ariba, or Oracle. This vendor will use its software and procedures and add partners as needed. Or, (2) use an integrator that will mix and match existing products and vendors to create "the best of breed" for your needs.

3. **Which model(s) should we use?** The availability of so many B2B models means that companies need to develop selection strategies based on preferred criteria. In addition to the company-centric models, there are several types of exchanges to consider (Chapter 6).

4. **Do we need B2B marketing?** Sell-side marketplaces may require advertising and incentives. Unless a company has a well-known name, like

Cisco, Dell, or IBM, it is likely that a company will need to heavily promote its site.

5. **Should we reengineer our procurement system?** If volume is heavy enough to attract the attention of major vendors, a company that is doing the purchasing might decide to reengineer the procurement (purchasing) process by establishing a buy-side marketplace on its server. Or, this buying company could join a third-party intermediary-oriented marketplace.

6. **What restructuring will be required for the shift to e-procurement?** Many organizations fail to understand that a fundamental change in their internal processes must be implemented to realize the full benefits of e-procurement. The two critical success factors that many organizations overlook are the need to cut down the number of routine tasks and the reduction of the overall procurement cycle through the use of appropriate information technologies such as workflow, groupware, and ERP software.

7. **What integration would be useful?** Trading in e-marketplaces is interrelated with logistics. Although this is particularly true in many-to-many exchanges (see Chapter 6), it is bene-

ficial to consider the benefits of integration with logistics and other support services in the company-centric marketplace.

8. **What are the ethical issues in B2B?** Because B2B EC requires the sharing of mutual infor-

mation, business ethics are a must. Employees should not be able to access unauthorized areas in the trading system, and the privacy of trading partners should be protected both technically and legally.

SUMMARY

In this chapter, you learned about the following EC issues as they relate to the learning objectives.

1. **The B2B field.** The B2B field comprises e-commerce activities between businesses. B2B activities account for about 85 percent of all EC, and the share is growing rapidly.

2. **The major B2B models.** The B2B field is very diversified. It can be divided into the following segments: sell-side marketplaces, buy-side marketplaces, trading exchanges, and collaborative commerce. Intermediaries play an important role in some B2B models.

3. **The characteristics of sell-side marketplaces.** Sell-side B2B EC is the direct sale, conducted online, by one seller (a manufacturer or an intermediary) to many buyers. The major technology used is electronic catalogs, but forward auctions are becoming popular, especially for selling surplus inventory. Sell-side activities include extensive customer service.

4. **Sell-side intermediaries.** Intermediaries use B2B primarily to provide value-added services to manufacturers and business customers. They can also aggregate buyers and conduct auctions.

5. **The characteristics of buy-side marketplaces.** Today, companies are moving to e-procurement to expedite purchasing, save on item and administrative costs, and gain better control over the purchasing process. A popular e-procurement model is the *reverse auction* (also known as tendering or bidding). Other models are internal marketplaces and group purchasing.

6. **Forward and reverse auctions.** Auctions play a major role in B2B. Forward auctions are used by sellers either as a new marketing channel or to liquidate surpluses and old equipment. A reverse auction is a tendering system used by buyers to collect bids electronically from suppliers.

7. **B2B aggregation and group purchasing.** Increasing the exposure and/or the bargaining power of companies can be done by aggregating either the sellers or the buyers. Buyer aggregation is very popular because it allows buyers to get better prices on their purchases.

8. **Collaborative EC.** Collaborative EC is conducted mainly among supply chain partners. A common collaborative model is to change the linear communications chain to a hub accessible by all partners. This model helps to speed communication and collaboration and eliminates errors made in paper-based systems. Joint design, planning, and control is done between manufacturers and their suppliers, and demand forecasts are developed jointly between retailers and their suppliers.

9. **Characteristics of Internet-based EDI and the role of XML.** Traditional EDI systems were implemented over VANs, limiting its accessibility to small companies. Internet-based EDI can replace traditional EDI or supplement it. Internet-based EDI provides several capabilities not available in traditional EDI. The Web uses the standard communication protocols of TCP/IP and HTTP, and Web pages are written in the standard notation of HTML. To improve compatibility between business partners' systems, standards organizations are pursuing XML, a standard for defining data elements.

KEY TERMS

Bartering exchange, p. 231
Business-to-business
e-commerce
(B2B EC), p. 203
Buy-side e-marketplace, p. 224
Collaborative commerce
(c-commerce), p. 232
Company-centric EC, p. 206
Direct materials, p. 204
E-procurement, p. 221
Electronic data
interchange (EDI), p. 237
Exchanges, p. 207

Extranets, p. 237
Group purchasing, p. 229
Horizontal marketplaces, p. 204
Indirect materials, p. 204
Intermediary-oriented
e-marketplace, p. 213
Internet-based EDI, p. 237
MROs, p. 204
Maverick buying, p. 221
Online intermediary, p. 204
Private e-marketplaces, p. 206
Procurement management, p. 220
Public e-marketplaces, p. 207

Request for quote
(RFQ), p. 224
Sell-side e-marketplace, p. 209
Spot buying, p. 204
Stickiness, p. 213
Strategic sourcing, p. 204
Trading exchanges (or
communities), p. 207
Value-added networks
(VANs), p. 237
Vertical marketplaces, p. 204
XML (eXtensible Markup
Language), p. 238

DISCUSSION QUESTIONS

1. Explain how a catalog-based sell-side e-marketplace works and discuss its benefits.

2. Distinguish sell-side e-marketplaces from buy-side e-marketplaces.

3. Discuss the advantages of selling through online auctions over selling from catalogs.

4. Discuss the role of intermediaries in B2B.

5. How can companies buying from a sell-side e-marketplace integrate order information with their corporation's procurement systems?

6. Discuss and compare all the mechanisms that aggregators of group purchasing can use.

7. How do companies eliminate the potential limitations and risks associated with Internet-based EDI? (Read the online appendix to the chapter.)

8. How can software agents work for multiple sellers and buyers?

9. Discuss the role of XML in B2B. Why is it so important?

INTERNET EXERCISES

1. Visit milacron.com and examine the site from the buyer's perspective. Find out how to place an order.

2. Enter gxs.com and review GSX Express's bidding process. Describe the preparations your company would make in order to bid on GE jobs.

3. Enter commerceone.com and review the capabilities of BuySite and MarketSite. Find out how Commerce One supports the integration of many sellers' electronic catalogs for a specific buyer.

4. Visit allsystem.com to review All-System Aerospace International, Inc., a company that

handles aircraft parts from several vendors. From an aircraft repair technician's point of view, evaluate whether this site can compete with Boeing's PART system.

5. Visit eventory.com, shop2gether.com, and biztobiz21.com. Compare the services offered by these businesses.

6. Examine the sites fastparts.com, ariba.com, trilogy.com, freemarkets.com, electricnet.com, peregrine.com, and ecweb.com. Match a B2B business model with each site.

7. Visit supplyworks.com and examine how the company streamlines the purchase process. How does this company differ from ariba.com?

8. Enter soho.org and onlinesoho.com and locate EC applications for small offices and home offices (SOHO). Also, check the business services provided by officedepot.com for small businesses.

9. Visit ebay.com and identify all activities related to its small business auctions (*business eXchange*). What services are provided by eBay?

10. Review information about GE's TPN (GXS) and answer the following questions.

   a. Describe the benefits of TPN to GE in terms of procurement processing time, labor costs, and purchase prices.

   b. List the benefits of linking with suppliers.

c. Visit gxs.com and find the services offered to companies that are invited to place RFQs on the public site.

d. What motivates suppliers to join the TPN?

e. What are the pros and cons of opening the TPN to other buyers?

11. Visit avnet.com and find how its supply chain is structured. Draw the chain, showing Marshall's role. (Hint: Look at Timmers 1999, and at Kalakota and Robinson 2001.)

12. Review the Cisco Connection Online (CCO) case.

   a. What is the CCO business model?

   b. Where are the success factors of CCO?

   c. What kinds of inquiries are supported when customers check their order status?

   d. What are the major benefits of CCO to Cisco and its customers?

TEAM ASSIGNMENTS AND ROLE PLAYING

1. Predictions about the future magnitude of B2B and statistics on its actual volume in various countries keep changing. In this activity, each team will locate current B2B predictions and statistics for different world regions (Asia, Europe, North America). Using at least five sources, each team will find the predicted B2B volume (in dollars) for the next 5 years in their assigned region. Some sources of data are listed in Exhibit 4.2 (page 149).

2. Your goal in this assignment is to investigate the major B2B vendors. A good place to start is with the B2B e-commerce report found at e-global.es/017/017_durlacher_b2b.pdf.com. Each team should investigate a major vendor (e.g., Ariba, Commerce One, Oracle, or IBM) or an application type (buy-side, sell-side, or auction). Find the major products and services offered, and examine customer success stories. Write a report of your findings. Convince the class that your vendor is the best.

REAL-WORLD CASE

EASTMAN CHEMICAL MAKES PROCUREMENT A STRATEGIC ADVANTAGE

Eastman Chemical (ECM), a multibillion-dollar, multinational corporation, operates in an extremely competitive environment. In response to competitive pressures, management decided to improve on the procurement of nonproductive (MRO) items. In their effort to do so, the company embarked on two interrelated activities: integrating the supply chain and introducing e-procurement. The objectives of the project, which started in late 1999, were:

- To increase compliance with purchasing policies (reduce maverick buying).
- To support frontline employees while maintaining existing rules.
- To reduce procurement transaction costs via elimination of non-value-added and redundant processes.
- To leverage corporate spending to negotiate favorable trading terms with channel supply partners.

Each year, the company purchases over $900 million in MROs from over 3,500 suppliers. The company used an SAP R/3 ERP system, part of the legacy system that interfaces with the e-procurement application that provided good control, but at a cost of $115 per order when a purchasing card (see Chapter 10) was used. The ERP helped to reduce the workload on accounts payable personnel and procurement approvers. However, purchasing from noncontracted suppliers increased. (The card made such purchasing easy.) This maverick buying reduced purchase volumes with the primary suppliers, thus reducing the company's negotiating power and increasing costs.

As part of its initiative to improve the MRO procurement process, Eastman Chemical established channel partnership relationships with its largest MRO suppliers. This increased the company's buying leverage and reduced costs and delays. Inventories and service levels were improved. In addition, Eastman Chemical introduced two new EC applications to its procurement system: Commerce One's BuySite e-procurement software for dealing with the suppliers and MarketSite for transaction management and value-added services.

Using BuySite, Eastman Chemical has created an *internal catalog* of all MRO products located in Eastman's storerooms. The e-commerce software checks availability and prevents redundant purchases. The software also supplies catalog-management features that ensure that all vendors' changes and updates are entered into the internal catalog.

The MarketSite application supported the creation of a portal that enables:

- Use of a common Web browser by all of Eastman Chemical's 16,000 employees.
- Different types of employees to use the system without need for additional training.
- Support for Windows NT platform, which was already in use.
- Ability to integrate the SAP R/3 with EC and the procurement card.
- An effective and efficient catalog management strategy.
- Maintenance of the existing systems infrastructure.
- Simplification of business processes.
- Flexibility and empowerment of frontline employees.

All of the previous points reduce costs, increase profitability, and competitiveness.

Source: Compiled by authors from *eastman.com*, *aberdeen.com*, *computerworld.com*, and *commerceone.com/news/releases/ eastman.html*.

Questions

1. Enter *commerceone.com* and find information about the capabilities of BuySite and MarketSite. How do the two applications differ?

2. Why did Eastman Chemical concentrate on e-procurement and not on the sell-side? You may want to visit *eastman.com* to learn more about the company.

3. In July 2000, Eastman Chemical introduced an EC project that enables buyers to participate in Eastman's private online price negotiations using LiveExchange from Moai (*moai.com*). Explain how the software works and why it is referred to as "dynamic commerce."

4. Which of the problems cited in this case can be solved by other EC applications? Relate your answer to Commerce One products.

PUBLIC B2B EXCHANGES

Content

ChemConnect: The World Chemical Exchange

Managerial Issues

Real-World Case:
Integration at *E-steel.com* (now *newview.com*)

Learning objectives

Upon completion of this chapter, you will be able to:

▶ Define e-marketplaces and exchanges.

▶ List the various types of e-marketplaces.

▶ Describe B2B portals.

▶ Describe third-party exchanges.

▶ Distinguish between e-procurement and e-selling consortia.

▶ Describe the various ownership and revenue models of exchanges.

▶ Describe the support mechanisms offered by exchanges, including auctions.

▶ Describe networks of exchanges and exchange management.

▶ Describe the critical success factors of exchanges.

▶ Discuss implementation and development issues of e-marketplaces and exchanges.

▶ Describe the major support services of B2B.

▶ Describe the extranet and its role in supporting marketplaces and exchanges.

CHEMCONNECT: THE WORLD CHEMICAL EXCHANGE

The Problem

The trading of raw and partially processed chemicals and plastics is done daily by thousands of companies in almost every country in the world. Before the Internet, the trading process was slow, fragmented, ineffective, and costly. As a result, buyers paid too much, sellers had high expenses, and there was a need for intermediaries to smooth the process.

The Solution

Today, buyers and sellers of chemicals and plastics can meet electronically in a large Internet marketplace called ChemConnect (*chemconnect.com*). Global chemical-industry leaders, such as British Petroleum, Dow Chemical, BASF, Hyundai, Sumitomo, and many more, make transactions here every day in real time. They save on transaction costs, reduce cycle time, and find new markets and trading partners around the globe.

ChemConnect provides a trading marketplace and an information portal for 12,000 members in 125 countries. In 2001, over 60,000 products were traded in this public e-marketplace, which was founded in 1995. This is an unbiased third-party marketplace that offers three trading places:

1. **A public exchange floor.** Here members can post items for sale or bid, for all types of products, at market prices. A large electronic catalog of "offers to sell" and "requests to buy," including starting prices and shipping terms, is organized by category. Buyers bid by changing the starting prices.

2. **The commodities floor.** Here top producers, intermediaries, and end users buy, sell, and exchange commodity products online, in real time, through regional trading hubs.

3. **Corporate trading rooms.** In these private online auction places, members negotiate contracts and spot deals (one-time, as needed purchases) and conduct private auctions managed by ChemConnect. Companies can negotiate online simultaneously with several suppliers or buyers.

ChemConnect is an independent intermediary, so it works within certain rules and guidelines that ensure an unbiased approach to trades. There is full disclosure of all legal requirements, payments, trading rules, and so on. (Click on "Legal and privacy issues" on the site for more information on disclosure policies.)

All three trading locations provide up-to-the-minute market information that can be translated into 30 different languages. Members pay transaction fees only for successfully completed transactions. Business partners provide several support services. For example, Citigroup and ChemConnect jointly offer several financial services for exchange members.

The Results

ChemConnect brings potential partners into the trading rooms. The trading rooms allow companies to save up to 15 percent in just 30 minutes of reverse auction, instead of over weeks or months, which was the case with manual bidding methods. For example, a company that placed an RFQ for 100 metric tons of acid to be delivered in Uruguay with a starting price of $1.10 per kilogram reduced the price to $0.95 in only six consecutive bids, offered in 30 minutes. (A demo for such a reverse auction is available on the site; click on "Corporate Trading Rooms, CTR Demo.") ChemConnect is growing rapidly, adding members and increasing trading volume each year.

What We Can Learn . . .

The ChemConnect vignette demonstrates an e-marketplace with many buyers and many sellers, all in one industry. These buyers and sellers, as well as other business partners, congregate electronically to conduct business. This type of a marketplace is an electronic exchange owned and operated by a third-party intermediary. As will be seen later in the chapter, ownership has some major implications for B2B marketplaces.

This opening vignette illustrates one interesting B2B model that is used in e-marketplaces. We will see additional models in the chapter. In contrast with the company-centric models that were the focus of Chapter 5, in this chapter the models include *many buyers* and *many sellers*. They are *public* e-marketplaces, known by a variety of names and having a variety of functions. For now, we will simply call them *exchanges*.

Source: Based on *Chemconnect.com*.

6.1   B2B ELECTRONIC EXCHANGES—AN OVERVIEW

As defined in Chapter 5, **public e-marketplaces (public exchanges)** are trading venues open to all interested parties (sellers and buyers) and usually run by third parties. The term **exchange** is often used to describe many-to-many e-marketplaces. According to *The New Shorter Oxford English Dictionary*, an *exchange* is a building, office, or other area used for the transaction of business or for monetary exchange. In the context of e-commerce, exchanges are *virtual* (online) trading venues, not physical locales. Exchanges are known under a variety of names: *e-marketplaces*, *e-markets*, and *trading exchanges*. Other terms that are used include *trading communities*, *exchange hubs*, *Internet exchanges*, *Net marketplaces*, and *B2B portals*, as well as several others. We will use the term *exchange* in this book to describe the general many-to-many e-marketplaces, but we will use some of the other terms in more specific contexts.

According to AMR Research, exchanges, in their various forms, are expected to account for over 50 percent of all B2B activities by 2004 and host over $3 trillion in transactions (amrresearch.com). All exchanges share one major characteristic: They are an electronic trading-community meeting place for many sellers and many buyers, and possibly for other business partners, as shown in Exhibit 6.1 (page 248). In the center of every exchange is a **market maker**, the third-party that operates an exchange (and in many cases, also owns the exchange).

In an exchange, just as in a traditional open-air marketplace, buyers and sellers can interact and negotiate prices and quantities. Generally, free-market economics rules the exchange trade community, as demonstrated by ChemConnect.

According to Forrester Research (2001), there were 2,500 exchanges worldwide—at several stages of operation—in the spring of 2001. Since then, more than 50 percent have folded due to a lack of customers and/or cash (e.g., Chemdex and MetalSite). However, the companies that use these exchanges, both as sellers and buyers, are generally pleased with them and plan to increase the number of exchanges they are participating in, from 1.7 to 4.1, on the average, within 2 years (Dolinoy, Cooperstein and Scaffidi, 2001). The traders expect to more than double the value of transactions that they do through the exchanges.

public e-marketplaces (public exchanges)
Trading venues open to all interested parties (sellers and buyers) and usually run by third parties.

exchange
A many-to-many e-marketplace. Also known as *e-marketplaces*, *e-markets*, and *trading exchanges*.

market maker
The third-party that operates an exchange (and in many cases, also owns the exchange).

EXHIBIT 6.1 Trading Communities: Information Flow and Access to Information

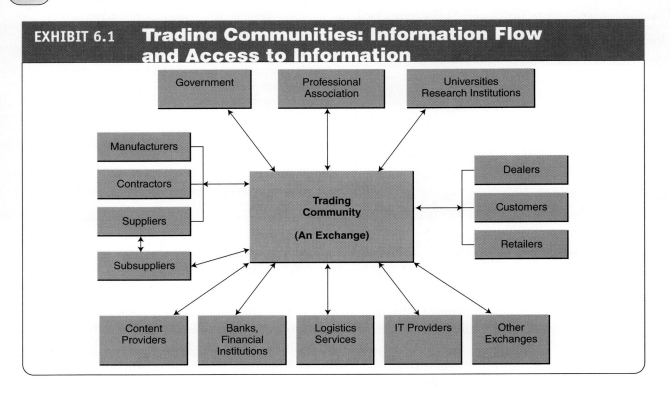

CLASSIFICATION OF EXCHANGES

There are several ways of classifying exchanges. We will use the approach suggested by Kaplan and Sawhney (2000) and by Durlacher (2000). According to this classification, an exchange can be classified into one of four cells in a matrix. The matrix is shown in Exhibit 6.2 and is composed of two dimensions. On the top, we distinguish two types of materials traded, either *direct or indirect* (MRO), as defined in Chapter 5. On the left, we see two possible sourcing strategies: systematic sourcing and spot sourcing. **Systematic sourcing** deals with purchasing made in long-term supplier–buyer relationships. **Spot sourcing** refers to unplanned purchasing, purchases made as the need arises. The intersection of these characteristics results in the four exchange classifications.

In spot sourcing, the prices are *dynamic*, based on supply and demand at any given time. A common example of dynamic pricing is a stock exchange. Spot sourcing of direct materials takes place in **vertical exchanges**, which are considered vertical because sales take place in one industry or industry segment. Examples of a vertical exchange are the trading rooms of ChemConnect and an exchange called e-steel.com (now newreview.com) (see the Real-World Case at the end of this chapter), which conducts online auctions and bids for steel. Spot sourcing of indirect materials takes places in **horizontal exchanges**. These exchanges are considered horizontal because they handle materials traded in several different industries. For example, light bulbs and office supplies might be purchased in a horizontal exchange by both an automaker and a steelmaker. (In these horizontal exchanges, MROs can include both products, such as office supplies, and services, such as temporary labor.) The

systematic sourcing
Purchasing done in long-term supplier–buyer relationships.

spot sourcing
Unplanned purchases made as the need arises.

vertical exchange
An exchange whose members are in one industry or industry segment.

horizontal exchanges
Exchanges that handle materials traded in several different industries.

EXHIBIT 6.2   Classification of B2B Exchanges

	Direct	Indirect (MRO)
Systematic Sourcing	Vertical Distributors *Plastics.com* *papersite.com* Methods: Aggregation, fixed/negotiated prices	Horizontal Distributors *MRO.com* Methods: Aggregation, fixed/negotiated prices
Spot Sourcing	Vertical Exchanges *eSteel.com* *ChemConnect.com* Methods: Matching, dynamic pricing	Horizontal Exchanges *EmployEase.com* Methods: Matching, dynamic pricing

market makers in both vertical and horizontal exchanges match supply and demand in their exchanges, and as a result, prices are determined.

If systematic sourcing is used, the market maker aggregates the buyers and/or the sellers and provides the framework for *negotiated* prices and terms of direct materials. Systematic sourcing of direct materials is frequently done with the aid of intermediaries. An example of this type of exchange is plastics.com, an exchange for the plastics industry. Using the speed, access, and ease of the Internet, it simplifies and streamlines the process of buying and selling, at substantially reduced costs.

In the fourth cell, systematic sourcing of indirect materials (MROs), the market maker basically aggregates the sellers' catalogs, as mro.com does. MRO.com provides tools and technology in a hosted environment that enables manufacturers and distributors of industrial parts—the "supply" of the industrial supply chain—to participate in e-commerce quickly and affordably. MRO.com creates one catalog containing products from multiple suppliers, connects the catalog to an order processing system, and offers different types of industrial buyers a single source from which to buy their MROs.

DYNAMIC PRICING

The previous classification of exchanges lists dynamic pricing as the major element of spot sourcing. **Dynamic pricing** refers to a rapid movement of prices over time, and possibly across customers, as a result of supply and demand at any given time. Stock exchanges, which can be considered spot sourcing, are an excellent example of dynamic pricing. Prices on the stock exchanges sometimes change minute by minute depending on how much buyers are willing to pay for a stock and how many sellers of that stock are willing to sell at various prices. Another good example of dynamic pricing occurs in *auctions*, where prices vary all the time. Dynamic

dynamic pricing
A rapid movement of prices over time, and possibly across customers, as a result of supply and demand.

pricing may mean that exactly the same product or service is sold to different customers at different prices.

Dynamic pricing is based on market information available to buyers and sellers. One of the reasons the U.S. stock exchanges are thought to work as well as they do is the amount of financial information generally available to investors. The Internet and certain market mechanisms (such as auctions) provide a large amount of such information, sometimes in real time. Therefore, the Internet facilitates many of the dynamic pricing models for both B2B and B2C. For example, priceline.com uses a reverse auction that results in dynamic pricing. In Chapter 5, we described group purchasing and forward auctions, which also employ dynamic pricing. When dynamic pricing is used with methods such as auctions, the process is referred to as *dynamic trading*. For example, IBM's WebSphere commerce suite includes a dynamic trading module (reverse auctions, exchanges, contract negotiations).

The typical process that results in dynamic pricing in most exchanges includes the following steps:

1. A company lists a bid to buy a product or an offer to sell one.
2. Buyers and sellers can see the bids and offers, but may not always see who is doing the buying or selling. Anonymity is often a key ingredient of dynamic pricing.
3. Buyers and sellers interact in real time with their own bids and offers. Sometimes buyers join together to obtain a volume discount price (group purchasing).
4. A deal is struck when there is an exact match between a buyer and a seller on price, volume, and other variables such as location or quality.
5. The deal is consummated, and payment and delivery are arranged.

Third-party companies outside the exchange provide supporting services such as credit verification, quality assurance, insurance, and order fulfillment. They ensure that the buyer has the money and that the product is in good condition. They also coordinate the delivery. These services are discussed in Chapter 10.

OWNERSHIP, GOVERNANCE, AND ORGANIZATION OF EXCHANGES

Let's look at the owners of exchanges and how exchanges are governed and managed.

Ownership of Exchanges

There are three basic types of ownership models for Internet exchanges:

1. **An industry giant.** One manufacturer, distributor, or broker sets up the exchange and runs it. An example is IBM, which established an exchange for the purpose of selling patents (delphion.com). IBM placed 25,000 of its own patents up for sale and invited others to sell their patents as well. This model is an extension of the sell-side model described in Chapter 5. General Electric's TPN is an example of a buy-side exchange controlled by an industry giant. In

the past, Samsung of Korea manually brokered various commodities; it currently has several online exchanges, including one for fish. The major potential problem for this type of exchange: Will the giant's competitors be willing to use the exchange?

2. **A neutral entrepreneur.** A third-party intermediary sets up an exchange and promises to run an efficient and unbiased exchange (e.g., ChemConnect). (These exchanges are discussed in Section 6.3.) The potential problem: Will anyone come?

3. **The consortia (or co-op).** Several industry players get together and decide to set up an exchange so that all can benefit. Covisint is an example of such as exchange. (These exchanges are discussed in Section 6.4.) The potential problem: Who is the boss?

Governance

Exchanges are governed by guidelines and rules, some of which are required by law. These must be very specific regarding how the exchange operates, what the requirements are to join the exchange, what fees are involved, and what rules need to be followed. Furthermore, the governance document needs to specify security and privacy arrangements, what will happen in cases of disputes and so forth. The contract terms between an exchange and buyers/sellers are also critical, as well as assurances that the exchange is fair.

Organization of Exchanges

Regardless of their ownership and governance structure, exchanges may include the following elements.

Membership. Membership refers to the community in the exchange. Many exchanges do not charge members a fee to join (e.g., alibaba.com, chemconnect.com). To generate revenue, the exchange collects transaction and other fees. Some exchanges charge registration fees and annual membership fees (e.g., chemconnect.com). Members may be either observing members, who can only view what is going on but not trade, or trading members, who can make offers and bid, pay, and arrange deliveries. Trading members usually need to go through a qualification process with the market maker. In some cases a cash deposit is required. Some exchanges set limits on how much each member can trade.

Site access and security. Exchanges must be secured. Members' activities can be very strategic, and information should be carefully protected, as competitors frequently congregate in the same exchange. In addition to the regular EC security measures, special attention should be made to prevent illegal offers and bids. Several exchanges have a list of individuals that are authorized to represent the participating companies.

Services. Exchanges provide many services to buyers and sellers. These depend on the nature of the exchange. For example, the services provided by a stock exchange are completely different from those provided by a steel or food exchange or by an intellectual property or patent exchange. However, there are some services that most exchanges provide. These are shown in Exhibit 6.3 (page 252).

EXHIBIT 6.3   Services in Exchanges

The Exchange

Sellers
A
B
C
D
•
•
•

- Buyer-seller registration, qualification, coordination
- Catalog management (conversion, integration, maintenance)
- Communication / protocol translation (EDI, XML, CORBA)
- Sourcing—RFQ, bid coordination (product configuration, negotiation)
- Security, anonymity
- Software: groupware, workflow
- Integration with members' back-office systems
- Auction management
- News, information, industry analysis
- Support services (financing, payment, insurance, logistics, tax, escrow, order tracking)
- Administration—profiles, statistics, etc.

Buyers
X
Y
Z
•
•
•

GAINS AND RISKS OF B2B EXCHANGE PARTICIPATION

The potential gains and risks of B2B exchanges for buyers and for sellers are summarized in Exhibit 6.4. As you can see, the gains outnumber the risks.

▶ Define B2B exchanges.

▶ Define systematic sourcing, spot sourcing, direct sourcing, and MRO.

▶ Describe the ownership and organization of exchanges.

▶ List the potential gains and risks of exchanges.

EXHIBIT 6.4   Gains and Risks in B2B Exchanges

	For Buyers	For Sellers
Potential gains	▶ One-stop shopping, huge variety ▶ Search and comparison shopping ▶ Volume discounts ▶ 24/7 ordering from any location ▶ Make one order from several suppliers ▶ Unlimited, detailed information ▶ Access to new suppliers ▶ Status review and easy reordering ▶ Fast delivery ▶ Less maverick buying	▶ New sales channel ▶ No physical store is needed ▶ Reduce ordering errors ▶ Sell 24/7 ▶ Reach new customers at little extra cost ▶ Promote the business via the exchange ▶ An outlet for surplus inventory ▶ Can go global more easily
Potential risks	▶ Unknown vendors; may not be reliable ▶ Loss of customer service quality (inability to compare all services)	▶ Loss of direct CRM ▶ Price wars ▶ Competition for value-added services ▶ Transaction fees (including on your existing customers) ▶ Possible loss of customers to competitors

6.2   B2B PORTALS

As you may recall, selling in B2C can be conducted in various types of public or private Web sites. Some of these public sites are *information portals* (often called just *portals*), such as Yahoo!, where information is intended for individual customers. In some portals you can place an order; but in most the buyer is transferred to a seller's storefront to complete the transaction. Other portals or e-malls provide extensive order-taking and order-fulfillment services.

Similar situations exist in B2B. **B2B portals** are information portals for businesses. Some exchanges act as pure information portals. They might have catalogs of products offered by sellers, lists of vendors and what they offer, lists of buyers and what they want, and other industry or general information. Buyers can then hyperlink to sellers' sites to complete their trades. Information portals have a difficult time generating revenues, and so they are starting to offer, for a fee, additional services that support trading. This brings them closer to being trading communities or *exchanges*. We can see the differences between portals and exchanges by looking at two examples.

B2B portals
Information portals for businesses.

THOMAS REGISTER

Thomas Register of America publishes a directory of millions of manufacturing companies. In 1998, it teamed up with GE's TPN (see Chapter 5) to create the TPN Register (now part of GXS), a portal that facilitates business transactions for MROs. TPN Register works with buyers and sellers to build electronic trading communities. Sellers can distribute information on what they have to sell; buyers can find what they need and purchase over a comprehensive and secure procurement channel that helps them reduce costs, shrink cycle times, and improve productivity. For-fee services are also available. However, the TPN Register is basically an *information portal*.

ALIBABA.COM

Another intermediary that started as a pure information portal and is moving toward becoming a trading exchange is Alibaba (alibaba.com). Launched in 1999, Alibaba.com initially concentrated on China, but today serves traders in over 200 countries. It includes a large, robust community of international buyers and sellers who are interested in direct trade without an intermediary. Initially, the site was a huge classified posting place, due to its incredible database. To understand the power of Alibaba.com you need to explore its marketplace, which is a collection of classified ads organized in a database.

The Database

The center of Alibaba.com is its huge database, which is basically a horizontal information portal with offerings in a wide variety of product categories. The portal is organized into 27 major product categories (as of 2002), including agriculture, apparel and fashion, automobiles, and toys. In each product category, one can find subcategories. For example, the toy category includes items such as dolls, electrical pets, and wooden toys. Each subcategory includes classified ads, organized into four groups: sellers, buyers, agents, and cooperation. Each group may include many companies. The ads are fairly short, as shown in Exhibit 6.5. Note that in all cases you can click on an ad for details. All ads are posted free (as of spring 2002). In some categories there are thousands of postings; therefore, a search engine is provided. The search engine works by country, type of advertiser, and how old the postings are.

Reverse Auctions

Alibaba.com allows buyers to post an RFQ. Would-be sellers can then send bids to the buyer, conduct negotiations, and accept a purchase order when one is offered. In January 2002, the process was not fully automated. (To see how the process works, go to "My trade activity" and take the tour, initiate a negotiation, and issue a purchase order.)

Features and Services

In spring 2002, the following features were provided: free e-mail, free e-mail alerts, a China club membership, news (basically related to importing and exporting), legal information, arbitration, and forums or discussion groups. Finally, a member can create a company Web page, as well as a "sample house" (for showing products). Certain other services are available for a fee. In the future, additional services will be added to increase the company's revenue stream. As of 2002, the site offers its services in English, Chinese, and Korean.

Revenue Model

As of spring 2002, the site's revenue stream was limited to advertisement and fees for special services. Alibaba.com competes with several global exchanges that provide similar services (e.g., meetworldtrade.com, chinatradeworld.com, and globalsources.com). The advantage of Alibaba.com is its low operational cost. Therefore, it can sustain losses much longer than its competitors. Someday in the future, Alibaba.com may be in a position that will enable it to make a great deal of money. Possible sources of future revenue are one-time registration fees, annual maintenance fees, transaction fees, and fees for services. Will Alibaba.com be strong

---

EXHIBIT 6.5 Sample B2B Classified Ads

- **Electronic Pets** (October 21, 2000) [SELLER]
  UMC group [China]
  We offer you electronic pets that can either be sound activated or remote controlled. These hot selling toys are welcomed all over the world. They come in different sizes. (*Click for details . . .*)
- **Electronic, Intelligent Pet** (October 23, 2000) [BUYER]
  Scheer Wholesale [United States]
  We are looking for electronic, intelligent pets like: Tekno, T-cat 2000, Clever dog 2000. Please forward your info for purchasing large quantities of these robot dogs. (*Click for details . . .*)
- **Toys/Electrical Pets Representation in India** (November 24, 2000) [AGENT]
  Penguin Exports [India]
  We are a marketing organization having a network of eight offices in India with representatives in most of the major cities and towns of India. We seek to represent manufacturers of toys/electrical pets.
  (*Click for details . . .*)
- **Looking for Partner of Rep-Ornament of 100 Percent Handmade** (January 06, 1999) [COOPERATION]
  Jogift Enterprise Corporation [Taiwan]
  Jogift Enterprise, we specialize in manufacturing delicate hand-crafted ornaments of the most characterized dolls in detailed leather. Our factory is located in the city of Shanghai in China.
  (*Click for details . . .*)

Note that in all cases you can click on details. All ads are posted free (spring 2001).
Source: *Alibaba.com*, 2001.

enough to sustain losses until that day? According to experts (see Section 6.7), there is a good chance it will.

MORE ON INFORMATION PORTALS

Information portals can be horizontal, like Alibaba, offering a wide range of products to different industries. Or, they can be vertical, focusing on a single industry or industry segment. Vertical portals are often referred to as **vortals**. You will find that some use the word portal as equivalent to an exchange. The reason is that many B2B portals are adding capabilities that make them look like a full exchange. Also, many exchanges include their own information portals.

vortals
B2B portals that focus on a single industry or industry segment; "vertical portals."

▶ Define B2B portals.

▶ List the major services provided by alibaba.com

▶ Distinguish a vortal from a horizontal portal.

6.3   THIRD-PARTY (TRADING) EXCHANGES

The opening vignette introduced us to ChemConnect, a neutral, public, third-party market maker. ChemConnect's initial success was well publicized, and dozens of similar third-party exchanges, mostly in specific industries, have been developed since. These exchanges are characterized by two contradicting properties. On one hand, they are *neutral*, not favoring either sellers or buyers. On the other hand, because they do not have a built-in constituency of sellers or buyers, they have a problem attracting enough buyers and sellers to attain financial viability.

Therefore, to increase their financial viability, these exchanges try to team up with partners such as large sellers or buyers, financial institutions that provide payment schemes, and logistics companies that fulfill orders, as ChemConnect did. The goal of such partnerships and alliances is to increase liquidity. **Liquidity** is the result of having a sufficient number of participants in the marketplace as well as a sufficient volume of transactions conducted (see Section 6.7). In a partnership that did not work, Chemdex, a pioneering exchange that was closed in late 2000, allied itself with VWR Scientific Products, a large brick-and-mortar intermediary. In the case of Chemdex, the liquidity was not large enough.

liquidity
The result of having a sufficient number of participants in the marketplace as well as a sufficient transaction volume.

Third-party exchange makers are electronic intermediaries. In contrast with a portal, such as Alibaba.com, the intermediary not only presents catalogs, but also tries to match buyers and sellers and encourage them to make transactions. Let's see how this is done by looking at two models of third-party exchanges: supplier aggregation and buyer aggregation.

THE SUPPLIER AGGREGATION MODEL

In the *supplier aggregation model*, virtual distributors standardize, index, and aggregate suppliers' catalogs or content and make this content available to buyers in a centralized location. The hosting can be done by an Internet service provider (ISP) or by a large telecommunications company such as NTT, Deutsche Telecom, or MCI. An example is Commerce One's catalog of MRO suppliers. Commerce One acts as the aggregator in this case. The supplier aggregation system is shown in Exhibit 6.6. Once catalogs are aggregated, they are presented to potential buyers. (This is similar to the sell-side e-marketplace described in Chapter 5, but with many sellers.)

Notice that the diagram shows two types of buyers: large and small (SMEs). Large buyers need software to support the purchase-approval process (e.g., workflow software), budgeting, and the tracking of purchases across the buying organization. This requires system integration with existing company regulations, contracts, pricing and so forth. Such integration may be provided by an ERP architecture. As you may recall from Chapter 5, bigboxx.com provided such a service to its large buyers using SAP software (see EC Application Case 5.1). Also, e-steel.com (now newview.com) (see the Real-World Case at the end of this chapter) is using integration as its major strategy. (For more on ERP integration, see Norris et al. 2000.) For smaller buyers, hosted workflow and applications are available from ASPs, which team up with aggregators such as Ariba and Commerce One.

The major problems encountered in this model are in recruiting suppliers and introducing the system to buyers. Solving these problems requires a strategy (see Cunningham 2000).

THE BUYER AGGREGATION MODEL

In the *buyer aggregation model*, buyers' RFQs are aggregated and then linked to a pool of suppliers that are automatically notified of the RFQs. The suppliers can then make bids. (This is similar to the buy-side e-marketplace described in Chapter 5). The buyers (usually small businesses) can benefit from volume discounts, especially if they use a group purchasing approach. The sellers benefit from the new source of pooled buyers. Exhibit 6.7 shows this process.

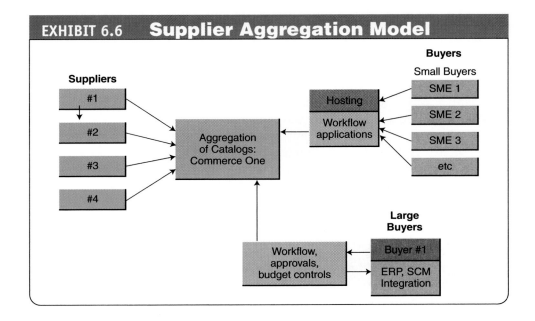

EXHIBIT 6.6 Supplier Aggregation Model

EXHIBIT 6.7   Buyer Aggregation Model

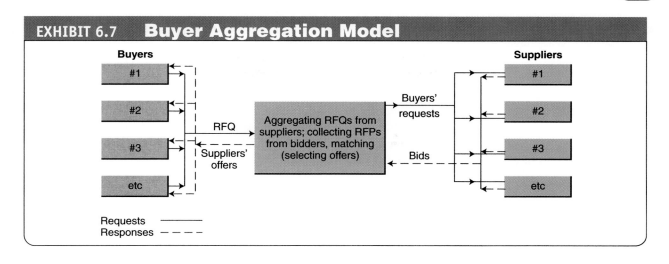

SUITABILITY OF THIRD-PARTY EXCHANGES

Aggregation models work best with MROs and services that are well defined and have stable prices and where the supplier or buyer base is fragmented. Buyers save on search and transaction costs and are exposed to more sellers. Sellers benefit from lower transaction costs as well as from an increase in their customer base.

Three basic types of participant involvement exist in markets, as listed below. The type of participant involvement affects which third-party exchange is most appropriate to use.

1. **Fragmented markets.** These markets have large numbers of both buyers and sellers. Examples include the life sciences and food industries. Where a large percentage of the market is fragmented, third-party-managed exchanges are mainly suitable for MROs.

2. **Seller-concentrated markets.** In this type of market, several large companies sell to a very large number of buyers. Examples are the plastics and transportation industries. In this type of market, consortia (see next section) may be most appropriate.

3. **Buyer-concentrated markets.** In this type of market, several large companies do most of the buying from a large number of suppliers. Examples are the automotive, airline, and electronics industries. Here, again, consortia may be most appropriate.

As in other types of e-marketplaces, the key to the success of any third-party exchange is the critical mass of buyers and sellers (the liquidity issue).

▶ What is a third-party exchange?

▶ Define liquidity.

▶ Describe the supplier aggregation exchange.

▶ Describe a buyer aggregation exchange.

▶ List the types of markets most suitable for third-party ownership.

6.4 CONSORTIUM TRADING EXCHANGES

consortium trading exchange (CTE)
An exchange formed and operated by a group of major companies to provide industry-wide transaction services.

A subset of third-party exchanges is a **consortium trading exchange (CTE)**, an exchange formed and operated by a group of major companies. The major declared goal of CTEs (also called *consortia*) is to provide industry-wide transaction services that support buying and selling. These services include links to the participants' back-end processing systems, as well as collaborative planning and design services. During 2000, hundreds of CTEs existed all over the world, but by 2002 many had folded or were inactive. Some are limited to one country, but many are international. Examples of some representative vertical consortia are listed in Exhibit 6.8.

There are four types of CTEs:

1. Purchasing-oriented, vertical
2. Purchasing-oriented, horizontal
3. Selling-oriented, vertical
4. Selling-oriented, horizontal

In the following sections we will describe the characteristics of each of these four types and then examine several examples and issues of concern.

PURCHASING-ORIENTED (PROCUREMENT) CONSORTIA

Purchasing-oriented consortia are by far the most popular B2B consortium model. The basic idea is that a group of companies join together in order to streamline the purchasing processes, and, as some claim, to pressure suppliers to cut prices. This model can be either vertical or horizontal.

Vertical Purchasing-Oriented CTEs

Most CTEs are *vertical*, meaning that all the players are in the same industry, such as in the case of Covisint, discussed in EC Application Case 6.1 on pages 260–261 (see Baker and Baker 2000). While the declared objective is to support buying *and* selling, it is very obvious that in a market owned and operated by large buyers, the orientation is toward purchasing. Many of the exchanges in Exhibit 6.8 are of this type (e.g., aerospace, airlines, hospitality, mining, retailers). Each exchange may have tens of thousands of suppliers.

Horizontal Purchasing-Oriented CTEs

In a *horizontal* purchasing-oriented CTE, the owner-operators are large companies from different industries that unite for the purpose of improving the supply chain of MROs used by most industries. An example of this kind of CTE is Corprocure in Australia (corprocure.com). Fourteen of the largest companies in Australia (Qantas, Telstra Communications, the Post Office, ANZ Banking Group, Coles Myer, Coca-Cola, etc.) created the Corprocure exchange to buy MROs.

EXHIBIT 6.8 Representative Vertical Consortia

Consortium (CTE)	Industry Participants
Aerospace Consortium	Boeing, Lockheed Martin, BAE Systems, Raytheon
Agricultural Commodities	Cargill, DuPont, Cenex Harvest Cooperative
Airlines Consortium	Air France, American Airlines, British Airways, Continental, Delta, United Airlines
AutoExchange	GM, Ford, DaimlerChrysler
CoNext (for MROs)	Ariba, EDS
Consumer Products Consortium	General Mills, Heinz, Kellogg's, Nestle, Procter & Gamble, Sara Lee
Development Tool	Hytex
Energy Consortium	Royal/Dutch Shell, BP Amoco, Conoco, Equilon, Occidental Petroleum, Phillips Petroleum, Repsol, Statoil, Tosco, Unocal
E-Procurement Hub	Covisint
Global Collaboration Network	E2Open
Global Transport Exchange	Hutchinson Port (Hong Kong)
GlobalNetXchange (retailers)	Sears, Carrefour (France)
Health Care Distributors Consortium	AmeriSource Health, Cardinal Health, Fisher Scientific International, McKesson, HBOC, Owens Minor
Health Care Insurance	Johnson & Johnson, GE Medical Systems, Baxter International, Abbott Laboratories, Medtronic
Food Products Industry	Food Trader, eFood Manager, Novopoint
Hospitality Consortium	Hyatt, Marriott
Medical Equipment	Samsung (Korea), Pepex Biomedical
Mining Consortium	Alcoa, Anglo American, Rio Tinto
Natural Gas & Electricity Consortium	American Electric Power, Aquila Energy, Duke Energy, El Paso Energy, Reliant Energy, Southern Company
Paper (Forestexpress.com)	International Paper, Georgia-Pacific, Weyerhaeuser
Petroleum	Chevron, Texaco
PC Components PC Makers	IBM, Nortel, LG Electronics, Matsushita, HP, Compaq, Gateway, NEC, Samsung, Hitachi
Plastics Consortium	DuPont, Dow Chemical, BASF, Bayer, Ticona
Real Estate/Project Constellation	Chase, Equity Office, Hick Muse, Jones Lang Lasalle, Kaufman & Broad, Simon Properties, Spieker, Trammell Crow
Rubber Network	Goodyear Tire & Rubber, Continental AG, Cooper Tire & Rubber, Groupe Michelin, Pirelli SpA, Sumitomo Rubber Industries
Star Alliance (airlines)	Air Canada, Lufthansa, Singapore Airlines, SAS, and others
Transportation (air and land)	Carriers, Hunt, Swift, US Xpress, Werner

EC APPLICATION CASE 6.1
Interorganization and Collaboration
COVISINT: THE E-MARKET OF THE AUTOMOTIVE INDUSTRY

There are only several automakers, but they buy parts, materials, and supplies from tens of thousands of suppliers, who frequently buy parts and materials from thousands of sub-suppliers. At times, the procurement process is slow, costly, and ineffective.

On February 25, 2000, General Motors Corporation, Ford Motor Company, and DaimlerChrysler launched a B2B integrated buy-side marketplace, Covisint. The goal was to eliminate redundancies from suppliers through integration and collaboration, with promises of lower costs, easier business practices, and marked increases in efficiencies for the entire industry.

The name Covisint (pronounced KO-vis-int) is a combination of the primary concepts of why the exchange was formed: The letters "Co" represent *connectivity, collaboration,* and *communication.* "Vis" represents the *visibility* that the Internet provides and the *vision* of the future of supply chain management. "Int" represents the *integrated* solutions the venture offers as well as the *international* scope of the exchange.

The purpose of the marketplace's connectivity is to integrate buyers and sellers into a single network. Visibility would provide real-time information presented in a way that speeds decision making and

enables communication through every level of a company's supply chain, anywhere in the world. By using the Web, a manufacturer's production schedule and any subsequent changes can be sent simultaneously and instantly throughout its entire supply chain. The result is less need for costly inventory at all levels of the supply chain and an increased ability to respond quickly to market changes.

To better understand the Covisint concept, look at the figure below. The left side shows an automaker's traditional supply chain. Typically, an automaker would buy parts from one supplier, who in turn would buy from its suppliers (sub-suppliers), who would buy from other suppliers (sub-sub-suppliers). In this traditional linear supply chain, the automaker communicates only with its top-tier (tier 1) suppliers.

Now, try to imagine that the auto manufacturer has hundreds of similar supply chains, one for each supplier, and that many of the suppliers, in all tiers, produce for several manufacturers. The flow of information (as shown by the connecting lines in the drawing) will be very complex. This complexity introduces inefficiencies in communication as well as dif-

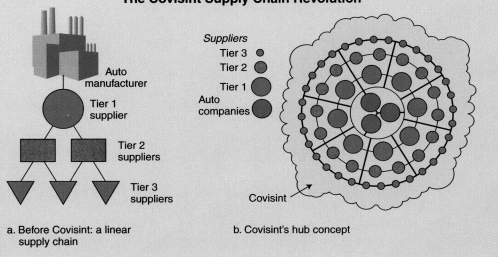

The Covisint Supply Chain Revolution

Auto manufacturer
Tier 1 supplier
Tier 2 suppliers
Tier 3 suppliers

Suppliers
Tier 3
Tier 2
Tier 1
Auto companies

Covisint

a. Before Covisint: a linear supply chain

b. Covisint's hub concept

ficulties for the suppliers in planning their production schedules to meet demand, resulting in supply chain problems.

The Covisint process greatly changed the supply chain communication in the automobile industry. Rather than being at the top point of a pyramid, as in the industry's traditional supply chain, the auto manufacturers now are at the center of a spoke-and-wheel arrangement. In 2001, there were six automakers in the Covisint marketplace—the three U.S. companies, Renault (France), Peugeot Citroen (France), and Nissan (Japan). Covisint has created a trading hub whereby any one of the automakers and the various suppliers and sub-suppliers can communicate directly with anyone else. Instead of an array of unorganized communication lines, it is all organized in one place.

One of the major objectives of the exchange is to facilitate product design. Covisint offers its customers best-of-breed functionality, in which customers take the best aspects from multiple technical providers. The ability to integrate providers across the supply chain creates a unique environment for collaborative design and development (collaborative commerce), enables e-procurement, and provides a broad marketplace of buyers and suppliers. It makes accessible a wealth of supply chain expertise and experience, ranging from procurement to product development. Covisint's potential membership is about 30,000 suppliers.

Source: Compiled from *covisint.com* and various press releases, 2000, 2001.

Questions

▶ Describe the concepts upon which Covisint is structured.

▶ Describe how Covisint changed the supply chain in the automobile industry.

SELLING-ORIENTED CONSORTIA

Selling-oriented consortia are less common than buying-oriented ones. Most selling-oriented consortia are vertical. Participating sellers have thousands of potential buyers within a particular industry. Here are some examples of selling-oriented consortia:

▶ Cargill, a producer of basic food ingredients, has a wide range of buyers and has major ownership in a food exchange (cargill.com).

▶ Several international airline consortia act like large travel agencies, selling tickets or travel packages to business buyers (e.g., lexres.com).

▶ Health care suppliers and health care distributors (e.g., ghx.com).

▶ Plastics consortia (e.g., trplastics.com).

LEGAL CHALLENGES FOR B2B CONSORTIA

B2B exchanges and other e-marketplaces typically introduce some level of collaboration among both competitors and business partners. In both cases, antitrust and other competition laws must be considered. The concept of consortia itself may lead to antitrust scrutiny by governments, especially for industries in which either a few firms produce most or all of the output (oligopolies or monopolies), or in which there are only a few buyers (monopsonies). This could happen in many countries, especially in European countries, the United States, Australia, Japan, Korea, Hong Kong, and Canada.

Gesilicones.com is an exchange for industrial sealants. GE Toshiba Silicone initiated this exchange and started discussions with other leading industrial sealant makers, such as Dow Corning, Wacker Chemical, and Shin-Etsu Chemical, about joining the marketplace. The initial group of participants controls over 80 percent of the world market of industrial sealants. The potential exists for the participants to deal with some sensitive business issues such as industry pricing policies, price levels, price changes, and price differentials in ways that may violate antitrust laws. Similarly, many fear that buyers' consortia will "squeeze" the small suppliers in an unfair manner.

Antitrust issues and investigations may slow the creation of CTEs, especially global ones. For example, the Covisint venture required approval in the United Kingdom, the United States, and Germany. The German antitrust investigation was very slow and delayed the project by several months.

CRITICAL SUCCESS FACTORS FOR CONSORTIA

The critical success factors for consortia, according to a Goldman Sachs report (2000), are the following:

Size of the industry. The larger the size of the industry, the larger the addressable market, which in turn means a greater volume of transactions on the site. This leads to greater potential cost savings to the exchange participants and ultimately more profitability for the exchange itself. The danger here is that industry size may spawn several competing consortia, which has happened in the banking, mining, and airline industries.

Ability to drive user adoption. Consortia must have the ability to provide immediate liquidity to an exchange. The more oligopolistic the consortium is, the more accelerated the adoption will be.

elasticity
The measure of the incremental spending by buyers as a result of the savings generated.

Elasticity. A critical factor for any exchange is the degree of elasticity the exchange fosters. **Elasticity** is the measure of the incremental spending by buyers as a result of the savings generated.

Standardization of commodity-like products. The breadth of the suppliers brought in to transact with the buyers will help standardize near-commodity products due to content management and product-attribute description needs of online marketplaces. The more commodity-like products become, the greater the market competition and the lower the prices.

Management of intensive information flow. An exchange has the ability to be a repository for the huge amounts of data that flow through supply chains in a given industry. It can also enable information-intensive collaboration between participants, including product collaboration, planning, scheduling, and forecasting. The more information the exchange has, the more added value the exchange provides the participants, and the more buyers will come to the exchange.

Smoothing of inefficiencies in the supply chain. It is important for the consortium-led exchange to help smooth inefficiencies in the supply chain such as those in order fulfillment, logistics, and credit-related services.

Section 6.7 discusses critical success factors for exchanges in general, many of which also apply to consortia.

▶ Define CTEs.

▶ Describe purchasing-oriented consortia and selling-oriented consortia.

▶ Describe potential legal issues for consortia.

▶ List the major critical success factors of consortia.

6.5   DYNAMIC TRADING: MATCHING AND AUCTIONS

Earlier in the chapter we talked about dynamic pricing, the rapid change in prices based on supply and demand. One of the major features of exchanges is dynamic trading. **Dynamic trading** occurs in situations when prices are being determined by supply and demand, and therefore changing continuously. Two major mechanisms are used in dynamic trading in exchanges: matching and auctions.

dynamic trading
Exchange trading that occurs in situations when prices are being determined by supply and demand (dynamic pricing).

MATCHING

An example of *matching* supply and demand is the stock market. While buyers place their bids and sellers list their asking prices, the market makers are conducting the matching, sometimes by buying or selling stocks from their own accounts. The matching may be more complex than in regular auctions (discussed next) due to the need to match both prices and quantities. In other cases, times and locations also need to be matched. Today, matching in stock exchanges is fully computerized. Most commodity exchanges (e.g., corn, oil, silver) are B2B, as are some financial markets.

AUCTIONS

As seen in the ChemConnect case, exchanges offer members the ability to conduct auctions or reverse auctions in *private trading rooms*. When this takes place, the one-to-many model is activated, as described in Chapter 5, with the hosting done *by the exchange*. The advantage of running an auction in an exchange is the ability to attract many buyers to a forward auction and many suppliers to a reverse auction. For small- or medium-size companies, finding auction participants is a major problem. By going to an exchange, this problem may be solved.

There are several arrangements for auctions. Two options are as follows.

1. An exchange offers auction services as one of its many activities, as ChemConnect does. Most vertical exchanges offer this option.

2. An exchange is fully dedicated to auctions. Examples of this auctions-only arrangement are General Electric's GXS, eBay for Businesses, and Ariba's Dynamic Trading.

An exchange can conduct many-to-many public auctions. These auctions may be vertical or horizontal and can run on the Internet or over private lines. Examples of auctions conducted over private lines are Aucnet in Japan, which is for selling used cars to dealers, and TFA, the Dutch flower market auction (described in EC Application Case 6.2 on page 264).

Exhibit 6.9 (page 265) summarizes the major B2B, many-to-many models discussed so far in the chapter.

EC APPLICATION CASE 6.2
Interorganization and Collaboration
NEW ENTRANT TO THE DUTCH FLOWER MARKET: TFA

The Dutch flower market auction is the largest in the world, attracting 11,000 sellers from dozens of countries, such as Thailand, Israel, and East Africa; 3,500 varieties of flowers are sold in 120 auction groups to about 5,000 buyers using the *Dutch auction* method. The auctions used to be semi-automated. Buyers and sellers had to go to one location, where the flowers were shown to the buyers. The auctioneer of each flower variety used a clock with a large hand, which was set at a high price. The price dropped as the time ticked off on the clock until a bidder stopped the clock by pushing an order button. Using an intercom, the quantity ordered was clarified; then the clock hands were reset at the starting price level for the next batch of flowers. The process continued until all of the flowers were sold.

In September 1994, the Dutch growers (DFA), who own the auction organization, decided to ban foreign growers from participating in the auction during the summer months in order to protect the Dutch growers against low prices from abroad. By March 1995, some foreign growers, together with some local buyers, created a competing auction called the TeleFlower Auction (TFA), an *electronic auction* that enables its initiators to penetrate the Dutch flower market.

In the TFA electronic auction, buyers can bid on flowers via their PCs at designated times from any location connected to the private network. The process is similar to the traditional Dutch auction, except that the auction clock is shown on the buyer's PC screen (see the figure below). The buyers can stop the clock by pushing the space bar on the keyboard. The auctioneer then converses with the buyers by telephone, and a sale is completed. After the sale, the clock on the PC is reset. One difference in the TFA auction is that the flowers are not physically visible to the buyers. However, to offset this potential drawback, a large amount of relevant information is available online. For example, buyers are alerted to a specific auction, in real time, when their item of interest is auctioned.

Initial results indicated that buyers and growers were enthusiastic about the new auction. Although

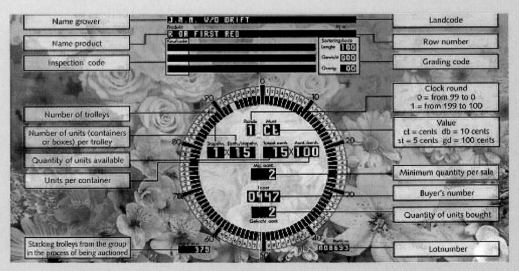

Source: Used with permission of *aquarius-flora.com*, 2002.

prices are about the same as in the DFA auctions, the process is much quicker and the after-sale delivery is much faster. Delivery starts within half an hour after the sale; nearby buyers can receive their flowers within that time. A major issue can be the quality of the flowers, because the buyers cannot see them. In fact, the quality of the flowers is actually better because the flowers are handled less frequently (no need to bring the flowers to an auction site) and the growers stand behind their products. As a result, there is enough trust so that everyone is happy.

The TFA has gained considerable market share at the expense of existing organizations and is a real new-entrant success story. Using IT, TFA quickly built a competitive advantage. This advantage impressed the DFA, but it took that group more than a year to

cancel the import restrictions and implement its own electronic clearinghouse for flowers. However, the TFA continues its own auctions.

Sources: Compiled from A. Kambil and E. Van Hack (March 1998); E. Van Hack et al., January 1997.

Questions

▶ Classify this exchange according to the categories presented in Section 6.1.

▶ What type of auction is used to sell flowers?

▶ With the TFA auction, once a bid is made, a telephone call follows, mainly for security. What mechanism could replace the telephone call and still fulfill the security function?

EXHIBIT 6.9   Comparing the Major B2B Many-to-Many Models

Name	Major Characteristics	Types
B2B catalog-based exchanges	▶ A place for selling and buying ▶ Fixed prices (updated as needed)	Vertical, horizontal ▶ Shopping directory, usually with hyperlinks (only) ▶ Shopping carts with services (payment, etc.)
B2B portals	▶ Community services ▶ Communication tools ▶ Classified ads ▶ Employment markets ▶ May sell, buy ▶ Fixed prices ▶ May do auctions	Vertical (vortals), horizontal ▶ Shopping directory, usually with hyperlinks
B2B dynamic exchanges	▶ Matches buyer/seller orders at dynamic prices, auctions ▶ Provides trading-related information and services (payment, logistics) ▶ Highly regulated ▶ May provide general information, news, etc. ▶ May provide for negotiations	Vertical, horizontal

▶ Explain how matches are made in exchanges.

▶ Explain how private and public auctions are conducted in public exchanges.

▶ Compare fully dedicated and partially dedicated auction exchanges.

6.6   BUILDING AND INTEGRATING MARKETPLACES AND EXCHANGES

BUILDING E-MARKETPLACES

Building e-marketplaces and exchanges is a complex process. It is usually performed by a major B2B software company such as Commerce One, Ariba, Oracle, or IBM. In large exchanges, a management consulting company such as Andersen Consulting (now Accenture), PriceWaterhouseCoopers, GartnerGroup, or McKinsey usually participates. Also, technology companies such as IBM, Oracle, EDS, i2, Intel, Microsoft, and SAP have major roles in building large exchanges. Most exchanges are built jointly by several vendors.

Most large B2B software vendors have specially designed e-marketplace packages. For example, Oracle, Microsoft, Ariba, and Commerce One each has a set of e-marketplace solutions (see online Chapter 12, prenhall.com/turban). Here we present a brief description of the development process that a market maker goes through in developing an e-marketplace, regardless of who the partnering vendors are. A typical process for building a vertical e-marketplace is shown in Exhibit 6.10.

THE INTEGRATION ISSUE

Seamless integration is needed between the third-party exchange and the participants' front- and back-office systems. This takes place through interfacing with applications and protocols. In addition, there is a need for integration across multiple, frequently incompatible exchanges, each with its own XML scheme. Tibco.com is the major infrastructure service provider for vertical exchanges.

The four most common elements of B2B integration solutions, discussed in the following sections, are external communications, process and information coordination, system and information management, and a shopping cart.

External Communications

External communications require the following:

▶ **Web/client access.** Businesses can use a Web browser, such as Internet Explorer, to interact with a Web server application hosted by other businesses.

▶ **Data exchange.** Information is extracted from an application, converted into a neutral data format, and sent to other businesses. Examples of data exchange include EDI over VANs and Internet-based EDI.

EXHIBIT 6.10 Steps in Building Vertical E-Marketplaces

Steps	Description of Activities
Step 1: Think ahead	▶ Think through what the current market environment is, how the e-market can make a change in the target industry, and what the monetary contribution for the players will be. ▶ Align the e-business with existing brick-and-mortar operations of companies in the industry. ▶ Clearly identify potential cost savings and revenue enhancement opportunities for both sellers and buyers. ▶ Find out if there is a competitor or a planned competitor in that industry. ▶ Outline the mission of the exchange.
Step 2: Planning	▶ Think through the vertical exchange's business scope, including how the exchange will operate in the target industry and what capabilities and benefits it will have for the players. ▶ Identify strategic objectives for the exchange such as financial returns and a target number of participants in the virtual market. ▶ Estimate the market potential, number of participants/players, and trading volume generated at different times. ▶ Plan details of how to build and implement the virtual exchange, including: functions for sharing industry information, for trading direct parts and materials, for improving communications among companies and their customers and business partners, and for automated bidding and offering processes. ▶ Be sure to address all relevant issues: financing, human resources, marketing, operations, payment, logistics, and their interface with the exchange.
Step 3: System analysis and design	▶ Start to design the exchange's technological platform, such as hosting, the hardware and software architecture, and databases. The platform should take into account scope, objectives, desired capabilities, and estimated trading volume at different time periods. ▶ Do not neglect the important issue of networking and integration of all exchange members. ▶ Formulate a development strategy either using a technology partner or outsourcing the construction of various components of the exchange.
Step 4: Building the exchange	▶ Build, test, and implement the exchange's platform. A good project management tool may be useful here. ▶ Be sure to consider how to connect exchange members to the exchange and the possibility of integrating members' systems. ▶ Decide whether the exchange will be hosted on the market maker's server, a Web hosting vendor, or a combination of the two.
Step 5: Testing, installation, and operation	▶ Conduct tests. ▶ Make needed improvements based on test results. ▶ Connect members. ▶ Open the exchange for business.
Step 6: System evaluation and improvement	▶ Monitor and evaluate the system on an ongoing basis. ▶ Make continuous improvements, which are common in most exchanges.

▶ **Direct application integration.** Application integration often requires middleware technologies, such as distributed object technologies, message queuing, and publish/subscribe brokers, to coordinate information exchange between applications (see tibco.com and peregrine.com).

▶ **Shared procedures.** Businesses can agree to use the same procedures for certain processes. For example, a supplier and a buyer may agree to use the same order management process.

Process and Information Coordination in Integration

Process and information coordination concerns how to coordinate *external communications* with *internal information systems*. This coordination includes external processes, internal processes, data transformation, and exception handling. For example, an online sales transaction must be processed directly to an internal accounting system.

System and Information Management in Integration

System and information management involves the management of software, hardware, and several information components, including partner-profile information, data and process definitions, communications and security settings, and users' information. Furthermore, because hardware and software change rapidly (i.e., upgrades or releases of new versions), the management of these changes is an essential element of B2B integration.

▶ List the steps in building a vertical exchange.

▶ Describe the integration issues for third-party exchanges.

6.7   MANAGING EXCHANGES

The topic of managing exchanges is very broad. Here we will describe three major management issues. (For further details on exchange management, see Schully and Woods 2000). We conclude the section with an examination of the critical success factors for exchanges.

REVENUE MODELS

Exchanges require revenue to survive. The following are potential sources of revenue:

▶ **Transaction fees.** Transaction fees are basically a commission paid *by sellers* for each transaction they make. Several methods exist for setting transaction fees. The most popular are fees based on a percentage of the total value of the sale (such as in real estate) or a flat fee per trade (as in discount stock brokering). Combinations of these two methods are also used. Sellers may object to transaction fees, especially when their regular customers are involved.

Exchanges charge relatively low transaction fees per order in order to attract sellers. Therefore, to cover its expenses, the exchange must generate sufficient volume (or be forced to raise its transaction fees).

▶ **Fee for service.** Some exchanges have successfully changed their revenue model from commission to "fee for service." Sellers are more willing to pay for value-added services than they are to pay commissions. Sometimes buyers will also pay some service charges.

▶ **Membership fees.** A membership fee is usually a fixed annual or monthly fee. It usually entitles the exchange member to get some services free or at a discount. In some countries, such as China, the government may ask members to pay annual membership fees, and then provide the participating sellers with free services and no transaction fees. This encourages members to use the exchange. The problem is that low membership fees may result in insufficient revenue to the exchange, whereas high membership fees discourage participants from joining.

▶ **Advertisement fees.** Exchanges can also derive income from fees for advertising on the information-portal part of the exchange. For example, some sellers may want to increase their exposure and will pay for special advertisements on the portal (like boxed ads in the yellow pages of telephone books).

NETWORKS OF EXCHANGES

With the increasing number of vertical and horizontal exchanges, it is logical to think about connecting them. Large corporations work with several exchanges, and they would like these exchanges to be connected in a seamless fashion. Today, most exchanges have different log-on procedures, separate sets of rules for fulfilling orders, and different business models for charging for their services.

At present, exchanges are created quickly so that they can be *first movers* in a market. The primary objective of these newly created exchanges is the acquisition of buyers and sellers. Integration with other companies or with another exchange is a low priority. However, some exchanges have begun to integrate in order to better serve their customers.

Commerce One and Ariba have developed a marketplace strategy that allows them to plug a broad range of horizontal exchanges into their main networks (such as the British Telecommunications' MarketSite), as well as an increasing number of connected vertical marketplaces (such as ChemConnect). Corporations can plug into Ariba or Commerce One networks and reach thousands of suppliers. Each time a new customer signs up with Ariba or Commerce One, the customer can bring its business partners into the network. These business partners are then connected to any other company that plugs into the network.

The joint network combining the Commerce One and Ariba networks is expanding rapidly, and the two companies are launching horizontal exchanges in several countries. These exchanges range from a marketplace for governmental and educational institutions (buysense.com) to a New Zealand marketplace for business (supplynet.co.nz). Ariba and Commerce One are also partnering with vertical exchanges such as ChemConnect. The network allows any customer to buy from any supplier connected to the network. Other large vendors, such as Oracle and SAP, may join the networks someday. (For further details, see Duvall 2000.) (See the textbook's Web site, prenhall.com/turban, for a diagram of connecting e-marketplaces.)

Exchanges can also be connected in an industry supply chain, as shown in Exhibit 6.11. Each exchange serves different participants, but some are members of different exchanges.

CENTRALIZED MANAGEMENT

Managing exchanges and providing services to participants on an individual basis can be expensive. Therefore, it makes sense to have "families" of exchanges managed jointly. This way, one market builder can build and operate several exchanges from a unified, centralized place. It manages all the exchanges' catalogs, auction places, discussion forums, and so on, thus centralizing accounting, finance, human resources, and IT services. Furthermore, dealings with third-party vendors that provide logistic services and payment systems may be more efficient if a vendor is supplying services for many exchanges instead of just one. Two such "families" of exchanges were those of VerticalNet (verticalnet.com) and Ventro (see Turban et al. 2002a). However, due to the large number of exchange failures in 2001, both VerticalNet and Ventro (now nexprise.com) changed their business models and became software providers.

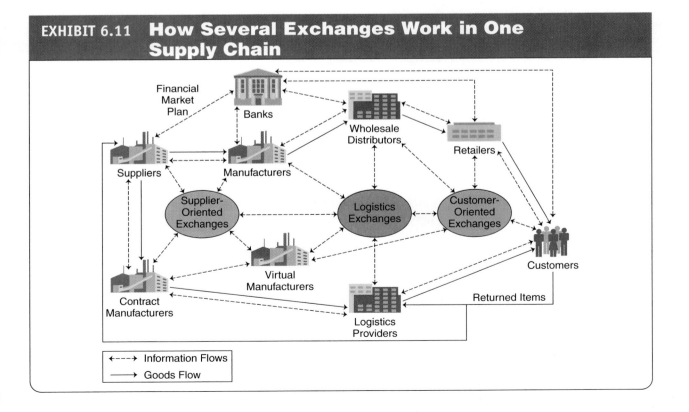

EXHIBIT 6.11   How Several Exchanges Work in One Supply Chain

CRITICAL SUCCESS FACTORS FOR EXCHANGES

By 2001, there were thousands of B2B exchanges. As in the B2C area, many, perhaps 90 percent, folded or will fail. There were dozens of failures in 2000, including that of chemdex.com. In certain areas or countries there are too many competing exchanges. For example, there is probably not room for three toy exchanges in Hong Kong. Therefore, there will be failures and consolidation in B2B exchanges. The question is, "What determines whether an exchange will survive?"

According to Ramsdell (2000) of McKinsey & Company, a major management consulting company, the following five factors will influence the outcome of what he believes will be a B2B shakeout:

1. **Early liquidity.** Recall that liquidity refers to the number of participants and the transaction volume. The *earlier* a business achieves the necessary liquidity level, the better its chances for survival. The more buyers that trade on an exchange, the more suppliers will come, which will lead to lower transaction fees, which in turn will increase the liquidity even more.

2. **The right owners.** One way to increase liquidity is to partner with companies that can bring liquidity to the exchange. For example, Covisint was founded by the big automakers, which are committed to buying via the exchange. The desire to have suitable partners is why many vertical exchanges are of the consortia type. In a situation where both the sellers and buyers are fragmented, such as in the bioscience industry, the best owner may be an intermediary who can increase liquidity by pushing both the sellers and the buyers to use the exchange.

3. **The right governance.** Good management and effective operations and rules are critical to success. The governance provides the rules for the exchange, minimizes conflicts, and supports decision making. Furthermore, good management will try to induce the necessary liquidity. Also, good governance will minimize conflicts among the owners and the participants. Owners may try to favor some of their trading partners, a situation that may hurt the exchange, if not checked by effective management. To succeed, good exchanges must be unbiased. Finally, good management of operations, resources, and people is mandatory for smooth operations and success.

4. **Openness.** Exchanges must be open to all, from both organizational and technological perspectives. Commitment to open standards is required, but there should be universal agreement on these standards. Using the wrong standards may hurt the exchange.

5. **A full range of services.** Although prices are important, buyers and sellers are interested in cutting their total costs. Therefore, exchanges that help cut inventory costs, spoilage, maverick buying, and so on, will attract participants. Many exchanges team up with banks, logistics services, and IT companies to provide support services. Furthermore, exchanges must be integrated with the information systems of their members—not a simple task (see the Real-World Case at the end of this chapter).

In addition to Ramsdell's five factors, there are a number of other factors that are critical to the success of an exchange. These are presented and discussed in the nearby Insights and Additions box.

In order to achieve these critical success factors, market makers must carefully select the vendors that design and build the exchanges. In addition, of utmost importance are the connecting networks, which we will examine next.

Insights and Additions   Other Critical Success Factors for Exchanges

▶ **Importance of domain expertise.** In order to meaningfully aggregate buyers and sellers in a community and subsequently enable transactions among them, operators should have knowledge of a given industry's structure and business processes, the nature of buyer and seller behavior in the industry, and government and policy stipulations that impact the sector.

▶ **Targeting inefficient industry processes.** The traditional business processes in most industries have many inefficiencies. These contribute to increased costs, time, and delays for businesses transacting with one another, and they create significant opportunities for vertical exchanges to add value.

▶ **Targeting the right industries.** The most attractive verticals to target typically are characterized by: (1) a large base of transactions; (2) many fragmented buyers and sellers; (3) difficulties in bringing buyers and sellers together; (4) high vendor and product search/comparison costs, which may be caused by information-intensive products with complex configurations and nonstandard specifications; (5) high process costs associated with manual processes based on paper catalogs, manual requisitioning, telephone or fax-based ordering, the need for credit verification, and order tracking; (6) strong pressure to cut expenses; and (7) a climate of technological innovation.

▶ **Brand building.** The low switching costs inherent in exchanges will make branding of exchanges of paramount importance to their long-term viability. Exchange operators must first invest in gaining brand awareness and getting businesses to use their exchange. For example, in Hong Kong, *bigboxx.com* even advertises on buses. Exchange operators must then focus on customer retention. Adding valuable features and functionality is one way to increase switching costs. (In this case, switching costs include the services the customer would lose by switching.)

▶ **Exploiting economies of scope.** Once a critical mass is reached, exchange operators must expand the services they provide to users. Value-added services such as industry news, expert advice, or detailed product specification sheets, and so on, can make an exchange even more compelling. As noted above, expanding the range of services may also increase switching costs. Better-developed exchanges are now offering services such as systems integration, hosting, financial services (e.g., payment processing, receivables management, credit analysis), and logistics services (e.g., shipping, warehousing, and inspection), as well as risk mitigation services.

▶ **Choice of business/revenue models.** Exchange operators should generate multiple revenue streams, including software licensing, advertising, and sponsorship, and recurring revenues from transaction fees, subscription fees, and software subscription revenues. Other value-added services and applications, such as auctions, financial services, business reporting, and data mining services, may provide other sources of revenue.

▶ **Blending content, community, and commerce.** Exchanges differ in their approaches—some originate from a content/community perspective, whereas others have an EC-transaction perspective. Though content and community features have the advantage of stimulating traffic, the ability to conduct EC transactions is thought to create a higher level of customer "stickiness" and greater value for the exchanges. A successful exchange should combine rich content and community with the ability to conduct EC transactions.

▶ **Managing channel conflict.** The movement of buyers to interact directly with sellers and the consequent disintermediation of the supply chain is invariably a hostile phase. Impacts on short-term revenues of both buyers and sellers may result from a backlash from existing fulfillment channels, resulting in price erosion that may affect a company's medium-term profitability. Exchanges are trying to minimize the conflict by utilizing existing services of the major buyers and/or sellers.

> List the revenue sources (models) of exchanges.

> Describe a network of exchanges.

> List the five critical success factors for exchanges cited by Ramsdell.

> Discuss other critical success factors for exchanges.

6.8   COMMUNICATION NETWORKS AND EXTRANETS FOR B2B

In Chapter 5, we pointed out the need for networks to support communication and collaboration among B2B business partners. We also described EDI and its supporting role in facilitating B2B communication and collaboration. Here we look at the networks needed for e-marketplaces and exchanges.

The major network structure used in e-marketplaces and exchanges is an *extranet*, or "extended intranet." It connects with both the Internet and individual companies' intranets. An extranet adds value to the Internet by increasing its security and expanding the available bandwidth. In order to better understand how an extranet interfaces with the Internet and intranets, let's turn our attention to the basic concepts of the Internet, intranets, and extranets.

THE INTERNET

Of course you have a working familiarity with the Internet, but here is the official definition: The **Internet** is a public, global communications network that provides direct connectivity to anyone over a local area network (LAN) via an Internet service provider (ISP) or directly via an ISP. This public network is connected and routed over gateways. The ISPs are connected to Internet access providers, to network access providers, and eventually to the Internet backbone. Because access to the Internet is open to all, there is a minimum level of control and security.

INTRANETS

An **intranet** is a corporate LAN or wide area network (WAN) that uses Internet technology and is secured behind a company's firewalls. (Chapter 9 discusses firewalls.) An intranet links various servers, clients, databases, and application programs, such as ERP, within a company. Although intranets are based on the same TCP/IP protocol as the Internet, they operate as a private network with limited access. Only authorized employees are able to use them.

Intranets are limited to information pertinent to the company and contain exclusive, often proprietary, sensitive information. The intranet can be used to enhance communication and collaboration among authorized employees, customers, suppliers, and other business partners. Because an intranet allows access through the Internet, it does not require any additional implementation of leased networks. This open and flexible connectivity is a major capability and advantage of intranets.

Internet
A public, global communications network that provides direct connectivity to anyone over a local area network (LAN) via an Internet service provider (ISP) or directly via an ISP.

Intranet
A corporate LAN or wide area network (WAN) that uses Internet technology and is secured behind a company's firewalls.

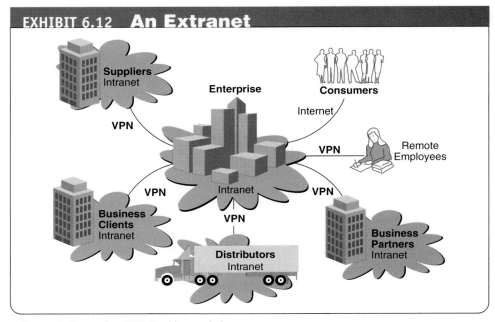

EXHIBIT 6.12   An Extranet

Source: B. Szuprowicz, 1998. Used by permission.

EXTRANETS

extrant
A network that uses a virtual private network (VPN) to link intranets in different locations over the Internet; an "extended intranet."

virtual private network (VPN)
A network that creates tunnels of secured data flows, using cryptography and authorization algorithms, to provide secure transport of private communications over the public Internet.

An **extranet** or "extended intranet," uses the TCP/IP protocol to link intranets in different locations (as shown in Exhibit 6.12). Extranet transmissions are usually conducted over the Internet, which offers little privacy or transmission security. Therefore, it is necessary to add security features. This is done by creating tunnels of secured data flows, using cryptography and authorization algorithms, to provide secure transport of private communications. An Internet with tunneling technology is known as a **virtual private network (VPN)**.

Extranets provide secured connectivity between a corporation's intranets and the intranets of its business partners, materials suppliers, financial services, government, and customers. Access to extranets is usually limited by agreements of the collaborating parties, is strictly controlled, and is available only to authorized personnel. The protected environment of an extranet allows partners to collaborate and share information and to perform these activities securely.

As an extranet allows connectivity between businesses through the Internet, it is an open and flexible platform suitable for supply chain management. To increase security, many companies replicate the portions of their databases that they are willing to share with their business partners and separate them physically from their regular intranets. However, even separated data needs to be secured. (See Chapter 9 for more on EC network security.) To see how an extranet functions, read the example discussed in EC Application Case 6.3.

EC APPLICATION CASE 6.3
Implementation and Strategy

A NETWORK LOADED WITH EXTRAS: ANX

In September 1997, the "Big Three" U.S. auto manufacturers and two dozen other auto industry companies piloted what is probably the world's largest extranet, the Automotive Network Exchange (ANX). ANX is an infrastructure for B2B applications, particularly Covisint, that promises to cut costs by billions of dollars and change the way the auto supply chain does business (Davis et al. 1997). Backed by General Motors, Ford, and Chrysler, ANX allows companies in the automotive market to swap supply and manufacturing data, buy, sell, and collaborate. The commercial network involves tens of thousands of companies and their counterparts globally. ANX was piloted on a small scale in 1997 and fully initiated on November 1, 1998, and is now operational as a start-up company, ANXeBusiness (*anx.com*), that is not affiliated with the major U.S. auto manufacturers.

Benefits of ANX

ANX applications include one-to-one and one-to-many connections, such as procurement, CAD/CAM file transfers, EDI, e-mail, and groupware. The ANX organizers believe that the network's EDI element alone slices $71 from the cost of designing and building a car. That translates into an industry-wide savings of $1 billion a year. Each of the "Big Three" automakers expects to save many millions of dollars by consolidating communications links onto ANX. Not only will the companies pay for fewer T1 lines and satellite connections, but standardizing the protocol will reduce support costs.

The extranet also helps auto suppliers reduce order turn-around time. The faster the parts and subassemblies come in, the faster the cars

leave the assembly line. Ford Motor Co., for example, hopes to compress some work-order communications from 3 weeks to 5 minutes. "We may well convert our entire WAN to ANX," says Rick Collins, a senior IS consultant at Paccar Inc., a maker of custom semi-trailer trucks. Today ANX is the infrastructure upon which the Covisint exchange operates.

A VPN for ANX

The ANX is probably the most visible B2B implementation of VPNs that run over the Internet across the country and the globe. As for security, all participants on the ANX must have tools compliant with Internet Protocol (IP) security standards, which cover authentication, encryption, and encryption key management. Each packet that travels over the ANX is encrypted and authenticated.

Overall, the ANX has successfully met participants' expectations. Similar networks exist in Europe, South America, and other parts of the world.

Source: Compiled from Dalton and Davis (1998), Davis et al., 1997, and *anx.com*.

Questions

▌ What are the differences between the ANX and Covisint?

▌ Can the ANX support exchanges that compete with Covisint? Why or why not?

▌ ANX is the infrastructure for Covisint. Could an alternative infrastructure be used?

▌ Can the ANX support company-centered transactions?

According to Szuprowicz (1998), there are five categories of extranet benefits. They are:

1. **Enhanced communications.** Improved internal communications; improved business partnership channels; effective marketing, sales, and customer support; and collaborative activities support.

2. **Productivity enhancements.** Just-in-time information delivery; reduction of information overload; productive collaboration between work groups; and training on demand.

3. **Business enhancements.** Faster time to market; simultaneous engineering potential; lower design and production costs; improved client relationships; and new business opportunities.

4. **Cost reduction.** Fewer errors; improved comparison shopping; reduced travel and meetings; reduced administrative and operational costs; and elimination of paper-publishing costs.

5. **Information delivery.** Low-cost publishing; leveraging of legacy systems; standard delivery systems; ease of maintenance and implementation; and elimination of paper-based publishing and mailing costs.

▶ What is an intranet?

▶ What is an extranet?

▶ List five benefits of extranets.

6.9 IMPLEMENTATION ISSUES

Large exchanges are supposed to bring together entire industry sectors, creating supply chain efficiencies and reducing costs for buyers and sellers alike. However, despite the fact that more than 1,500 exchanges were created between January 1999 and December 2000, only a few hundred were active by the end of 2001, and less than half of these were conducting a high volume of transactions (forrester.com, 2001). Let's look at some of the implementation issues that might explain these numbers.

PRIVATE VS. PUBLIC EXCHANGES

As described earlier, exchanges owned by a third party are referred to as *public exchanges*. In contrast, **private exchanges** are owned and operated by an industry giant or a consortium. (Note that we differentiate here between private exchanges, covered in this chapter, and private e-marketplaces, the company-centric marketplaces covered in Chapter 5.) Both types of exchanges have implementation and viability problems.

> **private exchanges**
> E-marketplaces that are owned and operated by an industry giant or a consortium.

Problems with Public Exchanges

Exchanges need to attract sellers and buyers. Attracting sellers, especially large businesses, to public exchanges is difficult for the following reasons:

▶ **Transaction fees.** One of the major reasons that large and successful suppliers refuse to join third-party exchanges is that they are required to pay transaction fees even when they engage in transactions with their existing customers.

▶ **Sharing information.** Many companies do not like to join public exchanges because they have to share key business data with their competitors.

▶ **Cost savings.** Many of the first-generation exchanges were horizontal, concentrating on MROs. These are low-value items. Although administrative costs can be reduced, the cost of the products to the buyers remains essentially the same. Thus the monetary savings may not be attractive enough to SME buyers.

▶ **Recruiting suppliers.** One of the major difficulties facing public exchanges is the recruitment of large suppliers. For example, GE Plastics, a major vendor of plastic materials, said that the company was asked to join plasticsnet.com, but it did not see any benefit in doing so. There was simply no business case for it. GE Plastics is working very hard to develop e-purchasing capabilities for its customers, which are working quite well. The company likes the direct contact with its customers, which it would lose if it were part of the public exchange. Also, some suppliers just want to wait and see how exchanges will fare before they make a commitment to join.

▶ **Too many exchanges.** When an exchange receives the publicity of being the *first mover*, as Chemdex did, it is sure to attract some competition. Competitors believe that they can do a better job than the first mover or that they have "deeper pockets" to sustain losses and survive. For example, in Hong Kong there were three competing toy exchanges in late 2000 (e.g., chinasite.com). Similarly, two chemical exchanges competed against Chemdex, which closed in 2000. (For more on competition among exchanges, see the newview.com case at the end of this chapter.)

▶ **Supply chain improvements.** Public exchanges prepare the entire infrastructure and ask suppliers to just plug in and start selling. However, companies are interested in streamlining their supply chains, which requires integration with internal operations, not just plugging in. This is why companies like i2 and Aspect, leaders in supply chain management (SCM), are partnering with some exchanges.

Problems with Private Exchanges

Private exchanges face several problems. First, they may not be trusted because they are run by an industry giant or a consortium. Such distrust can lead to liquidity issues. Second, as discussed earlier in the chapter, they may face legal problems. In 2001, some major manufacturers adopted private exchanges for the main supply chain, so the combined use of private and public exchanges is a new issue for manufacturers to consider. By combining private and public exchanges, the liquidity is increased, and also there are fewer legal problems.

SOFTWARE AGENTS IN B2B EXCHANGES

The use of B2B exchanges has fostered a need within the B2B community for an efficient infrastructure to provide real-time, tighter integration between buyers and sellers and to facilitate management of multiple trading partners and their transactions across multiple virtual industry exchanges. Such capabilities can be provided by software agents such as AgentWare's Syndicator. This software enables customized syndication of content and services from multiple sources on the Internet to any device connected to the Internet. Thus it allows access to real-time information on the exchange. (For further details, see agentware.net.) Another software agent, Dotcom-Monitor from dotcom-monitor.com, monitors traffic on a B2B exchange and takes appropriate actions when needed. (Some of the shopping agents in Chapter 4 can also be used for B2B purposes.)

DISINTERMEDIATION

Exchanges, especially consortia-like ones, could replace many traditional B2B intermediaries. Let's look at some examples of exchanges that might replace B2B intermediaries in certain industries.

▶ In September 2000, eight metal companies (e.g., Alcoa) created metalspectrum. com. The consortium offered a market for specialty metals and business services to the metal industry. The exchange could have eliminated traditional wholesalers and retailers. The participating companies tend to prefer the consortia sites over third-party exchanges such as e-steel.com. The consortium went out of business in 2001 due to difficulties enlisting enough buyers.

▶ Sun Microsystems, after publicly announcing that there was no need for third-party exchanges because they waste time, joined a consortium headed by IBM that develops and smoothes lines in the computer maker's supply chain. This exchange competes with a similar exchange created by Compaq, HP, AMD, and NEC.

▶ Marriott and Hyatt, large competing hoteliers, created an MRO exchange (avendra.com) that could eliminate wholesalers in that industry.

EVALUATING EXCHANGES

With the increased number of competing exchanges, companies need to carefully evaluate which ones work best for them. According to works.com, the following are some useful suggestions for evaluating exchanges.

▶ Analyze how much the company will really save and/or gain by using the exchange.

▶ Determine the viability of the exchange and check its ownership and management team.

▶ Look out for contracts and technology that lock a company into a long-term relationship.

▶ Look at the membership; find out who sits on the board.

▶ Determine who provides payment, logistics, and other services.

Specific questions that buyers and sellers should ask are shown in the Insights and Additions box on the next page.

Insights and Additions · Questions Buyers and Sellers Should Ask About Exchanges

QUESTIONS FOR BUYERS TO ASK	QUESTIONS FOR SELLERS TO ASK
▶ Does the B2B exchange have a critical mass of buyers and suppliers?	▶ Could the company acquire more buyers by being in the exchange?
▶ Can buyers and sellers hide their identities (anonymity feature)?	▶ How would participation affect the price of our goods?
▶ What kind of secret information does the company have? Will it be disclosed?	▶ What kind of information do we have? Would it be uncovered and exposed to others?
▶ How much will it cost to be online and to use the e-marketplace?	▶ How much does it cost to participate in e-trading?
▶ Can past trading records be traced?	▶ What is the transaction fee?
	▶ Could we sell independently in the future?
	▶ How severe is the competition in the exchange itself?

Source: Krammer, Hope-Ross and Spencer, 2001

▶ List the problems of public exchanges.
▶ List the problems of private exchanges.
▶ How can exchanges cause disintermediation?
▶ What are some of the questions one should ask when evaluating exchanges?

6.10 SUPPORT SERVICES FOR B2B AND EXCHANGES

In order to succeed in B2B, and particularly in exchanges, it is necessary to have support services. The Delphi Group (2001) (delphigroup.com) suggests that B2B services be organized into six major categories: e-infrastructure, e-process, e-markets, e-content, e-communities, and e-services. The details in each category are shown in Exhibit 6.13 (page 280). (A full description of each service can be found in Turban et al. 2002a.) In this section we will examine a few key support services. In Chapter 10 we will address e-process and e-content, and in online Chapter 12, the topic of e-infrastructure.

DIRECTORY SERVICES AND SEARCH ENGINES

The B2B landscape is huge, with thousands of companies online. Directory services can help buyers and sellers manage the task of finding potential partners. Some popular directories are listed and described in Exhibit 6.14 (page 281). Note that the last three entries in the exhibit are search engines, which can be used to discover information about B2B. Some of these are embedded in the directories.

EXHIBIT 6.13 E-Commerce Services

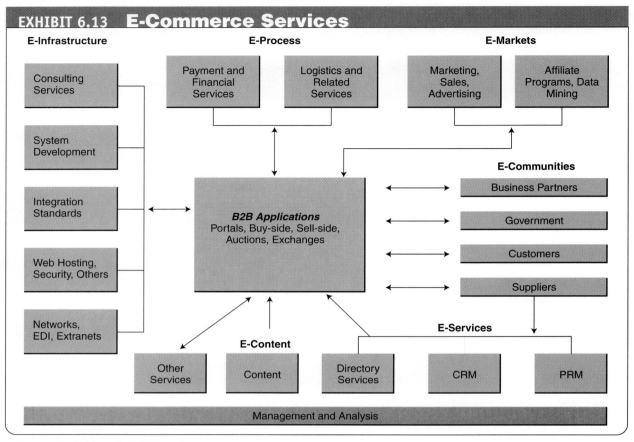

Source: Adapted from Choi, 1997, p. 18.

PARTNER RELATIONSHIP MANAGEMENT

Successful e-businesses carefully manage partners, prospects, and customers across the entire value chain, most often in a 24/7 environment. Therefore, one should examine the role of e-service solutions and technology, such as extranets, call centers, and collaboration tools, in creating an integrated online environment for engaging e-business customers and partners. The use of such solutions and technology appears under two names: CRM and PRM.

In Chapter 4, we introduced the concept of CRM in the B2C environment. Here our interest shifts to a situation where the customer is a business. Many of the customer service features of B2C are also used in B2B. For example, it may be beneficial to provide customers with a chat room and a discussion board. A Web-based call center may also be useful.

Corporate customers may require additional services. For example, customers need to have access to the supplier's inventory status report so they know what items can be delivered quickly. Customers may want to see their historical purchasing records, and they may need private showrooms and trade rooms. Large numbers of vendors are available for designing and build-

EXHIBIT 6.14	**B2B Directory Services and Search Engines**
Directory Services	
B2Business.net	A major resource for B2B professionals that provides listings of business resources in about 30 functional areas, company research resources (e.g., credit checks, customs research, financial reviews), and information on start-ups.
B2BToday.com	Contains listings of B2B services organized by type of service (e.g., Web site creation, B2B marketing, and B2B software) and product category (e.g., automotive, books).
Communityb2b.com	Offers many B2B community services, such as news, a library, events calendar, job market, and resource directory.
A2zofb2b.com	Company directory organized in alphabetical order or industry order. Specifies the type and nature of the company, the venture capital (VC) sponsor, and the stock market ticker (if it is an IPO).
I-stores.co.uk	A UK-based directory of online stores; provides validation of secure Web sites.
Dmoz.org/Business/	A large business directory organized by location and by product or service. Also provides listings by industry and sub-industry (according to SIC code).
Thomasregister.com	Directory of more than 150,000 manufacturers of industrial products and services.
Allnetresearch. internet.com	A comprehensive B2B guide for marketers that provides directories, news, auctions, and much more.
b2b.yahoo.com	Provides business directories that cover over 250,000 companies (as of 2001).
Line56.com/directory	Provides information about B2B software, services, and marketplaces.
Search Engines	
W.moreover.com	In addition to locating information, it also aggregates B2B (and other business) news.
Google.com	In addition to its search tools, it offers a directory of components for B2B and B2C Web sites (e.g., currency exchange calculators, server performance monitors, etc.).
Ientry.com	Provides B2B search engines, targeted "niche engines," and several industry-focused newsletters. Operates a network of Web sites and e-mail newsletters that reaches over 2,000,000 unique opt-in subscribers.

ing appropriate B2B CRM solutions. This type of e-service is sometimes called **partner relationship management (PRM)**. This strategy focuses on providing comprehensive quality services for business partners.

In the context of PRM, customers are only one category of business partner. Suppliers, partners in joint ventures, service providers, and others are also part of the B2B community in an exchange or company-centric B2B initiative.

partner relationship management (PRM)
Business strategy that focuses on providing comprehensive quality service for business partners.

Implementing PRM is different from implementing CRM with individual customers. Behavioral and psychological aspects of the relationships are less important in B2B, but trust, commitment, quality of services, and continuity are more important.

OTHER B2B SERVICES

Many other B2B service providers support e-commerce in different ways. Each seeks to provide a value-added service that will be of use to companies seeking to do business online. Here are some representative examples:

- **Trust services.** Trust is as important in B2B as in B2C. Some of the trust-ratings services used in B2C can also be used in B2B. Examples are TRUSTe, BBBOnline, and Ernst & Young's trust service.

- **Trademark and domain names.** A number of domain-name services are available to B2B companies. These services help in registering URLs, identify potential URL conflicts, and look at legal and global issues related to domain names. Some companies offering these services are register.com, easyspace.com, and dotster.com.

- **Digital photos.** Companies such as ipix.com provide innovative pictures for use on company Web sites.

- **Global business communities.** The eCommerce Portal from wiznet.net is a global, Web-based "business community" that supports the unique requirements of buying organizations. For example, it offers cross-catalog searches, RFQ development and distribution, and decision support; it also enables suppliers to dictate the content and presentation of their own product catalogs.

- **Client matching.** Techrepublic.com matches clients with firms that provide a wide variety of information technology services. Clients define what it is they want and Techrepublic performs the searching and screening, checking against some general parameters and criteria. This reduces the risk of making bad IT decisions.

- **E-business rating sites.** A number of services are available for businesses to research rankings of potential partners and suppliers. Bizrate.com, forrester.com, gomez.com, and shopnow.com all provide business ratings.

- **Promotion programs.** Some promotion programs of interest to B2B include NetCentives, ClickRewards, AirMiles, eCentives, and MyPoints.

- **Encryption sites.** VeriSign provides valuable encryption tools for B2B and B2C organizations.

- **Web-research services.** There are a number of Web-research providers that can help companies learn more about technologies, trends, and potential business partners and suppliers. Some of these are MMXI, WebTrack, IDG, ZDNet, and Forrester.

- What type of information of use to B2B is provided by directory services and search engines?
- How does PRM differ from CRM?

MANAGERIAL ISSUES

Some managerial issues related to this chapter are as follows.

1. **Have we "done our homework"?** Study the options and select the most secure and economical choice for exchange implementation. Consult the technical staff inside and outside of each partnering company. Planning is essential.

2. **Can we use the Internet?** Review the current proprietary or leased network and determine if it can be replaced by intranets and extranets via the Internet. Doing so may reduce costs and widen connectivity for customers and suppliers.

3. **Which exchange?** One of the major concerns of management is selecting exchanges in which to participate. At the moment, exchanges are not integrated, so there is a major start-up effort and cost for joining the exchanges. This is a multicriteria decision that should be analyzed carefully.

4. **Will joining an exchange force restructuring?** Joining an exchange may require a restructuring of the internal supply chain, which may be expensive and time-consuming. Therefore, this possibility must be taken into consideration when deciding whether or not to join an exchange.

5. **Will we face channel conflicts?** Channel conflicts may arise when a company joins an exchange. This issue must be considered, and an examination of its impact must be carried out.

6. **What are the benefits and risks of joining an exchange?** Companies must take the issues in Exhibit 6.4 very seriously. The risks of joining an exchange must be carefully weighed against the benefits.

SUMMARY

In this chapter, you learned about the following EC issues as they relate to the learning objectives.

1. **E-marketplaces and exchanges defined.** Exchanges are e-marketplaces that provide a trading platform for conducting business among many buyers, many sellers, and other business partners. Other names used are *trading portals* or *Net marketplaces*.

2. **The major types of e-marketplaces.** E-marketplaces include B2B portals, third-party trading exchanges (exchanges for short), consortium trading exchanges, and dynamic trading floors (for matching and auctions). They can be vertical (industry-oriented) or horizontal. They can target systematic buying (long-term relationships) or spot buying (for fulfilling an immediate need).

3. **B2B portals.** These portals are similar to B2C portals such as Yahoo!. B2B portals are gateways to B2B community-related information. They are usually of a vertical structure; those that are referred to as *vortals*. Some B2B portals offer product and vendor information and even tools for conducting trades.

4. **Third-party exchanges.** Third-party exchanges are owned by an independent company and usually operate in highly fragmented markets. They try to maintain neutral relations with both buyers and sellers. Their major problem is customer acquisition for liquidity.

5. **Consortium trading exchanges.** A consortium trading exchange (CTE) is an exchange formed and operated by a group of major companies. Buying-oriented consortia are established by several large buyers (e.g., automakers). Their major objective is to smooth the purchasing process. Selling-oriented consortia are owned and operated by several large sellers, usually in the same industry (e.g., plastics). Their major objective is to increase sales and smooth the supply chain to their customers.

6. **Dynamic pricing and trading.** Dynamic pricing occurs when prices are determined by supply and demand at any given moment. Dynamic trading refers to exchange trading in which prices are continuously changing. The two major dynamic pricing mechanisms are matching of supply and demand (such as in stock markets) and auctions (forward and reverse).

7. **Ownership and revenue models.** Exchanges may be owned by an intermediary (a third party), a large group of buyers or sellers (a consortium), or one large company. The major revenue models are annual fees, transaction fees (flat or percentage), fees for added-value services, and advertisement income.

8. **Exchange networks and management of exchanges.** It will benefit customers if exchanges are connected to one another. Such integration is complex and will take years to complete. Managing exchanges individually can be expensive; therefore, "families" of exchanges, such as VerticalNet, are emerging.

9. **Critical success factors for exchanges.** Some of the major critical success factors for ex-

changes are early liquidity, proper ownership, proper governance and management, openness (technological and organizational), lack of bias, and a full range of services.

10. **Extranets.** An extranet connects the intranets of business partners in an effective and efficient manner. Several extranets can be combined, even globally. Using a VPN provides security so that the Internet can be used rather than private lines. Extranets support both company-centric e-marketplaces and exchanges.

11. **E-marketplaces and exchange implementation and development issues.** E-marketplaces and exchanges are usually developed and implemented by vendors. Therefore, vendor selection and management is a critical issue.

12. **Support services.** Six categories of support services exist: e-infrastructure, e-process, e-markets, e-content, e-communities, and e-services. Directory services and B2B search engines are examples of e-services. Partnership relationship management (PRM) is facilitated by the various support services.

KEY TERMS

B2B portals,	p. 253	Horizontal exchanges,	p. 248	Public e-marketplaces (public exchanges),	p. 247
Consortium trading exchange (CTE),	p. 258	Internet,	p. 273		
		Intranet,	p. 273	Spot sourcing,	p. 248
Dynamic pricing,	p. 249	Liquidity,	p. 255	Systematic sourcing,	p. 248
Dynamic trading,	p. 263	Market maker,	p. 247	Vertical exchanges,	p. 248
Elasticity,	p. 262	Partner relationship management (PRM),	p. 281	Virtual private network (VPN),	p. 274
Exchange,	p. 247				
Extranet,	p. 274	Private exchanges,	p. 276	Vortals (vertical portals),	p. 255

DISCUSSION QUESTIONS

1. How does dynamic pricing differ from fixed pricing?

2. Suppose a manufacturer uses an outside shipping company. How can the manufacturer use

an exchange to arrange for the best possible shipping? How can a shipment's status be tracked?

3. Explain the legal concerns regarding consortia.

4. Which exchanges are most suitable for third-party ownership and why?

5. Compare and contrast the supplier aggregation model with the buyer aggregation model in an industry of your choice.

6. Describe the various issues of integration related to B2B exchanges.

7. Explain the logic for networks of exchanges.

8. Discuss the logic of companies such as VerticalNet.

9. Explain the importance of early liquidity and describe methods to achieve it.

10. Explain the relationships between Covisint (EC Application Case 6.1) and ANX (EC Application Case 6.3).

11. How do exchanges affect disintermediation?

12. What questions should buyers and sellers ask when evaluating exchanges?

13. Compare the viability of private exchanges over public exchanges.

INTERNET EXERCISES

1. Visit ariba.com and commerceone.com. Find the software tools they have for building e-markets. Check the capabilities provided by each and comment on their differences.

2. Go to alibaba.com and sign-up (free) as a member. Go to the site map and find the "sample house." Create a product and place it in the sample house. Tell your instructor how to view this product.

3. Compare the services offered by global sources.com with those offered by alibaba.com and meetworldtrade.com.

4. Enter chemconnect.com and view the demos for different trading alternatives. Evaluate the services from both the buyer's and seller's points of view. Also, examine the site policies and legal guidelines. Are they fair? Compare chemconnect.com with eglobalchem.com.

5. Most of the major exchanges use an ERP/SCM partner. Enter i2.com and view its solutions, such as TradeMatrix. What are the benefits of these solutions?

6. Enter fastparts.com and review all the services offered there. Write a report based on your findings.

7. Investigate the various auctions offered by freemarkets.com. Comment on the services provided.

8. Visit converge.com. What kind of exchange is this? What services does it provide? How do its auctions work?

TEAM ASSIGNMENTS AND ROLE PLAYING

1. Form two teams (A and B) of five or more members. On each team, Person 1 plays the role of an assembly company that produces television monitors. Persons 2 and 3 are domestic parts suppliers to the assembling company, and Persons 4 and 5 play foreign parts suppliers. Assume that the TV monitor company wants to sell televisions directly to business customers. Each team is to design an environment composed of membership in exchanges and present its results. A graphical display is recommended.

2. Investigate the status of Covisint, both in the United States and in Europe. What are the relationships between Covisint and the company-centered marketplaces of the large automakers? Relate Covisint with the European-based ENX

and the U.S.-based ANX. Have another team find similar industry-wide exchanges and compare them with Covisint.

3. Enter isteelasia.com, metalworld.com, lme.co.uk, and newview.com. Compare their operations and services. These exchanges compete in global markets. Examine the trading platforms, portal capabilities, and support services (e.g., logistics, payments, etc.) offered by each. In what areas do these companies compete? In what areas do they not compete? What are the advantages of isteelasia.com in dealing with Asian companies? Do we need regional exchanges? If it is good for Asia to have a regional exchange, why not have a Western European exchange, an Eastern European exchange, a Central American exchange, and so on? If we need these regional exchanges, can they work together? How? If there are too many exchanges, which are likely to survive? Research this topic and prepare a report.

REAL-WORLD CASE

INTEGRATION AT *E-STEEL.COM* (now *newview.com*)

The steel industry is well known for its cumbersome, paper-based supply chain. This is one of the reasons why the industry is unprofitable. E-steel.com (*newview.com*) decided to change this situation. Founded in 1998, E-steel.com initially wanted to bring buyers and sellers together to trade in an efficient manner over the Internet. Also, it wanted to connect with "difficult to reach" buyers and sellers. The site allows the various industry players, from steel mills to service centers, to submit RFQs for all types of steel products, compare prices and packages across multiple suppliers, negotiate prices, and complete transactions, all in a secure, global marketplace.

E-steel.com decided to support systematic sourcing, where transactions are negotiated among known parties. (In contrast, its primary rival, *metalsite.com*, supported auctions for spot purchasing. MetalSite.com folded in spring 2001.) To support systematic sourcing, E-Steel had to deal with the issue of integration, the process of linking participating companies' back-end financial, order entry, inventory, and manufacturing control systems to the exchange.

Integration is not simple to achieve, especially in light of the fact that one company may be a member of several (four to five) exchanges. The difficulties of integration are not only technical. One integration problem is that most exchanges are more concerned with liquidity than with integration. (This is true of most industries.) Also, with B2B EC, com-

panies need to rethink the global supply chain practices and institute a massive change—possibly a BPR. Companies must review existing processes and their interactions with the supply chains in which they are involved. This may be difficult if one company has several supply chains. Thus, companies need to make bold decisions about changes.

Companies also need to be able to connect the exchange to the ERP system if they have one in place. Otherwise, the exchange just automates paper transactions, which may not be sufficient incentive to attract members, particularly when they are asked to pay transaction fees (see Norris et al. 2000).

In contrast to other exchanges, E-steel.com approached integration as a high-priority initiative. It built an IT unit specializing in integration. It also selected consultants who were experts in providing integration services to steel companies and software that supported that goal. To help automate the process of loading inventory information into a marketplace, E-steel.com created DataJet—a free data mapping and uploading tool that helps customers upload inventory and product catalog information to the site without data format conversions. Also, E-steel.com helped the steel industry develop Steel Markup Language, a set of extensions to XML. In addition, it partnered with *webmethods.com*, a company that makes special hub-and-spoke software for integration, taking the software to a higher level. All in all, it took E-steel.com almost 18 months to prepare its integration solutions.

E-steel.com has about 3,500 members, including U.S. Steel Corp., which owns a minor part of E-steel.com and helps E-steel.com experiment with the new systems. To maximize efficiencies, E-steel.com has integrated U.S. Steel's operations with those of its customers, such as Ford Motor Co., so that these partners can seamlessly upload their purchasing requirements to the E-steel.com exchange. For this to happen, U.S. Steel had to redesign its databases and data collection procedures. To complete the integration, E-steel.com partnered with Ford, offering the automaker its ValueTrack program. The strategic alliance covers Ford's steel-supply program, and includes Ford's tier-1 suppliers. The joint program is aimed at eliminating manual processes and giving the complete supply chain access to the same database of inventory, ordering, and pricing information.

Sources: Compiled from Stackpole, 2000; *InteractiveWeek*, January 17, 2000; *steel-net.com*; and *worldsteel.org*.

Questions

1. A variety of smaller, or niche, exchanges compete with *e-steel.com*. These include *materialnet.com* and *isteelasia.com*. Investigate the services offered by and the nature of such competition.

2. *E-steel.com* deals with sellers, such as U.S. Steel, and buyers, such as Ford Motor Co. E-steel.com also reaches Ford's other tier-1 suppliers. At the same time, Ford, through Covisint, can reach not only U.S. Steel, but also U.S. Steel's suppliers and sub-suppliers. This could create confusion. Why not just merge E-steel.com into Covisint?

3. *E-steel.com* expects to generate revenue by building and selling specialized software applications for its exchange for a specific buyer's industry (e.g., automotive). How can it do this?

4. What value-added services can *E-steel.com* provide to sellers in the exchange?

INTRABUSINESS, E-GOVERNMENT, C2C, E-LEARNING, AND MORE

Content

Learning objectives

Upon completion of this chapter, you will be able to:

▶ Define intrabusiness e-commerce and describe its major activities.

▶ Describe the intranet and its use in organizations.

▶ Understand the relationship between corporate portals and intranets.

▶ Describe e-government to citizens (G2C) and to business (G2B).

▶ Describe various e-government initiatives.

▶ Understand how peer-to-peer technology works in intrabusiness, in B2B, and in C2C e-commerce.

▶ Discuss online publishing and e-books.

▶ Describe e-learning and virtual universities.

▶ Describe knowledge management and dissemination.

E-LEARNING AT CISCO

The Problem

Cisco Systems is one of the fastest growing high-tech companies in the world, selling devices that connect computers and networks to the Internet and other networks. Cisco's products are continuously being upgraded or replaced, so extensive training of employees and customers is needed. Cisco has recognized that its employees, business partners, and independent students seeking professional certification all require training on a regular basis. Traditional classroom training was flawed by its inability to scale rapidly enough. Cisco offered in-house classes 6 to 10 times a year, but the rapid growth in the number of students coupled with the fast pace of technological change made the training both expensive and ineffective.

The Solution

Cisco believes that *e-learning* is a revolutionary way to empower its workforce with the skills and knowledge needed to turn technological change to an advantage. Therefore, Cisco implemented e-learning programs that allow students to self-learn new software, hardware, and procedures. Cisco believes that once people experience e-learning, they will recognize that it is the fastest, easiest way to get the information they need to be successful.

To encourage its employees to use e-learning, Cisco:

- Makes e-learning "nonthreatening" by using an anonymous testing and scoring process that focuses on helping people improve rather than penalizing those who fail.
- Gives those who fail the tests precision learning targets (modules, exercises, or written materials) to help them pass and remove the fear associated with testing.
- Enables people to track, manage, and ensure employee development, competency change, and, ultimately, performance change.
- Offers additional incentives and rewards such as stock grants, promotions, and bonuses to employ-

ees who pursue specialization and certification through e-learning.

- Adds e-learning as a strategic top-down metric for Cisco executives, who are measured on their deployment of it in their departments.
- Makes e-learning a mandatory part of employees' jobs.
- Offers easy access to e-learning tools via the Web.

Cisco also wants to serve as a model of e-learning for its customers, hoping to convince them to use e-learning programs.

Cisco operates E-Learning Centers for Excellence that offer training at Cisco's center as well as at customers' sites via intranets and the Internet. Some of the training requires the use of partnering vendors. Cisco offers a variety of training programs supported by e-learning. For example, in 2001, Cisco converted a popular $4\frac{1}{2}$–day, instructor-led training (ILT) course on Cisco's signature IOS (interorganizational information system) technologies into an e-learning program that blends both live and self-paced components. The goal was to teach seasoned systems engineers (SEs) how to sell, install, configure, and maintain those key IOS technologies, and to do so in a way that would train more people than the 25 employees the ILT course could hold.

The Results

On the IOS course alone, Cisco calculated its return on investment as follows:

- It cost $12,400 for labor to develop the blended course.
- The course saved each SE 1 productivity day and 20 percent of the travel and lodging cost of a 1-week training course in San Jose. Estimating $750 for travel and lodging and $450 for the productivity day, the savings totaled $1,200 per SE.
- Seventeen SEs attended the course the first time it was offered, for a total savings of $20,400. Cisco

therefore recovered the development costs in the first offering—and saved $8,000 over and above the development costs. Since March 2001, the IOS Learning Services team has presented two classes of 40 SEs per month. At that rate, Cisco saves $1,152,000 net for just this one course every 12 months.

In 2001, there were 10,000 corporate salespeople, 150,000 employees of business partners, and 200,000 independent students all taking courses at Cisco learning centers. By 2002, Cisco had developed 75 e-learning courses and was planning to develop many more soon.

What We Can Learn . . .

This opening vignette demonstrates the application of e-learning as an efficient training tool. E-learning is frequently delivered over the corporate intranet, and the corporate portal is used as the gateway to this training. Cisco's application is also an example of intrabusiness e-

commerce. All of these topics—intrabusiness EC, intranets, corporate portals, and e-learning—are covered in this chapter. We will also examine e-government, C2C applications, and e-publishing.

Source: Miscellaneous news items at *Cisco.com* (2001).

7.1   INTRABUSINESS AND BUSINESS-TO-EMPLOYEE E-COMMERCE

As indicated in Chapter 1, e-commerce is conducted not only between business partners, but also *within* an organization. Such within-the-company EC activity is referred to as **intrabusiness EC**, or, in short, *intrabusiness*. Intrabusiness can be done:

> between a business and its employees.

> between units within the business.

> among employees in the same business.

intrabusiness EC
E-commerce activities conducted *within* an organization.

BUSINESS-TO-EMPLOYEE EC

Intrabusiness in which an organization delivers products or services to its employees is termed **business-to-employee (B2E)**. Some representative applications of B2E include:

> Training and education is provided over intranets.

> Employees electronically order supplies and material needed for their work using the corporation's electronic catalogs and ordering forms.

> Employees can make purchases via the corporate intranet for discounted insurance, travel packages, and tickets to events.

> Many companies have corporate stores that sell a company's products to its employees, usually at a discount. The employees place orders on the intranet, and the store will pack and deliver the items to the employees, at work or at home. Payment is then deducted from payroll or paid with the employee's personal credit card.

> Businesses disseminate information to employees on the intranet.

> Employees communicate with each other and share knowledge with teleconferencing applications, electronic discussion groups, and knowledge management systems.

> Businesses allow employees to manage their fringe benefits, take classes, and much more, all electronically.

business-to-employee (B2E)
Intrabusiness in which an organization delivers products or services to its employees.

Several other applications are described later in this chapter (Sections 7.2 and 7.3).

ACTIVITIES BETWEEN UNITS WITHIN A BUSINESS

Large corporations frequently consist of independent units, called strategic business units (SBUs), which "sell" or "buy" materials, products, and services from each other. Transactions of this type can be easily automated and performed over the intranet. An SBU can be either a seller or a buyer.

Many large corporations also have a network of dealerships that are usually wholly or partially owned by the corporation. In such cases, a special network is constructed to support communication, collaboration, and execution of transactions between headquarters and the dealerships. Such intrabusiness commerce is conducted by auto dealers, equipment manufacturers (e.g., Caterpillar), and most other large manufacturers. EC Application Case 7.1 discusses intrabusiness commerce at the consumer-products company Toshiba America.

EC APPLICATION CASE 7.1
Intraorganization and Collaboration

INTRABUSINESS E-COMMERCE AT TOSHIBA AMERICA

Toshiba America works with 300 dealers that sell its consumer-electronics products. Dealers who needed product parts quickly had to place a telephone or fax order by 2:00 P.M. for next-day delivery. To handle the express shipments, Toshiba's Electronic Imaging Division (EID), a maker of fax machines and copiers, spent $1.3 million annually on communications and charged $25 per shipment to the dealers. In addition, dealers had to pay the overnight shipping fee. A cumbersome order-entry system was created in 1993, but no significant improvement was achieved.

In August 1997, Toshiba created a Web-based order-entry system for product parts using an extranet/intranet. Dealers can now place orders for parts until 5:00 P.M. for next-day delivery. The company placed a physical warehouse in Memphis, Tennessee, near FedEx headquarters, to ensure quick delivery. On the intranet, dealers can also check accounts receivable balances and pricing arrangements and read service bulletins, press releases, and so on.

Once an order is submitted, a computer checks for the part's availability. If the part is available, the order is sent electronically to Toshiba's warehouse in Memphis. Once at the warehouse site, the order pops up on a handheld wireless radio frequency (RF) monitor for quick fulfillment. Within a few hours,

the part is packed, verified, and packaged for FedEx. (See the book's Web site, *prenhall.com/turban*, for a figure that illustrates this process.)

The intranet also allows sales reps to interact more effectively with dealers. The dealers can be kept up-to-date about orders and inventory and can manage their volume discount quotes online.

Using the intrabusiness system, Toshiba has cut the cost per express order to about $10. EID's networking costs have been reduced by more than 50 percent (to $600,000 a year). The low shipping cost results in overnight delivery of 98 percent of its orders, which increases customer satisfaction. The site processes more than 85 percent of all dealers' orders.

Source: L. McCreary, 1999.

Questions

▶ What are the benefits of Toshiba's intranet to the dealers?

▶ What are the wireless devices used for?

▶ What role does FedEx play in the order-fulfillment process?

ACTIVITIES AMONG CORPORATE EMPLOYEES

Many large organizations have classified ads on the intranet through which employees can buy and sell personal products and services from each other. This service is especially popular in universities, where it was conducted even before the commercialization of the Internet. In addition to buying and selling activities, employees collaborate and communicate using EC technologies.

As the various examples in this section have indicated, the most popular infrastructure for intrabusiness is the intranet, which is described in the following section.

▶ List the major intrabusiness EC categories.

▶ Describe B2E EC.

▶ Describe EC activities among business units.

▶ Describe EC among corporate employees.

7.2 INTRANETS

As we defined it in Chapter 6, an **intranet** is a corporate LAN or WAN that uses Internet technology and is secured behind a company's firewalls. This "internal network," or internal Web, is a network architecture designed to serve the internal informational needs of a company, using Web concepts and tools. An intranet uses Internet technology and capabilities, such as easy and effective browsing, search engines, and tools for communication and collaboration. Using a Web browser, managers can view employee resumes, business plans, and corporate regulations and procedures; they can retrieve sales data, review any desired document, and call a meeting. Employees can check availability of software for particular tasks and test the software from their workstations.

Intranets frequently have a secure connection to the Internet, enabling the company to conduct e-commerce activities, such as cooperating with suppliers and customers or checking a customer's inventory level before making shipments. Such activities are facilitated by *extranets*, as described in Chapter 6. Using screen sharing and other groupware tools, intranets can also be used to facilitate the work of groups. Companies also publish newsletters and deliver news to their employees on intranets and conduct online training. Intranets are fairly safe, operating within the company's firewalls (see Chapter 9). Employees can venture out onto the Internet, but unauthorized users cannot enter the intranet. Finally, intranets can change organizational structures and procedures and help reengineer corporations.

The cost of converting an existing client-server network to an intranet is relatively low, especially when a company is already using the Internet. Many computing facilities can be shared by both the Internet and intranets. An example of this is a client-server-based electronic conferencing software module from Pixion (pixion.com) that allows users to share documents, graphics, and video in real time. This capability can be combined with an electronic voice arrangement.

According to a Meta Group study (Stellin 2001), nearly 90 percent of all U.S. corporations have some type of intranet, and over 25 percent are using corporate

intranet
A corporate LAN or wide area network (WAN) that uses Internet technology and is secured behind a company's firewalls; designed to serve the internal informational needs of a company.

portals that perform functions well beyond just publishing material on the intranet (see Section 7.3).

Intranets are structured on one or several LANs. In multilocation corporations, WANs are used. EC Application Case 7.2 illustrates the use of a wireless LAN and the benefits it offers in accessing a hospital intranet and other applications.

MORE INTRANET EXAMPLES

Intranets can be used for a variety of business functions, as shown by the following examples.

- **Business intelligence.** In 2000, Financial Times (FT) Electronic Publishing implemented its online news and information service, FT Discovery, for 10,000 intranet users at KPMG Peat Marwick, one of the Big Five accounting firms. FT Discovery is integrated into the KPMG corporate intranet to provide immediate access to critical business intelligence from over 4,000 information sources. For example, corporate Navigator from Story Street Partners is integrated into the intranet to provide in-depth advice on where to go for information on the issues and companies of interest to KPMG (Firstcall.com, 1999).

- **Public services.** All the Hawaiian islands are linked by a state educational, medical, and public services network (htdc.org). This ambitious intranet provides quality services to residents of all the Hawaiian islands.

EC APPLICATION CASE 7.2

Implementation and Strategy

WIRELESS LANS SPEED HOSPITAL INSURANCE PAYMENTS

Bridgeton is a U.S. holding company that operates four hospitals in New Jersey. The company uses wireless LANs to process insurance documentation to reduce the number of claims denied by insurers. Nurses log on to the network using notebook computers to access the hospital's intranet, pharmacy, and labs and to use e-mail. The nurses aggregate all the documents needed by the insurance company and submit them electronically.

The network environment supports an intranet and broadcasts data over a distance of about 120 feet from nursing workstations. Nurses can move from the station into patient rooms while maintaining a network connection. As a nurse takes a notebook computer from one nursing station to another, the radio card in the notebook computer goes into a roaming mode similar to a cellular phone. The wireless environment enabled changes in business processes; many of these processes are now done faster and with fewer errors.

The company is getting a good return on investment, with savings in six-figure dollar amounts for the moderate cost of setting up the network (about $200 for each notebook computer radio card and $750 for each of 28 wireless access points).

Source: J. Cope, April 10, 2000.

Questions

- What role does the intranet play in the hospital?
- Can this case be classified as mobile commerce? Why or why not?

▶ **Corporate information.** Employees at IBM ranked the intranet as the most useful and credible source of corporate information. They use the intranet to order supplies, sign up for fringe benefits, take classes, track projects, and manage their retirement plans. IBM considers its intranet an extremely valuable source of information that helps increase productivity. For example, managers can post and read information about projects in progress without bothering people, making calls, or sending e-mails. IBM employees who telecommute can log onto the intranet from home and conduct work. In May 2001, IBM asked its employees to contribute ideas for solving some current problems. More than 6,000 suggestions were collected over the intranet in just 3 days (Holmesreport.com, 1999).

▶ **Customer service.** At Charles Schwab, 25,000 employees use the intranet (Sch Web) regularly. It helps employees provide better customer service, because it makes responding to customers' inquiries much easier. Using search engines, employees can quickly find the answers they need without asking other employees. It is now part of Schwab's culture to look at the intranet first in order to find answers. Schwab estimates tens of millions of dollars in savings due to its intranet (Informationweek.com News, 2001).

BUILDING INTRANETS

To build an intranet, a company needs Web servers, browsers, Web publishing tools, back-end databases, TCP/IP networks (LAN or WAN), and firewalls, as shown in Exhibit 7.1. A *firewall* is software and/or hardware that allows only those external users with specific characteristics to access a protected network (see Chapter 9). Additional software may be necessary to support Web-based workflow, groupware, and enterprise resource planning (ERP), depending upon the

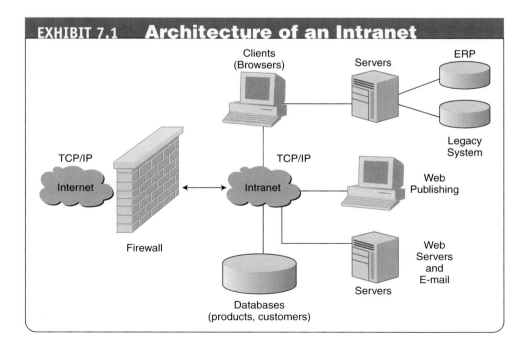

EXHIBIT 7.1   Architecture of an Intranet

individual company's needs. Security schemes, which are basically the same for intranets and for the Internet, are described in Chapter 9.

A company may have one intranet composed of many LANs. Alternatively, a company may have several interconnected intranets, each composed of only a few LANs. The decision of how to structure the intranet depends on how dispersed the LANs are and what technologies are involved.

In building an intranet, network architects need to consider and plan for the functionalities the network will need.

INTRANET FUNCTIONALITIES

Intranets have some or all of the following functionalities:

- Web-based database access for ease of use.
- Search engines, indexing engines, and directories that assist in keyword-based searches.
- Interactive communication tools such as chatting, audio support, and video-conferencing.
- Document distribution and workflow, including Web-based downloading and routing of documents.
- Groupware, including enhanced e-mail, bulletin boards, screen sharing, and other group support tools.
- Conduit for the computer-based telephony system.

In addition, intranets usually have the ability to integrate with EC applications and interface with Internet-based electronic purchasing, payment, and delivery applications. They also can be part of extranets, so that geographically dispersed branches, customers, and suppliers can access certain portions of the intranets. These functions provide for numerous applications that increase productivity, reduce costs, reduce waste and cycle time, and improve customer service, as discussed in the following section.

INTRANET APPLICATION AREAS

According to a survey conducted by *InformationWeek* in 1998, with nearly a thousand responding managers, the information that is most frequently included in intranets is in the form of product catalogs (49 percent of all companies), corporate policies and procedures (35 percent), purchase ordering (42 percent), document sharing (39 percent), corporate phone directories (40 percent), and human resource forms (35 percent) (McGee, 1998). Also included, in lower percentages, were training programs, customer databases, data warehouse and decision support access, image archives, and travel reservation services. These figures are probably much higher today, as intranets have matured over the past few years.

In addition to the many activities just discussed, intranets provide benefits in the following ways:

- **Search and access to documents.** The intranet provides access to information that can increase productivity and facilitate teamwork.

▶ **Personalized information.** The intranet can deliver personalized information via personalized Web pages and e-mail.

▶ **Enhanced knowledge sharing.** The Web-based intranet can encourage knowledge sharing among company employees.

▶ **Individual decision making.** Employees can make better decisions because they can easily access the right information and online expertise.

▶ **Software distribution.** Using the intranet server as the application warehouse helps eliminate many maintenance and support problems.

▶ **Document management.** Employees can access pictures, photos, charts, maps, and other documents regardless of where they are stored or where the employees are located.

▶ **Project management.** Most project management activities are conducted over intranets.

▶ **Training.** A corporate Web page is a valuable source of information for employees. Employee training can be done through online classes over the intranet.

▶ **Enhanced transaction processing.** Data can be entered just one time into a database connected to an intranet, thus eliminating errors and increasing internal control.

▶ **Paperless information delivery.** Elimination of paper by disseminating information on the intranet can result in lower costs, easier accessibility to information, less paper to maintain, and increased security.

▶ **Employees control their own information.** Employees can check their annual vacation-day status, change their postal address, tax status, or retirement fund allocation.

When intranets are combined with an external connection to create an extranet, these additional benefits occur:

▶ **Electronic commerce.** Intrabusiness marketing can be done online; selling to outsiders is done via the extranet, involving portions of the intranet.

▶ **Customer service.** UPS, FedEx, and other companies have shown that information about product shipment and availability increases customer satisfaction. Again, the intranet-extranet combination is used in such applications.

▶ **Enhanced group decision making and business processes.** Web-based groupware and workflow are becoming part of the standard intranet platform. These can also be part of the internal supply chain operation.

▶ **Virtual organizations.** Web technology removes the barrier of incompatible technology between business partners.

▶ **Improved administrative processes.** The internal management of production, inventory, procurement, shipping, and distribution can be effectively supported by linking these functions in a single threaded environment (the intranet). These functions can also be seamlessly integrated with interorganizational extranets.

INDUSTRY-SPECIFIC INTRANET SOLUTIONS

Intranet solutions are frequently classified by industry instead of by technology. According to *InformationWeek Online* (informationweek.com), the top 100 intranet and extranet solutions can be classified by industry as follows: financial services (banking, brokerages, other financial services, and insurance); information technology; manufacturing (chemicals and oil, consumer goods, food and beverage, general manufacturing, and pharmaceuticals); retail; and service providers (construction/engineering, education, environmental, health care, media, entertainment, telecommunications, transportation, and utilities). Internet applications are very diversified, as shown in the list of six industry-specific intranets in online Appendix 7.1 (see prenhall.com/turban).

▶ Define intranet.

▶ How is an intranet secured?

▶ Describe some intranet applications.

▶ List five intranet functionalities.

▶ List five intranet application areas.

7.3 ENTERPRISE (CORPORATE) PORTALS

Portals and corporate portals were presented in Chapter 2. Here we provide some examples of how corporate portals interface with the intranet to support B2E e-commerce.

CORPORATE PORTALS AND INTRANETS

corporate (enterprise) portal
A gateway for entering a corporate Web site, enabling communication, collaboration, and access to company information.

A **corporate (enterprise) portal** is a gateway to a corporate Web site, enabling communication, collaboration, and access to company information. Kounadis (2000) more formally defines a corporate portal as a personalized, single point of access through a Web browser to critical business information located inside and outside of an organization. In contrast with publishing and commercial portals such as Yahoo!, which are only gateways to general information on the Internet, corporate portals provide single-point access to specific enterprise information and applications available on the Internet, intranets, and extranets. Companies may have separate portals for outsiders and for insiders.

Corporate portals are an extended form of an intranet that offer employees, business partners, and customers an organized focal point for their interactions with the firm. Through the portal, these people can have structured and personalized access to information across large, multiple, and disparate enterprise information systems, as well as the Internet. A schematic view of a corporate portal is provided in Exhibit 7.2.

Many large organizations are already implementing corporate portals to cut costs, free up time for busy executives and managers, and add to the bottom line.

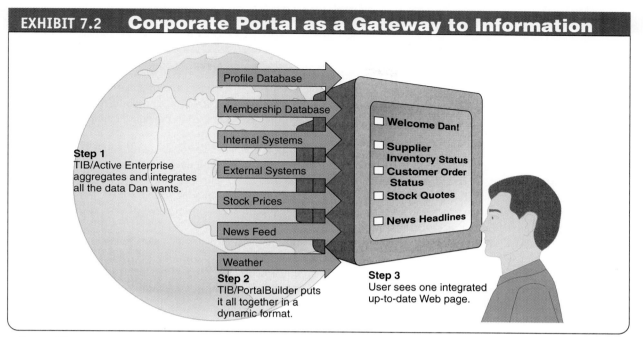

EXHIBIT 7.2   Corporate Portal as a Gateway to Information

Profile Database

Membership Database

Internal Systems

External Systems

Stock Prices

News Feed

Weather

Step 1
TIB/Active Enterprise aggregates and integrates all the data Dan wants.

Step 2
TIB/PortalBuilder puts it all together in a dynamic format.

□ **Welcome Dan!**

□ **Supplier Inventory Status**
□ **Customer Order Status**
□ **Stock Quotes**
□ **News Headlines**

Step 3
User sees one integrated up-to-date Web page.

Source: *Tibco.com*.

(See ROI white papers and report at plumtree.com.) Corporate portals are popular in large corporations, as shown in the Insights and Additions box on page 300.

CORPORATE PORTAL APPLICATIONS

According to a Delphi Group survey (delphigroup.com, 1999), the top portal applications, in decreasing order of importance, are as follows.

- Knowledge bases and learning tools
- Business process support
- Customer-facing sales, marketing, and services
- Collaboration and project support
- Access to data from disparate corporate systems
- Personalized pages for various users
- Effective search and indexing tools
- Security applications
- Best practices and lessons learned
- Directories and bulletin boards
- Identification of experts
- News
- Internet access

In Chapter 5, we described collaborative commerce (c-commerce) as taking place when employees of different organization work together. Note that intranets can

Insights and Additions   Corporate Portals at Procter & Gamble, DuPont, and Staples

Procter & Gamble's (P&G) IT division developed a system for sharing documents and information over the company's intranet. The scope of this system has expanded into a global knowledge catalogue to support the information needs of all 97,000 of P&G's employees worldwide. Although the system helped in providing required information, it also led to information overload.

To solve this problem, P&G developed a corporate portal that provides personalized information to each employee and that can be accessed through a Web browser without having to navigate through 14 different Web sites. P&G's corporate portal, implemented by Plumtree (*plumtree.com*), provides P&G's employees with marketing, product, and strategic information, and with industry-news documents numbering over 1 million Web pages. Employees can gain access to the required information through customized preset views of various information sources and links to other up-to-date information.

DuPont & Co. implemented an internal portal to organize millions of pages of scientific information stored in information systems throughout the company. The initial version of the portal was intended for daily use by over 550 employees to record product orders, retrieve progress reports for research products, and access customer-tracking information. DuPont plans to extend the portal to between 20,000 to 60,000 employees in 30 business units in various countries.

Staples' corporate portal, launched in February 2000, is used by 3,000 executives, knowledge workers, and store managers. Staples is expecting that the portal will grow to support 10,000 of its 46,000 employees and serve as their interface to business processes and applications. The portal is used by top management, as well as by managers of contracts, procurement, sales and marketing, human resources, and retail stores. It is also used by Staples' three B2B Web sites. The portal offers e-mail, scheduling, headlines on articles about the competition, new product information, internal news, job postings, and newsletters.

Sources: S. Konicki, May 1, 2000.

contribute to c-commerce efforts *within* organizations when employees from different units within one company collaborate using intranets and the corporate portal.

Exhibit 7.3 depicts a corporate portal framework. This framework illustrates the features and capabilities required to support various organizational applications using internal and external information sources.

Developing Portals

Before a company can develop a corporate portal, it must decide what the purpose and content of the portal will be. For some practical guidelines for determining a corporate portal strategy, see the Insights and Additions box on page 302. Many vendors offer tools for building government and corporate portals, as well as hosting services. Representative vendors are tibco.com (Portal Builder), Computer Associates (Jasmine II Portal at ca.com), and Plumtree (plumtree.com).

EXHIBIT 7.3   *Corporate Portal Framework*

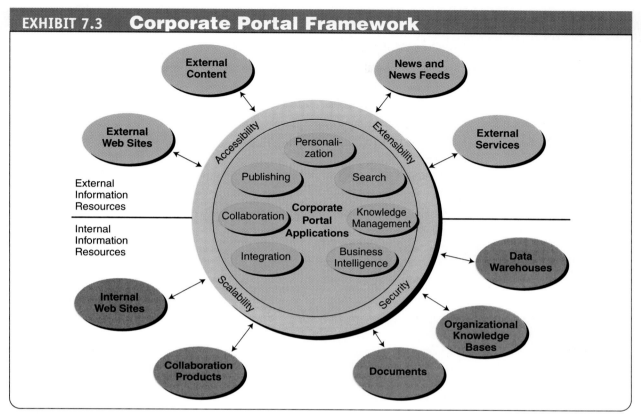

Sources: Compiled by N. Bolloju, City University of Hong Kong, from Aneja et al., 2000, and Kounadis, 2000.

INTRANET/PORTAL EXAMPLE: CADENCE DESIGN SYSTEMS

Here we present an extended example of the successful design and implementation of an intranet and a corporate portal by Cadence Design Systems, Inc. The company is a leading supplier of electronic design automation (EDA) software tools and professional services for managing and accelerating the design of semiconductors, computer systems, networking and telecommunications equipment, consumer electronics, and other electronics-related products. The San Jose-based company employs more than 3,000 people worldwide to support the development requirements of the world's leading electronics manufacturers.

The Business Challenge

Early in 1995, Cadence recognized that the business model for EDA products was beginning to evolve from a tools-oriented model to one where software and consulting services held the potential for the greatest revenue growth.

To understand and address this changing model, Cadence identified two areas of customer interaction: sales and logistics. The new sales strategy required the sales force to have an in-depth understanding of Cadence's product line of almost 1,000 products and services. With two separate organizations, sales and logistics,

Insights and Additions   Key Steps to Corporate Portal Strategy

▶ Identify the content that is or will be available and identify where this content resides.

▶ Leverage existing systems, resources, and repositories.

▶ Include both structured and unstructured information.

▶ Organize content into categories that can be browsed and searched.

▶ Integrate search functionality across multiple information repositories.

▶ Build a platform for publishing and subscribing to content.

▶ Deliver personalized content and services to users based on their responsibilities and roles.

▶ Develop the corporate portal in phases.

▶ Create online communities to connect people and enable collaborative work.

▶ Develop an extensible architecture that allows for extended functionality.

▶ Sustain a collaborative portal by institutionalizing it within daily business operations and weaving it into long-term strategies.

▶ Purchase an integrated portal product rather than building custom portal functionality.

Source: Extracted from A. Aneja, et al., 2000.

interacting with customers, coordination and communication were needed to ensure an effective and consistent relationship built on a real understanding of the customer's issues.

The Solution: Intranet and Portal Technology

For almost a year, Cadence worked with a consulting firm to create a corporate portal and intranet to support its sales organization. The system, called OnTrack, uses a home page with links to other pages, information sources, and custom applications to map each phase of the sales process with supporting materials and reference information.

With OnTrack, the sales representative now has a single unified tool that provides all the information and data needed for the sales process, from finding new clients to closing a deal to managing the account. In addition, global account teams have their own home pages where they can collaborate and share information. However, OnTrack is much more than a static road map. For example, information on a customer or competitor is now available instantly through access to an outside provider of custom news. The sales rep can also use a search engine to locate everything from financial information to recent news articles and press releases about clients or competitors. In addition, the intranet is used to disseminate Cadence news and other information.

All creators of information in the company, from sales reps to marketing and management personnel, are responsible for maintaining the information contained in OnTrack. With a wide range of people entering data, a simple-to-use information submission process was needed. To avoid the need to understand HTML, electronic forms were created to allow submission or modification of any part of the information in the OnTrack system. Anyone with appropriate access can now add a new message to the daily alerts, modify a step in the sales process, or update a customer presentation by using these custom tools.

Feedback is also a key part of OnTrack. Reports highlight frequently accessed pages and documents, and reviews of frequent searches identify new information to include in the system to make critical information even easier to access.

Lessons Learned

Managers who made the decision to implement the OnTrack system learned several lessons. First, balancing the cost of training against returns is a difficult task. Although the use of a browser and the navigation of a Web page required only minimal employee training, the application of the OnTrack system to the daily activities of the sales reps was not as easy. OnTrack supported a reengineering of the sales process, and Cadence now believes that demonstrating the use of OnTrack and its support of sales activities might have accelerated the use of the system.

A second key to success was the holistic approach Cadence took in unifying the technology with the process. Rather than mandate a new process or install a new software system, Cadence did both. The combination of an easy-to-use technology, a refined process, and the appropriate support systems created a single coherent system that could support the new sales paradigm.

Cadence also worked to design a process and infrastructure that could satisfy 80 percent rather than 100 percent of the sales situations. This strategy helped the company in two ways. First, it is often more effective to refine a system after gaining experience than to attempt to design the perfect system from the beginning. Second, a process that can address all possible exceptions is often an exercise in futility. One reason that the Cadence system has worked so well is its focus on supporting the bulk of the work process rather than the entire process.

OnTrack was implemented at a relatively low cost. Cadence leveraged its existing infrastructure and wisely hired outside experts to create the application rather than devoting internal resources to it. This choice allowed the company to focus its efforts on defining the process and tools needed to support the sales force rather than designing software. Cadence calculates that OnTrack has achieved a high return on investment, 1,766 percent!

Finally, the greatest impact of OnTrack has been the result of the shortened training time for new sales reps. A new salesperson stated that he had learned in two days from OnTrack what it took months to learn at a previous company. With 40 new reps hired in the first year, and 40 planned for each of the next 2 years, reducing the training time for new sales personnel has created additional profits for Cadence.

▸ What is a corporate portal?

▸ List the benefits of corporate portals.

▸ List five applications of portals.

▸ What did Cadence seek to achieve by implementing an intranet and corporate portal?

7.4 E-GOVERNMENT: AN OVERVIEW

SCOPE AND DEFINITION

As e-commerce matures and its tools and applications improve, greater attention is being given to its use to improve the business of public institutions and governments (country, state, county, city, etc.). Several international conferences were held in 2000 and 2001 to explore the potential of what is called e-government. **E-government** is the use of information technology in general, and e-commerce in particular, to provide citizens and organizations with more convenient access to government information and services and to provide delivery of public services to citizens, business partners, and those working in the public sector. It is also an efficient and effective way of conducting business transactions with citizens and other businesses and within the governments themselves. In short, e-government is the application of information technology and EC to the processes of government.

E-government in the United States was especially driven by the 1998 Government Paperwork Elimination Act and by President Clinton's December 17, 1999, Memorandum on E-Government, which ordered the top 500 forms used by citizens to be placed online by December 2000. The memorandum also directed agencies to construct a secure e-government infrastructure.

Some use the term e-government to mean an extension of e-commerce to government procurement. This use of the term views e-government only in the realm of B2G (business-to-government) transactions (International Trade Center-Executive Forum 2000, intracen.org/execforum/ef2000/eb200010.htm). However, we will use the term in the broader context given earlier—the bringing together of governments, citizens, and businesses in a network of information, knowledge, and commerce.

In that broader view, e-government is both the advent of a new form of government and the birth of a new market. It offers an opportunity to improve the efficiency and effectiveness of the functions of government, and to make government more transparent to citizens and businesses by providing access to more of the information generated by government.

Within our broad definition of e-government, there are several major categories: government-to-citizens, government-to-business, government-to-government, and government-to-employees. We will look at each of them, in turn, in the following sections.

GOVERNMENT-TO-CITIZENS

In the **government-to-citizens (G2C)** category of e-government, we include all the interactions between a government and its citizens that can take place electronically. As shown in the Real-World Case at the end of the chapter about Hong Kong, G2C involves dozens of different initiatives. The basic idea is to enable citizens to interact with the government from their homes. Citizens can ask questions of government agencies and receive answers, pay taxes, receive payments and documents, and so forth. Governments can disseminate information on the Web, conduct training, help citizens find employment, and more. In California, for example, drivers' education classes are offered online, and can be taken anytime, anywhere.

e-government
The use of IT and e-commerce to provide access to government information and delivery of public services to citizens and business partners.

government-to-citizens (G2C)
E-government category that includes all the interactions between a government and its citizens.

Government agencies and departments in many cities, counties, and countries are planning more and more diverse e-services. For example, many governments are now seriously considering electronic voting. In some countries, voters actually see their choice on the computer screen and are asked to confirm their vote, much as is done when purchasing a book online from amazon.com, transferring funds, or selling stocks. (For further discussion of online voting, see Schwartz 2000.)

Electronic Benefits Transfer

The United States government transfers more than $500 billion in benefits annually to its citizens. More than 20 percent of these transfers go to citizens who do not have bank accounts. In 1993, the U.S. government launched an initiative to develop a nationwide *electronic benefits transfer* (EBT) system to deliver government benefits electronically. When implemented, this approach will rely on the use of a smart card loaded with credits for cash and food benefits. Benefit recipients will be able to use the card at automated teller machines and point-of-sale locations, just like other bank card users do with their smart cards (see Chapter 10).

The U.S. federal government is implementing a nationwide EBT system for miscellaneous payments, such as those for Social Security and welfare. Agencies at the federal, state, and local levels are expanding EBT programs into new areas, including health, nutrition, employment, and education. Most states operate EBT systems for state-provided benefits.

The basic idea of EBT is that recipients will either get electronic transfers to their bank accounts or be able to download money to their smart cards. The advantage is not only the reduction in processing costs from 50 cents per check to 2 cents, but also the reduction of fraud. With biometrics coming to smart cards and PCs, officials expect fraud to be reduced substantially. Governments also use smart cards as purchasing media for procurement. For more information on EBT in government, see fns.usda.gov.

GOVERNMENT-TO-BUSINESS

Governments seek to automate their interactions with businesses. Although we call this category **government-to-business (G2B)**, the relationship works two ways: government-to-business and business-to-government. Thus G2B refers to e-commerce in which government sells to businesses and provides them with services, as well as to businesses selling products and services to government. Two G2B areas that receive a lot of attention are e-procurement and the auctioning of government surpluses.

government-to-business (G2B) E-government category that includes interactions between governments and businesses (government selling to businesses and providing them with services, and businesses selling products and services to government).

E-Procurement

Governments buy large amounts of MROs and other materials direct from many suppliers. In many cases, an RFQ or tendering system is mandated by law. For years, these requisitions were done manually; the systems are now moving online. In principle, the systems are basically *reverse auctions*, such as those described in Chapter 5 (buy-side systems). An example of a reverse auction used for G2B procurement in Hong Kong is briefly described in the Real-World Case at the end of the chapter (and at info.gov.hk). For additional information about such reverse auctions, see gsa.gov. Governments provide all the support for such tendering systems, as shown in EC Application Case 7.3.

E-Auctions

Many governments auction surplus goods ranging from vehicles to foreclosed real estate. Such auctions used to be done manually, then over private networks. These auctions are now moving online. Governments can use third-party auction sites

---

EC APPLICATION CASE 7.3
Individuals and Communities
CONTRACT MANAGEMENT IN AUSTRALIA

The focus of the Western Australian (WA) government agency Contract and Management Services (CAMS) is to develop online contract management solutions for the public sector. CAMS Online allows government agencies to search existing contracts to discover how to access the commonly used contracts across government. It also assists suppliers wanting to sell to the government. Suppliers can view the current tenders (bids) on the Western Australia Government Contracting Information Bulletin Board and download tender documents from this site.

CAMS Online provides government departments and agencies with unbiased expert advice on e-commerce, Internet, and satellite services, and how-to's on building a bridge between the technological needs of the public sector and the expertise of the private sector. The center offers various types of support for government procurement activities.

Support of E-Commerce Activities

WA's e-commerce activities include electronic markets for government buying. Government clients can purchase goods and services on the *CAMS Internet Marketplace*, which provides services ranging from sending a purchase order to receiving an invoice and paying for an item. The *WA government electronic market* provides online supplier catalogs, electronic purchase orders, and electronic invoicing, EFT, and check and credit card payments. Other e-commerce functions are *ProcureLink*, an established CAMS service that sends electronic purchase orders to suppliers for EDI, EDI Post (an online hybrid mail service),

facsimile, and the Internet; *SalesNet*, by which the government secures credit card payments for the sale of government goods and services across the Internet; and *DataLink*, which enables the transfer of data using a secure and controlled environment for message management. DataLink is an ideal solution for government agencies needing to exchange large volumes of operational information.

Training Online

In addition to G2B functions, the site also offers citizens online training. A service called *Westlink* delivers adult training and educational programs to remote areas and schools, including rural and regional communities. A videoconferencing service offers two-way video and audio links, enabling government employees to meet together electronically from up to eight sites at any one time.

Access to the Online Services Centre is given to government employees and businesses that deal with the government via the CAMS Web site at *business.wa.gov.au*.

Source: *wa.gov.au/business*, February 2001.

Questions

▶ How is contract management facilitated by e-commerce tools?

▶ What other e-commerce activities are performed by the government?

▶ Describe the WA online training program.

such as eBay, bid4assets.com, or freemarkets.com for this purpose. In January 2001, the U.S. General Services Administration (GSA) launched a property auction site online (auctionrp.com) where real-time auctions for surpluses and seized goods are conducted. Some of these auctions are restricted to dealers; others are open to the public (see govexec.com).

GOVERNMENT-TO-GOVERNMENT

The **government-to-government (G2G)** category includes all intragovernmental EC activities, primarily those among different units within one governmental body, but also those between governments. Some examples of G2G in the United States include:

government-to-government (G2G)
E-government category that includes activities within government units and those between governments.

▶ **Intelink.** Intelink is an intranet that carries classified information shared by the numerous U.S. intelligence agencies.

▶ **Procurement at GSA.** The GSA's Web site, gsa.gov, is an experiment in technologies such as demand aggregation and reverse auctions. This site seeks to apply innovative Web-based procurement methods to government buying.

▶ **Federal Case Registry (Department of Health and Human Services).** This service helps state governments locate information about child support, including data on paternity and enforcement. It is available at acf.dhhs.gov/programs/cse/newhire/fcr/fcr.htm.

▶ **Procurement Marketing and Access Network (Small Business Administration).** This service (pro-net.sba.gov) presents PRO-Net, a searchable database that contracting officers can use to find products and services sold by small, disadvantaged, or women-owned businesses.

For more examples of G2G services, see the Real-World Case at the end of the chapter and at govexec.com.

GOVERNMENT-TO-EMPLOYEES

Governments employ large numbers of people. Therefore, they are just as interested as private-sector organizations are in electronically providing services and information to their employees. Indeed, because employees of federal and state governments often work in a variety of geographic locations, **government-to-employees (G2E)** applications may be especially useful in enabling efficient communication. One example of G2E is the Lifeline services provided by the U.S. government to Navy employees and their families (see EC Application Case 7.4 on page 308).

government-to-employees (G2E)
E-government category that includes activities and services between government units and their employees.

▶ Define e-government.

▶ What are the four categories of e-government?

▶ Describe G2C.

▶ Describe how EBT works.

▶ Describe the two main areas of G2B activities.

EC APPLICATION CASE 7.4
Individuals and Communities
G2E IN THE U.S. NAVY

The U.S. Navy uses G2E to improve the flow of information to sailors and their families. Because long shipboard deployments cause strains on navy families, in 1995, the navy began seeking ways to ensure that quality-of-life information reaches navy personnel and their loved ones all over the world. Examples of quality-of-life information include self-help, deployment support, stress management, parenting advice, and relocation assistance.

Lifelines (*lifelines2000.org*) uses the Internet, simulcasting, teleconferencing, cable television, and satellite broadcasting to reach overseas personnel. The navy has found that certain media channels are more appropriate for different types of information.

Lifelines regularly features live broadcasts, giving forward-deployed sailors and their families welcome information and, in some cases, a taste of home. On the Web, an average of 2,000 people access the Lifelines site each day.

The government provides several other e-services to navy personnel. Notable are online banking, personal finance services, and insurance. Education and training are also provided online.

Sources: Compiled from online news items and *lifelines2000.org*, February 2001.

Questions

▶ Why is the navy using multiple media channels?

▶ Compare the G2E services provided by the navy with the B2E services discussed in Section 7.1.

7.5   IMPLEMENTING E-GOVERNMENT

As in any other organization, one can also find large numbers of EC applications in government organizations. Like any other organization, government entities want to move into the digital era. In this section, we take a look at some issues involved in implementing e-government.

THE TRANSFORMATION PROCESS

The transformation from traditional delivery of government services to full implementation of online government services may be a lengthy process. The business consulting firm Deloitte and Touche conducted a study (see Wong 2000) that identified six stages in the transformation to e-government, as shown in Exhibit 7.4 and described later.

Stage 1:   **Information publishing/dissemination.** Individual government departments set up their own Web sites. These provide the public with information about the department, the range of services it offers, and contacts for further assistance. At this stage, governments establish an electronic encyclopedia to reduce the number of phone calls customers need to make to reach the appropriate employee who can fulfill their service requests. Also, paperwork and help-line employees can be reduced.

Stage 2:   **"Official" two-way transactions.** With the help of legally valid digital signatures and secure Web sites, customers are able to submit per-

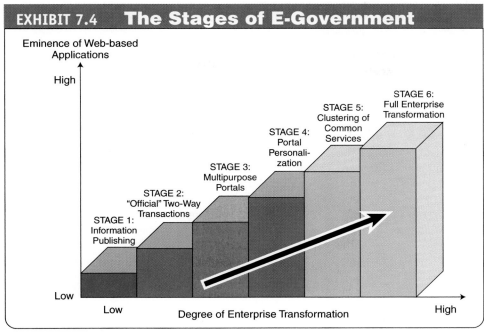

EXHIBIT 7.4   The Stages of E-Government

Source: Wong, 2001.

sonal information to—and conduct monetary transactions with—individual departments. At this stage, customers must be convinced of the department's ability to keep their information private and free from piracy. For example, the local government of Lewisham, United Kingdom, lets citizens claim income support and housing benefits using an electronic form. In Singapore, payments to citizens and from citizens to various government agencies can be performed online.

Stage 3: **Multipurpose portals.** At this point, customer-centric governments make a big breakthrough in service delivery. Based on the fact that customer needs can cut across department boundaries, a portal allows customers to use a single point of entry to send and receive information and to process monetary transactions across multiple departments. For example, in addition to acting as a gateway to its agencies and related governments, the government of South Australia's portal (sa.gov.au) features a "business channel," a link for citizens to pay bills (utilities, automotive), manage bank accounts, and conduct personal stock brokering (see EC Application Case 7.5 on page 310).

Stage 4: **Portal personalization.** Through stage 3, customers can access a variety of services at a single Web site. In stage 4, government puts even more power into customers' hands by allowing them to customize portals with their desired features. To accomplish this, governments will require much more sophisticated Web programming that permits interfaces to be manipulated by the users. The added benefit of portal personalization is that governments will get a more accurate read on

EC APPLICATION CASE 7.5

Individuals and Communities

E-GOVERNMENT IN THE STATE OF VICTORIA, AUSTRALIA

Titled Maxi, Victoria's e-government initiative went live online on December 9, 1997, with more than 30 government-related services. People can use the system to register vehicles, obtain drivers licenses, order birth certificates, notify the government of changes of address, and pay utility bills and fines. *Egov.vic.gov.au* is designed around the concept of "life events" (similar to the Hong Kong initiative in the Real-World Case at the end of the chapter). The site provides services 24 hours a day, every day of the year. The project is part of the "Victoria Government's Vic 21 strategy," which seeks to modernize government-to-citizen services. It embraces not only the government's relationship with citizens and the business sector, but also the different tiers of government.

The Internet portal features four service areas: (1) general information about Maxi, (2) bill payment and services by agencies, (3) life events (change of address, getting married, turning 18), and (4) a business channel. The business channel offers a range of private-sector-related services to help existing firms expand their services and to help new businesses start up.

Maxi kiosks are located in shopping centers, libraries, government offices, and other public locations around Victoria. Each kiosk has a touch screen, a bar code scanner, an A4 printer, a thermal-receipt printer, and full EFTPOS (electronic funds transfer at point-of-sale) capability for paying with debit or credit cards. Maxi employs SecureNet Certificates to provide customers with digital certificates of authenticity and public keys for digital signatures.

To encourage greater use, Maxi offered a lucky draw to users from July 1 to December 31, 2000. Anyone who used Maxi, even just one time, was entitled to participate in the lucky draw. The more transactions done on Maxi, the better the chance for a citizen to become a winner.

Customer adoption of Maxi has exceeded the government's expectations. One year after Maxi first went live, more than 24,000 transactions were conducted monthly over the network, tripling the initial target of 8,000 a month. Maxi has also given citizens new levels of convenience, with 40 percent of all transactions occurring outside normal 9-to-5 business hours.

Questions

▶ Discuss the role of Maxi kiosks in G2C.

▶ How can the government of Victoria justify its investment in G2C?

---

customer preference for electronic versus nonelectronic service options. As in industry, this will allow for true CRM in government. Such portals began in spring 2001, and many state and county governments either implemented them by spring 2002 or are planning to do so before 2004. Examples include the U.S. Department of Education (ed.gov) and the Internal Revenue Service (irs.gov).

Stage 5: **Clustering of common services.** Stage 5 is where real transformation of government structure takes shape. As customers now view once-disparate services as a unified package through the portal, their perception of departments as distinct entities will begin to blur. They will recognize groups of transactions rather than groups of agencies. To make this happen, governments will cluster services along common lines to accelerate the delivery of shared services. In other words, a business restructuring will take place.

Stage 6: **Full integration and enterprise transformation.** At stage 6, what started as a digital encyclopedia is now a full-service center, personalized to each customer's needs and preferences. At this stage, old walls defining silos of services have been torn down, and technology is integrated across the new government structure to bridge the shortened gap between the front and back offices. In some countries, new departments will have formed from the remains of predecessors. Others will have the same names, but their interiors will look nothing like they did before e-government.

IMPLEMENTATION ISSUES

Several issues are involved in implementing e-government programs. Some of these issues are:

▷ **Transformation speed.** The speed at which a government moves from stage 1 to stage 6 varies, but usually the transformation is very slow. Some of the determining factors are the degree of resistance to change by government employees, the adoption rate of applications by citizens, the available budget, and the legal environment. Deloitte and Touche found that in 2000, most governments were still in stage 1 (Wong 2000).

▷ **G2B implementation.** Implementation of G2B is easier than implementation of G2C. In some countries, such as Hong Kong, G2B implementation is outsourced to a private company that pays all of the start-up expenses in exchange for future transaction fees. As G2B services have the potential for rapid cost savings, they can be a good way to begin an e-government initiative.

▷ **Security issues.** Governments are concerned about maintaining the security and privacy of citizens' data. One area of particular concern is that of health care. From a medical point of view, it is necessary to have quick access to people's data, and the Internet and smart cards provide such capabilities; however, the protection of such data is very expensive (see Chapter 9). Many local and central governments are working on this topic.

NON-INTERNET E-GOVERNMENT

Today, e-government is associated with the Internet. However, governments have been using other networks, especially internal ones, to improve government operations for over 15 years. For example, on January 17, 1994, there was a major earthquake in Southern California. About 114,000 buildings were damaged and more than 500,000 victims turned to the Federal Emergency Management Agency (FEMA) for help. Initially, tired and dazed citizens stood hours in lines to register and have in-person interviews. To expedite the process, an e-government application was installed to expedite the issuance of checks to citizens. Citizens called an 800–number, and operators entered the information collected directly into online electronic forms. Then the data traveled electronically to the mobile disaster inspectors. Once checked, data went electronically to financial management and finally to check writing. The data never touched paper, and the cycle time was reduced by more than 50 percent. Another example of non-Internet e-government are auctions conducted over private, secured lines. Sooner or later, such non-Internet e-government initiatives will probably be converted to Internet-based ones.

▶ List the six stages of e-government development.

▶ Describe some e-government implementation issues.

▶ Provide an example of a non-Internet e-government service.

7.6 CUSTOMER-TO-CUSTOMER E-COMMERCE AND PEER-TO-PEER APPLICATIONS

CUSTOMER-TO-CUSTOMER E-COMMERCE

customer-to-customer (C2C)
E-commerce in which both the buyer and the seller are individuals (not businesses); involves activities such as auctions and classified ads.

Customer-to-customer (C2C) e-commerce refers to e-commerce in which both the buyer and the seller are individuals (not businesses). C2C is conducted in several ways on the Internet. The best known are auctions. Millions of individuals are buying and selling on eBay and hundreds of other Web sites worldwide. In addition to the major C2C activity of auctions, other C2C activities include classified ads, personal services, and exchanges.

Classified Ads

People sell to people every day through classified ads. Internet-based classified ads have several advantages over newspaper classified ads: They offer a national, rather than a local, audience. This greatly increases the supply of goods and services available and the number of potential buyers. For example, classifieds2000.com contains a list of about 500,000 cars, compared with the much smaller number you might find locally. Often, placing an ad on one Web site brings it automatically into the classified sections of numerous partners. This increases ad exposure, at no cost. To help narrow the search for a particular item, on some sites shoppers can use search engines. In addition, Internet-based classifieds often can be placed for free by private parties, can be edited or changed easily, and in many cases display photos of the product offered for sale.

The major categories of classified ads are similar to those found in the newspaper: vehicles, real estate, employment, general merchandise, collectibles, computers, pets, tickets, and travel. Classified ads are available through most Internet service providers (AOL, MSN, etc.), in some portals (Yahoo!, etc.), and from Internet directories, newspapers, and more. Once users find an ad and get the details, they can e-mail or call the other party for additional information or to make a purchase.

Personal Services

Numerous personal services are available on the Internet (lawyers, handy helpers, tax preparers, investment clubs, dating services). Some are in the classified ads but others are listed in specialized Web sites and directories. Some are for free, some for a fee. Be very careful before you purchase any personal services. Fraud or crime could be involved (e.g., a lawyer online may not be an expert in the area they profess, or may not deliver the service at all).

Exchanges

There are several C2C exchanges. These may be *consumer-to-consumer bartering exchanges* (e.g., fa-barterresource.com) in which goods and services are exchanged without monetary transactions. Or, they may be *consumer exchanges* that help buyers and sellers find each other and negotiate deals. For a complete list of exchanges, see Business2.com. Another form of C2C exchange is one in which consumers exchange information about products (e.g., consumerdemocracy.com, epinions.com).

PEER-TO-PEER NETWORKS AND APPLICATIONS

With C2C, B2C, B2B, and G2C, we described the relationship between parties in an EC transaction. We now introduce a similar-sounding term, but this one describes a computer architecture rather than a relationship between trading partners.

Peer-to-peer (P2P) computer architecture is a type of network in which each workstation (or PC) has similar capabilities. This is in contrast with *client-server* architecture in which some computers serve other computers. The peer computers share data, processing, and devices with each other directly, rather than through a central server.

The main benefit of P2P is that it can expand enormously the universe of information accessible from a personal computer—users are not confined to just Web pages. Additionally, some proponents claim that a well-designed P2P system can offer better security, reliability, and availability of content than the client-server model, on which the Web is based. Note that the acronym P2P also can stand for people-to-people, person-to-person, or point-to-point. Our discussion here refers to *peer-to-peer networks* over which files and other resources are shared.

peer-to-peer (P2P)
A network architecture in which each workstation (or PC) has similar capabilities; the networked peers share data and processing with each other directly rather than through a central server.

Characteristics of P2P Systems

Peer-to-peer systems have seven key characteristics:

1. User interfaces that load outside of a Web browser.
2. User computers can act as both clients and servers.
3. The overall system is easy to use and is well integrated.
4. The system includes tools to support users wishing to create content or add functionality.
5. The system provides connections with other users.
6. The system does something new or exciting.
7. The system supports "cross-networking" protocols such as SOAP or XML-RPC.

These characteristics of P2P computing show that devices can join the network from any location with little effort. Instead of dedicated LANs, the Internet itself becomes the network of choice. Easier configuration and control over the applications enables people without network savvy to join the user community. In fact, P2P signifies a shift in peer networking emphasis—from hardware to applications.

Peer-to-peer networking connects people directly to other people. It provides an easy system for sharing, publishing, and interacting that requires no knowledge of system administration. The system wraps everything up into a user friendly interface and lets people share or communicate with each other.

An example of a P2P network is graphically illustrated in Exhibit 7.5. The workstations shown in the drawing perform computer-to-computer communication directly through their own operating systems, and each resource can be shared by all devices. Let's look at some C2C P2P applications, the most well known of which is Napster.

Consumer-to-Consumer P2P Applications

Napster—The File-Sharing Utility. In Chapter 3, we introduced the case of Napster as an example of C2C e-commerce. By logging into the Napster system, people could enter files that other people decided to share. The network also allowed users to search other members' hard drives for a particular file (music and games were the most popular), including data files created by users or copied from elsewhere. Napster had more than 50 million members by the end of 2001.

The Napster server functioned as a directory that listed the files being shared by other users. Once logged into the server, users could search the directory for songs that they like and locate the file owner. They could then directly access the owner's computer and download the songs they had chosen. Napster also included chat rooms to connect its millions of users. Napsters is to be acquired by Bedelsomann, a major media company and shareholder of Napster (2002). (For more on Napster, see Chapter 9.)

In March 2002, Napster closed its free services after a U.S. federal court found the company to be in violation of copyright laws. Napster is still operational for file sharing—now for a fee, from which Napster makes payments to copyright owners.

Other file sharing programs. An even purer version of P2P is Gnutella, a P2P program that dispenses with the central database altogether in connecting the peer computers. To access games over P2P networks, try fusiongames.com and battle.net.

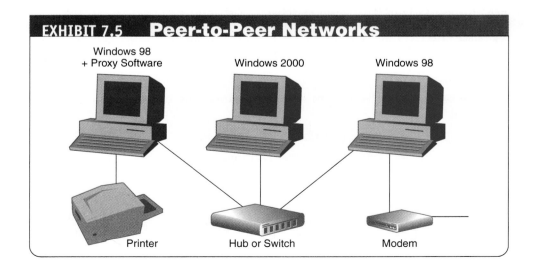

EXHIBIT 7.5 Peer-to-Peer Networks

Windows 98 + Proxy Software

Windows 2000

Windows 98

Printer

Hub or Switch

Modem

ICQ (the instant messenger-type chat room) can be considered a hybrid P2P technology because the chatters share the same screen.

Other commercial applications. With P2P, users can sell digital goods directly from their computers rather than going through centralized servers. If users want to sell on eBay, they are required to go through eBay's server, putting an item on eBay's site and uploading a photo. However, if an auction site uses *file sharing*, it can direct customers to the seller's PC, where buyers can find an extensive amount of information, photos, and even videos about the items being sold. In this case, an auction site serves as an intermediary, making the C2C link between the sellers and buyers.

Intrabusiness P2P Applications

Several companies are using P2P to facilitate internal collaboration. For example, in 1990, Intel wrote a file transfer program called NetBatch, which allows chip designers to utilize the additional processing power of colleagues' computers across sites in California, Arizona, and even foreign countries such as Israel. Intel saved more than $500 million between 1992 and 2001 (intel.com, 2001).

Business-to-Business P2P Applications

P2P could be a technology panacea for systems innovators building B2B exchanges. With P2P, people can share information, but they are not required to send it to an unknown server. Some companies fear that exchanges make it possible for unauthorized personnel to gain access to corporate data files. P2P applications enable such companies to store documents in-house instead of on an unknown, and possibly unsecured, server.

Several companies are using the P2P architecture as a basis for speeding up business transactions, as shown in the following examples.

▶ Hilgraeve of Monroe, Michigan, has a technology called DropChute that establishes a connection between two computers and allows users to transfer files. The company has won a U.S. patent for its P2P communication process that touts four levels of encryption and virus-scanning protection.

▶ Fort Knox Escrow Service in Atlanta, Georgia, which transmits legal and financial documents that must be highly secure, has leveraged DropChute to enable clients to deliver material electronically. "Instead of having to wait for an overnight package, we can do it all over the Internet," said Jeanna Israel, Fort Knox's director of operations (Lason, 2001).

▶ Certapay.com is a P2P e-mail payment platform that enables e-banking customers to send and receive money using only an e-mail address.

Peer networks effectively address the Web's B2B deficiencies. The model is a natural fit for the needs of business, as business relationships are intrinsically peer to peer. Peer networks allow businesses to communicate, interact, and transact with each other as never before by making business relationships interactive, dynamic, and balanced—both within and between enterprises.

However, the success of P2P in B2B is not guaranteed. It depends in part on the ability of the technology to address security and scalability issues. For additional information on P2P in B2B, see McAffee (2000).

Business-to-Consumer P2P Applications

There are several potential applications of P2P in marketing and advertisement. For example, fandango.com is combining P2P with collaborative filtering (Chapter 4). Assuming a user is conducting a search for a product, Fandango's product will work as follows:

1. The user enters a search keyword.

2. The keyword is sent to 100 peers, which search local indexes of the Web pages they have visited.

3. Those computers also relay the query to 100 of their peers, and that group submits it to 100 of theirs, yielding, in theory, up to 1 million computers queried.

4. The resulting URLs are returned to the user, weighted in favor of the most recently visited pages and peers with similar interests.

P2P enables new EC applications. Although sensitive information may require special security arrangements and many users may encounter scalability issues, P2P is a very promising technology.

▶ List the major C2C applications.

▶ Define P2P networks and list their major characteristics.

▶ Describe P2P applications in C2C.

▶ Describe P2P applications in B2B.

7.7 ONLINE PUBLISHING AND E-BOOKS

online publishing
The electronic delivery of newspapers, magazines, books, news, music, videos, and other digitizable information over the Internet.

One type of file that can be shared digitally is electronic books and other online materials. **Online publishing** is the electronic delivery of newspapers, magazines, books, news, music, videos, and other digitizable information over the Internet. Initiated in the late 1960s, online publishing was designed to provide online bibliographies and to sell knowledge that was stored in online commercial databases. Publicly funded online publishing was established for the purpose of disseminating medical, educational, and aerospace research information.

Today, online publishing has additional purposes. It is related to worldwide dissemination of knowledge and to advertisement (because it is sometimes provided free to attract people to sites where advertising is conducted). And publishers of traditional hard-copy media have expanded to add online operations. Magazine and newspaper publishers such as *Ad Week*, *PC Magazine*, the *Wall Street Journal*, and the *Los Angeles Times* all use online publishing to disseminate information online. Chicagotribune.com (the online version of the *Chicago Tribune*) provides not only the paper's hard-copy issue online for free, but in its a soft-copy version it also posts additional news details, jobs and housing listings, and community service information. Online publishing includes material either received free or by subscription fee; sometimes such material may be customized for the recipient. The potential of new interactive technologies and other Internet applications are expected to aid the growth of online publishing.

ONLINE PUBLISHING APPROACHES AND METHODS

Several online publishing methods are in use, including the following:

- **Online-archive approach.** The online-archive approach to online publishing is a digital archive. Such an archive may be a library catalog or a bibliographic database. With this approach, paper publications are converted to a digitized format and offered electronically.

- **New-medium approach.** The new-medium approach is used by publishers that seek to use the publication capabilities of the Web to create new material or add content and multimedia to paper publications. With this approach, publishers may provide extra analysis or additional information on any issue or topic online, offering more information than a traditional magazine or newspaper can offer. One way of doing this is by offering integrated hypertext links to related stories, topics, and graphics. The Web medium also allows for easy customization or personalization, which old publishing media do not. Taylor and Francis Publishing Co. placed more than 500 of its journals online. The company provides research services, hypertext links, summaries, and more to subscribers. The new-medium approach also offers up-to-date material, including breaking news. Examples of the new-medium approach include HotWired (hotwired.lycos.com), which complements a paper version of *Wired* magazine, and the *Wall Street Journal* Online (wsj.com).

- **Publishing-intermediation approach.** The publishing-intermediation approach can be thought of as an online directory for news services. Publishing intermediation is an attempt to help people locate goods, services, and products online. Netscape and other portals provide publishing-intermediation services.

- **Dynamic approach.** The dynamic approach (also referred to as the *just-in-time* approach, or *point casting*) personalizes content in real time and transmits it on the fly in the format best suited to the user's location, tastes, and preferences.

CONTENT PROVIDERS AND DISTRIBUTORS

Content providers and distributors are, as their name implies, those who provide and distribute content online. These services are offered by several specialized companies (e.g., akamai.com, digisle.com, mirror-image.com) as well as by news services such as the Associated Press and ABC News. Due to the difficulty of presenting multimedia, content providers face major challenges when operating in an environment of less-developed infrastructures. Also, the issue of intellectual property payments is critical to the success of content distribution. If authors do not receive payment for or recognition of their work, the content provider may face legal problems. If payments are made, the providers' costs may be too high.

In early 2002, more online content providers were starting to charge for content, as advertising that used to support content dried up. In addition, more readers appeared willing to pay for online publications (e.g., *South China Morning Post* started to charge for articles in 2002).

Of special interest in this area is digimarc.com, which provides a tool for linking print publications with the Web. Digimarc's model for content delivery is shown in Exhibit 7.6.

PUBLISHING OF MUSIC, VIDEOS, GAMES, AND ENTERTAINMENT

The Internet is an ideal media for publishing music, videos, electronic games, and related entertainment. As with content providers, a major issue here is the payment of intellectual property fees.

One of the most interesting new capabilities in this area, as discussed earlier, is P2P networks over which people swap digital files, such as music or video files. When such swapping is managed by a third-party exchange (e.g., Napster), the third party may be in violation of copyright law. (For more on the legal difficulties faced by Napster, see Chapters 3 and 9.)

Edutainment

edutainment
The combination of education and entertainment, often through games.

Edutainment is a combination of education and entertainment, often through games. One of the main goals of edutainment is to encourage students to become active rather than passive learners. With active learning, a student is more involved in the learning process, which makes the learning experience richer and the knowledge gained more memorable. Edutainment embeds learning in entertainment to help students learn almost without their being aware of it.

Edutainment covers various subjects, including mathematics, reading, writing, history, and geography. Edutainment is targeted at varying age groups ranging from preschoolers to adults, and it is also used in corporate training over intranets.

EXHIBIT 7.6   A New Content-Delivery Model

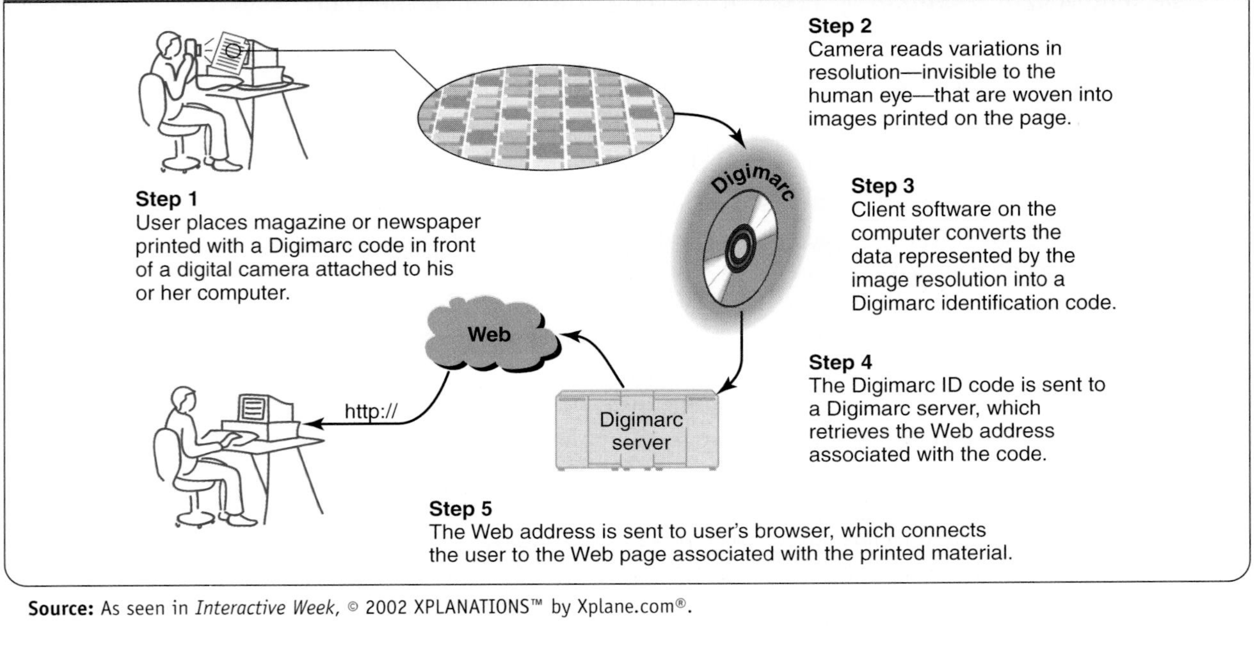

Step 1
User places magazine or newspaper printed with a Digimarc code in front of a digital camera attached to his or her computer.

Step 2
Camera reads variations in resolution—invisible to the human eye—that are woven into images printed on the page.

Step 3
Client software on the computer converts the data represented by the image resolution into a Digimarc identification code.

Step 4
The Digimarc ID code is sent to a Digimarc server, which retrieves the Web address associated with the code.

Step 5
The Web address is sent to user's browser, which connects the user to the Web page associated with the printed material.

Source: As seen in *Interactive Week*, © 2002 XPLANATIONS™ by Xplane.com®.

Software Toolworks (toolworks.com, now a part of The Learning Company at broderbund.com) is a vendor of edutainment products.

For over a decade, educational games have been delivered mostly on CD-ROMs. However, since 1998, increasing numbers of companies now offer online edutainment in a distance-learning format (e.g., Knowledge Adventure products at sunburst.com and education.com).

ELECTRONIC BOOKS

An electronic book, or **e-book**, is a book in digital form that can be read on a computer screen, including handheld computers. Readers must have an e-book reader to read an e-book. You can download either Adobe Acrobat eBook Reader or Microsoft Reader *for free* from Amazon.com or from other e-book sites. After installing the reader, you download the e-book, and within minutes you can enjoy reading it. The books are portable (e.g., see Pocket PC store at amazon.com) and convenient to carry; 70 e-books (on average) can be loaded onto one CD-ROM or a special storage disk. E-books can be updated frequently, contain up-to-the-minute information, and are easy to search.

e-book
A book in digital form that can be read on a computer screen.

A major event in electronic publishing occurred on March 24, 2000, when Stephen King's book *Riding the Bullet* was published exclusively online. For $2.50 readers could purchase the e-book at bn.com/ebook and other e-book providers. Several hundred thousand copies were sold in a few days. However, the publishing event did not go off without some problems. Hackers breached the security system and distributed free copies of the book. In addition to regular books, electronic *technical* documents are available from the eMatter division of Fatbrain (now a barnesandnoble.com company).

An increasing number of online publishers produce e-books. In addition to all the major textbook publishers that sell e-books directly, you can also buy e-books at electronic bookstores. E-books can be a major part of e-learning, the topic of our next section. (For more information on e-books see ebookconnections.com and netlibrary.com.)

▶ Define online publishing and list some advantages it offers over traditional media.

▶ List the major methods of online publishing.

▶ What issues are involved in content creation and distribution?

▶ Describe e-books and list their advantages.

7.8   E-LEARNING AND KNOWLEDGE MANAGEMENT AND DISSEMINATION

E-LEARNING

E-learning is the online delivery of information for purposes of education, training, knowledge management, or performance management. It is a Web-enabled system that makes knowledge accessible to those who need it, when they need it, anytime,

e-learning
The online delivery of information for purposes of education, training, knowledge management, or performance management.

anywhere. E-learning is useful both as an environment for facilitating learning at schools and as an environment for efficient and effective corporate training.

The Challenges of E-Learning

In order for it to be widely accepted, e-learning faces challenges from both the learning and the teaching perspectives. From the learner's perspective, the challenge is to simply change the mindset of how learning typically takes place. Learners must be willing to give up the idea of traditional classroom training (with its limitations and its strengths), and must come to understand that continual, lifelong learning will be as much a part of normal work life as voice mail and e-mail.

From the content provider's perspective, the challenge is to make learning more interactive and engaging. From the implementation side, converting ("tagging") all learning objects to a digital format can be challenging. Once objects are tagged, however, learners can retrieve the information they need, whenever they need it, from a learning management system that can track an individual's usage and progress.

The Benefits of E-Learning

E-learning is the great equalizer. It can eliminate barriers of time, distance, and socioeconomic status, and thus enable individuals to take charge of their own lifelong learning. In the information age, learning opportunities truly span a lifetime—from childhood through adulthood. Skills and knowledge need to be *continually updated* and refreshed to keep up with today's fast-paced culture. New content technologies and trends in e-learning will help countries and organizations adapt to the demands of the Internet economy by educating their citizens and training their workers.

E-learning provides a new set of tools that can add value to traditional learning modes—classroom experiences, textbook study, CD-ROM, and traditional computer-based training. E-learning does not usually replace the classroom setting, but enhances it, taking advantage of new content and delivery technologies. Retention of learning by students varies, depending on the individual student's learning style, the content type, and the delivery vehicle. The better the match of content and delivery vehicle to an individual's learning style, the greater the retention, and the better the results. New e-learning support environments, such as Blackboard and WebCT, add value to traditional learning (see the Insights and Additions box on the next page).

As the opening vignette about Cisco showed, e-learning also can be used in the business environment. E-learning provides a superior learning and communication model that increases access to learning, provides clear accountability for all participants, and reduces costs. More importantly, e-learning equips employees with the knowledge and information needed to help increase customer satisfaction, expand revenue and sales, and accelerate technology adoption. In short, e-learning enables companies to prepare their workforces for an increasingly competitive world marketplace.

Insight and Additions   Blackboard and WebCT

There is a good chance that you will use the Blackboard or WebCT frameworks when using this text. These competing products provide the Internet infrastructure software for e-learning, serving one of the fastest growing industry segments in the world. Eduventures.com, Inc., a leading independent e-learning industry analyst, projects that the higher education e-learning market will grow from $4 billion in 2001 to $11 billion by 2003.

With both frameworks, the publisher places a book's content, teaching notes, quizzes, etc. on the Blackboard or WebCT in a standardized format. Instructors can access modules and transfer them into their own specific Blackboard that can by accessed by their students.

Blackboard offers a complete suite of enterprise software products and services that power a total "e-education infrastructure" for schools, colleges, universities, and other education providers. Blackboard's two major lines of business are Course & Portal Solutions and Commerce & Access Solutions.

WebCT provides a similar set of tools, but uses a different vision and strategy. According to WebCT, technology-enabled learning has opened a new world of opportunities. WebCT uses advanced pedagogical tools to help institutions of higher education capitalize on the shift to e-learning. WebCT's innovations make distance learning courses possible, enabling institutions to expand campus boundaries, attract and retain students and faculty, and continually improve course and degree program quality.

Textbook publishers are embracing these tools by making their major textbooks Blackboard and/or WebCT enabled. Thus, your professor can easily incorporate this book's content into the software that is used by thousands of universities worldwide.

Source: Compiled from *webct.com* and *blackboard.com* (fall 2001).

Drawbacks of E-Learning

Offsetting the benefits of e-learning are some drawbacks. In the environment of higher education, the issues cited as possible drawbacks of e-learning are as follows:

- **Need for instructor retraining.** Some instructors are not competent in teaching by electronic means and may require additional training. It costs money to provide such training. Also, some instructors refuse retraining.

- **Equipment needs and support services.** Additional funds are needed to purchase multimedia tools to provide support services for its use and maintenance.

- **Lack of face-to-face interaction and campus life.** Many feel that the intellectual stimulation that takes places through classroom interactions and on campus cannot be fully replicated in e-learning.

- **Assessment.** There is criticism that professors may not be able to adequately assess student work completed at home. There is no guarantee, for example, of who actually completed the assignment or exam.

- **Maintenance and updating.** There are practical difficulties (e.g., cost, time of professors) in keeping e-learning materials up-to-date. No online course can deliver real-time information in the way a "live" instructor can.

- ▶ **Protection of intellectual property.** It is difficult to control the transmission of copyrighted works downloaded from the e-learning platform.
- ▶ **Computer literacy.** E-learning cannot be extended to those students who are not computer-literate.
- ▶ **Student retention.** It may be difficult to keep students mentally engaged and enthusiastic about e-learning over a long period of time.

Some of these drawbacks, several of which exist in any learning situation, not just in colleges, can be reduced by technology. For example, some online products have features that help stimulate student thinking, and the use of biometric controls will verify the identity of students who are taking examinations from home. However, these features add to the costs of e-learning.

Balancing the benefits and the drawbacks of e-learning, many people remain enthusiastic about its potential.

Virtual Teaching and Online Universities

Distance learning is formal education that takes place off campus, often from home. The concept is not new. Educational institutions have been offering correspondence courses and degrees for decades. Lately, IT in general and the Web in particular have expanded the opportunities for distance learning to the online environment.

The concept of **virtual universities**, online universities from which students take classes from home or an off-site location via the Internet, is expanding rapidly. Hundreds of thousands of students in dozens of countries from Great Britain to Israel to Thailand are studying in such institutions. Large numbers of existing universities, including Stanford University and other top-tier institutions, offer online education in some form. Some universities, such as California State University at Dominguez Hills, offer hundreds of courses and dozens of degrees to students worldwide, all online. Other universities offer limited online courses and degrees but use innovative teaching methods and multimedia support in the traditional classroom, as discussed in the Insights and Additions box on the next page. (For a list of schools that offer online courses, see distancelearn.about.com.) The forces that are driving the transition from traditional education to online learning are shown in Exhibit 7.7.

The virtual university concept allows universities to offer classes worldwide. Moreover, we may soon see integrated degrees, where students can customize a degree that will best fit their needs and take courses at different universities. Several new all-virtual schools include eschool-world.com, walden.com, and train ingzone.co.uk.

Online Training

A large number of organizations are using online training on a large scale. Many companies offer online training, as Cisco does, or even in-home universities, such as that offered by COX Industries. IBM Taiwan Corp. is using Web-based "electronic training" for new employees, and KPMG Peat Marwick offers e-learning to the company's customers. Some vendors of online training and educational materials are digitalthink.com, click2learn.com, and smartplanet.com.

Insights and Additions   Interactive MBA at City University of Hong Kong

As of May 1999, students in Hong Kong can study for their MBA anytime, anywhere, and at any pace. This unique program started by integrating two technologies—the Web and interactive television. The objective of the program is to provide participants with a high-tech, innovative, and interactive learning experience to improve their managerial and professional competence.

The program is composed of 17 standard courses: eight core courses, six advanced, and three cross disciplinary. Each course includes 45 lecture hours delivered on an interactive television (iTV or TV on demand). The students choose what lecture to watch and when they want to watch it. In addition to the lectures, all support material, exercises, and other resources are provided on the Web. Students can interact electronically with instructors and with each other using e-mail and chat rooms.

The program is supported by Hong Kong Telecom, which provides broadband access service at 1.5 Mbps download speed (about 30 times the speed of a fast regular modem). For details about the program and the technology, check *imba.cityu.edu.hk.*

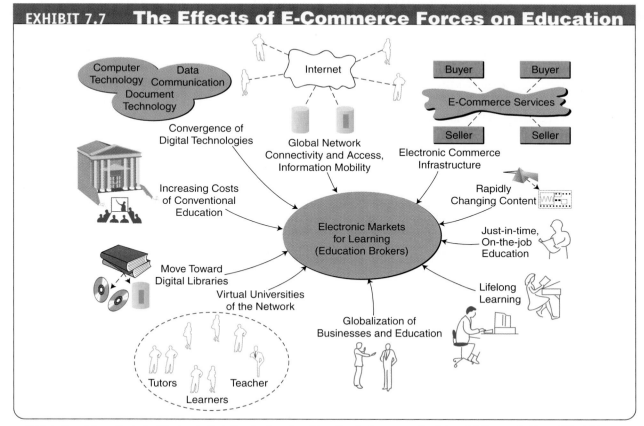

EXHIBIT 7.7   The Effects of E-Commerce Forces on Education

Source: Hamalainen M. et al., "Electronic Marketing for Learning: Education Brokerages on the Internet," *Communications of the ACM,* June © 1996 ACM, Inc., p. 52. Used with permission.

KNOWLEDGE MANAGEMENT

The term *knowledge management* is frequently mentioned in discussions of e-learning. Why is this so? To answer this question, one first needs to understand what knowledge management is.

Knowledge management and e-learning both use the same "coin of the realm"—knowledge. Knowledge is one of the most important assets in any organization, and so it is important to capture and apply it. Whereas e-learning uses that "coin" for the sake of *individual* learning, knowledge management uses it to improve the functioning of an *organization*. This is one of the major purposes of knowledge management. In our view, **knowledge management (KM)** refers to the process of capturing or creating knowledge, storing and protecting it, updating it constantly, and using it whenever necessary. Knowledge is collected from both external and internal sources. Then it is examined, interpreted, refined, and stored in what is called a **knowledge base**, the repository for the enterprise's knowledge.

The major purpose of an organizational knowledge base is to allow for *knowledge sharing*. Knowledge sharing among employees, with customers, and with business partners has a huge potential payoff in improved customer service, shorter delivery cycle times, and increased collaboration within the company and with business partners. Furthermore, some knowledge can be sold to others or traded for other knowledge.

Knowledge management promotes an *integrated* approach to the process of identifying, capturing, retrieving, sharing, and evaluating an enterprise's information assets, both those that are documented and the tacit expertise stored in individuals' heads. The integration of information resources is at the heart of KM. EC implementation involves a considerable amount of knowledge about customers, suppliers, logistics, procurement, markets, and technology. The integration of that knowledge is required for successful EC applications. These applications are aimed at increasing organizational competitiveness.

Knowledge management programs are frequently delivered via portals and can be integrated with EC and IT applications in enterprise computing. EC Application Case 7.6 shows a knowledge management portal that combines business intelligence capabilities. EC and KM also can be combined to offer collaborative communications and workflow. (For further discussion, see Raisch 2001.)

ONLINE ADVICE AND CONSULTING

Finally, another online use of knowledge can be to offer it in advice and consulting services. The online advice and consulting field is growing rapidly as tens of thousands of experts of all kinds sell their expertise on the Internet, for a relatively low price. Here are some examples:

- **Medical advice.** Companies such as webmd.com, kasamba.com, and keen.com provide health-advice consultations with top medical experts. You can ask specific questions and get an answer from a specialist in a few days.

- **Management consulting.** Many consultants are selling their accumulated expertise from knowledge bases. A pioneer in this area was Andersen Consulting (through its Web site knowledgespace.com). Another online management

knowledge management (KM)
The process of capturing or creating knowledge, storing it, updating it constantly, and interpreting and using it whenever necessary.

knowledge base
The repository for an enterprise's accumulated knowledge.

EC APPLICATION CASE 7.6

Implementation and Strategy

PORTAL SPEEDS PRODUCT R&D AT AMWAY

Through thousands of independent agents all over the world, Amway sells more than 450 home, nutrition and wellness, and personal products. To be effective, the research and development (R&D) department at Amway must develop new products in a streamlined and cost-efficient manner. The R&D department consists of 550 engineers, scientists, and quality-assurance staff, who have more than 1,000 projects in the works at any one time.

Fast and easy access to information such as product specifications, formulas, design criteria, production schedules, costs, and sales trends is required for supporting the design activity. Access to this information used to be difficult because the data sometimes resided in 15 to 20 disparate repositories. When scientists needed production or financial data, for instance, they had to request paper reports from each department, which could take days to be processed. Also the corporate knowledge and experience were scattered in a disorganized fashion over many different locations.

To meet the need for easier access to corporate knowledge, Amway developed a business intelligence and knowledge management portal, called Artemis. Tailored to the R&D division, Artemis is a browser-based intranet application that enables R&D staff to quickly find the information and knowledge they require. It also includes features such as collaboration tools and a database for locating company experts. Using the Lotus Notes/Domino search agent, Artemis

enables employees to pull data from disparate corporate sources and generate dynamic reports in response to user queries. This information is highly secured by Domino's superb security capabilities.

Artemis's collaborative features include a time-accounting function used to help the R&D staff calculate R&D tax credits. The Artemis event-reporting database also tracks project content and status.

After a staged rollout of Artemis, all employees now have access to the system. Time required to access information dropped from days to minutes or seconds, enabling fast "what-if" investigations by product developers. Initial user surveys indicated that 60 percent of the users were saving 30 minutes or more per week; that figure increased to 1 hour for most employees after additional links to more information sources were added and users gained comfort with the system. The target for the near future is a savings of 2 hours per employee each week. The system paid for itself ($250,000) in less than 6 months.

Source: C. Abbott, October 2000.

Questions

▷ Identify the KM elements in this case.
▷ What is the role of Artemis in KM?
▷ Relate this case to collaborative commerce.

consultant is aberdeen.com. Because of their high consultation fees, such services are used mainly by corporations.

▷ **Legal advice.** Delivery of legal advice to individuals and businesses by consultation services has considerable prospects. For example, Atlanta-based law firm Alston & Bird coordinates legal counseling with 12 law firms for a large health-care company and for many other clients. The company created a knowledge base that contains information from some of the best law firms in the country. This information is then made available to all 12 of the law firms in the consultation group. Many lawyers offer inexpensive consulting services online. Linklaters, a leading U.K. law firm, created a separate company (blueflag.com) to sell its legal services online. The company offers several products and also sells support technology to other law firms.

▶ **Gurus.** Several sites provide diversified expert services, some for free. One example is guru.com, which offers general advice and a job board for experts on legal, financial, tax, technical, lifestyle, and other issues. It aggregates over 200,000 professional "gurus." Expertise is sold at allexpert.com. At this site, one can post a required service for experts to bid on. Of special interest is sciam.com, which offers advice from science experts at *Scientific American* magazine.

▶ **Financial advice.** Many companies offer extensive financial advice. For example, Merrill Lynch Online (askmerrill.ml.com) provides free access to the firm's research reports and analyses.

One word of caution about advice: It may not be wise to risk your health, your money, or your legal status on free advice. Always seek more than one opinion, and carefully check the credentials of any advice provider.

MANAGERIAL ISSUES

Some managerial issues related to this chapter are as follows.

1. **Who's in charge of our intranet content?** Because the content delivered on the intranet is created by many individuals, two potential risks exist. First, proprietary corporate information may not be secure enough, so unauthorized people may have access to it. Second, appropriate intranet Netiquette must be maintained; otherwise unethical or even illegal behavior may develop. Therefore, managing intranet content, including frequent updates, is a must.

2. **Who will design the corporate portal?** Corporate portals are the gateways to corporate information and knowledge. Appropriate portal design is a must, not only for easy and efficient navigation, but also because portals portray the corporate image to employees and to business partners who are allowed access to it. Design of the corporate portal must be carefully thought out and approved by management.

3. **How can we "sell" the intranet to users?** In some companies, it is difficult to "sell" the intranet to users. If paper documents are replaced, then employees must check the intranet frequently. Depending on the organizational culture, in many cases employees often

are not using intranets to their fullest capacity. To promote intranet use, some companies make formal presentations to employees, including online and off-line training. Others provide incentives to users; some penalize nonusers. One approach is the creation of an Intranet Day (see *Internetweek*, May 3, 1999, p. 27).

4. **Who can access the intranet from the outside?** The more applications a company places on the intranet, the more important the need to allow employees to access it while they are outside the organization. This may create security problems, especially when employees try to access the intranet via a modem (see Chapter 9).

5. **What are the connectivity needs?** Intranets need to be connected to the Internet, and in many cases to extranets, for B2B applications. Because many partners may be involved, along with several communication and network protocols, careful planning is needed.

6. **What intranet applications?** Intranet technology is mature enough for its applications to have become fairly standard. Look at case studies at vendors' sites for ideas. Also look at

intranetjournal.com/casestudies and at *google.com* (search for "intranet case studies"). The material at this book's Web site, *prenhall.com/turban* (Chapter 7) and at *cio.com/research/ec/cases.html* are also good places to investigate.

7. **Are there e-government opportunities?** If your organization is doing business with the government, you will eventually do it online. You may find new online business opportunities with the government, because governments are getting serious about going online. Some even mandate it as the only way to conduct B2G and G2B.

8. **Are there P2P applications?** Watch for new developments in P2P tools and applications.

Some experts say a major revolution is coming for faster and cheaper online communication and collaboration. As with any new innovation, it will take time to mature.

9. **How well are we managing our knowledge?** Connecting e-commerce initiatives with a KM program, if one exists, is a very viable strategy. The knowledge is needed for the operation and implementation of EC projects.

10. **Are there e-learning opportunities?** Adding an e-learning component to your company's activities is useful when your employees need to retrain themselves and keep up with new knowledge.

SUMMARY

In this chapter, you learned about the following EC issues as they relate to the learning objectives.

1. **Intrabusiness EC defined.** Intrabusiness EC refers to all EC initiatives conducted within one organization. These can be activities between an organization and its employees, between SBUs in the organization, and among the organization's employees.

2. **The intranet and its use in organizations.** An intranet is an internal corporate network that is constructed with Internet protocols and tools, such as search engines and browsers. It is used for internal communication, collaboration, and discovery of information in various internal databases. It is protected by firewalls against unauthorized access.

3. **The relationship between the corporate portal and the intranet.** The corporate portal is the gateway through which users access the various applications conducted over the intranet, such as training, accessing databases, or receiving customized news.

4. **E-government to citizens.** Governments worldwide are providing a large variety of services to citizens over the Internet. Such initiatives increase citizens' satisfaction and decrease government expenses in providing customer service applications.

5. **Other e-government activities.** Governments, like any other organization, can use EC applications for great savings. Notable are e-procurement using reverse auctions, e-payments to and from citizens and businesses, auctioning of surplus goods, and using electronic travel and expense management systems.

6. **Applications of peer-to-peer technology.** Peer-to-peer (P2P) technology allows direct communication for sharing files and for collaboration. Although Napster gets a lot of publicity for its support of music and game sharing among millions of its members, the same technology is used in both B2B and in intrabusiness.

7. **Online publishing and e-books.** Online publishing of newspapers, magazines, and books is growing rapidly, as is the online publishing of other digitizable items such as software, music, games, movies, and other entertainment.

8. **E-learning, virtual universities, and knowledge management and dissemination.** E-learning is the delivery of educational content via electronic media, including the Internet and extranets. Degree programs, lifelong learning topics, and corporate training are delivered by thousands of organizations worldwide. E-learning delivers knowledge, an integral part of e-commerce.

KEY TERMS

Business-to-employee (B2E),	p. 291	E-learning,	p. 319	Intrabusiness EC,	p. 291
Corporate (enterprise) portal,	p. 298	Government-to-business (G2B),	p. 305	Intranet,	p. 293
Customer-to-customer (C2C),	p. 312	Government-to-citizens (G2C),	p. 304	Knowledge base,	p. 324
Distance learning,	p. 322	Government-to-employees (G2E),	p. 307	Knowledge management (KM),	p. 324
E-book,	p. 319	Government-to-government (G2G),	p. 307	Online publishing,	p. 316
Edutainment,	p. 318			Peer-to-peer (P2P),	p. 313
E-government,	p. 304			Virtual university,	p. 322

DISCUSSION QUESTIONS

1. Discuss the relationship between a corporate portal and an intranet.

2. Compare and contrast an Internet portal (such as Yahoo!) with a corporate portal.

3. Interest in intranets is returning. Discuss the reasons why.

4. Discuss the relationship between B2E and portals.

5. Which e-government EC activities are intrabusiness activities? Explain why they are intrabusiness.

6. Identify the benefits of G2C to citizens and to governments.

7. Some say that B2G is simply B2B. Explain.

8. Compare and contrast B2E with G2E.

9. Discuss the major properties of P2P.

10. Discuss some of the potential ethical and legal implications of people using P2P to download music, games, and so forth.

11. In what way can online publishing support a paper-based publication?

12. Discuss the advantages and disadvantages of e-books.

13. Will paper-based books and magazines be eliminated in the long run? Why or why not?

14. Discuss the advantages of e-learning for an undergraduate student.

15. Discuss the relationship between knowledge management and a portal.

16. In what ways does knowledge management support e-commerce?

17. Discuss the advantages of e-learning in the corporate training environment.

INTERNET EXERCISES

1. Enter whitehouse.gov/government/index and review the "Gateway to Government." Based on the stages presented in Exhibit 7.4, what stage does this site represent? Review the available tours. Suggest ways the government could improve this portal.

2. Enter oecd.org and identify the studies conducted by the Organization for Economic Cooperation and Development (OECD) on the topic of e-government. What are their major concerns?

3. Enter fcw.com and read the latest news on e-government. Identify initiatives not covered in this chapter. Check the B2G corner.

4. Enter ca.com/products and register. Then take the Clever Path Portal Test Drive at ca.com/solutions/product.asp?ID=262. (Flash Player from Macromedia is required.)

5. Enter xdegrees.com, centrata.com, and badblue.com and evaluate some of the solutions offered. Also, enter aberdeen.com to learn more about P2P operations. How can the operator of this site expedite a search for a song at gnutella.co.uk?

6. Enter knowledgespace.com. This knowledge base resides on Andersen's intranet. Sign up for the service if it is still available for a free trial period. Why is such a system better when used on the intranet? Why not use a CD-ROM-based technology?

7. Enter govexec.com/egov and explore the latest developments in G2C, G2B (and B2G), and G2G.

8. Enter plumtree.com. Find the white paper about corporate portals and their justification. Prepare a report based on your findings.

9. Enter worldstreet.com and go to "products." Identify all potential B2B applications and prepare a report about them.

10. Enter procurement.com and govexec.com. Identify recent e-procurement initiatives and summarize their unique aspects.

11. Enter fortune.com. How would you compare reading the electronic magazine against the print version?

12. Enter webct.com and blackboard.com. Compare the capabilities of the two products.

13. Enter e-learningcentre.com.uk and evaluate its resources and activities.

TEAM ASSIGNMENTS AND ROLE PLAYING

1. Assign each team to a different country. Each team will then explore the e-government offerings of that country. Have each team make a presentation to convince the class that its country's offerings are the most comprehensive.

2. Create four teams, each representing one of the following: G2C, G2B, G2E, and G2G. Each team will prepare a plan of its major activities in a small country such as Denmark, Finland, or Singapore. A fifth team will deal with the coordination and collaboration of all e-government activities in each country. Prepare a report based on the activity.

3. Have teams search for virtual universities (e.g., the University of Phoenix). Write a summary of the schools' e-learning offerings.

4. In this activity, teams will investigate e-books. Have each team represent one of the following sites: netlibrary.com, ebooks.bn.com, ebooks.com, and zanderebooks.com. Each team will examine the technology, legal issues, prices, and business alliances associated with its site. Each team will then prepare a report answering the question, "Will e-books succeed?"

E-GOVERNMENT INITIATIVES IN HONG KONG

The Hong Kong SAR government in China (HK) initiated several e-government projects under the Digital 21 IT strategy (*info.gov.hk/digital21*). The major projects of this initiative were the electronic service delivery scheme (ESD), the interactive government services directory (IGSD), the electronic tendering system (ETS), the HKSAR Government Information Center, and the HK post office certification service (Post e-Cert). The highlights of some of these initiatives are provided here. Further information can be found at the specific URLs presented at *info.gov.hk*.

The Electronic Service Delivery Scheme (ESD)

The ESD project provides a major infrastructure through which the public can transact business electronically with 38 different public services provided by 11 government agencies, as demonstrated by the following examples:

1. **Transport Department.** Applications for driving and vehicle licenses, appointments for vehicle examinations and road tests, change-of-address reports, and so forth.

2. **Immigration.** Applications for birth/death/marriage certificates, appointments for ID card issuance, applications for foreign domestic helpers, communication on any other issue concerning immigration.

3. **HK Tourist Association.** Tourist information, maps, answers to queries.

4. **Labour Department.** List of job openings, job searches for job seekers, searches for applicants by employers, FAQs regarding legal issues, information on employee-compensation plans.

5. **Social Welfare Department.** Applications for senior citizen cards and special program participation, welfare information, registration for volunteer activities, requests for charitable fund-raising permits.

6. **Inland Revenue Department.** Electronic filing of tax returns, electronic payment program, change of address forms, interactive tax Q&A, applications for sole proprietor certificate, applications for business registrations, purchase tax reserve certificates.

7. **Registration and Electoral Office.** Applications for voter registration, change of address forms, interactive Q&A.

8. **Trade and Industry Department.** Business license information and applications, SME information center.

9. **Treasury Department.** Electronic bill payment.

10. **Rating and Valuation Department.** Changes of rates and/or government rent payers' particulars, interactive Q&A.

11. **Innovation and Technology Commission.** Information on technology funding schemes, electronic applications for funding.

These services are provided in Chinese and English. The project is managed by ESD Services Limited (*esdlife.com*). For additional information, see *esd.gov.hk*.

In addition to these services, the Web site includes eight ESD clubs, or communities. The public can sign up for a club, get information, share experiences, or just chat. The eight clubs are ESDbaby (for new parents, family planning, etc.), ESDkids (how to raise kids), ESDteens (a meeting point for the teens on music, culture, learning, etc.), ESD1822 (lifestyle, education, jobs, etc., for adults aged 18 to 22), EDScouples (information on getting married and building a family), ESDprime (information on jobs, education, entertainment, investment, travel, for middle-aged adults, etc.), ESDsenior (health care, fitness, education, lifestyle), and ESDhospice (complete services for the end of life).

The Interactive Government Services Directory (IGSD)

IGSD is an interactive service that enables the public to access information and services not included in the ESD. For example, it includes:

▶ Telephone and Web site directory of public services containing information and links to hundreds of services.

- Interactive investment guide offered by Industry Department (for investing in Hong Kong)
- Interactive employment services.
- Interactive road traffic information.

The Electronic Tendering System (ETS)

ETS is a G2B Web site that manages the reverse auctions conducted by the government supplies department. It includes supplier registration, notification of tenders, downloading of tendering documents, interactive Q&A, submission of tender offers, and more. The HK government conducts more than 5,000 tenders a year. For further information, see *ets.com.hk*.

The HKSAR Government Information Center

The HKSAR Government Information Center is the official government Web site (*info.gov.hk*). This site enables people to view news, government notices, guides to major government services, information on leisure and cultural activities, and more.

The HK Post E-Cert

HK Post e-Cert is the home of the Hong Kong Public Certification Authority (*hongkongpost.com*). The Hong Kong Post created a PKI system (see Chapter 9), and issues digital certificates (Post e-Cert) to individuals and to organizations. It also maintains a certificate repository and directory of all certificates issued, so that the public can verify the validity of the certificates. The Post e-Cert also issues certificates to servers and to security systems.

Accessibility to this extensive e-government portal is available not only from PCs, but also from hundreds of kiosks placed in many public places in Hong Kong.

Source: Student interview at *info.gov.hk/digital21*, February 2001.

Questions

1. Identify each of the five initiatives as G2C, G2B, C2G, or G2E.
2. Visit *info.gov.hk/digital21* and identify the goals of the five e-government initiatives.
3. How will the role of the HK government change when the initiatives mature and are fully utilized?
4. Compare the services offered by Hong Kong with those offered in Singapore (*ecitizen.gov.sg*). What are the major differences between the two?
5. What applications could be added in the future by the HK government? (Use Exhibit 7.4 for ideas and insights.)

MOBILE COMMERCE

Learning objectives

Upon completion of this chapter, you will be able to:

▶ Describe the characteristics and attributes of m-commerce.

▶ Describe the drivers of m-commerce.

▶ Understand the technologies that support m-commerce.

▶ Describe wireless standards and transmission networks.

▶ Describe m-commerce applications in finance, marketing, and customer service.

▶ Describe the applications of m-commerce within organizations.

▶ Describe B2B and supply chain applications of m-commerce.

▶ Describe consumer and personal applications of m-commerce.

▶ Describe some non-Internet m-commerce applications.

▶ Describe location-based commerce (l-commerce).

▶ Describe the major limitations of m-commerce.

▶ Describe some m-commerce implementation issues.

Content

NEXTBUS: A SUPERB CUSTOMER SERVICE

The Problem

Buses in certain parts of San Francisco have difficulty keeping up with the posted schedule, especially in rush hours. Generally, buses are scheduled to arrive every 20 minutes, but, at times, passengers may have to wait 30 to 40 minutes. The scheduled times become meaningless.

The Solution

San Francisco bus riders carrying an Internet-enabled wireless device such as a cell phone or Palm (or other) PDA can quickly find out when a bus will actually arrive at a particular bus stop. They can find not only the scheduled arrival time, but also the actual one. The system tracks public transportation buses in *real time*. Knowing where each bus is and factoring in traffic patterns and weather reports, NextBus (*nextbus.com*) calculates the estimated arrival time of the bus to each bus stop on the route. The arrival times are also displayed on the Internet and on a screen at each bus stop.

The NextBus system is used successfully in several other cities around the United States, in Finland, and in several other countries. It is an example of location-based e-commerce, which is a major part of mobile commerce.

Exhibit 8.1 (page 334) shows how the NextBus system works. The core of the NextBus system is the GPS satellites that let the NextBus information center know where a bus is. Based on a bus's location, the scheduled arrival time at each stop can be calculated. Users can access the information from their cell phones or PCs, anytime, anywhere.

Currently, NextBus is an ad-free customer service, but in the near future advertising may be added. As the system knows exactly where you are when you request information and how much time you have until your next bus, it may send you to the nearest Starbucks for a cup of coffee, giving you an electronic $1 discount coupon.

The Results

Passengers in San Francisco are happy with the system; worries about missing the bus are diminished. Passengers may even discover they have time for a cup of coffee before the bus arrives! In rural areas in Finland, where buses are infrequent and it is very cold in winter, passengers can stay in a warm coffeehouse not far from the bus stop rather than waiting in the cold for a bus that may be an hour late. Also, using the system, a bus company can do better scheduling, arrange for extra buses when needed, and improve its operations.

What We Can Learn . . .

This opening vignette demonstrates an application of one of the most talked-about areas of EC, *mobile commerce*. Its most significant feature is that the service is provided to the customer wherever they are located. This capability, which is not available in regular EC, may change many things in our lives. The technological basis of mobile commerce, its major applications, and its limitations are the subject of this chapter.

Sources: Compiled from *Itsa.org/ITSNEWS.NSF*, August 10, 2001, P. Murphy, September 7, 1999, and *nextbus.com*.

EXHIBIT 8.1   NextBus Operational Model

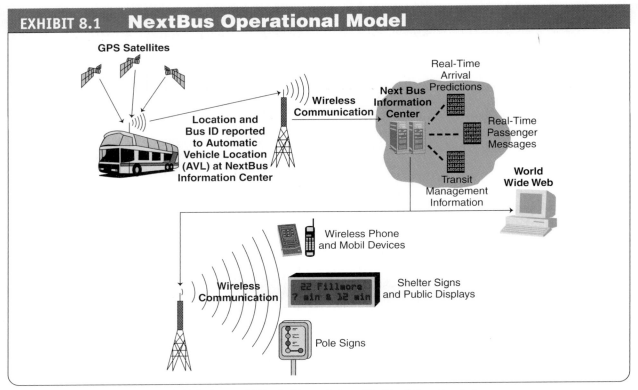

Source: *NextBus.com/corporate/works/index.htm*, 2002. Used with permission of NextBus Information Systems.

8.1   MOBILE COMMERCE: OVERVIEW, BENEFITS, AND DRIVERS

mobile commerce (m-commerce, m-business)
Any e-commerce done in a wireless environment, especially via the Internet.

Mobile commerce, also known as **m-commerce** and **m-business,** is basically any e-commerce or e-business done in a wireless environment, especially via the Internet. Like regular EC applications, m-commerce can be done via the Internet, private communication lines, smart cards, or other infrastructures.

M-commerce is not merely a variation on existing Internet services; it is a natural extension of e-business. Mobile devices create an opportunity to deliver new services to existing customers and to attract new ones. Varshney and Vetter (2001) classified the applications of m-commerce into 12 categories, as shown in Exhibit 8.2. This classification covers most of the applications that existed in 2001. (A classification by industry is provided at mobile.commerce.net. Also see mobiforum.org.)

M-COMMERCE TERMINOLOGY

We will begin our discussion by defining some common m-commerce terms. Common m-commerce terms include:

> ◗ **1G.** The first generation of wireless technology, 1G was in effect from 1979 to 1992. It was an analog-based technology.

EXHIBIT 8.2 Classes of M-Commerce Applications

Class of Applications	Examples
Mobile financial applications (B2C, B2B)	Banking, brokerage, and payments for mobile users
Mobile advertising (B2C)	Sending user-specific and location-sensitive advertisements to users
Mobile inventory management (B2C, B2B)	Location tracking of goods, boxes, troops, and people
Proactive service management (B2C, B2B)	Transmission of information related to distributing components to vendors
Product locating and shopping (B2C, B2B)	Locating/ordering certain items from a mobile device
Wireless reengineering (B2C, B2B)	Improvement of business services
Mobile auction or reverse auction (B2C)	Services for customers to buy or sell certain items
Mobile entertainment services (B2C)	Video-on-demand and other services to a mobile user
Mobile office (B2C)	Working from traffic jams, airport, and conferences
Mobile distance education (B2C)	Taking a class using streaming audio and video
Wireless data center (B2C, B2B)	Information can be downloaded by mobile users/vendors
Mobile music/music-on-demand (B2C)	Downloading and playing music using a mobile device

Source: U. Varshney and R. Vetter, "Recent Advances in Wireless Networking," *IEEE Computer*, June 2000. © 2000 IEEE.

▷ **2G.** The second generation of digital wireless technology, 2G is in existence today. It is based on digital radio technology and mainly accommodates text.

▷ **2.5G.** This is an interim technology based on GPRS and EDGE (see Section 8.3) that can accommodate limited graphics.

▷ **3G.** The third generation of digital wireless technology, 3G will support rich media such as video clips. It started in 2001 in Japan, reached Europe in 2002, and is expected to reach the United States in 2003.

▷ **4G.** The next generation after 3G, 4G will provide faster display of multimedia. The arrival of 4G is expected between 2006 and 2010.

▷ **Global positioning system (GPS).** A satellite-based tracking system that enables the determination of a GPS device's location. (See Section 8.9 for more on GPS.)

▷ **Personal digital assistant (PDA).** A small portable computer, such as a Palm m-500 or a Handspring Visor.

▷ **Short Message Service (SMS).** A technology that allows for the sending of short text messages (up to 160 characters in 2002) on certain cell phones. In

2G
The second generation of digital wireless technology; accommodates mainly text.

3G
The third generation of digital wireless technology; supports rich media such as video clips.

personal digital assistant (PDA)
A handheld wireless computer.

existence since 1991, data is borne by the radio resources reserved in cellular networks for locating mobile devices and connecting calls. SMS messages can be sent or received concurrently, even during a voice or data call. Used by hundreds of millions of users, it is known as the e-mail of m-commerce.

▶ **Enhanced Messaging Service (EMS).** An extension of SMS that is capable of simple animation, tiny pictures, and short melodies.

▶ **Multimedia Messaging Service (MMS).** The next generation of wireless messaging; this technology will be able to deliver rich media.

▶ **Wireless Application Protocol (WAP).** A technology that offers Internet browsing from wireless devices (see Section 8.3).

▶ **Smartphones. Smartphones** are Internet-enabled cell phones that can support mobile applications. These "phones with a brain" are becoming standard devices. They include WAP microprocessors for Internet access.

smartphones
Internet-enabled cell phones with attached applications.

THE ATTRIBUTES AND BENEFITS OF M-COMMERCE

Generally speaking, many of the EC applications described in this book can be done in m-commerce. For example, e-shopping, e-banking, e-stock trading, and e-gambling are gaining popularity in wireless B2C. Auctioning is just beginning to take place on cell phones, and wireless collaborative commerce in B2B is emerging. Wireless, non-Internet intrabusiness applications have been in use since the early 1990s. However, in addition to conducting regular EC in a wireless environment, there are several new applications that are possible only in the mobile environment. To understand why this is so, let's examine the major attributes of m-commerce.

The Specific Attributes of M-Commerce

M-commerce has two major characteristics that differentiate it from other forms of e-commerce: mobility and broad reach.

▶ **Mobility.** M-commerce is based on the fact that users carry a cell phone or other mobile device everywhere they go. Mobility implies portability. Therefore, users can initiate a *real-time* contact with commercial and other systems from wherever they happen to be.

▶ **Broad reach.** With m-commerce, people can be reached at any time. Of course, users can block certain hours or certain messages, but when users carry an open mobile device, they can be reached instantly.

These two characteristics break the barriers of geography and time. As shown in Exhibit 8.3, they create five value-added attributes. The benefits from these value-added attributes will drive the commercial development of m-commerce.

Ubiquity. Ubiquity refers to the attribute of being available at any location at any given time. A mobile terminal in the form of a smartphone or a PDA can fulfill the need both for *real-time information* and for communication independent of the user's location. It creates easier information access in a real-time environment.

EXHIBIT 8.3   The Characteristics of M-Commerce

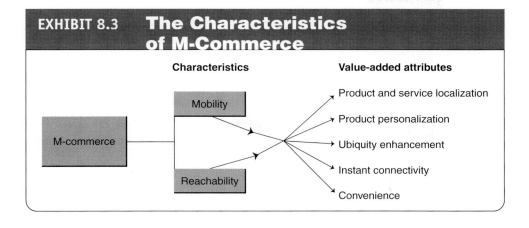

Convenience. It is very convenient for users to operate in the wireless environment. All they need is a smartphone. The technology is making rapid progress. Soon, using GPRS, it will be easier and faster to access information on the Web without booting up a PC or placing a call via a modem.

Instant connectivity. Mobile devices enable users to connect easily and quickly to the Internet, intranets, other mobile devices, and databases. Thus, the new wireless devices could become the preferred way to access information.

Personalization. Product personalization enables the preparation of information for individual consumers. For example, if a user is identified as someone who likes to travel, they might be sent travel-related information and advertisements. Product personalization is still limited on mobile devices. However, the emerging need for conducting transactions electronically, combined with availability of personalized information and transaction feasibility via mobile portals, will move personalization to new levels, leading ultimately to the mobile device becoming a major EC tool.

Localization of products and services. Knowing where the user is physically located at any particular moment is key to offering relevant services. Such services are known as location-based e-commerce or l-commerce. Precise location information is known when a GPS is attached to a user's wireless device. GPS may be a standard feature in mobile devices by 2004. When the mobile operator knows where the user is physically located, the operator can offer localized services. For example, you might use your mobile device to find the nearest ATM or FedEx drop box. Localization can be general, to anyone in a certain location (e.g., all shoppers at a shopping mall). Or, even better, it can be targeted so that users get messages that depend both on where they are and what their preferences are, thus combining localization and personalization. For instance, if it is known that you like Italian food and you are strolling in a mall that has an Italian restaurant, you might receive a SMS that tells you that restaurant's "special of the day" and gives you a 10 percent discount.

Vendors and carriers can *differentiate* themselves in the competitive marketplace by offering new, exciting, and useful services based on these attributes. These services will help vendors attract and keep customers and grow their revenues. In turn, the increasing number of value-added services will facilitate the use of m-commerce, as will the following business drivers.

DRIVERS OF M-COMMERCE

In addition to the value-added attributes just discussed, m-commerce is driven by the following factors.

Widespread availability of devices. The number of cell phones exceeded 1.1 billion in spring 2002 (mobiforum.org, 2001). That number is growing rapidly, and is expected to reach 1.3 billion by 2004 (Intex Management Services 2001). It is estimated that within a few years, about 70 percent of cell phones will have Internet access. Thus, a potential mass market is available for conducting m-commerce. Cell phones are spreading quickly in developing countries such as China, because there is no need for cables. In 2001, there were significantly more cell phone users than Internet users in most countries of the world. In some countries (e.g., Finland, Hong Kong), 80 percent of the population carries a cell phone (mobiforum.org, 2001).

No need for a PC. Because the Internet can be accessed via smartphone or other Internet-enabled wireless device, there is no need for a PC to access the Internet. Even though the cost of a PC that is used primarily for Internet access can be as low as $500 (or even less), it is still a major expense for the vast majority of people in the world. Furthermore, one needs to learn how to operate a PC, service it, and replace it every few years.

The handset culture. The widespread use of cell phones is becoming a social phenomenon, especially among the 15-to-25-year-old age group. These users are growing up and will constitute a major force of online buyers once they begin to make and spend reasonable amounts of money. For example, the use of SMS has been spreading like wildfire in several European and Asian countries. In the Philippines, SMS is a national phenomenon in the youth market.

Vendors' push. Both mobile communication network operators and manufacturers of mobile devices are advertising the many potential applications of m-commerce so that they can push new technologies, products, and services to buyers.

Declining prices. With the passage of time, the price of wireless devices is declining, and the per-minute pricing of mobile services is expected to decline by 50 to 80 percent before 2005. At the same time, functionalities are increasing.

Improvement of bandwidth. To properly conduct m-commerce, it is necessary to have sufficient bandwidth for transmitting text, however, bandwidth is also required for voice, video, and multimedia. The 3G technology is expected to do just that, at a data rate of up to 2 Mbps. This enables information to move seven times faster than when 56K modems are used.

The explosion of EC in general. Despite the failure of many Internet start-ups, the use of EC is growing rapidly, especially in B2B, some parts of B2C, e-government, and C2C. Therefore, more applications and opportunities are available online.

The drivers of m-commerce increase the demand for applications, whose execution requires an infrastructure.

▶ Define m-commerce.

▶ Define the following terms: 3G, PDA, WAP, SMS, GPS, and smartphone.

▶ List the value-added attributes of m-commerce.

▶ List at least five major drivers of m-commerce.

8.2 MOBILE COMPUTING INFRASTRUCTURE

Mobile computing requires hardware, software, and networks. The major components of mobile computing are described in this section.

M-COMMERCE HARDWARE

To conduct m-commerce, one needs devices for data entry and access to the Internet, applications, and other equipment. Several mobile computing devices are used in m-commerce. The major ones include the following:

- **Cellular (mobile) phones.** All major cell phone manufacturers are making or plan to make Internet-enabled cell phones. These cell phones are improving with time, adding more features, larger screens, keyboards, and more. You can even play games and download music files. An example of an Internet-enabled cell phone (as of 2002) is the Nokia 9290 Communicator (see the demo at nokia.com). It measures 158 × 56 × 27 mm, and it weighs 253 grams (about 0.6 lb.). The Nokia 9290 includes Internet access and fax capabilities, SMS, regular e-mail, digital camera connectivity, scheduling features, games, and more. Note that even phones without screen displays can be used to retrieve voice information from the Web (see tellme.com and the discussion of voice portals in Section 8.3).

- **Attachable keyboard.** Transactions can be executed with the regular handset entry keys, but it is fairly time-consuming to do so. An alternative is to use a larger cell phone such as the Nokia 9290 that contains a small-scale keyboard. Yet another solution is to plug an attachable keyboard into the cell phone. (Attachable keyboards are also available for other wireless devices, such as PDAs).

- **PDAs.** Personal Digital Assistants (PDAs) with Internet access are now available from several vendors, and their capabilities are increasing. One example of an Internet-ready PDA is Palm's i705. Using special software, one can connect the PDA to the Internet via a wireless modem. PDAs for corporate users include additional capabilities, such as e-mail synchronization and exchange of data and backup files with corporate servers. (Examples of such PDAs are Jornada from HP, 1Page from Compaq, and MobilePro from NEC.)

- **Interactive pagers.** Some two-way pagers can be used to conduct limited m-commerce activities on the Internet (mainly sending and receiving text messages, such as stock market orders).

- **Screenphones.** A telephone equipped with a color screen, possibly a keyboard, e-mail, and Internet capabilities is referred to as a **screenphone**. Initially, these were **wirelined**; that is, they were regular phones connected by wires to a network. As of 2000, wireless screenphones are available. Some are portable. They are used mainly for e-mail.

- **E-mail handhelds.** To enhance wireless e-mail capabilities, one can use devices such as the BlackBerry Handheld (blackberry.net). This device includes a keypad, making it easy to type messages. It is an integrated package, so there is no need to dial into an Internet provider for access. There are a variety of services for data communication, so you can receive and send messages from anywhere. A product demo is available at blackberry.net. Enterprise and home/personal solutions are available.

screenphone
A telephone equipped with a color screen, possibly a keyboard, e-mail, and Internet capabilities.

wirelined
Connected by wires to a network.

▶ **Other devices.** Notebooks, handhelds, and other mobile computers can be used in m-commerce. Many other wireless support devices are on the market. For example, SmartPad (seikosmart.com) allows you to write from a notepad instantly to a cell phone or PDA screen, overcoming the small screen size of these devices. Access from portable PCs to the Internet has been available since the early 1990s. Some new cell phones have built-in cameras; you can take a picture and e-mail it from your mobile location.

There is a clear trend toward the *convergence* of PDAs and cell phones. In 2001, Palm Corp. added a telephony attachment device that enabled Palm V to function like a cell phone. At the same time, Nokia, NEC, and other cell phone manufacturers added PDA functionalities. For example, Nokia's 9290 includes a calendar. The border between different mobile devices is beginning to blur. For example, phones with an integrated MP3 player and/or video player are coming to the market. For the state of the art, see the QCP smartphone at kyocera-wireless.com (check the demos).

In addition to the hardware described earlier, m-commerce also requires the following infrastructure hardware, most of which the user does not see or know about, but which is essential for wireless connectivity:

▶ A suitably configured wireline or wireless WAN modem, wireless LAN adapter, or wireless MAN (metro-area network) adapter.

▶ A Web server with wireless support, a WAP gateway, a communications server, and/or a mobile communications server switch (MCSS). Such a Web server provides communications functionality that enables the handheld device to communicate with the Internet or intranet infrastructure (see mobileinfo.com).

▶ An application or database server with application logic and a business application database.

▶ A large enterprise application server.

▶ A GPS locator that is used to determine the location of the person carrying the mobile computing device. This is the basis for location-based applications, as described in Section 8.9. The GPS locator can be attached or inserted into a mobile device.

SOFTWARE

Developing software for wireless devices is challenging because, as of 2002, there is no widely accepted standard for wireless applications. Therefore, software applications need to be customized for each type of device with which the application may communicate. The major software products required for m-commerce include the following:

▶ **Microbrowsers.** These browsers are designed with limited bandwidth and limited memory requirements. They can access the Web via the wireless Internet.

▶ **Mobile client operating system (OS).** This is the operating system software that resides in the mobile device. It may be Windows 2000/2001/NT, PalmOS, Win CE (or Pocket PC), EPOC, a specialized OS such as Black-Berry, or a Web browser.

▶ **Bluetooth.** **Bluetooth** (named after a famous Viking king) is a chip technology that enables voice and data communications between many wireless devices (e.g., between a digital camera and a PC) through low-power, short-range, digital two-way radio frequency (RF). Bluetooth is a Wireless Personal Area Network (WPAN) standard backed by most wireless-industry corporations and employed by major corporate users. It is deployed by placing a radio chip and special software into the devices that you want to communicate with each other. As of 2002, it is effective only up to 30 meters. The technology enhances ubiquitous connectivity and enables easy data transfer. For details see bluetooth.com.

▶ **Mobile application user interface.** The interface is the application logic in a handheld PDA, smartphone, Palm, or Wintel notebook. In the Internet world, it is often under the control of a browser or microbrowser.

▶ **Back-end legacy application software.** Legacy software that resides on large Unix servers (from vendors such as Sun, IBM, and HP) or on mainframes is a major part of m-commerce software because it provides the back-end systems (e.g., accounting, inventory).

▶ **Application middleware.** Middleware is a piece of software that communicates with back-end legacy systems and Web-based application servers. IBM's WebSphere is one such example.

▶ **Wireless middleware.** Wireless middleware that links multiple wireless networks to application servers is also needed.

Bluetooth

A chip technology and WPAN standard that enables voice and data communications between wireless devices over short-range radio frequency (RF).

NETWORKS AND ACCESS

A wireless network may be a private network used by police agencies and emergency health services. Such wireless local area networks (WLANs) can be created with one or more support technologies such as RF and Bluetooth. WLANs are easy and fast to install and to change. Because no cables are required, these networks allow organizations to quickly relocate or return to normal in case of a disaster.

Or, a wireless network may be a shared public network that is provided by a network provider such as Motient, Cingular, Verizon, Sprint, AT&T Wireless, Metricom, Nextel, Bell Mobility (Canada), Roger's AT&T (Canada), BT in United Kingdom, Deutsche Telecom, France Telecom, Vodafone, SK Telecom, NTT DoCoMo (Japan), and so on. Access to the Internet is provided by these companies or by specialized wireless ISPs on a regular subscription basis. Or, mobile users may use a wireless network for occasional connections, such as from hotels or airport VIP lounges.

Several wireless transmission media are in use, as shown in Exhibit 8.4 (page 342).

Wireless Systems

The various mobile infrastructure components need to be integrated into one system. Such integration may be done with a platform such as IBM's WebSphere, which integrates diverse data, applications, and processes. An example of such an application used by Delta Airlines is shown in Exhibit 8.5 (page 342). Through

EXHIBIT 8.4 Major Wireless Transmission Media

Medium	Description and Advantages	Limitations and Drawbacks
Microwave	▶ Point-to-point communication in line-of-sight path. ▶ Antennas are used (30 miles apart). ▶ Provide large capacity. ▶ Can be done quickly at lower cost.	▶ Must have visual contact between antennas. ▶ Susceptible to environmental interferences.
Satellites	▶ Can be at high, medium, or low orbit; used in GPSs. ▶ Complete global coverage is available. with three satellites.	▶ Expensive to build and maintain.
Radio/electromagnetic	▶ Effective for short ranges; used in LANs. ▶ Inexpensive and easy to install.	▶ Limited range; difficult to secure. ▶ Can create interference with communication devices. ▶ Susceptible to eavesdropping.
Cellular radio technology	▶ Defined cellular service areas around a radio transceiver and computerized control. ▶ All cell sites are connected to a mobile telephone switching office that provides connections and transfer calls between cells.	▶ Cellular areas are auctioned by governments who control them. During 1998–2001 prices were very high; some telecommunications companies took on too much debt by paying too much.

EXHIBIT 8.5 Delta Airlines' Wireless System

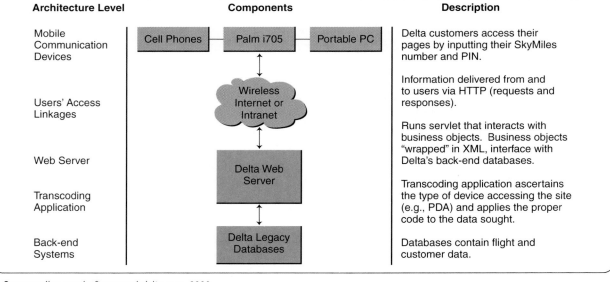

Sources: *ibm.com/software* and *delta.com*, 2000.

the use of such an application, Delta Airlines' customers can access their mileage accounts, flight information, and much more. For further details on WebSphere, see ibm.com/software.

- ❯ Describe the major hardware devices used for mobile computing.
- ❯ List the major software items used for mobile computing.
- ❯ Describe the four wireless transmission media.

8.3   WIRELESS STANDARDS AND SECURITY

M-commerce is supported by the infrastructure components described in the previous section and by the Internet infrastructure (when done on the Internet). It is also supported by standards, security, and voice systems, which are described briefly in the following sections.

STANDARDS

Wireless communications standards are developed by several organizations worldwide. A leading standards organization is ETSI (the European Telecommunications Standards Institute), which aims to create global wireless standards. The most important standards and technologies are:

- ❯ **Time Division Multiple Access (TMDA).** This technology divides each cellular telephone region into three time slots to increase the amount of data carried. It has been in use since 1992, mainly in Europe. Its capacity is limited to 9.6 to 14.4 Kbps.
- ❯ **General Packet Radio Services (GPRS).** A technology that will replace today's circuit-switching technology, making communications faster and with fewer interruptions.
- ❯ **Code Division Multiple Access (CDMA).** A technology that allows the reuse of scarce radio resources in adjacent areas.
- ❯ **CDMA one.** This is an interim wireless communication standard available commercially since October 2000. Considered a 2.75G technology, it is more advanced than 2.5G technologies.
- ❯ **Global System of Mobile Communication (GSM).** A wireless communication specification based on TDMA that has been in existence since 1992.
- ❯ **WLAN 802.11 (Wi-Fi).** A WLAN standard. In 2002 it was upgraded to 802.11g. Its 11e version is for multimedia and entertainment. Version 11a increased speed from 11 to 54 Mbps and frequency from 2.4 to 5 GHz.
- ❯ **Wideband-CDMA (W-CDMA) and CDMA 2000.** These are 3G technologies with up to 2 Mbps capacity. (The capabilities of CDMA, as envisioned by NTT of Japan, are shown in an exhibit at the book's Web site, prenhall.com/turban.)

wireless application protocol (WAP)
A set of communications protocols designed to enable different kinds of wireless devices to talk to a server installed on a mobile network, so users can access the Internet.

▶ **Wireless Application Protocol (WAP).** WAP is a set of communication protocols designed to enable different kinds of wireless devices (e.g., mobile phones, PDAs, pagers, etc.) to talk to a server installed on a mobile network so that users can access the Internet. It was designed especially for small screens and limited bandwidth. It enables the deployment of a microbrowser into mobile devices (see Redman 2000b). WAP is being challenged by several competing standards, including Java-based applications (the J2ME platform), which offer better graphics and security (see wapforum.org).

▶ **Subscriber Identification Module (SIM).** This is a smart card that holds a user's identity and includes it in an approved-subscribers telephone directory.

▶ **Wireless Markup Language (WML).** WML is the scripting language used for creating content in the wireless Web environment. It is based on XML, and it removes unnecessary content, such as animation. This simplification increases speed. WML works with WAP to deliver content. WML does not require a keyboard or a mouse.

▶ **Voice XML (VXML).** This is an extension of XML designed to accommodate voice.

▶ **Enhanced Data Rates for Global Evaluation (EDGE).** This is an extension of GSM that leverages TDMA and GPRS infrastructures.

▶ **Universal Mobile Telecommunications System (UMTS).** This is the 3G mobile standard. It allows different mobile systems to talk to each other across international borders.

▶ **IPv6.** This is the next-generation protocol for wireless Internet access (see the IPv6 Forum at nokia.com).

SECURITY ISSUES

A number of security issues affect wireless communications and m-commerce.

Viruses

Computer viruses have begun the migration to mobile devices as such terminals gain more processing power and intelligence. In 2001, the Gartner Group predicted a proliferation of viruses afflicting handheld computers and mobile phones as of mid-2002. This presents a significant security risk to mobile users.

The first computer virus that targeted mobile phones was identified in mid-2000. The virus was spread as an e-mail enclosure on conventional computers but was also designed to send prank SMS messages to randomly selected mobile phone numbers on a particular cellular network in Spain. Had the outbreak not been contained early, the flood of messages could have potentially crippled Spain's wireless network. Few mobile phones today handle e-mail attachments, but subsequent generations of better-equipped Internet-enabled devices that will receive attachments will be more vulnerable. Antivirus vendors have already begun shipping antivirus programs for handheld computers.

Smart Card Security Solutions

Many of the generic EC security issues that will be discussed in Chapter 9 are applicable to m-commerce. In addition, there are issues related mainly to m-commerce. For example, problems may result from the ease with which wireless voice communication can be intercepted by hackers. According to Baltimore Technologies (2000), it is more difficult to ensure confidentiality (privacy), authentication, integrity, and nonrepudiation in m-commerce than in e-commerce.

One practical solution is to use smart-card technologies embedded in cell phones. Smart cards with a biometric add-on feature can enhance cell phone security. The success of smart card/biometric applications on mobile phones for improved security depends on the existence of a standardized multiapplication card. This card would allow the incorporation of a number of different applications, including GSM-SIM, and security applications such as PKI (public key infrastructure), all on the same card. Such a card may be implemented in mobile phones by 2003 or 2004.

Back-End Security Solutions: PKI

A PKI system (see Chapter 10) can be adapted to m-commerce. Basically, PKI is a security system that uses two different keys, one public and the other private, one for encrypting data and the other for decrypting it. A PKI solution can be integrated with other security measures or applications in providing a comprehensive security framework. For example, PKI on a SIM card can be attached to a GSM phone (Muller-Veese 2000).

Alternatively, PKI solutions can be connected to the Transport Layer Security (TLS) (Baltimore Technologies 2000). TLS provides a secure network connection session between a client and a server. It is most commonly adopted between a Web browser and a Web server. The wireless version of the industrial standard of TLS, which is equivalent to SSL (Secure Socket Layer, an encryption protocol), is called Wireless Transport Layer Security (WTLS). PKI solutions can be connected to WTLS. Such security measures tightly bind digital identities to content providers and wireless customers, making their associated transactions more secure.

Security products and services are offered by companies such as VeriSign. Products include *wireless personal trust agents* (PTAs), a transparent microclient code that can be embedded in handheld devices to enable the use of private keys, digital certificates, and digital signatures; short-lived *wireless server certificates*, "mini-digital certificates" that provide authentication and real-time certificate validation; and *gateway-assisted SSL*, which enables network service providers to substitute wireless certificates for existing SSL certificates.

New wireless security services include subscriber trust services, which allow for secure messaging and transactions via wireless handhelds; server/gateway trust services to deliver secure applications over wireless networks; developer trust services to digitally protect downloadable content; enterprise trust services to provide wireless services such as e-banking, e-brokerage, e-healthcare, and e-messaging; and service provider platforms to offer a range of VeriSign-based wireless trust services.

For a comparative study of security in wireless systems in Europe, Japan, and the United States, see Macklin (2001).

VOICE SYSTEMS FOR M-COMMERCE

The most natural mode of human communication is voice. When people need to communicate with each other from a distance, they use the telephone more frequently than any other communication device. Voice communication can now also be done on the computer using a microphone and a sound card.

Voice and data can work together to create useful applications. For example, operators of PBXs (private branch exchanges, which are basically the command center of the intracompany phone systems) are letting callers give simple computer commands using interactive voice response (e.g., spelling the last name of the person one is calling). The number and type of voice technology applications is growing.

Voice technologies have the following advantages:

▶ Hand- and eyes-free operations increase the productivity, safety, and effectiveness of mobile computer users ranging from forklift drivers to military pilots.

▶ Disabled people can use voice commands to tell a computer to perform various tasks.

▶ Voice terminals are designed for portability; users do not have to go to the computer.

▶ Voice terminals are more rugged than keyboards; they operate better in dirty or moving environments.

▶ People can communicate about two-and-a-half times faster talking than typing.

▶ In most circumstances, speaking results in fewer data entry errors than does keyboard data entry, assuming a reliable voice recognition system is used.

One of the most popular conventional voice applications is interactive voice response.

Interactive Voice Response

interactive voice response (IVR)
A computer voice system that enables users to request and receive information and to enter and change data through regular telephone lines or through 1G cell phones.

Interactive voice response (IVR) systems enable users to interact with a computerized system to request and receive information and to enter and change data. These systems have been in use since the 1980s. The communication is conducted through regular telephone lines or through 1G cell phones. Examples of the application of this technology include the following:

▶ Patients can schedule doctor appointments.

▶ Users can request a pick-up from FedEx.

▶ Employees can find information about fringe benefits, select benefits, or make changes to their benefits package.

▶ Electric utilities can respond to customers who are calling to report power outages; the system then attempts to diagnose the problem and route it to the proper department.

Originally, IVR was conducted from a regular telephone, and the receiving system was hosted inside an organization (e.g., a call center). IVR systems are now moving to the Web, where they are incorporated into voice portals.

Voice Portals

A **voice portal** is a Web site with an audio interface. Voice portals are not really Web sites in the normal sense because they are designed to be accessed through a standard or a cell telephone. A certain phone number connects you to a participating Web site where you can request information verbally. The system finds the information, translates it into a computer-generated voice reply, and tells you what you want to know. Several of these new sites are in operation. An example of this application is the voice-activated 511 traveler information line developed by Tellme.com. Sites such as tellme.com and bevocal.com allow callers to request information about weather, local restaurants, current traffic, and other handy information.

In addition to retrieving information, some sites provide true interaction. iPing.com is a reminder and notification service that allows users to enter information via the Web and receive reminder calls. In addition, iPing.com can call a group of people to notify them of a meeting or conference call.

The real value for Internet marketers is that these voice portals can help businesses find new customers. Several of these sites are supported by ads; thus, the customer profile data they have available can deliver targeted advertising very precisely. For instance, a department-store chain with an existing brand image can use short audio commercials on these sites to deliver a message related to the topic of the call.

With the development of technical standards and continuing growth of wireless technologies, the number of m-commerce applications is growing rapidly. Applications are derived from providing wireless access to existing B2C, intrabusiness, and CRM applications and from creating new location-based and SMS-based applications. In the next six sections of the chapter, we will study m-commerce applications in a number of diverse categories.

> **voice portal**
> A Web site with audio interface, accessed by making a phone call.

- ▶ Describe the following terms: Bluetooth, microbrowser, WAP, and WLAN.
- ▶ Explain the need for technical standards. Describe several available standards.
- ▶ Describe security issues and solutions in m-commerce.
- ▶ Describe IVR.
- ▶ What are voice portals?

8.4 MOBILE FINANCIAL APPLICATIONS

Mobile financial applications are likely to be one of the most important components of m-commerce. These applications include mobile banking, bill payment services, m-brokerage services, mobile money transfers, and mobile micropayments. These services could turn a mobile device into a business tool, replacing banks, ATMs, and credit cards by letting a user conduct financial transactions with a mobile device.

WIRELESS ELECTRONIC PAYMENT SYSTEMS

Wireless payment systems transform mobile phones into secure, self-contained purchasing tools capable of instantly authorizing payments over the cellular network for goods and services consumed. For example, in Finland, SMS messages sent from GSM handsets are already being used to pay for food and drinks at some outlets. Users can also initiate automatic car washes and trigger vending machines into dispensing goods, all by simply dialing special phone numbers posted for those purposes.

MICROPAYMENTS

micropayments
Electronic payments for small-purchase amounts (generally less than $10).

Micropayments are electronic payments for small-purchase amounts (generally less than $10). For example, a mobile device can communicate with a vending machine, using a local wireless network, to make a micropayment for purchase of an item.

Micropayments can be implemented in a variety of ways. One way is that the user could make a call to a certain number where per-minute charges equal the cost of the vending item. This approach has been used by Sonera, a Finnish wireless provider, in its Coke (and now Pepsi) vending machine service (see Muller-Veerse 2000). In effect, this method transfers money from the user's telephone bill to the vending provider's account. Another way to perform micropayments is by using prepaid cards purchased from a service provider, bank, or credit card company. Attaching a smart card with prepaid money on it to a mobile device is another option.

An Israeli firm, TeleVend, Inc. (televend.com), has pioneered a secure platform that allows subscribers to make payments using mobile phones of any type on any cellular infrastructure. A customer places a mobile phone call to a number stipulated by the merchant to authorize a vending device to dispense the service. Connecting to a TeleVend server, the user selects the appropriate transaction option to authorize payment. Billing can be made to the customer's bank or credit card account or to the mobile phone bill. Micropayment technology has wide-ranging applications, such as making payments to parking garages, restaurants, grocery stores, and public utilities. The success of micropayment applications depends on the costs of the transactions. Transaction costs will be small only if there is a large volume of transactions. See Chapter 10 for more about micropayments.

WIRELESS WALLETS

m-wallet (mobile wallet)
A wireless wallet that enables cardholders to make purchases with a single click from their wireless devices.

Financial transactions can be made on the Web using what is called an *e-wallet*. As we will discuss in more detail in Chapter 10, an e-wallet is a piece of software that stores an online shopper's credit card numbers and other personal information so that they do not have to reenter that information for every online purchase.

Nextcard.com has developed a wireless wallet that enables cardholders to make purchases with a single click from their wireless devices. Called **m-wallet (mobile wallet)**, the service is offered by other companies as well (e.g., see the Nokia Wallet at nokia.com). The m-wallet is basically a single-click checkout. For instance, shoppers in certain Swedish stores can pay for their purchases with a virtual credit card (from Eurocard) that is stored in their Ericsson or Nokia handsets. Using Bluetooth technology, the handset interacts with the in-store payment terminal.

BILL PAYMENTS

In addition to paying bills with checks or through online banking, one can pay bills, such as a MasterCard or utility bill, directly from a cell phone. This can be done via a bank, a credit card, or a prepaid arrangement. Over 50 percent of Portuguese mobile phone customers are anonymous prepaid subscribers. They use ATM bill payment facilities to "reload" their mobile phones for more talk time. An example of how bill payments can be made using a mobile device is shown in Exhibit 8.6.

EXAMPLES OF FINANCIAL APPLICATIONS

As the following examples show, use of m-commerce financial applications is quite broad and varied.

▶ The Swedish Postal Bank (Postbanken) and Telia's Mobile Smart service allow consumers to make giro payments from their handsets. (Giro systems are payment systems run by a country's national postal system.) MeritaNordbanken's customers in Sweden can check their balances and transaction logs from their mobile phones and conduct some types of transactions.

▶ *Dagens Industri*, Europe's fourth-largest business daily, allows subscribers to use their handsets to receive financial data and trade on the Stockholm Exchange.

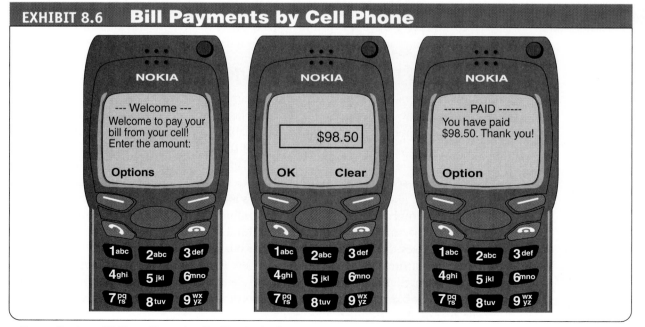

EXHIBIT 8.6 Bill Payments by Cell Phone

Source: Courtesy of Nokia, *nokia.com/pc_files/download.swf*, 2001.

- Citibank has a diversified mobile banking service. Consumers can use their mobile handsets to access account balances, pay bills, and transfer funds using SMS.

- Many banks in Japan allow for all banking transactions to be done via cell phone. For example, one online bank, Japan Net Bank, allows customers to pay for goods and services from their cell phones, debiting their purchases from their accounts.

- Hoover's Wireless (hoovers.com) can be accessed from mobile devices. Investors can access stock information, news, quotes, and more.

- ASB Bank (New Zealand) provides customers with a personalized service that alerts them with an SMS when a specific stock breaks a personally defined price threshold. The customer is then linked to his ASB account for possible trading.

- Vendors selling from portable carts at Boston's Faneuil Hall Marketplace did not have dedicated telephone lines, so they were unable to get real-time authorization for credit cards. Vendors used to lose about 15 percent of their annual sales due to fraud because they were able to check credit card purchases only after they went home for the day. Installing wireless point-of-sale terminals, the vendors can now process cards in 3 to 5 seconds, resulting in increased sales and decreased fraud.

- How are micropayments made?
- Describe the m-wallet and wireless bill payments.
- Discuss mobile banking, mobile stock trading, and other mobile financial applications.

8.5 MOBILE MARKETING, ADVERTISING, AND CUSTOMER SERVICE APPLICATIONS

M-commerce B2C applications are expected to be concentrated in three areas: retail shopping, advertising (possibly targeted), and personalized customer services.

SHOPPING FROM WIRELESS DEVICES

Many vendors allow customers to shop from wireless devices. For example, AT&T customers who use Internet-ready cell phones can shop at certain sites such as buy.com. Shopping from wireless devices enables customers to perform quick searches, compare prices, order, and view the status of their order using their cell phones. Wireless shoppers are supported by services similar to those available for wireline shoppers. For example, users have access shopping carts, as well as product search and price comparison tools. The wireless shopping process is shown on the left side of Exhibit 8.7.

Today, you can buy books or check online auctions at amazon.com via mobile devices; many more features will be added in 2002. Amazon.com's CEO, Jeff Bezos, believes that in 5 to 10 years most business will be wireless.

In the future, users will be able to view products in online showrooms (catalogs) and purchase them using handheld devices. These handheld devices may be enhanced by bar code scanners (see allnetdevices.com). Some customization may even be possible (e.g., if the vendor has a list of past purchases that can be used to predict future purchases).

EXHIBIT 8.7   Mobile Shopping Supported by CRM

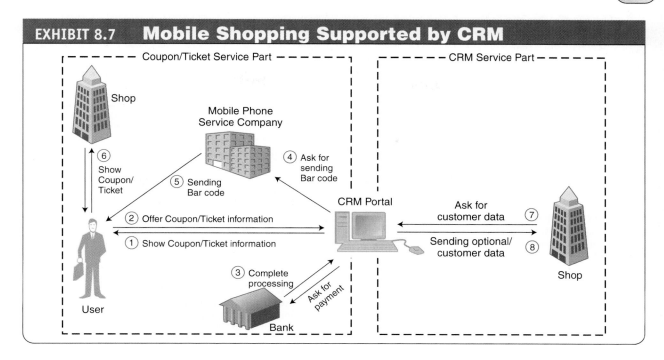

TARGETED ADVERTISING

Using demographic information collected by wireless services, barnesandnoble.com, which launched its wireless service for mobile devices in 1999, now provides more personalization of services and an enhanced user interface for its wireless Web page. In one improvement, the company added music clips to its wireless Web page so that customers can download and listen to the clips on their cell phones.

Knowing the current location of mobile users (using GPS) and their preferences or surfing habits, marketers can send user-specific advertising messages. Advertisements can also be location-sensitive, informing a user about various ongoing special sales in shops, malls, and restaurants close to where a potential buyer is. This type of advertising can be performed by sending SMS messages to a cell phone or short paging messages to pagers. Many companies are capitalizing on targeted advertising, as shown in the Insights and Additions box on the next page.

As more wireless bandwidth becomes available, content-rich advertising involving audio, pictures, and video clips will be generated for individual users with specific needs, interests, and inclinations. Also, depending on the interests and personality types of individual mobile users, the network provider may consider using "push" or "pull" methods of mobile advertising on a per user basis or to a class of users (segmentation). The number of ads pushed to an individual customer should be limited, to avoid overwhelming a user with too much information and also to avoid the possibility of congestion over the wireless networks. Wireless network managers may consider ad traffic to be of a lower priority compared with ordering or customer interaction. Finally, since ad pushers need to know a user's current location, a third-party vendor may be used to provide location services. This will require a sharing of revenues with a location service provider.

Insights and Additions   Wireless Advertising in Action

The following are a few examples of wireless advertisement in action.

Vindigo.com

Vindigo.com has a large database of customers (over 350,000 as of early 2002) willing to accept promotional materials on their wireless devices. This is known as *permission marketing*. The users download a special software on their PDAs that allows Vindigo.com to deliver timely, accurate information about places to go and things to do in their area. Along with every listing, the company can deliver a customized message to the users at a time and place where it is of most interest to them and they are most likely to act on it.

   The company targets ads by city (New York, San Francisco, Los Angeles, etc.) and channel (Eat, Shop, or Play). Vindigo.com tracks which ads a user sees and selects, and even allows a user to request information from an advertiser via e-mail. Vindigo.com determines a user's location through GPS or by asking with which neighborhoods they want to be matched. For example, if you own an Italian restaurant chain, you can use Vindigo.com to send a message to anyone looking for Italian food within a few blocks of one of your locations. You can give them directions to that restaurant and even offer them the list of specials on the menu.

GeePS.com

Location-based start-up geePS.com delivered coupons to the cell phones of shoppers at the Palisades Center Mall near New York City and mobile customers in upscale Summit, New Jersey. After finding coupons at the wireless version of New Jersey Online (*nj.com*), mobile customers showed store employees the digital coupon and claimed their discounts at local stores. GeePS.com planned to offer its location-based ads throughout Maryland, Ohio, Pennsylvania, and West Virginia, and also to offer location-based radio commercials when 3G is widespread. Before the company could expand, it succumbed to marketplace economics and folded.

Go2Online.com

Hoping to become the king of location-based Web domains, *go2online.com* helps mobile travelers find everything from lodging (choose *go2hotels*) to Jiffy Lube stations (choose *go2oilchanges*). Partnering with Sprint, NexTel, Verizon, and BellSouth, go2 services are available on every Web-enabled phone, Palm i705, and BlackBerry RIM pager in America. Entering "JiffyLube" or hundreds of other brand names into the go2 system will bring up the nearest location where a shopper can find that product or service.

Source: Compiled from Vindigo.com, GeePS.com and Go2Online.com

Paying Customers to Listen to Advertisements

Would you be willing to listen to a 10–second ad when you dial your cell phone if you were paid 2 minutes of free long-distance time? It depends on which country you are in. In the United States this service was a flop in most places and was discontinued. In Singapore it works very well. Within a few months of offering the ads, more than 100,000 people subscribed to the free minutes in exchange for listening to the ads offered by SingTel Mobile (Media Corp TV, Channel 5, 2001).

   SingTel operates its program in partnership with Spotcast. In exchange for Spotcast's software platform, SingTel paid the Maryland-based company $600,000 and will continue to pay ongoing maintenance fees. Spotcast's technology enables SingTel to build increasingly accurate profiles of subscribers and target ads to them. SingTel recouped its initial investment from ad revenues in about a year. By spring 2001, about 100 advertisers had signed up, but their ads are getting 10 times the response rate of an average Internet banner ad. Subscribers to SingTel's service fill out a personal questionnaire when they sign up. This information is fed into the Spotcast database and encrypted to shield subscribers' identities—Spotcast cannot match phone numbers to names, for example. To collect their free minutes—1 minute per call, up to 100 minutes a month—subscribers dial a four-digit code, then the phone number of the person they want to talk to. The code prompts SingTel to forward the call to Spotcast and, in an instant, Spotcast's software finds the best ad to send to the subscriber based on the subscriber's profile.

Advertising Strategies and Guidelines

On one hand, hundreds of millions of people have mobile devices, and the number is growing daily. On the other hand, marketers do not have much experience with wireless mobile advertising. The Wireless Advertising Association (waaglobal.org) is trying to establish wireless ad guidelines (e.g., opt-in ad programs involving mobile message alerts if, for instance, an open seat becomes available on a plane heading to a desired destination). The industry is currently addressing issues such as spamming and unethical strategies (e.g., confirmed opt-ins, personally identifiable information, and push advertising).

SUPPORTING CUSTOMERS AND BUSINESS PARTNERS (CONSUMER SERVICES)

Supporting customers and business partners is the essence of the CRM and PRM programs described earlier in this text. Wireless solutions complement the wireline solutions.

Look back at Exhibit 8.7, which showed the wireless shopping process. The right side of the figure shows the relationship of mobile shopping to CRM (customer service). Special CRM applications, called MobileCRM, have been developed by Siebel Systems and Accenture, Inc. (see nokia.com). These systems allow customers to interact with vendors while they are actually shopping inside a physical store. For example, shoppers equipped with an AT&T Internet-ready cell phone can access mysimon.com, a leading comparison shopping agent. Then, as they shop in a physical store, they will be able to compare the prices in the store to those available elsewhere.

Using Voice Portals in Marketing and Customer Service

Voice portal technology can be connected to legacy systems to provide enhanced customer service or to improve access to data for employees, as shown in the following examples.

- Customers who are away from the office could use a vendor's voice portal to check on the status of deliveries to a job site.
- Service technicians could be provided with diagnostic information, enabling them to diagnose more difficult problems.
- Sales people could check on inventory status during a meeting to help close a sale.

There are a wide variety of CRM applications for voice portal technology. The challenge is in learning how to create the navigation and other aspects of interaction that makes customers feel comfortable with voice-access technology.

Using Mobile Portals

mobile portal
A customer interaction channel that aggregates content and services for mobile users.

Similar to regular Internet portals, such as Yahoo!, we are seeing an increasing number of mobile portals, especially in Europe, where, according to Bughin et al. (2001), there are over 200 mobile portals. A **mobile portal** is a customer interaction channel optimized for mobility. It aggregates content and services for mobile users. Examples of pure mobile portals (those whose only business is to be a mobile portal) in Europe are Room 33, Halebop, and Iobox. Also, some telecommunications companies operate their own mobile portals (e.g., Zed from Sonera in Finland).

Mobile portals charge for their services. For example, you may be asked to pay 50 cents to get a weather report over your mobile phone. Alternatively, you may pay a monthly fee for the portal service and get the report free any time you want it. I-Mode in Japan (see Chapter 2) generates revenue mainly from subscription fees.

In addition to the public mobile portals, there are mobile *corporate* portals that serve a corporation's customers and/or suppliers (e.g., the major airline portals). For further discussion of mobile portals, see Kalakota and Robinson (2001).

▶ Describe how mobile devices can be used to shop.
▶ Explain targeted advertising in the wireless environment.
▶ Describe wireless CRM.
▶ Describe mobile portals.

8.6 MOBILE INTRABUSINESS AND ENTERPRISE APPLICATIONS

Although B2C m-commerce is getting considerable publicity, most of today's applications are used within organizations. Let's look at how mobile devices and technologies can be used within organizations.

SUPPORT OF MOBILE EMPLOYEES

The Gartner Group predicted in 2000 that by 2002 over 25 percent of all workers in many industries could be mobile workers. This prediction was proven to be too optimistic and was revised to be true by 2004. Examples of mobile employees are sales people in the field, traveling executives, telecommuters, people working in corporate yards and warehouses, and repair or installation employees who work at customers' sites or on utility lines. These mobile employees need the same corporate data available to employees working inside the company's offices. Using wireline devices may be inconvenient or even impossible when employees are away from their offices.

The solution is a myriad of smaller, simple wireless devices—the smartphones and handheld companions carried by mobile workers and the in-vehicle information systems installed in cars. Some mobile wireless applications used by employees are described in EC Application Case 8.1.

EC APPLICATION 8.1
Intraorganization
MOBILE WORKPLACE APPLICATIONS

The following are two scenarios of wireless applications for mobile employees.

Sales Support

Linda is a member of the field sales team at Theru Tools (a fictitious company name). Each day she drives out to her customers in a van stocked with products. For each sale, she has to note the customer, the number and type of products sold, and any special discounts made. This used to be done manually, and many errors were made, leading to customer complaints and lost sales.

The company was reluctant to invest in laptops for such a limited application, but Linda wanted the speed and reliability of automation. With the help of SAP, Theru was able to implement a system using low-cost but powerful handheld wireless devices.

Using Mobile Sales (an application for handhelds), accessed via the mysap.com Mobile Workplace, Linda and her coworkers in the field now have information at their fingertips, including updates on new products and special promotions. She can place orders without delay and get immediate feedback on product availability and delivery times. What's more, the system at headquarters can prompt Linda and make plausibility checks on the orders, eliminating many of the errors associated with the manual process. It can also check if she is giving the right discounts to the right customer, and immediately trigger the invoicing process or print out a receipt on the spot.

Customer Service Support

Michael works for Euroblast, Inc. (a fictitious company name) as a service engineer. It is his job to provide time-critical maintenance and support for the company's customers' electromechanical control systems. To do so, he needs to know immediately when a customer's system is faltering, what is malfunctioning, and what type of service contract is in effect for billing purposes.

Using SAP's Mobile Service, Michael does not need to carry all of this information in his head, but instead has it in the palm of his hand. With only a few taps of the stylus, Michael accesses the *mysap.com* Mobile Workplace for all the data he requires, including the name and address of the next customer he should visit, equipment specifications, parts inventory data, and so forth.

Once he has completed the job, he can report back on the time and materials he used, and this data can be employed for timely billing and service quality analysis. In addition, his company is able to keep track of his progress and monitor any major fluctuations in activities. As a result, both Michael and his supervisors are better informed and better able to serve the customer.

Sources: Compiled from "CRM and the *mySAP.com* Mobile Workplace," SAP AG Corp., 2000 (a publicly available brochure).

Questions

▶ How does SAP software help Linda do her job? How is m-commerce being applied in this case?

▶ What information does Michael need for his job? How do the m-commerce capabilities of SAP provide this information?

Wearable Devices

Employees who work on buildings, electrical poles, or other difficult-to-climb places may be equipped with a special form of mobile wireless computing devices called **wearable devices**. Examples of wearable devices include:

wearable devices

Mobile wireless computing devices for employees who work on buildings and other difficult-to-climb places.

- **Cameras.** A camera is mounted on a safety hat. Workers can take digital photos and videos and transmit them instantly to a portable computer nearby. Photo transmission to a wearable device or computer is made possible via Bluetooth technology.
- **Screen.** A computer screen is mounted on a safety hat, in front of the workers eyes, displaying information to the worker.
- **Keyboard.** A wrist-mounted keyboard enables typing by the other hand. It is an alternative to voice recognition systems, which are also wireless.
- **Touch-panel display.** In addition to the wrist-mounted keyboard, mobile employees can use a flat-panel screen, attached to the hand, which responds to the tap of a finger or stylus.

For an example of wearable devices used to support mobile employees, see EC Application Case 8.2 and wearable.com.au.

Job Dispatch

Mobile devices are becoming an increasingly integral part of groupware and workflow applications. For example, nonvoice mobile services can be used to assign jobs to mobile employees, along with detailed information about the task. The target areas for mobile delivery and dispatch services include the following:

- Transportation (delivery of food, oil, newspapers, cargo, courier services, tow trucks)
- Taxis (already in use in Korea and Singapore)
- Utilities (gas, electricity, phone, water)
- Field service (computer, office equipment, home repair)
- Health care (visiting nurses, doctors, social services)
- Security (patrols, alarm installation)

A dispatching solution allows improved response with reduced resources, real-time tracking of work orders, increased dispatcher efficiency, and a reduction in administrative work. An interesting solution is that delivered by edispatch.com. With a Web-based dispatching solution using smartphones, the company promises savings of about 30 percent in communication costs and increases in workforce efficiency of about 25 percent.

Mobile Sales Force Automation

The sales force automation (SFA) tools (e.g., those from microsoft.com/mobile) integrate software that is aimed at m-commerce applications. The mobile sales force is equipped with smartphones, providing them with easy access to cus-

EC APPLICATION 8.2

Implementation and Strategy

WEARABLE DEVICES FOR BELL CANADA WORKERS

For years mobile employees, especially those who had to climb trees, electric poles, or tall buildings, were unable to enjoy the new technologies designed to make employees work or feel better. Thus, their productivity and comfort were inferior, especially where computers were involved. That is all beginning to change.

On a cold, damp November day in Toronto, Chris Holm-Laursen, a field technician with Bell Canada (*bell.ca*), is out and about as usual, but this time with a difference: A small but powerful computer sits in a pocket of his orange mesh vest, a keyboard is attached to the vest's upper-left side, and a flat-panel display screen hangs by his waist. A video camera attached to his safety hat enables him to take pictures without using his hands and send them immediately to the office. A cell phone is attached as well, connected to the computer. A battery pack to keep everything going sits against his back.

Holm-Laursen and 18 other technicians on this pilot project were equipped like this for 10 weeks during fall 2000. The wearable devices enabled the workers to access work orders and repair manuals wherever they were. What is notable is that these workers are not typical of the group usually most wired up, that is, white-collar workers. The hands-free aspect and the ability to communicate anytime, from anywhere, represent major steps forward for these utility workers. A wide variety of employees—technicians, medical practitioners, aircraft mechanics, and contractors—are using or testing such devices.

So far, only a few companies make and sell wearables for mobile workers. Bell Canada's system was developed by Xybernaut, a U.S. company, which in 2002 had more than a thousand of its units in use around the world, some in operation and others in pilot programs. (See case studies at *xybernaut.com*.) Minneapolis-based ViA is another supplier, most of whose systems are belt-worn (*bell.ca*).

Meanwhile, Bell Canada was impressed with the initial results, and is equipping most of its technicians with wearables. Of course, a practical problem of wearable devices in many countries is the weather: What happens when the temperature is minus 50 degrees or the humidity is 99 percent? Other potential problems also exist: If you are wearing thick gloves, how can you use a keyboard? If it is pouring rain, will the battery short circuit? Various solutions are being developed, such as voice input, tapping on a screen instead of typing, and rainproof electrical systems.

Sources: Compiled from XyberFlash, "Wearable Computers for the Working Class," *New York Times*, December 14, 2000, and *xybernaut.com*, 2001.

Questions

▶ What are some other industrial applications of similar wearable devices? (Use *google.com* to find additional applications.)

▶ How do you think wearable devices could be used in entertainment?

---

tomer data at the central office. Key data that can be retrieved include contact-management information, product and spare part availability, and deal tracking. Using SFA tools, a traveling salesperson is able to check the latest status of a customer's account just before going to a customer's office, and is able to report a successful contract immediately after signing it. Sales forecasting and opportunity tracking could be done as well. For more on wireless SFA, see salesnet.com, nokia.com, and iconverse.com.

NON-INTERNET INTRABUSINESS APPLICATIONS

Wireless applications in the non-Internet enterprise environment have been around since the early 1990s. Examples of such applications include the following:

- Wireless networking is used to pick items out of inventory in warehouses via PCs mounted on forklifts, other vehicles, or carried by employees.
- Delivery and order status updates, entered on PCs inside distribution trucks.
- Online dispatching, online diagnosis support from remote locations, and parts ordering/inventory queries from service people in the field.
- Mobile shop-floor quality control systems that enable voice reports by inspectors, data collection from facilities, and transmission to a central processor.
- Sales people use their PDAs to access the corporate wireless network to report sales, competitors' inventories in stores, orders from customers' sites, and charges to customers' credit cards.
- Remote database queries regarding order status or product availability.

The variety of possible wireless applications is shown in Exhibit 8.8. Some of these are amenable to Web technologies and can be delivered on a wireless intranet. For details on intrabusiness applications, see mdsi-acvantex.com. The advantages offered by intrabusiness wireless solutions can be seen through an examination of workflow applications, shown in Exhibit 8.9 (page 360).

INTERNET-BASED INTRABUSINESS APPLICATIONS

A large number of Internet-based wireless applications have been implemented inside enterprises. Examples of such applications include the following:

- Employees at companies such as Sonera (Finland) get their monthly pay slips either by regular e-mail or via SMS sent to their mobile phone. The money itself is transferred electronically to a designated bank account. Both methods are much cheaper for Sonera and result in less paperwork than the old method of mailing monthly pay slips.
- At Chicago's United Center—home of the NBA's Bulls and NHL's Blackhawks—manual inventory systems were replaced with procedures that take advantage of mobile computing. In November 1999, the concessionaire, Bismarck Enterprises, deployed throughout the United Center 25 handheld devices from Symbol Technologies that run the Palm OS and custom applications on an intranet with Web technology (for searches, messages, etc.). Bismarck employees can now inventory a full warehouse of food items in about 3 hours. The company used to hand-count everything once a month, taking between 48 and 72 hours to do inventory. With the new system, employees can do reconciliation right on the spot. The system saves the company about $100,000 a year in labor.
- Express delivery companies, such as FedEx and UPS, have been employing handheld wireless devices for several years, but the units were usually connected to a private network and generally designed to serve one vertical industry and transfer a specific type of data, say, the location of a package on the

EXHIBIT 8.8 Intrabusiness Workflow Applications

Before Wireless	With Wireless
Work orders are manually assigned by multiple supervisors and dispatchers.	Work orders are automatically assigned and routed within minutes for maximum efficiency.
Field service technicians commute to dispatch center to pick up paper work orders.	Home-based field service technicians receive first work order via mobile terminal and proceed directly to first assignment.
Manual record keeping of time, work completed, and billing information.	Automated productivity tracking, record keeping, and billing updates.
Field service technicians call in for new assignments and often wait because of radio traffic or unavailable dispatcher.	Electronic transmittal of additional work orders with no waiting time.
Complete work orders dropped off at dispatch center at the end of the day for manual entry into the billing or tracking system. Uncompleted orders are manually distributed to available technicians. Overtime charges often result.	Technicians close completed work orders from the mobile terminals as they are completed. At the end of the shift, the technicians sign off and go home.

Source: From the publicly distributed brochure "RALI Mobile" from Smith Advanced Technology, Inc., 2001.

road. New wireless devices that access the Web using cellular or other wireless networks give employees access to the Web, e-mail, databases, and intranets or extranets (Redman 2000a).

▌ Bertelsmann AG of Germany gives junior-level executives wireless access to a company portal, JuniorNet, that is accessible from almost anywhere. When a manager is about to give a presentation and wants to pull up a profile on one of the company's employees or other piece of information, they can contact JuniorNet with a cell phone and get the information instantly. Bertelsmann's wireless feature integrates WAP with mobile phones and other wireless appliances so that users can access company intranets from Internet-enabled mobile phones and PDAs (such as the Palm i705).

▌ Kemper Insurance Company, which is based in Kentucky, has piloted an application that lets property adjusters report from the scene of an accident. Kemper attached a wireless digital imaging system to a camera that lets property adjusters take pictures in the field and transmit them to a processing center. The cameras are linked to Motorola's StarTac data-enabled cellular, which sends the information to a database. This application eliminates delays in obtaining information and in film processing that exist with conventional methods.

▌ The U.S. Internal Revenue Service is equipping 15,000 of its field employees with mobile devices that can connect them to the agency's secured intranet. With these devices, audits can be conducted anywhere, anytime.

Intelligent Offices

In many offices, wireless LANs are used to integrate all communications services like computers, fax machines, and e-mail without wires, as shown in Exhibit 8.10. This arrangement improves productivity and the quality of office operations.

EXHIBIT 8.9   Automated Wireless Workflow Applications

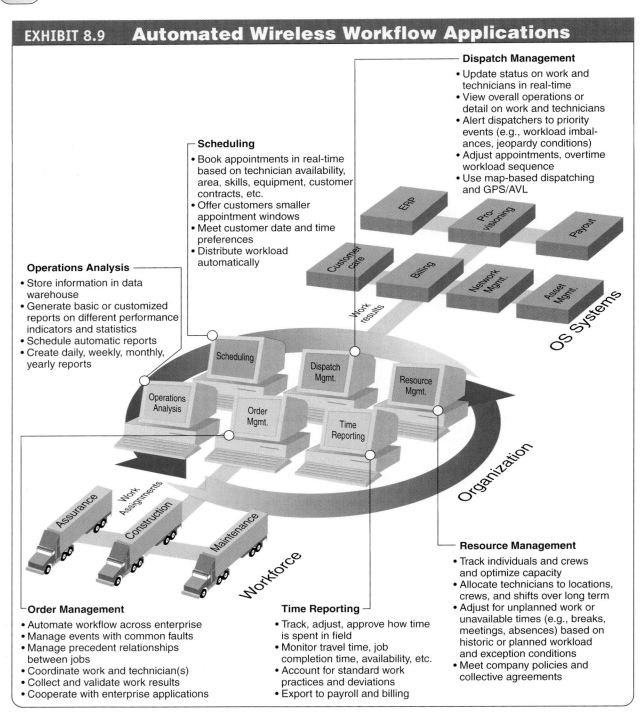

Dispatch Management
- Update status on work and technicians in real-time
- View overall operations or detail on work and technicians
- Alert dispatchers to priority events (e.g., workload imbalances, jeopardy conditions)
- Adjust appointments, overtime workload sequence
- Use map-based dispatching and GPS/AVL

Scheduling
- Book appointments in real-time based on technician availability, area, skills, equipment, customer contracts, etc.
- Offer customers smaller appointment windows
- Meet customer date and time preferences
- Distribute workload automatically

Operations Analysis
- Store information in data warehouse
- Generate basic or customized reports on different performance indicators and statistics
- Schedule automatic reports
- Create daily, weekly, monthly, yearly reports

Resource Management
- Track individuals and crews and optimize capacity
- Allocate technicians to locations, crews, and shifts over long term
- Adjust for unplanned work or unavailable times (e.g., breaks, meetings, absences) based on historic or planned workload and exception conditions
- Meet company policies and collective agreements

Order Management
- Automate workflow across enterprise
- Manage events with common faults
- Manage precedent relationships between jobs
- Coordinate work and technician(s)
- Collect and validate work results
- Cooperate with enterprise applications

Time Reporting
- Track, adjust, approve how time is spent in field
- Monitor travel time, job completion time, availability, etc.
- Account for standard work practices and deviations
- Export to payroll and billing

Source: MDSI Mobile Data Solutions, Inc., 2000, used with permission.

EXHIBIT 8.10   Intelligent Office Connected by Wireless LAN

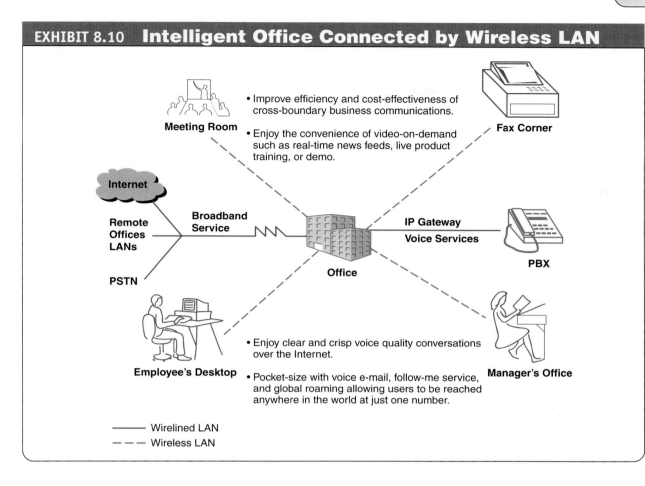

- Improve efficiency and cost-effectiveness of cross-boundary business communications.
- Enjoy the convenience of video-on-demand such as real-time news feeds, live product training, or demo.
- Enjoy clear and crisp voice quality conversations over the Internet.
- Pocket-size with voice e-mail, follow-me service, and global roaming allowing users to be reached anywhere in the world at just one number.

Meeting Room   Fax Corner

Internet

Remote Offices LANs   Broadband Service   IP Gateway / Voice Services   PBX

PSTN   Office

Employee's Desktop   Manager's Office

————— Wirelined LAN
‐ ‐ ‐ ‐ ‐ Wireless LAN

▶ Describe how mobile employees are supported by wireless applications.

▶ Describe wireless job dispatch.

▶ Describe mobile sales force automation.

8.7   MOBILE B2B AND SUPPLY CHAIN APPLICATIONS

Accurate and timely information is critical to business success. Companies must frequently respond in real time, and speedy response is especially important in managing the supply chain. Mobile computing solutions enable organizations to respond faster to supply chain disruptions by proactively adjusting plans or shifting resources related to critical supply chain events as they occur. With the increased interest in collaborative commerce comes the opportunity to use wireless communication to collaborate along the supply chain. For this, integration is needed.

Integration of business processes along the supply chain is a key issue in wireless B2B EC. As these processes become increasingly time sensitive and participants become more mobile, mobile devices will be integrated into information exchanges. The integration of mobile commerce is taking place on the buy-side as well as on the sell-side of ERP.

An integrated messaging system is at the center of B2B communications. By integrating the mobile terminal into the supply chain, it is possible to make mobile reservations of goods, check availability of a particular item in the warehouse, order a particular product from the manufacturing department, or provide security access to obtain confidential financial data from a management information system.

An example of an integrated messaging system is that made possible by wireless *telemetry*, which involves the integration of wireless communications, vehicle monitoring systems, and vehicle location devices. (See the opening vignette; telemetry is described further in Section 8.9.) This technology makes possible large-scale automation of data capture, improved billing timeliness and accuracy, reduced overhead associated with the manual alternative, and increased customer satisfaction through service responsiveness. For example, vending machines can be kept replenished and in reliable operation by wirelessly polling inventory and service status continually to avert costly machine downtime.

Collaboration among members of the supply chain also can be facilitated by mobile devices. There is no longer any need to call a partner company and ask someone to find certain employees who work with your company. Instead, you can call these employees directly, on their cell phones. A special organization, Global Commerce Forum (gmcforum.com) is an international cross-industry group that facilitates the use of m-commerce for collaboration. For example, engineers can work together from different locations; truck drivers can notify their destinations of exact arrival times.

3Com and Aether Technologies created OpenSky (now Omnisky), a service that gives smartphones and communicators mobile access to database applications. They provide support for better collaboration. Omnisky provides remote wireless access via PDAs to establish secure connections to applications such as Lotus Notes, Microsoft Exchange, ERP, and CRM.

▶ Describe wireless support along the supply chain.

▶ How can telemetry improve supply chain operations?

8.8 MOBILE CONSUMER AND PERSONAL SERVICE APPLICATIONS

A large number of applications exist that support consumers and provide personal services. As an example, let's look at the situation of a person going to an international airport. Exhibit 8.11 lists 12 problem areas that can be solved using mobile devices. The capabilities shown in the table are now possible in some places, and are expected to be widely available by 2004.

EXHIBIT 8.11 Traditional vs. Mobile Support at an Airport

Problem	Traditional Solution	Solution Enabled by the Local Mobile Network
Find a cart for your luggage.	You have to search for a cart; sooner or later you will find one.	Your PDA/cell will inform you where you are and where to find the closest available cart.
Find the right check-in desk.	Review all check-in desks and eventually find the right check-in desk. You could also find a monitor which, with luck, is close to where you are.	Your PDA/cell will, as soon as you have entered the departure hall, show you the way to the right check-in desk and inform you of your estimated check-in time.
Get in line and wait your turn at the check-in desk.	You visually try to find the quickest line.	Your PDA/cell has already shown you which check-in desk to go to.
Find the way to customs.	Check the signs that will lead you to customs.	Your PDA/cell will inform you of the way to customs.
Find the duty-free products for which you are looking.	Wander through the duty-free stores and find the products you are looking for. Hopefully, you will get a good price.	When close to the shopping area, your PDA/cell will inform you where to find the products you already pre-programmed to buy. You will also be informed about the price and "today's offering" for the product groups you are interested in.
Find a place to eat.	Review the different restaurants and their menus by walking through the airport.	You type in what you want to eat and the PDA/cell informs you where to find the food. The PDA/cell may also present alternative restaurants, their menu, prices, seat availability, and order time.
Find the closest washroom.	Walk around looking for signs with directions.	Your PDA/cell will show you the way to the closest washroom.
Find out if there are any delays and when you have to board the aircraft.	Find a monitor, which informs you of any delays and/or gate changes.	Your PDA/cell will beep and tell you when you have to go to the gate depending on where you are in the airport building.
Find where to get your luggage upon arrival.	Find a monitor, which informs you of the baggage claim location.	Your PDA/cell will inform you of the baggage claim location to pick up your luggage.
While waiting for the luggage at the baggage-claim, you want to use the time to make taxi and hotel reservations.	There are no options. You have to wait until you are in the arrival hall.	The local airport portal provides a number services. While waiting for your luggage you can make taxi and hotel reservations and other arrangements from your PDA/cell.
You are waiting for your luggage, but it never shows up.	You have to find a place to report the missing luggage and make a loss report.	The luggage will be identified when leaving the cargo space, your PDA/cell will inform you that the luggage has arrived and provide its estimated time to the baggage claim area. If the luggage is missing, you will be informed and a loss report will be generated.
You have a connecting flight and you want information about where to catch this flight.	Find a monitor, which informs you about connecting flights.	Your PDA/cell will tell you where to go after you have left the aircraft.

Source: From the publicly available brochure "Mobile Access by AXIS: Wireless Access Points" of AXIS Communications (*axis.com*), 2001. Reprinted with permission.

Other consumer and personal service areas in which wireless devices can be used are described in the following sections. (See also attws.com.)

MOBILE GAMING AND GAMBLING

Mobile games are available for PDAs, such as Handspring's Visor, which is equipped with a slot for an external Flash RAM (random access memory) card. Nintendo's Game Boy Advance, Sony's PocketStation, and Sega's portable device that connects with the Dreamcast controller also link to wireless networks. Nintendo Game Boy users, for example, can exchange game data with other users and send e-mails from the device.

Mobile betting could become a very interesting application for m-commerce because gambling is time-critical and may involve a lot of money. In Germany, the first online lottery company, fluxx.com, offers its service via mobile terminals, and in Hong Kong, betting on horse races via cell phones is popular.

More interesting perhaps are the opportunities that will emerge for *spread* betting, for instance, the odds on how many corners David Beckham (UK) might take in a particular soccer match, or how many he might take in the last 15 minutes of the match, or, if the match has already begun, how many he might make in the next 5 minutes. The type of bets offered over the network would correspond to the profile submitted by the mobile betting service provider.

MOBILE ENTERTAINMENT: MUSIC AND VIDEO

The availability of portable MP3 players has lead to the development of music devices integrated with mobile phones. Samsung Corp. has already developed an MP3-phone, which enables music titles to be stored locally on the mobile device. Korean consumer-electronics company HanGo sells a portable MP3 player that can hold up to 81 hours of music.

It is now possible to download streaming audio files from radio stations, record companies, and Web sites onto mobile devices. Streaming media enables the real-time playback of audio or video clips as they are being retrieved, without waiting for the entire file to be downloaded.

Music vendors can offer instant delivery of songs from their music libraries for online purchase. Location-based services can even be integrated to target subscribers with location-sensitive streaming content such as audio jingles promoting offers at retail outlets in the vicinity or movie trailer previews for films showing at the nearest theater.

The U.S.-based Packet Video Corporation pioneered real-time streaming video (see packetvideo.com) via wireless networks. Up to five frames per second can be delivered over the existing CDMA network. A new standard, MPEG-4, is emerging for video decoding. These technologies will make it possible for people to watch movies on their mobile phones. (This capability already exists in Japan.) For example, store-and-replay technology from Replay Networks and TiVo allows customers to download videos overnight or at preset times and play them from their phone-video player whenever they want.

HOTELS

There are many applications of m-commerce in the hotel industry. For example, hotel guests equipped with Bluetooth-enabled mobile devices are instantly recognized when they enter the hotel after being out for dinner, shopping, touring, and so on. With the system's confirmation that the guest is properly registered, the guest can use a password on the mobile device to open the door to their room, providing increased safety. The system can also be used for checkout, to make purchases from the hotel's vending machines and other stores in the hotel, and to track loyalty points (see tesalocks.com). A pioneering hotel in the use of m-commerce is Scanic Hotels (see case study at nokia.com). For a comparison of traditional and m-commerce hotel services, see Exhibit 8.12 (page 366). These capabilities are now available in some locations, and are expected to be widely available by 2005.

INTELLIGENT HOMES AND APPLIANCES

"Intelligent homes" include many appliances and devices, which can reside on a wireless LAN. Basically, in an intelligent home, all your appliances are accessible through the Internet, so they can be controlled from a distance via your cell phone and can be programmed to communicate with each other. By using the wireless system, you do not need all the cables and the wires typically found in a house, and your home security devices cannot be tampered with. An example of an intelligent home is shown in Exhibit 8.13 (page 367).

Of special interest are "smart" kitchen appliances that can be controlled from cell phones. Smart appliances are coming from Sharp Corp. and Sunbeam Corp. These appliances can "talk" to each other, coordinate tasks, and deliver convenience and safety. For more on smart appliances, see electronichouse.com and Norman (1998).

WIRELESS TELEMEDICINE

Wireless **telemedicine** refers to the use of mobile telecommunications infrastructures and multimedia technologies to provide medical information and deliver health care services remotely. For example, it facilitates the continuous monitoring of a patient's vital signs and condition by a hospital physician (see micromed.com.au). This allows a physician to manage a patient's treatment from a remote location when the patient is en route to a hospital in an ambulance fitted with a wireless transmission system. Research experiments have demonstrated the feasibility of simple implementations of this technology over 2G infrastructure.

Teleconsultations have traditionally been conducted between medical specialists in urban areas and doctors and patients in distant, rural areas over ISDN networks. With the impending introduction of broadband 3G mobile systems, the concept of mobile medical clinics on wheels may become commercially viable, leveraging 3G multimedia capabilities, potentially reducing costs, and improving delivery of quality health care in remote regions. Physical mobile clinics

telemedicine
The use of mobile telecommunications infrastructures and multimedia technologies to provide medical information and deliver health care services remotely.

EXHIBIT 8.12 Traditional vs. Mobile Support at a Hotel

Problem	Traditional Solution	Solution Enabled by the Local Mobile Network
Arrive at the hotel for a check-in.	Line up at the check-in desk and sign in, hand over your credit card, and receive the room key.	You send your personal information, preferences, and credit card details to the hotel system via your PDA/cell. The hotel system sends back the designated room number and the PIN-code to the room door.
Arriving at the room, you want to know what restaurants and facilities exist at the hotel.	Look in the hotel binder, call reception, or find the info on the hotel TV broadcast.	Information on what facilities are available and different restaurants with menus is automatically transferred to your PDA/cell upon arrival.
Review and order food from room service.	Look in the hotel binder and call the room service telephone number to place an order.	The room service menu is downloaded to your PDA/cell and you may directly order the food of your choice. Next day's breakfast selection can also be ordered at the same time.
Access the Internet and the corporate Internet with a high-speed connection from the hotel room, lobby, and conference facilities.	Find the analog telephone plug, connect your laptop through a wire and make a remote dial-up. At some hotels, a specific device is required to be connected to the telephone.	As you enter the room, you will have instant broadband access available on your laptop, and your PDA/cell will automatically update the latest news headlines, your private e-mail, and calendar information.
Make work-related telephone calls and call home from abroad.	Make the call on the available hotel phones and pay the local premium rates or use your mobile phone.	Specific discount telephony rates are offered by the hotel through Voice Over IP (VoIP) over your mobile phone with Bluetooth wireless technology.
Book a rental car.	Ask the concierge to book a car or call the rental car companies directly.	Information is available on your PDA/cell. You may book a car directly with a simple click and send the required personal information at the same time.
Order transportation to the office or to the airport.	Ask the concierge or reception to book taxi or bus transportation.	A selection of transportation means is presented on your PDA/cell. You may book and pay for your preference directly from your PDA/cell.

Source: From the publicly available brochure "Mobile Access by AXIS: Wireless Access Points" of AXIS Communications, (*axis.com*), 2001. Reprinted with permission.

make treatments accessible that are not otherwise available to remote doctors and clinics.

OTHER SERVICES FOR CONSUMERS

Many other services exist for consumers, in a variety of service categories. Examples include services providing news, weather, and sports reports; online language translations; information about tourist attractions (hours, prices); and emergency services.

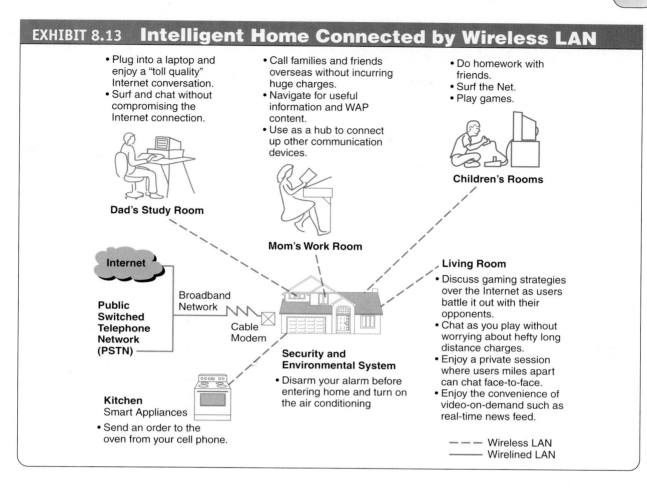

EXHIBIT 8.13   Intelligent Home Connected by Wireless LAN

- Plug into a laptop and enjoy a "toll quality" Internet conversation.
- Surf and chat without compromising the Internet connection.

Dad's Study Room

- Call families and friends overseas without incurring huge charges.
- Navigate for useful information and WAP content.
- Use as a hub to connect up other communication devices.

Mom's Work Room

- Do homework with friends.
- Surf the Net.
- Play games.

Children's Rooms

Internet

Public Switched Telephone Network (PSTN)

Broadband Network

Cable Modem

Living Room

- Discuss gaming strategies over the Internet as users battle it out with their opponents.
- Chat as you play without worrying about hefty long distance charges.
- Enjoy a private session where users miles apart can chat face-to-face.
- Enjoy the convenience of video-on-demand such as real-time news feed.

Security and Environmental System

- Disarm your alarm before entering home and turn on the air conditioning

Kitchen
Smart Appliances

- Send an order to the oven from your cell phone.

- - - Wireless LAN
——— Wirelined LAN

Other services are listed in an exhibit at the book's Web site (prenhall.com/turban); also, see the case studies at mobileinfo.com.

NON-INTERNET CONSUMER APPLICATIONS

Non-Internet EC applications for consumers, mainly those using smart cards, have existed since the early 1990s. Active use of the cards is reported in transportation where millions of "contactless" cards (also called *proximity cards*) are used to pay bus and subway fares and road tolls. Amplified remote-sensing cards that have an RF (radio frequency) of up to 30 meters are used in several countries for toll collection. See EC Application Case 8.3 (page 368) for more on the use of proximity cards for toll collection.

▶ Describe m-commerce applications in the following categories: gaming, gambling, and entertainment.
▶ Describe wireless auctions, wireless hotel services, and wireless home applications.
▶ Describe wireless telemedicine.

Individuals and Communities

THE HIGHWAY 91 PROJECT

Route 91 is a major eight-lane, east-west highway near Los Angeles. Traffic is especially heavy during rush hours. California Private Transportation Company (CPT) built six express toll lanes along a 10–mile stretch in the median of the existing Highway 91. The express lane system has only one entrance and one exit, and it is totally operated with EC technologies. Here is how the system works.

1. Only prepaid subscribers can drive on the road. Subscribers receive an automatic vehicle identification (AVI) device that is placed on the rearview mirror of the car. The device, about the size of a thick credit card, includes a microchip, an antenna, and a battery.

2. A large sign over the tollway tells drivers the current fee for cruising the express lanes. In 2000, it varied from $0.50 in slow traffic hours to $3.25 during rush hours.

3. Sensors in the pavement let the tollway computer know that a car has entered; the car does not need to slow or stop.

4. The AVI makes radio contact with a transceiver installed above the lane.

5. The transceiver relays the car's identity through fiber-optic lines to the control center, where a computer calculates the fee for that day's trip.

6. Surveillance cameras record the license numbers of cars without AVIs. These cars can be stopped by police at the exit or fined by mail.

7. Video cameras along the tollway enable managers to keep tabs on traffic, for example, sending a tow truck to help a stranded car. Also, through knowledge of the traffic volume, pricing decisions can be made. Raising the price as traffic increases ensures that the tollway will not be jammed.

8. The system accesses the driver's account and the fare is automatically deducted from the driver's prepaid account. A monthly statement is sent to the subscriber's home.

The system saves commuters between 40 and 90 minutes each day, so it is in high demand. An interesting extension of the system is the use of the same AVIs for other purposes. For example, they can be used in paid parking lots. Someday you may be recognized when you enter the drive-through lane of McDonalds and a voice asks you, "Mr. Smart, do you want your usual meal today?"

Sources: Compiled from *dot.ca.gov/fastrak/*, 2002 and *91expresslanes.com*, 2002.

Questions

▶ What is the role of the wireless component of this system?

▶ What are the advantages of the system to commuters?

8.9 LOCATION-BASED COMMERCE

location-based commerce (l-commerce)
E-commerce applications provided to customers based on a user's specific location.

As discussed in Section 8.1, **location-based commerce (l-commerce)** refers to the localization of products and services. With l-commerce, EC applications are specific to a user's location. L-commerce has been touted as the "next big thing." However, by 2002, there were only a few commercial applications of the technology.

L-COMMERCE TECHNOLOGIES

GPS

As discussed at the start of the chapter, a **global positioning system (GPS)** is a wireless system that uses satellites to enable users to determine their position anywhere on the earth. GPS equipment has been used extensively for navigation by commercial airlines and ships and for locating trucks and buses (as in the opening case study). GPS is supported by 24 U.S. government satellites that are shared worldwide. Each satellite orbits the earth once every 12 hours on a precise path, at an altitude of 10,900 miles. At any point in time, the exact position of each satellite is known, because the satellite broadcasts its position and a time signal from its onboard atomic clock, which is accurate to one-billionth of a second. Receivers also have accurate clocks that are synchronized with those of the satellites.

Knowing the speed of the signals (186,272 miles per second), it is possible to find the location of any receiving station (latitude and longitude) to within 50 feet by triangulation, using the distance from a GPS to three satellites to make the computation. GPS software then computes the latitude and longitude of the receiver. For an online tutorial on GPS, see trimble.com/gps.

global positioning system (GPS)
A wireless system that uses satellites to enable users to determine their position anywhere on the earth.

Geographical Information Systems

The location provided by GPS is expressed in terms of latitude and longitude. Therefore, it is necessary in many cases to relate those measures to a certain place or address. This is done by inserting the latitude and longitude onto an electronic map. (See Steede-Terry 2000 for an explanation of how this is done.) Companies such as mapinfo.com provide the *geographical information systems* (GIS) core spatial technology, maps, and other data content to power location-based GIS/GPS services, as shown in Exhibit 8.14 (page 370).

An interesting application of GPS/GIS is now available from several car manufacturers (e.g., Toyota, Cadillac) and car rental companies (e.g., Hertz, Avis). Some cars have a navigation system that indicates how far away the driver is from gas stations, restaurants, and other locations of interest. The GPS knows where the car is at at any time, so the application can map the route for the driver to a particular destination.

GPS Handsets

GPS handsets can be stand-alone units for applications such as tracking buses (NextBus case), tracking trucks on the roads, or finding your location in the outdoors. Or, they can be plugged into a mobile device or completely embedded in one. The manner in which the GPS device is connected to an l-commerce system is shown in Exhibit 8.15 (page 371).

E-911 EMERGENCY CELL PHONE CALLS

The U.S. Federal Communication Commission's E-911 directive, effective October 1, 2001, seeks to improve the reliability of **wireless 911 (e-911)** emergency services. Among its requirements is that U.S wireless carriers must provide a feature that allows carriers to identify the telephone number and location (within 100 meters) of a cell phone caller to 911 at least 67 percent of the time. (To give

wireless 911 (e-911)
Calls from cellular phones to providers of emergency services.

EXHIBIT 8.14 Location-based Services Involving Maps

**Location-based
Services & Solutions**

Find Location — Geocoding

Visualize — Mapping

Directions — Routing

Intelligence — Content

- Enhanced Billing
- Personalized Portals
- Buddy Finder
- Emergency Assistance
- Service Call Routing
- Find Nearest Services

Source: *Mapinfo.com*, 2001.

you an idea of the magnitude of this requirement, more than 55 million emergency calls were received on cell phones in the United States in 2001.) The FCC also requires that emergency calls be forwarded immediately by carriers to the appropriate public safety department. It is expected that many other countries will follow the example of the United States.

In the future, cars will have a device for **automatic crash notification (ACN)**. This device will automatically notify the police of an accident involving an ACN-equipped car and its location.

automatic crash notification (ACN)
Device (now experimental) that will automatically notify police of a vehicular accident.

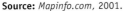

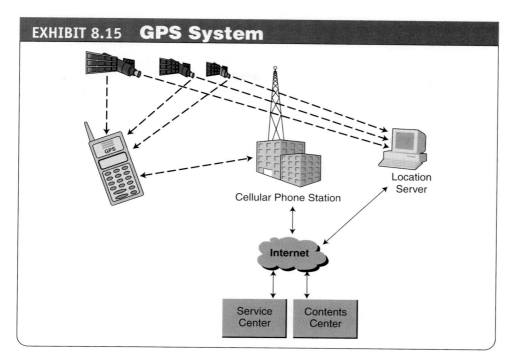

EXHIBIT 8.15 GPS System

GPS

Cellular Phone Station

Location Server

Internet

Service Center

Contents Center

TELEMATICS AND TELEMETRY APPLICATIONS

Telematics refers to the integration of computers and wireless communications in order to improve information flow. It uses the principles of *telemetry*, the science that measures physical remoteness by means of wireless transmission from a remote source (such as a vehicle) to a receiving station. The term telematics is often used to refer to vehicle monitoring systems and vehicle location devices. MobileAria (mobilearia.com) is a proposed standards-based telematics platform designed to bring multimedia services and m-commerce to automobiles. General Motors Corporation popularized automotive telematics with its OnStar system. With the OnStar system, a cellular phone, a handheld computer such as a PDA, and other appropriate hardware are integrated to provide personal information management, mobile Internet services, and entertainment right on the vehicle dashboard. Sophisticated text-to-speech and voice recognition capabilities minimize driver distraction during use of the service. For example, users can compose and send e-mail by dictation and have news read aloud to them.

Telematics offers diverse applications for cars. For example, one use is as a remote vehicle self-diagnostics tool. Field trials have been conducted by Daimler-Chrysler and Volvo to install GSM chip sets in cars to monitor performance and to provide an early warning system for potential problems. The chip sends a message to the manufacturer indicating what problem is occurring with the car (e.g., high temperature in the engine, brake problems, or "out of oil" alarm). The manufacturer's system is able to analyze the various data and provides a fix (via a software tool) to be sent to the car or asks the vehicle owner to go to a service station. Thus, developing faults can be found before they become critical and the continuous operation of the car can be ensured. The additional following applications are part of

telematics
The integration of computers and wireless communications to improve information flow using the principles of telemetry.

telematics: breakdown service when a vehicle has an immediate fault, emergency calls when the car breaks down in a deserted area, and, of course, positioning information about the exact location of the car. Similar services are already offered via a satellite network for high-end Chrysler customers in the United States.

Nokia has set up a business unit focusing solely on telematics called Smart Traffic Products. They believe that every vehicle will be equipped with at least one Internet Protocol (IP) address by the year 2010.

BARRIERS TO L-COMMERCE

What is holding back the widespread use of l-commerce? Basically, there are several main factors holding back l-commerce:

▶ **The accuracy of some of the location technologies**. GPS provides a location that is accurate up to 15 meters. Less expensive but less accurate technologies can be used instead to find an approximate location (within about 500 meters).

▶ **The cost-benefit justification.** For many potential users, the price of the hardware plus the time to acquire information are not yet greater than the benefits received from l-commerce.

▶ **M-spam.** Imagine the day when you walk into a shopping center, and your location-enabled cell phone rings 11 times, as five clothing stores, two shoe stores, two restaurants, a computer store, and a music store try to sell you something. The potential for annoying customers with too much information is enormous.

▶ **The bandwidth of GSM networks.** GSM bandwidth is currently limited; it will be improved as 3G technology spreads. (More on this point later.)

▶ Describe location-based commerce.
▶ Describe a GPS and GPS/GIS integration.
▶ Describe wireless 911.
▶ Describe telematics.

8.10 LIMITATIONS OF M-COMMERCE

Several limitations are slowing down the spread of m-commerce and/or leaving many customers disappointed or dissatisfied. The major ones are covered in the following discussion.

THE USABILITY PROBLEM

When mobile Internet users visit mobile Internet sites, the *usability* of the site is critical to attract attention and retain user stickiness. There are three dimensions to usability, namely *effectiveness*, *efficiency*, and *satisfaction*. However, users find current mobile devices to be ineffective, particularly with respect to restricted keyboards and pocket-size screens, limiting their usability. In addition, because of the limited storage capacity and information access speed of most smartphones and PDAs, it is often difficult or impossible to download large files to these devices.

Mobile visitors to a Web site are typically paying premium rates for connections and are focused on a specific goal (e.g., conducting a stock trade). Therefore, if customers want to find exactly what they are looking for, easily and quickly, they need more than text-only devices with small screens. In 2001, most WAP applications were text-based and had only simple black and white graphics. This made tasks such as mobile shopping difficult. Because all the transactions were essentially text-based, mobile users could not "browse" an online picture-based catalog. However, more and faster multimedia are becoming available as 3G spreads as of 2002.

TECHNICAL LIMITATIONS

A number of technical limitations have slowed the spread of m-commerce, as discussed in the following sections.

Lack of a Standardized Security Protocol

As of 2002, there is no consensus or standardization on the security methodologies that must be incorporated into all mobile-enabled Web sites. Because of this, customer confidence in the security of using their mobile phones or PDAs to make payments is low. In order for m-commerce to spread, confidence in its security must be raised.

Insufficient Bandwidth

A shortage of bandwidth limits the extent to which mobility can be viewed as a commodity (i.e., the extent to which mobility is characterized by widespread use, low cost, and little differentiation in service). This situation will exist until the global introduction of 3G.

For 3G technology to perform up to expectations, the availability of chipsets (sets of integrated circuits designed to perform one or more related functions) is vital (cdg.org, 1999 and 2001). However, these chipsets were still in development as of 2002, and a special 3G terminal was introduced only in late 2001 for UMTS. This resulted in delays in implementing 3G networks in some countries.

3G Licenses

The implementation of 3G technology is only one of the issues related to next-generation wireless. Another issue is 3G licenses, which are auctioned by governments. During the late 1990s, many licenses were sold at very high prices. However, starting in 2000, investors were unwilling to support such costly purchases. By 2001, in a number of countries, many 3G licenses remained to be sold. This means that certain countries or areas within countries cannot be served by 3G devices.

Transmission and Power Consumption Limitations

Depending on the media used, users of mobile devices may experience multipath interference, weather and terrain problems, and distance-limited connections. In addition, reception in tunnels and certain buildings may be poor. For example,

GPS may be inaccurate if the device is in a city with tall buildings. In addition, as bandwidth increases, power consumption increases. In a mobile device, this reduces battery life.

WAP Limitations

As of 2002, WAP is still unable to meet the following expectations of the mobile phone industry:

▶ **Speed.** Connections to WAP sites are still too slow. Also, it takes too long for a WAP site to build a screen. As Internet experience shows, most users abandon Web sites that take too long to load.

▶ **Cost.** Fees for mobile phone users are still too high for widespread adoption of m-commerce.

▶ **Accessibility.** A WAP phone is only able to access sites that are written in WML. As of spring 2002, there are fewer than 50,000 WAP-accessible sites worldwide (mobileinfo.com 2002) compared to the many millions of HTML-written sites.

POTENTIAL HEALTH HAZARDS

The issue of cellular radio frequency emissions and the fear that radiation from wireless mobile devices may induce cancer has been debated for several years. As of 2002, there is no conclusive evidence that links radiation from wireless devices with cancer (Rapid Interagency Committee 2001). However, drivers using mobile telephones have an increased of chance of being involved in a traffic accident, even if they are using hands-free kits. In addition, the use of cell phones may interfere with sensitive medical devices, such as pacemakers. Researchers are examining these topics. Results are expected in 2003 to 2005.

Lawsuits relating to the potential health hazards of wireless devices have already been filed against major vendors (Borland 2000). In the meantime, the public is advised to adopt a precautionary approach in using mobile phones (e.g., use an earphone device that keeps the phone's antenna away from your head).

▶ Why is usability important to the widespread adoption of m-commerce?

▶ List the technical limitations of m-commerce.

▶ Describe the potential health hazards of mobile devices.

8.11 IMPLEMENTING M-COMMERCE

The limitations of m-commerce just described are slowing its spread. However, these limitations are expected to lessen with time, as technology improves and new applications are developed. Certain other issues also need to be considered in implementing m-commerce, as illustrated in the following discussion.

REVENUE MODELS

Devising innovative m-commerce applications is one thing, but collecting revenues from them is something else altogether. In theory, there are several ways in which revenue can be generated: basic (fixed) fees and traffic fees by users, point-of-traffic fees, transaction fees, content and service charges, implementation and customer service fees, payment clearing, hosting fees, certification (PKI) fees, and maintenance fees.

On the wireline Internet, users pay a monthly fee for service. For wireless Internet services, users pay by the minutes of use. Although cell phone customers do not necessarily expect services to be free, there is a limit to how much they may be willing to pay. Also, collecting fees, especially micropayments, is not simple (see Kalakota and Robinson 2001).

CONSUMER CONFIDENCE AND TRUST

As in EC, consumer confidence and trust is a critical success factor in m-commerce. Consumers love free services and are willing to pay a small amount of money for SMSs and other services, such as those offered by i-Mode, but they have not demonstrated a willingness to spend large amounts of money until they trust the wireless system and its security. Confidence is expected to increase as payment mechanisms become more reliable.

Several companies and research institutions around the globe (e.g., Nokia and MIT) are conducting research on consumer adoption of m-commerce. Until we see the results of these studies and statistics about actual adoption, we will not know how widespread B2C m-commerce is.

THE M-COMMERCE VALUE CHAIN

The implementation of m-commerce involves many business partners, as shown in Exhibit 8.16 (page 376). The success of the implementation depends on coordination among all the participants and on sufficient compensation to each partner. Whereas some implementations involve only some of the members listed; other applications involve most or all of them. The value chain is improved by expediting production, reducing administrative costs, reducing errors, and better opportunities for collaboration.

This brings us to the issue of using ASPs to deliver m-commerce. ASPs can deliver comprehensive solutions. Alternatively, some large vendors such as IBM or Microsoft contract with other vendors that complement their services, offering customers comprehensive wireless systems. For a detailed discussion of ASPs, see Barnett et al. (2000).

▶ List some potential revenue sources for m-commerce.

▶ Describe the issue of consumer confidence and trust and how it affects the implementation of m-commerce.

▶ List the benefits of m-commerce to the value chain.

EXHIBIT 8.16   M-Commerce Value Chain

Value Chain Member		Role
Technology platform vendors	↓	Delivering operating systems and microbrowsers.
Infrastructure and equipment vendors	↓	Developing network infrastructure equipment and new technologies (WAP, GPRS, UMTS).
Application platform vendors	↓	Providing middleware infrastructure such as WAP gateways; contributing to standards.
Application developers	↓	Developing applications on Windows CE, PalmOS, and Symbian's EPOC32. Applications are for SMS, SIM, WAP, and more.
Content providers	↓	Internet content providers (e.g., Reuters) prepare content for m-commerce as well. Major issue: how to charge.
Content aggregators	↓	Repackaging available data for distribution to wireless devices, providing added value. See *digitallook.com* and *olympic-worldlink.co.uk*.
Mobile portal providers	↓	Aggregating applications and content to create mobile portals (e.g., Yahoo! mobile and MSN Wireless).
Mobile network operators	↓	Providing m-commerce services (e.g., Orange, Vodafone, Sprint). They try to become ISPs.
Mobile service providers	↓	Selling services of others to customers under their name. Large telecoms offer such services.
Handset vendors	↓	Manufacturing mobile devices. They are closest to the customers and they create value.
Customers	⟵⊣	Buying and paying. Mostly, 15–25 youth market or 25–36 business market: sales, service, logistics.

MANAGERIAL ISSUES

Some managerial issues related to this chapter are as follows.

1. **What's our timetable?** Large-scale m-commerce applications are not expected in the near future. Exceptions are some applications in e-banking, e-stock trading, e-gambling, emergency services, and some B2B tasks. This means that companies have time to carefully craft an m-commerce strategy. This will reduce the number of failed initiatives and bankrupted companies.

2. **Which applications first?** Finding and prioritizing applications is a part of a business's e-strategy (see Chapter 11 for methods). Although location-based advertising is logically attractive, its effectiveness may not be known for several years. Therefore, companies should be very careful in committing resources to m-commerce. However, "missing the boat" can be just as risky.

3. **Is it real or just a buzzword?** In the short run, m-commerce, and especially l-commerce, may be just buzzwords due to the many limitations they now face. However, in the long run, both concepts will fly. Management should monitor the technological developments and make plans accordingly.

4. **Which system to use?** The multiplicity of standards, devices, and supporting hardware and software can confuse a company planning to implement m-commerce. An unbiased consultant can be of great help. Checking the vendors and products carefully, as well as who is using them, is also critical. This issue is related to the issue of whether or not to use an ASP for m-commerce.

SUMMARY

In this chapter, you learned about the following EC issues as they relate to the learning objectives.

1. **Characteristics and attributes of m-commerce.** M-commerce is based on mobility and reach. These characteristics provide convenience, instant connectivity, product and service localization, ubiquity enhancement, and personalization.

2. **Drivers of m-commerce.** The following are the major drivers of m-commerce: large numbers of users of mobile devices, especially cell phones; no need for a PC; a developing "cell phone culture" in some areas; vendor marketing; declining prices; increasing bandwidth; and the explosion of EC in general.

3. **Supporting technologies.** M-commerce requires mobile devices (e.g., PDAs, cell phones) and other hardware, software, and wireless technologies. Commercial services and applications are still emerging. These technologies allow users to access the Internet anytime, anywhere. For l-commerce, a GPS receiver is needed.

4. **Wireless standards and technologies.** Standards are being developed by several organizations in different countries, resulting in competing systems. It is expected that with time some of these will converge. Transmission media include microwave, satellites, radio, and cellular radio.

5. **Finance and marketing applications.** Many EC applications in the service industries (e.g., banking, travel, and stocks) can be conducted with wireless devices. Also, shopping can be done from mobile devices. Location-based advertising and advertising via SMSs on a very large scale is expected.

6. **Intrabusiness applications.** Large numbers of intrabusiness applications, including inventory management, sales force automation, wireless voice, job dispatching, wireless office, and more are already evident inside organizations.

7. **B2B applications.** Emerging B2B applications are being integrated with the supply chain and facilitating cooperation between business partners.

8. **Consumer applications.** M-commerce is being used to provide entertainment, personalized information in emergency services, auctions, and delivery of education and medical services. Many other applications for individual consumers are planned for, especially targeted advertising.

9. **Non-Internet applications.** Most non-Internet applications involve various types of smart cards. They are used mainly in transportation, security, and shopping from vending machines and gas pumps.

10. **L-commerce.** Location-based commerce, or l-commerce, is emerging in emergency services. In the future, it will be used to target advertising to an individual based on their location. Use of GPS to calculate arrival time of buses is spreading rapidly. Other innovative applications are expected.

11. **Limitations of m-commerce.** The major limitations of m-commerce are small screens on mobile devices, limited bandwidth, high cost, lack of (or small) keyboard, transmission interferences, unproven security, and possible health hazards. Most limitations are expected to diminish over time.

KEY TERMS

2G,	p. 335	Bluetooth,	p. 341	Interactive voice response (IVR),	p. 346
3G,	p. 335	Global positioning system (GPS),	p. 369	Location-based commerce (l-commerce),	p. 368
Automatic crash notification (ACN),	p. 370				

DISCUSSION QUESTIONS

1. Discuss how m-commerce can solve some of the problems of the digital divide (the gap within a country or between countries with respect to people's ability to access the Internet). (See the 1999 report "Challenges to the Network" at itu.int.)

2. Discuss how m-commerce can expand the reach of EC.

3. Explain the role of protocols in m-commerce.

4. Discuss the impact of m-commerce on emergency medical services.

5. How do smartphones and screenphones differ? What characteristics do they share?

6. How are GIS and GPS related?

7. List three to four major advantages of wireless commerce to consumers presented in this chapter and explain what benefits they provide to consumers.

8. You can use location-based tools to help you find your car or find the closest gas station. However, some people see location-based tools as an invasion of privacy. Discuss the pros and cons of location-based tools.

9. Discuss how wireless devices can help people with disabilities.

10. Discuss the benefits of IVR.

11. Discuss the benefits of telemetry-based systems.

12. Describe m-commerce applications supported by smart cards.

13. Which of the current m-commerce limitations do you think will be minimized within 5 years? Which ones will not?

14. Describe some m-commerce B2B applications along the supply chain.

INTERNET EXERCISES

1. Learn about PDAs by visiting vendors' sites such as Palm, Handspring, Hewlett-Packard, IBM, Phillips, NEC, Hitachi, Compaq, Casio, Brother, Texas Instruments, and others. Start with a visit to 4pads.4anything.com. List the m-commerce devices manufactured by these companies.

2. Access progressive.com, an insurance company, from your cell phone (use the Go to. . . .

feature). If you have a Sprint PCS wireless phone, do it via the Finance menu. Then try to visit mobileprogressive.com from a wireless PDA. If you have a Palm i705, you can download the Web-clipping application from Progressive. Report on these capabilities.

3. Research the status of 3G and the future of 4G by visiting itu.int, mobiforum.org, and wapforum.org. Prepare a report on the status of 3G and 4G based on your findings.

4. Explore what AT&T (att.com), MCI (mci.com), and other telecommunications companies are doing in the area of mobile communications. Write a report based on your findings.

5. Enter nokia.com/corporate/wap/sdk.html and download (for free) the WAP Developer Toolkit. What can you do with this toolkit?

6. Enter kyocera-wireless.com. Take the smart tour and view the demos. What is a smartphone? What are its capabilities? How does it differ from a regular cell phone?

7. Enter ibm.com/software and click on the case studies. Read the two wireless-related stories and a story in an industry with which you are familiar. Prepare a summary of the capabilities of these wireless solutions.

8. Building m-commerce systems can be complex. Enter ibm.com and explore and document the capabilities of its WebSphere Suite.

9. Visit alcatel.com, siemens.com, and nortel networks.com. Locate the various m-commerce tools offered by these companies.

10. Enter ericsson.com and review all the available demos. Also play the stock-trading game.

11. Enter mapinfo.com and look for the location-based services demos. Try all the demos. Find all of the wireless services. Summarize your findings.

12. Visit ordersup.com, astrology.com, and similar sites that capitalize on l-commerce. What features do these sites share?

13. Enter packetvideo.com and microsoft.com/mobile/pocketpc. Examine their demos and products and list their capabilities.

14. Learn about intelligent home appliances by visiting x-home.com and sunbeam.com. List the capabilities of such devices.

15. Enter mdsi-advantex.com and review the wireless products for the enterprise. Summarize the advantages of the different products.

TEAM ASSIGNMENTS AND ROLE PLAYING

1. Each team should examine a major vendor of mobile devices (Nokia, Kyocera, Motorola, Palm, BlackBerry, etc.). Each team will research the capabilities and prices of the devices offered by each company and then make a class presentation, the objective of which is to convince the rest of the class why one should buy that company's products.

2. Each team should explore the commercial applications of m-commerce in one of the following areas: financial services, including banking, stocks, and insurance; marketing and advertising; manufacturing; travel and transportation; human resources management; public services; and health care. Each team will present a report to the class based on their findings. (Start at mobiforum.org.)

3. Each team will investigate a global organization involved in m-commerce, such as gmcforum.com, wapforum.com, etc. The teams will investigate the membership and the current projects the organization is working and then present a report to the class based on their findings.

4. Each team will investigate a standards-setting organization and report on its procedures and progress in developing wireless standards. Start with the following: atis.org, etsi.org, and tiaonline.org.

REAL-WORLD CASE

HERTZ GOES WIRELESS

The car rental industry is very competitive, and Hertz (*hertz.com*), the world's largest car rental company, competes against hundreds of companies in thousands of locations. The competition focuses on customer acquisition and loyalty. In the last few years, competition has intensified and profits in the industry have been drifting downward. Hertz has been a "first mover" to information technologies since the 1970s, so it has naturally looked for new technologies to improve its competitive position. In addition to data warehousing and mining, a superb executive information system, and e-commerce, Hertz has pioneered some mobile commerce applications:

▷ **Quick rentals.** Upon arrival at the airport, Hertz's curbside attendant greets you and transmits your name wirelessly to the renting booth. The renting-booth employee advises the curbside attendant about the location of your car. All you need to do is go to the slot where the car is parked and drive away. This system, which once operated over a WLAN, is now part of a national wireless network that can check credit cards, examine your rental history, determine which airline to credit your loyalty mileage to, and more.

▷ **Instant returns.** Pioneered by Hertz in 1987, a handheld device connected to a database via a wireless system expedites the car return transaction. Right in the parking lot, the lot attendant uses a handheld device to calculate the cost of the rental and print a receipt for the renter. You check out in less than a minute, and you do not have to enter the renting booth at all.

▷ **In-car cellular phones.** Starting in 1988, Hertz rents cell phones with its cars. Today, of course, this is not as "big a deal" as it was in 1988, when it was a major innovation.

▷ **NeverLost Onboard.** Some cars come equipped with an onboard GPS system, which provides route guidance in the form of turn-by-turn directions to many destinations. The information is displayed on a screen with computer-generated voice prompts. An electronic mapping system (GIS) is combined with the GPS, enabling you to see on the map where you are and where you are going. Also, consumer information about the locations of the nearest hospitals, gas stations, restaurants, and tourist areas is provided.

▷ **Additional customer services.** Hertz's customers can download city guides, Hertz's location guide, emergency telephone numbers, city maps, shopping guides, and even reviews of restaurants, hotels, and entertainment into their PDAs and other wireless devices. Of course, driving directions are provided.

▷ **Car locations.** Hertz is experimenting with a GPS-based car-locating system. This will enable the company to know where a rental car is at any given time, and even how fast it is being driven. Although the company promises to provide discounts based on your usage pattern, this capability is seen by many as an invasion of privacy. On the other hand, some may feel safer knowing that Hertz knows where they are at all times.

Hertz has been the top car rental company and still maintains that position. It is also a very profitable company that is expanding and growing continuously. Its success is attributed to being customer-centric, as facilitated by its use of wireless technologies and EC.

Source: *hertz.com* (2000).

Questions

1. Which of these applications are intrabusiness in nature?

2. Identify any finance- and marketing-oriented applications.

3. What are the benefits to Hertz of knowing exactly where each of its cars is? As a renter, how do you feel about this capability?

CHAPTER

9

LAW, ETHICS, AND CYBER CRIME

Content

MP3.com, Napster, and Intellectual Property Rights

Learning objectives

Upon completion of this chapter, you will be able to:

▶ Describe the differences between legal and ethical issues in EC.

▶ Understand the difficulties of protecting privacy in EC.

▶ Discuss issues of intellectual property rights in EC.

▶ Understand the conflict between free speech and censorship on the Internet.

▶ Document the rapid rise in computer and network security attacks.

▶ Understand the factors contributing to the rise of EC security breaches.

▶ Describe the key security issues facing EC sites.

▶ Discuss some of the major types of cyber attacks against EC sites.

▶ Describe some of the technologies used to secure EC sites.

MP3.COM, NAPSTER, AND INTELLECTUAL PROPERTY RIGHTS

The Problem

Before the advent of the Web, people made audiotape copies of music and videos. They either gave these copies to friends and family or used them for their own personal enjoyment. Few individuals had either the interest or the means to create and distribute copies to larger populations. For the most part, these activities were ignored by producers, distributors, and the artists who had the legal rights to the content (Spaulding 2000).

Then came the Web and a variety of enterprising sites such as *MP3.com* and Napster (*napster.com*). MP3.com enabled users to listen to music from any computer with an Internet connection without paying royalties. Utilizing peer-to-peer (P2P) technology, Napster supported the distribution of music and other digitized content among millions of users. When asked whether they were doing anything illegal, MP3.com and Napster claimed that they were simply supporting what had been done for years and, like most private individuals, were not charging for their services.

The popularity of MP3.com and Napster was too great for the content creators and owners to ignore. To them the Web was becoming a vast copying machine for pirated software, CDs, movies, and the like. If left undeterred, MP3.com's and Napster's services could result in the destruction of millions of jobs and revenue.

The Solution

In December 2000, emusic.com filed a copyright infringement lawsuit against MP3.com. They claimed ownership of the digital rights to some of the music made available at MP3.com. Warner Brothers Music Group, Inc., EMI Group PLC, BMG Entertainment, and Sony Music Entertainment, Inc. followed suit. A year later, Napster faced similar legal claims.

Copyright laws and copyright cases have been in existence for decades. By the year 2000, the laws should have been clear. However, the legal system can be picky. First, existing copyright laws were written for physical, not digital, content. Second, the Copyright Infringement Act stated, "the defendant must have willfully infringed the copyright and gained financially." With respect to the second point, an MIT student named David LaMacchia was sued for offering free copies of Excel, Word, and other software titles on the Internet. The suit was settled in his favor because there was no financial gain. This loophole in the act was later closed.

The Results

In 1997, the U.S. No Electronic Theft Act (NET) was passed, making it a crime for an individual to reproduce and distribute copyrighted works. The act further clarified that reproduction or distribution could be accomplished by electronic means, and that even if copyrighted products are distributed without charge, financial harm is experienced by the authors or creators of a copyrighted work.

Given the precedents and laws, MP3.com and Napster had little recourse but to capitulate. MP3.com suspended operations in April 2000 and settled the lawsuit against it, paying the litigants $20 million each. Napster suspended service and settled its lawsuits for $26 million dollars. With the backing of the record company Bertelsmann AG's BMG, Napster has been trying with little success to resurrect itself as an online music subscription service.

What We Can Learn . . .

All commerce involves a number of legal, ethical, and regulatory issues. Copyright, trademark, and patent infringement, freedom of thought and speech, theft of property, and fraud are not new to the world of commerce. As this opening case illustrates, EC adds to the scope and scale of these issues, and it also raises a number of questions about what constitutes illegal behavior versus unethical, intrusive, or undesirable behavior. This chapter examines some of the legal and ethical issues arising from EC and various legal and technical remedies and safeguards.

9.1 LEGAL ISSUES VS. ETHICAL ISSUES

In theory, one can distinguish between legal issues and ethical issues. If you break the law, you have done something illegal. Laws are enacted by governments and developed through case precedents (common law). Laws are strict legal rules governing the acts of all citizens within their jurisdictions. **Ethics** is a branch of philosophy that deals with what is considered to be right and wrong. Over the years, philosophers have proposed many ethical guidelines, yet what is unethical is not necessarily illegal.

ethics
The branch of philosophy that deals with what is considered to be right and wrong.

EC opens up a new spectrum of unregulated activity where the definition of right and wrong is not always clear. Businesspeople engaging in e-commerce need guidelines as to what behaviors are reasonable under any given set of circumstances. Consider the following scenarios:

▶ A Web site collects information from potential customers and sells it to its advertisers. Some of the profiles are inaccurate; consequently, people received numerous pieces of inappropriate and intrusive e-mail. Should junk e-mail of this sort be allowed? Should it come with a warning label?

▶ A company allows its employees to use the Web for limited personal use. Unknown to the employees, the IT staff not only monitors their messages, but also examines the content. If they find objectionable content, should the company be allowed to fire the offending employees?

Whether these actions are considered unethical (or even illegal) depends in large part on the value system of the country in which they occur. What is unethical in one culture may be perfectly acceptable in another. Many Western countries, for example, have a much higher concern for individuals and their rights to privacy than do some Asian countries. In Asia, more emphasis is placed on the benefits to society rather than on the rights of individuals. Some countries, such as Sweden and Canada, have very strict privacy laws; others have none. This situation may obstruct the flow of information among countries. Indeed, the European Community Commission issued guidelines in 1998 to all its member countries regarding the rights of individuals to access information about themselves and to correct errors.

▶ Define ethics and distinguish it from the law.
▶ Give an example of an EC activity that is unethical but legal.

9.2 PRIVACY

Privacy means different things to different people. In general, **privacy** is the right to be left alone and the right to be free of unreasonable personal intrusions. Privacy has long been a legal and social issue in the United States. The right to privacy is recognized today in virtually all U.S. states and by the federal government, either

privacy
The right to be left alone and the right to be free of unreasonable personal intrusions.

by statute or by common law. The definition of privacy can be interpreted quite broadly. However, the following two rules have been followed fairly closely in past court decisions: (1) The right of privacy is not absolute. Privacy must be balanced against the needs of society. (2) The public's right to know is superior to the individual's right of privacy. These two rules show why it is difficult, in some cases, to determine and enforce privacy regulations.

The complexity of collecting, sorting, filing, and accessing information manually from several different agencies was, in many cases, a built-in protection against misuse of private information. It was simply too expensive, cumbersome, and complex to invade a person's privacy. The Internet, in combination with large-scale databases, has created an entirely new dimension of accessing and using data. The inherent power in systems that can access vast amounts of data can be used for the good of society. For example, by matching records with the aid of a computer, it is possible to eliminate or reduce fraud, government mismanagement, tax evasion, welfare cheats, family support filchers, employment of illegal aliens, and so on. The question is: What price must every individual pay in terms of loss of privacy so that the government can better apprehend criminals?

The Internet offers a number of opportunities to collect private information about individuals. Here are some of the ways that it can be done (Rainone et al. 1998):

- By reading an individual's newsgroup postings.
- By looking up an individual's name and identity in an Internet directory.
- By recording an individual's actions as they navigate the Web with a browser.
- By reading an individual's e-mail.
- By asking an individual to complete a Web site registration.

Of these, Web site registration and recording an individual's Internet use through a browser are the most common ways of gathering information on the Internet.

WEB SITE REGISTRATION

Americans are a little schizophrenic when it comes to privacy and the Internet. In a poll conducted by the Pew Internet and American Life Project, 86 percent of the respondents said they were worried about online privacy. Yet, in another poll conducted by Jupiter Media Matrix (a market analysis firm), 50 percent said they would disclose personal information on a Web site for the chance to win a sweepstakes (Steinberg 2001).

Virtually all B2C and marketing Web sites ask visitors to fill out registration forms. During the process, customers voluntarily provide their names, addresses, phone numbers, e-mail addresses, sometimes their hobbies and likes or dislikes, and so forth, in return for information, for the chance to win a lottery, or for some other item of exchange. There are few restraints on the ways in which the site can use this information. The site might use it to improve customer service or its own business. Or, they could just as easily sell the information to another company, which could use it in an inappropriate or intrusive manner.

COOKIES

Another way that a Web site can gather information about an individual is by using cookies. In Internet terminology, a **cookie** is a small piece of data that is passed back and forth between a Web site and an end user's browser as the user navigates the site. Cookies enable sites to keep track of which users are which without having to constantly ask them to identify themselves.

Web sites use cookies for a variety of reasons. They use cookies to personalize the pages displayed to an individual or to improve online sales and service. For example, an airline may want to keep track of a customer's seating preferences so that it does not have to ask whether a window or aisle seat is desired each time a reservation is made. Cookies can be very handy for users, too. Some users do not mind having cookies used to make their Web browsing more convenient because they find it cumbersome to enter a password or fill out a form over and over again.

However, cookies can be used to invade an individual's privacy. Cookies allow Web sites to collect detailed information about a user's preferences, interests, and surfing patterns. The personal profiles created by cookies are more accurate than self-registration because users have a tendency to falsify information in a registration form. Again, the personal information collected via cookies has the potential to be used in illegal and unethical ways. EC Application Case 9.1 (page 386) details the resistance faced by online advertiser DoubleClick when it attempted to use cookies to better target its advertising. Although the use of cookies is still debated, concerns about cookies reached a pinnacle in 1997 at the U.S. Federal Trade Commission hearings regarding online privacy. Following those hearings, Netscape and Microsoft introduced options enabling users to block the use of cookies. Since that time, the furor has abated, and most users willingly accept cookies.

Users can protect themselves against cookies; they can delete them from their computers or they can use anticookie software such as Pretty Good Privacy's Cookie Cutter or Luckman's Anonymous Cookie. Anticookie software disables all cookies and allows the user to surf the Web anonymously. The problem with deleting or disabling cookies is that the user will be forced to keep reentering information and in some instances may be blocked from viewing particular pages.

Today, a new Microsoft component called **Passport** is beginning to raise some of the same concerns as cookies. Passport is an Internet strategy that lets consumers permanently enter a profile of information along with a password and use this information and password repeatedly to access services at multiple sites. Critics say that Passport affords the same opportunities as cookies to invade an individual's privacy. Critics also feel that the product gives Microsoft an upper hand in EC.

PROTECTION OF PRIVACY

Europe, Canada, and the United States share some of the same ethical principles when it comes to the collection and use of personal information. These principles include the following.

> ◗ **Notice/awareness.** Consumers must be given notice of an entity's information practices prior to collection of personal information. Consumers must be able to make informed decisions about the type and extent of their disclosures based on the intentions of the party collecting the information.

cookie
A small piece of data that is passed back and forth between a Web site and an end user's browser as the user navigates the site; enables sites to keep track of users' activities without asking for identification.

Passport
A Microsoft component that lets consumers permanently enter a profile of information along with a password and use this information and password repeatedly to access services at multiple sites.

EC APPLICATION CASE 9.1

Individuals and Communities

PRIVACY ADVOCATES TAKE ON DOUBLECLICK

DoubleClick is one of the leading providers of online advertising. Like other online advertisers, DoubleClick uses cookies to personalize ads based on consumers' interests. Although privacy advocates have long criticized the use of cookies, they have generally tolerated the practice because there was no way to tie the data collected by cookies to a consumer's identity. All this changed in January 1999 when DoubleClick bought catalog marketer Abacus Direct and announced plans to merge Abacus's offline database with DoubleClick's online data.

Following the announcement, several class action lawsuits were brought against DoubleClick, claiming that the company was "tracking Internet users and obtaining personal and financial information such as names, ages, addresses, and shopping patterns, without their knowledge" (Dembeck and Conlin 2000). Many of these suits were consolidated into a single suit brought in DoubleClick's home state of New York. A short time later, the Electronic Privacy Information Center (EPIC) filed a complaint with the Federal Trade Commission (FTC) alleging that DoubleClick was using unfair and deceptive trading practices. The Attorney General of Michigan also claimed that DoubleClick was in violation of the state's Consumer Protection Act and asked it to stop placing cookies on consumers' computers without their permission.

In January 2001, the FTC ruled that DoubleClick had not violated FTC policies. In March 2002, DoubleClick reached a preliminary settlement, clearing up a number of the class action suits brought by the states. As a consequence, DoubleClick agreed to enhance its privacy measures and to pay legal fees and costs up to $18 million. One of the key provisions of the settlement requires DoubleClick to "obtain permission from consumers before combining any personally identifiable data with Web surfing history" (Olsen 2002).

Prior to the settlement, DoubleClick had already appointed a chief privacy officer and substantially strengthened its privacy policies. (For a detailed listing of the policies see *doubleclick.com/us/corporate/privacy*). In spite of these changes and the proposed settlement, EPIC was still not satisfied. As Marc Rotenberg, EPIC's executive director, stated, "You have to keep in mind DoubleClick's unique position—its consumer profiles are collected from Web sites it supplies advertising to. For this reason, we should expect a much higher standard for privacy protection" (Olsen 2002).

Sources: Compiled from Dembeck and Conlin, 2000 and Olsen, 2002.

Questions

▶ What are some of the ways in which DoubleClick's use of cookies might infringe on an individual's privacy rights?

▶ What are some of the key elements in DoubleClick's new privacy policies?

▶ In its complaint, EPIC proposed a number of ways to curb DoubleClick's practices. What were some of EPIC's suggestions, and does the recent ruling enforce any of the proposed limitations?

▶ **Choice/consent.** Consumers must be made aware of their options as to how their personal information may be used, as well as any potential secondary uses of the information. Consent may be granted through *opt-out clauses* requiring steps to prevent collection of information. In other words, no action equals consent. Or, consumers may grant consent through *opt-in clauses*, which require steps to allow the collection of information.

▶ **Access/participation.** Consumers must be able to access their personal information and challenge the validity of the data.

▶ **Integrity/security.** Consumers must be assured that their personal data are secure and accurate. It is necessary for those collecting the data to take whatever precautions are required to ensure that data are protected from loss, unauthorized access, destruction, and fraudulent use, and to take reasonable steps to gain information from reputable and reliable sources.

▶ **Enforcement/redress.** There must always be a method of enforcement and remedy. Otherwise there is no real deterrent or enforceability for privacy issues. The alternatives are government intervention, legislation for private remedies, or self-regulation.

In the United States, these principles are supported by specific pieces of legislation. For example, the *Federal Internet Privacy Protection Act* prohibits federal agencies from disclosing personal records or making identifying records about an individual's medical, financial, or employment history. Probably the broadest in scope is the *Consumer Empowerment Act*, which requires (for instance) the Federal Trade Commission to enforce online privacy rights in EC, including the collection and use of personal data.

In 1998, the European Union passed a privacy directive (EU Data Protection Directive) reaffirming the principles of personal data protection in the Internet age. Member countries are required to put this directive into effect by introducing new laws or modifying existing laws in their respective countries. The directive aims to regulate the activities of any person or company that controls the collecting, holding, processing, or use of personal data on the Internet.

In many countries there is a continuing debate about the rights of the individual versus the rights of society. Some feel that self-regulation is the best alternative. However, some empirical data suggest that this approach does not work. For instance, in 1998 the U.S. Federal Trade Commission audited 1,400 commercial Web sites in the United States to measure the effectiveness of self-regulation (ftc.gov/opa/reports/privacy3/toc..htm). They found that privacy protection at these sites was poor and that few sites provided end users with the following privacy protections:

▶ Details about the site's information-gathering and dissemination policies.

▶ Choice over how their personal information is used.

▶ Control over personal information.

▶ Verification and oversight of claims made by the site.

▶ Recourse for resolving user complaints.

▶ Define privacy.

▶ List some of the ways that the Internet can be used to collect information about individuals.

▶ Describe cookies.

▶ List some of the ethical principles shared by Europe, Canada, and the United States relating to the gathering of personal information.

9.3 INTELLECTUAL PROPERTY RIGHTS

Intellectual property rights are one of the foundations of modern society. Without these rights, the movie, music, software, publishing, pharmaceutical, and biotech industries would collapse (Claburn 2001). According to the World Intellectual Property Organization (WIPO; wipo.int), **intellectual property (IP)** refers to "creations of the mind: inventions, literary and artistic works, and symbols, names, images, and designs used in commerce." There are three main types of IP in EC:

intellectual property (IP)
Creations of the mind, such as inventions, literary and artistic works, and symbols, names, images, and designs used in commerce.

▶ Copyrights

▶ Trademarks

▶ Patents

COPYRIGHTS

Copyrights usually exist in the following works:

▶ Literary works (e.g., books and computer software)

▶ Musical works (e.g., compositions)

▶ Dramatic works (e.g., plays)

▶ Artistic works (e.g., drawings, paintings)

▶ Sound recordings, films, broadcasts, cable programs

On the Web, copyrights can also be used to protect images, photos, logos, text, HTML, JavaScript, and other materials.

copyright
An exclusive grant from the government that allows the owner to reproduce a work, in whole or in part, and to distribute, perform, or display it to the public in any form or manner, including the Internet.

Copyright is an exclusive grant from the government that confers on its owner an essential exclusive right to: (1) reproduce a work, in whole or in part, and (2) distribute, perform, or display it to the public in any form or manner, including the Internet. In general, the owner has an exclusive right to export the copyrighted work to another country (Delgado-Martinez 2002).

Various international treaties provide copyright protection. Of these, the Berne Union for the Protection of Literary and Artistic Property (Berne Convention) is one of the most important. The Berne Convention dates to 1886. It is administered by WIPO and is supported by over 90 percent of the world's countries.

A copyright owner may seek a court injunction to prevent or stop any infringement and to claim damages. Certain kinds of copyright infringements also incur criminal liabilities. These include: commercial production of infringing works, selling or dealing in infringing works, possessing infringing works for trade or business, and manufacturing and selling technology for defeating copyright protection systems.

A copyright does not last forever; it is good for a fixed number of years after the death of the author or creator (e.g., 50 in the United Kingdom and in the United States in most cases). After that time, the copyright of the work reverts to the public domain.

Copyright Protection Techniques

In the United States, congressional legislation has been proposed that will make it "unlawful to manufacture, import, offer to the public, provide, or otherwise traffic in any interactive device that does not include and utilize certified security technology" (Nickell 2001) If this measure becomes law, the implication is that virtually any digital device—PC, MP3 player, digital camera, etc.—must include government-approved copy protection that makes it impossible to reproduce copyrighted material. It is possible to use software to produce digital content that cannot be copied.

Digital watermarks can also be used to provide copyright protection. Similar to watermarks on fine paper that indicate the maker of the paper, digital watermarks are unique identifiers that are imbedded in the digital content. Although they do not prevent an individual from making illegal copies, they do make it possible to identify pirated works. If a pirated copy is placed on the Internet, then sophisticated search programs, such as Digimarc's MarSpider, can be used to locate the illegal copies and notify the rightful owner.

digital watermarks
Unique identifiers imbedded in digital content that make it possible to identify pirated works.

TRADEMARKS

A **trademark** is a symbol used by businesses to identify their goods and services. The symbol can be composed of words, designs, letters, numbers, shapes, a combination of colors, or other such identifiers. Trademarks need to be registered in a country in order to be protected by law. To be eligible for registration, a trademark must be distinctive, original, and not deceptive. Once registered, a trademark lasts forever, as long as a periodic registration fee is paid.

The owner of a registered trademark has exclusive rights to:

trademark
A symbol used by businesses to identify their goods and services; government registration of the trademark confers exclusive legal right to its use.

▶ Use the trademark on goods and services for which the trademark is registered.

▶ Take legal action to prevent anyone else from using the trademark without consent on goods and services (identical or similar) for which the trademark is registered.

Trademark infringement carries criminal liabilities. In particular, it is a crime for anyone to fraudulently use a registered trademark, including the selling and importing of goods bearing an infringing trademark, and to use or possess equipment for forging registered trademarks.

On the Internet, fake brand names and products can be sold or auctioned from anywhere. In 1998, Playboy was able to shut down an adult Web site that was using the Playboy trademark. In the past, several private individuals were given the right by the governing bodies of the Internet to use Web site (domain) names that involved trademarked names (e.g., microsoft.com is a domain name). For example, in 1998 a New Jersey dealer named Russell Boyd applied for and was given the rights to 50 domain names, including juliaroberts.com and alpacino.com. He then proceeded to auction the names on eBay. In that same year, Julia Roberts complained to WIPO. In the summer of 2000, WIPO's Complaint and Arbitration Center, which coordinates international patents, copyrights, and trademarks, upheld the actress's claim. It ruled that Boyd had no rights to the domain name juliaroberts.com even though she was not using it at the moment.

PATENTS

A **patent** is a document that grants the holder exclusive rights on an invention for a fixed number of years (e.g., 17 years in the United States and 20 years in the United Kingdom). Patents serve to protect tangible technological inventions, especially in traditional industrial areas. They are not designed to protect artistic or

patent
A document that grants the holder exclusive rights on an invention for a fixed number of years.

literary creativity. Patents confer monopoly rights to an idea or an invention, regardless of how it may be expressed. An invention may be in the form of a physical device or a method or process for making a physical device.

Thousands of patents related to IT have been granted over the years. Examples of EC patents given to Open Market Corp., for example, are Internet Server Access Control and Monitoring (5708780), Network Sales Systems (5715314), and Digital Active Advertising (5724424). Juno Online Services received an interactive ad patent (5809242). IBM has several patents, including 5870717, a system for ordering from electronic catalogs, and 5926798, a system for using intelligent agents to perform online commerce.

Certain patents granted in the United States deviate from established practices in Europe. For example, amazon.com has successfully obtained a U.S. patent on its 1–Click book-ordering procedure. Using this patent, Amazon.com sued Barnes and Noble in 1999 and in 2000, alleging its rival had copied its patented technology. Barnes and Noble was enjoined by the courts from using the procedure. Similarly, in 1999 priceline.com filed a suit against expedia.com alleging that it was using its patented reverse auction business model. The suit was settled on January 9, 2001, when Expedia.com agreed to pay Priceline.com royalties for use of the model. In Europe, it is almost impossible to obtain patents on business methods or computer processes.

▶ List three types of intellectual property.

▶ List the legal rights covered by a copyright.

▶ What is the purpose of a digital watermark?

▶ List the legal rights of a trademark owner.

▶ Define patent.

9.4 FREE SPEECH AND CENSORSHIP ON THE INTERNET

Several surveys indicate that the issue of censorship is one of the most important to Web surfers, usually ranking as the number one or number two concern in Europe and the United States (see, for example, the GVU User Surveys at cc.gatech.edu/gvu/user_surveys). On the Internet, censorship refers to government's attempt to control, in one way or another, material that is broadcasted.

At a symposium on free speech in the information age, Parker Donham (1994) defined his own edict, entitled "Donham's First Law of Censorship." This semi-serious precept states: "Most citizens are implacably opposed to censorship in any form—except censorship of whatever they personally happen to find offensive" (see ei.cs.vt.edu/~wwwbtb/book/chap5/opine1.html). Take, for example, the question, "How much access should children have to Web sites, newsgroups, and chat rooms containing 'inappropriate' or 'offensive" materials, and who should control this access?" This is one of the most hotly debated issues between the advocates of censorship and the proponents of free speech.

The proponents of free speech contend that there should be no government restrictions on Internet content and that parents should be responsible for monitoring and controlling their children's travels on the Web. The advocates of censorship feel that government legislation is required to protect children from offensive material. The *Children's Online Protection Act (COPA)* exemplifies this approach. Passed in 1998, this law required, among other things, that companies verify a viewer's age before showing online material that is deemed "harmful to minors" and that parental consent is required before personal information can be collected from a minor. The fact that the act was ruled unconstitutional illustrates how hard it is to craft legislation that abridges freedom of speech in the United States.

The advocates of censorship also believe that it is the responsibility of the ISPs to control the content of the data and information that flow across their networks and computers. The difficulty is that ISPs have no easy way of monitoring the content or determining the age of the person viewing the content. The only way to control "offensive" content is to block it from children and adults alike. This is the approach that America Online (AOL) has taken, for instance, in blocking sites pandering to hate crime and serial killer enthusiasts.

CONTROLLING SPAM

Spamming refers to the practice of indiscriminately broadcasting messages over the Internet (e.g., junk mail). One major piece of legislation addressing marketing practices in EC is the *Electronic Mailbox Protection Act*. The primary thrust of this law is that commercial speech is subject to government regulation, and secondly, that spamming, which can cause significant harm, expense, and annoyance, should be controlled.

spamming
The practice of indiscriminately broadcasting messages over the Internet (e.g., junk mail).

At some of the largest ISPs, spam now comprises 25 percent to 50 percent of all e-mail (Black 2002). This volume significantly impairs an already-limited bandwidth, slowing down the Internet in general and, in some cases, shutting down ISPs completely. The Electronic Mailbox Protection Act requires those sending spam to identify it as advertising, to indicate the name of the sender prominently, and to include valid routing information. Recipients may waive the right to receive such information. Also, ISPs are required to offer spam-blocking software, and recipients of spam have the right to request termination of future spam from the same sender and to bring civil action if necessary.

▶ What is spamming?
▶ Describe the Electronic Mailbox Protection Act.

9.5 CYBER CRIME

There is no universally accepted definition of computer crime or computer crimes conducted on the Internet—what we label as *cyber crime*. Just because the Internet is used to perpetrate a crime does not mean it is a cyber crime.

fraud
Intentional deceit or trickery, often with the aim of financial gain.

Many traditional crimes are now carried out using computers and have moved to the Internet. Take fraud as an example. **Fraud** involves intentional deceit or trickery, often with the aim of financial gain. A few years ago, mail and fax were used to carry out frauds. Today, it is the Web. The most frequently perpetrated fraud on the Internet involves online auctions. Money is collected from the buyer in the auction, but the goods are never delivered. Fraud, child pornography, software piracy, and copyright violation are all acts that can be facilitated by the Internet. However, in most jurisdictions these are usually prosecuted as non-computer crimes.

This leaves the crimes of cyber intrusion and cyber vandalism. *Cyber intrusion* is similar to breaking and entering or criminal trespass, except that the entry point is the Internet. *Cyber vandalism* occurs when unauthorized access to the Internet results in damaged files, programs, or hardware. We use the term **cyber attack** to cover both types of acts. EC Application Case 9.2 introduces you to the "main players" in the world of cyber attacks.

cyber attack
An electronic attack, either criminal trespass over the Internet (*cyber intrusion*) or unauthorized access that results in damaged files, programs, or hardware (*cyber vandalism*).

Again, a distinction needs to be made between a cyber crime and simple misuse or abuse. As noted earlier, for an act to be a crime there must be a statutory prohibition. Because the law often lags technological innovation, there are few laws covering many of the undesirable or harmful behaviors that occur on the Internet. For example, the creator of the famous "ILOVEYOU" computer virus that caused millions (if not billions) of dollars in damage could not be prosecuted because the activity was not illegal in the country in which he lived (the Philippines).

▶ Define fraud.
▶ Describe a cyber attack.

9.6 INTERNET SECURITY

In 1988, a man named Robert Morris released a "worm" on the Internet that disrupted service on a number of networks for several days. Back then it was a newsworthy event, but it affected the lives of very few nontechnical people. For over 9 years, there were no significant viruses or worms released on the Internet. Then, in 1999, the security dam broke when the Melissa virus appeared on the scene. Since that time rarely a month has gone by without the announcement of some new kind of cyber attack. Exhibit 9.1 (page 394) chronicles some of the more infamous attacks. Unlike Morris's worm, these attacks have disrupted the lives of millions of nontechnical people, have resulted in millions (maybe billions) of dollars worth of damage, and are taken seriously by organizations of all sorts throughout the world.

Empirical evidence leaves no doubt that the rise in attacks against computers and networks has mirrored the growth of the Web. Since 1996, the Computer Security Institute (CSI) and the FBI Computer Intrusion Squad have conducted a survey of computer security practitioners in U.S. corporations and government agencies. The findings of their most recent survey (Computer Security Institute

EC APPLICATION CASE 9.2
Interorganization and Collaboration
THE PLAYERS: HACKERS, CRACKERS, AND OTHER ATTACKERS

Whenever the media reports about a large Internet security attack, there is a great deal of speculation about who perpetrated the attack and why. By now, most people have heard the term "hacker" bandied about in the media. Often, attacks are blamed on these so-called hackers. Who or what are hackers? What role do they play in Internet security, and what motivates them to do what they do?

Hackers

Originally, the term "hacker" referred to a shared culture of expert programmers and networking wizards who worked on the first time-sharing minicomputers and the earliest ARPANET experiments. This culture created the Unix operating system and helped build the Internet, Usenet, and the World Wide Web. The term did not then have the negative connotation it does now. Many hackers employ their skills to test the strength and integrity of computer systems for a wide variety of reasons: to prove their own ability, to satisfy their curiosity about how different programs work, or to improve their own programming skills by exploring the programming of others.

Over time, the term hacker came to be applied to rogue programmers or network wizards who illegally break into computers and networks. The term now has been adopted by the mass media to refer to all people who break into computer systems, regardless of motivation. Many in the Internet security community strongly disagree with the use of the term hacker to refer to people who hack illegally for criminal purposes. Sometimes the terms "white-hat" hackers and "black-hat" hackers are used to distinguish the two types of hackers.

Crackers

People within the Internet community tend to refer to people who engage in unlawful or damaging hacking as "crackers," short for "criminal hackers." The term cracker generally connotes a hacker who uses their skills to commit unlawful acts or to deliberately create mischief. Unlike hackers, whose motivations may be professional or computer-community enhancement, the motivation of crackers is generally to cause mischief, create damage, or to pursue illegal activities, such as data theft or vandalism.

Other Attackers

Some of the most highly publicized Internet security breaches, such as the denial of service (DoS) attacks discussed later in the chapter, are committed by middle-class teenagers, who seem to perpetrate mischief in order to make a name for themselves. Security experts often refer to this other category of computer-security attackers as "script kiddies."

Script kiddies are generally ego-driven, unskilled crackers who use information and software (scripts) that they download from the Internet to inflict damage on targeted sites. Script kiddies are generally looked upon with disdain by members of the hacking community, as well as by law enforcement authorities, because they are generally unskilled individuals with a lot of time on their hands who wreak havoc primarily to impress their friends.

Although there are differences among the various players, we use the term hacker throughout the chapter to denote someone who attacks a site, regardless of their motivations.

Source: Sager, 2000.

Questions

▶ What is the difference between a hacker and a cracker?

▶ A number of companies have used hackers to test the security of their networks. Is this a good idea? Why or why not?

EXHIBIT 9.1   Significant Cyber Attacks 1999–2000

Date	Attack	Description
March 1999	Melissa	The Melissa was a Microsoft World macro virus that was spread as an e-mail attachment. It arrived with the words, "Here is the document you asked for . . . don't show it to anyone else;)." The virus was first posted to the alt.sex newsgroup. When opened it would e-mail itself to the first 50 addresses in the recipient's address book. Melissa was significant because it was the first time in the 10 years since the Morris worm that a virus had infected a significant portion of the Internet.
May 1999	FBI vs. Hackers	After investigating several U.S. hacker groups and seizing the computer of a teenager, a DoS attack was launched against the FBI's Web site. As a result, the site was closed down for a week.
June 1999	Explorer.Zip	Similar to the Melissa virus, this virus was spread through e-mail that, when opened, automatically mailed itself out. The virus could also be spread without human intervention through various network-sharing vulnerabilities. Explorer.Zip created substantial problems for the e-mail systems at Microsoft, Intel, and NBC.
September 1999	Hotmail.hole	A Hotmail security hole was discovered by a Bulgarian hacker named Georgi Guninski that allows a JavaScript program to be injected into the user's systems via an e-mail message. The script could be used to display a fake login screen that stole the user's password. In this way the attacker could read the user's e-mail and send messages of any sort under the user's name.
November 1999	BubbleBoy	This e-mail virus differed from its predecessors because it only required the recipient to preview the message, not open it, in order to infect other computers.
January 2000	CDNow Attacked	A Russian cracker named Maxum stole 300,000 credit-card records from the CD Universe Web site, demanding $100,000 ransom for their return. When CD Universe refused, he started publishing the numbers one-by-one. Maxum's ISP shut him down when they learned about his criminal activity. Both Discover Card and American Express issued new cards to any of their cardholders shopping at CDNow.
February 2000	DDoS Attacks	From February 6 to February 7, Amazon.com, Buy.com, CNN.com, eBay, E*Trade, Yahoo!, and ZDNet were subjected to a series of distributed denial of service (DDoS) attacks. These sites were inundated with so many Internet requests that legitimate traffic was virtually halted. The combined attacks cost an estimated $1.2 billion.
Spring 2000	Credit Card Postings	A hacker named Raphael Gray (net name Curador) broke into EC sites in five countries—United States, Canada, Thailand, Japan, and the United Kingdom—and effortlessly obtained customer credit card numbers— 26,000 in all. His stated objective was to bring the security vulnerabilities to the attention of the Webmasters at the sites, which he did by posting the numbers on the Internet. The combined attacks cost an estimated $1.2 billion.
May 2000	ILOVEYOU	The VBS.LoveLetter.A virus originated in the Philippines, struck Hong Kong on May 4, and within hours had attacked computers worldwide. By the

EXHIBIT 9.1 (CONTINUED)

Date	Attack	Description
August 2000	Brown Orifice	time it had run its course, it had infected 1.2 million computers in North America and caused an estimated $80 million in damage. The virus was propagated virulently as an e-mail attachment that e-mailed itself to the contacts in the recipient's address book when opened. A computer consultant named Dan Brumleve announced that he had found two security flaws in the Netscape browser implementation of Java. The flaws enabled the distributor of a Java applet to view the file.
October 2000	Microsoft Source Code compromised	A cracker gained access to Microsoft's networks, enabling him or her to view the source code of applications under development. The cracker was able to penetrate the network through some "semi-retired" Web servers that hadn't been fixed to correct a vulnerability in Microsoft's Internet Information Server (i.e., Microsoft's commercial Web server product). Some security experts speculated that the hacker used the QAZ Trojan to spy on Microsoft's R&D division.

Source: Mell and Wack (2000).

and Federal Bureau of Investigation 2000), based on the responses of 643 practitioners, indicated the following.

- Cyber attacks are on the rise. In 2000, 70 percent of respondents indicated that their systems had experienced unauthorized use. This is up from 42 percent in 1996.

- Internet connections are increasingly a point of attack. The number of respondents indicating that their Internet connection is a frequent point of attack increased from 37 percent in 1996 to 59 percent in 2000.

- The variety of attacks is on the rise. Eleven percent detected financial fraud, 17 percent sabotage of data or networks, 20 percent theft of proprietary information, 25 percent penetration from the outside, 27 percent denial of service, 71 percent unauthorized access by insiders, 79 percent employee abuse of Internet access privileges, and 85 percent viruses.

Overall, the anecdotal and survey data indicate that security is a major issue for any EC Web site (B2C or B2B) and for consumers as well.

WHY NOW?

Years ago, a well-known bank robber named Willy Sutton was asked, "Why do you rob banks?" His response: "Because that's where the money is." Today, if you asked a hacker why they attack the Internet or Web, the hacker might offer a similar response: "Because that's where the money and information are."

Prior to the Web, the Internet was a research network. Most of the information was circulated through e-mail or FTP (File Transfer Protocol) from one researcher to another. Although there was certainly sensitive and proprietary information that could be compromised by a malicious hacker, much of the information was academic in nature and of little interest to the outside world. With the rapid growth of EC, things have changed. Consumers use their credit cards to purchase goods and services online, millions of individuals use their e-mail accounts to conduct business, B2B sites make sensitive business data available to trading partners, and, at a minimum, virtually every major business in the world has a marketing site that is open to the public at large. The sheer growth in EC has certainly made the Internet an enticing playground for hackers and crackers.

In addition, a number of other factors have contributed to the rise in cyber attacks. According to Marchany (2000), these include the following.

Security systems are only as strong as their weakest points. An EC system consists of a number of components, including security defenses such as firewalls, authentication schemes, and encryption. Yet, an intruder needs only a single weakness in order to attack a system.

Security and ease of use are antithetical to one another. The old adage says that if you want a really secure system, then shut the system off. Obviously this is ludicrous advice, but it does highlight the idea that security and usability tend to be inversely related. Take the case of passwords. If you are assigned a password like "#$8^-96–32," it is hard to remember and hard to use. In all likelihood, you will write it down somewhere. If you have a password like "johnsmith," it is easy to remember but not very hard to guess.

Security takes a back seat to market pressures. Most EC sites are built from components supplied by third-party vendors. Because of market pressures and rapidly evolving technologies, these vendors have often focused on time-to-market, paying little attention to security features.

Security of an EC site depends on the security of the Internet as a whole. The number of schools, libraries, homes, and small business sites directly connected to the Web continues to increase. Although larger companies and ISPs invest a substantial amount of time and effort securing their EC sites, the administration of these other sites often falls upon people with little or no training in network security.

Security vulnerabilities are mushrooming. In fact, vulnerabilities are increasing faster than they can be combated. As Mark Fabro, chief scientist at a vendor of security systems notes, "The hacker community is huge and very close-knit. They share their findings and post them 'in the wild,' where anyone can access them—and build on them" (Watson 2000). For an example of this, see livinginternet.com/?i/ia_hackers_sites.htm.

Security is compromised by common applications. Over the past few years, Microsoft has come to dominate not only the worlds of document processing (Word) and spreadsheets (Excel), but also the worlds of e-mail (Outlook), Web browsers (Internet Explorer), and presentations (PowerPoint). For most organizations, this set of common applications has eliminated a number of administrative costs and headaches and made it easier for people to share documents both inside and outside the organization. The problem is that once a hacker finds a hole in any of these products, the whole world is at risk. For example, the Melissa and ILOVEYOU macro worms were able to spread rapidly because of the widespread usage of Microsoft Outlook (Mell and Wack 2000).

BASIC SECURITY ISSUES

Major EC sites such as eBay, Yahoo!, and MSN are constantly on the alert for cyber attacks of all sorts, and rightfully so. The overall costs of the February 2000 DDoS attacks (see Exhibit 9.1) were estimated at $1.2 billion (Pappalardo 2000). The estimate was based not only on the person-hours required to restore service, but also on the dollar value of the number of purchases that were not made and the number of ads that were not seen. Based on a study by International Data Corporation (IDC), large organizations spent $6.2 billion on security consulting in 1999 and will more than double that amount to $14.8 billion by 2003 (Nieto et al. 2001).

Larger B2C and B2B sites are not the only ones that need to be concerned with security issues. Smaller business sites, as well as individual users, must be conscious of security. Consider, for example, the situation in which a user connects to a Web server at a marketing site in order to obtain some product literature (Loshin 1998). In return, the user is asked to fill out a Web form providing some demographic and other personal information in order to receive the literature. In this situation, what kinds of security questions arise?

From the user's perspective:

- How can the user be sure that the Web server is owned and operated by a legitimate company?
- How does the user know that the Web page and form do not contain some malicious or dangerous code or content?
- How does the user know that the Web server will not distribute the information the user provides to some other party?

From the company's perspective:

- How does the company know the user will not attempt to break into the Web server or alter the pages and content at the site?
- How does the company know that the user will not try to disrupt the server so that it is not available to others?

From both parties' perspectives:

- How do they know that the network connection is free from eavesdropping by a third party "listening in" on the line?
- How do they know that the information sent back and forth between the server and the user's browser has not been altered?

These questions illustrate the types of security issues that can arise in an EC transaction. For transactions involving e-payments, other types of security issues must be confronted. The following list summarizes some of the major security issues that can occur in EC:

- **Authentication.** When you view a Web page from a Web site, how can you be sure that the site is not fraudulent? If you file a tax return electronically, how do you know that you have sent it to the taxing authority? If you receive an e-mail, how can you be sure that the sender is who he or she claims to be? The process by which one entity verifies that another entity is who they claim to be is called **authentication**. Authentication requires evidence in the form of credentials, which can take a variety of forms, including something known (e.g., a password), something possessed (e.g., a smart card), or something unique (e.g., a signature).

authentication
The process by which one entity verifies that another entity is who they claim to be by checking credentials of some sort.

authorization
The process that ensures that a person has the right to access certain resources.

auditing
The process of collecting information about attempts to access particular resources, use particular privileges, or perform other security actions.

integrity
As applied to data, the ability to protect data from being altered or destroyed in an unauthorized or accidental manner.

nonrepudiation
The ability to limit parties from refuting that a legitimate transaction took place, usually by means of a signature.

▶ **Authorization.** Does a person or program have the right to access particular data, programs, or system resources (e.g., files, registries, directories, etc.) once authenticated? **Authorization** ensures that a person has the right to access certain resources. It is usually determined by comparing information about the person or program with access control information associated with the resource being accessed.

▶ **Auditing.** If a person or program accesses a Web site, various pieces of information are noted in a log file. If a person or program queries a database, the action is also noted in a log file. The process of collecting information about attempts to access particular resources, use particular privileges, or perform other security actions (either successfully or unsuccessfully) is known as **auditing**. Audits provide the means to reconstruct the specific actions that were taken and often the ability to uniquely identify the person or program that performed the actions.

▶ **Confidentiality (privacy).** Information that is private or sensitive should not be disclosed to unauthorized individuals, entities, or computer software processes. Some examples of things that should be confidential are trade secrets, business plans, health records, credit card numbers, and even the fact that a person visited a particular Web site. Confidentiality is usually ensured by encryption.

▶ **Integrity.** The ability to protect data from being altered or destroyed in an unauthorized or accidental manner is called **integrity**. Data can be altered or destroyed while it is in transit or after it is stored. Financial transactions are one example of data whose integrity needs to be secured. Again, encryption is one way of ensuring integrity of data while it is in transit.

▶ **Availability.** If you are trying to execute a stock trade through an online service, then the service needs to be available in near real time. An online site is available if a person or program can gain access to the pages, data, or services provided by the site when they are needed. Technologies such as load-balancing hardware and software are aimed at ensuring availability.

▶ **Nonrepudiation.** If you order an item through a mail-order catalog and pay by check, then it is difficult to dispute the veracity of the order. If you order the same item through the cataloger's "1–800" number and pay by credit card, then there is always room for dispute, although "caller ID" can be used to identify the phone from which the order was placed. Similarly, if you use the cataloger's Web site and pay by credit card, then you can always claim that it you did not place the order. **Nonrepudiation** is the ability to limit parties from refuting that a legitimate transaction took place. One of the keys to nonrepudiation is a "signature" that makes it difficult to dispute that you were involved in an exchange.

Exhibit 9.2 depicts some of the major components involved in most EC applications and indicates where these security issues come into play. It is safe to say that virtually every component in an EC application is subject to some sort of security threat.

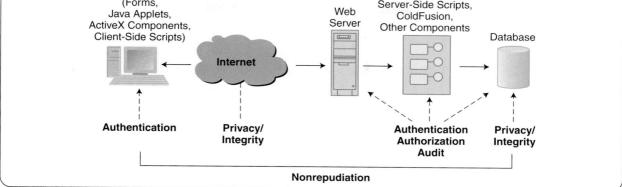

Source: Scambray et al., 2000.

TYPES OF CYBER ATTACKS

Security experts distinguish between two types of attacks—nontechnical and technical. **Nontechnical attacks** are also called *social engineering attacks*. In such attacks, a perpetrator uses chicanery or other form of persuasion to trick people into revealing sensitive information or performing actions that can be used to compromise the security of a network.

In contrast to a nontechnical attack, software and systems knowledge are used to perpetrate **technical attacks**. In conducting a technical attack, an expert hacker often uses a methodical approach. On the Internet, there are several software tools, which are readily and freely available, that enable a hacker to expose a system's vulnerabilities. Although many of these tools require expertise, a number of them can be easily used by novice hackers.

In 1999, Mitre Corporation and 15 other security-related organizations (cve.mitre.org) began to enumerate all publicly known **common vulnerabilities and exposures (CVEs)**. One of the goals was to assign standard and unique names to each of the known problems so that information could be collected and shared with the security community throughout the world. To date, there are over 1,900 known vulnerabilities. Almost all of these are very technical in nature and well beyond the scope of this book. For this reason we will confine our discussion to two types of attacks that are well known and have affected the lives of millions—distributed denial of service attacks (DDoS) and malicious code attacks (viruses, worms, and Trojan horses).

Distributed Denial of Service Attacks

In a **denial-of-service (DoS) attack**, an attacker uses specialized software to send a flood of data packets to the target computer with the aim of overloading its resources. With a **distributed denial of service (DDoS) attack**, the attacker gains illegal administrative access to as many computers on the Internet as possible. Once an attacker has access to a large number of computers, the hacker loads the

nontechnical attack
An attack in which a perpetrator uses chicanery or other form of persuasion to trick people into revealing sensitive information or performing actions that compromise the security of a network.

technical attack
An attack perpetrated using software and systems knowledge or expertise.

common vulnerabilities and exposures (CVEs)
Publicly known computer security risks or problems; these are collected, enumerated, and shared by a board of security-related organizations (*cve.mitre.org*).

denial-of-service (DoS) attack
An attack on a Web site in which an attacker uses specialized software to send a flood of data packets to the target computer with the aim of overloading its resources.

distributed denial of service (DDoS) attack
A denial-of-service attack in which the attacker gains illegal administrative access to as many computers on the Internet as possible and uses these multiple computers to send a flood of data packets to the target computer.

specialized DDoS software onto these computers. The software lays in wait, listening for a command to begin the attack. When the command is given, this distributed network of computers begins sending out requests to the target computer. The requests can be legitimate queries for information or very specialized computer commands designed to overwhelm specific computer resources. There are different types of DDoS attacks. In the simplest case, it is the magnitude of the requests that brings the target computer to a halt.

The machines on which the DDoS software is loaded are known as *zombies* (Heim and Ackerman 2001). Zombies are often located at university and government sites (see Exhibit 9.3). Increasingly, with the rise of cable modems and DSL modems, home computers that are connected to the Internet and left on all the time have become good zombie candidates.

Malicious Codes: Viruses, Worms, and Trojan Horses

malware
A generic term for malicious software.

Sometimes referred to as **malware** (for malicious software), malicious code is classified by the way in which it is propagated. Some malicious code is rather benign, but it all has the potential to do damage.

New variants of malicious code appear with amazing frequency. For example, the Computer Security Association's computer virus prevalence survey showed the number of different viruses doubling every year from 1997 to 1999. In the same vein, virtually every organization with e-mail has been the victim of a virus or worm. In the CSI survey described earlier (at the beginning of Section 9.6), 85 percent of the respondents said that their organizations were the victims of viruses.

EXHIBIT 9.3   Using Zombies in a DDoS Attack

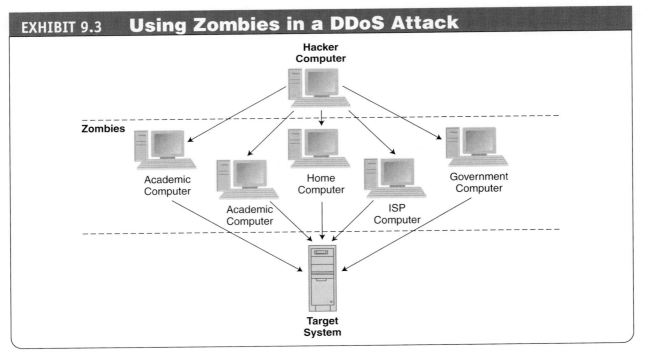

Source: Scambray et al., 2000.

Malicious code takes a variety of forms—both pure and hybrid. The names of such codes are taken from the real-world pathogens they resemble. Viruses are the best known. A whole industry has grown up around computer viruses. Companies such as Network Associates exist for the sole purpose of fighting viruses. The antivirus industry is extensive and profitable. Today, it has expanded beyond viruses and now also follows and catalogs worms, macro viruses and macro worms, and Trojan horses.

Viruses This is the best known of the malicious code categories. Although there are many definitions of a computer virus, the Request for Comment (RFC) 1135 definition is widely used: "A **virus** is a piece of code that inserts itself into a host, including the operating systems, to propagate. It cannot run independently. It requires that its host program be run to activate it."

A virus has two components. First, it has a propagation mechanism by which it spreads. Second, it has a payload that refers to what the virus does once it is executed. Sometimes the execution is triggered by a particular event. The Michelangelo virus, for instance, was triggered by Michelangelo's birth date. Some viruses simply infect and spread. Others do substantial damage (e.g., deleting files or corrupting the hard disk).

Worms The major difference between a worm and a virus is that a worm propagates between systems (usually through a network), whereas a virus propagates locally. RFC 1135 defines a worm in this way: "A **worm** is a program that can run independently, will consume the resources of its host from within in order to maintain itself, and can propagate a complete working version of itself onto another machine."

Macro Viruses and Macro Worms A **macro virus** or **macro worm** is usually executed when the application object (e.g., spreadsheet, word processing document, e-mail message) containing the macro is opened or a particular procedure is executed (e.g., a file is saved). Melissa and ILOVEYOU were both examples of macro worms that were propagated through Microsoft Outlook e-mail and whose payloads were delivered as a Visual Basic for Applications (VBA) program attached to e-mail messages. When the unsuspecting recipient opened the e-mail, the VBA program looked up the entries in the recipient's Outlook address book and sent copies of itself to the contacts in the address book. If you think this is a difficult task, note that the ILOVEYOU macro was about 40 lines of code.

Trojan Horses A **Trojan horse** is a program that appears to have a useful function but contains a hidden function that presents a security risk (Norton and Stockman 2000). The name is derived from the Trojan horse in Greek mythology. Legend has it that the city of Troy was presented, during the Trojan War, with a large wooden horse as a gift to the goddess Athena. The Trojans hauled the horse into the city gates. During the night, Greek soldiers, who were hiding in the hollow horse, opened the city gates and let in the Greek army. The army was able to take the city and win the war.

Two of the better-known Trojan horses are "Back Orifice" and "NetBus." Both are self-contained and self-installing utilities that can be used to remotely control and monitor the victim's computer over a network (e.g., execute commands, list files, and upload and download files on the victim's computer).

"Whack-A-Mole" is a popular delivery vehicle for NetBus. Whack-A-Mole is actually a game that is delivered as a self-extracting "Zip file." (For a nonmalicious

virus
A piece of software code that inserts itself into a host, including the operating systems, to propagate; it cannot run independently but requires that its host program be run to activate it.

worm
A software program that runs independently, consuming the resources of its host from within in order to maintain itself and propagating a complete working version of itself onto another machine.

macro virus or macro worm
A virus or worm that is usually executed when the application object (e.g., e-mail message) containing the macro is opened or a particular procedure is executed (e.g., a file is saved).

Trojan horse
A program that appears to have a useful function but that contains a hidden function that presents a security risk.

version of the game, see tomorrowfund.org/swgame09.html.) When a rogue version of the game is installed, so is NetBus. Once NetBus is installed, it provides a hacker with almost complete control over the user's computer.

EC Application Case 9.3 provides another example of a Trojan horse, one that even got past security experts.

SECURITY TECHNOLOGIES

Internet and EC security is a thriving business. International Data Corporation (IDC) estimates that the security software market reached $2 billion in 2002 and will grow to $14.6 billion in 2006 (Owens 2002).

The recent CSI/FBI survey and Information Security survey give some indication of where the money is being spent. The CSI/FBI survey combined respondents from both EC and non-EC sites. The results indicated that high on the list of security solutions were the following: antivirus software (90 percent of the sites); access control—basically user IDs and passwords (92 percent); physical

---

EC APPLICATION CASE 9.3

Implementation and Strategy

TROJAN HORSE ATTACK ON BUGTRAQ LIST

BugTraq is "a full disclosure moderated mailing list for the detailed discussion and announcement of computer security vulnerabilities: what they are, how to exploit them, and how to fix them" (Lemos 2000). The list has 37,000 subscribers and is moderated by security experts working at *SecurityFocus.com*, a leading provider of security information services for business. Well, it seems that even the experts get fooled sometimes. On February 1, 2000, someone sent SecurityFocus a program designed to identify four flaws in the Berkley Internet Domain Name (BIND) software. SecurityFocus had Network Associates (a security software maker) check out the code. Network Associates gave it their seal of approval.

Unfortunately, hidden in the code was a Trojan horse. The program was actually designed to use any computer on which it runs to send a simple form of Internet data to a single domain name server in an attempt to overwhelm the computer with information (a standard DDoS attack). In this case, the computer to which the data was to be sent was Network Associates' server. When SecurityFocus sent the code to its 37,000 BugTrac subscribers, Network Associates soon found itself under attack. Being

experts, though, it took Network Associates only 90 minutes to get back online.

SecurityFocus defended the list's posting procedure and said that despite the incident, the way the list is moderated will not change. According to a vice president at the firm, "The BugTraq moderation has never been in place to verify every single piece of information or exploits (incidents) that go through the list. There is no way we could have a lab or staff to do that. As always, we tell people to wait for other people to test the exploits before installing them themselves."

Source: Lemos, 2000.

Questions

▶ What information is provided by the messages in the BugTraq mailing list?

▶ There is a great deal of information on the Web about Trojan horse attacks. What are these attacks, and what measures can be used to guard against them?

security—controlling physical access to servers (90 percent); firewalls (78 percent); encrypted files (62 percent); encrypted log-ins (50 percent); and intrusion detection (50 percent).

In contrast, the Information Security survey focused specifically on EC sites and grouped the responses by type of site (B2C vs. B2B). The results from the survey are reproduced in Exhibit 9.4. One of the major differences between B2C and B2B sites is that B2B sites use a more layered approach to their security, with 70 percent employing more than four overlapping security technologies to secure communications and commerce. The main reason for this is that B2B is more mature, and more money is currently being spent on this form of EC.

Firewalls and Access Control

One of the major impediments to EC has been concern about the security of internal networks. A number of companies have sidestepped the issue by letting third parties host their Web sites. In this way, they eliminate the possibility of a hacker breaking into their internal systems, although hackers can still play havoc with the contents of the Web site. For those companies hosting their own sites, one of the immediate concerns is controlling access to network services, both inside and outside the company. Companies need to ensure that intruders cannot gain access to critical applications by tunneling through the Web site to exploit weaknesses in the internal network operating system, application software, and databases.

For most applications, the primary means of access control is *password* protection, the use of a special word or code for identification. Passwords are notoriously susceptible to compromise. Users have a habit of sharing their passwords with others, writing them down where others can see them, and choosing passwords that are easily guessed. On top of these problems, when the Web requests the user to enter a password to access protected documents or applications, the browser transmits the passwords in a form that is easily intercepted and decoded. One way to combat this problem is to make sure that even if the passwords are

EXHIBIT 9.4 **EC Security Controls**		
Tool	**B2C**	**B2B**
User IDs/Passwords	86%	85%
Firewalls/Packet Filtering	N/A	79%
Transactional Encryption (SSL/SET/SHTTP)	67%	60%
Server Segregation (DMZ)	50%	51%
Application-Specific Controls	44%	N/A
Authentication Servers (Kerberos, RADIUS, RAS)	40%	46%
Digital Certificate-Based Authentication/PKI	39%	45%
Point-to-Point Encryption (VPNs)	38%	56%
Dedicated Circuits	20%	36%
Authentication Tokens (hard or soft, including smart cards)	20%	29%
Other	3%	3%
None	3%	1%

Source: Briney, 2000. Used with permission of Information Security.

compromised, the intruder has restricted access to the rest of the network. This is one of the roles of a firewall.

firewall
A network node consisting of both hardware and software that isolates a private network from a public network.

A **firewall** is a network node consisting of both hardware and software that isolates a private network from a public network. Hazari (2000) provides a simple analogy to understand the general operation of a firewall: "We can think of firewalls as being similar to a bouncer in a nightclub. Like a bouncer in a nightclub, firewalls have a set of rules, similar to a guest list or a dress code, that determine if the data should be allowed entry. Just as the bouncer places himself at the door of the club, the firewall is located at the point of entry where data attempts to enter the computer from the Internet. Just as different nightclubs might have different rules for entry, different firewalls have different methods of inspecting data for acceptance or rejection."

Some firewalls filter data and requests moving from the public Internet to a private network based on the network addresses of the computer sending or receiving the request. Other firewalls block data and requests depending on the type of application being accessed. For instance, a firewall might permit requests for Web pages to move from the public Internet to the private network.

Intrusion Detection Systems

Even if an organization has a well-formulated security policy and a number of security technologies in place, it is still vulnerable to attack. For example, in 2000, 90 percent of the respondents to the CSI/FBI survey had antivirus software, yet 85 percent reported incidents of virus contamination. This is why an organization must continually watch for attempted, as well as actual, security breaches.

intrusion detection system (IDS)
A special category of software that can monitor activity across a network or on a host computer, watch for suspicious activity, and take automated action based on what it sees.

In the past, audit logs, produced by a variety of system components and applications, were manually reviewed for excessive failed log-on attempts, failed file and database access attempts, and other application and system violations. Obviously, this manual procedure had its flaws. For example, if intrusion attempts were spread out over a long period of time, they could be easily missed. Today, there is a special category of software that can monitor activity across a network or on a host computer, watch for suspicious activity, and take automated action based on what it sees. This category of software is called **intrusion detection systems (IDSs)**.

Security Risk Management

security risk management
A systematic process for determining the likelihood of various security attacks and for identifying the actions needed to prevent or mitigate those attacks.

It takes more than technology to secure a computer network. Those organizations with sound security practices rely on comprehensive risk management to determine their security needs (King 2001; Power 2000).

Security risk management is a systematic process for determining the likelihood of various security attacks and for identifying the actions needed to prevent or otherwise mitigate those attacks. It consists of four phases:

▶ **Assessment.** In this phase, organizations evaluate their security risks by determining their assets, system vulnerabilities, and the potential threats to these vulnerabilities.

▶ **Planning.** The goal of this phase is to arrive at a set of policies defining which threats are tolerable and which are not. A threat is deemed tolerable if the cost of the safeguard is too high or the risk too low. The policies also specify the general measures to be taken against those threats that are intolerable or high priority.

▮ **Implementation.** During implementation, particular technologies are chosen to counter high-priority threats. The selection of particular technologies is based on the general guidelines established in the planning phase. As a first step in the implementation phase, generic types of technology should be selected for each of the high priority threats. Given the generic types, particular software from particular vendors can then be selected.

▮ **Monitoring.** This is an ongoing process that is used to determine which measures are successful, which measures are unsuccessful and need modification, whether there are any new types of threats, whether there have been advances or changes in technology, and whether there are any new business requirements that need to be secured.

> ▮ List the major security issues in EC.
> ▮ Describe a nontechnical cyber attack.
> ▮ Describe the difference between a computer virus and a computer worm.
> ▮ Describe a firewall.
> ▮ List the basic phases of security risk management.

MANAGERIAL ISSUES

Some managerial issues related to this chapter are as follows.

1. **How can the global nature of EC impact business operations?** A large percentage of EC sites are global. Laws and ethics can vary radically from one culture and country to the next. What is illegal or unethical in one country may not be so in another country. It is essential that any enterprise with an EC site develop policies and measures that account for these differences—not only to protect the company's own property rights (copyrights, trademarks, and patents), but also to respect and ensure the rights of users and customers. Failure to enact these policies and measures can substantially erode profits (Hildebrand 1996) and open up an enterprise to potential litigation.

2. **What sorts of legal and ethical issues should be of major concern to an EC enterprise?** There is no set list of ethical and legal issues that are paramount in EC. However, some of the key issues to consider include the following: (1) What type of proprietary information should you allow on your site? (2) Who will have access to information that is posted by visitors to your the site? (3) Do the content and activities on your site comply with the laws in other countries? (4) Do you need to post disclaimers concerning the content of your Web site? (5) Are you inadvertently using trademarked or copyright materials without permission? Regardless of the specific issues, an attorney should periodically review the content on your site, and someone should be responsible for monitoring the legal and liability issues.

3. **What are the business consequences of poor security?** According to a 1998 Government Accounting Office (GAO) study (Merkow and Breihaupt 2000), the single most important factor in establishing an effective network security

program is the general recognition among senior management of the enormous risks to business operations associated with relying on highly interconnected computer systems. In a nutshell, ineffective security opens the door to computer and network attacks. Such attacks can result in damage to technical and information assets; theft of information and information services; temporary loss of a Web site and Internet access; loss of income; litigation brought on by dissatisfied organizational stakeholders; loss of customer confidence; and damaged reputation and credibility. In some cases, attacks can literally put an enterprise out of business, especially if EC is their sole source of revenue.

4. **Are we safe if there are few visitors to our EC site?** Suppose you decide to set up a B2B site in order to service your suppliers and partners. Because it is not a public site, the only ones who are likely to know of its existence are you, your suppliers, and your partners. Therefore you assume there is no need to institute strong security measures. Wrong! Because of the prevalence of automated scanning tools, it could be only a few days before hackers discover your site. Once discovered, it could be only hours or minutes before the hackers have compromised your site and taken control, if your system has known vulnerabilities. The moral of the story is that regardless of how obscure, uninteresting, or unadvertised a site

is, no EC site can afford to take security for granted. All sites should thoroughly review their security requirements and institute stringent measures to guard against high-priority threats.

5. **Is technology the key to EC security?** Most discussions about security focus on technology. You hear statements such as, "Firewalls are mandatory" or "All transmissions should be encrypted." Although firewalls and encryption can be important technologies, no security solution is useful unless it solves a business problem. Determining your business requirements is the most important step in creating a security solution. In turn, business requirements determine your information requirements. Once your information requirements are known, you can begin to understand the value of those assets and the steps that should be taken to secure those that are most valuable and vulnerable.

6. **Where are the security threats likely to come from?** As the Internet Security survey showed, EC sites are more likely than non-EC sites to encounter security breaches, both inside and outside the organization. Except for the prevalence of viruses and worms, breaches perpetrated by insiders are much more frequent than those perpetrated by outsiders. This is true for both types of sites. The point is that security policies and measures for EC sites need to address these insider threats.

SUMMARY

In this chapter, you learned about the following EC issues as they relate to the learning objectives.

1. **Describe the differences between legal and ethical issues in EC.** The legal framework for EC—both statutory and common law—is just beginning to solidify. To date, the major legal issues in EC have involved rights of privacy, intellectual property, freedom of speech and censorship, and fraud. In the absence of legal constraints, ethical codes help to fill the gap. The problem is that ethics are subjective and vary widely from one culture to the next.

2. **Understand the difficulties of protecting privacy in EC.** EC sites require customer information to improve products and service. Registration and cookies are two of the ways used to collect this information. The key privacy issues are who controls this information and how private it should remain. Although legal measures are being developed to protect the privacy of individuals, it is basically up to the EC companies to regulate themselves.

3. **Discuss the issues of intellectual property rights in EC.** It is extremely easy and inexpensive to copy or steal intellectual works on the Internet (e.g., music, photos, graphics, and the like) and to distribute or sell them without the permission of the owners—violating or infringing on copyrights, trademarks, and patents. Although the legal aspects are now fairly clear, monitoring and catching violators is difficult.

4. **Understand the conflict between free speech and censorship on the Internet.** There is an ongoing debate about censorship on the Internet. The proponents of censorship feel that it is up to the government and the various ISPs and Web sites to control inappropriate or offensive content. Others oppose any form of censorship; they believe that control is up to the individual. In the United States, most legal attempts to censor content on the Internet have been found unconstitutional. The debate is not likely to subside in the near term.

5. **Document the rapid rise in computer and network security attacks.** Anecdotal and survey data reported by organizations such as the Computer Security Institute indicate that there has been a substantial rise in cyber attacks of all sorts. The data also indicate that EC sites are much more vulnerable than others, reaffirming the notion that the rise in cyber attacks on the Internet is a direct result of the rise of EC.

6. **Understand the factors contributing to the rise of EC security breaches.** EC sites have proven to be particularly vulnerable to cyber attacks because they are built from a number of complex components and applications. Many of these components and applications are insecure. Unfortunately, all it takes is one vulnerable component or application to compromise the security of the whole system.

7. **Describe the key security issues facing EC sites.** EC sites need to be concerned with a variety of security issues, including authentication, authorization, auditing, confidentiality, integrity, availability, and nonrepudiation.

8. **Discuss some of the major types of cyber attacks against EC sites.** EC sites are exposed to a wide range of attacks. To date, the Common Vulnerabilities and Exposures group has identified 1,900 different types of cyber attacks. Among the most frequent types of attacks affecting both EC and non-EC sites are distributed denial of service attacks and malicious code attacks (i.e., viruses, worms, and Trojan horses).

9. **Describe some of the technologies used to secure EC sites.** Virtually all EC sites rely on some combination of antivirus software, user IDs and passwords, physical security, firewalls, encrypted files and transmissions, and intrusion detection to secure their sites. A major difference between the security of B2C and B2B sites is that B2B sites employ a wider variety of technologies.

KEY TERMS

DISCUSSION QUESTIONS

1. Provide two privacy examples in EC in which the situation is legal but unethical.

2. Distinguish between self-registration and cookies in EC. Why do you think Internet users are concerned about cookies?

3. What are some of the things that EC Web sites can do to ensure that personal information is safeguarded?

4. On the Internet, why is it difficult to protect intellectual property? Do you think that sites such as MP3.com and Napster should be able to operate without restrictions? Justify your answer.

5. Who should control the access of minors to "offensive" material on the Internet—parents, the government, or ISPs? Why?

6. Should spamming be illegal? Explain why or why not.

7. In exchange for receiving a free magazine article, you are asked to register at an EC site. What types of security issues can arise?

8. Cyber attacks are on the rise. Discuss the factors that have contributed to the increase. Do you expect the situation to get better or worse? Explain.

9. Discuss some of the major types of cyber attacks perpetrated against EC sites.

10. All EC sites employ security safeguards, yet there are differences between B2C and B2B sites in the safeguards they use. Discuss the similarities and differences between the two types of sites.

INTERNET EXERCISES

1. Two commonly used Internet terms are *flaming* and *spamming*. Surf the Web to find out more about these terms. How are they similar? How are they different?

2. Visit ftc.gov and identify some of the typical types of frauds and scams being run on the Internet.

3. You want to set up a personal Web site. Using legal sites such as cyberlaw.com, prepare a report summarizing the types of materials you can and cannot use (e.g., logos, graphics, etc.) without breaking copyright law.

4. Using google.com, prepare a list of industry and trade organizations involved in various computer privacy initiatives. One of these groups is the World Wide Web Consortium (W3C).

Describe its Privacy Preferences Project (w3.org/TR/2001/WD-P3P-20010928).

5. Visit the hacked pages at 2600.com (2600.com/hacked_pages/index.html). Construct a list of some of the famous sites that have been the object of hacker attacks.

6. Go to Network Associates Virus library (vil.nai.com/vil/default.asp). What are the general characteristics of a computer virus? How are risks of viruses assessed (see mcafeeb2b.com/avert/virus-alerts/avert-risk-assessment.asp)?

7. You have installed a cable modem at your home or apartment. You have heard that it makes your computer susceptible to DDoS attacks and you want to install a personal firewall to

guard against the threat. What sorts of commercial products are available? Which one would you choice and why?

8. Your B2C site has just been hacked. You would like to report the incident to the Computer Emergency Response Team (cert.org) at Carnegie Mellon University so they can alert other sites. How do you do this, and what types of information do you have to provide?

TEAM ASSIGNMENTS AND ROLE PLAYING

1. Over the past few years, there have been an increasing number of lawsuits in the United States and elsewhere involving EC. Have each team member prepare a list of 10 or more such cases. Relate the cases to the topics in this chapter. What have been the outcomes of these cases? If there has not yet been an outcome in certain cases, what is likely to happen and why?

2. Security experts have been especially critical of the security vulnerabilities of Microsoft's software and systems. Using the Web, collect a body of empirical evidence—survey data, reports in journals, data collected by various security Web sites—to support or refute this claim. Why are Microsoft's software and systems any more or less vulnerable than other software and systems? What is Microsoft doing to address these issues?

REAL-WORLD CASE

THE RISE OF SECURITY STANDARDS

As Rob Clyde, vice president and CTO at security vendor Symantec Corp., recently said, "On a scale of 1 to 10, in terms of security in the Internet infrastructure, we are probably about 3 or 4" (Lewis 2001). A key factor contributing to this low score is the absence of a set of practical, nonproprietary, widely accepted Internet security guidelines, detailing how systems ought to be configured and what sorts of safeguards should be present.

You could think of these guidelines as similar to the preflight maintenance checks used by airlines to ensure the safety of their aircraft before flight (Paller et al. 2000). Without standard guidelines, organizations, especially smaller businesses, will continue to build and maintain EC sites with little knowledge of the security hazards that await them.

On the B2C front, Visa is leading the charge for better security standards. In July 2000, the company issued a set of guidelines that each merchant partner must meet if it wants to keep the Visa logo. Included in the list of guidelines are the following:

1. Establish a hiring policy for staff and contractors.
2. Restrict access to data on a need-to-know basis.
3. Assign each person a unique identity to be validated when accessing data.
4. Track access to data, including read access, by each person.
5. Install and maintain a network firewall if data can be accessed via the Internet.
6. Encrypt data maintained on databases or files accessible from the Internet.
7. Encrypt data sent across networks.
8. Protect systems and data from viruses.
9. Keep security patches for software up to date.
10. Do not use vendor-supplied defaults for system passwords and other security parameters.

11. Do not leave papers/diskettes/computers with data unsecured.

12. Securely destroy data when it is no longer needed for business reasons.

13. Regularly test security systems and procedures.

14. Immediately investigate and report to Visa any suspected loss of account or transaction information.

15. Use only service providers that meet security standards.

In a pilot test, Visa worked with members to monitor compliance with these standards. Information Security Systems (*iss.net*), a supplier of intrusion-detection software and provider of managed security services, performed monthly vulnerability scans of merchant sites, ready to fix holes if they emerged. Eventually, enforcement of the standards could involve fines, restricting the dollar amount of sales that individual merchants could process through the network, or terminating their Visa membership.

To encourage widespread acceptance of security standards throughout the EC world, representatives from federal, state, and local government agencies are working with academics and corporations (led by representatives from Visa and Merrill Lynch) to convert the Visa effort into one global set of standards. Their not-for-profit organization is called the Center for Internet Security (*cisecurity.org*). These global standards will be aimed not only at B2C sites, but also at B2B sites.

Although most B2B firms are confident about safeguarding data residing on corporate premises, they are still very leery about exchanging in-process designs, demand forecasts, inventory management, logistics updates, and a host of other important information across the Internet. They are even more leery about doing contract negotiations across the Internet. These negotiations, which can involve billions of dollars, are still largely done over the phone or in person. In an effort to address a broad range of B2B security (at least in the electronics industry), Cisco Systems, IBM, Intel, Nortel Networks, and Symantec formed the Information Technology Information Sharing and Analysis Center (IT-ISAC) in January 2000. The aim of the center is to promote best practices in network security and, in turn, encourage the growth of B2B commerce.

Source: Visa (2000).

Questions

1. The standards proposed by Visa appear to be common sense. What types of businesses do you think the standards are aimed at? Why?

2. Visa is only one credit card vendor among many. Does the success of Visa's program rest on the adoption of these or similar standards by Visa's competitors? Explain.

3. What sort of impact will Visa's or any set of security standards have on the rise in cyber attacks?

CHAPTER 10

PAYMENTS AND ORDER FULFILLMENT

Content

LensDoc Organizes Payments Online

10.1 Electronic Payments: A Critical Element in EC Support Services

10.2 Security for E-Payments

10.3 Electronic Cards and Smart Cards

10.4 E-Cash and Innovative Payment Methods

10.5 E-Checking

10.6 Order Fulfillment and Logistics— An Overview

10.7 Problems in Order Fulfillment

10.8 Solutions to Order Fulfillment Problems

Managerial Issues

Real-World Case:

How Dell Computer Fulfills Customer Orders

Learning objectives

Upon completion of this chapter, you will be able to:

▶ Understand the crucial factors that determine the success of e-payment methods.

▶ Describe the key elements in securing e-payments.

▶ Discuss the players and processes involved in using credit cards online.

▶ Describe the uses and benefits of purchase cards.

▶ Discuss the different categories and potential uses of smart cards.

▶ Discuss various online alternatives to credit card payments and identify under what circumstances they are best used.

▶ Describe the processes and parties involved in e-checking.

▶ Describe the role of order fulfillment and back-office operations in EC.

▶ Describe the EC order fulfillment process.

▶ Describe the major problems of EC order fulfillment.

▶ Describe various solutions to EC order fulfillment problems.

LENSDOC ORGANIZES PAYMENTS ONLINE

The Problem

LensDoc (*lensdoc.com*), based in Hilton Head, South Carolina, is an online retailer of contact lenses, sun and magnifying glasses, and dental care and personal care products. As with most B2C retailers, there is only one way for a customer to pay for a purchase from LensDoc—with a credit card. Over 80 percent of the purchases made on the Web are done with credit cards—and over 90 percent for Web purchases made in the United States (eccho.org, 2002).

Although LensDoc relies on credit cards, they present a troubling dilemma for the retailer (Carr 2000). Credit cards make it easy for customers from all over the world to purchase items from online stores. They also make it easy for a customer to return an item and receive credit for the return. LensDoc has been the victim of a number of fraudulent charges from customers in Eastern Europe who have used other people's credit cards to buy expensive sunglasses. They also have had a problem with the return of contact lenses. People try them on and return them if they are not satisfied. The problem is that U.S. regulations prohibit the return of contact lenses that have been used, but the credit card companies are predisposed at the moment to allow the returns and simply discard the lenses, forcing LensDoc to take a loss on the return.

The Solution

LensDoc has implemented special handling procedures for authorizing credit card purchases. The company manually processes credit card orders and asks customers to fax a form that includes the cardholder's address as well as the shipping address. Obviously, the assumption is that if the card being used is a fraudulent one, the perpetrator is unlikely to know the cardholder's address.

The Results

LensDoc has investigated a number of alternative e-payment methods, including cash cards, special card-swiping peripherals, credit card processing services, and the like. Each has its advantages and disadvantages. To date, the disadvantages of each alternative seem to outweigh the advantages, or at least none seems more advantageous than credit cards.

What We Can Learn . . .

Most B2C purchases are paid by credit card, however, there is potential for considerable fraud when credit cards are used online. As recently as 2000, some 83 percent of online merchants surveyed said that online fraud is a serious problem. Merchants are responsible for fraudulent charges because online credit card purchases are treated as "card-not-present" transactions. Thus, the merchant must absorb the loss and also incur a "chargeback" fee of $25 to $100, as well as the initial transaction fee of 2 percent (or more) levied by the credit card company (Duvall 2000; Caswell 2000).

Therefore, it is necessary to secure the credit card payment process as well as to develop and encourage the use of alternative payment methods. In this chapter, we will explore some of the methods used to secure credit card transactions and examine the various alternative payment methods. We will also examine the problems related to the return of unwanted merchandise. In addition to payments and logistics, EC requires other support services, such as content creation, which are covered in the online appendix and Chapter 8 of Turban et al. (2002b).

10.1 ELECTRONIC PAYMENTS: A CRITICAL ELEMENT IN EC SUPPORT SERVICES

In the off-line world, consumers use cash, checks, and credit cards to make purchases. At a fast-food restaurant, we usually pay with cash. If we purchase an appliance at a discount store, we are likely to use a credit card. When we pay our bills, most of us use checks. How do we pay online?

PAYING WITH CREDIT CARDS ONLINE

A few years ago, it was generally believed that consumers would be extremely reluctant to use their credit card numbers on the Web. The assumption was that special forms of electronic or digital cash were required for B2C to survive and thrive. Today, EC is thriving, and, as noted earlier, the overwhelming majority of Web purchases are made with credit cards, not with digital cash.

However, some statistics indicate that the picture may change in the near future. First, two-thirds of the people who will be on the Internet in 2003 have not had even their first Web experience. Many of these users will come from countries outside the United States, where the use of credit cards is not as prevalent (Gazala and Shepard 2001). A good number of these users are also likely to be younger and have less access to credit and debit cards. Many of the purchases they make will involve currency values that are too small for credit cards (e.g., purchasing a single song or playing an online game).

Second, and more importantly, about 85 percent of the transactions that occur on the Web are B2B rather than B2C (forrester.com, 2001). Credit cards are rarely used in B2B transactions. Instead, more traditional methods of payment are used. In the future, a sizeable percentage of these payments will be electronic. However, these electronic payments are more likely to involve electronic funds transfers or electronic checks.

In addition to credit cards and funds transfers, electronic payments (e-payments) are another payment option. There are many types of e-payment methods. What these diverse e-payment methods share in common is the ability to transfer a payment from one person or party to another person or party over a network without face-to-face interaction.

Whatever the e-payment method, four parties are usually involved:

1. **Issuer.** The banks or nonbanking institutions that issue the e-payment instrument used to make the purchase.
2. **Customer/payer/buyer.** The party making the e-payment in exchange for goods or services.
3. **Merchant/payee/seller.** The party receiving the e-payment in exchange for goods and services.
4. **Regulator.** Usually a government agency whose regulations control the e-payment process.

Although usually behind the scenes, issuers play a key role in any online purchase for two reasons. First, customers must obtain their e-payment accounts from an

414 Part 5: Supporting EC Applications

issuer. Second, issuers are usually involved in authenticating a transaction and approving the amount involved (often in real time).

Because online buyers and sellers are not in the same place and cannot exchange payments and products at the same time, issues of trust come into play. The acronym PAIN (Privacy, Authentication, Integrity, and Nonrepudiation) has been devised to represent the key issues of trust that must be addressed by any e-payment method (see Cornwell 2000 and Chapter 9).

CHARACTERISTICS OF SUCCESSFUL E-PAYMENT METHODS

A number of factors come into play in determining whether a particular method of e-payment achieves widespread acceptance. Some of the crucial factors include:

- **Independence.** Some forms of e-payment require specialized software or hardware to make the payment. Almost all forms of e-payment require the seller or merchant to install specialized software to receive and authorize a payment. Those e-payment methods that require the payer to install specialized components are less likely to succeed.

- **Interoperability and portability.** All forms of EC run on specialized systems that are interlinked with other enterprise systems and applications. An e-payment method must mesh with these existing systems and applications and be supported by standard computing platforms.

- **Security.** How safe is the transfer? What are the consequences of the transfer being compromised? Again, if the risk for the payer is higher than the risk for the payee, then the method is not likely to be accepted.

- **Anonymity.** Unlike credit cards and checks, if a buyer uses cash, there is no way to trace the cash back to the buyer. Some buyers want their identities and purchase patterns to remain anonymous. To succeed, special payment methods such as e-cash or digital cash (discussed later) have to maintain anonymity.

- **Divisibility.** Most sellers accept credit cards only for purchases within a minimum and maximum range. If the cost of the item is too small—say, only a few dollars—a credit card won't do. On the other hand, a credit card will not work if an item or set of items costs too much—say, an airline company purchasing a new airplane. Any method that can address the lower or higher end of the price continuum or that can span one of the extremes and the middle has a chance of being widely accepted.

- **Ease of use.** For B2C e-payments, credit cards are the standard due to their ease of use. For B2B payments, the question is whether the online e-payment methods can supplant the existing off-line methods of procurement.

- **Transaction fees.** When a credit card is used for payment, the merchant pays a transaction fee of up to about 3 percent of the item's purchase price (above a minimum fixed fee). These fees make it prohibitive to support smaller purchases with credit cards, which leaves room for alternative forms of payment.

To date, the acceptance of various e-payment methods has been slow. There are some areas—online billing (Chapter 3) and online procurement—where e-payments are likely to make significant inroads in the near future. Several key business drivers are behind the growth of these alternatives. Using e-payment reduces transaction costs by 30 to 50 percent, compared to off-line payment. Another is speed. If you pay a bill by check, for example, it takes time to mail the bill, time to mail the check, and time to deposit and process the check. The whole process takes at least a week. If the bill is presented and paid online, it takes a couple of days at the most. E-payments also make it possible to conduct business across geographical and political boundaries, greatly enhancing the possibilities for international deals and transactions.

In this chapter, we consider various forms of e-payments for B2C, B2B, and C2C commerce. However, before we look at any specific payment methods, we will discuss the key foundational issue for any payment technology—security.

▶ Why is credit card payment so popular in EC? What are the problems with using credit cards for EC?

▶ List all of the parties involved in e-payment.

▶ List the various factors (characteristics) that determine the acceptance of an e-payment method.

▶ What are some of the benefits of e-payments?

10.2 SECURITY FOR E-PAYMENTS

When you use a credit card to make a purchase on the Internet, how can you be sure that someone will not intercept the card number as it traverses the network? If you contact an EC site with the intention of making a purchase, how can you be sure that it is a legitimate site? If one company sends a bill to another company over the Internet, how can the recipient be sure that the bill has not been changed? If a customer sends your company an e-check and later denies that they sent it, how can you refute the denial? These questions illustrate the issues of trust (or "PAIN") that arise with e-payment systems. A well-devised online security system provides the answer to many, but not all, of these and similar questions. Internet security is a very complex issue that was addressed in Chapter 9. The security of e-payments is the focus of this section.

PUBLIC KEY INFRASTRUCTURE

One element that has emerged as the cornerstone for secure e-payments is **public key infrastructure (PKI)**. PKI refers to the technical components, infrastructure, and practices needed to enable the use of *public-key encryption*, *digital signatures*, and *digital certificates* with a network application. PKI is also the foundation of a number of network applications, including supply chain management, virtual private networks, secure e-mail, and intranet applications.

Public Key Encryption

Encryption (or **cryptography**) ensures the confidentiality and privacy of a message as it moves across a network by scrambling (*encrypting*) a message in such a way that it is difficult, expensive, or time-consuming for an unauthorized person to

public key infrastructure (PKI)
A scheme for securing e-payments using public key encryption and various technical components.

encryption (cryptography)
The process of scrambling (*encrypting*) a message in such a way that it is difficult, expensive, or time-consuming for an unauthorized person to unscramble (*decrypt*) it.

unscramble (*decrypt*) it. In the case of e-payments, the message could be credit card information entered in a form or contractual terms between two companies.

All encryption has four basic parts:

plaintext
An unencrypted message in human-readable form.

ciphertext
A plaintext message after it has been encrypted into unreadable form.

encryption algorithm
The mathematical formula used to encrypt the plaintext into ciphertext and vice versa.

key
The secret code used to encrypt and decrypt a message.

1. **Plaintext.** The original message in human-readable form.
2. **Ciphertext.** The plaintext message after it has been encrypted into unreadable form.
3. **Encryption algorithm.** The mathematical formula used to encrypt the plaintext into ciphertext and vice versa.
4. **Key.** The secret code used to encrypt and decrypt a message. Different keys produce different ciphertext when used with the same algorithm.

There are two major classes of encryption systems: *symmetric systems*, with one secret key, and *asymmetric systems*, with two keys. In a *symmetric* system, the *same key* is used to encrypt and decrypt the plaintext (see Exhibit 10.1). The key must be shared by the sender and receiver of the text. Several algorithms may be used to encrypt a message, such as Data Encryption Standard (DES).

Even if the algorithm is known, the message is still secure as long as only the sender and receiver know the key. However, it is possible to guess a key simply by having a computer try all the encryption combinations until the message is decrypted. High-speed and parallel-processing computers can try millions of guesses in a second. This is why the length of the key (in bits) is the main factor in securing a message. If a key were 4 bits long (e.g., 1011), then there would be only 16 possible combinations (i.e., 2^4). One would hardly need a computer to crack the key. Now, consider the data shown in Exhibit 10.2. Based on the data in Exhibit 10.2, it is easy to see that 40–bit keys can be broken in seconds and 56–bit keys in a matter of days or faster, depending on the power of the computer being used.

Imagine trying to use one-key encryption to buy something offered on a particular Web server. If the sender's key were distributed to thousands of buyers, then the key would not remain secret for long. This is where public key encryption comes into play. **Public key encryption** uses a *pair* of keys—a public key to encrypt the message and a private key to decrypt the message, or vice versa. There

public key encryption
Method of encryption that uses a *pair* of keys—a public key to encrypt a message and a private key (kept only by its owner) to decrypt it, or vice versa.

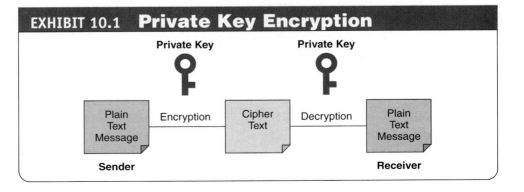

EXHIBIT 10.1 Private Key Encryption

Private Key — Plain Text Message (Sender) — Encryption — Cipher Text — Decryption — Plain Text Message (Receiver) — Private Key

EXHIBIT 10.2 Key Sizes and Time to Try All Possible Keys

Key Size	Number of Possible Keys (2x)	Time to Check All Keys at 1.6 million keys per second	Time to Check All Keys at 10 million keys per second
40	1,099,511,627,776	8 days	109 seconds
56	72,057,594,037,927,900	1,427 years	83 days
64	18,446,744,073,709,600,000	365,338 years	58.5 years
128	3.40282E + 38	6.73931E + 24 years	1.07829E + 21 years

Source: Based on Howard, 2000.

is only one copy of a **private key,** and it is kept by its owner. A **public key** is publicly available to anyone, and is frequently posted on the Internet.

The most common public key encryption algorithm is RSA. RSA uses keys ranging in length from 512 bits to 1024 bits. With public key encryption, if a Web site sends out its public key to a large group of prospective buyers, it does not matter because the only way to decrypt a message created with that public key is with the matching private key that only the Web site owner has.

The main problem with public key encryption is its speed. It cannot be used effectively to encrypt and decrypt large amounts of data. Symmetrical algorithms are significantly faster than asymmetric key algorithms. In practice, a combination of symmetric and asymmetric encryption is used to encrypt messages.

private key
Secret encryption code held only by its owner.

public key
Secret encryption code that is publicly available to anyone.

Digital Signatures: Authenticity and Nondenial

In the online world, how can you be sure that a message is actually coming from the person you think sent it? Similarly, how can you be sure that a person has no way of denying they sent a particular message? One part of the answer is a **digital signature**—the electronic equivalent of a personal signature that cannot be forged. Digital signatures are based on public keys. They can be used to authenticate the identity of the sender of a message or document. They can also be used to ensure that the original content of an electronic message or document is unchanged. Digital signatures have additional benefits in the online world. They are portable, cannot be easily repudiated or imitated, and can be time-stamped.

Exhibit 10.3 (page 418) shows how a digital signature works. Suppose you want to send the draft of a financial contract as an e-mail message to a company with whom you plan to do business. You want to assure the company that the content of the draft has not been changed en route, and that you really are the sender. To do so, you take the following steps:

digital signature
An identifying code that can be used to authenticate the identity of the sender of a message or document.

1. You create the e-mail message with the contract in it.
2. Using special software, you "hash" the message, which results in a special summary of the message, converted into a string of digits, called a message digest.
3. You use your private key to encrypt the hash. This is your digital signature. (No one else can do it because you are using your private key.)

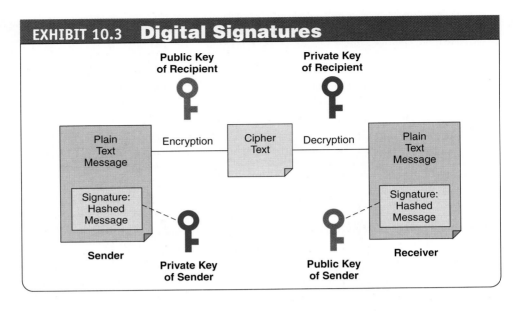

EXHIBIT 10.3 **Digital Signatures**

4. You e-mail the original message (to simplify the explanation, assume that it is not encrypted) along with the encrypted hash to the receiver.

5. Upon receipt, the receiver uses the same special software to hash the message they received.

6. Finally, the company uses your public key to decrypt the message hash (from step 3) that you sent. If their hash matches the decrypted hash, then the message is valid.

In this scenario, the company has evidence that it was really you that sent the e-mail because (theoretically) you are the only one with access to your private key. They know that the message was not tampered with, because if it had been, then the two hashes would not have matched.

According to the U.S. Federal Electronic Signatures in Global and National Commerce Act that went into effect on October 1, 2000, digital signatures in the United States now have the same legal standing as a signature written in ink on paper. Although PKI will certainly be the foundation of digital signatures, the act does not specify that any particular technology needs to be used. Several third-party companies are now exploring other methods to verify a person's legal identity, including the use of personal smart cards, PDA encryption devices, and biometric verifications (e.g., fingerprint, voice, or iris scans).

Digital Certificates and Certificate Authorities

digital certificate
Verification that the holder of a public or private key is who he or she claims to be.

certificate authorities (CAs)
Third parties that issue digital certificates.

If you have to know someone's public key to send them a message, where does it come from and how can you be sure of the person's actual identity? **Digital certificates** verify that the holder of a public and/or private key is who he or she claims to be. Third parties called **certificate authorities (CAs)** issue digital certificates. A certificate contains things such as the owner's name, validity period, subject's public key information, and a signed hash of the certificate data (i.e., hashed contents of the certificate signed with the CA's private key). Certificates are used to authenticate Web sites (*site certificates*), individuals (*personal certificates*), and software companies (*software publisher certificates*).

The number of third-party CAs is growing. VeriSign (verisign.com) is the best known of the CAs. VeriSign issues three classes of certificates. Class 1 verifies that an e-mail actually comes from the user's address. Class 2 checks the user's identity against a commercial credit database. Class 3 requires notarized documents. Companies such as Microsoft offer systems that enable companies to issue their own private, in-house certificates.

STANDARDS FOR E-PAYMENTS

If the average user had to figure out how to use encryption, digital certificates, digital signatures, and the like, there would be few secure transactions, and, in turn, few purchases made on the Web. Fortunately, all of these issues are handled in a transparent fashion by Web browsers and Web servers. As many different companies, financial institutions, and governments, in many countries, are involved in e-payments, it is necessary to have generally accepted protocols for securing e-payments. Two protocols are in use: Transport Layer Security (TLS) and Secure Electronic Transactions (SET).

Transport Layer Security

A special protocol called **Secure Socket Layer (SSL)** was invented by Netscape to utilize standard certificates for authentication and data encryption to ensure privacy or confidentiality. SSL became a de facto standard adopted by the browsers and servers provided by Microsoft and Netscape. In 1996, SSL was renamed the **Transport Layer Security (TLS)**.

Secure Socket Layer (SSL)
Protocol that utilizes standard certificates for authentication and data encryption to ensure privacy or confidentiality.

Transport Layer Security (TLS)
As of 1996, another name for the Secure Socket Layer protocol.

Secure Electronic Transactions

TLS makes it possible to encrypt credit card numbers that are sent from a consumer's browser to a merchant's Web site. However, there is more to making a purchase on the Web than simply passing a credit card number to a merchant. The number must be checked for validity, the consumer's bank must authorize the card, and the purchase must be processed. TLS is not designed to handle any of the steps beyond the transmission of the card number.

A cryptographic protocol that *is* designed to handle a complete online transaction is called the **Secure Electronic Transaction (SET)** protocol. It provides secure online credit card transactions for both consumers and merchants. Visa and MasterCard were instrumental in developing SET. Today, they manage the specifications for SET through a joint venture—SET Secure Electronic Transaction LLC (see setco.org).

Secure Electronic Transaction (SET)
A protocol designed to provide secure online credit card transactions for both consumers and merchants; developed jointly by Netscape, Visa, MasterCard, and others.

▶ Describe PKI and public key encryption.

▶ Compare symmetric key encryption with PKI.

▶ Describe how a digital signature works.

▶ Describe the roles of a digital certificate and a certificate authority.

▶ What are TLS and SET?

10.3 ELECTRONIC CARDS AND SMART CARDS

Electronic cards are plastic cards that contain information. This information can be used for payment purposes, in which case we refer to the electronic cards as **payment cards**. Electronic cards also can be used for other purposes, such as identification or to access a secure location. Some electronic cards are considered "smart" cards because they contain information that can be manipulated. In this section, we will discuss both types of electronic cards.

payment cards
Electronic cards that contain information that can be used for payment purposes.

PAYMENT CARDS

If you are an American, you are likely to have at least one electronic payment card. In the United States, there are over 700 million payment cards. They can be used at over 4 million merchants in the United States and another 11 million merchants around the world. Over the last few years Americans paid for over $850 billion worth of purchases with their payment cards. There are about 12 billion payment card transactions per year (Evans and Schmalensee 2000).

There are three types of payment cards:

1. **Credit cards.** A credit card provides the holder with credit to make purchases up to a limit fixed by the card issuer. Credit cards rarely have an annual fee. Instead, holders are charged high interest—the annual percentage rate—on their unpaid balances. Visa, MasterCard, and EuroPay are the predominant credit cards.

2. **Charge cards.** The balance on a charge card is supposed to be paid in full upon receipt of the monthly statement. Technically, the holder of a charge card receives a loan for 30 to 45 days equal to the balance of their statement. There are usually annual fees with charge cards. American Express's Green Card is the leading charge card, followed by the Diner's and the Discover cards.

3. **Debit cards.** With a debit card, the cost of a purchased item comes directly out of the holder's checking account (called a demand-deposit account). The transfer of funds from the holder's account to the merchant's takes place within 1 to 2 days. MasterCard, Visa, and EuroPay are the predominant debit cards.

Whether a credit card payment is processed off-line or online, the processes involved are essentially the same (see Exhibit 10.4). For example, suppose you want to buy some CDs from a Web site with your credit card. You add the CDs to your shopping cart and go to the checkout page. On the checkout page, you select a method of shipping and enter your credit card information. The checkout page is usually secured, so that the credit card and other information are protected by TLS encryption. When you hit "Submit," the page is transmitted to the merchant. From there, the information, along with the merchant's identification number, is passed on to the merchant's *acquirer* (or third-party processor). The acquirer sends the information on to the customer's *issuing bank* for approval. The issuer sends its response (approve or disapprove) back to the acquirer, from where it is passed on to

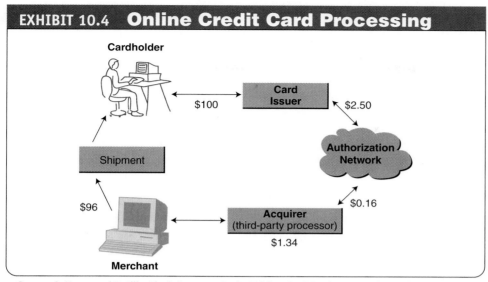

EXHIBIT 10.4   Online Credit Card Processing

Source: S. Korper and J. Ellis, *The E-Commerce Book: Building the E-Empire.* © 2000 by Academic Press. Used with permission.

the merchant. Finally, the customer is notified. The entire process takes place in seconds. After the transaction is complete, the issuer settles the transaction. Typically, for a $100 purchase, the merchant receives $96, the acquirer $1.34, the authorization network $0.16, and the issuer $2.50.

It takes time, skill, money, software, and hardware to establish an online connection between the merchant's EC systems and the merchant's acquirer or third-party processor. Recognizing the difficulties associated with this task, several vendors now offer credit card gateways. A **credit card gateway** ties the merchant's systems to the back-end processing systems of the credit card issuer. A few of the vendors offering credit card gateway software are Authorize.net (authorizenet.com), First Data (firstdata.com), SurePay (surepay.com), and VeriSign (verisign.com). For additional vendors, see Carr (2000).

One innovation in online credit cards is a **virtual credit card**. This is an e-payment system in which a credit card issuer issues a special number that can be used in place of regular credit card numbers to make online purchases. This allows users to use a credit card online without having to disclose the actual credit card number. The user gives a transaction number instead of a credit card number. The Insights and Additions box on page 422 has more on virtual credit cards.

credit card gateway
An online connection that ties a merchant's systems to the back-end processing systems of the credit card issuer.

virtual credit card
An e-payment system in which a credit card issuer gives out a special transaction number that can be used online in place of regular credit card numbers.

E-WALLETS

Most of the time when you make a purchase on the Web you are required to fill out a form with your name, shipping address, billing address, and credit card information. Doing this a few times is fine, but having to do it every time you shop on the Web is an annoyance. Some merchants solve the problem by having you fill out a form once and then saving the information on their servers for later use. For

Insights and Additions   Virtual Credit Cards

For those who are still leery of using their credit cards online, American Express has a new virtual credit card service called Private Payment. With this service, when a user shops online and wants to use an American Express card for a payment, the user enters a user name and password, which logs the user into a special site run by American Express. Next, the user selects the particular American Express card to be used for the purchase. At this point, American Express will generate a one-time, limited-life transaction number, good for anywhere from 30 to 67 days. Now, instead of the user entering their American Express number, the shopper enters the transaction number. The transaction number is tied to the specific card. The merchant who receives the transaction number will pass it on to American Express in order to receive an authorization for the purchase. The transaction number operates just like a real credit card, except that it is good for only one purchase. If the number is stolen or intercepted, it will do little harm as it can only be used once.

Similar virtual credit card services are available through many banks (e.g., see *cyota.com* and *orbiscom.com*).

Sources: Comiled from American Express press releases (2000), *cyota.com*, and *orbiscom.com*.

instance, this is what Amazon.com has done with its "One-Click" shopping. Of course, even if every merchant provided "one-click" shopping, you would still have to set up an account with every merchant. This would also increase the possibility that the information might fall into the hands of a merchant who wanted to use this information for some other purpose.

One way to avoid the problem is to use an **electronic wallet (e-wallet)**. An e-wallet is a software component that a user downloads to their desktop PC and in which the user stores credit card numbers and other personal information. When a user shops at a merchant who accepts the e-wallet, the user clicks the e-wallet, which automatically fills in all the necessary information.

Credit card companies such as Visa and MasterCard offer e-wallets. So do Yahoo!, AOL (Quick Checkout), and Microsoft (Passport). Of these, Yahoo! has the largest number of participating merchants, with over 11,000 as of 2000 (Angwin, 2000).

electronic wallet (e-wallet)
A software component in which a user stores credit card numbers and other personal information; when shopping online; the user simply clicks the e-wallet to automatically fill in information needed to make a purchase.

SECURITY RISKS WITH CREDIT CARDS

Even though TLS is used to secure the transaction between the Web browser and Web server, there are still risks with using credit card payments online. For the most part, *the merchant* bears the responsibility for the following risks:

- **Stolen cards.** If someone steals a credit card and the valid cardholder contests any charges made by the thief, the issuer will credit the cardholder's account and "charge back" the merchant.

- **Reneging by the customer.** A customer can authorize a payment and later deny it. If the denial is believable to the issuer, the merchant will bear the loss. Merchants can avoid such a situation by showing evidence that the cardholder confirmed the order and received the goods. The purchase can also be handled with a digital signature; but this form of verification is expensive and cumbersome for most online credit card transactions.

▸ **Theft of card details stored on the merchant's computer.** There have been cases where hackers have electronically broken into a merchant's computer where credit card details were stored. The key to protecting this information is to isolate the computer or files storing this information so that it cannot be accessed directly from the Internet.

PURCHASING CARDS FOR B2B

Though credit cards are the instrument of choice for B2C payments, this is not the case for the B2B marketplace. Traditionally, payments between companies have been handled by checks, electronic data transfer (EDI), and electronic funds transfer (EFT).

The problem is that the traditional B2B payment methods may be too expensive for small to medium-sized businesses. Today, the major credit card players—Visa, MasterCard, and American Express—are trying to convince companies to utilize *purchasing cards* instead of checks for high-volume, low-cost purchases. According to an American Express study conducted by Ernst & Young in 1999, moving from paper checks to purchasing cards can lower the average processing cost per buying transaction from 90 cents to 22 cents.

Purchasing cards are special-purpose payment cards issued to a company's employees. They are to be used solely for the purpose of purchasing and paying for nonstrategic materials and services (e.g., stationery, office supplies, computer supplies, repair and maintenance services, courier services, and temporary labor services) up to a limit (usually $1,000 to $2,000).

Purchase cards operate essentially the same as any other charge card. They are used both for off-line and online purchases. However, the company's account with the merchant is maintained on a *nonrevolving* basis, meaning that it needs to be paid in full each month, usually within 5 days of the end of the billing period. Exhibit 10.5 (page 424) shows how a purchase card is used.

Several benefits accrue from the use of purchasing cards (Jilovec 1999):

▸ **Productivity gains.** Purchasing departments are freed from day-to-day procurement activities and can focus on developing and managing relationships with suppliers.

▸ **Bill consolidation.** Small purchases from many cardholders can be consolidated into a single invoice that can also be paid electronically through EDI or EFT.

▸ **Payment reconciliation.** Data from the card vendors can be more easily integrated with a corporation's general ledger system, making the process of payment reconciliation simpler, more efficient, and more accurate.

▸ **Preferred pricing.** Settlement of accounts can occur in 5 days or less (rather than the traditional 30 days). This enables companies to negotiate with their suppliers for more favorable prices.

purchasing cards
Special-purpose payment cards issued to a company's employees to be used solely for purchasing nonstrategic materials and services up to a preset dollar limit.

EXHIBIT 10.5 The Participants and the Process of Using a Purchasing Card

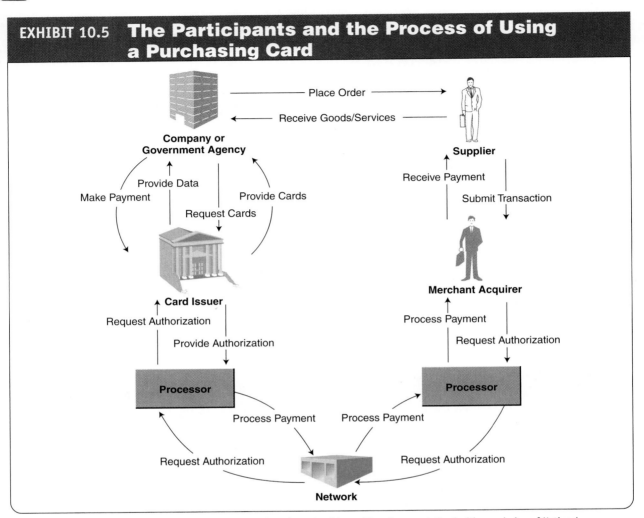

Source: *napcp.org/napcp/napcp.nsf/NavigationAll/P-Card+Basics+-+Participants?OpenDocument*. Used with permission of National Association of Purchasing Card Professionals.

> **Management reports.** The financial institutions issuing the cards provide the using organizations with detailed reports of purchasing activities. This makes it easier for a company to analyze the spending behavior of its purchasing agents and to monitor supplier compliance with agreed-upon prices.

> **Control.** Companies can control the unplanned purchases by limiting the authorized amount per purchase.

smart card
An electronic card containing an embedded microchip that enables predefined operations or the addition, deletion, or manipulation of information on the card.

SMART CARDS

A **smart card** looks like any plastic payment card but it is distinguished by the presence of an embedded microchip (see Exhibit 10.6). The embedded chip can either be a microprocessor and a memory chip combined or just a memory chip with nonprogrammable logic. The microprocessor card can add, delete, and otherwise manipulate information on the card, whereas a memory-chip card can undertake

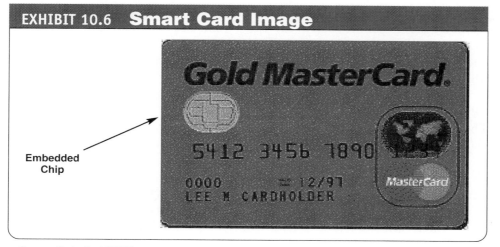

EXHIBIT 10.6 Smart Card Image

Source: MasterCard (2000).

only predefined operations. Although the microprocessor is capable of running programs like a computer, it is not a stand-alone computer. The programs and data must be downloaded from some other device (such as a card reader or an ATM machine).

Smart cards can be categorized by the way in which data (and applications) are downloaded and read from the card. Under this scheme there are two major types of smart cards. The first type is a **contact card**, a card that is inserted in a smart card reader. These cards have a small gold plate about 1/2 inch in diameter on the front; when the card is inserted in the reader, the plate makes contact and data are passed to and from the chip. The second type is the **contactless (proximity) card**. Besides the chip, a contactless card has an embedded antenna. In this case, data (and applications) are passed to and from the card through the card's antenna to another antenna attached to a card reader unit or other device. Contactless cards are used for those applications where the data must be processed very quickly (e.g., mass-transit applications).

Securing Smart Cards

Smart cards house or provide access to either valuable assets (e.g., e-cash) or to sensitive information (e.g., medical records). For this reason they must be secured against theft, fraud, or misuse.

In general, smart cards are more secure than conventional payment cards. If someone steals a payment card, the number of the card is clearly visible, as is the owner's signature. Although it may be hard to forge the signature, there are many situations where only the number is required to make a purchase. The only protection the cardholder has is that there are usually limits on how much they will be held liable for (e.g., in the United States it is $50). If someone steals a prepaid, **stored-value card** (a card that has monetary value loaded onto it, such as a phone card, and is usually rechargeable,), the original owner is out of luck. On the other hand, if someone steals a smart card, they are out of luck. Some smart cards show account numbers, but others do not. Before the card can be used, the holder may be required to enter a PIN (personal identification number) that is stored on the card.

contact card
A smart card containing a small gold plate on the face that when inserted in a smart-card reader makes contact and so passes data to and from the embedded microchip.

contactless (proximity) card
A smart card with an embedded antenna, by means of which data and applications are passed to and from a card reader unit or other device.

stored-value card
A card that has monetary value loaded onto it, and is usually rechargeable.

Theoretically, it is possible to "hack" into a smart card. Most cards, however, can now store the information in encrypted form. The same cards can also encrypt and decrypt data that is downloaded or read from the card. Because of these factors, the possibility of hacking into a smart card is classified as a "class 3" attack, which means that the cost to the attacker of doing so far exceeds the benefits.

Applications of Smart Cards

The growth in smart card usage is being driven by applications. Today, the vast majority of smart cards are being issued in Europe, South America, and Asia. Over the next few years, their use in United States and Canada will expand. Although disposable, prepaid phone cards are the most widely used smart cards, there are a number of applications where smart cards are making significant inroads. A thorough discussion of these applications can be found at the Smart Card Industry Association Web site (scia.org/knowledgebase/default.htm). The following are some of the more important applications.

Loyalty Retailers are using smart cards to identify their loyal customers and reward them. Both Boots (wellbeing.com) and Shell Company have deployed millions of cards that allow customers to collect points that can be redeemed for rewards.

Financial Financial institutions, payment associations, and credit card and charge card issuers are using smart cards to extend traditional card payment services. Multiple applications such as loyalty programs, digital identification, and electronic money are securely offered. In fact, in many countries, there are tens of millions of smart bankcards in use.

Information Technology It won't be long before many PCs will contain smart card readers. All card issuers will utilize the underlying security of the smart card to extend relationships from the physical world to the virtual world. Smart cards will allow individuals to protect their privacy, and card issuers will be able to ensure that only valid customers access services.

Health and Social Welfare Many countries with national health care systems are evaluating or deploying smart card technology to reduce the costs associated with delivering health services and government social services. The largest deployed system is in Germany, with over 80 million cards. The program was introduced in 1993 with the primary purposes of identification, eligibility verification, and electronic claims processing. France, Italy, and the United Kingdom implemented a similar card-based system, Adicarte. Local authorities use this system to monitor and distribute social services in home-care programs, eliminating the fraud and misuse of funds that previously plagued such programs.

Transportation The availability of low-cost, single-chip contactless smart card technology has many mass transit agencies implementing or evaluating the technology, especially for collecting fares. One of the first large projects to deploy contactless card technology was the Seoul Bus Association, which won the SCIA 1998 Outstanding Smart Card Application award.

Identification Smart cards are a natural fit in the identification market and are being used in applications such as college IDs, driver's licenses, and immigration cards. In the United States, several million smart cards are issued annually in the college market alone.

▶ List the common types of payment cards.

▶ Describe how online credit card processing works.

▶ List security issues related to payment cards.

▶ Describe how a purchase card works.

▶ Define smart cards and list some major applications.

10.4 E-CASH AND INNOVATIVE PAYMENT METHODS

It was the mid-1990s, and EC was in its infancy. At the time, most pundits and analysts were saying that consumers would be unwilling to use their credit cards on the Internet, and that other digital money schemes would be needed. Up stepped DigiCash, offering a product called eCash—the digital equivalent of paper currency and coins. During its short life, DigiCash was able to convince only one U.S. bank, Mark Twain Bank of St. Louis, to participate. A few months later DigiCash ran out of money and filed for bankruptcy. A similar fate befell other early electronic payment and e-cash schemes.

Conceptually, **e-cash** makes a lot of sense. The digital equivalent of paper currency and coins, it is secure and anonymous, and it can be used to support payments that cannot be economically supported with payment cards. From a practical standpoint, however, the inconvenience of opening an account and downloading software and the difficulty of obtaining a critical mass of users seems to have outweighed the benefits of e-cash. In spite of these hurdles, though, new e-cash schemes, or at least alternatives to payment cards, appear with some regularity. These schemes can be grouped into four categories: e-cash and credit card alternatives, stored-value cards, e-loyalty and rewards programs, and person-to-person (P2P) payments. In addition, special payment arrangements must be made for global B2B payments.

e-cash
The digital equivalent of paper currency and coins, which enables secure and anonymous purchase of low-priced items.

E-CASH AND ALTERNATIVES TO CREDIT CARDS

Consider the following online shopping scenarios:

▶ You go to an online music store and purchase a single CD that costs $8.95.

▶ You go to a leading newspaper or news journal (such as *Forbes* or *Business Week*) and purchase a copy of an archived news article for $1.50.

▶ You go to an online gaming company, select a game, and play for 30 minutes. You owe the company $3.00 for the playing time.

▶ You go to a site selling digital images and clip art. You purchase a couple of images at a cost of $0.80.

These are all examples of **micropayments**, which are small payments, usually under $10. Credit cards do not work well for such small payments. Vendors who accept credit cards typically must pay a minimum transaction fee that ranges from 25 cents to 35 cents, plus 2 to 3 percent of the purchase price. These fees are relatively insignificant for credit card purchases above $10, but are cost-prohibitive for

micropayments
Small payments, usually under $10.

smaller transactions. Also, when the purchase amount is small, consumers are unwilling to type in credit card numbers or wait for a standard credit card authorization. Micropayments are one area where e-cash and other payment card schemes come into play. Here are examples of a few innovative methods.

eCoin

A modern-day e-cash system that is currently struggling to survive is eCoin, run by eCoin.net (ecoin.net). The system consists of three participants: the user, the merchant, and the eCoin server. The user opens an account with eCoin.net, downloads a special e-wallet to their desktop PC, and then purchases some eCoins with a credit card. An eCoin is a digital string, 15 bytes long, that is worth 5 cents. Each string is unique so that it can be easily identified. The eCoins are downloaded into the e-wallet. To accept eCoins, a merchant simply has to embed a special eCoin icon in its payment page. The eCoin server operates as a broker that keeps customer and merchant accounts, accepts payment requests from the customer's e-wallet, and computes embedded invoices for the merchant. (For a demonstration of how eCoin works, see the company's Web site at ecoin.net.)

In an eCoin purchase, the identity of the user is hidden from the merchant. Only eCoin.net is aware of the user's identity. The communications between the user, the merchant, and eCoin.net are all secured with TLS. The eCoin system also addresses the issue of double spending. Because eCoins are just collections of bytes and bits, they could be forged or duplicated. To prevent this, the eCoin server has a database of all the tokens that have been issued. When an eCoin is spent, the copy on the server is deleted. If anyone tries to use the same eCoin, they will be refused.

Although eCoin is easier to use than some of the earlier e-cash systems, it suffers some of the same problems, requiring users and merchants to download specialized software and to repeat a series of steps with every purchase, no matter how small the purchase price. Like its predecessors, the adoption rate of eCoin has been slow, and at the moment (spring 2002), eCoin.net is no longer issuing U.S. dollar-based coins. It is likely that eCoin will suffer the same fate as its predecessors.

Wireless Payments

An ideal way to pay for certain types of micropayments is to use wireless devices (see Chapter 8 and Deitel et al. 2002). Vodafone, for example, has an "m-pay bill" system that enables wireless subscribers to use their mobile phones to make payments of $10 or less. The m-pay bill system is based on reverse billing: Users respond to a telephone number posted on a Web site by sending a text message (SMS) from their cell phones. A message is then sent back, confirming the payment arrangement and including a PIN number that acts as a password to the specific customer's account (at vodafone.com). The customer then proceeds with the transaction, and the charge shows up on their monthly Vodafone bill.

Qpass

One micropayment system that avoids some of the e-cash problems and has enjoyed some success is Q pass (qpass.com). Q pass is used primarily to purchase content from participating news services and periodicals such as the *New York*

Times, *Wall Street Journal*, and *Forbes*. The user sets up a Q pass account, creating a user name and password and specifying a credit card against which purchases will be charged. Then, when a purchase is made at a participating site, the user simply enters their Q pass user name and password and confirms the purchase. Instead of immediately billing the user's credit card account, the charges are aggregated into a single monthly transaction, which is billed to the user's credit card.

STORED-VALUE CARDS AND OTHER INNOVATIONS

Stored-value cards have found greater usage than e-cash schemes as an alternative to credit cards. When used to store cash downloaded from a bank or credit card account, smart cards can be used to purchase items with values ranging from a few cents to hundreds of dollars. Various types of vendors worldwide accept stored-value cards: fast-food restaurants, convenience stores, vending machines, gas stations, transportation, sundries stores, cinemas, parking garages, grocery stores, department stores, taxis, parking meters, cafeterias, and video stores. A leading vendor of stored-value cards is Visa.

Visa Cash

Visa Cash is a stored-value card designed to handle small purchases or micropayments. This chip-based card can be used in the physical (off-line) world or on the Internet. When a purchase is made, the cost of the purchase is deducted from the cash loaded on the card. Visa Cash can be used only at vendors having special terminals displaying the Visa Cash logo.

There are two types of Visa Cash: disposable and reloadable. *Disposable cards* are loaded with a predetermined value. These cards typically come in denominations of local currency, such as $10. When the value of the card is used, the card is discarded, and a new card may be purchased. *Reloadable cards* come without a predefined value. Cash value is reloaded onto the card at specialized terminals and at ATMs. When the value is used up, users can reload the card.

Visa Cash cards can be obtained from financial institutions, special card dispensing machines, and kiosks. These cards are widely used outside the United States. They were initially introduced in Hong Kong in 1996, and they can now be used at more than 1,500 merchants and reloaded at over 300 ATMs. For PCs with a Visa Cash card reader, it is also possible to make payments across the Internet. The card may be combined with a regular Visa credit card.

Visa Cash
A stored-value card designed to handle small purchases or micropayments; sponsored by Visa.

Mondex

The **Mondex** microchip card is the MasterCard product similar to Visa Cash. It is administered and developed by Mondex International, a subsidiary of Master-Card. Cash is downloaded onto the card through cash dispensers, pay phones, and home phones. Payments can be made wherever the Mondex sign is displayed. In addition, using a Mondex Wallet, two cardholders can transfer cash between their cards. A Mondex Telephone can also be used to transfer cash from one party to the next. Unlike Visa Cash, a Mondex card can store up to five currencies at the same time. Mondex is currently being tested in the United Kingdom, Canada, the

Mondex
A stored-value card designed to handle small purchases or micropayments; sponsored by Mondex, a subsidiary of MasterCard.

United States, Hong Kong, and New Zealand. There were about 150,000 Mondex cards in use in 2001.

E-LOYALTY AND REWARDS PROGRAMS

Some B2C sites spend hundreds of dollars acquiring new customers. Yet, the payback only comes after a customer has made several purchases. These repeat customers are also more likely to refer other customers to a site. In the off-line retail world, companies often use *loyalty programs* to generate repeat business. In the United Kingdom, for example, the Airmiles program is one of the best-known rewards programs. Airmiles can be earned at over 10,000 locations worldwide and exchanged for airline tickets and other merchandise (Cassy 2000). Loyalty programs are also appearing online. Beenz, MyPoints-CyberGold, and RocketCash are three of the better-known loyalty programs. The currency used by loyalty programs is **electronic script**. This is a form of electronic money (or points), issued by a third party, that can be used by consumers to make purchases at participating stores.

Beenz is a form of electronic script. Beenz.com sells a quantity of beenz to a Web site. A consumer earns beenz by visiting, registering, or making purchases at participating sites. The beenz are deposited into a private account maintained by Beenz.com. Later, a consumer can redeem their beenz for products at the same sites. It is estimated that Beenz.com had 300 participating sites and 3.5 million accounts in 2001.

In 2001, Beenz.com partnered with MasterCard to offer Rewardzcard, a stored-value card that can be used in the United States and Canada to make purchases wherever MasterCard is accepted. The Rewardzcard is a way to transfer beenz that you earn on the Web into money you can spend on the Web, for mail or phone orders, and at physical store locations. The conversion rate is about 200 beenz to the dollar.

MyPoints-CyberGold (mypoints.com) is the result of the merger of two separate loyalty programs—MyPoints and CyberGold. In this program, customers earn cash by visiting, registering, or making purchases at affiliated MyPoints merchants. The cash can be used to make purchases at participating sites or can be transferred to a credit card or bank account.

electronic script
A form of electronic money (or points), issued by a third party as part of a loyalty program; can be used by consumers to make purchases at participating stores.

beenz
A form of electronic script offered by *beenz.com* that consumers earn at participating sites and redeem for products or services.

Prepaid Stored-Value Cards

Another innovative payment approach is the use of prepaid cards, such as prepaid telephone cards. These can be used both online and off-line. Obviously, if the customer has a prepaid stored-value card, they are more likely to be loyal to the card sponsor, at least until the stored value runs out.

Several companies attempting this approach offer cards that are sold in kiosks, supermarkets, and even the post office. Starbucks, for example, offers a prepaid stored-value card, intended to keep customers coming back for more coffee products. One company that is offering a stored-value-card program for use online is Internetcash, whose story is described in EC Application Case 10.1.

INTERNETCASH—SOLVING THE CHICKEN-AND-EGG PROBLEM IN THE TEENAGE MARKET

Harris Interactive and Nickelodeon Online estimated in 2001 that 68 percent of all 13- to 18-year-olds in the United States go online. About 50 percent spend an average of 8.5 hours a week on the Internet. What are they doing there? The primary reason for going online is communicating with friends via e-mail and chat rooms. Other reasons include doing homework, researching information, playing games, and downloading music or videos. The picture is similar in most other countries.

One thing that most youngsters are not doing online is shopping. They spend time researching potential purchases, but they do not spend much money online.

Teenagers cite a number of reasons for why they do not shop online—they cannot touch the products, it is difficult to return items purchased on the Web, they do not have the money, and the transaction may be insecure. The number one reason, however, is that their parents will not let them. Or, more specifically, parents won't let teens use *their* credit cards online. Only 10 percent of U.S. teenagers have their own credit cards (Quittner 2000). The fact that teenage consumers are not financially independent creates challenges for online merchants. It also creates opportunities for firms who can come up with creative ways for teenagers to make purchases without relying on credit cards.

One firm that is addressing this opportunity is InternetCash. InternetCash offers at retail outlets prepaid stored-value cards sold in amounts of $10, $20, $50, and $100. Like prepaid phone cards, they must be activated to work. Activation is a two-step process. When a card is purchased, the seller of the card swipes it through a specially programmed POS terminal to activate it. Next, the user logs on to the InternetCash Web site (*internetcash.com*), enters the 20-digit code from the back of the card, and creates a personal identification number (PIN). That gives the user shopping privileges at designated online stores, which carry an InternetCash icon. Purchases are automatically deducted from the value of the card. When the value is used up, consumers throw it away, or link an amount not used to another card. As with cash, InternetCash's transactions are anonymous.

InternetCash has a number of competitors, including *splashplastic.com* and *rocketcash.com*, who have already signed some major online retailers such as CDNow, *amazon.com*, and *barnesandnoble.com*. Even if they did not have any competitors, InternetCash would still be facing enormous obstacles. It is the old "chicken-and-egg" problem: First, they have to find retailers willing to sell the cards. InternetCash is aiming for 30,000 outlets. The bait for the retailers is that it costs the retailers nothing to handle the cards. Instead, they receive 6 percent of the value of the card sold.

The second obstacle is trying to persuade merchants to accept the card for online purchases. This is a harder task, as InternetCash charges commissions of 2.25 to 10 percent of sales. In 2001, InternetCash had signed 200 merchants, the bulk of which were smaller businesses.

InternetCash and other vendors of e-cash products could also face some serious legal issues. For the moment, they exist in a gray area regulated by individual laws of the state in which the cards are used. But the Federal Reserve is looking into treating these companies more like banks, which would open them up to a whole series of banking and depository institution regulations.

Other InternetCash ventures in the works include U.S.-to-Mexico money transfers through the Internet using plastic cards with transferable balances and a partnership for kiosk-based EC and money transfer using convenience store and check cashing outlet locations as a base.

Sources: Compiled from J. Quittner, March 7, 2000, and *internetCash.com*.

Questions

▶ What are the biggest obstacles that InternetCash needs to overcome in order to succeed?

▶ Is InternetCash's strategy of trying to sign up small businesses likely to entice teenagers to use InternetCash's cards?

▶ Are there other demographic segments that are likely to use a stored-value card for online shopping?

Similarly, RocketCash (rocketcash.com) combines an online cash account with a rewards program. A user opens a RocketCash account and adds funds to the account with a money order, a credit card, beenz, or MyPoints. The cash account can then be used to make purchases at participating merchants. Purchases earn RocketCash rewards that can also be redeemed for merchandise.

PERSON-TO-PERSON PAYMENTS

person-to-person (P2P) payments
E-payment schemes (such as *paypal.com*) that enable the transfer of funds between two individuals.

Person-to-person (P2P) payments are one of the newest and fastest-growing e-payment schemes. They enable the transfer of funds between two individuals for a variety of purposes, such as repaying money borrowed from a friend, paying for an item purchased at an online auction, sending money to students at college, or sending a gift to a family member.

One of the first companies to offer this service was PayPal (paypal.com). PayPal has several million customer accounts; it handles 25 percent of all transactions on eBay (Crockett 2000). It funnels about $3.5 billion in payments annually (in 2002) through its servers. This kind of activity has drawn the attention of a number of other companies who are trying to get in on the action. Citibank C2IT (c2it.com); AOL QuickCash (aol.com), which is a private-branded version of c2it; Bank One's eMoneyMail; Yahoo! PayDirect; and WebCertificate (webcertificate.com) are all PayPal competitors.

Virtually all of these services work the same way. Assume you want to send money to someone over the Internet. First, you select a service and open an account with it. Basically, this entails creating a user name and a password, giving them your e-mail address, and providing the service with a payment card or bank account number. Next, you add funds to your account with your payment card or bank account. Once the account has been funded, you are ready to send money. You access the account with your user name and password. You then specify the e-mail address of the person to receive the money, along with the dollar amount that you want to send. An e-mail is sent to the specified e-mail address (see Exhibit 10.7). The e-mail will contain a link back to the service's Web site. When recipients clicks on the link, they will be taken to the service and asked to set up an account to which the money that was sent will be credited. Recipients can then transfer the money from that account to their credit card or bank account.

Although the various services all work in similar ways, there are differences. For example, in 2001 c2it charged $2 per transaction, offered no insurance against fraud, and required paperwork sent by snail mail if the money had to be moved into a bank account. On the other hand, PayPal charged no fees, offered insurance against fraud, and did not require any paperwork for bank transfers.

GLOBAL B2B PAYMENTS

Payment schemes are more complex when they involve B2B payment, because large amounts of money are involved and global payments may need to be made. Here we describe two alternative global B2B payment methods, one that is close to a form of cash payment, and another that is an innovative e-payment method that uses a payment card.

EXHIBIT 10.7 Sending Money with PayPal

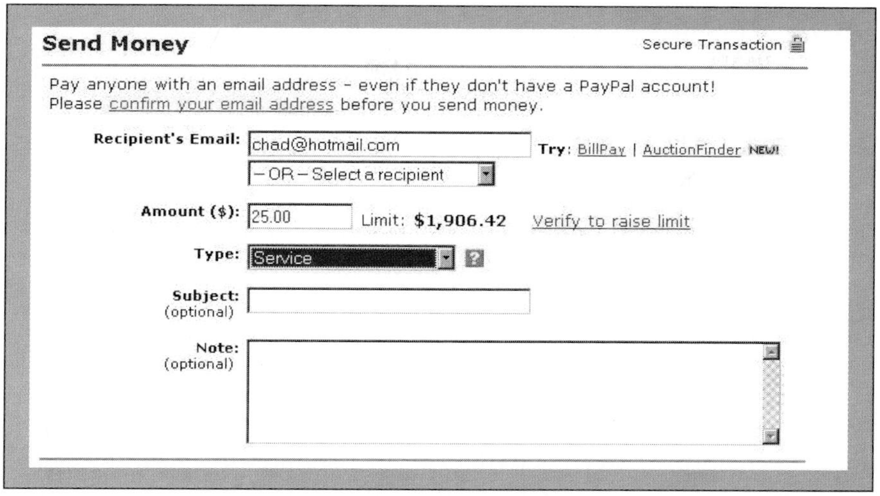

Send Money   Secure Transaction 🔒

Pay anyone with an email address – even if they don't have a PayPal account!
Please confirm your email address before you send money.

Recipient's Email: chad@hotmail.com   **Try:** BillPay | AuctionFinder **NEW!**
– OR – Select a recipient

Amount ($): 25.00   Limit: **$1,906.42**   Verify to raise limit

Type: Service ❓

Subject:
(optional)

Note:
(optional)

Source: *paypal.com*.

Electronic Letters of Credit

A **letter of credit (LC)** is a written agreement by a bank to pay the beneficiary (the seller) on account of the applicant (the buyer) a sum of money upon presentation of certain documents. The LC gives precise instructions concerning the documents that must be produced by the beneficiary for payment or acceptance before the LC expiration date.

LCs benefit both sellers and buyers. The benefits of LCs to the seller are:

▶ Credit risk is reduced because payment is accessed via the creditworthiness of the issuing bank.

▶ Payment is highly assured if all the terms and conditions stipulated in the LC are met.

▶ Political/country risk is reduced if the LC is confirmed by a bank in the seller's country.

The benefits of LCs to the buyer are:

▶ An LC may allow the buyer to negotiate for a lower purchase price, because credit risk is reduced.

▶ The buyer may expand its source of supply, as certain sellers are willing to supply goods only under LC arrangements.

▶ Funds will be withdrawn from the buyer's account only after the documents have been inspected by the issuing bank.

Many financial institutions offer LCs online (e.g., anz.com.au and royalbank.com). LCs are also used in auctions, such as those at ebay.com. The major advantage

letter of credit (LC)
A written agreement by a bank to pay the seller, on account of the buyer, a sum of money upon presentation of certain documents.

of LCs is that payments are guaranteed in a short time (sometimes even minutes).

TradeCard Payments in B2B Global Trading

Letters of credit may be too expensive or too complicated, especially for SMEs. An alternative solution, introduced by MasterCard and TradeCard, Inc., allows businesses to effectively and efficiently complete B2B transactions whether large or small, domestic or cross-border, or in multiple currencies. Buyers and sellers become TradeCard members, a process that entails evaluation of their creditworthiness and a check that they have not been involved in money-laundering activities. The buyers and sellers then interact with each other via the TradeCard system, which checks purchase orders for both parties, awaits confirmation from a logistics company that deliveries have been made and received, and authorizes payment to complete the financial transaction between the buyer and seller.

The service can be integrated with B2B exchanges and marketplaces, which currently (spring 2002) have no similar comprehensive online payment solution for handling different sizes and types of transactions. Businesses can pay for spot transactions or track larger, more complicated corporate purchase orders through their transaction cycle and then pay for them when the contract terms have been satisfied. Companies are able to receive integrated payment information, including transaction-level detail, via secure Web access. (For more information, see tradecard.com.)

▶ Describe the drivers of e-cash.

▶ Define micropayments. Why are they suitable for e-cash?

▶ What are stored-value cards?

▶ Describe e-loyalty programs.

▶ Describe P2P payment methods.

▶ Describe two B2B payment methods.

10.5 E-CHECKING

According to U.S. government statistics, over 70 percent of all noncash payments in the United States are made by checks. In 2002, U.S. consumers, businesses, and government entities wrote about 80 billion checks. It costs about 1 percent of the U.S. gross domestic product (GDP) to process these checks. This percentage does not count the costs associated with check fraud, which is estimated to be $60 billion annually (in 2002), with banks absorbing about $1.45 billion in losses and retailers and other payees about $60 billion. These costs are one of the driving forces behind the move to electronic checks (e-checks). According to the Electronic Check Clearing House Organization (eccho.org, 2002), a not-for-profit clearinghouse, e-checks can yield industry-wide savings and benefits in the United States of $2 to $3 billion per year.

e-check
The electronic version or representation of a paper check.

An **e-check** is the electronic version or representation of a paper check. E-checks contain the same information as a paper check, can be used wherever paper checks are used, and are based on the same legal framework. E-checks work essentially the same way a paper check works, but in pure electronic form, with fewer manual steps. Simply put, they are faster and cheaper.

E-checks fit within current business practices, eliminating the need for expensive process reengineering and taking advantage of the competency of the banking industry. Using state-of-the-art security techniques, e-checks can be used by all bank customers who have checking accounts, including small and mid-size businesses that otherwise have little access to electronic payment systems (see echeck.commerce.net).

eCheck Secure (from flagship.vantaguard.com) and checkfree.com provide software that enables the purchase of goods and services with an e-check. The processes that are supported are fairly common, regardless of the Web site used.

In situations such as B2B e-commerce or e-government purchases, where the dollar values are likely to be in the hundreds of thousands of dollars, more secure procedures are required. The eCheck Project Consortium (echeck.commerce.net), a team of over 15 banks, government agencies, technology vendors, and industry associations, has worked to develop e-check standards that will support B2B and e-government payments. The standards are currently being tested in pilot projects by the U.S. Treasury Department. (For further information on e-checking, see the online addition to this chapter at prenhall.com/turban.)

▶ Define e-check.

▶ List some of the benefits of e-checks.

▶ Why are e-checks used in B2C? In B2B?

10.6 ORDER FULFILLMENT AND LOGISTICS—AN OVERVIEW

Taking orders over the Internet could well be the easy part of B2C EC. Fulfillment and delivery to customers' doors are the sticky parts. As a matter of fact, many e-tailers have experienced fulfillment problems since they started EC. Amazon.com, for example, which initially operated as a totally virtual company, added physical warehouses in order to expedite deliveries and reduce order fulfillment costs.

Several factors can be responsible for delays in deliveries. They range from an inability to accurately forecast demand to ineffective e-tail supply chains. Several such problems also exist in off-line businesses. One factor typical for EC is that EC is based on the concept of "pull" operations that begin with an order, frequently a customized one. This is in contrast with traditional retailing, which usually begins with a production to inventory that is then pushed to customers (see Exhibit 10.8 on page 436). In the pull case, it is more difficult to forecast demand due to lack of experience and changing consumer tastes. Another delay factor is that in a B2C pull model, the goods need to be delivered to the customer's door, whereas in brick-and-mortar retailing, the goods are shipped in large quantity to stores.

Before we analyze the order fulfillment problems and describe some solutions, we need to introduce some basic concepts relating to order fulfillment and logistics.

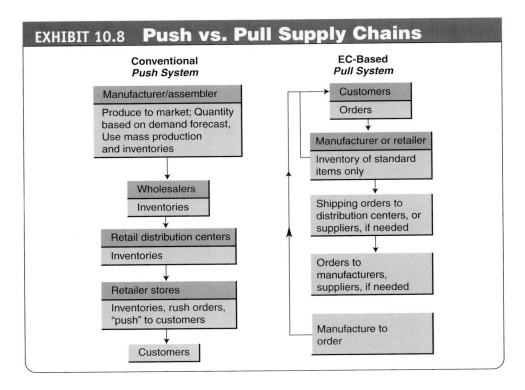

EXHIBIT 10.8 **Push vs. Pull Supply Chains**

OVERVIEW OF ORDER FULFILLMENT

Order fulfillment refers not only to providing customers with what they ordered and doing it on time, but also to providing all related customer services. For example, the customer must receive assembly and operation instructions with a new appliance. This can be done by including a paper document with the product or by providing the instructions on the Web. (A nice example of this is available at livemanuals.com.) In addition, if the customer is not happy with a product, an exchange or return must be arranged. Thus, although order fulfillment is basically a part of the **back-office operations** (the activities that support fulfillment of sales, such as accounting and logistics), it is also strongly related to the **front-office operations** (the business processes, such as sales and advertising, that are visible to customers).

OVERVIEW OF LOGISTICS

Logistics is defined by the Council of Logistics Management in the United States (clm1.org) as "the process of planning, implementing, and controlling the efficient and effective flow and storage of goods, services, and related information from point of origin to point of consumption for the purpose of conforming to customer requirements." Note that this definition includes inbound, outbound, internal, and external movement and return of materials and goods. It also includes *order fulfillment*. However, the distinction between logistics and order fulfillment is not always clear, and the terms are sometimes used interchangeably (as in this textbook).

Obviously, the key aspect of order fulfillment is delivery of materials or services in the right time, to the right place, at the right cost.

THE EC ORDER FULFILLMENT PROCESS

In order to understand why there are problems in order fulfillment, it is beneficial to look at a typical EC fulfillment process, as shown in Exhibit 10.9. The process starts on the left when an order is received. Several activities take place, some of which can be done simultaneously, whereas others must be done in sequence. These activities are:

1. **Making sure the customer will pay.** Depending of the payment method and prior arrangements, an investigation must be made regarding the validity of the payment. This activity may be done in B2B by the company's finance department and/or a financial institution (i.e., a bank or a credit card issuer such as Visa). Any delay may cause a shipment delay, resulting in a loss of goodwill or a customer.

2. **Checking for in-stock availability.** Regardless of whether the vendor is a manufacturer or a retailer, an inquiry needs to be made regarding stock availability. Several scenarios are possible here that may involve both the material management and production departments, as well as outside suppliers or warehouse facilities. In this step, the order information needs to be connected to the information about in-stock availability.

EXHIBIT 10.9 **Order Fulfillment and Logistics System**

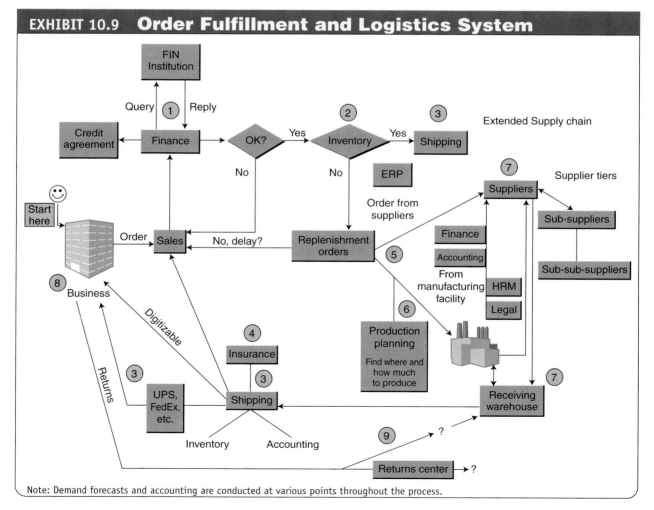

Note: Demand forecasts and accounting are conducted at various points throughout the process.

3. **Arranging shipments.** If the product is available, it can be shipped to the customer (otherwise, go to step 5). Products can be digital or physical. If the item is physical and it is readily available, packaging and shipment arrangements need to be made. Both the packaging/shipping department and internal shippers or outside transporters may be involved. Digital items are usually available because their "inventory" is not depleted. However, a digital product, such as software, may be under revision, and thus unavailable for delivery at certain times. In either case, information needs to flow among several partners.

4. **Insurance.** Sometimes insurance for the shipment is needed. Both the finance department and an insurance company could be involved, and again, information needs to flow frequently not only inside the company, but also to and from the customers and insurance agents.

5. **Production.** Customized orders will always trigger a need for some manufacturing or assembly operation. Similarly, if standard items are out of stock, they need to be produced. Production can be done in-house or by contractors. In-house production needs to be planned. Production planning involves people, machines, financial resources, and possibly suppliers and subcontractors. Manufacturing involves the acquisition of materials and components. The suppliers may have their own suppliers. The actual production facilities may be in a different country from where the company's headquarters or retailers are. This may further complicate the flow of information and communication.

6. **Plant services.** In the case of assembly and/or manufacturing, several plant services may be needed, including possible collaboration with business partners. Services may include scheduling of people and equipment, shifting other products' plans, or working with engineering on modifications.

7. **Purchasing and warehousing.** If the seller is a retailer, such as in the case of amazon.com or walmart.com, purchasing from manufacturers is needed. Several scenarios may exist. Purchased items can be stocked in warehouses, which is what Amazon.com does with its best-selling books. However, Amazon.com does not stock books for which only a few orders are received. In such cases, special deliveries from the publishers or other sources must be made. This requires appropriate receiving and quality assurance of incoming materials and products.

Once production (step 5) or purchasing (step 7) is completed, shipments (step 3) are arranged.

8. **Contacts with customers.** The salespeople need to keep in constant touch with customers, starting with notification of orders received and ending with notification of a shipment or change in delivery date. These contacts are usually done via e-mail, and are frequently generated automatically.

9. **Returns.** In some cases, customers want to exchange or return items. Such returns can be a major problem, as up to 30 percent of all items purchased in the United States are returned to a vendor. The movement of returns from customers to vendors is called **reverse logistics**.

reverse logistics
The movement of returns from customers to vendors.

Two other major activities are related to the order fulfillment process. The first is *demand forecasting*. In the case of noncustomized items, such as toys, a demand forecast must be done in order to determine appropriate inventories at various points in the supply chain. Such a forecast is difficult in the fast-growing field of EC. In the case of customized products, it is necessary to forecast the demand for the components and materials required for fulfilling customized orders. Demand forecasting must be done with business partners along the supply chain, as will be discussed later.

A second major activity related to order fulfillment is *accounting*. In many cases, the accounting department is involved in generating invoices and/or receipts, auditing internal transactions and inventories, monitoring payments, and updating the accounting records. The accounting department also handles tax and customs issues. Therefore, information flow and communications are required for every transaction.

Order fulfillment processes may vary, depending on the product and the vendor. There are also differences between B2B and B2C activities, as well as between the delivery of goods and of services, and between small and large products. Furthermore, additional steps may be required in certain circumstances, such as in the case of ordering perishable materials or foods.

Order Fulfillment and the Supply Chain

The processes of order fulfillment (Exhibit 10.9) and order taking are integral parts of the supply chain. The flows of orders, payments, and materials and parts need to be coordinated among all the company's internal participants, as well as among the external partners. The principles of supply chain management (Chapter 2 and Handfield and Nichols 1999) must be considered in planning and managing the order fulfillment process.

▶ Compare the push and pull production processes.

▶ Define order fulfillment and logistics.

▶ Describe the steps of the order fulfillment process.

10.7 PROBLEMS IN ORDER FULFILLMENT

During the 1999 holiday season, the B2C e-tailers, especially those that sold toys, were plagued with logistics problems. Price wars boosted the demand, and supplies were late coming from manufacturers. Toys 'R' Us, for example, had to stop taking orders around December 14, and many customers did not get their holiday gifts on time (see the Insights and Additions on page 440). The manufacturers, warehouses, and distribution channels were not in sync with the e-tailers.

Several other corporate problems have been observed in EC: Some companies grapple with high inventory costs; quality problems exist due to misunderstandings; shipments of wrong products, materials, and parts occur frequently; and there is a high cost to expedite operations or shipments. The chance that such problems will occur in EC is higher due to the lack of appropriate infrastructure and e-tailing experience, as well as the special characteristics of EC. For example, most warehouses are designed to ship large quantities to stores; they cannot optimally pack and ship many small packages to customers' doors.

TYPICAL PROBLEMS

The problems along the EC supply chain stem mainly from *uncertainties* and from the need to *coordinate* several activities and/or internal units and business partners.

The major source of the uncertainties in EC is the demand forecast. Demand is influenced by factors such as consumer behavior, economic conditions, competition, prices, weather conditions, technological developments, customers' confidence, and more, and so may change quickly. As mentioned earlier, the demand forecast should be conducted frequently with collaborating business partners along the supply chain in order to correctly gauge demand and make plans to meet it. As we will soon show, companies attempt to achieve accurate demand forecasts by methods such as collaborative commerce.

Other uncertainties that lead to fulfillment problems are delivery times, which depend on many factors ranging from machine failures to road conditions; quality problems of materials and parts, which may create production time delays; and labor troubles (such as strikes), which may interfere with shipments.

Insights and Additions Order Fulfillment Troubles in Toyland

While the entire world watched the transition into the third millennium occur without any major Y2K problems, the B2C industry in general, and online toy retailers in particular, experienced a major logistics problem at the end of 1999.

According to reports by many popular media and EC research companies, overall satisfaction with online shopping declined significantly in December 1999 and January 2000, driven by consumer frustration with late deliveries and with poor customer service before, during, and after purchases (Brooker, 2000). In general, e-tailers struggled to meet the demands of last-minute shoppers. It became clear during the period of peak demand that the order fulfillment infrastructure of most e-tailers was weak.

The situation was especially critical in the toy business, where competition was fierce. Many toy e-tailers promised to pay delivery charges and even gave $20 discount coupons. *Toysrus.com* averaged 1.75 million visiting customers a day, and *etoys.com* averaged 1.9 million. The number of toy orders far exceeded the companies' projections.

As a result, Toysrus.com notified customers that only orders made prior to December 14 would arrive in time for the holidays. For orders made after that date, customers would have to pay a premium for priority shipping. A few days prior to Christmas, Toysrus.com notified some customers that the toys they ordered for the holiday (even some ordered before December 14) probably would not arrive in time, and offered these customers $100 coupons as compensation. eToys and other e-tailers experienced similar problems. *Amazon.com* was forced to ship multiproduct orders in several shipments instead of one, substantially increasing its expenses. It is no wonder that consumer satisfaction with online retailing fell. The e-tailers themselves undoubtedly felt considerable dissatisfaction with their order fulfillment record.

Pure EC companies are likely to have more problems because they do not have a logistics infrastructure already in place and so are forced to use external logistics services (third-party logistics suppliers, rather than in-house departments for these functions). Going out-of-house for such services can be expensive, and it requires more coordination and dependence on outsiders who may not be reliable. For this reason, large virtual retailers such as amazon.com are developing their own physical warehouses and logistics systems. Other virtual retailers are creating strategic alliances with logistics companies or with experienced mail-order companies that have their own logistics systems.

In addition to uncertainties, EC order fulfillment problems are created by lack of coordination and inability or refusal to share information. One of the most persistent order fulfillment problems is known as the bullwhip effect.

The Bullwhip Effect

The **bullwhip effect** refers to large fluctuations in inventories along the supply chain that result from small fluctuations in demand for finished products. These erratic shifts can occur in orders up and down both the regular and the EC supply chain (Lee et al. 1997).

The bullwhip effect was initially observed by Procter & Gamble (P&G) with its disposable diapers product, Pampers, in off-line stores. Although actual sales in stores were fairly stable and predictable, orders from distributors had wild swings. An investigation revealed that distributors' orders were fluctuating because of poor demand forecasts, price fluctuations, order batching, and rationing within the supply chain. All of this resulted in unnecessary inventory buildup in various areas along the supply chain, fluctuations of P&G orders to suppliers, and the flow of inaccurate information. Distorted information can lead to tremendous inefficiencies, excessive inventories, poor customer service, lost revenues, ineffective shipments, and missed production schedules.

bullwhip effect
Large fluctuations in inventories along the supply chain, resulting from small fluctuations in demand for finished products.

▶ Describe the 1999 holiday-toy-order fulfillment problem.

▶ Explain how uncertainties create order fulfillment problems.

▶ Describe the problem of the bullwhip effect.

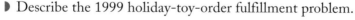

10.8 SOLUTIONS TO ORDER FULFILLMENT PROBLEMS

Many EC logistics problems are generic; they can be found in the non-Internet world as well. Therefore, many of the solutions that have been developed for these problems for brick-and-mortar retailers also work for e-tailers. Most of these solutions are facilitated by IT and by EC technologies, as shown in Exhibit 10.10. In this section, we will discuss some of the solutions to order fulfillment problems.

IMPROVEMENTS IN THE ORDER-TAKING PROCESS

One way to improve order fulfillment is to improve the order-taking process and its links to fulfillment and logistics. Order taking can be done on EDI, EDI/Internet, or an extranet, and it may be fully automated. For example, in B2B, orders are generated and transmitted automatically to suppliers when inventory levels fall below certain levels. The result is a fast, inexpensive, and more accurate (no need to rekey data) order-taking process. In B2C, Web-based ordering using electronic forms expedites the process, makes it more accurate (intelligent agents can check the input data and provide instant feedback), and reduces the processing cost for sellers. When EC order taking can interface with a company's back-office system, such an interface, or even integration, shortens cycle time and eliminates errors.

Order-taking improvements can also take place *within* an organization, for example, when manufacturers order parts from a warehouse. When delivery of such parts runs smoothly, disruptions to the manufacturing process are minimized, reducing losses from downtime. For example, as detailed in the Real-World Case at the end of the chapter, Dell has improved the flow of parts in its PC repairs operations, resulting in greater efficiency and cost savings.

Implementing linkages between order-taking and payment systems can also be helpful in improving order fulfillment. Electronic payments can expedite both the order fulfillment cycle and the payment delivery period. With such systems, payment processing can be significantly less expensive and fraud can be better controlled.

EXHIBIT 10.10 IT Solutions to Supply Chain Problems

Order Fulfillment Problem	IT Solution
Linear sequence of processing is too slow.	Parallel processing, using workflow software.
Waiting times between chain segments are excessive.	Identify reason (DSS software) and expedite communication and collaboration (Intranets, groupware).
Existence of non-value-added activities.	Value analysis (SCM software), simulation software.
Slow delivery of paper documents.	Electronic documents and communication system (e.g., EDI, e-mail).
Repeat process activities due to wrong shipments, poor quality, etc.	Electronic verifications (software agents), automation; eliminating human errors, electronic control systems.
Batching; accumulate work orders between supply chain processes to get economies of scale (e.g., save on delivery).	SCM software analysis, digitize documents for online delivery.
Learn about delays after they occur, or learn too late.	Tracking systems, anticipate delays, trend analysis, early detection (intelligent systems).
Excessive administrative controls such as approvals (signatures). Approvers are in different locations.	Parallel approvals (workflow), electronic approval system. Analysis of need.
Lack of information or too slow a flow of information.	Internet/intranet, software agents for monitoring and alerts. Bar codes, direct flow from POS terminals.
Lack of synchronization of moving materials.	Workflow and tracking systems. Synchronization by software agents.
Poor coordination, cooperation, and communication.	Groupware products, constant monitoring, alerts, collaboration tools.
Delays in shipments from warehouses.	Use robots in warehouses, use warehouse management software.
Redundancies in the supply chain: too many purchase orders, too much handling and packaging.	Information sharing via the Web creating teams of collaborative partners supported by IT (see Epner 1999).
Obsolescence of parts and components that stay too long in storage.	Reducing inventory levels by information sharing internally and externally, using intranets and groupware.

INVENTORY MANAGEMENT IMPROVEMENTS

Inventories can be minimized by introducing a make-to-order (pull) production process and by providing fast and accurate demand information to suppliers. By allowing business partners to electronically track and monitor orders and production activities, inventory management can be improved and inventory levels, as well as the administrative expenses of inventory management, can be minimized. In some instances, the ultimate inventory improvement is to have no inventory at all: For products that can be digitized (e.g., software), order fulfillment can be instantaneous.

Automated Warehouses

Large-volume EC fulfillment requires automated warehouses. Regular warehouses are built to deliver large quantities to a small number of stores and plants. In B2C e-commerce, however, businesses need to send small quantities to large numbers of individuals. Automation of warehouses can minimize the order fulfillment problems that arise from this need.

Automated warehouses may include robots and other devices that expedite the pick-up of products. An example of a company that built such a warehouse is amazon.com (Cone 1999). The largest EC/mail-order warehouse in the United States was operated by a mail-order company, Fingerhut. This company handled the logistics of mail orders (including online orders) for Wal-Mart, Macy's, KbKids, and many others. The order fulfillment process at the Fingerhut warehouse involved eight steps (Duvall 1999):

1. Retailers contracted with Fingerhut to stock products and deliver orders they received from their Web sites, by phone, or by fax.

2. Retailers' merchandise was stored by SKU (stock-keeping unit) at Fingerhut's warehouse.

3. Incoming orders were transferred to Fingerhut's mainframe computer.

4. To optimize the work of pickers, a special computer program consolidated the orders from all vendors (including Fingerhut's own catalog) and organized them into "picking waves." These waves were organized so that pickers did not have to run from one end of the warehouse to another to prepare an order. Some picking was done by robots.

5. The "picked" items were moved by conveyors to the packing area. The computer configured the size and type of box (or envelope) needed for packaging and types special packaging and delivery instructions.

6. Packages passed on a conveyor belt through a scanning station where they were weighed. (The actual weight had to match the SKU projected weight.).

7. From the bar code scanner a destination was identified, and at an appropriate time each package was pushed onto one of 26 destination conveyer belts that carried the package directly to a waiting truck.

8. Once trucks were full they departed for local postal offices in 26 major cities, dramatically cutting shipping costs.

Fingerhut was sold to Federated Department Stores in 1999. With the purchase, Federated hoped to create a fulfillment giant, but unexpectedly large numbers of deadbeat customers and a less-than-perfect IT system resulted in a financial loss for Federated on its investment (forbes.com/2001/08/06/0806federated_2.html). However, as of spring 2002, a turnaround company was considering a revival of the Fingerhut warehouse (news.mpr.org/features/200203/05_haega_fingerhut).

Other companies (e.g., submitorder.com and rubyglen.com/s/h2.htm) provide similar services. The key to inventory management in terms of order fulfillment is speed and efficiency.

SPEEDING DELIVERIES

In 1973, a tiny company initiated the concept of "next-day delivery." It was a revolution in door-to-door logistics. Today, this company, FedEx, is moving over 3 million packages a day all over the globe using several hundred airplanes and several thousand vans. FedEx introduced the "next-morning delivery" service a few years later. Incidentally, by one report (Pickering 2000), 70 percent of these packages are the result of EC.

Same Day, Even Same Hour Delivery

In the digital age, however, even the next morning may not fast enough. Today we talk about *same-day delivery*, and even delivery within an hour. Deliveries of urgent material to and from hospitals are an example of such a service. Two of the newcomers to this area are efulfillmentservice.com and owd.com, which created networks for rapid distribution of products, mostly EC-related ones. They offer a national distribution system across the United States in collaboration with shipping companies such as FedEx and UPS.

Delivering groceries is another area where speed is important, as discussed in Chapter 3. Quick pizza deliveries have been available for a long time (e.g., Domino's Pizza). Today, many pizza orders can be placed online. Many restaurants deliver food to customers who order online, a service called "dine online." Examples of this service can be found at food.com, gourmetdinnerservice.com.au, and anniesdinners.com. Some companies even offer aggregating services, processing orders from several restaurants and making deliveries (e.g., dialadinner.com.hk in Hong Kong).

Supermarket Deliveries

Supermarket deliveries are difficult, especially when fresh food is to be transported, as discussed in Chapter 3. Buyers need to be home at certain times to accept the deliveries. Therefore, the distribution systems for such enterprises are critical. For an example of an effective distribution system, see the EC Application Case about Woolworths of Australia at the book's Web site, prenhall.com/turban.

PARTNERING EFFORTS

Another effective way to solve order fulfillment problems is for an organization to partner with other companies. For example, *collaborative commerce* among members of the supply chain can be done in many areas, ranging from product design to demand forecasting. The results are shorter cycle times, minimal delays and work interruptions, lower inventories, and less administrative cost. Also, the bullwhip effect problem can be minimized by such collaboration.

One partnering example is a marketplace managed by relysoftware.com that helps companies with goods find "forwarders"—the intermediaries that prepare goods for shipping. The company also helps forwarders find the best prices on air carriers, and helps the carriers fill up empty cargo space by bidding on it.

Another partnering method is demonstrated by the joint venture of MailBoxes Etc. (now a subsidiary of UPS) with a fulfillment services company, Innotrac Corp., and with a logistics firm, accuship.com. The three companies developed a comprehensive logistics system that used software connecting e-tailers and order management systems to Return.com's intelligent system. The system determined whether a customer who wanted to make a return might do so and if they were entitled to a refund. If allowed to make a return, customers had the option of doing so using the kiosks in MailBoxes Etc.'s physical franchises.

ORDER FULFILLMENT IN B2B

Order fulfillment in B2B is different from that of B2C due to the larger quantities delivered to businesses. Some representative B2B fulfillment players and challenges are listed in Exhibit 10.11.

Using E-Marketplaces and Exchanges to Ease Order Fulfillment Problems

In Chapter 6, we introduced a variety of e-marketplaces and exchanges. One of the major objectives of these is to improve the operation of the B2B supply chain. Let's see how this works with different business models.

EXHIBIT 10.11 Players and Challenges in B2B Fulfillment

Players	Challenges
Shippers (sellers)	Mix of channels, choice of logistics partners, solo or go with aggregation, what to outsource, integration of strategic/tactical/operational decisions
Receivers (buyers)	Solo and/or consortia buy sites, supply chain collaboration, total delivered costs, when to buy
Carriers	Self-service Web sites, links to verticals and transportation marketplaces, institutional drag
Third-party logistics providers	Cooperation from carriers, breadth of modes/services, IT resources, customer acquisition
Warehouse companies	Location, operational intensity, capital investment, mode of automation, choice of builders
Vertical e-marketplaces	Where's the "ship-it" button? Who's behind it? What services are offered?
Transportation e-marketplaces	Moving beyond spot transactions to ASPs and value-added services, neutrality versus alignment, market mechanisms (e.g., bidding)
Logistics software application vendors	Comprehensive solutions, e-marketplace involvement, strategic partnerships, integration with existing software

▶ One business model is that of an e-procurement system controlled by one large buyer where the suppliers adjust their activities and information systems to fit the information system of the buyer. Such a system is especially suitable for a multinational corporation or a government that deals with many suppliers. With this system, the cycle time and the administrative costs are reduced by going to an e-market.

▶ A company-centric marketplace can solve several supply chain problems. For example, CSX Technology developed an extranet-based EC system for tracking cross-country train shipments as part of its supply chain initiative, and was able to effectively identify bottlenecks and more accurately forecast demand.

▶ Using an extranet, Toshiba America provides an ordering system for its dealers to buy replacement parts for Toshiba's products. The system smoothes the supply chain and delivers better customer service.

▶ Another model is a vertical exchange, such as that of covisint.com in the automotive industry, which connects thousands of suppliers with automakers. Hundreds of vertical exchanges exist all over the world; many of them deal with both buying and selling. The direct contact between buyers and sellers in e-marketplaces reduces communication and search problems in the supply chain.

For additional discussion on how fulfillment is done in B2B, see Chapter 8 in Turban et al. (2002b), fedex.com, and ups.com.

HANDLING RETURNS

Allowing for the return of unwanted merchandise and providing for product exchanges are necessary to maintain customers' trust and loyalty. The Boston Consulting Group (2001) found that the "absence of a good return mechanism" was the number two reason shoppers cited for refusing to buy on the Web frequently. A major logistics problem merchants face is how to deal with returns. Several options exist (Trager 2000):

▶ **Return the item to the place where it was purchased.** This is easy to do with a purchase from a brick-and-mortar store, but not a virtual one. To return a product to a virtual store you need to get authorization, pack everything up, pay to ship it back, insure it, and wait up to two billing cycles for a credit to show up on your statement. The buyer is not happy, and neither is the seller, who must unpack, check the paperwork, and resell the item, usually at a loss. This solution is workable only if the number of returns is small.

▶ **Separate the logistics of returns from the logistics of delivery.** In this option, returns are shipped to an independent returns unit and are handled separately inside the company. This solution may be more efficient from the seller's point of view, but it does not ease the returns process for the buyer.

▶ **Completely outsource returns.** Several outsourcers, including UPS, provide logistics services, as described in EC Application Case 10.2. The services deal not only with shipments, but with the entire logistics process.

▶ **Allow the customer to physically drop the returned item at a collection station.** Offer customers locations (such as a convenience store or at MailBoxes Etc.)

EC APPLICATION CASE 10.2
Interorganization and Collaboration
UPS PROVIDES BROAD EC SERVICES

UPS is not only a leading transporter of goods sold on the Internet, but it is also a provider of several other EC-support services, ranging from supply chain activities such as inventory management to electronic bill payment.

UPS has a massive infrastructure to support these efforts. For example, it has an over 120 terabyte (10^{12} byte) database containing customer information and shipping records. Here are some of its EC initiatives:

- Electronic tracking of packages.
- Electronic supply chain services for corporate customers, by industry. This includes a portal page with industry-related information and statistics.
- Calculators for computing shipping fees.
- Helping customers manage their electronic supply chains (e.g., expediting billing and speeding up accounts receivable).
- Improved inventory management, warehousing, and delivery. The first major corporate client was Ford Motor Co.
- A shipping management system that integrates tracking systems, address validation, service selection, and time-in-transit tools with Oracle's ERP application suite (similar integration with SAP and PeopleSoft exists).
- Notification of customers by e-mail about the status and expected arrival time of incoming packages.

REPRESENTATIVE TOOLS

UPS's online tools—a set of seven transportation and logistics applications—lets customers do everything from track packages to analyze their shipping history using customized criteria to calculate exact time-in-transit for shipments between any two postal codes in the continental United States.

The tools, which customers can download to their Web sites, let customers query UPS systems to get proof that specific packages were delivered on schedule. For example, if a company is buying supplies online and wants them delivered on a certain day, a UPS customer can use an optimal-routing fea-

ture to ensure delivery on that day, as well as to automatically record proof of the delivery into its accounting system.

UPS is offering logistics services tailored for certain industries. For example, UPS Logistics Group provides supply chain reengineering, transportation network management, and service parts logistics to vehicle manufacturers, suppliers, and parts distributors in the auto industry worldwide. UPS Autogistics improves automakers' vehicle delivery networks. For example, Ford reduced the time to deliver vehicles from plants to dealers in North America from an average of 14 days to about 6. UPS Logistics Group offers similar supply chain and delivery tracking services to other kinds of manufacturers.

UPS is also expanding into another area important to e-business—delivery of digital documents. The company was the first conventional package shipper to enter this market in 1998 when it launched UPS Document Exchange. This service monitors delivery of digitally delivered documents and provides instant receipt notification, encryption, and password-only access.

UPS offers many other EC-related services. These include the ability to enter the UPS system from wireless devices, helping customers configure and customize services, and providing for electronic bill presentation and payment (for B2B), electronic funds transfer, and processing of COD payments.

Sources: Compiled from B. Violino, May 4, 2000 and *ups.com*, press releases, 2000, 2001.

Questions

- Why would a shipper such as UPS expand to other logistic services?
- Why would shippers want to handle payments?
- Why does UPS provide software tools to customers?
- What B2B services does UPS provide? (*Note:* Check *ups.com* to make sure that your answers are up-to-date.)

where they can drop off returns. In Asia and Australia, returns are accepted in convenience stores and at gas stations. For example, BP Australia Ltd. (gasoline service stations) teamed up with wishlist.com.au, and Caltex Australia is accepting returns at the convenience stores connected to its gasoline stations. The accepting stores may offer in-store computers for ordering, and may also offer payment options, as at Japanese 7–Eleven (7dream.com, see Chapter 1).

▶ List the various order-taking solutions.

▶ List solutions for improved delivery.

▶ Describe same-day shipments.

▶ Describe how the return of items can be effectively managed.

MANAGERIAL ISSUES

Some managerial issues related to this chapter are as follows.

1. **What B2C payment methods should we use?** Only accepting credit cards rules out a number of potential market segments. Teenagers, non-U.S. customers, and customers who do not want to use credit cards online are examples of market segments for whom credit cards are of little use. Here, e-cash, virtual credit cards, and stored-value cards are possibilities. Also, when the purchase price is less than $10, credit cards are not a viable solution. Again, e-cash and stored-value cards are possibilities. Third-party companies such as PayPal also can handle payment transactions via secure e-mail. In all of these cases, merchants and other sellers need to be aware of the volatility of the alternatives they are adopting and their true costs. Because the various alternatives do not yet enjoy widespread use, there is always the possibility that they will not exist tomorrow.

2. **What B2B payment methods should we use?** Keep an open mind about online alternatives. When it comes to paying suppliers or accepting payments from partners, most large businesses have opted to stick with the tried-and-true method of EFT over an EDI. As an alternative to traditional checks, companies can use purchasing cards. For global trade, electronic letters of credit are popular. The use of e-checks is another area where costs savings can accrue. With all of these methods, a key factor is determining how well they work with existing accounting systems.

3. **Should we use an in-house payment mechanism or outsource it?** It takes time, skill, money, software, and hardware to integrate the payment systems of all the parties involved in processing any sort of e-payment. For this reason, even a business that runs its own EC site should consider outsourcing the e-payment component. There are many third-party vendors who provide payment gateways designed to handle the interactions among the various financial institutions that operate in the background of an e-payment system.

4. **How secure are e-payments?** Security of payment continues to be a major issue in making and accepting e-payments of all kinds. Measures that are employed to ensure the security of e-payments have to be part of a broader security scheme that weighs risks against issues such as the ease of use and the fit within the overall business context.

5. **Have we planned for order fulfillment?** Order fulfillment is a critical task, especially for virtual EC vendors. Even for brick-and-mortar retailers with physical warehouses, delivery to customers' doors is not always easy. The problem is not just the physical shipment, but the efficient execution of the entire order fulfillment process, which may be complex along a long supply chain.

6. **How should we handle returns?** Dealing with returns can be a complex issue. The company should estimate its percentage of returns and design and plan the process of receiving and handling them. Some companies completely separate the logistics of returns from that of order fulfillment and outsource its execution.

7. **Do we want alliances in order fulfillment?** Partnerships and alliances can improve logistics and alleviate supply chain problems. Many possibilities and models exist. Some are along the supply chain, whereas others are not related to it.

8. **What EC logistics applications would be useful?** One should think not only about how to create logistical systems for EC, but also how to use EC applications to improve the supply chain.

SUMMARY

In this chapter, you learned about the following EC issues as they relate to the learning objectives.

1. **Crucial factors determining the success of an e-payment method.** A crucial element in the success of an e-payment method is the "chicken-and-egg" problem: How do you get sellers to adopt a method when there are few buyers using it? And, how do you get buyers to adopt a method when there are few sellers using it? At a minimum, overcoming this hurdle requires that the e-payment method needs little specialized hardware or software, integrates well with existing EC and legacy systems, is secure, maintains the anonymity of the buyer and seller, supports products and services with varying prices, is easy to use, and costs little for both the buyer and seller to use.

2. **Key elements in securing an e-payment.** In B2C, B2B, and C2C EC, issues of trust are paramount. These issues are summarized by the acronym PAIN—privacy, authenticity, integrity, and nonrepudiation. Public key infrastructure (PKI) is the base of secure e-payments. PKI uses encryption (through a combination of private and public encryption keys) to ensure privacy and integrity and digital signatures to ensure authenticity and nonrepudiation. Digital signatures are themselves authenticated through a system of digital certificates issued by certificate authorities. For the average consumer and merchant, the security of e-payments is simplified because it is built into Web browsers and Web servers. Here, the security comes about because vendors can rely on protocols such as the secure socket layer/transport security layer (SSL/TSL) and secure electronic translation (SET) in communicating with each other.

3. **Online credit card players and processes.** Credit cards dominate the online B2C world in the United States and a few other countries. The players in online credit cards are the same as they are in the off-line world: cardholders, merchants, card issuers (that establish the cardholder's account), acquirers (e.g., financial institutions), and card associations of issuers and acquirers (e.g., Visa.)

4. **The uses and benefits of purchasing cards.** Businesses spend billions of dollars each year purchasing low-cost goods and services (e.g., office supplies). Purchasing cards are special-purpose charge cards issued to employees solely for purchasing these nonstrategic goods and services up to a certain limit. Use of these cards substantially reduces the paperwork and cycle time associated with such purchases.

5. **Categories and potential uses of smart cards.** Smart cards look like credit cards but contain embedded chips. They can be categorized by their underlying technologies. Cards that contain microprocessor chips can be programmed to handle a wide variety of tasks. Other cards have memory chips to which data can be written and from which data can be read. Most of these memory cards are disposable, but others—smart cards—can hold large stores of data and are rechargeable. Smart cards have been and will be used for a number of purposes, including generating loyalty among shoppers (loyalty cards), holding e-cash, ensuring secure payment card usage with digital signatures and certificates, maintaining health and social welfare records, paying for mass transit services, and identifying the cardholder (e.g., holding driver's licenses and immigration status). Smart cards are increasingly being used for shopping, both off-line and online.

6. **Online alternatives to credit card payments.** When an item or service being sold costs less than $10, credit cards are too costly. In such micropayment situations, various other payment methods can come into play: e-cash loaded to stored-value cards (smart cards with e-cash), specialized electronic script such as beenz, or e-rewards such as MyPoints. These alternatives can also serve certain market segments (e.g., teenagers) that do not have their own credit cards but still want to make online purchases. Some buyers simply do not trust using their credit cards online. In this instance, special systems allow a consumer to set up accounts that assign a special name and number that can be used in place of the consumer's own credit card number. Finally, there are cases where the seller cannot really obtain a merchant account with an acquirer. A number of alternatives for such situations, such as PayPal, have been established to handle C2C transactions and transactions between parties without credit cards.

7. **E-check processes and involved parties.** E-checks are the electronic equivalent of paper checks. E-checks are employed in situations where consumers do not want to use their credit cards, in B2B EC, and in cases when the payments are too large for credit cards. E-checks are handled in much the same way as paper checks, but are processed electronically in 2 days or less. When e-checks are used by a business to pay suppliers, more stringent security is required because of the size of the payments and the sensitivity of the information. The eCheck Consortium has been working on establishing standards for these larger payments. These standards are currently being tested by the U.S. Treasury.

8. **The role of order fulfillment and back-office operations in EC.** Taking orders is necessary, but not sufficient in EC. On-time delivery to customers may be a difficult task, especially in B2C. Fulfilling an order requires several activities, ranging from credit and inventory checks to shipments. Most of these activities are part of back-office operations and are related to logistics.

9. **The order fulfillment process.** The order fulfillment process varies from business to business and also depends on the product. Generally speaking, however, the following 11 steps are recognized: payment verification, inventory checking, shipping arrangement, insurance, production (or assembly), plant services, purchasing, demand forecasting, accounting, customer contacts, and return of products.

10. **Problems in order fulfillment.** It is difficult to fulfill B2C orders due to uncertainties in demand and potential delays in supply and deliveries. Problems also result from lack of coordination, as in the bullwhip effect.

11. **Solutions to order fulfillment problems.** Automating order taking (e.g., by using EDI) and smoothing the supply chain are two ways to solve order fulfillment problems. Several other innovative solutions exist, most of which are supported by software that facilitates correct inventories, coordination along the supply chain, and appropriate planning and decision making.

KEY TERMS

Back-office operations,	p. 436	Encryption (cryptography),	p. 415	Public key,	p. 417
Beenz,	p. 430	Encryption algorithm,	p. 416	Public key encryption,	p. 416
Bullwhip effect,	p. 441	E-wallet,	p. 422	Public Key Infrastructure (PKI),	p. 415
Certificate authority (CA),	p. 418	Front-office operations,	p. 436	Purchasing card,	p. 423
Ciphertext,	p. 416	Key,	p. 416	Reverse logistics,	p. 438
Contact card,	p. 425	Letter of credit (LC),	p. 433	Secure Electronic Transaction (SET),	p. 419
Contactless (proximity) card,	p. 425	Logistics,	p. 436	Secure Socket Layer (SSL),	p. 419
Credit card gateway,	p. 421	Micropayment,	p. 427	Smart card,	p. 424
Digital certificates,	p. 418	Mondex,	p. 429	Stored-value card,	p. 425
Digital signature,	p. 417	Order fulfillment,	p. 436	Transport Layer Security (TLS),	p. 419
E-cash,	p. 427	Payment cards,	p. 420	Virtual credit card,	p. 421
E-check,	p. 434	Person-to-person payment (P2P),	p. 432	Visa Cash,	p. 429
Electronic script,	p. 430	Plaintext,	p. 416		
		Private key,	p. 417		

DISCUSSION QUESTIONS

1. Online credit cards were able to overcome the "chicken-and-egg" problem. However, to date, various e-cash methods have failed. What are some of the reasons for their failures? What does an e-cash company need to do to break the barrier?

2. A small business owner wants to sell handcrafted jewelry to teenagers on the Web. What methods of e-payment would you recommend and why?

3. Recently, a merchant who accepts online credit card payments has experienced a wave of fraudulent purchases. What sorts of security measures can the merchant impose without hindering legitimate customers?

4. You receive an online e-check. What security methods can be used to ensure the identity of the sender?

5. You invite a group of friends to lunch. At the end of lunch, you pick up the check and your friends agree to repay you later. How could they pay you online?

6. Discuss why it is safe to post a public key on the Internet. If it is not a secret, why is a public key needed?

7. A business wants to gain better control of its office supply purchases. What sort of e-payment could it use to solve this problem? What types of control would the method afford?

8. A business that purchases millions of dollars in goods and services from its suppliers would like to substitute an Internet-based e-payment system for its older EDI system. A consultant has recommended that it use e-checks. How would this work and what sorts of security issues would arise?

9. Discuss the problems of reverse logistics in EC. What types of companies may suffer the most?

10. Explain why UPS defines itself as a "technology company with trucks," rather than a "trucking company with technology."

11. Chart the supply chain portion of returns to a virtual store. Check with an e-tailer to see how they handle returns. Prepare a report based on your findings.

12. Compare solutions such as PayPal to Internet-Cash.

INTERNET EXERCISES

1. Visit verisign.com and take their guided tour of e-payment processing solutions. While at VeriSign, sign-up for a digital ID that can be used with e-mail. Use the ID to encrypt and e-mail a message to your instructor.

2. Go to checkfree.com and run the e-billing demo. What features and functions does CheckFree provide?

3. Go to the RocketCash site (rocketcash.com). What is RocketCash? What is RocketFuel? Approximately how many stores accept RocketCash? What types of stores are they, and who do they cater to?

4. Visit the following Web sites: toysrus.com, kbkids.com, amazon.com, lego.com, and dogtoys.com. Find out what delivery options are offered by each company. Then examine delivery options offered by starbucks.com and carsdirect.com. Prepare a report based on your findings.

5. The U.S Postal Service is also in the EC logistics field. Examine its services and tracking systems at usps.com/shipping. What are the potential advantages for EC shippers?

6. Enter rawmart.com and find what information they provide that supports logistics. Also find what shipment services they provide online.

7. Visit ups.com and find its recent EC initiatives. Compare them with those of fedex.com.

8. Visit relysoftware.com and the sites of one or two other online freight companies. Compare the features offered by these companies for online delivery.

9. Enter efulfillmentservice.com. Review the products you find there. How does the company organize the network? How is it related to companies such as FedEx? How does this company make money?

10. Enter akamai.com and examine its latest content-maximization solutions. Examine customers' stories. What kinds of customers are most likely to use the service? For what purpose?

11. Enter points.yahoo.com and examine its loyalty/reward system. Compare it to mypoints.com. How do you get points? How you can redeem them in each system?

TEAM ASSIGNMENTS AND ROLE PLAYING

1. Select some B2C sites that cater to teens (e.g., alloy.com) and some sites that cater to older consumers (e.g., seniorcitizens.com and snow-bird.net). Have team members visit these sites. What types of e-payment methods do they provide? Are there any differences among the methods used on different types of sites? What other types of e-payment would you recommend for the various sites and why?

2. Several sites now support P2P or C2C payments. Locate as many of these sites as you can. What other types of services do they provide? Not all of these sites will be successful in the long run. Which of the sites do you think will be long-term players? Why? (Base your answer mostly on their payment and logistic services.)

3. Each team should investigate the order fulfillment process of an e-tailer, such as amazon.com, staples.com, or landsend.com. Contact the company, if necessary, and examine related business partnerships if they exist. Based on the content of this chapter, prepare a report with suggestions for how the company can improve its order fulfillment process. All the groups' findings will be discussed in class. Based on the class's findings, draw some conclusions about how order fulfillment can be improved.

4. FedEx, UPS, the U.S. Postal Service, and others are competing in the EC logistics market. Each team should examine one such company and investigate the services it provides.

Contact the company, if necessary, and aggregate the findings into a report that will convince the reader that the company in question is the best. (What are its best features?)

HOW DELL COMPUTER FULFILLS CUSTOMER ORDERS

One of Dell Computer's success factors is its superb logistics and order fulfillment systems. Customer orders, which are received mostly online, are automatically transferred to the production area, where configuration is done to determine which components and parts are needed to create the customized computer that the customer wants. Once configuration is done, the problem becomes how to get all the needed components so that a computer can be ready for shipment the next day. As part of the solution, Dell created a network of dedicated suppliers for just-in-time deliveries, as well as a sophisticated computerized global network of components and parts inventories. The global network is also used for product services (e.g., repairs per warranty commitments, upgrades, demanufacturing, etc.)

Let's examine how Dell provides service when a computer that is in the customer's possession needs to be repaired. Dell is trying to achieve for repairs, upgrades, and other services the next-day shipment that it uses for new computers. For repair activities, Dell needs parts and subassemblies to be delivered to hundreds of repair stations, worldwide, from internal warehouses or external vendors. The search for the parts and their delivery must be done very quickly. To facilitate this, Dell is using an online intelligent inventory optimization system from LPA software (*xelus.com*). The system can reconcile the demand for parts, with the action needed (e.g., repair, upgrade, transfer, or demanufacture). For example, the system allows Dell to factor the yield on reusable parts into its supply projection. This allows Dell to use repairable parts to compress time and reduce costs, enabling a team of about 10

employees to successfully process more than 6,000 service orders every day.

The online system generates timely information about demand forecast, the cost of needed inventory, and "days of supply of inventory." It compares actual to forecasted demand. This enables Dell to communicate critical information to external and internal customers, reducing order fulfillment delays.

Producing or acquiring the required parts through component substitution, upgrades, and engineering change orders must be effective in order to provide superb customer service at a low inventory cost. The system also provides an online standard body of knowledge about parts and planning strategies.

Sources: Compiled from an advertising supplement in *CIO Magazine*, October 1, 1999, *xelus.com*, June 2000, and *dell.com*.

Questions

1. What portions of order fulfillment are improved by this process?
2. Enter *xelus.com* and find information about its inventory optimization and other SCM-related products. List the major capabilities of the products it offers.
3. Enter *dell.com* and find information about how Dell conducts repair (warranty) customer service.
4. Relate this case to the discussion of "returns" in this chapter.
5. What competitive advantage is provided by this Dell system?

CHAPTER 11

E-STRATEGY, INTERNET COMMUNITIES, AND GLOBAL EC

Content

IBM's E-Business Strategy

Managerial Issues

Real-World Case:

Learning objectives

Upon completion of this chapter, you will be able to:

▶ Describe the importance and essentials of EC strategies.

▶ Describe the strategy planning and formulation process for EC.

▶ Understand how EC applications are discovered, justified, and prioritized.

▶ Describe strategy implementation and assessment, including the use of metrics.

▶ Understand EC failures and lessons for success.

▶ Describe the role and impact of virtual communities on EC.

▶ Evaluate the issues involved in global EC.

▶ Analyze the impact of EC on small businesses.

▶ Describe the relationship between EC and BPR, knowledge management, and virtual corporations.

▶ Describe the future of EC.

IBM'S E-BUSINESS STRATEGY

The Problem

IBM has been a huge presence in the computer industry since its inception in the 1940s. In the face of increased competition over the years, IBM has continually revamped its business strategy. Even more important, though, is the need to capture new business opportunities and technologies, such as EC, and to develop a business strategy for that purpose. IBM's current declared strategy is to transform itself into an e-business in order to provide business value to the corporation and its shareholders. IBM views e-business as being much broader than EC because it serves a broader constituency and offers a variety of Web-based processes and transactions.

The Solution

To ensure successful implementation of its e-business strategy, IBM formed an independent division, called Enterprise Web Management, that has the following four goals:

- To lead IBM's strategy to transform itself into an e-business and to act as a catalyst to help facilitate that transformation.

- To help IBM's business units become more effective in their use of the Internet, both internally and with their customers.

- To establish a strategy for the corporate Internet site. This includes a definition of how it should look, feel, and be navigated—in short, to create an online environment most conducive to customers doing business with IBM.

- To leverage the wealth of e-business information accumulated in case studies to highlight the potential of e-business to customers.

Like many other companies, IBM first used the Internet as a static digital brochure, basically a tool for posting information. IBM is now moving towards comprehensive e-business, carrying out business transactions of all kinds over the Internet, intranets, and extranets between IBM and its suppliers, among members of its Business Partner network, among its employees, and so on. IBM wants to become truly e-business-oriented and to focus on how it can use powerful networking technology to fulfill the diverse needs of its customers and partners.

One of the major issues in moving to e-business was the redesign of many of its core business processes on the Internet—including sales, procurement, customer care, and knowledge management. Implementing EC frequently requires such a redesign. The company targeted for redesign those areas in which IBM can earn the biggest return on investment. It focused its activities initially around seven key initiatives:

1. Selling more goods over the Web—*e-commerce*.

2. Providing customer support online, from technical support to marketing backup—*e-care for customers*.

3. Support for IBM's business partners over the Web—*e-care for business partners*.

4. Dedicated services providing faster, better information for IT analysts and consultants, financial analysts, media, and stakeholders—*e-care for influencers*.

5. Improving the effectiveness of "IBMers" by making needed information and services available to them—*e-care for employees*.

6. Working closely with customers and suppliers to improve the tendering process and to better administer the huge number of transactions involved—*e-procurement*.

7. Using the Internet to better communicate IBM's marketing stance—*e-marketing communications*.

The Results

Some of these initiatives have already borne fruit. For example, IBM implemented an e-procurement system that spans IBM globally, and that saved the company almost $5 billion in 3 years (Ashton, 1999). However, there is more to e-business than just how many dollars per day IBM sells or saves on the Web. In the procurement area, for example, IBM is invoicing electronically, to reduce the millions of paper invoices it sends out and to enable fast, competitive tendering from its suppliers. IBM has evaluated every step of the procurement process to determine where the use of the Web can add value. This has resulted in the identification of more than 20 initiatives—including collaboration with suppliers, online purchasing, and knowledge-management-based applications—in which the company is already reducing cost and improving purchasing. (For more information, see Bonnett 2000.)

As a result of its e-business initiatives, IBM's profitability has been solid, withstanding the economic problems of 2000 to 2002 better than any other large IT company.

What We Can Learn . . .

The opening vignette raises some interesting issues related to strategic planning for EC. First, IBM had a mission—to become a premiere e-business. Second, it identified over 20 EC initiatives or applications to consider. In addition, IBM implemented the following e-business strategies: It created an independent EC division; introduced EC as a corporate culture; leveraged its existing strengths; tied EC with the reengineering of its processes; began with only 7 out of the 20 EC initiatives; and finally, employed an evaluation metric (return

on investment, ROI) as a criterion for selecting the EC projects. All of these activities are typical for companies embarking on a new e-business initiative. And, for EC, as with any other significant project, it is necessary to relate the EC strategy to the corporate strategy. How to create an EC strategy is the subject of this chapter. We will also present the related topics of global EC, EC and small businesses, virtual communities, and introducing EC projects into organizations.

Sources: *ibm.com*, 2000, Ashton, 1999, Howard, Hamilton and Polinsky, 2001, and Bonnett, 2000.

11.1 EC STRATEGY: CONCEPTS AND OVERVIEW

STRATEGY DEFINED

A **strategy** is a broad-based formula for how a business is going to compete, what its goals should be, and what plans and policies will be needed to carry out those goals. Strategy means a search for actions that will significantly change the current position of a company, shaping its future.

Porter (1996) has further said that strategy is about finding the position in the marketplace that best fits a firm's skills. If there is no fit among activities, there is no distinctive strategy and little sustainability. Strategy can also be seen as a company's choice of a new position, which must be driven by its ability to find new trade-offs and leverage a new system of complementary activities into a sustainable advantage.

strategy
A broad-based formula for how a business is going to compete, what its goals should be, and what plans and policies will be needed to carry out those goals.

THE ELEMENTS OF A STRATEGY

Strategy involves several elements or activities. Some of the most important include:

▶ **Forecasting.** Forecasting the business, technological, political, economic, and other relevant environments.

▶ **Resource allocation.** Organizational resources are those owned, available to, and controlled by a company. They can be human, financial, technological, managerial, or knowledge-based. Resources must be allocated for the strategy to be successful.

▶ **Core competency.** Core competency refers to the unique combination of the resources and experiences of a particular firm. It takes time to build these core competencies, and they are difficult to imitate. For example, a core competency of amazon.com is to sell books online.

▶ **Environmental (industry) analysis.** Environmental analysis involves scanning the business environment and collecting and interpreting relevant information. It is usually confined to the industry where the business belongs, and thus is often referred to as industry analysis.

▶ **Company analysis.** Company analysis includes the business strategy, the capabilities, the constraints, and the strengths and weaknesses of the specific company.

▶ **Business planning.** Business planning refers to the plan of how to get from the current position to the desired one.

TYPES OF EC STRATEGIES

EC strategy (e-strategy)
An organization's strategy for use of e-commerce or e-business.

EC strategy (or simply, **e-strategy**) is an organization's strategy for e-commerce or e-business. Different types of companies use different types of EC strategies. The major ones are:

▶ **Click-and-mortar companies that use many EC applications.** Large companies may consider an EC strategy that uses as many EC applications as possible, and they usually use a comprehensive strategy that determines the portfolio of applications, their priorities, and more. IBM and Qantas Airways (see Chapter 1) are examples of companies that use this EC strategy.

▶ **Click-and-mortar companies that use only one or two EC applications.** In the late 1990s, many companies started EC by using it as an additional selling channel or for intrabusiness purposes. Over time, they may or may not add more applications. In such a case, a major strategic issue is when to add more applications, and in what order. For example, a small business may use the Web for promotion and perhaps for e-procurement, but not sell products because of their market and customers. After a few years it may employ a comprehensive EC strategy that takes the company into a strategy that uses many EC applications.

▶ **Click-and-mortar companies that use one EC application that fundamentally changes their business.** In such a case, the major strategic issue is basically "go or no go" on the EC application. An example is stockbroker Charles Schwab, which changed its business by deciding to sell online, as described in EC Application Case 11.1.

▶ **Pure-play EC companies.** Companies such as Amazon.com and E*TRADE that do business only online are pure-play EC companies. In such cases, the major strategy issue is how to survive and grow.

WHY DOES A COMPANY NEED AN E-STRATEGY

Is an e-strategy always needed? No, a formal strategy is not always needed. Even some large companies can sometimes do without a strategy (see Semler 2000). For SMEs in particular, formal strategic planning may be too expensive, and it also

EC APPLICATION CASE 11.1
Implementation and Strategy
CHARLES SCHWAB'S EC STRATEGY

Charles Schwab is the world's second largest discount stockbroker. On January 15, 1998, after conducting an opportunity analysis, Schwab launched *schwab.com*, making the company one of the first click-and-mortar stockbrokers.

In making this major change to its business format, the company decided to significantly drop its commission to $29.95 per transaction, changing the company pricing structure radically. In doing so, the company decided to take a short-term revenue loss of $125 to $150 million in order to gain a long-term strategic gain. The strategy paid off, and within a year Schwab handled over $81 billion on the Internet. This increased revenues by over $100 million a year and funded the 1,500 staff members and new technology required for the project. The EC strategy fit well with the company's overall strategy that emphasizes a one-to-one relationship with its customers. Now Schwab can convey personalized information in real time.

When Schwab embarked on EC, its competitors were offering significantly lower prices (Ameritrade, $8/transaction; E*TRADE, $15/transaction). However, Schwab had the first-mover advantage in securing key partnerships that would produce a competitive advantage. For example, in November 2000, Schwab and Nextel agreed to build an infrastructure that would let customers perform investment functions through Web-enabled mobile phones or wireless handheld devices.

Schwab decided to target existing off-line customers, trading customers with incomes over $150,000 a year, and those customers that buy and hold. It further decided its key benefits would be innovative products, superior service, and low fees, offered in conjunction with cutting-edge technology.

Schwab next considered specific products and services, offering a large number of financial services online (e.g., life insurance, tax strategies, retirement planning, bill payment, after-hours trading, and even a college planner), as well as community and personalized services (e.g., chat rooms and updated information on customer investment portfolios). To provide these services, Schwab partnered with content providers and technology companies.

To ensure financial viability, Schwab developed a *financial* and *revenue model* composed of three parts:

1. **The revenue model.** The specific sources of revenue (e.g., transaction fees, interest on margin loans to customers).

2. **The value model.** The features and functions that would provide value to customers (its value proposition). Schwab is known as a superb provider of the best information online, including personalized stock analysis, diversified stock analysis, and other services.

3. **The growth model.** Ideas for future expansion and extension of the business (e.g., plans to create an online investment bank, online educational activities, and more) of these extensions will be provided by business partners.

Sources: Pottruck and Pearce, 2000 and *schwab.com*.

Questions

▶ Describe Schwab's value proposition.

▶ Describe Schwab's revenue model.

may inhibit quick adaptation to changing environments. In general, though, in EC it may be too risky not to have an e-strategy. Many of the EC failures in 2000–2001 can be at least partially attributed to lack of strategy. The fast changes in the business and technological environments are so vigorous that both the opportunities and the threats can change any minute. Therefore, any company considering EC must have at least some EC strategy that includes a contingency plan. Before we look at the various dimensions of e-strategy, let's take a panoramic view of the strategy landscape.

THE E-STRATEGY LANDSCAPE

Because there are different types of e-strategies and implementation methods, it is difficult to have a single coherent view of the field of e-strategy. However, there are some major activities that are found in most formal strategic plans. These activities can be organized into four major phases, as shown in Exhibit 11.1. (Note that the phases in Exhibit 11.1 correspond to section numbers in this chapter.) The major phases of EC strategy are:

▶ *Strategy initiation*. In this phase, the organization prepares information about its vision, mission, purpose, and the contribution that EC could make to the business. This phase also includes environmental and company analyses, and it attempts to clarify the need for a formal strategy and tries to determine its major goals.

▶ *Strategy formulation*. This phase includes all the activities necessary to formulate a strategy, notably, identification of EC applications, cost-benefit analysis, and risk analysis. In the end, a list of candidate EC applications is created.

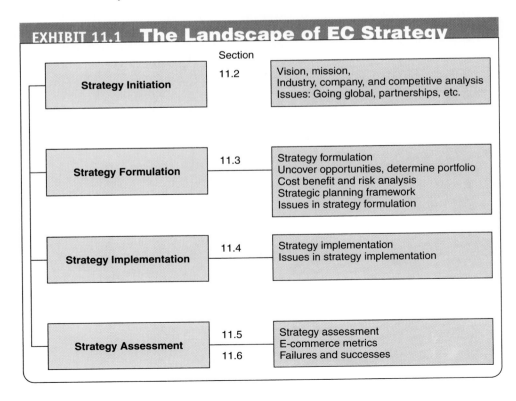

EXHIBIT 11.1 The Landscape of EC Strategy

	Section	
Strategy Initiation	11.2	Vision, mission, Industry, company, and competitive analysis Issues: Going global, partnerships, etc.
Strategy Formulation	11.3	Strategy formulation Uncover opportunities, determine portfolio Cost benefit and risk analysis Strategic planning framework Issues in strategy formulation
Strategy Implementation	11.4	Strategy implementation Issues in strategy implementation
Strategy Assessment	11.5 / 11.6	Strategy assessment E-commerce metrics Failures and successes

▶ *Strategy implementation.* Here, the organization's resources are analyzed, and a plan is developed for attaining the goals of the strategy. Decision makers evaluate options, establish specific milestones, plan budgets, and allocate resources.

▶ *Strategy assessment.* Periodically, the organization should assess progress toward the strategic goals. Based on the results, actions are taken and the strategy is reformulated as needed. This phase involves the development of EC metrics (discussed in Section 11.5).

Methodologies and tools are available to support these phases, many of which are described in this chapter.

An EC strategy can be very simple or it can cover many topics. In EC Application Case 11.1 we provided an example of the EC strategy used by Charles Schwab. A comprehensive EC strategy for Skymall is provided on the book's Web site, prenhall.com/turban (Chapter 11). Details of e-strategy in the private sector are usually considered propriety information and are not disclosed. Or, if the company is publicly traded, only the minimum required by the Securities and Exchange Commission is disclosed. In contrast, public organizations such as governmental units and not-for-profit organizations regularly disclose their EC strategies.

▶ What is a strategy? What are the elements of a strategy?

▶ Explain why e-strategy is needed.

▶ Describe the four phases of e-strategy.

▶ Describe Schwab's e-strategy.

11.2 STRATEGY INITIATION

In **strategy initiation**, the organization prepares information about its vision, mission, purpose, and the contribution that EC could make to the business. The steps in strategy initiation are to review the organization's vision and mission, to analyze its industry, company, and competitive position, and to consider various initiation issues.

VISION AND MISSION

The first step in any strategy initiation is to review the organization's vision and mission, both for its business in general and for its IT initiatives specifically. From there, the organization can generate its vision and mission for EC. For example, for IBM, part of the EC mission is, "IBM plans to transform itself into an e-business in order to provide business value to the corporation and its shareholders" (ibm.com). Although vision and mission statements are usually very vague, they do provide a springboard for generating more specific goals and objectives that are needed to initiate the strategy process.

Strategy initiation usually begins with industry, company, and competitive analysis.

strategy initiation
The initial phase of e-strategy in which an organization prepares information about its vision, mission, purpose, and the contribution that EC could make.

INDUSTRY, COMPANY, AND COMPETITIVE ANALYSES

The purpose of this step is to analyze the position of the company in its industry with respect to the competition. This analysis is required for assessing the changes that the EC project may introduce and the chance for its success. There are several methodologies for conducting such an analysis (e.g., see David 1998; Shapiro and Varian 1998; Kaplan and Norton 2000). A common methodology is to divide the analysis into three parts: industry assessment, company assessment, and competitive assessment.

In an industry assessment, an organization asks such questions as the following: Who are the customers (today and tomorrow)? What are the industry's current practices of selling and buying? Who are the major competitors? How intense is the competition? What e-strategies are used and by whom? What are the major opportunities and threats for EC projects? Are there any metrics or best practices in place? What are existing and potential partnerships for EC? Who are the major EC vendors in the industry?

An organization may use special software for conducting the industry, company, and competitive analyses. See Tutorial T-3 available at the book's Web site, prenhall.com/turban. (For additional details and examples, see Hackbarth and Kettinger 2000 and Plant 2000.)

In a company assessment, the organization investigates its own business strategy, performance, customers, partners, and so on. It will look at everything that has an impact on its operations—its processes, people, information flows, and technology support. (See Hackbarth and Kettinger 2000 and Tennant 2000 for details.)

Finally, data collected in the industry and company assessments are combined for evaluation, and the result is the competitive assessment. A popular methodology for competitive assessment is SWOT analysis.

SWOT Analysis

SWOT is an acronym for Strengths, Weaknesses, Opportunities, and Threats. **SWOT analysis** is a methodology that surveys the opportunities and threats in the external environment and relates them to the organization's particular strengths and weaknesses. The relationships between the opportunities and threats and the corporate strengths and weaknesses can be shown graphically in a four-cell matrix. This matrix, a sample of which is shown in Exhibit 11.2, is referred to as the *SWOT matrix*. Its elements (shown in salmon) are:

> In the Opportunities (O) block, the external opportunities available to the company now and in the future.
> In the Threats (T) block, the external threats facing the company now and in the future.
> In the Strengths (S) block, the specific areas of current and future strengths for the company.
> In the Weaknesses (W) block, the specific areas of current and future weakness for the company.

There are four cells that result from the intersection of the SWOT elements in the matrix (shown in green):

SWOT analysis
A methodology that surveys the opportunities and threats in the external environment and relates them to the organization's particular strengths and weaknesses.

EXHIBIT 11.2 SWOT Matrix

Internal Factors / External Factors	Strengths (S)	Weaknesses (W)
Opportunities (O)	**OS Strategies** **1** Generate strategies here that use strengths to take advantage of opportunities	**OW Strategies** **2** Generate strategies here that take advantage of opportunities by overcoming weaknesses
Threats (T)	**TS Strategies** **3** Generate strategies here that use strengths to avoid threats	**TW Strategies** **4** Generate strategies here that minimize weaknesses and avoid threats

Source: *Strategic Management and Business Policy: Entering 21st Century Global*, 7/e by Wheelen and Hunger © 1996. Reprinted by permission of Pearson Education Inc., Upper Saddle River, NJ.

1. The *opportunities* as they relate to the company's *strengths* (OS).

2. The *opportunities* as they relate to the company's *weaknesses* (OW).

3. The *threats* as they relate to the company's *strengths* (TS).

4. The *threats* as they relate to the company's *weaknesses* (TW).

For example, IBM's "captive" (existing) customers provide an opportunity for IBM to introduce sell-side EC using IBM products. A threat for IBM is that because the company is so large, it may be less innovative in creating new business models and may be slower to implement them than its smaller competitors.

In conducting the industry and competitive analyses, it is useful to employ some kind of competitive intelligence. This can be facilitated by using the Internet.

Competitive Intelligence on the Internet

Competitive intelligence refers to the collection of information regarding marketplace competition. It is an integral part of strategic planning and can be conducted by conventional methods and by using the Internet. The competitive analysis methods can be conducted using Internet-based tools:

▶ **Review competitors' Web sites.** Visits to competitors' sites can reveal information about new products or projects, potential alliances, trends in budgeting, advertising strategies, financial strength, and much more.

▶ **Examine publicly available financial documents.** This can be accomplished by entering a number of databases. Although some databases charge nominal fees, others are free. The most notable repository of publicly available financial

competitive intelligence
The collection of information regarding marketplace competition; conducted both by conventional methods and by using the Internet.

information in the United States is the database of the Securities and Exchange Commission, EDGAR (sec.gov/edgar.shtml).

- **Ask the customers.** You can give prizes to those visitors at your Web site who best describe the strengths and weaknesses of your products and of your competitors.
- **Analyze related discussion groups.** Internet discussion groups can help businesses find out what people think about a company and its products. For example, discussion group participants can state what they like or dislike about products provided by you and your competitors. You can also examine people's reactions to a new idea by posting a question.
- **Use an information delivery service.** Services such as Info Wizard, My Yahoo!, or Webcast can be used to find out what is being published on the Internet, including discussion group correspondence, about your competitors and their products.
- **Corporate research companies.** For a fee, companies such as Dun & Bradstreet and Standard and Poor's provide information ranging from risk analysis to stock market analysts' reports about a company's competitors. These are available electronically.
- **Chat rooms.** A company can solicit opinions in chat rooms about the company and its competitors.

ISSUES IN E-STRATEGY INITIATION

Representative issues in e-strategy initiation are covered in the following sections.

Be a First Mover or a Follower?

Is there a real advantage to being the first mover in an industry or market segment? In EC the answer is "maybe." Pioneering companies such as PointCast, eToy, and Chemdex went bankrupt or changed their operations. On the other hand, pioneers such as Ariba, eBay, VeriSign, and others have done extremely well. For other pioneering companies, it is too soon to say; amazon.com, for example, might go either way. The first-mover role may be taken on either by new Internet companies or by established companies assuming a leadership role. A comparison between leader and follower strategies is provided in Exhibit 11.3.

The major advantages of being a first mover are the chance to capture large market share, to establish a brand name, and to establish exclusive strategic alliances. The major disadvantages of being a first mover are the high cost of developing EC initiatives, the high likelihood of failure, the risk of the first system being made obsolete by the second wave of arrivals, and the lack of available support services at the beginning of an initiative.

Large companies such as IBM, Oracle, Intel, and SAP are more likely to be first movers, but they may lack the flexibility and the innovation of start-ups.

Going Global

Going global on a large scale is a strategic issue. For example, Lego of Denmark elected to go global selectively (i.e., in a few countries, with a few products). The issues involved in deciding whether or not to go global are discussed in Sec-

EXHIBIT 11.3	**Comparing a Follower vs. a Leader Position in EC**	
	Be a Follower	**Be a Leader**
Customer Service	▶ Significant capability to increase customer service/intimacy	▶ New dimension in customer care
Price	▶ Reduced by cost efficiencies passed through to the customer	▶ Significant decrease ▶ Source of competitive advantage for entire value chain
Quality	▶ Somewhat of an increase due to customer self-service	▶ Increased through standardized customer interface and automated processes
Fulfillment Time	▶ Decreased due to internal process theoretical minimum	▶ Drastically increased ▶ Source of customer loyalty
Agility	▶ Increased through standardization of data formats and interoperability	▶ New strategies enabled
Time to Market	▶ Decreased through knowledge management and extended access to information throughout the company	▶ Greatly enhanced ▶ Long-term advantages gained in the short term
Market Reach	▶ Increased ▶ Defense of current reach likely	▶ Rapid geographic increase ▶ Incremental penetration of "markets of one" served by competitors as market segments

Source: Raisch, 2000, pp. 202–203.

tion 11.8. The decision whether or not to go global is for many companies important enough to be a part of the strategy initiation.

Should You Have a Separate Online Company?

When the volume of e-business is large, the temptation to create a separate company increases, especially if you can take it to the stock market as a separate company with its own stock offering. Barnes and Noble did just that with its online company barnesandnoble.com. Similarly, the ASB Bank in New Zealand created BankDirect (bankdirect.co.nz) as a separate online company for virtual banking.

The advantages of creating a separate company are: reduction or elimination of internal conflicts; more freedom for the online company's management in pricing, advertising, and other decisions; the ability to create a new brand quickly; the opportunity to build new, efficient information systems that are not burdened by the legacy systems of the old company; and an influx of outside funding, if the market likes the idea of the e-business and buys the initial public offering of stock. On the other hand, the disadvantages of creating an independent division are that it may be very costly and/or risky, collaboration with the off-line business may be difficult, and the new company may lose the expertise of the business functions (marketing, finance, distribution), unless it gets superb collaboration from the parent company.

Several spin-offs, including Barnesandnoble.com, are not doing well, and grainger.com (a large industrial-supply company) has merged back into its parent company. Very few spin-off online companies have succeeded thus far.

▶ Briefly describe company, industry, and competitive analyses.

▶ How can the Internet aid a company in conducting a competitive analysis?

▶ Describe the first mover issue.

▶ What are the advantages and disadvantages of creating separate online companies?

11.3 STRATEGY FORMULATION

strategy formulation
The development of long-range and strategic plans to exploit opportunities and manage threats in the business environment in light of corporate strengths and weaknesses.

Based on the results of the industry and competitive analyses, the company can formulate more specific EC strategies and plans. **Strategy formulation** is the development of long-range and strategic plans to effectively exploit opportunities and manage threats in the business environment, in light of corporate strengths and weaknesses, identified in the previous phase. It includes examining or redefining the EC mission by specifying achievable objectives, developing strategies, and setting implementation guidelines for EC. Strategy formulation is relevant both for the decision to undertake an EC initiative in general and for individual EC projects. It should be noted that "going EC" can be done in many ways, as demonstrated throughout this book. Strategy formulation includes a number of topics, the most significant of which we deal with here.

DISCOVERING EC OPPORTUNITIES

Finding appropriate EC opportunities may not be an easy task. There are dozens of possible applications, and companies must decide which ones to adopt and in what order. It is well known that only a few business investments are 100 percent safe, and in the digital economy the uncertainty level is high, so even the most robust traditional planning tools may not work. As a result, according to Tjan (2001), companies often make one of the following three mistakes in selecting EC projects:

1. **"Let a thousand flowers bloom."** In this context, this phrase means that an organization funds many projects indiscriminately, hoping that the majority will succeed. Widespread success seldom happens.

2. **Bet it all.** The company bets everything on a single high-stake initiative. This strategy is very risky. If you wager it all, you can lose it all.

3. **Trend-surf.** The company follows the crowd toward the next "big thing," the most fashionable new idea. In this strategy, too much capital ends up pursuing too few opportunities or too much competition is created.

These types of mistakes can be very costly. Therefore, companies need to use a systematic approach to discover appropriate opportunities, as described in this section, and then evaluate them and prioritize them.

Generally speaking, companies use one of the following four approaches for identifying EC opportunities:

1. **Problem-driven.** When an organization has a specific problem (such as excess inventory or delays in deliveries), an EC application to solve the problem may be attempted. An example is General Motors, whose problem of disposing of old equipment was solved by implementing forward e-auctions (see the GM vignette in Chapter 5, page 202–203).

2. **Technology-driven.** In this case, the company wants to put certain existing technology to use. An example is shown in the IBM opening vignette: IBM had the technology (i.e., hardware, networks) on hand, and the strategy was to find as many areas to apply it to as possible. This approach is usually used by first movers and industry leaders. In taking this approach, the company may stumble over problems that no one knew existed, and solving them may bring a big reward.

3. **Market-driven.** In this approach, the company waits to see what the competitors in the industry do. When one or more competitors start to use EC, and it seems that they are doing well, then the company decides it is time to follow suit. ToysRUs.com followed eToys, barnesandnoble.com followed amazon.com, brick-and-mortar banks moved online following the virtual banks, and Merrill Lynch's online operations followed E*TRADE and Ameritrade.

4. **Fear- or greed-driven.** In this approach, companies are either so scared that if they do not practice EC they will be big losers or they think that they can make lots of money by going EC. In such cases, afraid they will "miss the boat," companies frequently jump into inappropriate ventures.

Finding the right EC initiative is critical. Between 1997 and 2000, many companies dumped large amounts of money into ill-fated EC initiatives. Two interrelated strategic issues are involved here. The first, which we just discussed, is uncovering potential opportunities. The second is deciding upon an appropriate application portfolio, namely, which initiatives to pursue and when.

DETERMINING AN APPROPRIATE EC APPLICATION PORTFOLIO

For years, companies have tried to find the most appropriate *portfolio* (group) of projects among which an organization should share its limited resources. The classical portfolio strategy attempted to balance investments with different characteristics. For example, the company would seek to combine long-term speculative investments in new potentially high-growth businesses with short-term investments in existing, profit-making businesses. The most well-known framework of this strategy is Boston Consulting Group's matrix with its "cash cows," start-ups, questionable projects, and "dogs." A similar portfolio approach specifically for EC was developed by Tjan (2001).

Tjan's Portfolio Strategy

Tjan (2001) adopted the Boston Consulting Group's approach to create what he called an "Internet portfolio." However, instead of trading-off industry growth and market position, here the strategy is based on *company fit*, which can be either low or high, and the *project's viability*, which also can be low or high. Together these create an Internet portfolio map.

Viability can be assessed by four criteria: market value potential, time to positive cash flow, personnel requirements, and funding requirements. EC initiatives such as B2B procurement sites, B2C stores, portals for kids, etc., can be evaluated on a scale of 1–100 (or on a qualitative scale of high, medium, low), based on their ranking on each criterion. Then, an average score per criterion is computed (a simple average).

For *fit*, the following criteria are used: alignment with core capabilities, alignment with other company initiatives, fit with organizational structure, fit with the company's culture and values, and ease of technical implementation. Again, each EC initiative is assessed on a scale of 1–100, and an average is computed.

The various initiatives are then mapped on what is called an *Internet portfolio matrix*, based on the two average scores for viability and fit. The Internet matrix is divided into four cells as shown in Exhibit 11.4. If both viability and fit are low, the project is *killed*. If both are high, then the project is *adopted*. If fit is high, but viability is low, the project is *sent to redesign*. Finally, if the fit is low but the viability is high, the project is to be *sold to someone*, or spun off. Exhibit 11.4 shows how several applications were rated for an e-marketplace for toys.

This method introduces a systematic approach to EC project selection. The assessment of the points per criteria can be done by several experts to ensure quality. Cases where there is more agreement on rankings can be considered with more confidence. Organizations can add their own criteria to the methodology. Also, one can place importance weights on the criteria, calculating a *weighted* rather than a simple average.

CHOOSING WHICH BUSINESS MODEL TO USE

The issue of uncovering opportunities is related to the issue of which EC business model(s) to use. EC implementation can be done in several ways. A typical choice is that used by the Chubb Group of Insurance Companies, which is shown in EC Application Case 11.2 (page 470).

MAKING THE BUSINESS CASE FOR EC

Executives need to be sure that EC initiatives can truly enhance their company's ability to generate revenues and reduce cost, thereby increasing competitiveness and profits. The process of doing so is referred to as making the business case for EC. As defined in Chapter 1, the *business case* is a written document that is used by managers to garner funding for specific applications or projects by providing justification for investments. The business case provides the bridge between the EC plan (or blueprint) and the execution. A good business case provides the foundation for tactical decision making and technology risk management. The business case helps to clarify how the organization will use its resources in the best way to accomplish the e-strategy. A business case is done for each EC project, individually. A business case can be done for a new online company (as a whole) as well. (See the online Tutorial T-3 at prenhall.com/turban for a demonstration of how to prepare a business case.)

The Content of an E-Business Case

The content of an e-business case includes an assessment of the project's feasibility, the preliminary scope of the project, and the justification. It should show that the EC investment is consistent with the company's overall business strategy. It should

EXHIBIT 11.4 Application Portfolio Map for Hypothetical Toy Manufacturer (Tjan)

Viability Metric

EC Application	Market-Value Potential	Time to Positive Cash Flow	Personnel Requirement	Funding Requirement	Average
E-marketplace (A)	85	70	20	20	49
Sell-side (B)	70	70	60	50	63
MRO procurement (C)	80	60	80	90	60

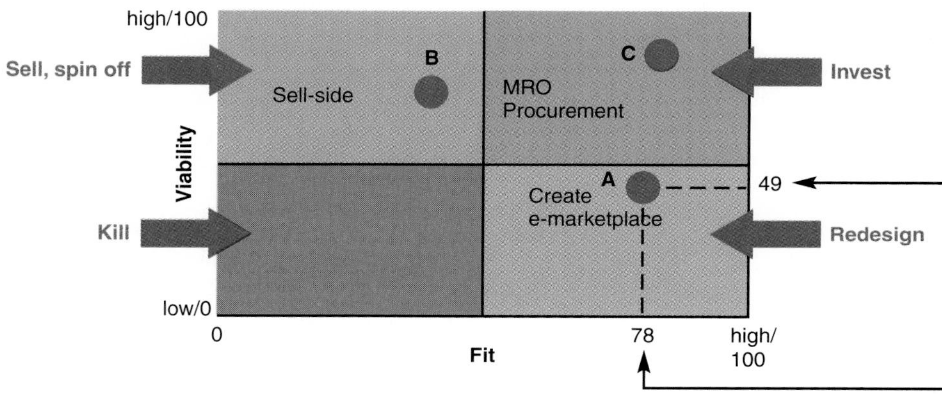

Fit Metric

EC Application	Alignment with Core Capabilities	Alignment with Other Company Initiatives	Fit with Organizational Structure	Fit with Company's Culture and Values	Ease of Technical Implementation	Average, Overall Fit
E-marketplace (A)	90	60	90	70	80	78
Sell-side (B)	10	30	30	40	60	35
MRO procurement (C)	90	60	90	80	80	84

Source: Reprinted by permission of *Harvard Business Review*. From "Finally, a Way to Put Your Internet Portfolio in Order" by A. K. Tjan, February 2001.

also show that the initiative will be managed efficiently. Kalakota and Robinson (2001) suggest the following four interrelated dimensions for an e-business case:

1. **Strategic justification—"Where are we going?"** Capabilities, competitive landscape, market gap, and more. What is the idea, how will customers be selected, and what value will be added (value proposition)?
2. **Generational justification—"How will we get there?"** What will be done and how improvements will be made.
3. **Technical justification—"When will we get there?"** How EC will support the organization's technology strategy.
4. **Financial justification—"Why will we win?"** What the costs and benefits are, what measurements and metrics are used, and how our business is different.

EC APPLICATION CASE 11.2
Implementation and Strategy
STRATEGIC DIRECTIONS AT CHUBB

The Chubb Group of Insurance Companies (*chubb.com*), a 115-year-old property and casualty insurance company, reviewed three possible EC strategies:

▶ Create a completely new business model with EC as the major driver of sales.

▶ Spawn an additional business model around EC according to which insurance products would be sold directly to consumers without the use of insurance agents and brokers as intermediaries. The company would maintain the traditional sales organization.

▶ Use EC as a tool within the existing business model.

The first option was quickly discarded; the company had a successful business model with products matching distribution systems. The company sells differentiated products that require some degree of explanation and a deep understanding of customers' needs, which Chubb's insurance agents provide. There was no logic in discontinuing a successful model.

The second model looked promising, but management did not want to disrupt the excellent relationship Chubb had with its agents and brokers. This model also required building a new infrastructure—a fully staffed around-the-clock call center, technologies for processing tasks that agents and brokers traditionally did, and more.

The company opted for the third alternative. This EC initiative helped Chubb to further differentiate its products and services, basically by providing superb customer service over the Internet. Chubb opened several Web sites, each targeted at a special interest group (e.g., wine collectors wishing to insure their collections).

With the new EC initiative, customers can view the status of their claims, and commercial clients can view their policies in full. Also, commercial customers have access to the data warehouse to view and use analytical tools to examine their policy-usage records.

The Web enabled speedy communication with agents and business partners and allowed business expansion into 20 countries. Online services include form creation, certification, validation, and more. A special value is the service to multinational corporations, which must be insured in several countries with different insurance regulations.

Source: *cio.com*, May 1, 1999.

Questions

▶ What added value was provided by EC?

▶ Discuss the strategy of using EC to improve an existing business model.

In addition, according to Kalakota and Robinson (2001), the following steps may be considered in preparing an e-business case: Develop a goal statement; set measurable goals; set objectives; develop short- and long-term action plans; and gain management approval and support.

The Revenue Model

One of the most critical success factors is to properly plan the revenue model. Many of the EC failures in 2000 and 2001 can be attributed to an incorrect revenue model. For example, many portals expected large revenues to come from advertising, but this did not happen. (The companies probably overestimated the amount of advertising revenue they could obtain, and in some cases, just failed to find the ad revenue that might have been available.) In addition, revenues from sales depend on customer acquisition. In many cases, the expenses for customer acquisition were larger than the revenues obtained from customers, resulting in large losses.

COST-BENEFIT AND RISK ANALYSIS

Like any other investment, investment in EC, either in an EC start-up or as an EC project in a click-and-mortar company, must go through the scrutiny of cost-benefit analysis and justification.

It is difficult to justify EC investment due to the many intangible variables involved. Various methods of justifying EC, such as return on investment (ROI) and/or discounted cash flow, are used (see Turban et al. 2002; Rayport and Jaworski 2001). Here we look at two common methods: value proposition and risk analysis.

Value Proposition

Value proposition refers to the benefit a company can derive from implementing a new project, such as EC, usually by increasing its competitiveness and by providing better service to its customers. For example, when customers use the Internet to conduct business, a new value for the selling company is created. If the customers move to the company from a competitor, the competitor may suffer a loss in value.

value proposition
The benefit a company can derive from implementing a new project, such as EC, usually by increasing its competitiveness and by providing better service to its customers.

Risk Analysis

It is extremely important to conduct risk analysis as part of an e-strategy formulation. The first chance to deal with risk is when a SWOT analysis is done and the threats are diagnosed. Then, when the strategy is formulated and specific initiatives are identified, a conventional risk analysis can be conducted. In general, in a risk analysis, the company should identify all potential risks, assess the potential damage if they occur, evaluate the possibility of protection (e.g., buying insurance), and measure the cost of protection versus the benefits.

A comprehensive discussion of risk in EC is provided by Deise et al. (2000), who identified the following e-business risks:

▶ **Strategic risks.** These include a competitive environment, wrong strategic direction, dependence on others (suppliers, buyers), wrong corporate culture, lack of reputation, regulatory changes, and poor governance.

▶ **Financial risks.** These include currency management and changes, unclear tax situations, and uneven or insufficient cash flow.

▶ **Operational risks.** These include technological changes and the use of poor technology; security problems; poor project management; business process controls; poor operations management; problems with employees, including a lack of skilled people.

Various methods can be used to conduct risk analysis (e.g., see Porter 1996; Wheelen and Hunger 1998; Kaplan and Norton 2000). One method that can be used to support risk analysis, for example, is *scenario planning* (see Levinson 1999/2000; Hutchinson 1997).

ISSUES IN STRATEGY FORMULATION

A variety of issues exist in strategy formulation depending on the company, industry, nature of applications, and so forth. Some representative issues are discussed in this section.

How to Handle Channel Conflicts

As we discussed in Chapter 3, channel conflicts may arise when an old-economy company creates an additional distribution channel online. Several options exist for handling channel conflicts. These include:

▶ Let the established old-economy dealers handle e-business fulfillment, as the auto industry is doing, even for customized cars. The ordering can be done online or directions to dealers can be provided online.

▶ Sell some products only online, such as lego.com is doing. Other products may be advertised online, but sold off-line.

▶ Help your intermediaries (e.g., by building portals for them). Provide services to your intermediaries and encourage them to reintermediate themselves.

▶ Sell online and off-line, as the airlines are doing.

▶ Do not sell online. With no online selling, there will be no channel conflict (conflict avoidance). Of course, in such a case, a company could still have an EC presence by offering promotion and customer service online (see Ritchey Design Inc., in Chapter 4).

How to Handle Conflict Between the Off-Line and Online Businesses

In a click-and-mortar situation, the allocation of resources between off-line and online activities can be very difficult. In some organizations, the two are viewed as competitors (in sell-side projects). Therefore, they may behave as competitors and not help each other. This conflict may cause problems when the off-line side needs to handle the logistics of the online side or when prices need to be determined. For example, when Schwab started e-Schwab, it was experimenting with different prices for online and off-line customers, making off-line customers angry. However, in 1997, the company merged its online services with the off-line, resulting in one price for all of its stock trades (Pottruck and Pearce 2000).

Corporate culture, the ability of top management to introduce change properly, and the use of innovative processes that support collaboration will all determine the degree of collaboration between off-line and online businesses. Clear support by top management for both the off-line and online operations and a clear strategy of "what and how" each unit will operate are essential. Some companies handle the situation by creating an independent division or subsidiary, enabling independent decisions to be made, thus reducing the conflict.

Pricing Strategy

Pricing products and services available online may be a difficult decision for any click-and-mortar company (Choi and Whinston 2000). Setting prices lower than those offered by the off-line business may lead to internal conflict, whereas setting prices at the same level will hurt competitiveness. Another strategic decision is how to price customized products and services. Dewan et al. (2000) and Prasad and Harker (2000) have developed quantitative economic models for making pricing decisions.

Should You Get Financing from Venture Capital Firms?

When EC first started, it was very easy to get capital from a venture capital (VC) firm. Now, because of the many recent failures, it has become increasingly difficult. Assuming such financing is available, a strategic issue is: Should an entrepreneur get VC financing and lose control over the idea and the business or try to get funding from other sources? One benefit of VC funding is access to VC experts whose managerial experience can be very helpful.

> ▶ Describe how a company can identify potential EC applications.
> ▶ Explain Tjan's portfolio model.
> ▶ Describe the content of a business case.
> ▶ Describe risk analysis for EC applications.
> ▶ Discuss some of the major issues in strategy formulation.

11.4 STRATEGY IMPLEMENTATION

The execution of the e-strategy plan takes place in the **strategy implementation** phase, in which detailed, short-term plans are developed for attaining the strategic goals. Decision makers evaluate options, establish specific milestones, plan budgets, and allocate resources. Introducing EC applications creates a major change in most organizations, and therefore it is also necessary to plan for an effective change-management program.

The implementation plan outlines the steps to follow during implementation. Typically, the first step is to establish a *Web team*, which then continues the execution of the plan. In this section, we deal with some topics related to the implementation process.

strategy implementation
The execution of the e-strategy plan, in which detailed, short-term plans are developed for attaining strategic goals.

CREATING A WEB TEAM AND ASSIGNING FUNCTIONAL SKILLS TO SUBPROJECTS

In creating a Web (project) team, the organization should carefully define the roles and responsibilities of the team leader, team members, Webmaster, and technical staff. The project leader often has the strategic challenge of being a "visionary" regarding the tasks of aligning business and technology goals and implementing a sound enterprise EC plan. Such a plan is best arrived at by negotiation with those knowledgeable about particular data and information and how they should be structured.

STARTING WITH A PILOT PROJECT

Implementing EC often requires significant investments in infrastructure. Therefore, a good way to start is to undertake one or a few small EC pilot projects. As pilot projects help uncover problems early, the pilot project can be considered a part of the planning process. Modifications in the plan after the pilot is completed are likely.

General Motors' pilot program (GM BuyPower) is an example of the successful use of a pilot project. On its Web site, gmbuypower.com, shoppers can choose car options, check local dealer inventory, schedule test drives, and get best-price quotes by e-mail or telephone. This pilot project has been in existence since 1997, starting in four western U.S. states and expanding to all states in 1999. Chrysler also went nationwide with its pilot Get-a-Quote program, carinfo.com. Similarly, when Home Depot decided to go online in 2000, it started in six stores in Las Vegas, then moved to four other cities in the western United States, and eventually went nationwide.

PLANNING FOR RESOURCES

In strategy formulation, decisions must be made on specific initiatives. The resources needed depend on the information requirements and the capabilities of each project. However, the infrastructure that is shared by many applications, such as databases, the intranet, and possibly an extranet, needs to be evaluated at this time. Some of the required resources will be in place, others will not be.

All relevant resources need to be planned for, especially people and money. Other resources may be a physical space for the EC unit, a physical warehouse for storage and packaging, and specific hardware and software. Standard system design tools can help in executing the resource-requirement plan. Obviously, the analysis of required resources is related to the organization's outsourcing strategy.

STRATEGY IMPLEMENTATION ISSUES

There are many strategy implementation issues, depending on the circumstances. Here we describe some common ones.

Evaluating Outsourcing

Implementing EC requires access to the Web, building the site, and connecting it to the existing corporate information systems (front-end for order taking, back-end for order processing). At this point, the company is faced with the decision of whether or not to outsource: Should it build an in-house EC infrastructure, purchase a commercial EC software package or EC suite, or use a Web hosting company?

Partners' Strategy

Another important issue is that many EC applications involve business partners with different organizational cultures and their own EC strategies. It is important to choose a partner whose strategy aligns with, or complements, your own. There are many potential partners. For example, companies that make B2B e-marketplaces may consider logistics, technology, and e-payment partners. What partners one chooses depends on a mutual meshing of strategic needs and also on one's out-sourcing strategy.

How to Coordinate B2B and B2C

Many companies are conducting both B2B and B2C e-commerce. One example of this is lego.com, which sells some products direct to customers but sells most of its products to retailers. The coordination between the two can be done in various ways, and it is important to make a strategic decision on how to do it during the implementation stage. For example, when you order one piece of software from Microsoft (a B2C transaction), your order will be fulfilled by a contractor. Large sales (B2B transactions) are handled directly by Microsoft.

- ▶ Describe a Web (project) team and its purpose.
- ▶ What is the purpose of a pilot project?
- ▶ Discuss the major strategy implementation issues.

11.5 STRATEGY AND PROJECT ASSESSMENT

The last phase of e-strategy is assessment, which is done periodically after the EC application is up and running. **Strategy assessment** involves the periodic formal evaluation of progress toward the organization's strategic goals. Based on the results, actions are taken and, if necessary, the strategy is reformulated. This phase involves the use of EC metrics.

strategy assessment
The periodic formal evaluation of progress toward the organization's strategic goals; may include needed actions and strategy reformulation.

THE OBJECTIVES OF ASSESSMENT

Strategic assessment has several objectives. The most important ones are:

- ▶ Find out if the EC project and strategy delivers what they were supposed to deliver.
- ▶ Determine if the EC project and strategy are still viable in the current environment.
- ▶ Reassess the initial strategy in order to learn from mistakes and improve future planning.
- ▶ Identify failing projects as soon as possible and determine why they failed to avoid the same problems on subsequent systems.

Web applications grow in unexpected ways, often expanding beyond their initial plan. For example, Genentec Inc., a biotechnology giant, wanted merely to replace a homegrown bulletin-board system. It started the project with a small budget, but soon found that the internal Web had grown rapidly and become very popular in a short span of time, encompassing many applications. Another example is Lockheed Martin, which initially planned to put its corporate phone directory and information about training programs on the intranet. Within a short time, many of its human resources documents were placed on the intranet as well, and soon thereafter, the use of the Web for internal information expanded from administrative purposes to collaborative commerce and partnership relationship management applications.

MEASURING RESULTS AND USING METRICS

Each company measures success or failure by different sets of standards. Some companies may find that their goals were unrealistic; that their Web server was inadequate to handle demand, or that expected cost savings were not realized. On the other hand, some may experience such a success that they have to respond to exploding application requests from various functional areas in the company.

Assessing EC is not simple because of the many configurations and impact variables involved. However, a review of the requirements and design documents should help answer many of the questions raised during the assessment. It is important that the Web team develop a thorough checklist to address both the evaluation of project performance and the assessment of a changing environment. One way to measure an organization's performance is to use *metrics*, which include benchmarks in different areas related to EC implementation and strategy.

EC Metrics

metric
A measurable standard or a target against which actual performance is compared.

A **metric** is a measurable standard, or a target against which actual performance is compared. Metrics can produce very positive results in organizations by driving behavior in a number of ways. According to Rayport and Jaworski (2001), metrics can help define and refine business models by specifying concrete goals with precise measurement. They also communicate strategy by specifying performance measures, helping to track performance, and increasing accountability by linking metrics to performance-appraisal programs. Finally, metrics help align objectives of individuals, departments, and organizations.

An example of EC metrics can be found in Voss (2000), where the following metrics for customer relationship management (CRM) are suggested:

- Response time to customers' enquiries (e.g., 24–hour limit)
- Response quality (percentage of the time that customers say they are satisfied with the company response)
- Security/trust level (how confident the customers are in the company's performance/service)
- Download time, especially of important material
- Timeliness of fulfillment
- How up-to-date information on products, prices, and services is
- Availability (how often customers are able to have what they want, when they want it, and where they want it)
- Site effectiveness, ease of use, and navigability (percentage of satisfied customers, number of complaints)

Note that metrics can be set as a strategy (e.g., "We respond in 12 hours, compared to the industry standard of 24"). For examples of other metrics, see Plant (2000) and metricnet.com.

Using Metrics: The Balanced Scorecard

An interesting proposal was made by Kaplan and Norton (1996) to use metrics to measure the health of organizations. In a structured methodology they call the **balanced scorecard**, they advocate that managers focus not only on short-term financial results, but also on four other areas for which metrics are available. These areas are:

> **Finance** (including both short- and long-term measures)

> **Customer** (how customers view the company)

> **Internal business process** (finding areas in which to excel)

> **Learning and growth** (ability to change and expand)

An implementation of the scorecard approach in EC was proposed by Plant (2000). He offered seven sets of metrics, covering the following areas: financial, markets, service, brand, competitive leadership, technology, and Internet site. For each of these, an organization can devise a subset of metrics and then compare actual results with goals and industry best practices. The scorecard can then be used to compute an overall score in each set of metrics, which can be tracked over time and related to strategies and modifications in strategies. The use of metrics is especially popular in e-marketing due to the ease with which Web site measurements (such as page views and click throughs) can be made (see Chapter 4 and Plant 2000).

balanced scorecard
A structured methodology for measuring performance in organizations, using metrics in four areas (finance, customers' assessments, internal business processes, and learning and growth).

Using Metrics: The Performance Dashcard

The balanced-scorecard approach has some limitations when applied to EC. Rayport and Jaworski (2001) have proposed a more suitable model called the **performance dashboard**. This model is divided into five desired outcomes and five corresponding metrics (see Exhibit 11.5 on page 478). Metrics are then mapped with leading and lagging indicators of performance, leading to calculated targets. Once performance measures are done, strategies can be evaluated and reformulated.

performance dashboard
A structured methodology proposed by Rayport and Jaworski (2001) for measuring EC performance using desired outcomes, corresponding metrics, and leading and lagging indicators of performance.

> Describe the need for assessment.

> Define metrics and provide some examples.

> Describe the scorecard approach.

> Describe the performance dashboard.

11.6 EC FAILURES AND LESSONS LEARNED

EC initiatives and EC companies are likely to fail. The reasons why they fail vary and depend on the circumstances. In this section we will look at some failures and attempt to identify the most common reasons for failure. Then we will try to derive from these lessons conclusions for avoiding such failures. This section is divided into three categories: e-tailing failures, failures of exchanges, and failures of individual EC initiatives. Remember as you read about the various failures that there is a domino

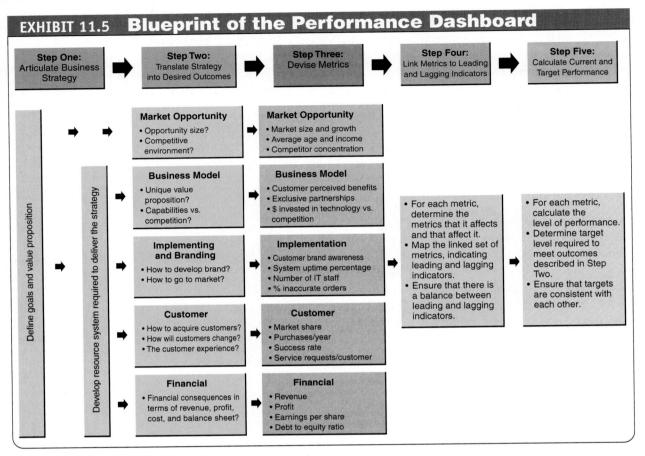

EXHIBIT 11.5 Blueprint of the Performance Dashboard

Source: Rayport and Jaworski, 2001, p. 270.

effect: With every dot-com failure, support companies and consultants that worked for dot-com companies suffered losses, or even failed too (Glater 2000).

FAILED E-TAILERS

E-tailing is the most publicized area of failure. During 2000 and 2001, several hundred e-tailers and related companies went out of business or were struggling, trying to prevent failure. For some examples of failed ventures, visit startupfailures.com and ghostsites at disobey.com.

One e-tailing area in which there have been numerous failures is the retail toy industry. Not only did a large number of companies fail (e.g., eToys), but even successful click-and-mortar companies such as Toys 'R' Us sustained heavy losses. Incidentally, the solution employed by Toys 'R' Us, moving e-tailing to a joint venture with amazon.com (see Chapter 3 for details), is a promising, but not guaranteed, strategy. And eToys is now back in business, with an affiliate program (eToys.com).

E-tailing failures have been recorded in many countries and industries, especially in commodity products such as toys, CDs, or books. Some of the reasons for failure were provided in Chapter 3: lack of profitability, excessive risk exposure, the high cost of branding, poor performance, and static Web site design. Two additional reasons are:

▶ **Lack of funding.** It takes a few years to acquire a large enough customer base to support an e-tail venture. Most of the failed companies "burned" (used up) all the cash they had before they had enough customers. Additional funding became very difficult to obtain. Investors in 2000 and 2001 were not willing to wait a long time for profits, figuring that the risk was too high. Typical examples of companies that ran out of funds are boo.com, garden.com, living.com, and etoys.com (now back in business with an affiliate program model; see etoys.com/affiliates/AffiliateLanding2.html).

▶ **Incorrect revenue model.** In the late 1990s, many companies used a business model in which the company would spend as much as it could on customer acquisition. The idea was that if you had millions of hits and visitors per month, advertisers would rush to your site. This model was proved to be incorrect; the advertising money did not come. Instead, the amount of advertising money on the Internet, which had been growing at an annual rate of over 100 percent, stopped growing, and even declined in late 2000 and 2001, due to a slowing economy and the disappearance of many dot-com companies. Also, the competition for advertising money grew rapidly, because hundreds of companies were trying to get some portion of it. With little revenue from sales or outside advertisers and big expenses, companies reached bankruptcy quickly.

FAILED EXCHANGES

In late 2000, the EC community was shocked to learn that chemdex.com had closed down. Chemdex was the "granddaddy" of the third-party exchanges, attracting lots of publicity and venture capital. The reasons for failure provided by Ventro.com, its parent company, were that the revenue growth was too slow and that they wanted to move to a new business model. (As reported at ventro.com, by 2002, Chemdex was mainly in the B2B software business.) It is predicted that as many as 90 percent of all exchanges will collapse (Ulph, Favier and O'Connell 2001). The major reason is the difficulty in obtaining enough buyers and sellers fast enough (before the cash disappears). See more in Chapter 6.

FAILED EC INITIATIVES

Whereas failing companies, especially publicly listed ones, are well advertised, failing EC initiatives within companies, especially within private companies, are less known. However, news about some failed EC initiatives has reached the media and been well advertised. For example, Levi Strauss stopped online direct sales of its apparel (jeans and its popular Dockers brand) on its Web site (levistrauss.com) after its major distributors and retailers put pressure on the company not to compete with their brick-and-mortar outlets. Furthermore, the site itself was poorly organized and managed. Another EC initiative that failed was a joint venture between Intel and SAP, two world-class companies, which was designed to develop low-cost solutions for SMEs. It collapsed in August 2000.

In addition to such channel conflict, initiatives fail due to poor planning, fast changing conditions, lack of cooperation from involved business partners, and lack of technical support.

ARE EC AND THE INTERNET DOOMED?

Some think that the EC failures and the fall of technology stocks in 2000 and 2001 means that EC is doomed (e.g., Mandel 2000). We do not believe that this is the case. We view the failures as a normal consolidation of an industry that was over-optimistic and driven by greed between 1996 and 2000. We see the failures as an example of history simply repeating itself: Between 1904 and 1908, more than 240 companies entered the then-new automobile business in the United States. In 1910 there was a shakeout, and today there are only three U.S. automakers. But the size of the auto industry has grown by *several hundredfold* since then. It is our belief that EC will go through a similar process.

Let's look at some success stories to see what it might take to be an Internet survivor.

SUCCESS STORIES AND LESSONS LEARNED

There are hundreds of EC success stories, primarily in specialty and niche markets. One example is puritan.com, a successful vitamin and natural heath care product store. Another one is campusfood.com, which serves take-out food to college students. Monster.com is doing very well, and so is Southwest Airlines Online (iflyswa.com). Alloy.com is a successful shopping and entertainment portal for young adults. For a comparison of how these and other thriving online businesses have translated critical success factors (CSFs) from the old economy into EC success, see Exhibit 11.6.

Here are some of the reasons for EC success and some suggestions from EC experts on how to succeed:

▶ Thousands of brick-and-mortar companies are slowly adding online channels, with great success. Examples are uniglobe.com, staples.com, homedepot.com, clearcommerce.com, 1–800 FLOWERS (800flowers.com), and Southwest Airlines (iflyswa.com).

▶ As of late 2000, more companies were pursuing mergers and acquisitions (e.g., ivillage.com with women.com, though each maintains its separate Web site). Mergers seem to be a growing trend (see Bodow 2000).

▶ Peter Drucker, the management guru, provides the following advice: "Analyze the opportunities, go out to look, keep it focused, start small (one thing at a time), and aim at market leadership" (Daly 2000).

▶ A group of Asian CEOs recommend the following CSFs: select robust business models, understand the dot-com future, foster e-innovation, carefully evaluate a spin-off strategy, co-brand, employ ex-dot-com staffers, and focus on the e-generation as your market (e.g., alloy.com and bolt.com) (Phillips 2000).

▶ Consultant PriceWaterhouseCoopers (pwcglobol.com) suggests avoiding technology malfunctions (e.g., inability to handle a surge of orders quickly enough), which erode consumer trust.

EXHIBIT 11.6 Critical Success Factors for EC

CSFs in the Old Economy	CSFs for EC Success
Vertically integrate or do it yourself	Create new partnerships and alliances, stay with core competency
Deliver high-value products	Deliver high-value service offerings that encompass products
Build share to establish economies of scale	Optimize natural scale and scope of business, look at mass customization
Analyze carefully to avoid missteps	Approach with urgency to avoid being locked out; use proactive strategies
Leverage physical assets	Leverage intangible assets, capabilities, and relationships—unleash dormant assets
Compete to sell product	Compete to control access and relationships with customers; compete with Web sites

▶ Many experts (e.g., emarketer.com, 2002) recommend contingency planning and preparing for disasters.

▶ Agrawal et al. (2001) suggest that companies should match a value proposition with customer segmentations, control extensions of product lines and business models, and avoid expensive technology.

▶ Huff et al. (1999) suggest the following critical success factors for e-commerce: add value, focus on a niche and then extend that niche, maintain flexibility, get the technology right, manage critical perceptions, provide excellent customer service, create effective connectedness, and understand Internet culture.

▶ Useem (2000) uncovered "12 truths" about how the Internet really works by analyzing the dot-com crash. You can find these "truths" on the book's Web site, prenhall.com/turban.

▶ What are the three major areas in which EC failures have occurred?

▶ List some reasons why B2C (e-tailing) companies fail.

▶ What are some CSFs in EC?

11.7 VIRTUAL COMMUNITIES

At this point in the chapter, we turn our attention from the EC strategy process to some topics related to its formulation and implementation. The first of these topics is virtual communities, which may be used as a major advertising and marketing vehicle.

A community is a group of people with some interest in common who interact with one another. A **virtual community** is one in which the interaction is done by

virtual community
A group of people with similar interests who interact with one another using the Internet.

using the Internet. Virtual communities, also known as *electronic communities* or *Internet communities*, parallel typical physical communities such as neighborhoods, clubs, or associations. Virtual communities offer several ways for members to interact, collaborate, and trade (see Exhibit 11.7). Similar to the click-and-mortar model, many physical communities have a Web site for Internet-related activities.

CHARACTERISTICS OF COMMUNITIES

Internet communities may have thousands or even millions of members. This is one major difference from physical communities, which are usually smaller. Another difference is that off-line communities are frequently confined to one geographical location, whereas only a few online communities are of this type.

Many thousands of communities exist on the Internet. Several communities are independent and are growing rapidly. For instance, GeoCities grew to 10 million members in less than 2 years, and has over 45 million members in 2002 (geocities.yahoo.com). GeoCities members can set up personal home pages on the site, and advertisers buy ad space targeted to community members. In order to understand the economic impact of electronic communities, let's see what they really are. We will start with some examples, shown in the nearby Insights and Additions box.

Internet communities can be classified in several ways. One possibility is to classify members as *traders*, *players*, *just friends*, *enthusiasts*, or *friends in need*. The most common classification is the one proposed by Armstrong and Hagel (1996) and Hagel and Armstrong (1997), who recognize four types of Internet communities, as shown in Exhibit 11.8 (page 484). (For a different, more complete classification, see that proposed by Schubert and Ginsburg 2000.)

EXHIBIT 11.7	**Elements of Interaction in a Community**
Category	**Element**
Communication	Bulletin boards (discussion groups)
	Chat rooms/threaded discussions (string Q&A)
	E-mail and instant messaging
	Private mailboxes
	Newsletters, "netzines" (electronic magazines)
	Web postings
	Voting
Information	Directories and yellow pages
	Search engine
	Member-generated content
	Links to information sources
	Expert advice
EC Element	Electronic catalogs and shopping carts
	Advertisements
	Auctions of all types
	Classified ads
	Bartering online

Insights and Additions   Examples of Communities

The following are examples of online communities.

▷ **Associations.** Many associations have a Web presence. These range from PTAs (Parent-Teacher Associations) to professional associations. An example of this type of community is the Australian Record Industry Association (*aria.com.au*).

▷ **Ethnic communities.** Many communities are country- or language-specific. An example of such a site is *elsitio.com*, which provides content for the Spanish- and Portuguese-speaking audiences in Latin America and the United States. Chinadotcom at *hongkong.com*, *sina.com*, and *sohu.com* cater to the world's large Chinese-speaking community.

▷ **Gender communities.** *Women.com* and *ivillage.com*, the two largest female-oriented communities, merged in 2001 in an effort to cut losses and to become profitable.

▷ **Affinity portals.** These are communities organized by interest, such as hobbies, vocations, political parties, unions (*workingfamilies.com*), and many, many more.

▷ **Catering to young people (teens and people in their early 20s).** Many companies see unusual opportunities here. Three communities of particular interest are *alloy.com*, *bolt.com*, and *blueskyfrog.com*. Alloy.com is based in the United Kingdom and claims to have over 10 million members. Bolt.com claims to have 4 million members and operates from the United States. Blueskyfrog.com operates from Australia, concentrating on cell phone users, and claims to have more than 1 million devoted members.

▷ **Mega communities.** GeoCities is one example of a mega community divided into many subcommunities. Owned by Yahoo!, it is by far the largest online community.

▷ **B2B online communities.** In Chapter 6 we introduced the "many-to-many" B2B exchanges. These are referred to by some as communities (e.g., Raisch, 2001 and *commerceone.com*). B2B exchanges support community programs such as technical discussion forums, interactive Webcasts, user-created product reviews, virtual conferences and meetings, experts' seminars, and user-managed profile pages. Classified ads can help members to find jobs or employers to find employees. Many also include industry news, directories, links to government and professional associations, and more. For example, PlasticsNet's 35,000 registered users generate thousands of classified advertisements every year. PlasticsNet also has searchable user profiles that allow users to submit contact information, Web links, and any personal or company information that they choose.

Rheingold (1993) believes that the Web is being transformed from just a communication and information-transfer tool into a social Web of communities. He thinks that every Web site should incorporate a place for people to chat. A community site should be an interesting place to visit, a kind of virtual community center. He believes it should be a place where discussions may range over many controversial topics.

EXHIBIT 11.8	Types of Communities
Community Type	**Description**
Transactions	Facilitate buying and selling (e.g., *ausfish.com.au*; see Real-World Case). Combine information portal with infrastructure for trading. Members are buyers, sellers, intermediaries, etc. Focused on a specific commercial area (e.g., fishing).
Purpose or interest	No trading, just exchange of information on a topic of mutual interest. Examples: The Motley Fool (*fool.com*) for investors; rugby fans congregate at the Fans Room at *nrl.com.au*; music lovers go to *mp3.com*. *City411.com* is a directory for cities and their entertainment, weather reports, etc., organized by city. *Geocities.com* is a collection of several areas of interest in one place.
Relations or practice	Members are organized around certain life experiences. Examples: *ivillage.com* caters to women; *seniornet.com* to senior citizens, and chinadotcom at *hongkong.com* to Chinese-speaking people. Professional communities also belong to this category. Examples: *isworld.org* for information systems faculty, students, and professionals; *energycentral.com* for energy-industry traders.
Fantasy	Members share imaginary environments. Examples: sport fantasy teams at *espn.com*; Geocities members can pretend to be a medieval barons at *geocities.com/timessquare/4076*. See *games.yahoo.com* for many more fantasy communities.

Sources: Armstrong and Hagel (1996) and Hagel and Armstrong (1997).

Internet communities also are closely related to EC. For example, Champy et al. (1996) describe online, consumer-driven markets in which most of the consumers' needs, ranging from finding a mortgage to job hunting, are arranged from a community Web site. This enables vendors to sell more and community members to get discounts. Internet communities will eventually have a massive impact on almost every company that produces consumer goods or services, and they could change the nature of corporate advertisement and community sponsorship strategy and the manner in which business is done. Although this process is slow, we can see some of the initial commercial development changes.

COMMERCIAL ASPECTS OF COMMUNITIES

Forrester Research conducted a survey in 1998 that found the following expected payback for organizations that sponsor online communities (in descending order of importance): increases in (1) customer loyalty, (2) sales, (3) customer participation and feedback, (4) repeat traffic to the site, and (5) new traffic to the site (Chatham, et al. 1998).

A logical step as a community site grows in number of members and influence may be to turn it into a commercial site. Examples of such community-commercial sites include ivillage.com and geocities.yahoo.com. *Interactive Week* (May 11, 1998) provides the following suggestions on how to make the transformation from a community site to a commercial one:

- Understand a particular niche industry, its information needs, and the step-by-step process by which it does the research needed to do business.
- Build a site that provides that information, either through partnerships with existing information providers or by gathering it independently.
- Set up the site to mirror the steps a user goes through in the information-gathering and decision-making process (e.g., how a chip designer whittles down the list of possible chips that will fit a particular product).
- Build a community that relies on the site for decision support.
- Start selling products and services that fit into the decision-support process (such selling sample chips to engineers).

Electronic communities can create value in several ways, as summarized in Exhibit 11.9. Members input useful information to the community in the form of

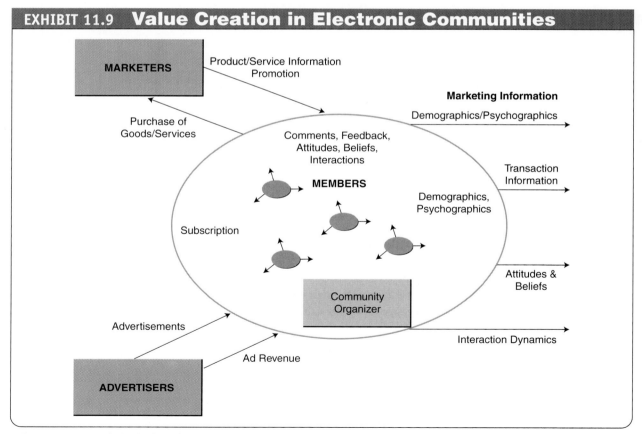

EXHIBIT 11.9 Value Creation in Electronic Communities

Source: Kannen et al. "Marketing Information on the I-Way," Vol. 41, No. 3, March © 1998, ACM, Inc., p. 35–40. Used with permission.

comments and feedback, elaborating on their attitudes and beliefs and information needs. This information can then be retrieved and used by other members or by marketers. The community organizers may also supply their own content to communities, as America Online does.

Also, some communities charge members content fees for downloading certain articles, music, or pictures, thus producing sales revenue for the site. Finally, since community members create their own home pages, it is easy to learn about them and reach them with targeted advertisements and marketing.

Financial Viability of Communities

The revenue model of communities is one based on sponsorship, sales commissions, and advertising. The expenses for communities are very high due to the need to provide fresh content and free services. In addition, most communities initially provide free membership. The objective is to have as many registered members as possible in order to attract advertisers.

This model has not worked very well. Several communities that were organized for profit, such as ivillage.com and elsitio.com, sustained heavy losses. Several other communities ceased operations in 2000 and 2001 (e.g., esociety.com). The trend toward mergers and acquisitions among communities, started in 2001, is expected to improve the financial viability of some communities.

KEY STRATEGIES FOR SUCCESSFUL ONLINE COMMUNITIES

The management consulting company Accenture outlined the following eight critical factors for community success (see details in Duffy 1999):

1. Increase traffic and participation in the community.
2. Focus on the needs of the members; use facilitators and coordinators.
3. Encourage free sharing of opinions and information—no controls.
4. Financial sponsorship is a must. Significant investment is required.
5. Consider the cultural environment.
6. Communities are not just discussion groups; provide several tools and activities for member use.
7. Community members must be involved in activities and recruiting.
8. Communities need to guide discussions, provoke controversy, and raise sticky issues.

Examples of some interesting communities that use one or more of these principles of success include the following: earthweb.com, icollector.com, webMD.com, terra.es, eslcafe.com, tradingdirect.com, icq.com, letsbuyit.com, barclays.co.uk, paltalk.com, radiolinja.fi, and projectconnections.com. (For more details and discussion of communities, see Raisch 2001; Preece 2000; and McWilliam 2000.)

▶ Define virtual (Internet) communities and describe their characteristics.

▶ List the major categories of communities.

▶ Describe the commercial aspects of communities.

▶ Describe the CSFs for communities.

11.8 GOING GLOBAL

A global electronic marketplace means access to larger markets, mobility (e.g., to minimize taxes), and flexibility to employ workers and manufacture products anywhere using a worldwide telecommuting workforce. The potential for a global economy is certainly here. However, going global may be complex due to a multiplicity of issues. Although geographical borders are falling, artificial borders are being erected through local language preferences, local regulations, access limitations, and so on. Thus the decision about going global is usually a strategic one.

BENEFITS AND EXTENT OF OPERATIONS

Global electronic activities have existed for more than 25 years, mainly in support of B2B financial and other repetitive, standard transactions. Most well known are the EFT and EDI. However, these activities were supported by expensive and inflexible private telecommunications lines and, therefore, were limited mostly to large corporations. The emergence of the Internet and extranets has resulted in an inexpensive and flexible infrastructure that can greatly facilitate global trade.

The major advantage of EC is the ability to do business at any time and from anywhere, and to do so rapidly at a reasonable cost. Indeed, we have seen some incredible success stories in this area. For example:

▶ You can buy and sell stocks in several countries using E*TRADE or boom.com as your broker.

▶ Exchanges such as e-Steel and ChemConnect have members in dozens of countries.

▶ Amazon.com sells books to individuals and organizations in over 190 countries.

▶ Small companies, such as Evineyard, Inc. (virtualvin.com), sell to hundreds of customers worldwide. Hothothot, for example, which has both a physical and online stores (hothothot.com), reported its first international trade only after it went online. Within 2 years, Hothothot's global sales climbed from zero to 25 percent of its total sales.

▶ Major corporations, such as General Electric and Boeing Inc., reported an increasing number of out-of-the-country vendors participating in their electronic requests for quotes. These electronic bids resulted in a 10 to 15 percent cost reduction and an over 50 percent reduction in cycle time.

▶ Many international corporations considerably increased their success in recruiting employees for foreign locations when online recruiting was utilized.

▶ Several global trading exchanges have been created in the last few years. A successful collaboration of B2B exchanges is described in the Insights and Additions box on the next page.

Insights and Additions   The Global Trading Web

The Global Trading Web (GTW) exemplifies globalization in the context of e-marketplaces. The Global Trading Web, founded by Commerce One, is the world's largest global online B2B trading community (more than 150,000 suppliers; see Global Trading Web at *commerceone.com*). It connects businesses via regional e-marketplaces located in the United States, Asia, Europe, the Middle East, and Africa. As of spring 2002, the GTW comprised about 100 global e-marketplaces. It enables companies to interact and conduct business with anyone, any time, anywhere. Linked together, the GTW e-marketplaces provide a common infrastructure that is similar to the Internet. As the number of users increases, so does its liquidity.

GTW provides global trading efficiencies through online aggregation. Each e-marketplace has access to the products, sources, and services of others, extending the market of buyers and suppliers bidirectionally. These ad hoc partnerships enable e-marketplaces to share economic advantages, such as access to trading partners and value-added services, in order to eliminate redundant development efforts. They speed time-to-market and increase return on investment. Through GTW, local markets in different parts of the world can be addressed in their native languages and according to their culture.

Some major players in GTW are:

▶ Asia: Asia2B (China), NTT Marketsite (Japan), *sesami.net* (Singapore).

▶ Europe: BT MarketSite (United Kingdom), DT Marketplace (Germany), Opciona (Spain), PT Electronic (Portugal), Swisscom (Switzerland).

▶ North America: City Group, *commerceone.com*, Enporion, eScout, Exostar, Pantellos (all from the United States); TD MarketSite (Canada), Artikos (Mexico).

▶ Multiple countries: Covisint, Concert, Metique, Trade Alliance Trade-Ranger, and *gtwa.net*.

Source: *commerceone.com*.

BARRIERS TO GLOBAL EC

Despite the trend toward globalization, there are many barriers to global EC. Some are similar to barriers to any EC venture (Chapter 1). We divide our discussion of those specific to global EC into four categories: legal, market-access, financial, and other issues.

Legal Issues

The U.S. government and major international organizations such as the European Union, the United Nations Commission on International Trade Law (UNCITRAL), the Organization for Economic Cooperation and Development (OECD), and the World Trade Organization (WTO) are presently engaged in discussions pertaining to the development of domestic and global legal frameworks that will facilitate global EC. Among these organizations there seems to be a consensus only to the extent that uncoordinated actions must be avoided and that an international policy of cooperation should be encouraged.

Market-Access Issues

Market-access issues, if not addressed, could impede the growth of global EC. Building a telecommunications infrastructure capable of accommodating all users and all types of data is a necessity. Companies starting EC need to evaluate bandwidth needs by analyzing the data required, time constraints, access demands, and user technology limitations. Monitoring and complying with technical standards will also minimize, if not eliminate, the possibility of incompatible technologies between the company and the user.

Financial Issues

Financial issues encompassing global EC include tariffs and customs, taxation, and electronic payment systems.

It is difficult to administer tariffs for products ordered over the Internet and delivered electronically. Many countries may want to add tariffs to the products, increasing the price to the consumer or business. All products delivered the traditional way still must go through customs, which lengthens the amount of time it takes for the customer to receive the merchandise. The biggest time savings are reached in delivery of digitized products. Thus far, such purchases are not subject to sales taxes and tariffs. However, the tax freeze is on for only a few years, and its future is uncertain. This issue may have a large impact on the success of global EC.

Pricing is another issue. The same products from the same vendors may carry different prices in different countries because prices are set by considering local prices and competition. If a company has one Web site, what price will it charge people in different countries? What currencies will be used for payment?

This brings us to the issue of currency exchange. All electronic payment systems will need to be able to exchange currency at current rates. (This issue is minimized for customers when credit cards are used, as credit card issuers generally take care of the currency exchange for international purchases.) Also important is the integration of the EC transaction with the accounting/finance internal information system of the sellers.

Another issue related to finance is the financial justification and the initial investment required to go global. Even assuming the financial justification can be made, the initial investment can so load the company with debt that it cannot survive unless it has immediate market success. An example of this is boo.com, which expanded to 18 countries but folded in 2000 as a result of the cost of its expansion. (It was revived in 2001.)

A final interesting issue related to finance is that, with the proper planning, even the smallest businesses can go global with unprecedented low costs. EC Application Case 11.3 (page 490) discusses one such example. The global marketspace erases national borders and gives even the smallest companies worldwide reach. For example, Schwartz (1997) reported that a small company in Gilbert, Arizona, generated half of its international trade on the Web during its first year, and that its international trade

EC APPLICATION CASE 11.3
Interorganization and Collaboration
A SMALL BUSINESS GOES GLOBAL

Cardiac Science of Irvine, California, had been trying to break into the international market for years. The company makes cardiac medical devices, and within 2 years after the Internet inception in the company, it was shipping its products to 46 countries. Today, 85 percent of the company's revenue is international, and much of this is executed over its Web site (*cardiacscience.com*). The company answers inquiries within 24 hours, linking product information to promising sales leads.

Small businesses need a great deal of advice in going global. Cardiac found the following Web sites to be useful:

▶ Universal Business Exchange (*unibex.com*) offers trade leads with the added capability of matching buyers and sellers automatically.

▶ Several government agencies provide online information for nominal fees (e.g., National Trade Data Bank, Economic Bulletin Board, and Globus; all can be accessed from *stat-usa.gov*).

The global Web business is not as simple as some may think. In a TV interview, Cardiac's CEO said that "crafting a solid export strategy takes a lot more commitment than putting up a snazzy Web site and waiting for the world to show up at our door. It's all about building relationships." The Internet is important for introductions, but you must follow it up properly.

Source: cardiacscience.com.

Questions

▶ What are the CSFs of the online operations of this company?

▶ Visit the sources of data suggested in the case and describe their usefulness.

was growing at a rate of 50 percent per year. Going global may be attractive, yet very risky, to small- and medium-sized companies (see Hornby et al. 2000).

Other Issues

Several other issues need to be considered in global EC. Some of these are EC-generic, and have been discussed in earlier chapters: authentication of buyers and sellers (Chapter 9), trust (Chapter 4), order fulfillment and delivery (Chapter 10), security (e.g., protection against viruses) (Chapter 9), and domain names (Chapter 9). Others are unique to global EC. In the remainder of this section, we will look at three such issues: language and translation, localization, and cultural diversity.

Language and Translation The language barrier between countries and regions presents an interesting and complicated challenge for global EC. Although English is widely accepted as the primary language of the Internet, in some cases an effective Web site may need to be specifically designed and targeted to the country that it is trying to reach. EC Application Case 11.4 discusses, for example, ways to target Japanese customers. (Also, see the discussion at tradecompass.com.)

The primary problems with language translation, especially with regards to customization, are cost and speed. It currently takes a human translator about a week to manually translate a medium-size Web site into just one language, and it

Implementation and Strategy

ATTRACTING JAPANESE CUSTOMERS TO YOUR SITE

The Japanese love to shop online, however, most Japanese do not read English. When William Hunt tried to market his earthquake kit in Japan's largest department stores, he had very few buyers. So his wife, a native of Hiroshima, helped him develop a Web site in Japanese. Now the Hunts have moved into a new business: They help small companies market online to Japan in Japanese.

The company, English-Japanese Promotion (now *ajpr.com*), helps clients avoid the mistakes entrepreneurs often make when they try to sell to the Japanese. Forget about scoring big with an English-only Web site. "You wouldn't market a car in Japan using an English ad campaign," the Hunts say. Also, they note, people too often overlook Japanese-only Web search engines. It is not hard to see why those listings are critical. The more your target audience sees your site, the better.

Of course, the site should be inviting to the visitors when they get there. For example, the Hunts encourage clients to state their return policies on their Web site. The Japanese are understandably leery of overseas companies, and an explicit return policy seems to ease their worries. Also, the company's translators are quick to alert companies when their logos or themes are likely to strike a sour chord with Japanese sensibilities. Finally, the Hunts may well suggest that clients have mascots. Japanese

audiences, it seems, respond positively to the use of symbols or characters.

The Hunts caution that if your product is not one that will fly with Japanese males in their twenties and thirties, there probably isn't much the Web can do for you. What are the hottest Web-marketed products in Japan? Outdoor sporting goods, computer software, popular music CDs, and gourmet-cooking items.

The company also provides help to Japanese companies who want an English version of their site. It provides localization advice as well. In 2002, services available included advertising, document translation, and various consulting services.

Sources: *Interactive Week*, February 2000 and *ajpr.com*.

Questions

▶ How is *ajpr.com* related to i-Mode (*nttdocomo.com/imode*)? (Visit both sites.)

▶ What are the particular benefits of *ajpr.com* to small businesses?

▶ What are the advantages of using *ajpr.com*'s services over automatic Web-page translation? What are the disadvantages?

costs about $2,000 to do so. For larger sites the cost ranges from $10,000 to $500,000, depending on the complexity of the site and languages of translation.

WorldPoint (worldpoint.com) presents a creative solution to these translation issues with its WorldPoint Passport multilingual software tool, which allows Web developers to create a Web site in one language and deploy it in several other languages. The cost of translation using the software is estimated at 24 to 26 cents per word. In a 1999 demonstration of the software's power, WorldPoint translated Japan's primary telephone company's (NTT) Web site into 10 different Asian languages in only 3 days (Lloyd, 1999).

Traditionally, automatic translation has been inaccurate. Therefore, many experts have advocated manual translation with the help of the computer as a productivity booster. However, as time passes, automatic translation is improving.

Localization In Chapter 4, we introduced the concept of localization as it relates to advertising. Companies are realizing that just translating Web content from one language to another is woefully inadequate to attract a global audience. In response, some Web sites are opting to localize content, including adapting local business practices for employees, partners, suppliers, and customers within the target country or ethnic group. This factor is particularly important as more users worldwide begin using Web browsers, cell phones, pagers, PDAs, and wireless systems to access an enterprise's Web site. For example, marketing and sales messages must be adapted to appeal to specific audiences, and purchasing data (e.g., product prices calculated in local currencies and terms and conditions based on local laws) must be made available. And because no successful online enterprise remains static, companies must keep their multiple international sites synchronized as content changes.

Many companies offer different sites in other countries. For example, there is an eBay site and a Yahoo! site in the United Kingdom, different from the sites for those companies in the United States. Chinadotcom at hongkong.com and sina.com ask users on the main menu to select a country, and the user finds sites customized by country. For more on localization, see Fessenden and Dwyer (2000) and tradecompass.com.

Culture Increasingly, the Internet is becoming a multifaceted marketplace made up of users from multiple cultures. These multiple cultures warrant different marketing approaches—something that marketers may overlook. Even the way different groups access the Internet plays a significant role in deciding how to target them. Whether they access from home, work, or Internet cafes is often linked to the GDP and availability of the Internet in a specific country. The culture also has an impact on how consumers prefer to do business and pay for it.

To tap the potential of the various cultures shopping on the Internet, marketers must adapt their efforts to the ways different groups of people make online purchase decisions. Although credit cards are widely used in the United States, many European and Asian customers complete online transactions with off-line payments. Even within the category of off-line payments, companies must offer different options depending on the country. For example, French consumers prefer to pay with a check, Swiss consumers expect an invoice by mail, Germans commonly pay for products upon delivery, and Swedes are accustomed to paying online with debit cards.

For further discussion of cultural issues, see DePalma (2000). DePalma introduces the concept of *cultural* or *ethnic marketing*, a strategy for meeting the needs of a culturally diverse population.

BREAKING DOWN THE BARRIERS TO GLOBAL EC

Experts from Idiom, Inc. (idiomtech.com) have made the following suggestions on how to break down the barriers to global EC that have been discussed (Josephson, 2001). Some of their suggestions include:

- **Value the human touch.** Trust the translation of your Web site content only to human translators, not automatic translation programs or machine translation tools.

- **Be strategic.** Identify your starting point and lay out a globalization strategy. Remember that Web globalization is a business-building process. Consider what languages and countries it makes sense for you to target and how you will need to support the site for each target audience.

▶ **Know your audience.** Carefully consider whom it is you want to reach. Be fully informed of the cultural preferences and legal issues that matter to your customers in a particular part of the world.

▶ **Be a perfectionist.** Involve several language and technical editors in your quality assurance process. One slight mistranslation or one out-of-place graphic will turn off your customers.

▶ **Remember, it is the Web.** One of the many things people have come to expect from the Internet is up-to-date information. This means that any Web site—especially global Web sites—should be kept current.

▶ **Integrate properly.** Web globalization should integrate seamlessly into the existing Web development architecture, complementing and enhancing existing content management and workflow systems.

▶ **Keep the site flexible.** Flexibility is the key to successful globalization. The site must respond to change.

▶ **Synchronize content.** Global online businesses must synchronize the publication of content, product offerings, interactive applications, and other corporate information across their multiple international sites.

A final bit of advice on breaking down the global barriers to EC is to consult the OECD. A major OECD report, "Dismantling the Barriers to Global Electronic Commerce," is available online at tradedata.net/cibre/tinfo/industry/e-com.htm. This report touches on all the issues discussed in this chapter and more.

▶ Describe globalization in EC and the advantages it presents.

▶ Describe the major limitations and barriers to global EC.

▶ Discuss the removal of barriers to global EC.

11.9 EC IN SMALL- AND MEDIUM-SIZE ENTERPRISES

Some of the first companies to take advantage of EC on the Web were, in fact, small companies (SMEs), many of which were start-ups. Prime examples are virtualvin.com, hothothot.com, and happypuppy.com. In this section we explore the advantages and opportunities, the disadvantages and risks, and the critical success factors for small- and medium-size enterprises in the Web economy. The major advantages and disadvantages of EC for SMEs are listed in the Insights and Additions box on page 494.

In a survey conducted in Hong Kong in 2002, of 2,033 SMEs surveyed, about 55 percent said they had implemented EC (Luk 2002). This was a 48.6 percent increase over a study conducted 6 months earlier. However, 39 percent of those surveyed use the Internet only for e-mail. Of the 45 percent that do not have EC, most (96 percent) said that they simply do not need EC.

Insights and Additions — Advantages and Disadvantages of EC for Small- and Medium-Size Businesses

ADVANTAGES/BENEFITS	DISADVANTAGES/RISKS
▶ Inexpensive source of information	▶ Inability to use the expensive EDI, unless it is EDI/Internet
▶ Inexpensive way of advertising	▶ Lack of resources to fully exploit the Web
▶ Inexpensive way of conducting market research	▶ Lack of expertise in legal issues, advertisement, etc.
▶ Inexpensive way to build (or rent) a storefront	▶ Less risk tolerance than a large company
▶ Lower transaction costs	▶ Disadvantage when a commodity is the product (e.g., CDs)
▶ Niche market; specialty products (cigars, wines, sauces) are the best	▶ No personal contact with customers (normally a strong point of a small business)
▶ Image and public recognition can be generated quickly	▶ No advantage of being in a local community
▶ Inexpensive way of providing catalogs	
▶ Inexpensive way and opportunity to reach worldwide customers	

There are basically two contradictory opinions regarding EC and SMEs. The first one is that EC is a blessing (e.g., see O'Connor and O'Keefe 1997 for arguments and success stories). The second is that SMEs will not be able to benefit from EC or even survive in the digital economy. There undoubtedly is some truth in both opinions, depending on variables such as the type of business, the industry in which it competes, and the predisposition of the owners to take risk (or not).

CRITICAL SUCCESS FACTORS FOR SMES

EC success for small businesses is not a just matter of chance. Considerable research has been done to allow us to identify the critical success factors that help determine whether a small business will succeed in EC. One very important factor is the choice of the product or service a company offers online. The Insights and Additions box at the top of page 495 lists typical products and services successfully sold online by small businesses.

Critical success factors for small EC businesses can also include the use of certain business strategies. Many of the small businesses that have succeeded on the Internet, either as click-and-mortar or as virtual businesses, have the following strategies in common:

▶ Capital investment should be kept to a minimum to keep the company's overhead and risk low.

▶ Inventory should be minimal or nonexistent.

▶ Electronic payments must be transmitted using secure means to reassure customers. Small businesses can work with vendors to provide this service.

Insights and Additions   Products and Services Successfully Sold Online by Small Businesses

Small businesses have had online success mainly by selling specific products or services, such as the following.

▶ Niche products, such as those with a low volume that are not carried by regular retail stores (e.g., *dogtoys.com*).

▶ Specialty books (e.g., old or technical books; see *powells.com*, which sells old and new technical books).

▶ International products that are not easily available off-line to consumers (e.g., ethnic foods; see *sunshinefoods.com*).

▶ A wide spectrum of companies offer information online. Smaller companies may choose to provide specialized information such as home and gardening pages. Revenue could come from home and garden retailers who place advertisements on the small business's Web page.

▶ Localized markets (e.g., *ausfish.com.au*).

▶ Payment methods must be flexible to accommodate different levels of users. Some customers prefer to mail or fax in a form or talk to a live agent rather than transmit a credit card number over the Internet.

▶ Logistical services must be quick and reliable. Many small businesses have successfully subcontracted out their logistical services to FedEx, which is an expert in the field.

▶ The Web site should be submitted to directory-based search engine services such as Yahoo!

▶ The company should become a member of an online service or mall, such as AOL or ViaWeb's Viamall.

▶ A Web site must be designed to be functional and provide all the services needed by consumers. In addition, the Web site should look professional enough to compete with larger competitors and be updated on a continual basis to maintain consumer interest.

For further discussion of EC and SMEs, including global aspects, see workz.com.

Although there are many risks associated with EC, overall, the level of risk associated with starting an online operation would be less for a small business than for a brick-and-mortar business (which requires much more capital). In addition, many businesses that could not have survived outside of the Internet have been able to thrive due to the lower cost of entry (e.g., cattoys.com or ausfish.com.au). Finally, small businesses can combine forces, for example, by jointly developing a storefront. They also may share the use of EC applications through group purchasing, as described in Chapter 5.

SUPPORTING SMALL BUSINESSES

There are many ways in which support is provided to small businesses. For example, technical support can be provided by IBM (for a fee of only $25 per month; see Small Business Center at ibm.com); Digital's virtual stores; and Microsoft's Personal

Web Server (PWS). Governments even provide support for small-business EC. For example, the U.S. government is encouraging small businesses to take advantage of EC opportunities (see ecommerce.gov).

In addition, Gartner Group, an IT research company, provides access to online research material about EC to which users can subscribe. Such material may be of help to small businesses.

▶ What are the advantages of being small in cyberspace?

▶ What are the disadvantages?

▶ What are the CSFs for small businesses online?

11.10   BPR AND VIRTUAL CORPORATIONS

As you may recall from the opening vignette about IBM, it is sometimes necessary to restructure business processes before installing EC applications. Furthermore, the introduction of EC may significantly change not only the organizational climate, but also the manner in which the entire organization operates. In other words, old-economy organizations sometimes must change to meet the new economy. When such a change is drastic, this process of changing an organization to a new mode of operation may be referred to as an **organizational transformation**.

REDESIGN OF ENTERPRISE PROCESSES AND BUSINESS PROCESS REENGINEERING

Some people believe that before introducing EC, it is necessary to conduct a comprehensive redesign of an enterprise's processes in a methodology called **business process reengineering (BPR)**. This is rarely the case. However, as in many other IT projects, it is frequently necessary to restructure *individual* processes.

Redesign or BPR may be needed in the following cases:

▶ It does not make sense to automate poorly designed processes.

▶ It may be necessary to change processes so they will fit commercially available software.

▶ A fit is required between systems and processes of different companies that are partnering in e-commerce.

▶ It is necessary to change processes to fit the procedures and standards of public e-marketplaces.

▶ It is necessary to adjust procedures and processes so they will be aligned with e-services such as logistics, payments, or security.

▶ It is necessary to make changes to assure flexibility and scalability.

Such restructuring may be very complex when many business partners are involved in one exchange. A major tool used in conjunction with redesign is workflow technology.

organizational transformation
The process of completely or drastically transforming an entire organization to a new mode of operation.

business process reengineering (BPR)
A methodology for comprehensive redesign of an enterprise's processes.

WORKFLOW TECHNOLOGIES

Workflow is the movement of information as it flows through the sequence of steps that make up an organization's work procedures. A **workflow system** is a set of software programs that manage all the steps in a business process from start to finish, including all exception conditions. Workflow applications are usually based on the organization's established business rules. The key to workflow management is the tracking of process-related information and the status of each activity of the process as it moves through an organization.

workflow system
Software programs that manage all the steps in a business process from start to finish, including all exception conditions.

Workflow applications fall into two categories:

▶ **Collaborative workflow.** This type of workflow refers to those products that address project-oriented and collaborative types of processes. They are administered centrally, yet they are capable of being accessed and used by knowledge workers from different departments and even from different physical locations. The focus of an enterprise solution for collaborative workflow is on allowing workers to communicate and collaborate within a unified environment. Some leading vendors of collaborative workflow applications are Lotus, JetForm, FileNet, and Action Technologies.

▶ **Production workflow.** Production workflow tools address mission-critical, transaction-oriented processes. They are often deployed only in a single department or to a certain set of users within a department. Often, these applications include document image storage and retrieval capabilities. They also can include the use of intelligent forms, database access, and ad hoc capabilities. The leading vendors of workflow applications are FileNet and Staffware.

A major area for EC workflow applications is the aggregation of sellers or buyers, which was described in Chapter 5. When large suppliers or buyers are involved, a workflow system is needed for both the collaborative efforts and for supply chain and production improvements.

VIRTUAL CORPORATIONS: NETWORKING BETWEEN BUSINESS PARTNERS

One of the most interesting EC-related organizational structures is the virtual corporation (VC). There are several types of virtual corporations, as well as several definitions. Some define a virtual corporation as a pure-play (purely online) EC company such as E*TRADE, amazon.com, or AOL. In the conventional economy, a **virtual corporation** is an organization composed of several business partners sharing costs and resources for the production or purchasing of a product or service. The partners can come to one physical place or they may be in different locations. Some can be pure-play EC players. We will use this definition because it is more accepted in the business community.

virtual corporation
An organization composed of several business partners (some of whom may be pure-play EC players) sharing costs and resources for the production or purchasing of a product or service.

It is common to distinguish between *permanent* virtual corporations and temporary ones. Permanent virtual corporations are designed to create or assemble productive resources rapidly, frequently, or concurrently, or to create or assemble a broad range of productive resources. In contrast, a temporary virtual corporation is created for a specific purpose and exists only for a short time.

Virtual corporations are not necessarily organized along the supply chain. For example, a business partnership may include several partners, each creating a portion of products or a service in an area in which its has special advantage, such as expertise or low cost. The modern virtual corporation can be viewed as a network of creative people, resources, and ideas connected by online services and/or the Internet.

The major attributes of virtual corporations are:

▶ **Excellence.** Each partner brings its core competence, creating an all-star winning team.

▶ **Utilization.** Resources of the individual business partners are frequently underutilized. A VC can utilize them more profitably.

▶ **Opportunism.** A VC can find and meet market opportunity better than an individual company.

▶ **Lack of borders.** It is difficult to identify the boundaries of a virtual corporation—it redefines traditional boundaries.

▶ **Trust.** Business partners in a VC must be far more reliant on each other and require more trust than ever before.

▶ **Adaptability to change.** The virtual corporation can adapt quickly to environmental changes because its structure is relatively simple.

▶ **Technology.** Information technology makes the VC possible. A networked information system is a must.

Another important critical success factor for virtual corporations is superb collaboration, which is provided by B2B technologies and collaborative commerce.

▶ Describe BPR and organizational transformation.

▶ Define workflow and relate it to BPR.

▶ Describe virtual corporations.

11.11   THE FUTURE OF EC

Generally speaking, the consensus regarding the future of EC is that it is bright. Analysts differ in their predictions about the anticipated growth rate of EC and the identification of industry segments that will grow the fastest. However, based on the following factors and trends, there is general optimism about the future of EC.

NONTECHNICAL SUCCESS FACTORS

The rosy scenario for the future of EC is based partially on the following nontechnical factors and trends.

1. **Internet usage.** The number of Internet users is increasing exponentially. With the integration of computers and television, cheaper PCs, Internet access via mobile devices, increased availability of access kiosks, and increased publicity,

there will be more and more Internet surfers. As younger people grow older, the usage will grow even faster. There is no question that sooner or later there will be a billion people who surf the Internet. By 2002, the number of worldwide Internet users was estimated to be 450 million, including more than half of the U.S. population (ipsos-reid.com/us/services/dsp_little_net_book.cfm, 2002).

2. **Opportunities for buying.** The number of products and services available online is increasing rapidly with improved trading mechanisms, intermediary services, presentations in multiple languages, and the willingness of more sellers and buyers to give EC a try. It is logical to expect significantly more purchasing opportunities. Several Web sites are reporting 50 to 60 percent annual sales increases.

3. **M-commerce.** With over 1.1 billion people using cell phones (2002) (emarketer. com, 2001) (Casonato, 2002), the ease with which one can connect from them to the Internet, and the forthcoming 3G capabilities, it is clear that m-commerce will play a major role in EC. The fact that you do not need a computer to go online will bring more and more people to the Web. M-commerce, as discussed in Chapter 8, has special capabilities that will result in new applications as well as in more people using traditional applications.

4. **Purchasing incentives.** The buyers' advantages described in Chapter 1 are likely to increase. Prices will go down, and the purchasing process will be streamlined. Many innovative options will be available, and electronic shopping may even become a social trend. For organizations, e-procurement is becoming the most attractive EC initiative.

5. **Increased security and trust.** One of the major inhibitors of B2C growth is the perception of poor security and privacy and a lack of trust. As time passes, we expect significant improvements in these areas.

6. **Efficient information handling.** More information will become accessible from anywhere, in real time. Using data warehouses, data mining, and intelligent agents, companies can constantly learn about their customers, steering marketing and service activities accordingly. The notion of real-time marketing might not be so far away. This will facilitate the use of EC.

7. **Innovative organizations.** Organizations are being restructured and reengineered with the help of IT (Turban et al. 2002, Hammer and Stanton 1995). Using different types of empowered teams, some of which are virtual, organizations become innovative, flexible, and responsive. The trend for process reengineering is increasing, as is organizational creativity. Innovative organizations will probably be more inclined to use EC.

8. **Virtual communities.** Virtual communities of all kinds are spreading rapidly, with some already reaching several million members. Virtual communities can enhance commercial activities online. Also, some communities are organized around professional areas of interest and can facilitate B2B commerce.

9. **Payment systems.** The ability to use e-cash and make micropayments online is spreading quickly; when these systems are implemented on a large scale, many EC activities will flourish. As international standards become the norm, electronic payments will extend globally, facilitating global EC.

10. **B2B EC.** Figures about the growth of B2B are being revised frequently. In some cases, industry-type extranets are forcing almost everyone to participate. B2B will continue to dominate the EC field (in terms of volume traded) for the intermediate future. There will be more sellers, more buyers, and more services; the rapid growth will continue. The success of B2B (as well as B2C) will depend upon the success of integrating EC technology with business processes and with conventional information systems.

11. **B2B exchanges.** In 2000, the number of B2B exchanges exploded. After the collapse of many exchanges in 2001, a few are maturing, providing the infrastructure for $5 to $8 trillion of B2B trade forecasted by 2005 by Forrester.com, in 2001. However, company-centric marketplaces will account for the majority of the B2B trade.

12. **Auctions.** The popularity of auctions and reverse auctions is increasing rapidly in B2B, B2C, G2B, and C2C. This is an effective and efficient EC business model.

13. **Going global.** One of the most appealing benefits of EC is the ability to go global. However, many barriers exist to global EC. These are expected to be reduced with time, but at a fairly slow pace.

14. **E-government.** Starting in 1999, many governments launched comprehensive G2C, G2B, G2G, and G2E projects. By 2002 over 120 countries had established e-government programs.

15. **Intrabusiness EC.** Many companies are starting to discover opportunities for using EC in-house, particularly in improving the internal supply chain and communications.

16. **E-learning.** The fastest-growing area in EC in 2002 was e-learning. Large numbers of companies were installing e-learning programs, and many universities were experimenting with distance-learning programs. We expect e-learning to grow even faster in the near future.

EC TECHNOLOGY TRENDS

The trend in EC technologies generally points toward significant cost reduction, coupled with improvements in capabilities, ease of use, increased availability of software, ease of site development, and improved security and accessibility. Some specifics include the following:

1. **Clients.** PCs of all types are getting cheaper, smaller, and more capable. The concept of a network computer (NC), also known as a *thin client*, which moves processing and storage off the desktop and onto centrally located servers running Java-based software on UNIX (Windows on Microsoft's version), could bring the price of a PC to that of a television.

2. **Embedded clients.** Another major trend is the movement toward *embedded clients*. A client, in such a case, can be a car or a washing machine with an embedded microchip. In many cases, an expert system is embedded with rules that make the client "smarter" or more responsive to changes in the environment.

3. **Servers.** A major trend is to use Windows NT as the enterprise operating system. Among NT's capabilities is clustering. Clustering servers can add processing power in much smaller increments than was previously possible. Clustering servers is very economical, resulting in cost reductions.

4. **Networks.** The use of EC frequently requires rich multimedia (such as color catalogs or samples of movies or music). A large bandwidth is required to accomplish this. Several broadband technologies (such as XDSL) will increase bandwidth manyfold. This could help in replacing expensive WANs or VANs with the inexpensive Internet. Security on the Internet can be enhanced by the use of VPNs.

5. **Wireless communications.** For countries without fiber-optic cables, wireless communication can save considerable installation time and money. In 1998, wireless access reached T1 speed (about 1.5 mbps), with cost savings of over 80 percent. However, wireless networks may be too slow for some digitized products in the future (see Chapter 8).

6. **EC software and services.** The availability of all types of EC software will make it easier to establish stores on the Internet and to conduct all types of trades. Already, hundreds of sites offer pages for inexpensive rent for a variety of activities ranging from conducting your own auctions to selling in a foreign language. Other support services, such as escrow companies that support auctions and multiple types of certifications, are developing rapidly. Also, a large number of consultants are being trained to assist in specialty areas.

7. **Search engines.** Search engines are getting smarter and better. This will enable consumers and organizational buyers to find and compare products and services easier and faster.

8. **P2P technology.** This technology is developing rapidly and is expected to have a major impact on knowledge sharing, communication, and collaboration by making these better, faster, and more convenient.

9. **Integration.** The forthcoming integration of the computer and the TV and the computer and the telephone, including Wireless One Inc., will increase Internet accessibility (e.g., see Silberman 1999).

10. **Wearable devices.** With advances in pervasive computing and artificial intelligence, we will see a large increase in wearable computing devices (Chapter 8). These will enhance collaborative commerce, B2E, and intrabusiness EC.

THE DIGITAL DIVIDE

Despite the factors and trends that contribute to future EC growth, since the inception of technology in general and the Internet and e-commerce in particular, we have witnessed a gap between those who have and those who do not have the ability to use the technology. This gap is referred to as the **digital divide**. According to UN and ITU reports, more than 90 percent of all Internet hosts are in developed countries, where only 15 percent of the world's population resides. In 2001, the city of New York, for example, had more Internet hosts than the whole continent of Africa.

digital divide
The gap between those who have and those who do not have the ability to access electronic technology in general, and the Internet and EC in particular.

The gap exists both within and between countries. The U.S. federal and state governments are attempting to close this gap (see ecommerce.gov) within the country, by encouraging training and supporting education and infrastructure. The gap among countries, however, may be widening rather than narrowing. Many government and international organizations are trying to close the digital divide.

INTEGRATING THE MARKETPLACE AND THE MARKETSPACE

Throughout this book we commented on the relationship between the physical marketplace and the marketspace. We pointed out conflicts in certain areas, as well as successful applications and cooperation. The fact is that from the point of view of the consumer, as well as most organizations, these two entities exist, and will continue to exist, together.

Probably the most noticeable integration of the two concepts is in the click-and-mortar organization. For the foreseeable future, the click-and-mortar organization will be the most prevalent model (e.g., see Otto and Chung 2000), though it may take different shapes and formats. Some organizations will use EC as just another selling channel, as most large retailers do today. Others will use EC for only some products and services, selling other products and services the conventional way (e.g., lego.com). As experience is gained on how to excel in such a strategy, more and more organizations, private and public, will move to this mode of operation.

A major problem in the click-and-mortar approach is how to cooperate in planning, advertising, logistics, resource allocation, and so on, and how to align the strategic plans of the marketspace and marketplace. We discussed some of the solutions earlier in this chapter. Another major issue is the conflict with existing distribution channels (i.e., wholesalers, retailers).

Another area of coexistence is in many B2C ordering systems, where customers have the option to order the new way or the old way. For example, you can do your banking both online and off-line. You can trade stocks via the computer, by placing a call to your broker, or just by walking into a brokerage firm and talking to a trader. In the areas of B2B and G2B, this option may not be available much longer; some organizations may discontinue the old-economy option as the number of off-line users will decline below a certain threshold. However, in most B2C activities the option will remain, at least for the foreseeable future.

In conclusion, many people believe that the impact of EC on our lives will be as much as, and possibly more than, that of the Industrial Revolution. No other phenomenon since the Industrial Revolution has been classified in this category. It is our hope that this book will help you move successfully into this exciting and challenging digital revolution.

▶ Describe nontechnical EC trends.

▶ Describe technological trends for EC.

▶ Define the digital divide and suggest ways to close it.

▶ Discuss the integration of marketplaces and marketspaces.

MANAGERIAL ISSUES

Some managerial issues related to this chapter are as follows.

1. **What is the strategic value of EC to the organization?** Management needs to understand how EC can improve marketing and promotions, customer service, and sales. Furthermore, new business opportunities may be found in EC. To capitalize on the potential of EC, management needs to view EC from a strategic perspective, not merely as a technological advancement.

2. **What are the benefits and risks of EC?** Strategic moves have to be carefully weighed against potential risks. Identifying CSFs for EC and doing a cost-benefit analysis should not be neglected. Benefits are often hard to quantify, especially when they are more strategic than operational cost savings. In such an analysis, risks should be addressed with contingency planning (deciding what to do if problems arise).

3. **What metrics should we use?** The use of metrics is very popular, but the problem is that you must compare "apples with apples." Companies first must choose appropriate metrics for its situation and then exercise caution in deriving conclusions whenever gaps between the metrics and actual performance are seen.

4. **Can we do a pilot project?** When a company decides to go for a pilot project, creating a Web team representing all functional areas of the company is an important part of the implementation plan. After the pilot project is completed, it is necessary to reexamine the EC project strategies to assess the EC strategic planning effort and its results.

5. **Do we have a community?** Although sponsoring a community may sound like a good idea, it may not be simple to execute. Community members need services and these cost money. The most difficult task is to find a community that matches your business.

6. **How can we go global?** Going global is a very appealing proposition, but may be difficult to do, especially on a large scale. In B2B, one may create collaborative projects with partners in other countries, which will last for a long time. Once such partners are discovered, exchanges and third-party marketplaces that promote global trade may lose business.

7. **Can we learn to love smallness?** Small can be beautiful to some; to others it may be ugly. Competing on commodity-type products with the big guys is very difficult, even more so in cyberspace. Finding a niche market is advisable, but it will usually be limited in scope. More opportunity exists in providing specialized support services than in trading.

8. **Is restructuring needed?** Frequently, it may be necessary to restructure business processes to ensure the success of EC. This may be a long and expensive proposition. But, as IBM found out, if you do it properly, the rewards can be enormous.

SUMMARY

In this chapter, you learned about the following EC issues as they relate to the learning objectives.

1. **Importance of strategic planning for EC.** Strategic planning clarifies what an EC project should do or focus on with respect to the company's mission and the given business environment. Because of the comprehensiveness of EC, conducting formal strategic planning is a must.

2. **The strategy planning and formulation process.** This process is composed of four major phases: initiation, formulation, implementation, and assessment. A variety of tools are available to execute this process. The strategy formulation phase involves understanding the industry

and competition, as well as analyzing costs-benefits. It provides guidance on whether to compete against others or to cooperate, for example, by forming an alliance in the market.

3. **Application discovery, justification, and prioritization.** Uncovering EC applications can be done in several ways, from finding solutions to problems to finding problems for proven solutions. Building the correct portfolio can be facilitated by special methodologies. Applications need to be justified (cost-benefit, risk analysis) and then ranked as to their overall importance.

4. **EC strategy implementation and assessment.** Creating a Web team representing various functional areas and planning for resources are important parts of an implementation plan. A major implementation issue is whether or not to outsource. A strategy must be monitored and assessed periodically. Corrective actions and strategy reformulation must follow. Metrics serve as guidelines to the various EC areas, from e-marketing strategy to e-budgeting. In assessment, one compares actual performance to metrics.

5. **Understanding failures and learning from them.** Many EC initiatives and companies failed in 2000 and 2001. The major reasons for failure were lack of appropriate planning and neglect of the business side of the e-business.

6. **The role and impact of virtual communities.** Virtual communities create new types of business opportunities—people with similar interests that are congregated in one Web site are a natural target for advertisers and marketers. Using chat rooms, members can exchange opinions about certain products and services. Of special interest are communities of transactions, whose interest is the promotion of commercial buying and selling. The communities help to foster customer loyalty, increase sales of related vendors, and increase customers' feedback for improved service and business.

7. **Issues in global EC.** Going global with EC can be done quickly and with a relatively small investment. However, businesses must deal with a number of different issues. These include legal issues such as jurisdiction and contracts, intellectual property, government regulations regarding export/import, tariffs and taxation, payment mechanisms, Web site presentation, language translation, and currency conversions. The U.S. government policy is to make electronic global trade free from restrictions. There is little international agreement on such a policy as well as on the necessary payments and other standards.

8. **Small businesses and EC.** Depending on the circumstances, innovative small companies have a tremendous opportunity to enter EC with little cost and to expand rapidly; others may be eliminated by larger online competitors. Being in a niche market provides the best chance for small businesses. Going after high-volume, commodity-type products (e.g., CDs, books, or computers) can be too risky for a small company.

9. **Restructuring and virtual organizations.** When implementing EC applications it is frequently necessary to redesign processes or even to perform a BPR. This may require the use of workflow tools. EC applications frequently support virtual corporations.

10. **The future of EC.** EC will continue to expand fairly rapidly for a number of reasons. To begin with, its infrastructure is becoming better and less expensive with time. Consumers will be more experienced and will try different products and services and tell their friends about them. Security, privacy protection, and trust will be much higher, and more support services will simplify the transaction process. Legal issues will be clarified, and more and more products and services will be online at reduced prices. The fastest growing area is B2B EC, and company-centric systems (especially e-procurement) and auctions will spread rapidly. The development of exchanges and other many-to-many e-marketplaces will be much slower.

KEY TERMS

DISCUSSION QUESTIONS

1. How would you start an industry analysis for a small business that wants to launch an EC project?

2. How would you apply the SWOT approach to a small, local bank evaluating its e-banking services?

3. What might be typical competitive activities done online for a company trying to launch a an online bookselling business?

4. Explain the logic of Tjan's application portfolio approach.

5. Amazon.com decided not to open physical stores, whereas First Network Security Bank (FNSB), which was the first online bank, opened its first physical bank in 1999. Compare and discuss the two strategies.

6. Discuss the relationship between virtual communities and doing business on the Internet.

7. Discuss the pros and cons of going global with a physical product.

8. Find some SME EC success stories and identify the common elements in them.

9. Discuss the issue of the digital divide and how to deal with the problem (see ecommerce.gov and google.com).

INTERNET EXERCISES

1. Survey several online travel agencies (e.g., travelocity.com, orbitz.com, cheaptickets.com, priceline.com, expedia.com, bestfares.com, and so on) and compare their business strategies. How do they compete against physical travel agencies?

2. Enter digitalenterprise.org and find Web metrics. Read the material on metrics and prepare a report on the use of metrics for measuring advertising success.

3. Check the music CD companies on the Internet (e.g., CDNow.com). Do any focus on specialized niche markets as a strategy?

4. Enter ibm.com/procurement and go to the e-procurement section. Read IBM's e-procurement strategy and the "Consultant's Report—

Best Practices." Prepare a report on the best lessons you learned.

5. Compare the following recording industry associations: aria.com.au (Australia), bpi.co.uk (United Kingdom), and riaa.com (United States). Consider the services offered, functionality of the site, use of multimedia, search capabilities, timeliness, range, links, customization (languages), product information, EC activities, etc., and prepare a report based on your findings.

6. One of the most global companies is amazon.com. Find stories about its global strategies and activities (try fortune.com and

forbes.com). What are the most important lessons you learned?

7. Visit abcsmallbiz.com and find some of the EC opportunities available for small businesses. Also, visit the Web site of the SBA (Small Business Administration) office in your area. Finally, check abcsmallbix.com on Saturdays and look for Applegate's column on small businesses. Summarize recent EC-related topics.

8. Enter alloy.com and bolt.com. Compare the sites on functionality, ease of use, message boards, home page layout, etc. Prepare a report based on your findings.

9. Find out how Web sites such as tradecard.com facilitate the conduct of international trade over the Internet. Prepare a report on your findings.

10. Use a currency conversion table (e.g., xe.com/ucc) to find out the exchange rate of $100 (U.S.) with the currencies of Brazil, Canada, China, India, Sweden, the European Union, and South Africa.

11. Enter the Web site of an Internet community (e.g., tripod.com or geocities.yahoo.com). Build a home page free of charge. You can add a chat room and a message board to your site using the free tools provided.

12. Investigate the community services provided by Yahoo! to its members (groups.yahoo.com). List all the services available and assess their potential commercial benefits to Yahoo!.

13. Conduct research on small businesses and their use of the Internet for EC. Visit sites such as success.com, webcom.com, and uschamber.org. Also, enter google.com or yahoo.com and type "small businesses and electronic commerce." Use your findings to write a report on current small business EC issues.

TEAM ASSIGNMENTS AND ROLE PLAYING

1. Have three teams represent the following units of one click-and-mortar company: (1) an off-line division, (2) an online division, and (3) top management. Each team member represents a different functional area within the division. The teams will develop a strategy in a specific industry (a group of three teams will represent a company in one industry). Teams will present their strategies to the class.

2. The relationship between manufacturers and their distributors regarding sales on the Web can be very strained. Direct sales may cut into the distributors' business. Review some of the strategies available to handle such channel conflicts. Each team member should be assigned to a company in a different industry. Study the strategies, compare and contrast them, and derive a proposed generic strategy.

3. Each team must find the latest information on one global EC issue (e.g., legal, financial, standards, etc.). Each team will offer a report based on their findings.

4. Survey google.com, electronicmarkets.org, and isworld.org to find out about EC efforts in different countries. Assign a country or two to each team. Relate the developments to each country's level of economic development and to its culture.

REAL-WORLD CASE

THE AUSTRALIAN FISHING COMMUNITY

Recreational fishing in Australia is popular both with residents and with international visitors. Over 700,000 Australians fish regularly. The Australian Fishing Shop (AFS) (*ausfish.com.au*) is a small e-tailer, founded in 1994, initially as a hobby site carrying information for the recreational fisherperson. Over the last few years the site has featured a fishing portal that has created a devoted community behind it.

A visit to the site will show immediately that the site is not a regular storefront, but actually provides considerable information to the recreational fishing community. In addition to the sale of products (rods, reels, clothing, and boats and fishing-related books, software, and CD-ROMs) and services (fishing charters and holiday packages), the site provides the following information:

▷ Hints and tips for fishing.

▷ What's new?

▷ A photo gallery of visitors' prize catches.

▷ Chat boards—general and specialized.

▷ Directions from boat builders, tackle manufacturers, etc.

▷ Recipes for cooking fish.

▷ Information about discussion groups and mailing lists.

▷ Free giveaways and competitions.

▷ Links to fishing-related government bodies, other fishing organizations (around the globe and in Australia), and daily weather maps and tide reports.

▷ General information site and FAQs.

▷ List of fishing sites around the globe.

▷ Contact details by phone, post, and e-mail.

▷ Free e-mail and Web page hosting.

In addition, there is an auction mechanism for fishing equipment, and answers are provided for customer inquiries.

The company is fairly small (gross income of about AU$500,000 a year). How can such a small company survive? The answer can be found in its strategy of providing value-added services to the recreational fishing community. These services attract over 1.6 million visitors each month, from all over the world, of which about 1 percent make a purchase. Also, several advertisers sponsor the site. This is sufficient revenue to survive. Aiming at the global market is another interesting strategy. Most of the total income is derived from customers in the United States and Canada who buy holiday and fishing packages.

The company acts basically as a referral service for vendors. Therefore, it does not have to carry an inventory. AFS does business with a small number of suppliers, thus they are able to aggregate orders from suppliers and then pack and send them to customers. Some orders are shipped directly from vendors to the customers.

Source: *Ausfish.com.au*, February 2002.

Questions

1. Why is this site considered a community site?
2. Which of the services offered are typical of online communities?
3. List the CSFs of the company.

REFERENCES

CHAPTER 1

Afuah, A., and C. L. Tucci. *Internet Business Models and Strategies.* New York: McGraw-Hill, 2000.

Applegate, L. M. "E-business Models." In *Information Technology for the Future Enterprise: New Models for Managers,* edited by G. W. Dickson and G. DeSanctis, pp. 49–101. Upper Saddle River, NJ: Prentice Hall, 2000.

"Australian Case Studies," Orbis brochure, 2002, orbis global.com/pdf/Orbis_CaseStudies.pdf.

Boyett, J. H., and J. T. Boyett. *Beyond Workplace 2000: Essential Strategies for the New American Corporation.* New York: Dutton, 1995.

Callon, J. D. *Competitive Advantage Through Information Technology.* New York: McGraw-Hill, 1996.

Choi, S. Y., and A. B. Whinston. *The Internet Economy, Technology and Practice.* Austin, TX: Smartecon.com, 2000.

Choi, S. Y., et al. *The Economics of Electronic Commerce.* Indianapolis, IN: Macmillan Technical Publishing, 1997.

Clinton, W. J., and A. Gore, Jr. "A Framework for Global Electronic Commerce," iitf.nist.gov/eleccomm/ecomm.htm, 1997.

Cochrane, N. "Image Bank Shows the Right Picture," February 1, 2000, orbisglobal.com/frameset.asp?articleID=13&ns=N&sSection=c&b=newsArticle.

Cunningham, M. S. *B2B: How to Build a Profitable E-Commerce Strategy.* Cambridge, MA: Perseus Publishing, 2001.

Eglash, J. *How to Write a .com Business Plan.* New York, McGraw-Hill, 2001.

Evans, P., and T. S. Wurster. *Blown to Bits: How the New Economics of Information Transforms Strategy.* Boston: Harvard Business School Press, 2000.

Farhoomand, A., and P. Lovelock. *Global E-Commerce.* Singapore: Prentice Hall, 2001.

Fingar, P., et al. *Enterprise E-Commerce.* Tampa, FL: Meghan-Kiffer Press, 2000.

Hoffman, D. L., and T. P. Novak. "How to Acquire Customers on the Web." *Harvard Business Review,* Vol. 78, No. 3 (May–June 2000): 179–187.

Huff, S. L., et al. *Cases in Electronic Commerce.* New York: McGraw-Hill, 2001.

Kalakota, R., and A. B. Whinston. *Electronic Commerce: A Manager's Guide.* Reading, MA: Addison Wesley, 1997.

Kalakota, R., and M. Robinson. *e-Business 2.0.* Boston: Addison Wesley, 2001.

Lederer, A. L., et al. "Using Web-Based Information Systems to Enhance Competitiveness." *Communication of the ACM,* Vol. 41, No. 7 (July 1998): 94–95.

Lipnack, J., and J. Stamps. *Virtual Teams—Reaching Across Space, Time, and Organizations with Technology.* New York: John Wiley & Sons, 1997.

Orbis. "The ProductBank Facts," August 17, 2001, orbisglobal.com/frameset.asp?articleID=15&ns=MR&sSection=c&b=newsArticle.

Pine, B. J., and J. Gilmore. "The Four Faces of Mass Customization." *Harvard Business Review,* Vol. 75, No. 1 (January–February 1997): 91–101.

Rao, B., et al. "Building World-Class Logistics, Distribution, and E-Commerce Infrastructure." *Electronic Markets* Vol. 9, No. 3 (1999). electronicmarkets.org/netacademy/publications.nsf/all_pk/1376.

Rosen, A. *The E-Commerce Q and A Book: A Survival Guide for Business Managers.* New York: AMACOM, 1999.

Rugullis, E. "Power to the Buyer with Group Buying Sites." *e-business Advisor,* Vol. 18, No. 2 (February 2000): 10.

Shaw, M. J., et al. *Handbook on Electronic Commerce.* Berlin: Springer-Verlag, 2000.

Slywotzky, A. J., and D. J. Morrison. *How Digital Is Your Business?* London: Nicholas Brealy Publishing, 2001.

Tapscott, D., et al., eds. *Blueprint to the Digital Economy: Wealth Creation in the Era of E-Business.* New York: McGraw-Hill, 1998.

Timmers, P. *Electronic Commerce.* New York: Wiley, 1999.

Turban, E., et al. *Electronic Commerce 2002.* Upper Saddle River, NJ: Prentice Hall, 2002b.

Turban, E., et al. *Information Technology for Management,* 3d ed. New York: John Wiley & Sons, 2002a.

Useem, J. "Dot-Coms: What Have We Learned?" *Fortune* (October 30, 2000): 82–104.

Wetherbe, J. C. *The World on Time.* Santa Monica, CA: Knowledge Exchange, 1996.

Wiegram, G., and H. Koth. *Custom Enterprise.com.* Upper Saddle River, NJ: Financial Times/Prentice Hall, 2000.

CHAPTER 2

Anonymous. "Business and the Internet." *The Economist* (June 26, 1999): 12.

Bakos, Y. "The Emerging Role of Electronic Marketplaces on the Internet." *Communications of the ACM* (August 1998).

bcop.com/about/ecommerce.shtml, 2001.

Beato, G. "Online Piracy's Mother Ship." *Business 2.0* (December 12, 2000).

Bloch, M., Y. Pigneur, and A. Segev. "Leveraging Electronic Commerce for Competitive Advantage: A Business Value Framework." *Proceedings of the Ninth International Conference on EDI-IOS,* Bled, Slovenia, June 1996.

"Boise Cascade Saves $1 Million in First Year of Web Catalog," wp.netscape.com/solutions/business/profiles/boisecascade.html, 2001.

Carr, N. G. "On The Edge." *Harvard Business Review* (May–June 2000).

Choi, S. Y., and A. B. Whinston. *The Internet Economy: Technology and Practice.* Austin, TX: Smartecon.com, 2000.

Choi, S. Y., et al. *The Economics of Electronic Commerce.* Indianapolis, IN: Macmillan Technical Publishing, 1997.

Davidson, J., "Driving Logistics Online Markets," April 9, 2001, nte.com/dynamic/articles/TW0401.pdf.

Dollardex.com, 2002.

"dollarDEX Launches Reverse Auction on Mortgages," March 28, 2000, Moneyq.com.hk.

Helmstetter, G., and P. Metivier. *Affiliate Selling: Building Revenue on the Web.* New York: John Wiley and Sons, 2000.

Various Inc. Staff. "Web Awards 2000: Innovation," November 15, 2000, inc.com/magazine/20001115/21019.html.

Kalakota, R., and M. Robinson. *M-Business: The Race to Mobility.* New York: McGraw-Hill, 2001.

Klein, S. "Introduction to Electronic Auctions." *Electronic Markets* Vol. 7, No. 4 (1997).

KPMG Consulting. "Virtual Close—A Financial Management Solution," cisco.com/warp/public/756/partnership/kpmg/enterprise_solutions/vcsolutionbrief.pdf, pp. 1–4.

Lim, G. G., and J. K. Lee. "Buyer Carts for B2B EC: The B-Cart Approach." *Organizational Computing and Electronic Commerce* (2002).

Lorek, L. "Trade Ya? E-Barter Thrives." *InteractiveWeek* (August 14, 2000).

Pine, J., II. *Mass Customization.* Boston: Harvard Business School Press, 1999.

Porter, Michael E. *Competitive Advantage: Creating and Sustaining Superior Performance.* Rev. ed. New York: The Free Press, 2001.

Porter, M. E. "Strategy and the Internet." *Harvard Business Review* (March 2001).

PRNewswire. "Boise Cascade Office Products Launches Industry-Leading Service," December 10, 2001.

Ramsdell, M. "The Real Business of B2B." *McKinsey Quarterly,* Third Quarter 2000.

Sadeh, N. *Mobile Commerce: New Technologies, Services and Business Models.* New York: John Wiley & Sons, April 2002.

Strader, T. J., and H. J. Shaw. "Characteristics of Electronic Markets." *Decision Support Systems,* No. 21 (1997).

"TDC and LINE Launch Transact Link: A Global E-Commerce Solution for Hong Kong's Trade

Community," March 26, 2001, portsnportals.com/press010326.html.

Turban, E., et al. *Information Technology for Management,* 3d ed. New York: Wiley, 2002.

Werbach, K. "Syndication—The Emerging Model for Business in the Internet Era." *Harvard Business Review* (May–June 2000).

Additional Readings

Beam, C., et al. "On Negotiations and Deal Making in Electronic Markets." *Information Systems Frontiers* Vol. 1, No. 3 (1999).

Beiser, D. "Cisco Chief Pushes 'Virtual Close:' Intranets Allow Up-to-Minute Look at Books." *USA Today,* October 12, 1999.

Elliot, A. C. *Getting Started in Internet Auctions.* New York: John Wiley & Sons, 2000.

Evans, P. B., and T. S. Wurster. *Blown to Bits: How the New Economics of Information Transforms Strategy.* Boston: Harvard Business School Press, 1999.

Fickel, L. "Bid Business." *CIO WebBusiness Magazine* (June 1, 1999).

Hamel, G. *Leading the Revolution.* Boston: Harvard Business School Press, 2000.

Kelly, K. *New Rules for the New Economy.* New York: Penguin USA, 1999.

Lim, E. P., and K. Siau. "Mobil Commerce." *Journal of Database Management* (April 2001).

Lisse, W. C. "The Economics of Information and the Internet." *Competitive Intelligence Review* (April 1998).

Ludorf, C. "Carriers and Online Load Matching Services," July 2001, net.com/dynamic/articles/TTT0701.pdf.

McKeown, P. G., and R. T. Watson. "Manheim Auctions." *Communications of the Association for Information Systems* (June 1999).

Phifer, G., and N. Mikula. "Enterprise Portals." *Informationweek.com* (September 20, 2001).

Prince, D. L. *Auction This!: Your Complete Guide to the World of Online Auctions.* Roseville, CA: Prima Publishing, 1999.

Ranadive, V. *The Power of Now.* New York: McGraw-Hill, 1999.

Strobel, M. "On Auctions as the Negotiation Paradigm of Electronic Markets" *Electronic Markets*, Vol. 10, No. 1 (2000).

Swass, V. "Structure and Macro-Level Impacts of Electronic Commerce." In *Emerging Information Technologies*, edited by K. E. Kendall. Thousand Oaks, CA: Sage Publishing, 1999.

Tapscott, D., et al. *Digital Capital.* Boston: Harvard Business Review Press, 2000.

U.S. Department of Commerce. "The Emerging Digital Economy II," ecommerce.gov/ede, June 1999.

Westland, J. C. "Ten Lessons That Internet Auction Markets Can Learn from Securities Market Automation." *Journal of Global Management* (January–March 2000).

Wharton School at the University of Pennsylvania. "Dynamic Pricing: What Does It Mean?" ebizchronicle.com/wharton/19-digitalfuture (October 18, 2000).

CHAPTER 3

Anonymous. *Computerworld Hong Kong* (January 14, 1999).

Bank of America. free-online-banking-internet-checking.com/security.html (June 2002). Press releases.

Berghel, H. "Predatory Disintermediation." *Communications of the ACM* (May 2000).

Bloch, M., and A. Segev. "The Impact of Electronic Commerce on the Travel Industry." *Proceedings, HICSS,* Maui, HI, January 1997.

Bloch, M., et al. "Leveraging Electronic Commerce for Competitive Advantage: A Business Value Framework." *Proceedings of the Ninth International EC Conference*, Bled, Slovenia, June 1996.

Bose, K. "Intelligent Agents Framework for Developing Knowledge-Based DSS for Collaborative Organizational Processes." *Expert Systems with Applications* Vol. 11, No. 3 (1996).

Calem, R. E. "Deal Clinchers: How to Get from Brochureware to Online Business." *Industry Standard* (February 14, 2000).

Carr, N. G. "Hypermediation: Commerce as Clickstream." *Harvard Business Review* (January–February 2000).

Giaglis, G. M., et al. "Disintermediation, Reintermediation, or Cybermediation." *Proceedings of the Twelfth International EC Conference*, Bled, Slovenia, June 1999.

Gilbert, J., et al. *Online Investment Bible.* Berkeley, CA: Hungry Minds, Inc., 2000.

Gosling, P. *Changing Money: How the Digital Age Is Transforming Financial Services.* Dulles, VA: Capital Books, Inc., 2000.

Karpinski, R. "E-Business Risk Worth Taking on Path to Success." *B to B* 85 (August 28, 2000).

Kauffman, R., et. al. "Analyzing Information Intermediaries in Electronic Brokerage." *Proceedings 33rd HICSS*, Maui, HI, January 2000.

Kruger, J. Interview by Merrill Warkentin, fall 2000.

landsend.com/cd/fp/help/0,,1_26215_26859_26908___,00.html?refer=/cd/frontdoor/0,,,00+en-USS_01DBC.html&sid=2272040784316151870#landsenddotcom.

MacSweeney, G. "Dual Strategy." *Insurance and Technology* (July 2000).

Matthew, K. O. Lee. *Internet Retailing in Hong Kong China*. City University of Hong Kong, 2001.

Peffers, K., and V. K. Tunnainen. "Expectations and Impacts of a Global Information System: The Case of a Global Bank from Hong Kong." *Journal of Global Information Technology Management* Vol. 1, No. 4 (1998).

Rafter, M. V. "Trust or Bust?" *Industry Standard* (March 6, 2000).

Schonfeld, E. "Schwab—Put It All Online." *Fortune* (December 7, 1998).

Schwartz, E. "Amazon, Toys R Us in E-Commerce Tie-Up." *InfoWorld* 22 (August 14, 2000).

Simison, R. L. "GM Retools to Sell Custom Cars Online." *Wall Street Journal*, February 22, 2000.

Tyson, E. *Personal Finance for Dummies*, 3d ed. San Francisco: Hungry Minds, Inc., 2000.

Van der Heijden, J. G. M. "The Changing Value of Travel Agents in Tourism Networks: Towards a Network Design Perspective." In *Information and Communication Technologies in Tourism*, edited by Stefan Klein, et al., 151–159. New York: Springer-Verlag, 1996.

Vandermerwe, S. "The Electronic 'Go-Between Service Provider': A New Middle Role Taking Center." *European Management Journal* (December 1999).

Warkentin, M., et al. "The Role of Mass Customization in Enhancing Supply Chain Relationships in B2C E-Commerce Markets." *Journal of Electronic Commerce Research* Vol. 1, No. 2 (2000): 1–17.

Additional Readings

Baghai, R., and B. E. Cobert. "The Virtual Reality of Mortgages." *McKinsey Quarterly* (summer 2000).

Boss, S., et al. "Will the Banks Centralize Online Banking?" *McKinsey Quarterly* (summer 2000).

Clemons, E. K., and H. Hann. "Rosenbluth International: Strategic Transformation." *Journal of MIS* (fall 1999).

Drummond, M. "Big Music Fights Back (Against Napster)." *Business 2.0* (December 2000).

Hagel, J., III, and M. Singer. *Net Worth: Shaping Markets When Customers Make the Rules*. Cambridge, MA: Harvard Business School Press, 1999.

Hanson, W. *Internet Marketing*. Cincinnati, OH: South-Western College Publishing, 2000.

Jandt, F. E., and M. B. Nemnich, eds. *Using the Internet and the Web in Your Job Search*, 2d ed. Indianapolis, IN: Jistwork, 1999.

Kare-Silver, M. D. *E-Shock: The Electronic Shopping Revolution: Strategies for Retailers and Manufacturers*. New York: AMACOM, 1999.

Kleindl, B. A. *Strategic Internet Marketing: Managing E-Business*. Cincinnati, OH: South-Western College Publishing, 2001.

Maes, P., et al. "Agents That Buy and Sell: Transforming Commerce as We Know It." *Communications of the ACM* (March 1999).

Richardson, P. *Internet Marketing: Readings and Online Resources*. New York: McGraw-Hill/Irwin, 2001.

Strauss, J., and R. Frost. *E-Marketing*, 2d ed. Upper Saddle River, NJ: Prentice Hall, 2001.

Warkentin, M., and A. Bajaj. "The On-Demand Delivery Services Model for E-Commerce." In *Managing Business with Electronic Commerce: Issues and Trends*, A. Gangopadhay, ed. Hershey, PA: Idea Group Publishing, 2001.

CHAPTER 4

Berry, J. A., and G. Linoff. *Data Mining Techniques for Marketing, Sales, and Customer Support*, 2d ed. New York: Wiley, 2000.

Brown, S. A. *Customer Relationship Management: Linking People, Process, and Technology*. New York: Wiley, 2000.

Camp, L. J. *Trust and Risk in Internet Commerce*. Cambridge, MA: MIT Press, 2000.

Chase, L. *Essential Business Tactics on the Net*. New York: Wiley, 1998.

Clow, K., and D. Baack. *Integrated Advertising, Promotion, and Marketing Communication*. Upper Saddle River, NJ: Prentice Hall, 2002.

Compton, J. "Instant Customer Feedback." *PC Computing* (December 1999).

Doubleclick.com/us/corporate/about/overview.asp, 2002.

Doyle, K., A. Minor, and C. Weyrich. "Banner Ad Placement Study," University of Michigan, 1997.

Extempo Systems Inc. "Smart Interactive Characters: Automating One-To-One Customer Service," September, 1999, extempo.com/company_info/press/webtechniques.shtml.

Fingar, P. "A CEO's Guide to E-Commerce Using Intergalactic Object-Oriented Intelligent Agents," commerce.net/reports (July 1998).

Georgia Institute of Technology. Graphics, Visualization, and Usability (GVU) Center, *8th WWW User Survey*, gvu.gatech.edu, Eighth Survey (1998).

Georgia Institute of Technology. Graphics, Visualization, and Usability (GVU) Center, *9th WWW User Survey*, gvu.gatech.edu, Tenth Survey (1999).

Giannoni, G. *E-Promotions: The Value of E-Mail Marketing.* New York: Inter-American Development Bank, 2000.

Hasan, H., and G. Ditsa. "The Impact of Culture on the Adoption of IT: An Interpretive Study." *Journal of Global Information Management* (January–February 1999).

Hayes-Roth, B., et al. "Web Guides." *IEEE Intelligent Systems* (March–April 1999).

Helm, S. "Viral Marketing." *Electronic Markets* Vol. 10, No. 3 (2000).

Helmstetter, G., and P. Metivier. *Affiliate Selling: Building Revenue on the Web.* New York: Wiley, 2000.

Hoffman, D. L., and T. P. Novak. "How to Acquire Customers on the Web." *Harvard Business Review* (May–June 2000).

Information Week (October 3, 1994): p. 26.

Kalakota, R., and M. Robinson. *E-Businesses: Roadmap for Success.* Reading, MA: Addison Wesley, 2001.

Keen, P., et al. *Electronic Commerce Relationships: Trust by Design.* Upper Saddle River, NJ: Prentice Hall, 2000.

Kotler, P., and G. Armstrong. *Principles of Marketing*, 9th ed. Upper Saddle River, NJ: Prentice Hall, 2002.

Lazar, J., and J. Preece. "Designing and Implementing Web-Based Surveys." *Journal of Computer Information Systems* (April 1999).

Levinson, M. "Customer Segmentation: Slices of Lives." *CIO Magazine* (August 15, 2000).

Meeker, N. *The Internet Advertising Report.* New York: Morgan Stanley Corporation, 1997.

Nobles, R., and S. O'Neil. *Streetwise Maximize Web Site Traffic: Build Web Site Traffic Fast and Free by Optimizing Search Engine Placement.* Holbrook, MA: Adams Media Corporation, 2000.

O'Keefe, R. M., and T. McEachern. "Web-Based Customer Decision Support System." *Communications of the ACM* (March 1998).

Parsa, I. "Web Mining Crucial to E-Commerce Success." *DM News* (December 7, 1999).

Peppers, D., et al. *The One-to-One Fieldbook.* New York: Currency and Doubleday, 1999.

Petersen, G. S. *Customer Relationship Management Systems: ROI and Results Measurement.* New York: Strategic Sales Performance, 1999.

Plant, R. T. *E-Commerce: Foundation of Strategy.* Upper Saddle River, NJ: Prentice Hall, 2000.

Reichheld, F. *Building Loyalty in the Age of the Internet.* Boston: Harvard Business School Press, 2001.

Reichheld, F., and P. Schefter. "E-Loyalty—Your Secret Weapon on the Web." *Harvard Business Review* (July–August 2000).

Reichheld, F., and W. Sasser. "Zero Defections: Quality Comes to Services." *Harvard Business Review* (September-October 1990).

Rothenberg, Randall. "An Advertising Power, but Just What Does DoubleClick Do?" *New York Times*, September 22, 1999.

Seybold, P. B., and R. Marshak. *Customer.com: How to Create a Profitable Business Strategy for the Internet and Beyond.* New York: Times Books, 1998.

Shapiro, D., et al. "Business on a Handshake." *The Negotiation Journal* (October 1992).

Sindell, K. *Loyalty Marketing for the Internet Age.* Chicago: Dearborn Trade, 2000.

"Smart Interactive Characters: Automating One-to-One Customer Service," extempo.com/company_info/press/webtechniques.shtml (September 1999).

Solomon, M. R. *Consumer Behavior.* Upper Saddle River, NJ: Prentice Hall, 2002.

Strauss, J., and R. Frost. *Internet Marketing*, 2d ed. Upper Saddle River, NJ: Prentice Hall, 2001.

Taylor, C. P. "Is One-to-One the Way to Market?" *Interactive Week* (May 12, 1997).

Tedeschi, B. "E-Commerce Report: New Alternatives to Banner Ads." *New York Times*, February 20, 2001.

Tiedrich, A. "Business Intelligence Tools: Perspective," October 9, 2001, gartner.com.

Todor, J. I., and W. D. Todor. *Winning Mindshare: The Psychology of Personalization and One-to-One Marketing.* New York: Perseus Books, 2001.

UCLA Center for Communication Policy. "UCLA Internet Report 2001: Surveying the Digital Future," November 2001, ccp.ucla.edu/pdf/UCLA-Internet-Report-2001.pdf.

Vassos, J. *Strategic Internet Marketing.* Indianapolis, IN: Que Publishing, 1996.

Voss, C. "Developing an eService Strategy." *Business Strategy Review* Vol. 11, No. 11 (2000).

Wang, S. "Analyzing Agents for Electronic Commerce." *Information Systems Management* (winter 1999).

Wong, T. *101 Ways to Boost Your Web Traffic.* New York: Intersync, 2000.

Yan, Y., et al. "A Multi-Agent Based Negotiated Support System." *Proceedings 33rd HICSS*, Maui, HI, January 2000.

Additional Readings

Benassi, P. "TRUSTe: An Online Privacy Seal Program." *Communications of the ACM* Vol. 42, No. 2 (1999).

Churchill, G. *Marketing Research*, 7th ed. Fort Worth, TX: Dryden Press, 1999.

Dickson, G. W., and G. DeSanctis, eds. *Information Technology and the Future Enterprise: New Models for Management.* Upper Saddle River, NJ: Prentice Hall, 2001.

Hanson, W. *Principles of Internet Marketing.* Cincinnati, OH: South-Western Publishing, 2000.

Kinnard, S. *Marketing with E-Mail.* Gulf Breeze, FL: Maximum Press, 2000.

Liang, T. P., and H. S. Doong. "Effect of Bargaining on Electronic Commerce." *International Journal of Electronic Commerce* (spring 2000).

Maes, P., et al. "Agents That Buy and Sell." *Communications of the ACM* (March 1999).

McDaniel, C., and R. H. Gates. *Marketing Research: The Impact of the Internet.* Cincinnati, OH: South-Western Publishing, 2001.

O'Keefe, S. *Publicity on the Internet.* New York: Wiley, 1997.

Orzech, D. "Call Centers Take to the Web." *Datamation* (June 1998).

Ratnasingham, P. "The Importance of Trust in Electronic Commerce." *Internet Research* Vol. 8, No. 4 (1998).

Reichheld, F. *The Loyalty Effect.* Boston: Harvard Business Press, 1996.

CHAPTER 5

ariba.com (2001).

Bunnell, D., and A. Brate. *Making the Cisco Connection.* New York: John Wiley & Sons, 2000.

cisco.com, 2002.

DiCarlo, L. "Case Study: Webcor Builders," *P C Computing*, December 1999, Vol. 12, No. 12, 108–120.

El-Sawy, O., et al. "Intensive Value Innovation in the Electronic Economy: Insight from Marshall Industry." *MIS Quarterly* (September 1999).

Fickel, L. "Online Auctions: Bid Business." *CIO Web Business Magazine* (June 1, 1999).

Forrester Research. "Estimates of the B2B Market," Forrester.com (March 7, 2001).

Freemarkets.com, 2002.

Goldman Sachs Group. Special Report, gs.com (February 15, 2001).

Intel Corp. "Franchising Meets the Internet." Intel.com/ebusiness/ (then go to Industry solutions), (March 4, 1999a).

Intel Corp. "Marriott International Checks In," Intel.com/ebusiness/ (then go to Industry solutions), (March 4, 1999b).

Jahnke, A. "How Bazaar." *CIO Magazine* (August 1, 1998).

Li, S. T., and L. Y. Shue. "Towards XML-Enabling E-Commerce Infomediary—A Case Study." *Proceedings of the 34th Hawaii International Conference on System Sciences,* Maui, HI, January 2001.

Lim, G., and J. K. Lee. "Buyer-Carts for B2B EC: The B-Cart Approach." *Organizational Computing and Electronic Commerce* (June 2002).

nygard.com/corporate/nygard_history.html, 2001.

Retter, T., and M. Calyniuk. *Technology Forecast: 1998.* Menlo Park, CA: Price Waterhouse, 1998.

Rudnitsky, H. "Changing the Corporate DNA," *Forbes Global,* July 24, 2000, forbes.com/global/2000/0724/0314099a.html.

Schram, P. *Collaborative Commerce: Going Private to Get Results,* special report. New York: Deloitte Consulting, dc.com, 2001.

Skinner, S. "Business to Business E-Commerce Investment Perspective," Durlacher Research Ltd., e-global.es/017/017_durlacher.beb.pdf (2002).

Stauffer, D. *Nothing But the Net: Business the Cisco Way.* Oxford, UK: Capstone Ltd., 2000.

Stephenson, W. "Nygard Goes Electronic." *Winnipeg Sun,* June 3, 1999.

Timmers, P. *Electronic Commerce: Strategies and Models for B2B Trading.* Chichester, UK: John Wiley & Sons, 1999.

Trading Process Network. "Extending the Enterprise: TPN Post Case Study—GE Lighting" (gegxs.com), 1999.

Webcor.com, 2000.

Wilson, T. "Marshall Industries: Wholesale Shift to the Web," *InternetWeek* (July 20, 1998).

Additional Readings

Andrew, S. M. "Collaborate for Better B2B." *e-Business Advisor* (October–November 2001).

Blankenhorn, D. "GE's E-Commerce Network Opens up to Other Marketers." *NetMarketing,* netb2b.com, May 1997.

Cone, E. "Building a Stronger Economy." *Interactiveweek* (January 24, 2000).

Cunningham, M. J. *B2B: How to Build a Profitable E-Commerce Strategy.* Cambridge, MA: Perseus Book Group, 2000.

E-Supply Chain and Logistics: Special Vendors' Section. *Fortune,* Fortune.com/fortune/sections/esupply, 2000.

Economist. Special issue on electronic commerce (June 26, 1999).

Fabris, P. "EC Riders (GE's TPN)." *CIO Magazine* (July 15, 1997).

Frook, J. E. "Web Links with Back-End Systems Pay Off." *InternetWeek* (July 13, 1998).

Gugullis, E. "Power to the Buyer with Group Buying Sites." *e-Business Adviser* (February 2000).

Hampe, J. F. "Standards and XML: Special Section." *Electronic Markets* Vol. 11, No. 4 (2001).

Handfield, R., and E. Nicols. *Supply Chain Management.* Upper Saddle River, NJ: Prentice Hall, 1999.

"High Technology Helps Garment Firms Compete," June 1999, nygard.com/corporate/high_technology_helps_garment_.html.

Hoque, F. *E-Enterprise.* Cambridge, UK: Cambridge University Press, 2000.

Kalakota, R., and M. Robinson. *E-Business 2.0.* Reading, MA: Addison Wesley, 2001.

Kaplan, S. "The Right Fit." *CIO Magazine* (December 1, 2001).

Lawrence, E., et al. *Internet Commerce. Digital Models for Business.* New York: John Wiley & Sons, 1998.

Lee, J. K., and W. Lee. "An Intelligent Agent Based Contract Process in Electronic Commerce: UNIK-AGENT Approach." *Proceedings of the 13th Hawaii International Conference on System Sciences,* Maui, HI, January 1997.

Linthicum, D. S. *B2B Application Integration.* Boston: Addison Wesley, 2001.

Maes, P., et al. "Agents That Buy and Sell." *Communications of ACM* (March 3, 1999).

McGagg, B. *The Essential Guide to Selling Surplus Assets.* Valhalla, NY: Tradeout.com, 1999.

Monczka, R. M., et al. *Purchasing and Supply Chain Management,* 2d ed. Cincinnati, OH: South-Western, 2002.

O'Connell, B. *B2B.com: Cashing in on the B2B EC Bonanza.* Holbrook, MA: Adams Media Corp., 2000.

Ragusa, J., and G. M. Bochenek. "Collaborative Design Environments." *Communications of the ACM* (December 2001).

Reimers, K. "Standardizing the New E-Business Platform: Learning from the EDI Experience." *Electronic Markets* Vol. 11, No. 4 (2001).

Senn, J. A. "B2B E-Commerce." *Information Systems Management* (spring 2000).

Silverstein, B. *Business-to-Business Internet Marketing.* Gulf Breeze, FL: Maximum Press, 1999.

Sullivan, D. "Extending E-Business to ERP." *e-Business Advisor* (January 1999).

Teasdale, S. "Boeing Extranet Speeds Ordering Process for Spare-Parts Buyers." *Net Marketing* (June 1997).

Trading Process Network. "Extending the Enterprise: TPN Post Case Study—GE Lighting," gegxs.com, 1999.

Turban, E., et al. *Information Technology for Management,* 3d ed. New York: John Wiley & Sons, 2002.

Webber, D. R. "Introducing XML/EDI Frameworks." *Electronic Markets* Vol. 3, No. 2 (1998).

CHAPTER 6

Alibaba.com, 2002.

Aquarius-flora.com, June 24, 2002.

Baker, S., and K. Baker. "Going Up! Vertical Marketing on the Web." *Journal of Business Strategy* (May–June 2000).

Bermudez, J., B. Kraus, L. Lapide, D. O'Brien, and B. Parker. "B2B Commerce Forecast: $5.7T by 2004," *AMR Research,* April 1, 2000, amrresearch.com/Content/view.asp?pmillid=13106&docid=380.

Chemconnect.com, 2002.

Choi, S. Y., et al. *The Economics of Electronic Commerce.* Indianapolis: Macmillan Technical Publications, 1997.

Covisint. "Supply Chain Management: Supplyconnect," February 2001, covisint.com/downloads/print/supplier_conn.pdf.

Cunningham, M. J. *B2B: How to Build a Profitable E-Commerce Strategy.* Cambridge, MA: Perseus Book Group, 2000.

Dalton, G., and B. Davis. "ANX Gets Certified Net-work Providers," *InformationWeek* (August 31, 1998).

Davis, B. G., et al. "Automotive Extranet Set for Test Drive," *InformationWeek* (September 1, 1997).

Delphi Group (2001).

Dolinoy, M., D. Cooperstein, and G. Scaffidi, "Customer Defined Networks," April 2001, forrester.com/ER/Research/Report/Summary/0,1338,11071,FF.html.

Durlacher Research Ltd. "Business to Business E-Commerce Report: An Investment Perspective," durlacher.com/fr-research.htm, May 6, 2000.

Duvall, M. "E-Marketplaces Getting Connected." *Interactive Week* (January 10, 2000).

Gartner Group (2001).

Goldman Sachs. "Internet: B2B E-Commerce," gs.com, May 8, 2000.

Interactive Week (January 17, 2000).

Kambil, A., and E. Van Hack. "Reengineering the Dutch Flower Auctions." *Information Systems Research* (March 1998).

Kaplan, S., and M. Sawhney. "E-Hubs: The New B2B Market Places." *Harvard Business Review* (May–June 2000).

Krammer, M., D. Hope-Ross, C. Spencer. "Attention SMBs: E-Markets Offer Rewards and Pitfalls." Gartner Group, September 5, 2001.

Norris, G., et al. *E-Business and ERP*. New York: John Wiley & Sons, 2000.

Ramsdell, G. "The Real Business of B2B," McKinsey & Company, October 2, 2000, techupdate.zdnet.com/techupdate/stories/main/0,14179,2635155-2,00.html.

Schully, A. B., and W. W. Woods. *B2B Exchanges*. New York: ISI Publications, 2000.

Stackpole, B. "Apps of Steel." *CIO Magazine*, October 15, 2000.

"Structural Material Manager: Complete Software Information," June 2002, steel-net.com/eje/softinfo.html.

Szuprowicz, B. *Extranet and Intranet: E-Commerce Business Strategies for the Future*. Charleston, SC: Computer Technology Research Corp., 1998.

Stackpole, B. "Apps of Steel." *CIO Magazine* (October 15, 2000).

Turban, E., et al. *Electronic Commerce 2002*. Upper Saddle River, NJ: Prentice Hall, 2002a.

Turban, E., et al. *Information Technology for Management*, 3d ed. New York: John Wiley & Sons, 2002b.

Van Heck, E., et al., "New Entrants and the Role of IT—Case Study: The Tele Flower Auction in the Netherlands." *Proceedings of the 30th Hawaiian International Conference on Systems Sciences*, Maui, HI (January 1997).

Worldsteel.org.

Additional Readings

Chan, S., and T. R. V. Davis. "Partnering on Extranets for Strategic Advantage." *Information Systems Management* (Winter 2000).

Cronin, C. "Five Success Factors for Private Trading Exchanges." *e-Business Advisor* (July–August 2001).

Cunningham, M. J. *B2B: How to Build a Profitable E-Commerce Strategy*. Cambridge, MA: Perseus Book Group, 2000.

Dalton, G., and B. Davis. "ANX Gets Certified Network Providers." *InformationWeek* (August 31, 1998).

Devine, D. A., et al. "Building Enduring Consortia." *McKinsey Quarterly*, no. 1 (2001).

Grimes, B. "The Rise and Fall (and Rise?) of E-Markets." *PC World* (June 2001).

Kobielus, J. G. *Biz Talk: Implementing B2B E-Commerce*. Upper Saddle River, NJ: Prentice Hall, 2001.

Krivda, C. D. "Internet Trading Exchanges," fortune.com/fortune/sections/emarketplaces, 2001.

Linthicum, D. S. *B2B Application Integration*. Boston: Addison Wesley, 2001.

Miner, R. C. *Dynamic Trading*. Tucson, AZ: Dynamic Trading Group, 2000.

O'Connell, B. *B2B.com: Cashing-In on the B2B E-Commerce Bonanza*. Avon, MA: Adams Media Publishing Co., 2000.

Radeke, M. "Understanding B2B Online Exchanges," Workz.com Corp., workz.com/content/1694.asp, January 2001.

Riggins, F. J., and H. S. Rhee. "Toward a Unified View of E-Commerce." *Communications of the ACM*, Vol. 41, No. 10 (October 2000): 88–95.

Sara, E. "E-Marketplaces: Opportunity or Threat?" *e-Business Advisor* (July 2000): S18–S21.

Silverstein, B. *Business-to-Business Internet Marketing*. Gulf Breeze, FL: Maximum Press, 1999.

Timmers, P. *Electronic Commerce: Strategies and Models for B2B Trading*. Chichester, U.K.: John Wiley & Sons, Ltd., 1999.

Weinberg, N. "B2B Grows Up." *Forbes* (September 10, 2001).

CHAPTER 7

Abbott, C. "At Amway, BI Portal Speeds Product R&D." *DM Review* (October 2000).

Aneja, A., et al. "Corporate Portal Framework for Transforming Content Chaos on Intranets." *Intel Technology Journal* (2000).

Bb. "Blackboard Learning and Community Portal System," June 2002, products.blackboard.com/cp/bb5/index.cgimway.html.

Bb. "Blackboard: Transaction System," June 2002, products.blackboard.com/ca/index.cgi.

Campbell, I. "The Intranet: Slashing the Cost of Business," cis.gsu.edu/~shong/teaching/cis849/idc/roi_reg.html.

Cope, J. "Wireless LANs Speed Hospital Insurance Payments." *Computerworld* (April 10, 2000).

Delphi Group. "Business Portals: Applications & Architecture," delphigroup.com/research/reports/bus-port-excerpt.htm (2001).

Hamalainen, et al. "Electronic Marketing for Learning: Education Brokerages on the Internet." *Communications of the ACM* (June 1996).

"How Communications Helped Turn IBM Around," *Holmes Report Knowledge*, holmesreport.com/holmestemp/story.cfm?edit_id=89&typeid=2, 1999.

International Trade Centre. "Export Development in the Digital Economy." *Executive Forum 2000*, September 2000.

Internetweek (May 3, 1999).

Konicki, S. "The New Desktop: Staples' Corporate-Portal Strategy Spells Productivity," *Information Week.com*, informationweek.com/784/porta4.htm, May 1, 2000.

Kontze, T. "Curing the Content Migrane: Managing Content is Becoming a Gigantic Pain, But It Doesn't Have to Be That Way." *InformationWeek.com News*, May 28, 2001.

Kounadis, T. "How to Pick the Best Portal." *e-Business Advisor* (August 2000).

Lason. "Fort Knox Escrow Service—A Lason Company—Unveils Escrow Direct," March 20, 2000, lason.com/press_releases/2000/3_20_00.htm.

McAffee, A. "The Napsterization of B2B." *Harvard Business Review* (November–December 2000).

McCreary, L. "Intranet Winners 1999." *CIO Web Magazine* (July 1, 1999).

McGee, M. K. "Strategic Applications: Companies are Forging a Unique Blend of Custom and Commercial Software to Gain a Competitive Advantage," informationweek.com/710/10prstr.htm, November 12, 1998.

McGregor, S. "The e-Learning Curve." *Profit Magazine*, oracle.com/oramag/profit/01-may/index.html?21ecurve.html, May 2001.

MyAPlus.com: A Return-on-Investment Study: A META Group White Paper, plumtree.com/webforms/MoreInfo_FormActionTemplate.asp, November 12, 2001.

myKGN: A Return-on-Investment Study: A META Group White Paper, plumtree.com/webforms/MoreInfo_FormActionTemplate.asp, June 19, 2001.

"Netscape Boosts Sales Effectiveness and Productivity at Cadence Design Systems," netscape.com/comprod/at_work/customer_profiles/cadence.html.

"Partner E-Learning Connection—Celebrates One Year," Cisco Partner Summit, Las Vegas, NV, cisco.com/warp/public/10/wwtraining/elearning/press/Final_PEC_release3_271.pdf, April 2001.

"Peer-To-Peer: Spreading the Computing Power," intel.com/ebusiness/products/peertopeer/ar011102.htm, June 2002.

Plumtree. "A Framework for Assessing Return on Investment for a Corporate Portal Deployment: The Industry's First Comprehensive Overview of Corporate Portal ROI," plumtree.com/webforms/MoreInfo_FormActionTemplate.asp, updated April 2002.

Raisch, W. D. *The eMarketplace*. New York: McGraw-Hill, 2001.

Schwartz, J. "E-Voting: Its Day Has Not Come Just Yet." *New York Times*, November 27, 2000.

"Solution Series: Intranet/Extranet 100," *Information Week* Online, informationweek.com/703/03sslist.htm, October 1998.

Sonicki, S. "The New Desktop: Powerful Portals," Informationweek.com, May 1, 2000.

Stellin, S. "Intranets Nurture Companies from the Inside." *New York Times*, January 29, 2001.

"Thomson Financial's First Call Acquires Story Street Partners: Acquisition Allows First Call to Continue Meeting Exploding Global Demand for its Customized Intranet and Portal Solutions," firstcall.com/press/news/1999/08_18.shtml, August 18, 1999.

WebCT. "WebCT Learning Transformations," June 2002, webct.com/transform.

WebCT. "WebCT: About Us," June 2002, webct.com/company.

Wong, W. Y. *At the Dawn of E-Government*. New York: Deloitte Research, Deloitte & Touche, 2000.

Additional Readings

Abramson, M. A., and G. E. Means, eds. *E-Government 2001*. Lanham, MD: Rowman and Littlefield, 2001.

Bacon, K., et al. *E-Government: The Blue Print*. New York: John Wiley & Sons, 2001.

Choi, S. Y., and A. B. Whinston. *The Internet Economy: Technology and Practice*. Austin, TX: SmartEcon Publishing, 2000.

Collins, H. *Corporate Portals*. New York: AMACOM, 2000.

Davenport, T. H., and L. Prusak. *Working Knowledge*. Boston: Harvard Business School Press, 2000.

Davydov, M. M. *Corporate Portals and eBusiness Integration*. New York: McGraw-Hill, 2001.

Hart-Teeter. *E-Government: The Next American Revolution*. Washington, D.C.: Council for Excellence in Government, 2001.

Hartley, D. E. *On-Demand Learning: Training in the New Millennium*. Amherst, MA: HRD Press, 2000.

Holmes, D. *Egov: E-Business Strategies for Government*. Yarmouth, ME: Nicholas Brealey, 2001.

Horton, W. *Evaluating E-Learning*. New York: American Society for Training and Development, 2001.

Koulopoulos, T. M. "Corporate Portals: Make Knowledge Accessible to All." *InformationWeek* (April 26, 1999).

McNurlin, B. "Experts Offer 5 Keys to Successful Portals." *F/S Analyzer Case Studies* (February 2000).

Palmer, N. "Transform Your Business into a B2B Portal." *e-Business Advisor* (April 2000).

Persson, C., and C. Perrson. *Administrator's Guide to Extranet/Internet*. Clifton Park, NY: Delmar Publishing, 2001.

Robinson, B. "Shopping for the Right B2G Model." *Federal Computer Week* (August 28, 2000).

Rosenberg, M. J. *E-Learning: Strategies for Delivering Knowledge in the Digital Age*. New York: McGraw-Hill, 2000.

Schubert, P., and U. Hausler. "E-Government Meets E-Business: A Portal Site for Start-up Companies in Switzerland." *Proceedings 34th HICSS*, Maui, HI, January 2001.

Tapscott, D. *Digital Capital: Harnessing the Power of Business Webs*. Boston: Harvard Business School Press, 2000.

Tiwana, A. *Knowledge Management Toolkit*. Upper Saddle River, NJ: Prentice Hall, 2001.

Watson, J., and J. Fenner. "Understanding Portals." *Information Management Journal* (July 2000).

CHAPTER 8

91 expresslances.com, 2002.

AXIS Communications. "Mobile Access by Axis: Wireless AccessPoints," axis.com, 2001. axis.com/documentation/brochure/wireless/mobile_access.pdf.

Baltimore Technologies PLC. "Wireless E-Security." Telepathy WST White paper, baltimore.com, 2000.

Barnett, N., et al. "M-Commerce: An Operator's Manual." *McKinsey Quarterly*, No. 3 (2000).

Bell, M., and C. Ross. "Workplace Transformation: A Business Imperative." Gartner Group, June 19, 2000.

Borland, J. "Technology Tussle Underlies Wireless Web," CNET News.com (cnet.com), April 19, 2000.

Bughin, J. R. et al. "Mobile Portals." *McKinsey Quarterly*, No. 2 (2001).

"Case Study—Xybernaut® Mobile Assistant®: Productivity Gains in the Telecommunication Field, Bell Canada: Time Savings of 50 Minutes per Day per Technician," xybernaut.com, 2001.

CDMA Development Group. "Kyocera Wireless Corp. Provides Prototype cdma2000 1X Handsets to Lucent Technologies for 3G Demonstration at CTIA," cdg.org/hot_news/index.asp?hnYY=2001&hnMM=03#032001_ven_n.html, March 20, 2001.

"CRM and the *mySAP.com* Mobile Workplace," SAP AG Corp., 2001.

Delta.com, 2000.

Delta Airlines. IBM, Modem Media Set to Deliver Travel Service, December 7, 1999, houns54.clearlake.ibm.com/solutions/travel/trapub.nsf/detailcontacts.

dot.ca.gov/fastrak, 2002.

Hertz Pressroom. "Hertz Announces New, Elite Levels for #1 Club Gold Members in the US—Revamps its #1 Club Membership with Free Upgrade to #1 Club Gold Service," hertz.com, July 11, 2000.

Ibm.com/software, 2000.

Intex Management Services. "One Billion Cellular Handsets Are to Be Shipped Yearly by 2004," gsmbox.co.uk, February 23, 2001.

Kalakota, R., and M. Robinson. *M-Business: The Race to Mobility*. New York: McGraw-Hill, 2001.

Macklin, B. "The Global Wireless Market—Benchmarking Europe with Japan and the U.S.," emarketer.com/analysis/wireless, April 17, 2001.

Mapinfo.com, 2001.

MDSI Wireless Work. "Dispatch Management," 2000, mdsi-advantex.com/workforce/docs/MDSI_Dispatch_Fact_Sheet.pdf.

Media Corp TV, Channel 5, 2001.

Mobileinfo.com. "Wireless Application Protocol—WAP: Future Outlook for WAP," mobileinfo.com/WAP/future_outlook.htm, 2001.

Muller-Veerse, F. "Mobile Commerce Report," durlacher.com, 2000.

Murphy, P. "Running Late? Take the NextBus," Environmental News Network, September 7, 1999, enn.com/enn-features-archive/1999/09/090799/nextbus_4692.asp.

"NextBus Expands Real-Time Transit Information in the Bay Area with AC Transit," ITS Access, August 10, 2001, itsa.org/ITSNEWS.NSF.

Nokia.com, 2001.

Norman, D. A. *The Invisible Computer*. Boston: MIT Press, 1998.

"Qualcomm CDMA Technologies Announced 500 Million Chips Shipped," cdg.org, August 27, 2001.

"Qualcomm Delivers 30 Million MSM Chips; Chipset Demand Fueled by Dramatic Increase in Use of CDMA Systems Worldwide," cdg.org, January 27, 1999.

Rapid Interagency Committee. "Mobile Phones, Cancer Not Linked in Two Short-term Studies." *Micro Wave News*, Vol. 21, No. 1, January/February 2001. microwavenews.com/j-f01ahf.html.

Redman, P. "Access Corporate Data on Your Wireless Phone." *e-Business Advisor* (March 2000a).

Redman, P. "Tap WAP for Enterprise Mobile Solutions." *e-Business Advisor* (May 2000b).

Smith Advanced Technology. "RALI Mobile," 2001, rali.com/Products/Mobile/htm.

Steede-Terry, K. *Integrating GIS and the Global Positioning System*. Redlands, CA: Environmental Systems Research Institute, 2000.

Varshney, U., and R. Vetter. "A Framework for the Emerging M-Commerce Applications." *Proceedings 34th HICSS*, Maui, HI, January 2001.

Wireless Communication Alliance (WCA), wca.org/Year2000/oct00.htm, October 17, 2000.

XyberFlash. "Wearable Computers for the Working Class." *New York Times*, December 14, 2000.

Additional Readings

Bergeron, B. *The Wireless Web: How to Develop and Execute a Winning Wireless Strategy*. New York: McGraw-Hill, 2001.

Berry, N. "Get Ready for the Wireless Web." *e-Business Advisor* (September 2000).

deChernatony, L., et al. "Added Value: Its Nature, Roles, and Sustainability." *European Journal of Marketing*, Nos. 1 and 2 (2000).

Durlacher Research. "UMAT Research Report," durlacher.com, 2001.

Evans, N. D. *Business Agility: Strategies for Gaining Competitive Advantage Through Mobile Business Solutions*. Upper Saddle River, NJ: Financial Times/Prentice Hall, 2002.

Goldman Sachs. "Wireless Data II: The Data Wave Unplugged," goldmansachs.com, 2000.

IBM Global Service. "A Wireless World Awaits: Nine Moves That Mobilize E-Business," ibm.com/services/innovations/ber.html, 2001.

Joshi, J. B. D., et al. "Security Models for Web-Based Applications." *Communications of the ACM* (February 2001).

Kannan, P. K. "Wireless Commerce: Marketing Issues and Possibilities." *Proceedings 34th HICSS*, Maui, HI, January 2001.

Macomber, C. "Mobile Solutions Success in Five Steps." *e-Business Advisor* (May 2001).

May, P. *Mobile Commerce*. Cambridge, UK: Cambridge University Press, 2001.

Raisinghani, M. S. "WAP: Transitional Technology for M-Commerce." *Information Systems Management* (summer 2001).

Sadeh, N. M. *M-Commerce: Technologies, Services, and Business Models*. New York: John Wiley and Sons, 2002.

Smith, M. "M-Commerce: What's Missing." *e-Business Advisor* (February 2001).

Synchrologic Corp. "Improving Account Manager Productivity at Cisco Systems, Inc.," Customer white paper, synchrologic.com, 2001.

Varshney, U. "Recent Advances in Wireless Networking." *IEEE Computer* (June 2000).

Vetter, R. "The Wireless Web." *Communications of the ACM* (February 2000).

Walters, D., and G. Lancaster. "Value and Information—Concepts and Issues for Management." *Management Decision*, No. 8 (2000).

CHAPTER 9

Black, Jane. "The High Price of Spam," *BusinessWeek Online*, businessweek.com, March 1, 2002.

Briney, A. "Security Focused: Survey 2000." *Information Security* (September 2000): 40–68.

CERT Coordination Center. "CERT/CC Statistics 1988–2001," cert.org/stats/cert_stats.html, 2000.

CERT Coordination Center. "2001 Annual Report," www.cert.org/annual_rpts/cert_rpt_01.html, 2001.

Claburn, T. "Intellectual Property: Harder to Protect than Ever." *Smart Business* 14 (December 1, 2001).

Computer Science Institute and Federal Bureau of Investigation. "Computer Crime and Security Survey," gocsi.com, 2000.

Delgado-Martinez, R. "What Is Copyright Protection?" whatiscopyright.org, 2002.

Dembeck, C., and R. Conlin. "Beleaguered DoubleClick Appoints Privacy Board." *E-Commerce Times* (May 17, 2000).

Donham, P. "An Unshackled Internet: If Joe Howe Were Designing Cyberspace," *Proceedings of the Symposium on Free Speech and Privacy in the Information Age, University of Waterloo*, gopher://insight.mcmaster.ca/00/org/efc/doc/sfsp/donham.txt, November 26, 1994.

Federal Trade Commission. *Privacy Online: A Report to the Congress*, www.ftc.gov/reports/privacy3, June, 1998.

Hancock, D. "What's in a Name?" everydayliving.com/archives/what_in_a_name.htm, 2000.

Haney, K. "Priceline Settles Microsoft Expedia Suit," digitrends.net. January 11, 2001.

Hazari, S. "Firewalls for Beginners," securityfocus.com/focus/basics/articles/fwbeg/htm, November 6, 2000.

Heim, K., and E. Ackerman. "'Zombie' Attacks Blamed in New Online Outages." *San Jose (CA) Mercury News,* January 26, 2001.

Hildebrand, C. "Privacy vs. Profit." *CIO* (February 15, 1996).

King, C. "Protect Your Assets with This Enterprise Risk-Management Guide." *Business Security Advisor* (February 2001): 14–16.

Lemos, R. "Hackers Infiltrate BugTraq List—Experts Send Malicious Code to 37,000 Users," zdNet.com (February 1, 2000).

Lewis, N. "Beyond the Firewall: Data Sharing Stirs Privacy Fears." *EBN* (February 12, 2001).

Loshin, P. *Extranet Design and Implementation.* San Francisco: Sybex Network Press, 1998.

Marchany, R. "The Top 10 Internet Security Vulnerabilities Primer," sans.org/topten.htm, December 2000.

Mell, P., and J. Wack. "Mitigating Emerging Hacker Trends." *ITL Bulletin* (June 2000).

Merkow, M., and J. Breithaupt. *Internet Security: The Complete Guide.* New York: AMACOM, 2000.

Nickell, J. "Legislation: Privacy, Telecom, Copyrights, and Taxes." *Smart Business* 14 (December 1, 2001).

Nieto, T., et al. *E-Business and E-Commerce: How to Program.* Upper Saddle River, NJ: Prentice Hall, 2001.

Norton, P., and M. Stockman. *Network Security Fundamentals.* Indianapolis, IN: SAMS, 2000.

Olsen, S. "DoubleClick Nearing Privacy Settlements." CNET News.com, cnet.com, March 31, 2002.

Owens, S., and E. Traudt. "Worldwide Internet Security Software Market Expected to More than Double by 2006." *IDC Press Release* (March 4, 2002).

Paller, A., et al. "Consensus Roadmap for Defeating Distributed Denial of Service Attacks," sans.org/ddos_roadmap.htm, February 23, 2000.

Pappalardo, D. "Avoiding Future Denial-of-Service Attacks," cnn.com/2000/TECH/computing/02/23/isp.block.idg, February 23, 2000.

Power, R. *Tangled Web.* Indianapolis, IN: Que, 2000.

Rainone, S. H., et al. "Ethical Management of Employee E-Mail Privacy." *Information Strategy: The Executive Journal* 14 (spring 1998): 34–40.

Sager, I. "The Players." *Business Week* (February 21, 2000).

Scambray, J., et al. *Hacking Exposed*, 2d ed. New York: McGraw-Hill, 2000.

Spaulding, M. "The ABC's of MP3: A Crash Course in the Digital Music Phenomenon." In *Signal or Noise? The Future of Music on the Net.* Berkman Center for Internet & Society at Harvard Law School and the Electronic Frontier Foundation, asc.upenn.edu/courses/comm334/Docs/Net%20music%20brief.pdf, August 23, 2000.

Steinberg, D. "Privacy: Surveillance vs. Freedom." *Smart Business* 12 (December 1, 2001).

Visa. "Visa Account Information Security Standards," visa.com/nt/gds/standards.html, 2000.

Watson, J. "E-Security: E-Defense Against Hackers, Crackers, and Other Cyber-Thieves." *Fortune* (Special Technology Section) (July 10, 2000).

CHAPTER 10

American Express. "American Express Continues 150-Year Tradition of Protecting Customers with New Suite of Online Privacy and Security Products." Press Release, home3.americanexpress.com/corp/latestnews/payments.asp, September 2000.

Angwin, J. "And How Will You Pay For That?," Special e-commerce report, *Wall Street Journal Europe*, fininter.net/payments/pmnt_systems.htm, October 23, 2000.

Boston Consulting Group. "Winning the Online Consumer: The Challenge of Raised Expectations," 2001, bcg.com/publications/search_view_ofas.asp?pubID=632.

Brooker, K. "The Nightmare Before Christmas." *Fortune* (January 24, 2000), 24–26.

Carr, J. "The Problem with Plastic." *eCommerce Business* (December 2000).

Cassy, J. "No Just Rewards in E-Heaven." *Business 2.0* (November 2000).

Caswell, S. "Credit Card Fraud Crippling Online Merchants." *E-Commerce Times* (March 2000).

"CLM Definitions," clm1.org/about/purpose.asp, 2002.

"Companies Can Pare Process Costs by 95 Percent When Purchasing Supplies," americanexpress.com/corp/latestnews/purch-process.asp, May 25, 1999.

Cone, E. "E-Com Meets Logistical Web." *Interactive Week* (July 26, 1999).

Cornwell, A. "Commerce Service Providers and Future Internet Payment Methods," *World Market Series Business Briefings*, wmrc.com, 2000.

Council of Logistics Management, clm1.org.

Crockett, R. "No Plastic? No Problem." *BusinessWeek* (October 2000).

"Cyota's SecureClick Allows Customers to Shop Without Revealing Their Credit Card Number," cyota.com/viewReleases.cfm?id=30, May 16, 2000.

Darden, C. "E-Commerce from the Back End: Why Logistics Is Where It's @." Parcel Shippers and Logistics Conference in Chicago, Illinois (October 2000).

Deitel, H., et al. *Wireless Internet and Mobile Business.* Upper Saddle River, NJ: Prentice Hall, 2002.

dell.com/us/en/gen/services/service_servicesportfolio.htm, 2002.

Duvall, M. "Retailers Predict Increased Credit Card Theft." *Interactive Week* (November 2000).

Duvall, M. "Santa's Helpers Get Their Feet Webbed." *Interactive Week* (September 13, 1999).

Electronic Check Clearing House Organization. "Managing Value in the Transition to Electronic Payments: Executive Summary," April 11, 2002, eccho.org.

Epner, S. "The Search for a Supply Team." Industrial Distribution, December 1999, findarticles.com/cf_0/

PI/search.jhtml?type=all&magR=m3263&key=The+Search+for+a+Supply+Team.

Evans, D., and R. Schmalensee. *Playing with Plastic: The Digital Revolution in Buying and Borrowing.* Cambridge, MA: MIT Press, 2000.

Gazala, M., and A. Shepard. "Credit Card Security Fears Wane," Forrester Research, forrester.com, September 1999.

Handfield, R. B., and E. L. Nichols, Jr. *Introduction to Supply Chain Management.* Upper Saddle River, NJ: Prentice Hall, 1999.

Howard, M. *Designing Secure Web-Based Applications.* Redmond, WA: Microsoft Press, 2000.

"InternetCash™ Launches First of Its Kind Private Label Gift Certificate Program for E-Merchants," internetCash.com/go/0,1190,159,00.html, October 24, 2000.

Jenkins, E. "Private Digital Currencies: Survey and Critique," Standard Reserve Holdings Limited, standardtransactions.com/a_survey_and_critique1.html, 2001.

Jilovec, N. *E-Business: Thriving in the Electronic Marketplace.* Loveland, CO: 29th Street Press, 1999.

Korper, S., and J. Ellis. *The E-Commerce Book: Building the E-Empire.* New York: Academic Press, 2000.

Lee, L. H., et al. "The Bullwhip Effect in Supply Chains." *Sloan Management Review* (spring 1997).

MasterCard. "SET Secure Electronic Transaction Setting the Stage for Safe Internet Shopping," mastercard.com/shoponline/set, 2000.

"NCL Survey Shows Consumers Face Online Holiday Shopping Season with Credit Card Worries: National Consumers League Launches New Tips for Safe Shopping Online," orbiscom.com/press/releases/051001.html, October 5, 2001.

"Nickelodeon Online and Harris Interactive Launch Syndicated Kid Poll: Nickelodeon/HarrisKidPulse to Continuously Survey 8 to 12 Year-Olds," harrisinteractive.com/news/allnewsbydate.asp?NewsID=45, January 24, 2000.

Orbis.com.

Pickering, C. "New Power Centers—FedEx Hub." *Business 2.0* (January 2000).

Quittner, J. "How Can Kids Buy Stuff on the Web? Ask InternetCash," *BusinessWeek Online,* businessweek.com, March 7, 2000.

Trager, L. "Not So Many Happy Returns." *Interactive Week* (March 20, 2000).

Turban, E., et al. *Electronic Commerce 2002.* Upper Saddle River, NJ: Prentice Hall, 2002b.

Turban, E., et al. *Information Technology for Management,* 3d ed. New York: John Wiley & Sons, 2002a.

United Parcel Service. "E-Logistics: Your Inventory is Worth More than Money," ec.ups.com/ecommerce/clicks/e_Logistics.html, August 1, 2001.

United Parcel Service. "UPS e-Logistics Gives Power Boost to Back-End Fulfillment Solution," upslogistics.com/news/news_052201_1.html, May 22, 2001.

Visa. "Visa Cash," visa.com/nt/visacash/main.html, 2000.

Xelus, Inc. "Case Study: Dell," xelus.com/CaseStudies/cs_dell.asp, 1999.

Additional Readings

Ayers, J. "A Primer on Supply Chain Management." *Information Strategy: The Executive's Journal* (winter 2000).

Borths, R., and D. Young. "E-Billing, Today and Beyond." *Information Strategy: The Executive's Journal* (winter 2000).

Coupey, E. *Marketing and the Internet.* Upper Saddle River, NJ: Prentice Hall, 2001.

Deitel, H., et al. *E-Business and E-Commerce: How-to Program.* Upper Saddle River, NJ: Prentice Hall, 2001.

Johnston, R. B., et al. "An Emerging Vision of Internet-Enabled Supply-Chain Electronic Commerce." *International Journal of Electronic Commerce* (summer 2000).

Menasce, D., and V. Almeida. *Scaling for E-Business.* Upper Saddle River, NJ: Prentice Hall, 2000.

Perry, G., and J. Perry. *Electronic Commerce.* Cambridge, MA: Thomson Learning, 2000.

Poirier, C. C., and M. J. Bauer. *E-Supply Chain: Using the Internet to Revolutionize Your Business.* San Francisco, CA: Berrett-Koehler, 2000.

Rigney, P. "Eliminate Fulfillment Problems." *e-Business Advisor* (March 2000).

Sandoe, K., et al. *Enterprise Integration.* New York: John Wiley & Sons, 2001.

Violino, B. "Supply Chain Management and E-Commerce." *Internet Week* (May 4, 2000).

Xelus, Inc. "Case Study: Dell," xelus.com/CaseStudies/cs_dell.asp, 1999. dell.com/html/us/corporate/brochure/index.htm.

CHAPTER 11

Agrawal, V., et al. "E-Performance: The Path to Rational Exuberance." *McKinsey Quarterly* 1 (2001).

Ajpr.com, 2002.

Armstrong, A. G., and J. Hagel. "The Real Value of Online Communities." *Harvard Business Review* (May–June 1996).

Ashton, H. "Best Practices for E-Procurement: IBM Becomes an E-Business from the Inside Out," Hurwitz Group, Inc., ibm.com/procurement/html/eprocurement/consultantsreport.html#lessons, March 31, 1999.

Ausfish.com.au, 2002.

Bodow, S. "Getting Hitched." *Business 2.0* (November 28, 2000).

Bonnett, K. R. *An IBM Guide to Doing Business on the Internet*. New York: McGraw-Hill, 2000.

Chatham, B., L. Orlov, E. Howard, B. Worthen, and A. Coutts. "The Customer Conversation," Forrester Research, forrester.com/ER/Research/ Report/Summary/0,1338,9510,FF.html, June 2000.

Casonato, R. "Gartner Predicts 2002: Wireless and Mobile," gartner.com/1_researchanalysis//focus/wireless2002.html, February 1, 2002.

Champy, J., et al. "The Rise of the Electronic Community." *InformationWeek* (June 10, 1996).

Choi, S. Y., and A. B. Whinston. *The Internet Economy: Technology and Practice*. Austin, TX: SmartEcon Pub., 2000.

CIO Communications. "The Means to an Edge—E-Commerce," *CIO* Special Advertising Supplement, cio.com/sponsors/050199_2.html, May 1, 1999.

Daly, J. "Sage Advice." *Business 2.0* (August 22, 2000).

David, F. *Strategic Management: Concepts and Cases*, 7th ed. Upper Saddle River, NJ: Prentice Hall, 1998.

Deise, M. V., et al. *Executive's Guide to E-Business—From Tactics to Strategy*. New York: Wiley, 2000.

DePalma, D. "Meet Your Customers' Need Through Cultural Marketing." *E-Business Advisor* (August 2000).

Dewan, R., et al. "Adoption of Internet-Based Product Customization and Pricing Strategies." *Proceedings 33rd HICSS*, Maui, HI, January 2000.

Duffy, D. "It Takes an E-Village." *CIO Magazine* (October 25, 1999).

"E-business: New Reality. New Rules. New Responses," -1.ibm.com/services/whitepapers/ebiz_new_reality_112900.html, 2000.

EMarketer. "Unwired and Online Around the World," emarketer.com/estatnews/estats/wireless/20010910_accent.html, September 10, 2001.

Fessenden, K., and T. Dwyer. "Going Global with E-Business," Aberdeen Group, aberdeen.com, September 2000.

Forrester.com, 1998.

Forrester.com, 2001.

Glater, J. D. "A High-Tech Domino Effect: As Dot-com's Go, So Go the E-Commerce Consultants." *New York Times*, December 6, 2000.

Hackbarth, G., and W. J. Kettinger. "Building an e-Business Strategy." *Information Resource Management* (summer 2000).

Hagel, J., and A. Armstrong. *Net Gain*. Boston: Harvard Business School Press, 1997.

Hammer, M., and S. A. Stanton. *The Reengineering Revolution: A Handbook*. New York: HarperCollins, 1995.

Hornby, G., et al. "Export Through E-Business: Cultural Issues Faced by SMEs." *Proceedings*, *PACIS 2000*, Hong Kong, May 2000.

Howard, P., D. Hamilton, and M. Polinsky. "Creating a Paragon of E-business Success," -1.ibm.com/services/whitepapers/paragon.html, 2001.

Huff, S., et al. "Critical Success Factors for Electroni Commerce," in *Cases in Electronic Commerce*. Irwin/McGraw-Hill, 1999.

Hutchinson, A. "E-Commerce: Building a Model." *Communications Week* (March 17, 1997).

Ibm.com, 2000.

Interactive Week (May 11, 1998)

Interactive Week (February 2000).

Josephson, M. "Why a Content Management System Won't Take You Global," diominc.com/us/solutions/gls_doc/GLS_september2001.pdf, September 2001.

Kalakota, R., and M. Robinson. *E-Business 2.0—Roadmap for Success*. Reading, MA: Addison Wesley, 2001.

Kannen, et al. "Marketing Information on the I-Way." *Communications of the ACM*, Vol. 41, No. 3, March 1998, 35–40.

Kaplan, R., and D. Norton. *The Balanced Scorecard: Translating Strategy into Action*. Cambridge, MA: Harvard Business School Press, September 1996.

Kaplan, R. S., and D. P. Norton. "Having Trouble with Your Strategy? Then Map It." *Harvard Business Review* (September–October 2000).

"Leading E-Marketplace Operators Leverage the Commerce One Global Trading Web to Expand Global E-Commerce," commerceone.com/news/releases/gtw_interoperability.html, July 10, 2001.

Levinson, M. "Don't Stop Thinking About Tomorrow." *CIO Magazine* (December 1999/January 2000).

Lloyd, R. "Translation Services Key to Global Internet," October 15, 1999, cnn.com/TECH/computing/9910/15/translation.

Luk S. "Hong Kong Firms Wary of E-Commerce," *South China Morning Post*, scmp.com.hk, February 9, 2002.

Mandel, M. J. *The Coming Internet Depression*. New York: Basic Book, 2000.

McWilliam, G. "Building Stronger Brands Through Online Communities." *Sloan Management Review* (spring 2000).

O'Connor, G. C., and B. O'Keefe. "Viewing the Web as a Marketplace: The Case of Small Companies." *Decision Support Systems*, Vol. 21, No. 3, November 1997, 171–183.

Organization for Economic Co-operation and Development. "Dismanteling the Barriers to Global Electronic Commerce," Organization for Economic Co-operation and Development, oecd.org, December 4, 1997.

OneWorld.net. "Campaigns: Digital Divide," May 17, 2002, oneworld.net/campaigns/digitaldivide.

Otto, J. R., and O. B. Chung. "A Framework for Cyber-Enhanced Retailing: Integrating EC Retailing with Brick-and-Mortar Retailing." *Electronic Markets* Vol. 10, No. 3 (2000).

"Our Evolution," aboutschwab.com/sstory/evolution.html.

Phillips, M. "Seven Steps to Your New E-Business." *Business Online* (August 2000).

Plant, R. T. *E-Commerce: Formulation of Strategy*. Upper Saddle River, NJ: Prentice Hall, 2000.

Porter, M. *Competition in Global Industries*. Boston, MA: Harvard Business School Press, 1996.

Pottruck, D., and T. Pearce. *Clicks and Mortar*. San Francisco: Jossey-Bass, 2000.

Prasad, B., and P. Harker. "Pricing Online Banking Services Amid Network Externalities." *Proceedings 33rd HICSS*, Maui, HI, January 2000.

Preece, J. *Online Communities*. Chichester, U.K.: John Wiley & Sons, 2000.

Raisch, W. D. *The E-Marketplace*. New York: McGraw-Hill, 2001.

Raisch, W. D. *The eMarketplace Strategies for Succeeding in B2B*. New York: McGraw-Hill, 2000.

Rayport, J., and B. J. Jaworski. *E-Commerce*. New York: McGraw-Hill, 2001.

Rheingold, H. *The Virtual Community: Homesteading on the Electronic Frontier*. Reading, MA: Addison-Wesley Publishing Co., 1993.

Schubert, P., and M. Ginsburg. "Virtual Communities of Transaction: The Role of Personalization in E-Commerce." *Electronic Markets* Vol. 10, No. 1 (2000).

"Schwab Alliance with Nextel Provides Wireless Investing Via Nextel Online (SM) Wireless Internet Service," San Francisco: *Businesswire*, businesswire.com, November 9, 2000.

Schwartz, E. I. *Webonomics*. New York: Broadway Books, 1997.

Semler, R. "How We Went Digital Without a Strategy." *Harvard Business Review* (September–October 2000).

Shapiro, C., and H. Varian. *Competitive Strategy for the Information Age*. Boston: Harvard Business School Press, 1998.

Silberman, S., "Just Say Nokia Wired," wired.com/wired/archive/7.09/nokia_pr.html, September 1999.

Spivey, C., et al. "Orchestrating Service Providers," *Tech Strategy Report*, forrester.com/ER/Research/Report/Summary/0,1338,10978,FF.html, January 2001.

Tennant, H. R. *Effective E-Strategies: The Themes and Strategies at Work on the Web*. Dallas, TX: Stanbury Press, 2000.

Tjan, A. K. "Finally, a Way to Put Your Internet Portfolio in Order." *Harvard Business Review* (February 2001).

Turban, E., et al. *Information Technology for Management*, 3d ed. New York: John Wiley & Sons, 2002.

Ulph, R., J. Favier, and P. O'Connell. "Integrated Marketing Needs Hubs," *Tech Strategy Report*, forrester.com/ER/Research/Report/Summary/0,1338,13712,00.html, December 2001.

Useem, J. "Dot-Coms: What Have We Learned?" *Fortune* (October 2000).

Voss, C. "Developing an eService Strategy." *Business Strategy Review* (spring 2000).

Wheelen, T., and J. Hunger. *Strategic Management and Business Policy*, 8th ed. Reading, MA: Addison-Wesley, 2002.

World Business Report, 2000.

Additional Readings

Baker, W., et al. "Price Smarter on the Net." *Harvard Business Review* (February 2001).

Barash, J., et al. "How E-Tailing Can Rise from the Ashes." *McKinsey Quarterly* 3 (2000).

Bressler, S. E., and C. E. Grantham. *Communities of Commerce*. New York: McGraw-Hill, 2000.

Clinton, W. J., and A. Gore. "A Framework for Global Electronic Commerce," iitf.nist.gov/eleccomm/ecomm.htm, November 1997; also in ecommerce.gov.

CommerceNet Survey. *Barriers to Electronic Commerce*. Palo Alto, CA: CommerceNet, 2000.

Cunningham, M. J. *B2B: How to Build a Profitable E-Commerce Strategy*. Cambridge, MA: Peruses, 2000.

DePalma, D. "International E-Commerce." *E-Business Advisor* (October 2000).

Earle, N., and P. Keen. *From .com to Profit*. New York: Jossey-Bass, 2000.

El Sawy, O. *Redesigning Enterprise Processes for E-Business*. New York: McGraw-Hill, 2001.

Gulati, R., and J. Garino. "Get the Right Mix of Bricks and Clicks." *Harvard Business Review* (May–June 2000).

Kaplan, R. S., and D. P. Norton. *The Strategy-Focused Organization*. Boston, MA: Harvard Business School Press, 2000.

Kaplan, R. S., and D. P. Norton. *The Balanced-Scoreboard*. Boston, MA: Harvard Business School Press, 1996.

Shaw, J., and J. Sperry. *eCommerce as a Business Strategy: An Overview*. Marietta, GA: E-Commerce Strategies, 2000.

Venkatraman, N. "Five Steps to a Dot-Com Strategy: How to Find Your Footing on the Web." *Sloan Management Review* (spring 2000).

Index

Q

R